A Missional Leadership History

The journey from Wycliffe Bible Translators

... to the Wycliffe Global Alliance

Kirk J Franklin and Susan Van Wynen

with Deborah Crough

First published 2022 by Regnum Books International

in partnership with Wycliffe Global Alliance

Regnum is an imprint of the Oxford Centre for Mission Studies
St. Philip and St. James Church, Woodstock Road
Oxford, OX2 6HR, UK
www.regnumbooks.net

Wycliffe Global Alliance
www.wycliffe.net

09 08 07 06 05 04 03 8 7 6 5 4 3 2 1

Design and typeset by Wes Franklin, wjfranklin.com

British Library Cataloguing in Publication Data
A catalogue record for this book is available from the British Library

ISBN: 978-1-5064-9756-3
eBook ISBN: 978-1-5064-9757-0

Distributed by Fortress Press in the US, Canada, India, and Brazil

Contents

Abbreviations 8
Introduction 9
Dedication 14
PART 1 CHRONOS EVENTS 16
Chapter 1 Founding: 1942–1965 17
Historical Context 17
Founding Wycliffe Bible Translators 20
Very Early Years 22
Expansion 24
Westernizing 29
Conclusion 43
Leadership Theories and Practices 44
Journey Reflections (A New Path) 45
Chapter 2 Expanding: 1966–1980 47
Historical Context 47
Organizational Growth 49
Relating to SIL 64
Forming Wycliffe International 69
Table 1: Distinctions of WBT and SIL 71
Conclusion 73
Leadership Theories and Practices 74
Journey Reflections (Natural Tensions) 76
Chapter 3 Creating: 1981–1990 77
Historical Setting 77
Renewing Vision 80
Milestones 88
Carrying on Despite Challenges 95
Moving Forward 99
Conclusion 104
Leadership Theories and Practices 105
Journey Reflections (Influences and New Terrain) 106
Chapter 4 Maturing: 1991–2000 109
Historical Setting 109
Immediate Challenges 112
Implications of Reorganization 127
Increasing Internationalization 136
Birthing of Vision 2025 145

Conclusion 151
Leadership Theory and Practice 152
Journey Reflections (Being and Becoming) 153
Chapter 5 Moving: 2001–2010 155
Historical Setting 155
Strategic Direction 158
Vision 2025 Three Years On 161
The Word in a Changing World 176
Discovering the Mission of God 188
New Era Begins 190
Understanding and Knowing 194
Conclusion 213
Leadership Theories and Practices 215
Journey Reflections (We've Never Been This Way Before) 217
Chapter 6 Birthing: 2011–2015 219
Introduction 219
New Name 220
Look What God is Doing! 229
Developing Community 239
Institution to Movement 241
Friendship in God's Mission 254
Voting Organizations 257
Table 2: Types and Numbers of Organizations 257
Conclusion 262
Leadership Theory and Practice 263
Journey Reflections (People with a Purpose) 265
Chapter 7 Flourishing: 2016–2020 267
Introduction 267
Preparing to Celebrate 269
The New Community 271
Table 3: The 15 Third Table Gifts 275
Assessing Participation 284
Table 4: Participation in Funding Stream 284
Table 5: Participation in Bible Translation Programs Stream 284
New Directions in Bible Translation 285
Ministering in a VUCA World 296
Table 6: Overview of a Decade of Development 298
Table 7: Overview of Models and Characteristics of Governance 301
A Shalom Community 302

Table 8: Revision of Participation Streams 303
Cancellations 305
Conclusion 306
Table 9: Shifts in Structure and Leadership 307
Leadership Theory and Practice 308
Journey Reflections (A Journey that Keeps on Going) 310
PART 2 KAIROS MOMENTS 312
Chapter 8 Embedding: National Bible Translation Organizations 313
Introduction 313
Call for a Moratorium 314
Nationalism and Western Missions 317
Complexities in Relationships 323
Growth and Development in National Contexts 325
Overview of Historic NBTOs 329
Evolving Structures and Relationships 339
Conclusion 343
Chapter 9 Perceiving: Vision 2025 345
Introduction 345
Audacious Goal 349
Vision, Mission, and Strategic Plan 353
Missiological Implications 356
Urgency in Service of our Patient God 364
Missiological Affirmations 369
Missiological Reflections 374
The Alliance Journey in Response to Vision 2025 375
Conclusion 376
Leadership Reflections 377
Chapter 10 Defining: Missiological Consultations that Shaped the WGA 381
Introduction 381
Characteristics of a Missiological Consultation 381
First Missiological Consultation, 2006 383
Second Missiological Consultation, 2007 385
Third Missiological Consultation, 2008 390
Last Languages Initiative, 2009 392
Community Within the Alliance, 2012 394
Funding God's Mission, 2013 396
Regional Funding Consultations, 2014 399
Our Response to the Mission of God in Local Context, 2013 403

Our Participation in Missio Dei, 2014 405
Bible Translation Philosophy, 2013 407
Leaders Journeying Together, 2013 411
Bible Translation Philosophy Joint Consultation, 2014 413
Global Leadership Team Future, 2015 416
Leaders Journeying Together—Third Table, 2015 417
Review of Principles of Community, 2016 420
Global Leadership in Community, 2017 422
Regional Global Leadership in Community, 2017 424
Together in the Mission of God in Europe, 2017 425
First Ecclesiology Consultation, 2017 427
Second Ecclesiology Consultation, 2017 428
Third Ecclesiology Consultation, 2018 430
Third Space Forum, 2018 431
Graphic 1: Third Spaces 432
People Serving in God's Mission, 2018 433
Task Force on Funding, 2019 435
Africa-Europe Funding, 2019 437
Young Leaders Initiatives, 2019 441
Exploring Generosity as a Way of Life, 2019 443
Transformation as an Expression of the Mission of God, 2019 445
Makings of a Missiological Consultation 446
Journey Thoughts 448
Chapter 11 Mapping: A Case Study of the Americas Area Journey 449
Introduction 449
Context 451
Journey Identity, Vision, and Values 453
People 455
Resources 457
Principles 459
Mindset 460
Decisions 463
Behaviours 465
Milestones 466
Lessons Learned 469
Discernment and Goals 472
Conclusion 474

Chapter 12 Measuring: Missional Intent of the Alliance Board 477
Introduction 477
Reflection and Realignment 478
Early Days 479
Realignment and Revision 480
Qualitative Reporting 481
Refining Measurements 482
Redefining Progress 483
New Way of Reporting 485
Refining Reporting 486
Missional Intent 487
Summary 488
Epilogue 491
Timeline 495
Bibliography 501
Index 507

Abbreviations

ALT	Alliance Leadership Team
AO	Alliance Organization
APO	Associated Partner Organization
COMIBAM	Cooperación Misionera Iberoamericana
EVP	Executive Vice President
GLT	Global Leadership Team
IFMA	International Foreign Mission Association (Victoria, Australia)
ILC	International Linguistics Centre
JAARS	Jungle Aviation and Radio Service
LLI	Last Languages Initiative
MO	Member Organization
NBTO	National Bible Translation Organization
PO	Participating Organization
SIL	Summer Institute of Linguistics
STA	Short-Term Assistant
STM	Short-Term Mission
TSC	The Seed Company
UBS	United Bible Societies
WA	Wycliffe Associates
WAO	Wycliffe Affiliate Organization
WBT	Wycliffe Bible Translators
WBT, Inc.	Wycliffe Bible Translators, Incorporated (in the state of California)
WBTI	Wycliffe Bible Translators International
WBTI, Inc.	Wycliffe Bible Translators International, Incorporated (in the state of California)
WEA	World Evangelical Alliance
WGA	Wycliffe Global Alliance
WO	Wycliffe Organization
WMO	Wycliffe Member Organization
WPO	Wycliffe Partner Organization

Introduction

This book is like no other! The reason for this claim is that the history of this particular mission has never been told before in this way. An appreciation for telling this story grew from authors Kirk Franklin and Susan Van Wynen when they had the privilege of doing their PhD research at the University of Pretoria in South Africa. There, the faculty of theology houses the library of the late missiologist David Bosch. Bosch did some of his theological studies at this university, therefore a fitting home for his collection. Bosch suggested that missiology—the theological study of God's mission—is a 'gadfly' to mission. It plays the annoying role of questioning the status quo.[1] The way this works, according to Bosch, is that missiologists 'accompany the missionary enterprise, to scrutinize its foundations, its aims, attitude, message, and methods.'[2]

Franklin and Van Wynen have tried to achieve Bosch's lofty aim through this book, exploring whether Wycliffe International had from its formation a vision and plan to become a worldwide movement for Bible translation. If it did, who were the people and organizational structures that made this possible? What challenges did they overcome along the way? What are the lessons of leadership and life that we gain from their journey? How is this journey relevant to mission today, that is, the *missio Dei*, the mission of God?

This book is distinct because of several important reasons, including the sources of the material, the purposes for the research and writing of the book, and the subject matter itself. This book is intentionally unusual in how it speaks from the past and is less 'filtered' than many histories of organizations. As a reader, you will observe how Wycliffe International thought and spoke and how that changed over time. You will have numerous opportunities to learn from and reflect on these happenings.

One of the audiences for this book is leaders of mission, especially leaders within the Bible translation movement, and more specifically, current, new, emerging, and future leaders within what is now the Wycliffe Global Alliance. John Johnson, who is also committed to leadership development across the world, makes a compelling case for why this is important: 'Every person and every organization has a history, and it needs careful attention. People need to read their ancestors, and organizations need to read their pasts.' [3] We believe that the history presented in this book captures the faith and vision of ancestors of the recent past and their organizations. Johnson also observes how people, especially leaders, tend to 'ignore

[1] David Bosch, *Transforming Mission: Paradigm Shifts in Theology of Mission* (Maryknoll: Orbis, 1991), 496.

[2] Bosch, 496.

[3] John Johnson, *Mission Voices: Learning to Lead Beyond Our Horizons* (Carlisle: Langham Global Library, 2019), 239.

the past' because they want to 'scrap what's in place and charge into the future.'[4] It is our conviction in writing this book that we no longer want to ignore or neglect our history. We want to see a foundation laid for learning, observing, and growing for all who go on the journey described throughout this book.

Let's be clear about what you're going to read and experience. Picture yourself travelling in a hot air balloon that is surveying mission history and especially Wycliffe's history. So, you are doing this from a distance, and you gain the big-picture perspective. Throughout this journey, you zoom in on particulars that serve as examples. Occasionally, reaching out and touching moments, you realize, 'oh, this is like something I've experienced.' Coming back down to the ground, you consider leadership trends and how this journey relates to your own journey or that of your organization. As you read, look for God's grace and guidance throughout the story.

The book's primary source material is the minutes of the meetings of the Wycliffe Bible Translators, Inc. Board that later became the Wycliffe International Board and then the Wycliffe Global Alliance Board. Also in the official archives were the minutes of all the international conferences for WBT. These sources raise the credibility of accuracy. As he worked through all the board minutes from 1942 to 2020, Franklin was alert for any indications that these boards had held a worldwide, or international, or global vision. Was it there from the start, or did it emerge over time? Was it just one leader developing such a vision if there was one, or was it several named people, or dozens of nameless people, who served on these boards over the years?

Assisting in the research by making board minutes available to Franklin, Wycliffe Global Alliance Board Secretary Matt Dawson, with his wife Janet, painstakingly scanned all the minutes that existed before the electronic age—originally typed copies, often carbon copies, and therefore hard to read. From the 1990s on, the minutes were already in electronic form. Accessing all the minutes as electronic versions made the task more feasible. The board met monthly in the early years, and the early conferences occurred every two years, providing ample material to identify key discussions and decisions that took place.

The board and conference minutes are probably not compelling reading to most people. But they proved to be a treasure, not just of facts, but of insights into how people were thinking. Finding treasure, however, takes some digging. Franklin often had to skim through page after page just to find one relevant entry that would help the research process. Admittedly, this introduces some level of subjectivity. Franklin and Van Wynen were also indirectly part of the history. From the 1990s onwards, both attended various WBT meetings and gatherings.

---

[4] Johnson, 239.

Van Wynen worked for Wycliffe International, then participated on Wycliffe Global Alliance's leadership team starting in 2008. Franklin joined the Wycliffe International Board in 2002 and then later became its executive director in 2008. Thus, the authors' perspectives came from an insider's vantage point.

Reading through the minutes and reports gave insights into the foundations of Wycliffe. As John Johnson states, this is important because they provide 'the lens of values, traditions, history, dreams, experience, competencies [and] culture.'[5] Wycliffe's history starts with its founder William Cameron Townsend, known to friends and colleagues as Cameron Townsend. He was not the kind of person that one might have imagined for such a task. As biographer William Svelmoe points out, Townsend was 'not the typical evangelical Bible institute graduate burning with a long and zealously nurtured passion for the lost heathen.'[6] Townsend himself admitted he was not a serious student of missions. He had read a pamphlet and the biography of David Livingstone, but that was about it.[7] Townsend did, however, believe he was obligated to go to Guatemala. He understood that he was obeying a calling from God, and that was all that mattered. He felt so strongly about this that he suspended his undergraduate studies with only a year to go. Townsend had no formal cross-cultural missionary training, spoke only broken, high school level Spanish, and his knowledge of the Bible was learned at church and from his parents. Svelmoe explains Townsend's lack of training by today's standards: 'Years of college and seminary were not required to tell the simple gospel story to souls perceived as lost. Linguistic and anthropological training was therefore virtually non-existent for prospective missionaries.'[8]

Townsend, and his southern California church friend and retired businessman William (Bill) Nyman, founded Wycliffe Bible Translators in 1942. Townsend asked Nyman for help to address the growing challenge of the lack of a US office to support Townsend's expanding field organization founded in 1934 and working in Mexico called the Summer Institute of Linguistics (SIL, now called SIL International). Nyman set up the first headquarters for WBT in his Glendale home. It had one main purpose: to be the resourcing organization for SIL.[9]

Another foundational factor is that Wycliffe started after the age of colonialism had peaked. The era was a time of nations repositioning themselves after the world wars and other calamities. Colonialism still existed, but it was already a time of questioning it and not just assuming colonial power and imperialism were here to stay. Wycliffe was born at the dawning of a new era of Christian mission.

---

5 Johnson, 239.

6 William Svelmoe, *A New Vision for Missions* (Tuscaloosa: University of Alabama Press, 2008), 1.

7 Svelmoe, 8.

8 Svelmoe, 630.

9 SIL's history is well-documented in other works and therefore is outside the scope of this book.

Historian Brian Stanley states, 'History is all about change, and the writing of history seeks to explain processes of change.'[10] Missiologist Pablo Deiros adds, 'Historical research helps us to know and understand what the Church has done in the fulfilment of its God-given mission, and thus what that mission is.'[11] Documenting the history of Wycliffe International becoming the Wycliffe Global Alliance serves the wider purpose of strengthening and deepening our understanding of how Christians and their ministries in nations around the world participate in global bodies and movements. Through the lenses of history, this journey gives an outline of 'the place to which we have been brought now' as Andrew Walls describes, and what may take shape in the future.[12] This book reminds us of the past and how we got to where we now stand. Our past gives us pointers and viewpoints to discern how we adjust and lead moving forward. The insights gained provide guidance toward future development of the Bible translation movement.

The Māori of New Zealand (*Aotearoa*) have a saying: '*Kia whakato muri te haere whakamua*', meaning we are 'travelling backwards in time to the future, with the present unfolding in front as a continuum into the past',[13] or paraphrased, I walk backwards into the future with my eyes fixed on my past. Stop and think about that for a moment. Looking into Wycliffe's past, we gain insights into what may lie ahead. This is relevant to our journey of exploring how Wycliffe grew from its US roots to a global movement during its nearly 80-year history.

Another aspect of the Māori proverb, according to Lesley Rameka, is how one's 'ancestors are ever present... existing both within the spiritual realm and in the physical, alongside the living as well as within the living.' Māori culture recognizes and takes pride in its 'ancestral heritage and... the contributions ancestors have made to tribal culture, etiquette and values.'[14] The folk religion of animism that has been prevalent among the Pacific Islands has associations with ancestral spirits of the dead. They may be malevolent or benevolent and, in both cases, must be respected. Without causing concerns of syncretism with animism and Christianity, the Pacific Islander worldview of honouring ancestors is worth considering in a study of the world Christian movement and the role of mission agencies. Ancestors of Wycliffe are ever-present, even though most have left this earth. We have their words in reports, board minutes, and other meeting records. We observe which

---

[10] Brian Stanley, *Christianity in the Twentieth Century: A World History* (Princeton: Princeton University Press, 2018), 313.

[11] Pablo A. Deiros, "Historical Research," in *Introduction to Missiological Research Design*, ed. Edgar Elliston (Pasadena: William Carey Library, 2011), 139.

[12] Andrew Walls, "Demographics, Power and the Gospel in the 21st Century," 2002.1.

[13] Ranginui Walker, *Ngā Pepa a Ranginui: The Walker Papers* (Auckland: Penguin, 1996), 14.

[14] Lesley Rameka, "Kia WhakatōMuri Te Haere Whakamua: 'I Walk Backwards into the Future with My Eyes Fixed on My Past'," *Contemporary Issues in Early Childhood* 17, no. 4 (2016): 388, https://dx.doi.org/10.1177/1463949116677923.

individuals played key roles and what the initial outcomes looked like. Learning from those who went before us, noting the historical markers they left and how they shaped the journey so far, we gain wisdom and understanding, and discover pointers to where our journey will take us. John Johnson observes, 'unless a leader goes back to the original vision, the initial steps of faith and the earliest dreams, and retells them, the leader will always be an outsider. One might charge into the future only to find that no one is following.'[15] Our ancestors in the Bible translation movement are ever present with us. We have their words in biographies, reports, and even board minutes. We want to understand how God worked through them—and in spite of them at times—as he does with all of us. We take our heritage from these ancestors. Learning from our predecessors is learning about how they sought to follow God. We want to continue to learn from them and how they shaped our journey. One day, we will be some of those ancestors.

In this book, we have used a hybridized (UK and US) English style. The source materials were predominantly in a US-style of spelling. Meanwhile, there was much UK English influence, and Regnum, our publisher, is British. Many acronyms are used throughout the book, though in general, we have tried to avoid them because multiple languages are used within Wycliffe, and also to refrain from exclusiveness. However, now as an alliance of organizations, we also must respect the many organizations known by their acronyms.

The book is structured in two parts. Part one contains the first seven chapters, is chronological, and covers eras of time. The Greek word *chronos* refers to the sequential measurement of time that moves in one direction from past to present. Typically, we measure time with our watches, diaries, and calendars. Each chapter presents a specific time frame, with the early chapters encompassing a decade or more and the later chapters covering five-year intervals due to more materials available to the authors in more recent years. There were no longer only minutes of board meetings and international conferences but reports and other unpublished works that mapped out Wycliffe's journey from Western to international to global. Material from the board minutes, reports to the board, and some correspondence gives the picture of developments that point to how and why Wycliffe started making decisions that would forever change its course in mission history. Each chapter begins by placing the era covered in context alongside the church, mission, and geopolitical factors of that time. Each chapter ends by aligning the era's prevalent leadership theories, indicating how they manifested in Wycliffe. The final part of each chapter presents reflections on features of Wycliffe's journey.

Part two, with the remaining five chapters, focusses on special opportune moments. Each chapter is such a moment. We've called this the *kairos* section

[15] Johnson, 240.

after the Greek word, which appears a few times in the New Testament. Kairos literally means the right time, an opportune time, a favourable moment, such as when chaos and courage collide. For example, in Matthew 16:1–3, Jesus is unhappy with some Pharisees and Sadducees because he observed that they could read the seasons they experienced but they didn't know how to 'interpret the signs of the times' (NIV). These chapters are topical (though some may also be chronological). Each of the five chapters in this section focus on *kairos* moments of Wycliffe's journey, which shaped the organization in profound ways. Thus, the topics covered here merit their own space and treatment.

In conclusion, this book seeks to address the concern that Pablo Deiros calls for in such work: 'Our identity as the body of Christ in mission in the world depends on our historical research on what we have done in the past to obey God's mission.'[16] We are very aware, as authors of this book, of how 'historical work invites humility as current conclusions can be adjusted by fresh research into the past, and current and future experimentation and thought. Integrity, critical thinking, and perseverance can, however, lead to warranted insights that both inform and inspire.'[17] It is our hope that you will experience such insights.

Dedication

A book like this would have been a dream to oversee for our friend and colleague, Dave Crough. He and his wife, Deborah (who edited this book), oversaw the editing and production of the precursor to this book, *Towards Global Missional Leadership*. Sadly, we lost our friend, brother in the Lord, and husband to Deborah. In 2019, Dave learned he had a rare form of cancer. His brave battle with the disease was brief. The Lord received him home in February 2020. We know that were he still alive, Dave would have wanted to be part of crafting this book, and to do so alongside Deborah, as they always had done.

We dedicate this book to Dave, who brought insights into Wycliffe's leadership at a critical time. He joined the leadership team in 2011, and with his inquisitive mind, kept asking, 'what is this "Alliance-ness" anyhow?' He was referring to the journey that Wycliffe had been on from its inception until then. Dave's probing became our gadfly. After much keen observation and pointed questioning, he got it, and became one of the greatest advocates for 'Allianceness'. Our hope for you, our readers, as you pursue this book with that same inquisitiveness, is that you will also come to understand 'Allianceness' and God's amazing work as he continues to allow us all to participate in his mission on paths and with plans we could never expect.

---

16 Deiros, in *Introduction to Missiological Research Design*, 140.

17 Charles E. Self, "Historical Research," in *Missiological Research: Interdisciplinary Foundations, Methods, and Integration*, ed. Marvin Gilbert, Alan R. Johnson, and Paul W. Lewis (Pasadena: William Carey Library, 2018), 155.

PART 1

CHRONOS EVENTS

Chapter 1
Founding: 1942–1965

Historical Context

People and organizations are products of their eras, influenced by the generations that precede them. Some organizations carve out a space and try to stay put, while others forge ahead as if compelled by the next horizon. Historical context, philosophies, ideas, trends, and the people involved all make their mark on any enterprise. In this book's chronological chapters, we look at the context and influences of the formation and ongoing shaping of WBT.

At the turn of the century, in 1900, approximately 95% of Christians lived in Europe and North America. At the 1910 Edinburgh Missionary Conference, there was a noticeable optimism concerning mission flowing through the discussions and plans for worldwide evangelization. The Great Commission was 'an inner principle of church faith and life' that gave freedom to churches and missions in how they interpreted and carried it out.[1] As Western mission became a formidable force, this conference 'represented the all-time high-water mark in Western missionary enthusiasm, the zenith of the optimistic and pragmatic approach to mission.'[2] It was no wonder since 'Christianity appeared to be ascending and moving from triumph to triumph.'[3]

Those present at the Edinburgh conference would be responsible for initiating a comprehensive plan for evangelization that was supposed to see the world 'reached' in the foreseeable future. The language of world dominion echoed through the corridors, with references, strategies, and plans that used military metaphors, such as crusade, conquest, and advance, based on the prevailing mood that fulfilling God's mission would signify Christianity's occupation of the world. There is also historical evidence which indicates the conference laid a foundation of 'co-operation and unity' for the ecumenical movement in mission that followed.[4]

South African missiologist David Bosch, recognizing the influences on modern missions, spoke of this era starting 'in the wake of the Enlightenment' and the

[1] David Hesselgrave, "The Great Commission," in *Evangelical Dictionary of World Missions*, ed. Scott Moreau (Grand Rapids: Baker Books, 2000), 413.

[2] Bosch, 338.

[3] John Mark Terry, and Robert Gallagher, *Encountering the History of Missions: From the Early Church to Today* (Grand Rapids: Baker Academic, 2017), 276.

[4] David Kerr, and Kenneth Ross, Edinburgh 2010: *Mission Then and Now* (Oxford: Regnum, 2009), 3.

Age of Reason.[5] That earlier age was still making its mark and causing ripples in academic, church, and societal circles. Though conservative Christendom rejected Darwinism and biblical higher criticism that, according to Edward Smither, 'caused many Christians to embrace liberal theology', it was still influenced by the rhetoric of the times that revered science and removed the limits to human endeavours.[6] Historian Stephen Neill observed, 'the wave of Western prestige and power' carried Christianity forward.[7] Just as British merchant ships had carried missionaries throughout the mighty Empire in the 1800s, secular thinking of the late 19th and early 20th centuries transported Christendom thinking to new places as well.

Innovation and new approaches marked the era as missionaries held 'a near legendary role' in their pioneering efforts.[8] Churches were planted, medical services provided, and educational institutions established. Most of this activity was 'closely patterned on Western models, funded by Western money, and controlled by Western personnel.'[9] The combination of the Student Volunteer Movement, the rapidly growing Bible institutes, and the nondenominational or interdenominational faith mission agencies focussed on historic tenets of the Christian faith. They were motivated by the Great Commission text of Matthew 28:18–20 (with some influence from Matthew 24:14 and Mark 16:15). Brian Stanley notes how 'fundamentalists and, later, evangelicals tended to define the goal of mission as the universal confession of Christ as Lord, with comparatively little attention being paid either to the hidden agency of the Spirit or to the achievement of the Father's redemptive purpose, extending to the renewal of creation.'[10]

This vision of what God could do through a nation, a missionary agency, and an individual devoted to furthering the Great Commission greatly influenced Cameron Townsend in 1917 as he left the US and headed by ship to Guatemala to sell Spanish Bibles. Anything was possible. But just as Townsend was optimistically venturing out, the tone of optimism around the world was being subdued by World War I (1914–1918) and the clash between the Allies and the Central Powers that swept Europe, involving the US and other parts of the Western world. The Russian Revolution in 1917 saw the rapid rise of Marxist Communism, an ideology that would impact generations to come.

Of course, Townsend wasn't the first to leave US shores with a vision for participating in the Great Commission. Many had gone before him. For example, in 1793, William and Dorothy Carey left the UK for India with the Particular Baptist

---

5 Bosch, 262.

6 Edward Smither, *Christian Mission: A Concise Global History* (Bellingham: Lexham Press, 2019), 149.

7 Stephen Neill, *A History of Christian Missions*, 2nd ed. (London: Penguin, 1986), 414.

8 Svelmoe, 18.

9 Stanley, 196.

10 Stanley, 196.

volunteer society, later called the Baptist Missionary Society, which introduced what became known as the modern missionary movement. In 1812, under the auspices of the American Board of Commissioners for Foreign Missions, 'the first American mission board',[11] Adoniram and Ann Judson, Samuel and Harriet Newell, Luther Rice, and Gordon Hall sailed for India. Later, other denominations joined in. The British led Western missions for well over a century. In 1922, at its height, the Great British Empire constituted about one-fifth of the world's population. Established over three centuries, this worldwide system of dependencies—colonies, protectorates, and other territories included almost a quarter of the world's landmass. 'The sun never sets on the British Empire' was an appropriate description. Then, as the British Empire decreased, the 'American Century' was just coming into its own.

The rise of American influence brought both positive and negative impacts. The Great Depression, triggered by the US stock market crash of 29 October 1929, spread to other Western countries over the next decade. Though Townsend was undoubtedly affected by these world events, his primary focus was elsewhere. As he developed a deeper understanding of the context in Latin America and developed rich relationships with local people, Townsend's convictions grew concerning those who did not speak Spanish. He started a linguistic school and training camp in 1934 with Leonard Livingstone (L. L.) Legters that grew into an academic organization called SIL. In 1942, he founded WBT. Based on Christian values, WBT would support Bible translation and fulfill Townsend's desire to reveal something of God's character and interaction with this world. The timing was God-ordained, as this took place during World War II (1939–1945). The war involved the great powers aligned in two opposing military groupings, the Allies and the Axis. At its peak, more than 100 million people served in military units. World maps were redrawn as territories were newly defined and conquered by nations including France, Germany, Japan, and Russia. The US emerged from World War II as the leading world power, although the USSR soon proved to be a strong rival and a threat to world peace. During the war, thousands of Allied young men and women had seen the world, its people, and their needs. Many Christians who served were just happy to be home again, while others started preparing to serve in missions. What began as the 'Great Century for Protestant Mission' eventually became a 'tumultuous century'.[12] There was no moving from 'triumph to triumph' as envisioned at Edinburgh.[13]

The early 20th-century optimism of Townsend, the growing global awareness brought by World War I, the persistence called for to get through the Depression,

[11] Terry, and Gallagher, 250.
[12] Terry, and Gallagher, 276.
[13] Terry, and Gallagher, 276.

and the influences and impact of World War II all combined to take Townsend and WBT forward on a path only God could know.

Founding Wycliffe Bible Translators

The turbulent 1930s–1940s were not the best times to start a new organization. But this did not deter Cameron Townsend. His faith was his defining attribute. In time, he became known for trusting God for the impossible.

When Townsend and his good friend and organization co-founder William (Bill) Nyman discussed names for the new organization, they thought of 'Pioneer Translation Agency' and 'Bible Translation Movement' but settled on Wycliffe Bible Translators.[14] The name was in honour of John Wycliffe (or Wyclif), who 'inspired, instigated and supervised the translation of the Bible into English from the [Latin] Vulgate.'[15] Historian William Svelmoe gives his opinion of the outcome of Townsend's decision, describing it as

> an unwieldy merger of three different organizations: (1) Camp Wycliffe, founded to train missionaries [under] any [mission] board to undertake pioneer work in Indian languages; (2) the Summer Institute of Linguistics, initially founded to provide an organization for translators from Camp Wycliffe who were not already committed to other boards and chose to join 'the Townsend group' in Mexico; and (3)... Wycliffe Bible Translators, which took over promotion and fundraising for both Camp Wycliffe and the Summer Institute of Linguistics....[16]

In reality, Townsend created two distinct organizations, SIL and WBT. The first, SIL, was based on the Camp Wycliffe courses initiated in 1934 that became a linguistics training institute and, at the time, operated exclusively in the summer. Townsend described SIL as a scientific linguistic organization that researched minority linguistic groups in many countries. Eventually, SIL also conducted academic courses at the University of Oklahoma and other institutions. Though focussed on linguistic research, the SIL staff was motivated by a desire to see the Scriptures available in these languages.

Before WBT began, there were already 46 members in SIL. Originally, Townsend had no intention of setting up a sending and support agency for SIL. Pioneer Mission Agency (PMA) of Philadelphia, a small mission, was willing to

---

[14] Svelmoe, 295.

[15] Kirk Franklin, "How Can the Reformation's Focus on Faithfulness to Scripture Inspire Us for Mission?," *HTS Teologiese Studies/Theological Studies* 74, no. 1 (2018): 2, https://dx.doi.org/10.4102/hts.v74i1.4817.

[16] Svelmoe, 252.

provide a US base and sponsorship for SIL's work. However, by 1942, SIL had added another 51 members, exceeding PMA's ability to support SIL, at which time Townsend decided to form WBT as the sending organization for SIL.

The new US-based WBT would facilitate the Christian public's understanding of what Townsend expressed as his 'burden of getting the Word of God to every tribe in its own tongue and a real concern of hastening the return of our Lord and the coming of that Great Day when we can look out on the throne of the redeemed from every tribe and nation and language, singing praises to God.'[17] In other words, WBT represented what this vision required (people, prayer, and finances) to the Christian public. Townsend's burden for 'hastening the return...' would continue to add to the appeal of supporting the Bible translation ministry. Over the years that followed, some supporters held to the idea that completion of Bible translations would clear the way for Christ to return.

As the two organizations continued to grow, Townsend understood that the dual nature of WBT and SIL confused the Christian public. Consequently, he and his colleagues regularly tried to clarify the relationship and the distinct identities of the two organizations, though often referred to as WBT-SIL, Wycliffe/SIL, SIL/WBT or SIL-WBT.

When the WBT Board granted membership to a recruit, it did so into what Townsend referred to as 'our group', meaning *both* WBT and SIL. At times, these same recruits became confused about the duality, and Townsend often had to tell his team something like this:

> Wycliffe is a little more peculiar than most. We're not sectarian, we're not promoting any denomination, any foreign institution. We are working on the languages and helping the governments that want to use our linguistic knowledge in... bilingual instruction and literacy, and... health matters. But our whole drive is directed toward giving the Bible to these language groups in their own tongues.[18]

Townsend wrote a position paper to clarify the distinctive of WBT, stating:

> Wycliffe Bible Translators, Inc. is not a mission.... We are a fellowship of scientific pioneers who are determined to see the Great Commission carried out and are willing to leave lesser details to ecclesiastical organizations. We are two organizations with a single vision. Or we can say we are one organization with three aspects: (1) the academic courses each summer; (2) the scientific linguistic research in many lands, and (3) the giving of the Word of God

[17] Cal Hibberd, Correspondence from W. Cameron Townsend, 1977.

[18] Cal Hibberd, Correspondence from W. Cameron Townsend, 1978.

> wherever we go. In a word, we are Wycliffe Bible Translators at the service of all.[19]

One might ask why Townsend emphasized his organization was a group of scientific pioneers. We must remember this was still in the Age of Reason when humans 'had faith... in themselves and in reason.'[20] Theological debates were swirling around the relationship between theology and science, and Christians were enamoured with science and took different positions on the discussion. Likewise, at the time, Townsend was positioning his work as a science and leaving theology in the hands of the theologians. From what we know of the time, some churches did not have a vision for translation as part of their ministry or mission endeavours, which may have influenced Townsend's thinking.

Very Early Years

The official name for WBT was Wycliffe Bible Translators, Incorporated (in the state of California), or abbreviated as WBT, Inc. Therefore, that is how we refer to it in the early years of this history. In looking at the development of WBT, Inc., we need to be aware of how it conducted its official business (such as with its board) and how it interacted in its close relationship with SIL. This is complex when reviewing WBT's historical documents because (1) WBT, Inc. Board minutes from 1942 onwards record discussions and actions that also refer to SIL and include Camp Wycliffe; (2) even though SIL was formed in 1934, it didn't hold its first board meeting until 1942. It then met at the same time, place, and with the same four directors as WBT. The same people were on both boards until 1996; and (3) although SIL and WBT created separate board meeting minutes, sometimes they were the same, and other times there were slight modifications between the two.

The WBT, Inc. Board's first meeting was in Mexico City on 15 September 1942, the same day and date that SIL and WBT incorporated as non-profit corporations in the state of California. Attending were William Cameron Townsend (general director), Kenneth Pike, William Nyman (secretary), and Eugene Nida. Decisions included:

- Granting an official charter to the Mexican Branch (of SIL).
- Commencing a 'perpetual written agreement with the Summer Institute of Linguistics... in which the personnel of its Directors shall be the same, both in name and numbers, and that the quorum required for doing business in both Corporations shall always be the same.'[21]

[19] Hugh Steven, *Doorway to the World* (Wheaton: Harold Shaw, 1999), 169.

[20] Bosch, 269.

[21] WBT, "Board Minutes," September 1942.

- Maintaining the headquarters for both organizations at Room 908, 357 South Hill Street, Los Angeles.
- Reading and adopting the new Corporation By-Laws and authorizing the secretary to contact three possible new board members.

The new bylaws stipulated there would be two categories of membership. The first consisted of 'Regular Members', described as people

> over the age of 21 who professed faith in the Lord Jesus Christ as their personal savior; who have satisfied themselves as to the principles and practices of this corporation and cordially approve of them and heartily desire to carry them out; have accepted without mental reservation the doctrinal statement of this corporation as herein set forth, both in letter and spirit; and are voting members of the Branch.[22]

This category included board directors from the time they were elected and for the length of their term of office. The second category was 'Honorary Members', people of 'eminence and distinction' who could be elected at the board's will but were not entitled to vote or hold any office in the corporation.[23]

The doctrinal basis of the corporation was

> formed under a deep sense of the world's pressing need, and with an earnest desire, constrained by the love of Christ and the hope of His coming, to obey His command to preach the gospel to every creature. Its aim is, by the help of God, to bring the Word of God, the Holy Bible, to all people in their own language.[24]

The board's second meeting was on 1 October 1942 at Glendale, California. Present were John Hubbard, Dawson Trotman (founder of the Navigators), E.S. Goodner, and William Nyman. The board decided that Townsend, as general director, would also be the board chairman. In his absence (which was most of the time since he lived in Mexico), Hubbard would fill in.[25] Subsequent meetings were held monthly in homes of board members in the Los Angeles area. Eventually, from 1949, the board members were elected from among their peers at the WBT, Inc. annual, and then biennial, Corporation Conference.

At the Glendale board meeting of 8 August 1943, there were 16 people welcomed as members of WBT, Inc., all from the US and all single—a good indicator

[22] WBT, "By-Laws," 1942, 2.

[23] WBT, 1942, 2.

[24] WBT, 1942, 2.

[25] WBT, "Board Minutes," October 1942, 1.

of how Townsend's work a year earlier was steadily growing.[26]

One of the values stated by the general director and discussed regularly was that SIL was to be 'field led'. The membership reinforced this when they stated positions such as: 'we continue our policy of direction on the field.'[27] Townsend formed this perspective from his earlier years serving as a missionary under the Central America Mission (CAM). CAM practised a form of governance where all decisions, including those on the field directly affecting missionaries and their work, were made by the executive council back in the US. Townsend disapproved of this approach. In practice, this meant WBT, Inc.'s primary purpose was to respond to the needs, requests, and opportunities it was regularly receiving from Townsend and his fellow leaders in SIL on the field. The WBT, Inc. Board adopted as policy the practice, from incorporation in 1942, of giving funds to SIL to enable it to finance its field work.[28]

Seeking to promote the work in the US, board member E.S. Goodner encouraged all WBT-SIL members to take prayer seriously through supporting WBT's work of starting prayer meetings in cities around the US. He also requested that every member do 'deputation work' (prayer and financial support raising) whenever they returned to the US. The board already had a policy of members spending a third of their furlough time doing deputation. Goodner also wanted to see interesting, well-written articles and stories about the linguistics-translation in Christian magazines such as *Moody Monthly*. These were indicators of a growing presence among the US Christian public.

Expansion

The first Annual Meeting of the WBT, Inc. Board (including the SIL Board) was held on 6 September 1943 at Cuernavaca, Mexico. Because the meeting was in Mexico, Townsend was also present, and he opened the meeting with a time of prayer, in which all the board members took part. The focus of the meeting was to discuss Townsend's and other members' ideas of expanding the work in South America. The board created basic policies to guide the expansion into and establishment of work in new fields. SIL policies important to WBT, Inc. as it related to the US Christian audience included: at least a portion of Scripture was translated 'for the tribe'; a group of people were taught to read the Word of God; and a 'nucleus of believers... were instructed in the Word'.[29]

WBT would seek cooperation with any evangelical mission or evangelical

[26] WBT, "Special Board Minutes," August 1943, 1.

[27] WBT, "Annual Meeting Motions," 1947, 3.

[28] WBT, "Board Minutes," December 1958, 3.

[29] WBT, "Board Minutes," September 1943, 2.

indigenous group if this collaboration met these conditions:

› The group had a doctrine compatible with Wycliffe.
› The group maintained a conservative financial policy (the board was concerned about financial extravagance).
› WBT held exclusive authority over the missionary.
› WBT approved all publicity for such work.
› WBT through SIL would provide 'every facility possible for the training of translators for all acceptable groups.'[30]

Townsend reminded the board of the organizations' call to 'pioneer work in so-called closed areas without encroaching on missionary boards now labouring in those fields, but rather cooperating with the missionary boards.'[31] He didn't want SIL competing with other missions working in the same locations. Furthermore, he was already receiving new missionaries who had joined other mission boards but now wanted to work with SIL.

At the 21 November 1943 WBT, Inc. Board meeting, held in Los Angeles, the board recommended that Townsend join Kenneth Pike in exploring the possibilities for other branches for the work in South America. Pike had already been to Peru, Bolivia, and Ecuador on a fact-finding visit. This follow-up trip was for Townsend to join Pike and determine whether SIL should expand, which it eventually did.

In 1944, Elvira Townsend died after a long illness. While greatly saddened at the loss of his wife, Townsend continued his quest to serve the Indian groups of Latin America. Two years later he met and married a Wycliffe member, Elaine Mielke. A few weeks after their honeymoon, they led a group of 20 recruits into the eastern rain forests of Peru to start a new work where there were at least 40 indigenous groups that had unwritten languages.

Growth and success brought new challenges for WBT, SIL, and Townsend. The Board of Directors based in the US and the WBT office in the Los Angeles area under Bill Nyman were functioning well. Likewise, SIL's work was growing in influence and impact. One challenge was that the team back in the US wanted Townsend to visit the US as often as possible to promote the ministry. During the board meeting of February 1944, they proposed that Townsend fit in a trip to the US to speak at various mission conferences. This became more and more of a juggling act as Townsend was general director over both US-based organizations, but living in Mexico. Other leaders within the two organizations, such as George Cowan, Eugene Nida, and Kenneth Pike, were increasingly called upon to speak at churches and mission conferences in the US.

[30] WBT, September 1943, 2.

[31] WBT, September 1943, 2.

In 1949, WBT joined the Interdenominational Foreign Missions Association (IFMA) in the US. However, in a reversal of this type of decision and to remain separate from US ecclesiastical bodies, the board decided in 1950 to decline an invitation to join the National Association of Evangelicals (NAE), citing 'the policy of our group... is not to affiliate in any way with organizations of this kind.'[32] Similarly, the board rejected a request for WBT to join the International Council of Christian Churches (ICCC) in 1952. Both actions are examples of Townsend and the board's desire to keep WBT's profile as a scientific organization rather than mission agency.

Growth with People

As WBT continued to grow, with more people wanting to join in linguistics and Bible translation for minority people groups, the board spent additional time during its monthly meeting making decisions about applicants. For example, in one of its meetings in 1949:

› Four single people were accepted 'without restrictions'.
› One was accepted 'with restrictions' (due to questionable physical health).
› Three couples and one single became 'approved candidates' because they had more training to do (Bible college or other formal education).
› Applications from nine individuals were postponed due to a variety of reasons (academic 'grades somewhat low', 'lack of training beyond high school', health checks not completed, or the applicant had applied to another mission at the same time).
› Ten people were rejected (because of 'lack of emotional stability', 'lack of personal adaptability', 'age differential—wife thirty-six, husband twenty-five', and because a candidate spoke in tongues, which at the time violated WBT's doctrinal policy of not accepting people who 'believe in speaking with tongues as evidence of the baptism of the... Holy Spirit').
› Applications of two individuals were withdrawn and one person resigned.[33]

New members were called Junior Members until they had served successfully for two years and passed a language assessment test. Then they became Senior Members, which allowed them to vote in legislative matters for WBT and SIL. In 1952, the board decided to allow 'properly qualified translators... into membership regardless of race, colour or nationality.'[34]However, the board's policy at the time was that it looked 'with disfavour on inter-marriages between racial groups'

[32] WBT, "Board Minutes," June 1950, 2.
[33] WBT, "Board Minutes," August 1949, 1.
[34] WBT, "Board Minutes," June 1952, 1.

without the prior consent of the board.[35]

While there was a steady stream of people wanting to join WBT and SIL in a longer-term capacity, the board also wanted to find people who could go for shorter-terms and fill critical needs assisting in the work. It created a category called Temporary Collaborators, later defined as Short Term Collaboratorship, for people who could go to the field for either three months or less, or three months to a year maximum.[36] Any stint longer than that required applying as a longer-term member.

Meanwhile, at the SIL courses (still called Camp Wycliffe) in Norman, Oklahoma, 235 students attended the first and second semesters in 1951, compared with 292 in 1950, and 205 in 1949. There were also 33 students from Canada in 1951, 38 in 1950, and 43 in 1949.

Growth through Promotion

The WBT Glendale office managed publicity to raise awareness of SIL's work and the resources required to sustain that work. This included the film *Oh for a Thousand Tongues* in 1950 and *Translation* magazine. A second film, *Each in His Own Tongue*, was launched in 1952, and a third film, *Unsheathed*, in 1957. The first two films used Moody Institute of Science's footage of SIL's work in Mexico and South America.

Townsend's biography on his friend Lazaro Cardenas, President of Mexico, was doing well among audiences in the US and Mexico. Other early books that helped WBT promote the vision of linguistics and Bible translation were *Not Alone* by Eunice Pike, and *He Purposeth a Crop* by Ethel Wallis (3,000 copies sold out in seven months). By 1959, the board created a Wycliffe film program and a perpetual fund with $25,000 through gifts and income generated from film showings. The fund would cover the production of films. A creative committee of four members approved the story content of any authorized film. In 1959, Clarence Hall authored a book titled *Adventurers for God*, which included a chapter on Townsend and WBT called 'Two Thousand Tongues to Go' and was featured in *Reader's Digest* magazine. At that time, with more than 10 million subscribers in the US and many more around the globe, the magazine had the largest circulation of any in the world.[37] In response, within a few months, WBT received 2,049 letters and gifts totalling $14,528. In 1965, Bob Russell released his book, *Farewell to Eden*, featuring the work among the Amahuaca people. WBT sold copies of the book at the World's Fair Pavilion in 1965.

---

35 WBT, June 1952, 1.

36 WBT, "Board Minutes," August 1960, 3.

37 New York Times, https://www.nytimes.com/2010/10/03/nyregion/03bookwe.html (accessed 21 August 2020).

These and other forms of literature helped spread the vision among US Christians. Not only did this result in more people registering to attend SIL schools as a prerequisite for linguistic and Bible translation ministry, but it also saw an increase in funds given to WBT for the work. For example, the WBT Treasurer reported in June 1951 that donations in May totalled $21,420. Of this, $3,000 was undesignated, and the rest was for members' support. However, the undesignated amount was insufficient because it only met 69% of the needs that month for the home office and all the work it did to promote SIL's needs on the field. Funding the growing organizations created challenges for the WBT Board. Quite simply, the 5% of the 10%-member income that was retained for the Glendale office was inadequate (the other 5% went to the field where members were assigned). In response, the board wanted to amend the Constitution to raise the assessment of all gifts from 10% to 11%. The rationale was that the 1% increase would enable salaries for headquarters staff and allow the team to increase as necessary. The membership at the 1959 Corporation Conference rejected the change.

Leadership Appointments

In 1957, at the election of officers for the WBT Corporation, Cameron Townsend was reappointed as general director for another five years, Richard Pittman as deputy general director, George Cowan as president (i.e., chairman of the board), E.S. Goodner as vice president, William (Bill) Nyman as secretary, Kenneth Watters as treasurer, George Cowan as extension director, and Otis Leal as candidate secretary. Earlier in 1949, Kenneth Pike became executive director of the Summer Institute of Linguistics (Camp Wycliffe), and Eugene Nida, associate director of the SIL school at Norman, Oklahoma.

In May 1960, Nyman resigned as secretary from WBT and SIL due to ill health and 'advanced years'.[38] This concluded a fruitful 18-year term of service, particularly with WBT in its formative years. Kenneth Watters, treasurer, was given the additional responsibilities Nyman held. After Nyman's passing in 1961, the board expressed 'profound gratitude to God for the many years of faithful service... on behalf of our 1,124 members scattered throughout the world.'[39]

The next appointments were made in 1963, with Richard Pittman as deputy general director for the Far East and South Pacific, Benjamin Elson as deputy general director for the North American Continent (from Panama to Canada), and George Cowan as deputy general director for Europe and Africa. Cameron Townsend continued as general director and Cowan as president. Lorin Griset was elected as vice president, Philip Grossman as secretary, and Kenneth Watters as treasurer.

---

[38] WBT, "Board Minutes," May 1960, 1.

[39] WBT, "Board Letter to family of William Nyman," January 1961.

Westernizing

Canada

Expansion outside of the US started when the WBT Board approved the creation of 'Canada Wycliffe' in December 1943.[40] In 1944, SIL linguists accepted an invitation to run an SIL training school in Canada with 40 students. In 1949, the board appointed George Cowan, a Canadian, as executive director of SIL in Canada (Canadian Camp Wycliffe) and Richard Pittman as associate director. In September 1950, Pittman brought the application of 14 Canadians to the WBT, Inc. Board. Most were given membership in WBT, Inc. (meaning the US), with a few delayed or rejected for various reasons.

At the 1953 Biennial Meeting of WBT, Inc., the delegates asked the general director (Townsend) to investigate the procedure of incorporating WBT in Canada, to strengthen the Moose Jaw Committee (First Nations work), to strengthen the Toronto Committee (promoting Bible translation), and to 'study more seriously the possibility of using the Advance Linguistics Workshop in Canadian SIL to train prospective workers.'[41] Within a year, Wycliffe in Canada was exploring incorporation.

The Canadian government's Deputy Minister of National Affairs suggested the incorporation of WBT of Canada with the Glendale Board as the parent organization. The benefits were owning property and having a presence with the Christian public. The WBT US Board tabled the recommendation but authorized the Glendale office to incorporate a branch in Canada called Wycliffe Bible Translators of Canada. In 1955, WBT, Inc. appointed the Board of Canada SIL and Wycliffe Bible Translators of Canada as misters Whittaker, Blager, Murihead, and George Cowan.

At the 1963 WBT, Inc. Corporation Conference, the Canadian representatives asked the WBT, Inc. Board to pursue: '1. ... [an] organized group of responsible men promoting Wycliffe interests in Canada; 2. a serious search, looking to the Lord, for such men who might be recommended to the Board for appointment to a Canadian Council.'[42]

The fact that the WBT, Inc. Board was still in charge of Wycliffe in Canada was noted in May 1959 when the board approved that a Canadian be appointed as Eastern Canada representative after the incumbent had resigned. The Canada operations were listed on the WBT, Inc. budget. For example, in 1965, the budget showed the Calgary Office was allocated $5,400 for its annual operations in Fiscal Year 1966.

[40] WBT, "Board Minutes," December 1943, 1.

[41] WBT, "Board Minute Extracts," 1953, 5.

[42] WBT, "Corporation Conference Extracts of Minutes," May 1963, 3.

Australia

In 1949 the IFMA invited Kenneth Pike and his wife Evelyn to come to Melbourne, Australia and head up the Wycliffe School for Linguistics for Missionaries. The WBT, Inc. Board prayed for the Pikes at a special service and prayer meeting at Calvary Bible Church in Santa Ana, California, as the trip came together. The board called this trip the 'Australia Advance',[43] and gave US $200 from the WBT Glendale office's fund. The first Australian SIL course ran in the early 1950. Richard Pittman visited the second course in early 1951 and reported to the WBT, Inc. Board about the 'success of the school in Melbourne and the splendid cooperation received from all of our friends in that part of the world.'[44] The WBT, Inc. Board started calling this work the 'Australian Wycliffe'.[45]

Pittman made another visit to Australia in 1954 to communicate the WBT, Inc. Board's decisions: endorsed the operation of the Australian Branch of Wycliffe Bible Translators, Inc., in Melbourne; approved the first officers and members of the Australian Home Council; approved the acceptance of the first five candidates for service (Harland and Marie Kerr, Howard and Lynette Oates, Mary Short) to be assigned to SIL's new work in the Philippines. The Australian Council accepted four more new members in 1955 for assignments in the Philippines.

The WBT, Inc. Board retained its responsibilities for the Australian operations, evidenced when 'Mr J.H. McCracken [was appointed] as Acting Chairman of the Australian Branch during Mr Hepburn's absence.'[46]

As the Australian work grew, the WBT, Inc. Board decided that 5% 'of all funds assessed that emanates from Australia should be returned to Australia to finance their office' and 5% 'of all funds assessed, regardless of the source, is to be given to the field office [i.e., SIL operations].'[47] This was an example of the 10% assessment policy as Wycliffe became more internationalized.

Robert Story, who headed up the Australian Council, actually worked for the Unevangelized Fields Mission (UFM). After hearing Story share at the 1955 WBT Corporation Conference, this cable message was sent to the Australian Council: 'Story's presentation [of] translation needs [in] New Guinea challenges tremendously. Please loan him to us till November 30th to recruit volunteers among Bible institutes, seminaries. Story in agreement. Signed, Pike, Nyman, Townsend.'[48]

Later in 1955, representing the Australian Council, Story went on a 'deputation tour' of the US and Canada. While in the US, he told the WBT, Inc. Board:

---

43 WBT, "Board Minutes," December 1949, 1.

44 WBT, "Board Minutes," May 1951, 2.

45 WBT, "Board Minutes," August 1951, 1.

46 WBT, "Board Minutes," June 1954, 1.

47 WBT, "Board Minutes," September 1954, 1.

48 WBT, "Corporation Motions," September 1955, 3.

> [In Australia,] Christian leaders and school staff instructors, as well as students, were usually favourably impressed with the challenge to carry God's Word to the Bibleless tribespeople of the South Pacific regions, assuring continuing interest in the needy area should it be possible to follow up with contacts made, with further information, or [as] the advance is launched.[49]

By agreement between WBT, Inc. and the Australian Council, SIL's work spread to the South Pacific through the 'New Guinea Advance' because Australia was the colonial government administering the then Territory of New Guinea (along with the Territory of Papua, which became the independent nation of Papua New Guinea in 1975). While the Australian Council oversaw the new work, the WBT, Inc. Board sought to appoint the first director, James Dean from Canada, and the Council agreed. Seeking to have a good relationship with the Council, the board sent Richard Pittman to visit the Council to finalize policies of 'handling the quota between Australian and US personnel, the division of personnel on the field, the directorship of the branch, and any other matters relating to the relationship between the US and Australian directorship.'[50]

At the 1957 WBT Corporation Meeting (in the US), a comprehensive agreement was prepared for negotiation with the Australian Council to formalize Wycliffe Bible Translators, Inc. Australia. Alfred Coombe represented Australia. From this meeting, a critical clause resulted: 'While it is mutually agreed that the WBT, Inc., Australia, be allowed a fair measure of autonomy, the WBT, Inc., Australia, recognizes the final authority of the WBT, Inc., California.'[51]

The subsequent development occurred in 1958 as an agreement between the WBT, Inc. Board and the Australian Council concerning how the two bodies would cooperate with the 'South Pacific Division' which was Australia, it's territories (e.g., New Guinea), and New Zealand.[52] Pittman reported to the board in March 1958 from his visit to Australia: 'The school was the largest that had yet been enrolled and... it looked as though we would be receiving a dozen or more WBT members there.' While in Australia, Pittman also discussed 'a possible advance into the aboriginal tribes' with the leaders.[53] The board set up an Australian Emergency Support scheme of US funds to assist Australian members who lacked adequate financial support. All members of Wycliffe, not just the Australians, benefited from an Emergency Support Fund that brought up their monthly financial quota to a pre-determined amount, based on available and undesignated funds

49 WBT, "Board Minutes," November 1955, 1.

50 WBT, "Board Minutes," January 1956, 1.

51 WBT, "Corporation Motions," September 1957, 3.

52 WBT, "Board Minutes," February 1958, 1.

53 WBT, "Board Minutes," March 1958, 1.

that were under the authority of the Glendale, California office. Money for this fund also came from a gift of $100,000 held in trust and included the interest from this gift. The WBT, Inc. treasurer reported at the October 1959 board meeting that the surplus of the fund was decreasing, although those in need had seen the fund pay up to 80% of their financial quota. Due to general demands on this fund, by 1961, it could only pay for 65% of a member's quota.

In 1958, the WBT, Inc. Board welcomed 12 new Australian members, and a year later, there were 14 more, including David and Ruth Cummings. David Cummings would later become Wycliffe Australia's first director. All were assigned to New Guinea.

In May 1964, the WBT, Inc. Board granted charter to the Australian Home Branch (not to be confused with the SIL Australian Aborigines Branch). This meant Wycliffe Australia could be formally represented at the Corporation Conferences. At the same time, a 'South Pacific Division' was established. It consisted of 'representatives from Australia, New Zealand, Territory of New Guinea, and other islands south of the equator (not the Philippines, which would [be included in] a North Pacific or Asia division).'[54] Richard Pittman was appointed the deputy general director for the Pacific and India.

New Zealand

In 1963, the WBT, Inc. Board rejoiced to hear how Christians in New Zealand had a 'burden of reaching Bibleless tribes' and local plans to start a New Zealand Council.[55] The board gave these plans its full endorsement, suggesting that it should happen in concert with the Australian Council and School. The board recommended that the New Zealand Council send a representative to the Australian Council meetings whenever New Zealand candidates from the SIL School were under consideration for membership. The board looked to the Australian Council, because of its long experience and closer proximity, to support the development of New Zealand as a sending country for Bible translators.

Great Britain

At the Corporation Meeting of SIL in 1951, delegates went on record to give 'priority to the establishment of an institute in Europe, presumably in Great Britain.'[56] This began to happen in 1953 when several mission agencies and churches in

[54] WBT, "Board Minutes," June 1965, 4.

[55] WBT, "Board Minutes," May 1963, 3.

[56] SIL, "Corporation Motions," 1951, 1.

Great Britain invited SIL to hold an 11-week school called the Wycliffe Language Course, hosted at the London Bible College. Ken Pike and George Cowan taught its 14 students. In 1956, the WBT, Inc. Board accepted the first eight people from the course as Approved Candidates or Junior Members. The board expected all candidates to attend the Jungle Training Camp in Mexico.

One of the first students to catch the vision for linguistics and Bible translation was John Bendor-Samuel. In 1957, the WBT, Inc. Board appointed him to be assistant director for Wycliffe Bible Translators, Inc. in England (where George Cowan was director from 1957 to 1960).

In 1956, as interest continued to grow, the WBT, Inc. Board discussed a report from Mr Hoxham, WBT's representative in England, to consider incorporating the Wycliffe Language Course to benefit from English income tax laws appropriate to English controlled charitable organizations.

WBT, Inc. and the Wycliffe Language Course developed an agreement in 1957 that spelled out procedures for candidates from Great Britain. This included the roles of the British Wycliffe Advisory Committee and the British WBT Director and Assistant Director in processing candidates and recommending them to the WBT, Inc. Board in the US. In April 1958, Cowan worked out with the board a 'temporary ruling by the British Committee... to expedite and avoid any delay in the US for [new] British members... who have already sailed from England', where the members concerned were able to 'draw upon... British undesignated funds in Glendale for their passage money to their permanent fields.'[57] This plan meant that new British members wouldn't get financially stranded in the US while attending further SIL summer school training and then Jungle Camp in Mexico.

Subsequent negotiations addressed the concern from the British office about the financial difficulty for their members to return to the UK to raise additional funds, once they had arrived in the US, received their training, and proceeded to assignments in South America. This was difficult because of the length of travel, which at the time was by ship. Later it was decided that, when accepted as candidates or Junior Members, British members would receive tentative field assignments, to be reviewed after completing training in North America, addressing any issues which might prevent advancement to field assignment.

In September 1959, growth from the UK continued when the WBT, Inc. Board accepted nine single people as candidates from England. The board was also active in other aspects of the work in the UK. It approved new members and their terms of service on the British Advisory Council and received annual audited financial reports, which, when signed by the chairman, were approved by the board. Upon Cowan's recommendation, the board approved the policy that British members

[57] WBT, "Board Minutes," April 1958, 2.

address their prayer letters with the London headquarters address, rather than the US address, including on their letterheads the phrase 'Headquarters in the U.S.A'.[58] This was later changed to simply state, 'British Office—Wycliffe Bible Translators, Inc'.[59] In 1962, WBT, Inc. loaned the British Council $10,000 at 4.75% interest to purchase 'headquarters property in England for use for both Wycliffe Bible Translators and Wycliffe Language Course facilities.'[60] The council agreed to repay the loan within ten years.

The WBT, Inc. Board, at its May 1963 meeting, expressed its appreciation for the fellowship with the British Advisory Council in the work of Bible translation. The council was encouraged to proceed with its Memorandum of Articles of Association for a Wycliffe Bible Translators Limited Company and a Constitution for a Branch of Wycliffe Bible Translators in Great Britain. The board would approve these documents and processes when the council had them endorsed by their British membership.

In 1961, the WBT, Inc. Board encouraged the British Council to take steps toward becoming a chartered Home Council and legal incorporation in Great Britain. Due to closer proximity and the involvement of John Bendor-Samuel in visiting West Africa, the board requested that the British Council 'make the West Africa advance an area for which they... accept special administrative participation.'[61]

Western Europe

In 1957, Kenneth Pike spoke at the 8th International Congress of Linguistics in Oslo, Norway. The WBT, Inc. Board wanted Pike, while there, to 'probe future possibilities for schools or other ways of implementing... future advances in that area of the world.'[62]

The WBT, Inc. Board authorized Paul Lilienberg of Sweden in 1961 to open a bank account in WBT's name for the withdrawal and deposit of funds for his work representing WBT in Sweden. In 1965, Marinus Wiering became the Wycliffe Representative for Holland.

Paul Meier became the Swiss representative of WBT, Inc. in Switzerland in 1959. He commenced his application for membership to WBT through the British Advisory Council in 1961 and attended the Bible Training Institute of Glasgow. Similarly, Erika Wiesmann, from Germany, also saw her candidacy processed through the British Advisory Council. In 1964, Friedhelm Frische from Switzerland

---

58 WBT, "Board Minutes," July 1958, 2.

59 WBT, "Board Minutes," October 1958, 1

60 WBT, "Board Minutes," June 1962, 2.

61 WBT, "Board Minutes," September 1961, 17.

62 WBT, "Board Minutes," August 1956, 4.

was accepted by the WBT, Inc. Board as an approved candidate, pending completion of Bible school training.

In 1958, Wilfried Zibell contacted WBT about serving as a representative in Germany, using Wycliffe films and literature from the US to promote the ministry. Later the same year, Hugo Schrieber was approved as Wycliffe's official representative in Germany.

In 1961, delegates of the WBT Corporation Conference made this statement of support—signed by George Cowan of WBT, Inc. and Kenneth Pike of SIL, Inc.—to the sponsoring committee and staff of the proposed linguistic school in Germany:

> Resolved that in dependence upon God for His guidance, and with deep appreciation of our brethren who have accepted the long-range responsibility of sponsoring a linguistic school in Germany... we are acutely aware of the tremendous task of giving the Word of God to two thousand tribes. We well know that one national group alone cannot shoulder this heavy burden. We welcome, therefore, the efforts of those of like mind and spirit who will help to train students for this task and enrol some of them, in addition, into the field program of the Wycliffe Bible Translators, Inc., and the Summer Institute of Linguistics, Inc., toward this end. [63]

In 1961, several Germans attended the annual SIL course in the UK. Eventually, SIL set up a course in Germany, and in 1962, Wycliff e.V. (eingetragener Verein, registered association) was founded to handle the administrative responsibilities. In the same year, Wycliff e.V. registered with the German authorities to further the work of WBT and SIL. The WBT, Inc. Board expressed its gratitude to Wycliff e.V. for taking this action, and to all who had worked hard on developing the German equivalent of the SIL course. Wilfried Zibell was appointed as the director until his departure for a field assignment, at which point Gerhard Fast took his place.

In summary, the training offered by SIL spread to Australia and Great Britain, then to Germany. Christians from these and other nations, such as Switzerland, undertook the training, applied to WBT, and were accepted for field assignments with SIL. The emerging structures of Australia and the UK were legally registered as Wycliffe in those countries and had formal recognition as subsidiaries of WBT US. Internally, this meant they were initially called Branches of WBT, Inc., with the US as headquarters. Later, they were called Divisions of WBT, Inc. As interest in Wycliffe and Bible translation grew in Western Europe, new Divisions of WBT were formed, such as Wycliff e.V. (Germany) in 1963, and Wycliffe Switzerland in 1964.

---

[63] WBT, "Corporation Conference Motions," September 1961, 20.

West Africa

In 1961, the WBT Corporation Conference discussed the involvement of nationals (the term used at that time to refer to people working in translation in their own countries) where there was no SIL or WBT presence. They considered ideas such as encouraging local citizens to form their own national Bible translation agencies comparable to WBT; WBT members helping to form and operate national organizations without becoming members of those organizations; and SIL Branches assigning nationals to serve with them. However, the conference didn't reach a consensus, and further discussion on the topic was postponed. We learn more about this in chapter 8.

In 1959, Ghanaian statesman John Agama asked SIL to help translate the Bible into Ghanaian languages. In December 1961, John Bendor-Samuel arrived in Ghana and worked out a cooperative agreement between SIL and the Institute of African Studies at the University of Ghana.

Bendor-Samuel also travelled to other West African countries in 1960–61 under the auspices of the WBT UK Home Council. He gave a written report to the WBT, Inc. Board outlining all the opportunities for Bible translation in Ghana and West Africa. Consequently, the board responded with this support:

> Under a deep sense of our responsibility to press on until every tribe is reached with the Scriptures, and reminded [by] many factors of the urgency of the situation in Africa today, together with the danger of unnecessarily delaying positive action on the preliminary survey report of Dr. John Bendor-Samuel to West Africa, and in view of the unanimity of feeling expressed by our General Director, British Advisory Council, and others of our leaders, [we] authorise... steps to implement the advance. [64]

This advance included appointing leadership oversight, assigning new personnel to the region, and informing the Christian public of this opportunity to enter Africa.

Standardizing English

As WBT's work was growing inside and outside of the US, the WBT, Inc. Board requested a study of operations of the candidate application process by countries where WBT operated, aiming to standardize and improve candidate procedures.

Many new WBT enquirers were from countries whose national language wasn't English. WBT was an international organization, and by historical precedent, kept

[64] WBT, "Board Minutes," September 1960, 1.

all records and issued all corporation level communications in English. In 1964, the WBT, Inc. Board decided to make English the official language of WBT. The board also required an adequate knowledge of English as a universal requirement for Senior membership. A new member was only assigned to a specific field when it was clear that the member could adequately communicate with colleagues.

International Board Idea

In 1960, the WBT, Inc. Board discussed a proposal from John Bendor-Samuel regarding establishing an International Board of Directors. The board felt there were these merits to the idea:

› The highest governing body was the Corporation Conference, and it was international in membership.
› Council members from countries other than the US were seated at the Corporation Conference as delegates.
› There could be additions of non-Americans to the board of directors (in addition to Canadian George Cowan), since the leadership of chartered branches could be in the hands of members from countries other than the US from time to time.
› An international board's members could be spread around the world, which meant in practice that the board met less often, such as every two years. Since this coincided with the Corporation Conference, the board could handle the same decisions as the Conference (this was before the age of frequent international air travel).[65]

While these reasons were compelling, the board didn't take any action, and it would be another 20 years before the concept gained attention.

International Procedures

Recognizing that there would likely be further growth of WBT in new countries, in 1961, the board set up the following procedures regarding the opening of WBT offices:

› Initial materials such as literature and films came from and were paid for by the headquarters office in Santa Ana.
› Finances were to be handled according to the pattern established in Great Britain.
› New Wycliffe work was under the responsibility of the WBT Extension Director until the WBT, Inc. Board could establish a Home Council.[66]

---

[65] WBT, "Board Minutes," May 1960, 3.
[66] WBT, "Board Minutes," March 1961, 1.

The WBT, Inc. Board updated the representation of WBT in a new country in 1965. Where WBT was known, but no work existed, the process was:

- A representative of the WBT, Inc. Board could seek out a suitable male candidate to head up a council (at this time only male applicants were considered; there was no reference to women).
- The council prayerfully invited the person to consider joining the council.
- Those invited included people who had already shown interest in Wycliffe.
- They were to be 'sound in the faith' in whatever church they worshipped.
- They had to sign the WBT doctrinal statement.
- They needed to be of good reputation in the circles in which they moved.
- They were to be appointed for a limited term by the WBT, Inc. Board on the recommendation of the WBT Deputy General Director.

If Wycliffe was unknown, the process was:

- A WBT, Inc. Board representative searched for suitable persons and invited them to prayerfully consider acting in specific functions on behalf of Wycliffe.
- Each person was appointed for a limited term by the board on the recommendation of the deputy general director.

If it was appropriate to establish a Wycliffe Home Council, then the WBT, Inc. Board had this procedure:

- The new council was authorized to use Wycliffe Bible Translators' name and to act for it, subject to the control of the WBT Deputy General Director.
- The deputy general director could also approve the new council to operate under the auspices of another chartered or authorized branch of WBT in its area.
- Any authority given to a home council by the WBT, Inc. Board could vary according to local, geographical, and cultural conditions.
- The council would direct a local candidate program (e.g., recruit, orient, recommend to the WBT, Inc. Board to accept or reject an applicant); handle publicity (news releases, prayer bulletins, arrange speakers for churches and student groups, distribute Wycliffe films, arrange exhibits); oversee activities of personnel in their home area (supervise deputation of new workers, arrange furlough programs, etc.); develop prayer circles; develop local representatives; promote the financial welfare of the members with a view of raising local support for local workers; consider discipline cases with people from its area and make recommendations to the WBT, Inc. Board.[67]

[67] WBT, "Corporation Conference Minutes," 1963, 3-4.

Separating Domestic from International

At the 1963 Corporate Conference, there was a lengthy discussion on the concept of a US (domestic) operational structure distinct from an international one. The suggestion of separate home councils in the US and Canada rather than the then-current joint one, which also handled matters from Australia and the UK and the occasional interests from other Western countries, triggered this response.

Interestingly, 21 years earlier in the incorporation of WBT, provision was made for the appointment by the WBT, Inc. Board of various kinds of councils or representative groups to help in presenting, supporting, and gaining confidence for the work. An example was WBT representatives in the US and Canada. However, the growing challenge WBT was facing was how its representatives lacked the status of formal participation in the Corporation Conference or access to the WBT, Inc. Board. When discussed in 1963, this aroused feelings of 'taxation without representation' and the 'need of "belonging" to [WBT] in some deeper way.'[68] Others thought the system was working since WBT, Inc. (therefore the US) supported those who represented WBT in Canada.

Reassessment of the system was forced with the advent of the representative work in Australia. It was so far away (this was before the age of mass commercial international air travel) that it was 'essential that a much greater measure of control of local matters be placed in the hands of the Australians themselves.'[69] Practically, this meant there were subtle differences in wording made by the Australians in materials, documents, policies, application forms, etc., from the US office. The work in Australia was initially under IFMA and the committee representing Wycliffe consisted of the same people. Therefore, a comprehensive agreement was drawn up between WBT, Inc. and this committee, later called the Australian Council, to represent Wycliffe and act on behalf of WBT, Inc. in Australia.

The work started differently in the UK, with WBT, Inc. taking full authority and responsibility for the Wycliffe Language School and the Wycliffe representative work. However, when it came time to hold the biennial Corporation Conference, WBT leaders noted how it was an 'embarrassment... not to give a voice to our Australian and British helpers' so WBT, Inc. took extra-constitutional action to appoint these people as official representatives to the Corporation Conference.[70]

The WBT, Inc. Board noticed how it had to give greater attention to 'international matters' initially presumed to be 'domestic'.[71] As it grew domestically in the

---

68 WBT, 1963, 1.

69 WBT, 1963, 2.

70 WBT, 1963, 2.

71 WBT, 1963, 3.

US and internationally through other WBTs, regardless of whether or not there were home councils, the difference between international and domestic functions needed clarification for WBT to operate efficiently.

Up to this point, WBT made the difference between international and domestic functions in this way:

- International: responsible for publicity materials, library file of all types of publications, candidates (setting of policies, ratification of candidates after Home Council's approval), members in training (assignments to the fields), financial oversight (uniform financial procedures, audit of Corporation finances, control of emergency support), and general oversight of SIL schools.
- Domestic: responsible for local publicity matters, promotion of the work, handling candidates, handling and transmission of local funds, and oversight of local SIL schools.[72]

The 1963 Corporation Conference identified these levels of home councils:

- Advisory Home Council, unchartered: primarily as a board of reference in a given country; no representation on the WBT, Inc. Board.
- Home Council, chartered: limited to WBT representative functions in a given country; one council member could sit on the International Board.
- Home Council with charter, limited to representative functions: represented Wycliffe in a given country and processed initial enquiries through to application for membership; one council member was able to sit on the International Board.
- Home Council with charter limited to representation, promotion, recruitment, and candidate processing functions: represented Wycliffe in a given country, processed initial enquiries, application for membership, and granting of provisional membership; one council member was able to sit on the International Board.
- Home Council with full charter: represented Wycliffe in a given country; processed initial enquiries, application for membership, granting of membership, and complete handling of personnel and financial matters; one council member was able to sit on the International Board.[73]

The 1963 Corporation Conference delegates recognized multiple advantages of having various WBT Home Councils: to spread the workload from the WBT, Inc. Board; to extend the sense of responsibility for the future of the ministry; to share the financial burden of the growing international administrative and board level support; to increase the pool of people with executive responsibility; to better

---

[72] WBT, 1963, 4-5.

[73] WBT, "Conference Supplement Minutes," 1963, 7-8.

represent the home constituency; and to better facilitate functioning because of geographical distance from the US. Disadvantages included: a growing number of Home Councils would be harder for the WBT, Inc. Board and leadership to manage; a more significant financial burden because not all Home Councils would be self-supporting; the burden of paying for an international administration; the necessity of training Home Council members would greatly increase; sorting out what was domestic (i.e. US) and international would be more complex; and shifting from the current international operations to domestic operations could mean few people would remain to serve in the international office.

International Headquarters Search

Facing the fact that WBT and SIL were growing rapidly, general director Cameron Townsend had the WBT, Inc. Board's approval in 1959 to write to A.J. McFadden, president of The Irvine Ranch Company of Santa Ana, California. In his letter, Townsend wanted McFadden to look with favour on Townsend's request for an international headquarters because it wasn't going to be long until WBT and SIL had 'several thousand members abroad.'[74] Townsend wanted to keep this in the Orange County area, near greater Los Angeles, because it was where the 'project of giving alphabets and the Bible to all the primitive tribes of the world was first planned.'[75] The current and too small Glendale office was in the greater Los Angeles area. Ranch land and former orchards across Orange County were now on the real estate market as Southern California entered a boom era. Townsend wanted

> 150 acres... to subdivide and sell to members and their close relatives or financial backers.... Within ten or twenty years [there] would be a community of 2,000 people and 750 homes, besides our own buildings and staff. This unique little city would be called BIBLE TOWN and might well become an attraction for Bible lovers from all over the U.S.A. and Canada when visiting California.

The plan called for an 'attractive museum' of artefacts from around the world where WBT members worked.[76] Townsend further envisioned a small airport that would serve JAARS and the wider community. He wasn't sure how this ambitious project could be funded, so he considered charging rent that would go towards the title deed for the 200 acres.

While the board and Townsend waited to hear from McFadden, they investigated other properties in southern California—in Costa Mesa, Ventura, and

---

[74] Cameron Townsend, correspondence, 24 February 1959, 1

[75] Townsend, 1.

[76] Townsend, 1.

Eagle Rock near downtown Los Angeles.[77] The board wrote to the Secretary of Health, Education, and Welfare requesting to purchase property owned by the US government on the Santa Ana Army Air Base, located in Costa Mesa. The letter was signed 'Board of Directors, Summer Institute of Linguistics, affiliated with Wycliffe Bible Translators, Inc.'[78]

Right before Townsend died in 1982, he conveyed to a friend that he couldn't understand why the board didn't see the pursuit of the Irvine Ranch property as a good thing. McFadden's company said that they would give Townsend the land just across the street from the small grass airstrip which is now John Wayne Airport (SNA). Today that busy airport and the real estate in the vicinity is considered a prime location. But, at the time, the WBT, Inc. Board had several good reasons to turn it down. The area was swamp land, far from Glendale, and not considered a desirable place to live. However, Townsend's ideas lived on because much of what he eventually inspired at the JAARS' centre at Waxhaw, North Carolina, was based on his vision in California.

Feeling the urgency of finding suitable space was not a new task for the WBT, Inc. Board. For example, at its September 1959 meeting, it noted possibilities in Orlando and Tulsa. The necessity for an international headquarters became an official project coinciding with SIL's 25th anniversary celebrations. WBT planned to allocate $225,000 towards purchasing property in Santa Ana, but this fell through, and in March 1960, the headquarters moved to a larger rented space in Santa Ana, while the board searched for a smaller three-acre space. A short time later, it became clear that the owner of the Santa Ana property was interested in selling the whole building to WBT.

In 1965, the WBT, Inc. Board recommended to the Corporation Conference that the time had come to develop a new national and international headquarters at one site in the US. This would 'include, if feasible, such units as administrative offices, auditorium, museum, library, staff housing, transient housing, retirement housing, children's home, warehouse, hangar and airstrip.' [79] The board held complete control so that the development never exceeded the funds raised for this purpose.

Re-stating the Importance of Bible Translation

The need to expand facilities was motivated by a greater desire. At the 1965 Corporation Conference, the WBT, Inc. Board re-stated the commitment of WBT to Bible translation with a sense of urgency stated in this policy:

[77] WBT, "Board Minutes," June 1959, 2.

[78] WBT, "Board Resolution," April 1958, 1.

[79] WBT, "Board Minutes," June 1965, 1.

> Granting the right of every Christian to have the whole Bible, [because] of the prior urgency in our estimation of reaching more tribes with some Scripture rather than reaching fewer tribes with more Scriptures for each, moved that we re-affirm our goal of giving each tribe as soon as practically possible, if not the whole New Testament, at least a sizable portion of it, at the same time allowing the branches and members latitude for translating or paraphrasing part or all of the Old Testament Scriptures. In statements to the public, it should be emphasized that our name Wycliffe Bible Translators (rather than Wycliffe New Testament Translators) emphasizes the Bible is our chief translating goal as distinct from all other books which might be translated and is not meant to draw contrast between [the] Bible and New Testament.[80]

These roots demonstrate the emphasis on expediting translation of the New Testament and then parts or all of the Old Testament.

Conclusion

The era under review started in the early 1940s. Founder Cameron Townsend's trait of trusting God for the impossible was foundational to what developed. Townsend didn't plan to set up an organization to resource people and funds for the work taking place through SIL. Nonetheless, pragmatism was valued and therefore, whatever it took to get the job done was the process followed. Believing a new organization was called for, Townsend and his friend William Nyman founded Wycliffe Bible Translators. They named it after John Wycliffe's translation work of the English Bible.

The interrelationship between SIL and WBT was key to the growth of both organizations. They enjoyed an interdependent bond that was not always understood within or without, but this didn't affect WBT's ability to recruit people to work under SIL. SIL's training programs were key to recruits becoming equipped for their future work.

As the vision for Bible translation spread, new WBT offices sprang up in the Western world of the US, Canada, parts of Western Europe, Australia, and New Zealand. Their responsibility was to promote the vision and recruit and evaluate personnel sent to serve under SIL if suited.

WBT and SIL developed various institutional structures to support this growth along the way. Sometimes this was unplanned, but usually, it involved extensive discussion within both organizations. In the process, WBT figured out

[80] WBT, "Board Minutes," June 1964, 2.

how to operate as an international ministry in its governance, headquarters, and leadership structure.

God was blessing the vision and efforts of WBT through its leaders, board, and members. They never lost their focus or reason for being, and it was always about the importance of translating God's Word and making this available to the peoples of the earth.

Leadership Theories and Practices

The era in focus in this chapter spans two traditional leadership approaches popular at the time: Traits-based and Charismatic. The era was marked by the fact that most leadership roles were held by Western men. Peter Northouse notes how the Trait theory formed in the early 20th century, and its basis was to determine what leadership behaviours made 'certain people great leaders'.[81] Also referred to as the Great Man theory (which presumes only males), these 'certain people' were born with attributes that caused them to stand out from others. Researchers identified the traits in these leaders as drive, vigour, risk-taking, initiative, self-confidence, influence, and capacity to structure social interaction systems for the purpose at hand. Individuals were 'born with these traits, they [could] learn them, or both.'[82]

Closely related was the Charismatic leadership theory which, as its name implies, was a leader's charisma—the inbuilt ability to 'magnify their impact' on other people through their inspiring personality, communication skills, or impressive accomplishments.[83] What made these leaders extraordinarily effective was their 'presence' that compelled people to follow their lead, a gift used to infuse organizations with meaning. [84] According to James MacGregor Burns, the potential weaknesses of this leadership included being 'confusing', 'undemocratic', or a 'type of tyranny'.[85]

Viewing this era of WBT's history from a leadership theory perspective, it is worth considering the attributes and behaviours of its leaders of this era. There was evidence of some characteristics of Trait and Charismatic theories. Therefore, think about how these characteristics helped WBT's leaders achieve their goals. Did this help develop WBT over the 25 years addressed here? Did this hinder WBT's development in any way? Reflecting on these questions helps us think about how one's context influences one's leadership.

---

81 Peter Northouse, *Leadership: Theory and Practice*, 8th ed. (London: SAGE Publications, 2019), 19.

82 Northouse, 22.

83 James Scouller, *The Three Levels of Leadership* (Cirencester: Management Books, 2011), 65.

84 Bernice Ledbetter, Robert Banks, and David Greenhalgh, *Reviewing Leadership: A Christian Evaluation of Current Approaches*, 2nd ed. (Grand Rapids: Baker Academic 2016), xix.

85 James MacGregor Burns, *Transforming Leadership* (New York: Gove Press, 2003), 27.

Journey Reflections (A New Path)

Cameron Townsend's original vision for the world's indigenous communities led to the creation of SIL, JAARS, and WBT. Both SIL and JAARS have been well documented in other works.[86] In this text, our focus is WBT. More digging, analysis, and reflection is necessary to see how this vision for Bible translation grew into WBT. When George Cowan, as President Emeritus of Wycliffe Bible Translators International, spoke about Townsend (internally often referred to as 'Uncle Cam') with the WBTI Board in 2003, he stated:

> Uncle Cam started a revolution in the world's perspective on minority languages. He was characterized by amazing sensitivity to the needs and motives of government leaders, although not by great abilities in writing, linguistics, etc. His leadership style was truly unique, but nonetheless powerful. In the early days, unusual obstacles faced the organization: untrained, weak, raw recruits; opposition from church and mission leaders; extreme poverty amid the Great Depression; lack of training materials; opposition from Communism and other ideologies. We can look back and see God's miracles abounding.... Through everything, God's hand is evident and may He get the glory![87]

As we reflect on the journey thus far, we may want to note the new terrain, challenges, and opportunities along the way. What changes do we begin to see regarding the role and expectations of mission organizations and mission workers? How might these changes impact the future? How do we see God at work? We can note here some of the early steps:

Strategies

- A deliberate attempt is made to avoid being characterized as a traditional US Christian mission agency.
- The founder maintains firm influence over the organization while proving to be a visionary and a maverick in what he is called to do.
- The vision of giving the small and forgotten indigenous language communities at least some books of the New Testament is an appealing way for Western Christians to participate in missions.

---

86 For example, see Hugh Steven, Doorway to the World (Wheaton: Harold Shaw, 1999), Hugh Steven, Yours for Finishing the Task (Orlando: Wycliffe Bible Translators, 2004) and Boone Aldridge, *For the Gospel's Sake: The Rise of Wycliffe Bible Translators and the Summer Institute of Linguistics* (Grand Rapids: Wm B. Eerdmans, 2018).

87 George Cowan, "Presentation to WBTI Board," May 2003.

Relationships

- Along the way, godly men (no evidence of women in leadership in this time frame) join the founder to give leadership and administrative support to make things happen.
- Christians who want to participate in the ministry of Bible translation must be strong individuals, especially in initiating new work and structures.

Form and function

- The work expands and more people want to be involved; leadership and administrative structures develop organically and are tweaked along the way.
- A complex organizational structure is formed with WBT's 'sister' organization, SIL.
- The division of labour and responsibility between WBT and SIL, between home office and field office, becomes increasingly complex and represents uncharted territory (because there were few other examples of this way of working).
- The idea of an international operation is not a large focus because most resources are from the US.
- A US founded mission agency finds itself having to think beyond its borders.
- The unique SIL training method opens the door for people of other Western countries to participate.

These first steps in WBT's journey echoed the era and context in which it began. There was great energy, exploration, and expansion. But WBT was already much more than a product of its times. One can see the hand of God providing for leaders of WBT, encouraging and challenging them to respond to His mission.

Chapter 2
Expanding: 1966–1980

Historical Context

From the 1950s to the 1960s, theological discussions concerning Christian mission's ownership, responsibility, and task increased. Did it belong to God, the church, or some other institutional structure? In his 1958 book *Missio Dei* (translated into English and published in 1965 as *The Mission of God* [1]), German theologian Georg Vicedom offered insight into this issue. With the Latin phrase *missio Dei,* which translates as 'the sending of God', Vicedom sought to clarify an understanding of mission within ecumenical circles. Vicedom was an experienced missionary in New Guinea and a professor in theological institutions in his homeland. The term *missio Dei* had already been introduced into theological circles by Karl Hartenstein when he mentioned it at the International Missionary Council (IMC) meeting in 1952 in Willingen, Germany. Theologians' discussions looked at how 'mission was understood as being derived from the very nature of God.'[2] Ownership of mission rested entirely with God, 'with the ultimate goal of establishing the reign of God over all creation.'[3] Vicedom emphasized the triune God's ownership of mission rather than the church or other institutions such as mission agencies.

By the time the IMC met again in Mexico City in 1963, it had become part of the World Council of Churches (WCC). The themes of mission and evangelism, previously considered separately to describe work at home and overseas, were now brought together. 'Mission, it was recognized, was taking place not only from the West to the rest but in "six continents", that is, everywhere in the world, including the so-called Christian nations.'[4] Mission was no longer limited to the church sending cross-cultural missionaries overseas and no longer based primarily on geography. Instead, mission profoundly represented 'what the Christian community is sent to do, beginning right where it is located'[5] (referring to Acts 1:8).

The Second Vatican Council (1962–65) influenced Bible ministry in Roman

---

1 Original German title was Georg Vicedom, *Die Mission Gottes: Einführung in Eine Theologie Der Mission* (Munich: Kaiser Verlag, 1958).

2 David Bosch, *Transforming Mission: Paradigm Shifts in Theology of Mission* (Maryknoll: Orbis Books, 2011), 399.

3 Francis Anekwe Oborji, *Concepts of Mission: The Evolution of Contemporary Missiology* (Maryknoll: Orbis Books, 2006), 140.

4 Kirsteen Kim, *Joining in with the Spirit: Connecting World Church and Local Mission* (London: Epworth, 2009), 25.

5 Andrew Kirk, *What Is Mission?* (Minneapolis: Fortress Press, 2000), 24.

Catholicism. For example, the Council approved cooperation with local Bible agencies in printing and distributing Bibles. As an outcome of this, Roman Catholics in the majority world had the opportunity to have their own Bibles. The Council also 'lifted many... traditional restraints on lay Catholic engagement with the biblical text.'[6] Before this, Latin was the official church language for all Bible reading, study, and teaching. Now, local parishes worldwide 'could offer masses in the local language rather than in Latin.'[7] This factor contributed to Brian Stanley calling the 20th century—'the century of the Bible' because 'more peoples received the Scriptures in their own languages than in any preceding century.'[8]

While these theological discussions give insights into the broader knowledge of mission at the time, they were not directly shaping WBT's understanding of its purpose. Instead, WBT's impetus came from the Great Commission text of Matthew 28:18–20, the primary motivational basis for evangelical missions in the US during this era. Theological reflection on this text came much later. For example, theologian Timothy Tennent points out that the Great Commission was and continues to 'frequently [be] treated as an isolated pericope, separated from the rest of the gospel as well as the larger biblical context of the *missio Dei*.'[9]

The importance of the Great Commission as a motivation for mission goes further back to William Carey (1761–1834), known as the father of the modern missionary movement. He developed his views in his booklet, *Enquiry into the Obligation of Christians to Use Means for the Conversion of Heathens* (1792). Carey wanted to determine whether 'the commission given by our Lord to His disciples [is] still binding on us; [to] consider the practicability of doing something more than is done; and [to] discuss the duty of Christians in general on this matter.'[10] Carey himself used the term commission, never Great Commission. Nevertheless, he concluded that Christians needed to work together to take the gospel to unevangelized people, and his booklet motivated Christians to be active in the Great Commission. A related command came from Matthew 24:14 (KJV), 'And this gospel of the kingdom shall be preached in all the world for a witness unto all nations; and then shall the end come.' The Matthew 24 and 28 texts inspired Western Christians, including those involved with WBT, to serve with and hasten the pace of missions as they could be part of completing the Great Commission.

Historian Andrew Walls observes two simultaneous approaches to mission contributing to the expansion of the Christian faith during this era—the

---

[6] Stanley, 9.

[7] Terry, and Gallagher, 305.

[8] Stanley, 9.

[9] Timothy Tennent, *Invitation to World Missions: A Trinitarian Missiology of the Twenty-First Century* (Grand Rapids: Kregel Academic & Professional, 2010), 127.

[10] Robert Hunt, *The Gospel among the Nations: A Documentary History of Inculturation* (Maryknoll: Orbis Books, 2010), 83.

'crusading mode and the missionary mode'.[11] The former referred to missionary efforts aligned with colonial Christendom governments, and God's mission was like a military conquest and an expansion of territory. Christianity was thought to be superior and would Christianize entire people groups. The latter occurred when missionaries sought to proclaim the gospel and seek out new followers to disciple in their faith sincerely and truthfully. However, the line often blurred between the two approaches.

WBT held to an intentional commitment towards the Great Commission by viewing Bible translation as a task to be accomplished using all means available. At the time, this primarily involved human and financial resources from the West. The language and practices of military strategy continued in use. For example, in 1970, the WBT Board instructed the leaders to make a Global Strategy Study that included a plan for 'occupying the remaining areas of the world and completing the task in each branch', as well as defining when the 'task... can be considered complete.'[12] The intention was that WBT's people resources for SIL were used in a given place only for as long as needed to get the task done and then reassigned to another area.

Many WBT recruits in the 1950s and 1960s had served in World War II or the Korean War. They and much of the rest of the Western world were accustomed to military terminology, which found its way into missions and business contexts. The term division also came from military language and specified an organizational unit. That's why WBT called its organizations divisions. This use of military expressions, including base, target, and furlough, was used widely in mission organizations. Because businesses also used the same language, many people didn't make a military connection to these terms.

All these factors set the stage for WBT's continued development from its 1942 formation in California, to a US-wide organization, to related offices in some other Western nations, to greater international participation. This chapter looks at milestones along this part of the journey.

Organizational Growth

At the 1967 WBT and SIL Corporation Conference, Executive Director Ben Elson reported the administration's recruitment goals for WBT offices in the US, Canada, UK, Australia, Germany, Switzerland, and New Zealand. Elson stated the aim for the number of new members was 225 for 1967, 300 by 1970, 400 by 1978, and 500 by 1984.

---

[11] Andrew Walls, "Afterword: Christian Mission in a Five Hundred Year Context," in *Mission in the 21st Century*, ed. Andrew Walls and Cathy Ross (Maryknoll: Orbis Books, 2008), 196.

[12] WBT, "Board Minutes," November 1970, 18.

The number of existing and new members projected by 1985 totalled 7,250. Two years after Elson announced the recruitment goal, board secretary Phil Grossman informed the 1969 Corporation Conference that there were 1,953 members, including 75 single men, 452 single women, and 713 married couples. WBT planned to grow to 9,200 people by 1985—an increase of 470% or about 29% per year. However, WBT never reached this goal. Nonetheless, this showed an intention by WBT leaders to recruit an increasing stream of people.

Within a few months of setting the growth goal, the leadership of Jungle Camp—a training course for recruits—expressed concerns about the projections of rapidly rising numbers of recruits. The camp staff trained and evaluated new members through basic living, language learning, and cultural situations before releasing them for an assignment with WBT or SIL. The staff wanted to ensure that Christian commitment remained a fundamental characteristic sought when recruiting people. The 'essential prerequisite' was 'a truly Christ-centred motivation [as] the basis of acceptance of any candidate and not just a desire to fill a particular work slot.'[13]

A decade after setting the growth goal, the board reaffirmed the necessity for more recruits to fill the continuing worldwide need. The plan had been for 425 recruits annually by 1979. The goal was re-adjusted in 1977 when the board asked all WBT organizations to pray for 270 new members in 1978 and 320 in 1979. While the board didn't explain the lower numbers, the momentum of exceptional growth was tapering off.

As more WBTs were forming in Western countries, the WBT International Administration began grappling with the tension between what it centralized and decentralized and left up to individual WBTs. For example, in 1978, the board decided that the administration would set the annual recruitment goals based on SIL field and WBT division requests, prioritizing the most widespread and urgent needs. The divisions had to set their own recruitment goals in response to the total requirement.

The numeric growth goals set for new members demonstrated WBT leaders' faith that God would lead them to these recruits. These plans also captured the realization by WBT leaders of how large the task of Bible translation was becoming and, therefore, the urgent need for additional personnel. At the same time, while initial recruitment looked solid, those numbers began to decline within a decade and required adjustment. In addition, the US operations where WBT started had little control over the recruitment programs of WBTs outside of the US. Instead, it relied on assuming the goodwill of these WBT's commitment to the vision and purpose of WBT set out in the US context.

13 WBT, "Board Minutes," September 1967, 1.

Strengthening Leadership

The WBT, Inc. Board appointed Frank Robbins at its November 1975 meeting to replace Ben Elson, who had decided to retire as the first Executive Director of WBT and SIL, a position he had held since the mid-1960s. The board commended Elson for being WBT's first 'chief executive officer', also thanking Elson's wife Adelle for 'her sterling support and faithful service as Ben's wife and secretary.'[14]

Significant growth of WBT and SIL took place under Elson's leadership. It included:

› Developing the Wycliffe US Home Division and its headquarters building in Huntington Beach, California.
› Creating the International Administration for WBT and SIL and moving it to the ILC at Dallas.
› Working on the WBT Inc. Board's governance process.
› Working out relationships with Wycliffe Associates.
› Establishing year-round academic and field orientation programs at the Dallas Center.

During Elson's tenure, WBT's membership had doubled, field work expanded into many more languages in several new countries, more home divisions formed, and the publication of translated Scripture had 'accelerated'.[15]

It is worth looking at the board's choice of the word 'accelerated' to describe aspects of the work of Bible Translation. For example, those who served in the Bible translation movement since the adoption of Vision 2025 in 1999 became familiar with the heavily promoted concept of accelerating or acceleration, particularly when describing the current rate of progress in the ministry. They could have thought this was a newer term or concept. But this is not so. The idea of mission 'accelerating' appeared nearly 25 years earlier in official WBT Board records.

Elson received praise for his steady and quiet handling of things, especially when taking over for Cameron Townsend when he stepped aside as general director (though as WBT founder, Townsend continued to play an influential role). This requires further explanation, going back to the 1969 WBT and SIL Corporation Conference. Considerable discussion occurred about Townsend's general director role and whether the position was still necessary to both organizations. In response, Townsend pointed out some of the critical roles he had played in the past. This included raising over US$200,000 for equipment for the fields, promoting the annual Bible Translation Day, his presence at the 1964–65 World's Fair in New York, and publicity through books such as *The Tariri Story* and *Now God Speaks Tzeltal.*

Townsend wasn't sure if SIL needed a general director, but he was adamant

14 WBT, September 1967, 1.

15 WBT, "Board Minutes," November 1975, 1.

WBT did. In the debate among the delegates, some pointed out that Townsend achieved these outstanding developments as the founder, and coincidently, the founder was also the general director. Another pointed out that there were 'two kinds of authority involved: 'legislative authority' that belonged to the executive director, and 'respect authority' which belonged to Townsend.[16] Subsequent concerns centred around the consequences of having both an executive director and a general director. That would mean two people led WBT since both reported to the board. There was agreement this wasn't a workable situation.

Earlier in 1966, when Elson was appointed, he was the principal administrative officer of the Corporation and served under the General Director (Townsend) and the WBT, Inc. Board. His duties included defining the lines of responsibility within the international and North America home offices and bringing to the board's attention new and ambiguous situations. Elson functioned as the executive officer for the international office, and he also coordinated departments and programs. Until there was a North America Home Council, Elson also served as the North America home functions leader in Canada and the US, relinquishing this involvement when others were appointed to those roles. In 1974, Elson's Executive Director title changed to Executive Vice President.

When Townsend retired as General Director in May 1971, the WBT and SIL Boards gave him two titles: Founder and General Director Emeritus of WBT and SIL. In doing so, the boards stated their deep love and esteem for Townsend, for his vision imparted for Bible translation work, for the wisdom he had shown in leading them over the years, and for the wise and daring policies and strategy he had taught them.

The ability to work under this unconventional leadership structure of a general director, founder, and executive director all reporting directly to the same board explains why Elson was commended for his steady and quiet handling of things when working with and under Townsend.

Publicity and Recruitment

WBT promoted and publicized its work in part through its slogan 'Each in his own tongue'. In 1974 this motto was replaced with 'Every tribe by '85', which included a date to help motivate action. A standardized WBT logo was developed to allow for translation into other national languages. It incorporated the word 'Wycliffe', an open Bible, and an outline map of the world.[17] This also demonstrated the strength of the Wycliffe brand in the US and some Western countries.

---

16 WBT, "Corporation Conference Minutes," May 1967, 16.

17 WBT, "Board Minutes," October 1974, 6.

Armed with outcomes of the Global Strategy Study and the slogan of 'Every tribe by '85' and covered by the grace of God, WBT continued to grow, with recruits filling both support and translation assignments. Considering the growth in assignments, the board realized it needed to clarify some of the preferred qualities administrators were looking at when evaluating new applicants. For support personnel, these were dedication to the task, potential or actual record-keeping ability, good management of time, ability to follow a system, or better yet, to create a system, and supervisory ability where a role required this. For translation personnel, the qualities included dedication to the task, good management of time, and the ability to carry on to a finish with only moderate supervision.

The board was very hands-on in its role in approving assignments of new people to a specific SIL Branch or WBT Home Division. These entities assigned the new member to a particular location and role within their areas of jurisdiction. Through this process the board tried to minimize any misunderstandings new people had about the roles they would fill.

As new WBT offices continued to emerge, the International Administration in 1973 clarified the steps for processing applicants for membership after they had attended an SIL school. Various scenarios were described:

› When there was a WBT Division and an SIL training school in the same location, this required a local candidate secretary to directly supervise the processing of all the recruits from the division.
› When there was a WBT Division but not an SIL training school in the same location, the international candidate secretary decided whether new personnel were processed from their home country or by another candidate office, usually where the applicant attended SIL training.
› When there wasn't a WBT Division, SIL training school, or SIL Branch in the same location, the international candidate secretary determined which local candidate office should handle the applicant.

Governance

At its May 1971 meeting, the board appointed an executive committee that included George Cowan, General Director, Ben Elson, Executive Director, David Cummings, Director of Australia, and David Bendor-Samuel, Director of Great Britain. There were also two field directors from SIL: Frank Robbins and Morris Cottle. This structure demonstrates that the Chartered Home Divisions of Australia and Great Britain (those able to vote) were represented on the board's executive committee. In contrast, others weren't included because they weren't yet chartered, such as the US and Canada.

From its inception in 1942, the board met monthly, usually in southern California. Board members were very hands-on, which helped the board manage the fledgling operations. However, after 30 years, this was no longer sustainable as more WBT offices formed outside of North America. In a wise move in 1973, the board began meeting twice a year instead of monthly and held some meetings outside of California.

This process indicated the growing maturity of the board, operating less like a working management committee and more as a board of governors or trustees acting on behalf of the growing US and international bodies. The board refined its objective to have final authority for the ongoing business and program of the WBT corporation and serve as the guardian of policy and practice. Its responsibilities were to:

- appoint officers, administrators, and committees for the corporation.
- grant charters to branches and divisions.
- set policies between corporation conferences.
- carry out the corporation's legal business.
- review agreements with other organizations.
- monitor and oversee the corporation's program through reports from the president and executive vice president.
- approve the operating budget.
- approve new geographical advances.
- approve major projects that required funding.
- review actions of divisions, branches, subsidiaries, and departments.
- review actions of standing committees.

This deliberate move towards a governing board required the establishment of various board committees. For example, an administrative committee acted on behalf of the board with the corporation's ongoing business. The finance committee gave general oversight for the control and investment of funds and reviewed the overall fiscal condition of the corporation. The personnel committee managed HR-related policies for members and staff. A strategy committee evaluated and recommended goals, plans and priorities. These committees were active between board meetings and made reports at each board meeting.

There were two other notable developments with the board during this time. First, it gave an age limit to the office of the president (i.e., chairman of the board). People holding this role had to retire at the age of 70. And second, in 1976, for the first time in the 34 years since WBT's founding, a woman—Mildred Larson—was appointed to serve on the board. The rest of the 18 board members were men. A subsequent board election in 1977 returned the board to its former all-male status. No explanation or rationale is given for the lack of women board members. This mirrored the number of those who held international administration leadership roles at the time, also predominantly men, even though the total membership of WBT included hundreds of accomplished women. One assumes this reflected the cultural norms of the Western church and mission scene at the time.

Headquarters Search

In 1966, the board set up an internal committee to find a suitable location for WBT's US and international headquarters. The committee considered several factors in this decision: the location of the majority of WBT's donors, potential sources of recruits, operational practicality, upkeep costs, local taxes, preferences of existing staff, and accommodation for US members on furlough.

Within a year, the board decided on Dallas, Texas, as the preferred location for the international headquarters. The International Administration held two gifts totalling $120,000 to purchase a property. By 1969, the executive director engaged an architect for the site plan development that followed the board's vision for the Dallas operations.

The board projected that US membership would grow and reach 6,000 by 1985. Envisioning a much larger WBT US headquarters with numerous regional centres, the board considered it necessary to separate the much smaller International Administration from WBT US.

In 1969 the board approved the purchase of 35 acres of land in Dallas in addition to 20 acres already donated. The building project was restricted to a maximum of forty acres until paid for, and the excess land could be sold off to pay for any debt. The board could borrow WBT and SIL funds for the project at the going rate of interest, with the 55 acres serving as collateral. Various titles were used for this development and the JAARS Center, under construction at Waxhaw, NC: National Administrative Center, Coordinating Center, and Major Center.

In 1973, plans for the Dallas Center, that included a joint international headquarters for WBT and SIL, were finalized. The site would include academic and administration facilities; classrooms; academic departments; services for finance, mail, reception, and printing; an auditorium to seat 400 people; and childcare facilities. There would be housing for students, members in training, families on furlough, longer-term residents (500 people in all), and land for private housing for members. The US Division would have space for a regional office. Also included were a retirement centre, mobile home park, and museum. The International Linguistics Center (ILC) Board planned to raise funds for the development.

Early Internationalization

In the early 20th century, more than 80% of the total number of Christians worldwide lived in Western countries. As a result, Western influence significantly shaped WBT's leadership and strategy from the start, particularly in terms of its human and financial resources.

Some internationalization was taking place for WBT at this time. The term 'international' is tied semantically to a Western concept of territorial expansion. Mission agencies used the word international in their name to identify them with a broader reach. However, the location of their headquarters and the nationalities of their leadership teams indicated that international still reflected that the agency was Western-based—usually in the US or UK—although it may have had affiliate offices in other countries. The purpose of this section is to explore how WBT was becoming more international.

Consolidation in Europe

In 1968, the board approved promotional activities in Scandinavia on a modest scale to encourage serious enquirers to study SIL courses in England or Germany. Scholarships could be offered to those considered eligible to join the organization. Other acceptable activities included developing a financial and prayer support team, performing linguistic demonstrations, screening promotional WBT films, and producing publicity and recruitment materials in Norwegian, Swedish, Danish, and Finnish.

In 1970, the board authorized Wilson Stiteler, WBT Regional Secretary for Europe, to begin legal work to create Stichting (Foundation) Wycliffe Bijbelvertalers (Bible translators) in the Netherlands. An organizing board was made up of Marinus Wiering, Piet Koen, Hans Keijzer, and Wilson Stiteler. Until this formation, WBT only had a representative in the country. Four years later, the WBT Executive Vice President appointed Piet Koen as the Netherlands Business Manager, Helmut Gaertner as Germany Business Manager, and Tony Williams as South Africa Business manager.

Developments in Asia

In March 1966, WBT, Inc. Board member Dan Piatt (also working with the Billy Graham Evangelical Association) visited the US AID office in Tokyo to discuss acquiring surplus equipment, including ex-military vehicles and communications equipment, which would be useful to SIL's field work in Asia. In March 1968, WBT leader John McIntosh travelled to Japan to meet with Christian leaders about WBT's work. Soon after, Executive Director Ben Elson informed the board that WBT was gaining new members from other countries such as Japan. Training and support for new Japanese recruits greatly interested Elson since Japan represented the first country outside the Western world to show interest in WBT's vision and purpose. By 1968, the first Japanese member, Sueyoshi (Tim) Toba was assigned to the SIL India/Nepal Branch. In November 1975 WBT gave Japan Non-Chartered Division status. An eight-member advisory body called the Japan Contact Committee took shape, and included Takashi Fukuda, who later served in WBT International roles and with the Wycliffe Global Alliance. The Committee became the Japan Division Council.

In October 1978, the WBT Board invited the Korea Translation Mission to function as the WBT committee in South Korea. By 1980, WBT representatives Steve and Marilyn Thrasher from the US were instructors at the East-West Centre in Seoul and liaised between Korea Translation Mission and WBT. Earlier, Bus Dawson from the International Administration served on an advisory committee planning the East-West Centre.

Africa and Latin America

Through leaders like John Bendor-Samuel, WBT's mission was becoming known in some regions of Africa. For example, in March 1969, the board divided the West Africa SIL Branch into the Nigeria-Cameroon Branch and the Ghana-Togo Branch. Strictly speaking, these were SIL field operations. But WBT believed that Africans should lead the emerging work in Africa. For instance, John Agamah became WBT's representative in Ghana.

In 1975, the WBT Board approved the formation of a WBT Brazil Home Office to be named Associação Wycliffe de Tradutores da Biblia. Eventually, in 1982, this transitioned into the Associação Linguistica Evangélica Missionária (ALEM) and was categorized as a National Bible Translation Organization (NBTO) (see chapter 8) in the 1980s. Another instance of internationalization in Latin America occurred in November 1979, when the board recognized the services of Celedonio and Gloria Gasca as WBT representatives in Mexico in the presentation of the Bible Translation task to the Mexican Church.

Internationalization

The realities of internationalization were pressing upon the board. Therefore, it proactively set up a committee comprised of John Taylor, John Bendor-Samuel, F.B. Dawson, and Donald Van Wynen to study the challenges of integrating non-English speaking members into field operations. New members were anticipated from Switzerland and Germany coming to South America to serve with SIL and its largely mother-tongue English speaking members.

In a different context, the board noted in 1970 that it was proving impossible for people from non-Commonwealth countries to secure visas to work in India. Consequently, the board decided that the program in India and Nepal would need to be conducted only with members from Commonwealth countries. This gave some impetus to those WBT countries (e.g., New Zealand, Australia, Canada and the UK) to focus on that region.

The board remained actively involved in the approval process of new members from other countries. For example, in December 1970, it rejected a candidate from New Zealand because his doctrinal statement conflicted with WBT's constitutional statement on doctrine regarding eternal punishment. Also, regarding an applicant serving on Germany's Home Council, the board rejected that person's doctrinal statement because it did not comply with WBT's statement on scriptural inerrancy.

In 1977, the board decided not to have an international logo for WBT. Instead, each division could have its own logo appropriate for the national context and approved by the International Administration.

Guiding New Wycliffe's

The board maintained active jurisdiction over the other WBTs that were forming or operating in Western countries, as illustrated here:

- In January 1966, the board decided that WBT in Canada should apply for incorporation in Canada.
- Also in 1966, the board appointed Ernst Wyss, Heribert Wolfensberger, Thomas Weismann, Klaus Detwyler, and Hanna Greber as members of a WBT Swiss Advisory Council, once they each signed the WBT, Inc. doctrinal statement.
- In May 1973, the board approved the appointment of Peter Warkentin of Winnipeg and Chester Fisher of Peterborough to the Canadian Council.
- In December 1968, the board approved the reappointment of three new members to the Canadian Home Council and accepted the resignation of another.
- In 1968, the board approved amendments to the constitution of the British Division.
- In 1973, the board approved for service on the Finland Committee: Laina Aho; France Committee: four new people; Germany Wycliffe Council: ten people, including four alternatives, all of whom had been elected by the German Division members; Japan Representative Committee: seven people; the Netherlands

Council: six people; Switzerland Council: five people; USA Council: four new people, two departures, and Clarence Church (US Director) was appointed to the International Linguistic Center Board (Dallas).

- In preparation for selecting delegates to the 1975 International Conference, the board decided that the home countries of Canada, Finland, Germany, the Netherlands, New Zealand, Switzerland, and the US were classified as Unchartered Divisions (whereas Australia and Great Britain were already Chartered Divisions).
- Also in 1975, the WBT, Inc.'s Constitution Committee approved the governing documents for the future US Division.
- In May 1979, the Norway Home Office was recognized as an Unchartered Division.

Appointing candidates for leadership in divisions began with nomination by the division's council, WBT Area Director, and WBT Executive Director (later called Executive Vice President). Then nominees were referred to the WBT, Inc. Board for final approval. Serving on a home council was seen as equivalent to being a senior member in WBT. For example, the board approved these appointments at its November 1979 board meeting: Canada Division Director: reappointment of Jim Dean; Germany Division Director: extension of term of Andreas Holzhausen; the Netherlands Division Director: reappointment of Piet Koen; New Zealand Division Director: Keith Sayers; and Switzerland Division Director: Martin Kruesi.

Centralization-Decentralization

At the 1965 Corporation Conference, amendments to the WBT Constitution were made that enabled the board to revise the candidate procedures for accepting new members by the British and Australian Councils. These councils' candidate programs remained under the general supervision of the Corporation Candidate Secretary, but the councils were now approved to appoint Junior Members, and in the case of the British Council, this included Western European countries over which it had jurisdiction. Functionally, this was limited decentralization of authority over new people joining in the UK and in Australia. Locally, the respective organization's home council held more authority in the process under the oversight of the International Administration's Corporation Candidate Secretary.

As another of its responsibilities, the board acknowledged the service of WBT leaders worldwide. Such care was illustrated when, in 1968, the board sent its condolences to Australian Lynette (Lyn) Oates and her family on the untimely death of her husband Bill. The board recalled how Bill and Lyn carried the load of starting the SIL Aborigines Branch, and how much Bill did to enlighten the Australian

Christian public and academic world concerning WBT's methods and the needs of the Australian Aborigines. Similarly, the board expressed its deep gratitude to God for giving the WBT British Council the inspiring fellowship, prayerful concern for people groups needing Bible translation, and effective leadership of Haddon Long as Chairman.

Financial Controls

The board influenced the financial matters of individual WBTs. Some examples include:

- Approval of German members setting up a voluntary hospitalization and surgery fund.
- Approval in 1968 of the British Director's request that financial quotas for British based personnel be set in Pounds rather than US Dollars. The board recommended the amount set at 41 Pounds (US$99).
- Consent to the quota for home assigned and furloughed members in New Zealand set at NZ$81 (US$90) per month. The board thought a higher quota based on the WBT Quota Committee's formula was called for. However, it respected the New Zealand Council's desire to keep the quota in line with the average New Zealand income.
- Discontinue the use of 50% of undesignated funds from Swiss and German donors to subsidize the *Seminar fuer Sprachmethodik* (SSm) linguistics course in Germany. Instead, these funds were to go to Swiss and German field members on low financial support.

These are illustrations of the growing financial responsibilities of WBT learning to operate beyond its original US borders.

The project funding approval process is another illustration. The board, wanting the various SIL Branches to be more involved, gave the branches authority to create any necessary projects. The projects then had to be approved by the International Administration and reported to the board. Approved projects could then be shared with interested WBT Divisions, who took responsibility for fundraising, including holding Faith Promise events. The SIL Branch could release personnel to the division to help with the efforts until all the funds were raised or the branch wanted the personnel back.

The board was integrally involved in WBT home council operations. For instance, it approved a request from the New Zealand Council to divide proceeds of its 1973 Faith Promise dinner rallies with one third designated to the Emergency Support Fund, one third for radio communications for the Indonesia Advance, and one third for various expansion ideas in New Zealand. Two years earlier, the board asked the New Zealand Division to prayerfully consider developing a centre in Auckland for translation work among the 40,000 South Pacific Polynesians who lived there. Meanwhile, plans were proceeding to establish the British Division headquarters with a $10,000 grant from WBT, Inc. legacy funds.

At its May 1980 meeting, the board approved the retirement plans for the Swedish, Swiss, and US Divisions, plans that highlighted the financial maturity of these organizations.

Categories of Home Country Operations

The structures and categories of organizations within WBT continued to be refined as internationalization increased. In November 1975, these were the structures:

- *Home Office:* A representative(s) appointed by the WBT Board could serve the WBT home office. The person(s) had the authority to use the name, mailing address, office, and functions necessary to fulfil the purpose set out by the International Administration for the Home Office. The primary purpose was to develop recruitment, prayer, and financial support in each country.
- *Non-Chartered Division:* This status was given to a Home Office when it had at least five members (excluding candidates) and either a Director or a Council in place—all approved by the WBT Board.
- *Chartered Division:* A Non-Chartered Division could progress to being approved by the WBT Board as Chartered after it had: at least 20 people in field service; a functioning administration and Council; a process for accepting, supervising, and sending new personnel to field assignments; and provided a means for linguistic training for new personnel.

When the board invited Unchartered Divisions to send a representative to the 1979 International Conference, it demonstrated how these categories functioned. These divisions included: Canada (the board granted Canada Charter status later in November 1980 when it was also recognized as a Canadian Religious Order), Finland, Germany, the Netherlands, New Zealand, Sweden, Switzerland, and Japan. These were in addition to the Chartered Divisions of Australia, UK, and the US. The Charter was approved for the US Division in October 1978, and the board recognized in 1980 that WBT, Inc. (i.e., the US) was a Religious Order. The Conference met in Dallas, Texas, from 20–29 May 1979, with 127 delegates in attendance. George Cowan was re-elected as president, David Cummings as vice president.

Relating to WBT US

WBT US continued to be integrated into an increasingly international operation, representing an ongoing concern for both the WBT Board and the US home operations. A second concern regarded whether to give Canada greater autonomy from the US. Support for creating two separate councils existed three years earlier, at the 1963 Corporation Conference. By 1966, the board encouraged its Executive Committee to study, and if feasible, implement the first phase of the USA Home Council and the Canadian Home Council. Respecting the developments in these two countries, in 1967, the board appointed Clarence Church as US Home Director and Ray Nicholson as Canada Home Director.

In November 1968, the board set up a committee consisting of the WBT Executive Director and the US home department heads to: (1) approve the US home program to be carried out by the various departments; (2) develop and approve the home budget; (3) coordinate the activities of the Santa Ana headquarters; and (4) evaluate the Wycliffe Associates program on behalf of the board. This new committee functioned in place of a US Home Council and its budget comprised the 5% of member's income normal to any Home Council's operations.

Developing a headquarters for the US Division was also becoming a great concern of the WBT Board. By September 1970, the board began negotiations with the Welch Foundation regarding their property in Huntington Beach, California, with the understanding that WBT would use the office buildings as the home office. Four years later, as obtaining the property was becoming a reality, the board approved a master plan for the US Headquarters. This included transient housing and an auditorium-museum-display building. The headquarters was called the William G. Nyman Administration Building in honour of William (Bill) Nyman, considered the co-founder of WBT with Cameron Townsend, who faithfully served as the board's first secretary and treasurer for 18 years.

Up until 1975, Wycliffe US was still classified as an Unchartered Division, even though newer Divisions such as Australia and Great Britain had become Chartered. This began to change when in 1975 the board asked its Constitution Committee to approve the governing documents for the future US Division.

In May 1976, the WBT Board approved a range of financial rights and powers to the US Division. This gave the latter significant financial and operational autonomy over its programs. In 1978, the WBT Board decided to have one of its members, Rey Johnson, serve on the US Division Council as the WBT Board representative.

At the 1979 International Conference, a historic moment came when the delegates approved the US Division as a legal entity. It now had the authority to use 'WBT, Inc of California' as its legal name. This action concluded the changing situation, since 1942, of the US operations, and it was recognized finally as a Chartered Division. The use of 'WBT, Inc.' from this point referred only to the US Division or US operations of WBT.

Forming Wycliffe Associates

Wycliffe Associates (WA) received permission from WBT to start operations on 16 December 1967. WA's purpose was to create means for volunteers who held the necessary skills to provide practical support, often on short-term projects, to WBT and SIL worldwide. WA would also raise funds for WBT and SIL's programs. The WBT Board appointed the first WA Board of Trustees: Paul Sutherland, Jim Beam, Evertt Sweem, Lorin Griset, Claes Wyckoff, Joseph Profita, and Rudolf Refer. In September 1968, the WBT Board encouraged WA to seek legal counsel. Unless they identified distinct advantages in remaining part of WBT, they should incorporate separately, leaving control of 'Wycliffe' with Wycliffe Bible Translators.

Later in 1973, the WBT Board set up a committee of Ben Elson, Bus Dawson, Clarence Church, and Earl Adams to meet with WA to review and formulate mutually agreeable guidelines. These guidelines would encourage closer cooperation and shared goals between WBT and WA, protect WBT and SIL international policies and government relations, identify ways WBT wanted WA's support, and find ways of informing WBT's members and constituencies of the programs and results of WA. The WBT Board decided that to maintain close and cordial relationships with WA, the WA Board should provide a quarterly written report to the WBT US Division Director. The report was to cover WA's operations, finances, policy changes, and any significant problems.

The WBT Board approved a revised agreement with WA for WA's promotional efforts for 1975–77. The agreement stipulated in part that the banquets WA was committed to running were to be held solely for the benefit of WBT, and the main speakers for these banquets required approval from by WBT.

In May 1976, the WBT Board gave a citation to William and Betti Butler for their vision and initiative in the founding of WA, and thus providing a means whereby laypeople could be more personally related to and involved in the worldwide WBT program. The Butlers were commended for 'their commitment to the furtherance of Bible translation through the Wycliffe Bible Translators for the language groups still without the Scriptures.'[18]

[18] WBT, "Board Minutes," May 1976, 11.

Relating to SIL

As WBT continued to grow through its home offices and divisions worldwide, the board became concerned about WBT and SIL's reputation since SIL received criticism from anthropologists and governments over its activity with indigenous groups. Therefore, the WBT Board wanted the Executive Director informed about publicity produced by divisions potentially misrepresenting work of SIL Branches that might be damaging to field relationships. The branches concerned were encouraged to provide the divisions with publicity guidelines to help orient their future publications without interrupting the free flow of communication about the work to the supporting constituency.

Managing crises between the two organizations had its challenging moments. For example, during the Vietnam War, the WBT Board approved the SIL Vietnam Executive Committee's recommendation that members who were mothers, along with their children, immediately leave Vietnam. The WBT Board also wanted to reduce the potential for criticism and harm to the worldwide cause of Bible translation should there be further tragedy associated with the war. The board naturally felt concerned about the organization's reputation.

Regarding names for their respective groupings, the WBT and SIL Boards decided that the term 'Branch' would be used when referring to SIL's field work. In contrast, WBT's work was called 'Division', meaning a 'Division of WBT, Incorporated in California.'

The two boards met at the same time and location but kept separate minutes. Occasionally, it may not have been clear which set of minutes should contain particular items. For example, the 9 March 1968 WBT Board minutes showed an SIL Board item, concerning the SIL Brazil Branch Constitution, placed in the WBT minutes and later scratched out.

The pathway to membership with and between the two organizations happened as follows: When a person was accepted for membership by the appropriate WBT body, they automatically became a member of the parent WBT Corporation. All members automatically became members of the Division of their home country. If there wasn't a Division in the home country, the International Personnel Committee assigned the member to an existing Division. Being granted membership in the Corporation and Division didn't automatically mean the person also had membership in an SIL Branch. Branch membership was given to people when they arrived for service. When members qualified for Senior Membership, they were given voting rights in their respective Division or Branch meetings. The category of Associate Membership was created for people aged 50–59 applying for membership. There were certain restrictions on this category, including not being eligible to vote and not being eligible for Emergency Funds. Before anyone could be assigned to language roles, the board decided in 1971 that all such personnel must attend two SIL courses before proceeding to the field.

In 1970, the WBT Board reiterated that WBT's policies had always been to pioneer, and therefore the SIL Branches were asked not to assign new people to

> language groups that already have the New Testament in a form sufficiently accurate and understandable to be used in active evangelism and teaching as long as there are still hundreds of tribes that have nothing of God's Word. This does not however, preclude participation in the provision of translations where existing scriptures are not in [a] sufficiently accurate and understandable form.[19]

Another critical discussion at the WBT Board level surfaced around the term missionary. As a result, the board declared:

> In view of the negative, imperialistic connotation attached to the use of the term 'missionary' in many developing nations, moved to advocate the increased use of other terms such as 'member' (or translator, linguist, pilot, mechanic, bookkeeper, etc. as appropriate) in WBT/SIL publications and correspondence, especially *Translation* magazine.[20]

The WBT Board in its September 1969 meeting informed the Director of the Ecuador Branch of WBT 'that the new preamble to the Ecuador Statement of Goals' was acceptable to the Board.'[21] Referencing the Ecuador Branch of Wycliffe illustrates the confusing relationship between WBT and SIL since field work was SIL's area of responsibility.

Another example comes from March 1970 when the board decided it needed a legal opinion regarding the simplest method to recognize delegates at the 1971 WBT and SIL Corporate Conference. There were two issues: the first was to have SIL delegates recognized as WBT delegates; the second was the further intricacies of recognizing SIL delegates from those SIL Branches that didn't have a WBT Division operating in the same geographical location. Such complexities of determining how the various parts of SIL and WBT would be represented at corporate meetings took considerable time and effort for the boards to sort out. The WBT Board handled this for the 1979 Conference by declaring at the beginning of WBT's sessions that all duly appointed SIL delegates to the SIL International Conference were automatically delegates to the WBT International Conference.

---

19 WBT, "Board Minutes," May 1970, 42.

20 WBT, "Board Minutes," May 1969, 42.

21 WBT, "Board Minutes," September 1969, 82.

The challenge of practical dynamics in the relationship between WBT and SIL was evident when the former sought in 1978 to make a more definite separation of WBT and SIL accounting in the employment of US members and other members residing in the US. The process involved figuring out who was an employee of WBT and a member of WBT, and possibly of SIL because this distinction had legal and financial implications.

There were also complications in how WBT and SIL related to Christian bodies. For instance, the WBT Board noted that SIL, though organized as non-religious, was seen by others as Christian because of its members' Christian commitment and close association with WBT. However, SIL usually avoided having contracts or formal agreements with religious organizations.

These examples illustrate why the WBT Board sought to clarify the relationship with SIL. This guideline was endorsed by the 1979 WBT and SIL International Conference:

> The distinction between SIL and WBT is essentially a functional one: they do not do the same things. The distinctions in function can be spelled out in great detail, but for our purpose here the essential thing to note is that WBT never works on the field, i.e., never does field work as such. Rather, WBT agrees to the assignment of its members to SIL for field work, or assigns its members to some other entity or organization for sponsorship of field work.[22]

The terms 'membership' and 'assignment' also needed clarification. Therefore, the board noted how 'most' members of WBT were assigned to SIL, and therefore were members of both WBT and SIL. Their WBT membership entitled them to elect representatives to the WBT International Conference, vote on WBT constitutional amendments, and have rights as members of WBT Divisions. Their assignment to SIL meant they reported to SIL. Furthermore, some SIL members were assigned to WBT. They retained their SIL membership entitlements such as voting for representatives to SIL's International Conference and SIL constitutional amendments.

WBT members could be assigned elsewhere beyond SIL, such as a co-operating organization. These individuals would have both WBT and SIL membership. Where a co-operating organization didn't exist, the board recommended a field entity other than SIL be created for this purpose. The board also thought that it could be helpful to set up an international organization as a subsidiary of WBT to link such entities.

At the 1979 WBT International Conference, the delegates 'unanimously agreed that [WBT] enter into a perpetual written agreement with the Summer Institute

[22] WBT, "International Conference Minutes," May 1979, 20.

of Linguistics [SIL]... in which the personnel of its Directors shall be the same, both in name and numbers.'[23] However, clear demarcation between WBT and SIL was called for. This was spelled out as follows:

> WBT and SIL will continue to function as separate organizations, neither one subordinate to the other, but with very close links such as the following:
>
> - The same people are members of both except for honorary members.
> - The same people are members of both boards of directors.
> - They have partly overlapping board officers.
> - The same people fill the same positions in the administration of both organizations.
> - Their goals are complementary although different in some respects.[24]

What WBT was responsible for was not always clear. It was responsible for the home office or division operations, with SIL taking responsibility for the field work through its branches. However, there were some discrepancies, such as when WBT Board decided in 1968 to recognize WBT members serving with Australian Aborigines as an unchartered branch of WBT, Inc. Another example was WBT members in Colombia, India/Nepal, Suriname, and West Africa recognized as unchartered branches of WBT. In November 1974 the WBT Board revoked the WBT charter of the Mexico Branch. While there may have been good reasons for this move, it added to the confusion between WBT and SIL regarding their roles and responsibilities since the field work in these examples was SIL's responsibility.

Relating to Churches and Missions

WBT certainly saw itself needing to relate to the church and the Christian public and therefore used language familiar to the evangelical movement. An example was in 1973 when the board made a 'Great Commission Declaration' which stated

> It is an alarming fact that the Great Commission has never been carried out. It cannot be carried out until dedicated translators learn at least 2,000 more languages and express in them the Way of Life.
>
> Pioneer translators of the Scriptures, meeting in Mexico City... and representing 25 different areas of the world, have been challenged anew by these facts and passed the following DECLARATION:
>
> - Every language group in the world must receive the message of God's love in its own tongue soon.

[23] WBT, 1979, 6.

[24] WBT, 1979, 20.

- Some in each group must be taught to read and therefore literacy material must be prepared.
- Some must be taught to teach their own people to read and to expound the Word.
- Other loving service must be given as needs demand and circumstances permit.
- This service must be carried out in cooperation with local governments, universities, missions, and others interested in the welfare of the needy language groups.[25]

WBT wanted to engage directly with the Christian public. In 1966, Cameron Townsend informed the board that Billy Graham intended to announce WBT's prayer request for 300 new recruits for that year on his radio broadcast.

Also noted, WBT leaders attended high profile Christian events. For instance, George Cowan participated in a missions conference in Berlin in the mid-1960s with Rachel Saint and two Waorani from Ecuador: Kimo and Kani. Cowan commented on 'the spiritual impact these men made on the Congress and other groups before which they appeared.'[26] In 1974, Cowan as WBT President attended the Lausanne International Congress on World Evangelism.

The board supported an outward-looking posture for WBT with other mission organizations and churches. In 1975, this included the desire to develop a close friendship and working relationship with Evangel Bible Translators (EBT), an organization founded by Reverend Syvelle Philipps, with support from Cameron Townsend, inviting Assembly of God and other Pentecostals into Bible translation. By April 1978, the board encouraged people of charismatic-Pentecostal backgrounds who wanted to serve in Bible translation but preferred not to do this through WBT to join EBT instead. The board also wanted WBT to have a good relationship with the newly established Pioneer Bible Translators. In addition, WBT made a formal partnership with the Mission to the World of the Presbyterian Church of America. The WBT President and Vice President developed guidelines for cooperative agreements with other Christian organizations.

In May 1976, the board asked the US Division to take the initiative to provide a solid intercessory prayer program for Bible translation for the US Christian public, presenting an international prayer focus when conducted in consultation with the other Wycliffe Divisions. At the request of the WBT Board, the WBT President declared an annual worldwide day of fasting, prayer, and thanksgiving, starting on November 11, 1976.

In 1979, under the direction of the Africa Area Director, WBT and the Ethiopian

---

[25] WBT, "Board Minutes," May 1973, 86.

[26] WBT, "Corporation Conference Minutes," May 1967, 14.

Evangelical Church Mekane Yesus (EECMY) signed an agreement for the joint responsibility of Bible translation. EECMY could ask WBT for the necessary expatriate personnel to serve under EECMY.

In 1979, the board authorized the Executive Vice President to have WBT apply for membership in the Evangelical Council for Financial Accountability (ECFA). This decision caused some controversy. Out of the 16 people voting, one voted against it, and there were three abstentions. The proposal passed, but not unanimously. WBT felt this tension at times when publicly associated with Christian organizations since they maintained a close relationship with SIL that, at the time, didn't associate in such ways.

Forming Wycliffe International

A growing sense of optimism and possibilities was noticeable in 1976 when the International Administration used its publicity channels for public and internal membership to highlight the changing aspects of the work. There was 'continued need for workers', the 'exciting new development of national involvement', and the obligation 'to find ways to help national translators get the training and support' required for their 'share of the task'.[27]

By 1980, under Frank Robbins as Executive Vice President of WBT, 'national involvement' growth became an ongoing objective. Partnerships were growing in Africa, Asia, and the Pacific. WBT faced difficulties as it learned how to relate with local Christians committed to Bible translation in their languages in terms acceptable to the local culture and political situation, and at the same time, compatible with WBT's nature.

The 1979 International Conference approved establishing a non-profit, tax-exempt US corporation called Wycliffe Bible Translators International, Inc (WBTI). The corporation would 'carry out the international functions' of WBT, serving as WBT's policy-setting body at the international level. It would also act as a worldwide membership entity for Wycliffe personnel and provide an organizational structure for the administration of WBT's international responsibilities. The purposes of this new organization were as follows:

- The translation of the Word of God into all those languages of the world where it is needed.
- The advancement of the Kingdom of God on earth, and the creation of a larger Christian fellowship to provide a vehicle by means of which Christian people can be involved in Bible translation.
- The formation of other organizations to promote the translation of the Word

[27] WBT, "Board Minutes," May 1976, 4.

of God into all those languages of the world where it is needed.[28]

WBTI was given the exclusive right by WBT, Inc. to authorize the use of Wycliffe Bible Translators for any promotional, recruiting, fundraising, translation need, or other purposes. To keep the new corporation closely connected to SIL, WBTI 'would be controlled in connection with SIL [and] the two Corporations would be governed by the same persons; and that except for honorary members, the membership of the Corporation would be identical.'[29]

Dynamic Between WBT and SIL

Due to the importance of clarifying the WBT and SIL relationship, Executive Vice President Frank Robbins stated:

> There is a basic unity of WBT and SIL. The members comprise one group of people. That group has one set of motivations, one compatible set of goals, activities and relationships (both internal and external). The group has one life view, one faith (reflected in a doctrinal statement), one commitment to obey God and serve such that each language group may have and use the Scriptures in the language of the heart.
>
> Because these goals and activities cover a broad range, including activities normally carried out in religious contexts and organizations... and activities normally carried out in secular contexts and organizations... the one group has formed two organizations and carried out separate activities appropriate to each under the separate, but closely related organizations. The two organizations complement and support each other, but fill distinct roles in meeting the goals the group has set for itself. The relationships are spelled out in a series of agreements between the two organizations.[30]

Robbins mentioned shared elements between WBT and SIL. These included purpose, membership, international and area meetings, legislation, spiritual fellowship, and boards. The International Administration was one as well, with JAARS being an exception because it was part of SIL and related closely to the Wycliffe US Division. Another was the NBTOs, whose formation both WBT and SIL encouraged. Robbins also described the Distinctions summarized in table 1:

[28] WBT, "International Conference Minutes," May 1979, 13.

[29] WBT, 1979, 13.

[30] WBT, 1979, 23.

WBT	SIL
Organized as Divisions or Home Offices	Organized as Field Branches or Area Sections
Recruits, orients, guides people into membership, and trains them in relating to their constituency	Runs SIL schools for academic training for applicants, members, and others
Receives financial support from the Christian public, and transmits support to SIL for field work and training	Receives minimal support from secular grants
Promotes field work and raises prayer support for this from the Christian community; does not engage in field work (where it isn't feasible to work under SIL, a person can be seconded to another organization)	Carries out field work (e.g., language learning, linguistic analysis and production, literacy, Bible translation and distribution, community development and anthropology)
Assigns members to serve under national translation organizations or church and mission organizations on the field	Promotes interest in field work and linguistics on the field and provides training and assistance to local citizens
Relates to Christian organizations; does not have formal relationships with secular, academic organizations, or governments	Relates to university and academic organizations and governments; does not normally have relationships with religious organizations
President and Vice President of Board are different people from SIL	President and Vice President are different people from WBT

Table 1: Distinctions of WBT and SIL

Robbins pointed out that 'when we speak of Wycliffe doing this or that on the field, we are appropriately referring to WBT's purposes being met, but strictly speaking, through some other organization [such as SIL].'[31]

In summary, the delegates of the 1979 International Conference recognized 'SIL as basically an academic organization oriented to field work, and WBT as basically a support organization oriented to the Christian community, with SIL and WBT sharing motivation, membership, and formal organizational ties.'[32]

Wycliffe International Administration

To ensure that both WBT and SIL had sufficient administrative funds for operation, the 1979 International Conference adopted this policy: The 10% assessment drawn from all members' support income (will) be distributed as follows: Branches 4%, Divisions 5% (including 1% for publicity costs), International Administration both WBT and SIL 0.7%, and WBT and SIL International Conference 0.3%.

In November 1979, the WBT Board approved the Articles of Incorporation and By-Laws of Wycliffe Bible Translators International, Inc., and authorized for them

[31] WBT, 1979, 25.

[32] WBT, 1979, 26.

to be filed with the State of California and US Internal Revenue Service. This was the next step towards the development of a legal structure for WBTI.

On 1 May 1980, the WBTI, Inc. Board was formally constituted, and the various executive and administrative positions were established. This meant that the WBT Divisions that were subsidiaries of WBT, Inc. now transferred to being under WBTI, Inc., and WBT, Inc. became the legal body of the US Home Division. George Cowan, as the first President of WBTI, operated from rented space in the Wycliffe US Division Headquarters in Huntington Beach, California.

International Growth and Development

At its last WBT Board meeting for 1980, the International Administration gave a progress report. John Bendor-Samuel, Africa Area Director, described more robust local participation and responsibility-sharing in several African contexts. Of note, he stated, 'In Ghana, full responsibility for linguistic, translation and literacy work has been assumed by the Ghana Institute of Linguistics [with] very good working relationships between the Ghanaian and expatriate members of GIL.'[33] Bendor-Samuel also reported the following developments. In Cameroon, community participation increased, and SIL set up a local organization. A slowly evolving national Bible translation organization emerged in Ivory Coast and the Sudan Bible Translation and Literacy Association also began to function. The Executive Committee of the Nigeria Bible Translation Trust asked Bendor-Samuel to find consultant assistance and expatriate teams as soon as possible.

At the same board meeting, Asia Area Director Dan Weaver reported that in Indonesia, six prominent Christians formed a National Bible Translation Committee. Also, eight students attended a cross-cultural communications course. Weaver said that in May 1980, the Translation Committee of Sabah (organized in November 1979) sponsored a translation seminar to acquaint young people in local churches of the needs and opportunities for involvement in Bible translation. The Committee continued to actively function and planned another seminar later that year. Meanwhile, in the Philippines, the SIL Branch acted as rapidly as was practical to involve Filipinos in all areas of its program, including turning over promotion aspects to Filipinos.

Weaver reported that the focus in Singapore involved developing an interest in Wycliffe within the Christian community. Key people interested in Bible translation had been identified and a local committee would be set up within a few months. Some contacts were made in Taiwan, but it was unlikely for there to be division-type activity in the near future. Contacts were also being made in Hong Kong.

---

[33] WBT, "Board Minutes," November 1980, 6.

Earl Adams, Europe Area Director, reported to the board on the total number of eleven European Divisions. He identified three sub-areas: 'Free Europe' (WBT Division activity), Middle East (primarily SIL type field activity, diverse enough to be considered for a separate Area at some point), and Communist Europe (no strategy at that time). He noted a general spirit of optimism, and a sense of potential availability of recruits and support, once opportunities could be made known among the European Divisions. Adams observed, for instance, how the Netherlands had 40 members and eight applicants, Finland had 21 members and five applicants, and France had three members and four applicants. The newly established SIL school in France had 29 students attend, and it could 'serve Francophone countries of Africa as well as Europe.' Adams also detailed negative publicity from anthropologists speaking against SIL's activities in Latin America. This publicity had spread across Europe, and WBT Divisions attempted to handle these issues, leading to a profitable dialogue with antagonists.

Kemp Pallesen, Area Director for the Pacific, reported to the board the increasing interest and responsibility in Bible translation occurring in the newly formed Bible Translation Association (BTA) of Papua New Guinea.

In summary, WBTI was growing. By the time it became a legal body in 1980, WBTI could list an impressive gathering of affiliated organizations. For example, those established in Europe: Wycliffe UK, 1955; Wyclif e.V. (Germany), 1962; Wycliffe Switzerland, 1964; Wycliffe Bijbelvertalers (Netherlands), 1970; Association Traduire la Bible (France), 1971; Wycliffe Raamatunkääntäjät (Finland), 1972; Wycliffe South Africa (under the then Apartheid years, this was administratively handled by Wycliffe Europe Area), 1973; Wycliffe Sweden, 1975; Wycliffe Denmark, 1976; Wycliffe Belgium, 1977; and Wycliffe Norway, 1979. Those recognized elsewhere in the Western world: Wycliffe US, Wycliffe Canada, Wycliffe Australia, and Wycliffe New Zealand. Those located in Asia: Wycliffe Japan, and a new organization developing in South Korea.

Independence movements in Africa and elsewhere and the growth of national involvement in the post-colonial days of the mid-1970s to 1980 saw the formation of many NBTOs, usually in close cooperation with SIL, but with interest in and some growing affiliation with WBT. These organizations were developing in Nigeria, Ghana, Cameroon, India, the Philippines, Indonesia, Papua New Guinea, and Brazil.

Conclusion

The famous evangelization slogan—from the 'West to the rest'—characterized the era from 1966 to 1980, describing how the Gospel message would reach the whole world. In many ways, WBT epitomized mission organizations at this time.

The divisions managed the distribution of resources (personnel, funds, prayer support, frameworks, and strategies) through SIL's overseas structures. The process assumed that the task was dependent upon Western resources. The system would, by default, keep Westerners in charge because their financial resources and academic expertise brought them to the field contexts in the first place.

With its headquarters still located in the US and most of its leadership coming from the US (with a few from the UK, Australia, and a handful of other Western nations), WBTI continued as a Western organization with a strong US influence. Even though in 1980 'International' was added to WBT's name, it still primarily reflected the 'West to the rest' mission context of the era. The journey towards being genuinely global had, however, begun. The WBT structure shifted from being solely a US-based mission agency. Wycliffe US became its own entity, numerous WBT home offices and divisions arose in non-Western countries, and WBTI embraced new divisions in Asia, and new national organizations in Papua New Guinea, Brazil, and parts of Africa.

WBTI had not yet encountered the slow decline in recruitment of the next generation of Western Christians, nor the growing retirement rate of its predominantly Western workforce. It also had not yet been affected by a trend in some Western countries towards shorter terms of service. But it was facing a growing dichotomy from the fruit of its intention to embrace national involvement. As these new NBTOs were born, WBTI hadn't done enough to figure out how to partner with them and welcome them into WBTI. These challenges and opportunities lay ahead as the 1980s–1990s took shape. WBTI's continuing journey would take it beyond its Western roots and deeper into the changing global context, providing increased insight for participating in mission. The Great Commission would continue to be a significant motivator for WBT's missional intent for some time. The awakening to what God was doing in the church worldwide influenced WBTI to an awareness of *missio Dei* even though the term was not yet part of its vocabulary.

Leadership Theories and Practices

Three leadership theories characterize this era of WBT's early development: Behavioural, Situational, and Path-goal. These theories illustrate how WBT's leaders led and why these individuals often acted independently rather than functioning as cohesive groups or teams.

The first leadership theory is a Behavioural approach that focusses on tasks and relationships. Through tasks, leaders 'influence followers in their efforts to reach a goal.'[34] Relationship behaviours 'help followers feel comfortable with themselves, each other, and with the situations in which they find themselves.'[35] A criticism of this theory is that it is 'US-centric' because it mirrors the ideals of US culture.[36] The theory is relevant to WBT and WBTI since its leaders came mainly from the US during this era.

The second theory is Situational and refers to how different conditions call for various types of leadership.[37] A leader observes what followers need to meet the organization's objectives and adapts the leadership style by being directive or supportive. A leader must be flexible for this theory to work in a wide range of settings and circumstances. For example, in WBT and WBTI, the nature of Bible translation meant personnel were generally well educated and did not expect or want to have directive leadership. Whenever leaders were not sensitive to this and unable to adapt their style, they faced resistance from those they were trying to lead.

Path-goal is the third theory and focusses on motivating followers and achieving their tasks. The leader gives followers what is required to reach the organization's goals. The leader compensates for deficiencies in the followers or their environment by 'designing and facilitating a healthy and productive work environment to propel followers toward success.'[38] This theory is difficult to achieve because it uses different aspects of leadership to address a wide variety of contexts. It also assumes leadership will focus on coaching, guidance, and direction for the followers, helping them overcome obstacles to achieve their goals. Because of the high turnover of leaders in WBT and WBTI, there were no apparent long-term plans for leadership development of emerging and current leaders. Individuals in WBT and WBTI frequently expressed their opinions—their voice—not as a collective group, which presented another challenge. Acting in this individualistic manner was a value held from the beginning of WBT's history. WBT and WBTI's leaders found this hard to address—how individuals had their say within the contexts of an organization of organizations.

In summary, these three theories originated from social science research and did not specifically have Christian mission organizations in mind. However, we see the influences of these theories on leadership in WBT and WBTI. We also see the industrious Protestant work ethic and a solid spiritual motivation, not tied to financial or productivity rewards nor necessarily influenced by a leader's effectiveness or ineffectiveness, as motivational factors.

[34] Northouse, 73.

[35] Northouse, 73.

[36] Northouse, 83.

[37] Northouse, 95.

[38] Northouse, 118.

Journey Reflections (Natural Tensions)

1966-1980 were formative years for Wycliffe as a whole, leading to the creation of WBTI as an international organization. As the organization grew, leaders sought to deal with the natural tensions that would accompany the organization on its journey for years to come. How to ensure flexibility and accountability, make decisions regarding centralization and/or decentralization, and discover methodology that could be contextually adapted to fit the increasingly multinational body of participants. This was the beginning of sorting out the complicated from the complex. WBTI leadership would need to find ways to create helpful processes and structures to reduce complications while also learning to accept and embrace complexity. This would not be an easy journey.

› What are some of the natural tensions in your context? How does the leadership acknowledge and approach these tensions?
› How do you identify and distinguish between the complicated and complex issues and situations in your context? Are there times you may have mistaken one for the other? Consider how such a situation could be approached differently and how that might help.

Chapter 3
Creating: 1981–1990

Historical Setting

Within a few years of WBTI's formation in May 1980, opportunities emerged that did not exist when its predecessor, WBT, Inc., was founded. That was 38 years earlier, in 1942, when Cameron Townsend and William Nyman formed it as the resourcing organization for SIL, which Townsend and L.L. Legters had founded in 1934. Barely two years after WBTI's start in 1980, on 23 April 1982, Townsend went to be 'in the presence of Jesus Christ whom he loved and served.'[1] Would WBTI be able to flourish past the founder's years? Would Townsend's spirit of pioneering and trusting God for the impossible continue through the next generation of leaders?

The decade of the 1980s was pivotal for the new WBTI. Significant developments were ahead, including WBTI's first International Conference in 1981. The symbiotic relationship between WBTI and SIL became more complex. Already an international administration managed the two organizations, based at the headquarters in Dallas, Texas. While the same people served on the WBTI and SIL boards, each board had a different president. Each president was also the board chair and had some public relations responsibilities.

Both WBTI and SIL would face the new challenge and opportunity of working with the emerging NBTOs located in the majority world. Discussions and decisions about this would take various turns over the decade. Structurally, where did the NBTOs fit? They needed help with their development. WBTI leaders had to balance support and avoid having too much influence in response.

Another challenge towards the end of the decade was when the WBT European divisions had to respond to the changing laws of their own countries. They required greater legal separation from WBTI. Navigating this issue would test WBTI's resolve to find the proper organizational structure to enable a worldwide Bible translation movement.

Looking back towards the start of the twentieth century, Scott Sunquist described Christianity as 'a confident, strong, imperial religion of the West.'[2] By the end of that century, more Christians existed outside the Western world than

[1] Hugh Steven, *Yours for Finishing the Task* (Orlando: Wycliffe Bible Translators, 2004), 267.

[2] Scott Sunquist, *The Unexpected Christian Century* (Grand Rapids: Baker Academic, 2015), xvi.

within. 'Christianity became more truly a world religion' in the twentieth century.[3] The shift happened during 'political change and upheaval, wars, violence, and suffering.'[4] It was the passing of 'the era of Western Christianity' and the dawning of 'Southern Christianity'.[5] This 'southern' phenomenon showed how terminology changed to describe the shifts. Various phrases were used at the time to describe this: 'global South', 'non-Western', 'third-world', 'two-thirds world', and 'developing world' Christianity.[6] In summary, after heading Christendom for a thousand years, and though it was the Western world that has led the modern missionary movement for the past 200 years and well into the twentieth century, the West was losing its predominance in global Christianity. As Sunquist states, 'No scholar [or] madman' could have predicted this new composition of Christianity in the 'unexpected' Christian century of global mission.[7]

At the start of the 1980s, this shift of worldwide Christianity was less noticeable within the composition of WBTI. The organization had yet to see a significant increase in participants from the regions where the church grew the most. However, this was changing by the end of the decade, especially with new organizations in Africa, Asia, and the Pacific becoming part of WBTI.

As the century ended, mission theology and the *missio Dei* were reviewed. Lesslie Newbigin was influential through his 'prophetic realization about the need for a Trinitarian missiology.'[8] He noted the authority of the Triune God in mission as the starting point for the church's understanding of mission. An example was in John 20:21–22, where God's mission involves all members of the Triune God through the interconnection 'between the Father's mission and Jesus's mission and the ongoing mission of the Holy Spirit in the life and witness of the church.'[9] As Newbigin elaborated, Jesus is the 'presence' who provides the 'possibility of repentance and freely given faith.'[10] The active Holy Spirit 'is the presence of the reign of God.'[11] On earth, 'the mission of the Church to all the nations... is itself the mighty work of God, the sign of the inbreaking of the kingdom.'[12] Mission under Christendom was affected by these trinitarian perspectives.[13]

---

3 Stanley, 11.

4 Smither, 164.

5 Philip Jenkins, *The Next Christendom*, Third ed. (New York: Oxford University Press, 2011), 8.

6 Smither, 165.

7 Sunquist, xvi.

8 Timothy Tennent, *Invitation to World Missions: A Trinitarian Missiology for the Twenty-First Century* (Grand Rapids: Kregel, 2011), 68.

9 Tennent, 67.

10 Lesslie Newbigin, *The Open Secret: An Introduction to the Theology of Mission, Revised* (Grand Rapids: Wm. B. Eerdmans, 1995), 118.

11 Newbigin, 118.

12 Newbigin, 119.

13 Tennent, 67.

This theological review of the *missio Dei* did not appear to have any influence on WBTI's understanding of its participation in God's mission. There was no evident expression of Bible translation as part of the Triune missionary God's plans. Nevertheless, it presented a task to complete to fulfill the Great Commission.

In 1974, the LCWE (Lausanne I), initiated by Billy Graham, was a significant event with outcomes influencing mission practice through Ralph Winter's belief that 'unreached people groups should be given priority in mission' and Rene Padilla and Samuel Escobar's 'call for a more holistic approach to mission.' [14] The resulting *Lausanne Covenant* set a course for evangelical theology of mission for decades to come. In 1976, Winter established the US Center for World Mission. He brought attention to 'the key to completing the Great Commission' that shifted focus from reaching countries to 'engaging people groups'.[15] Winter interprets the Genesis 12:1–2 reference to 'families of the earth' and the Matthew 28:18–20 reference to 'nations' to signify 'ethno-linguistic peoples'.[16] These were a 'grouping of individuals who perceive themselves to have a common affinity with one another.'[17] Reaching these groups with the gospel could entail establishing a church planting movement.

When Lausanne II met in 1989 in Manila, there was momentum to build upon Winter's people group focus. Luis Bush wanted mission efforts to address the unreached people groups who primarily lived in the '10/40 Window'—the region between 10 degrees and 40 degrees latitude between North Africa and Asia. The terminology 'unreached' and '10/40 Window' appeared in conversations within WBTI, especially in the Wycliffe organizations, who saw it as an opportunity for increasing interest in this challenging region through publicity and promotion.

Evangelical mission was strengthened in 1983 and 1986 when Billy Graham sponsored conferences for itinerant evangelists as part of his calling to bring 'together evangelical streams within global Christianity.'[18] The first COMIBAM Ibero-America Mission Conference in São Paulo in 1987 was another example of conferences emphasizing world mission. COMIBAM gathered over 3,000 evangelical leaders from across Latin America. 'As the conference organizers had hoped, the delegates affirmed that Latin America was becoming an active participant in world missions.'[19] The involvement of COMIBAM in the Bible translation movement would take time to develop, and it would not be in this decade.

At the Lausanne II Congress, 'hundreds of mission partnerships emerged to

---

[14] Smither, 174.

[15] Smither, 168.

[16] Smither, 168.

[17] Smither, 168.

[18] Sunquist, 64.

[19] Todd Hartch, *The Rebirth of Latin American Christianity* (Oxford: Oxford University Press, 2014), 186.

face the issues of mission at the end of the twentieth century.'[20] One such collaborative effort was an informal gathering of Bible translation and Bible distribution leaders. At the time, the world of the Bible agencies was known for its lack of collaboration and even disunity. During the time together, the Bible agency leaders wanted to meet again. That happened in 1990 when these same leaders gathered at Wycliffe UK's Horsleys Green Centre for a meeting co-hosted by Fergus Macdonald, then General Secretary of the Scottish Bible Society, and John Bendor-Samuel, then EVP for SIL and WBTI, and was later known as the inaugural meeting of the Forum of Bible Agencies International (FOBAI). Leaders from WBTI, SIL, and UBS gathered as founding members, with leaders from Open Doors, Scripture Union, Living Bible International (now Tyndale House Publishers), Bible League International, and Gideons UK, among others. The Forum became 'the world's only community for international Bible ministry leaders designed to benefit member agencies, individually, and through the partnerships they create.'[21]

Another development that positively impacted the Bible translation movement was the Jesus Film, a non-print medium for Scripture. Initially released in 1979 as a dramatization of the life of Christ based on Luke's gospel, it eventually became known as the Jesus Film Project. The film's soundtrack was—and continues to be—translated into hundreds of languages.

At the geopolitical level, late 1989 saw a sequence of 'popular revolutions in Eastern Europe that terminated the communist regimes of Poland, Hungary, East Germany, Bulgaria, Czechoslovakia, and Romania' and then the break-up of the Soviet Union in December 1991.[22] This meant that the churches in these lands had greater freedom from their governments to participate in worldwide mission. There would be Wycliffe organizations formed in many of these countries within a decade.

In summary, the decade under review was significant for WBTI and the Bible translation movement, occurring during what Brian Stanley called 'the century of the Bible' because 'more peoples received the Scriptures in their own languages than in any preceding century.'[23] WBTI, through its organizations and partnerships, played a growing role, especially in the second half of the century.

Renewing Vision

WBTI's first International Conference took place in 1981 in Dallas, Texas, chaired by George Cowan, president. The Conference objectives were (1) to confirm and

[20] Smither, 175.

[21] FOBAI, https://forum-intl.org/about/history/, accessed 23 September 2020.

[22] Stanley, 218.

[23] Stanley, 9.

renew WBTI's vision, (2) to decide on and agree to how WBTI implemented that vision, and (3) to provide interaction among those in attendance representing the entire membership.

In attendance were one or two delegates from each of 16 organizations representing three categories: (1) the unchartered divisions of Finland, Germany, Japan, New Zealand, Norway, Sweden, and Switzerland; (2) the chartered divisions of Australia, British Isles, Canada, the Netherlands, and the US; and (3) the emerging divisions with 'observer' status of Austria, Belgium, Denmark, and France. Additionally, SIL invited representatives from all its field entities plus the International Administration and WBTI and SIL Board members.

Electing the board of directors was a vital function. There were two boards—one for SIL and one for WBTI, the same people served on both boards, and each board had its own president. The WBTI President's objective was to provide vision and stimulus for the development of the overall program and completion of the task. Responsibilities included:

› communicating WBTI's vision and goals internally and externally;
› chairing the board, its meetings, and the International Conference;
› reviewing and monitoring of WBTI's programs and policies;
› attending global strategic planning sessions with the International Administration;
› advising and consulting divisions and monitoring the health and programs of the divisions;
› strengthening partnerships and relationships with global bodies;
› collaborating with the SIL President, the Executive Vice President, and International Administration (joint WBTI-SIL).

In other words, the role of president involved far more than chairing the board and constituted a full-time position.

Three constituency members were also to be elected (defined as those who were not members of the corporation, though they became members when they were appointed to the board); five people 'elected at large', assumedly from the general membership of SIL and Wycliffe Divisions; five SIL Branch Directors; and two WBT Division Directors. The election was implemented from a slate of candidates submitted to the WBTI and SIL Corporation Conference delegates by a nominating committee. The WBTI President was elected from a slate of at least two nominees.

Board members elected in 1981 to serve for the next two years were Cameron Townsend (Founder); David Cummings (WBTI President); Kenneth Gregerson (SIL President); Piet Koen and Andreas Holzhausen (WBT Division Directors);

Karl Franklin, Paul Meier, Al Pence, Bob Gunn, and Len Newell (SIL Branch Directors); Emmanuel Njock, Joseph Profita, and Alan Bergstedt (Constituency Representatives); Rey Johnson, Cyril Brigland, Thomas Wiesmann, Peter Warkentin, and Don Lindholm (members at large).

Faith goals (a term used to describe goals set in faith rather than concrete commitments) for the 1980s were adopted by both WBTI and SIL: publication of 500 more New Testaments; work to be started in 800 new languages, with substantial involvement by SIL members; 3,000 new members recruited through Wycliffe Divisions; progress towards identifying the remaining Bible translation needs; completion of the task in the majority of SIL Branches in the Americas; and strategies formulated for serving in the unreached areas of the world.

Towards the end of the Conference, George Cowan handed the leadership baton to David Cummings as the new WBTI President. Cowan was given President Emeritus status in recognition of his 24 years of distinguished service as president of WBTI. He received a standing ovation from all in attendance. With his unique and impactful manner, Cowan was urged to continue encouraging people to commit to the Bible translation movement worldwide. Cowan's further entitlements included a permanent invitation to attend all WBTI Board meetings with the 'privilege of the floor' and travel costs covered by WBTI. Later, in its December 1981 meeting, the board made Cowan a permanent observer to all future Conferences because of his long tenure as WBTI President.

Developing the International Board

Soon after taking the office of president, David Cummings expressed to the board his concerns over the high turnover among board officers and those in other leadership positions. He believed that continuity between leaders was lacking, and he advocated for longer terms of service for board members rather than the customary two years.

Five years into operating as WBTI, the board reviewed its make-up. It decided to keep the current configuration of five SIL Branch Directors (who also served on the SIL Board), two WBT Division Directors (who also served on the SIL Board), two members representing the supporting public, known as the Constituency (one of whom also served on the SIL Board), and three members at large who came from the broader pool of members of WBT and SIL (one of whom also served on the SIL Board). This composition showed how the WBTI Board was tied to the SIL Board.

As WBTI continued to grow, the role of president called for clarification. At the December 1981 board meeting, Cummings sought clarification for expectations of him in this role. SIL's president had been active all along in the promotion of SIL's work in the field of linguistics. Therefore, the board decided that the WBTI president needed to assist the divisions and NBTOs in the areas of (1) a collecting point for message outlines, modules, and other helpful materials for communicating about Bible translation with home and church audiences 'in a culturally relevant way'; and (2) carrying out research and production of materials that would inform the International Administration, divisions, and NBTOs 'to help them develop appropriate strategies and keep current with missiological progress.'[24]

From Councils to Divisions

As previously mentioned in this chapter, the growth of the worldwide church helps explain the also growing interest in establishing Wycliffe Divisions in new sending countries and the necessity to set goals for those divisions. These were: recruitment, fund-raising, ministering to the constituency, and care of members. Starting Wycliffe work in a new sending country relied on volunteers to represent Wycliffe and handle inquiries. It also involved a legal basis for operating an organization. For prospective recruits, additional requirements included raising prayer and financial support and the ability to interact and communicate well with their home churches. It entailed procedures for transmitting funds. Training opportunities for prospective new workers in field-related roles had to be provided—often in partnership with larger divisions and SIL training courses.

The next development step for a viable division included motivated leadership at the administrative and governance levels who shared the vision of Bible translation in the church's life. While preferable for local citizens to fill these leadership roles, sometimes, for a specified time, it was advantageous for experienced Wycliffe leaders from other countries to fill those roles. Within three years of a division's beginning, a responsible support committee must be in place, along with a constitution accepted by the governing body and membership, and legal or formal registration according to national laws (demonstrated through statutes, articles of incorporation, registration, or other evidence of legal registration). For a division to function, it needed members to join the organization, staff employment policies, and retirement and pension plans. It required a growing prayer and financial support base, demonstrating its financial accountability through annual audited financial accounts and current budget statements. After showing sustainability and growth, it could move toward achieving its final goal as a chartered division.

Until a division achieved chartered status, the WBTI Board continued its

[24] WBTI, "Board Minutes," November 1987, 9.

direct involvement in governance oversight. For example, in November 1985, the board approved the reappointment of five members of the Austria Council and made four new appointments to the Singapore Board. The WBTI Board was also involved in operational matters such as approving the Norway Division's retirement plan for its members.

Once a division was operational, it was necessary to clarify its purpose. Cummings outlined functions to be carried out by a division: ministry, public relations, developing resources, managing personnel, and operating the administration. WBTI was responsible for providing sufficient training and staffing for each division to carry out these functions. However, Cummings was concerned that the divisions were not engaging enough with the constituency church in achieving WBTI's goal of reaching the Bibleless peoples. According to Cummings, the 'task of Bible translation [was] the responsibility of the church' and WBT was 'a God-given instrument to draw alongside the local church and make it successful in its task of sharing the Word with those who do not have it.'[25]

Relationships with Divisions

The WBTI Board was also responsible for appointing new division directors. At the December 1981 board meeting, Andreas Holzhausen was reappointed as German Division Director, Martien de Groot as acting director of the Netherlands, and Sam McBride as New Zealand Division Director. Having been nominated by both the WBTI Executive Vice President and the WBTI Europe Area Director, the German Division Director was reappointed to the role. This pattern was the same for the other appointments, coming from the Executive Vice President and the respective Area Director. The WBTI Board continued to have a representative on the WBT, Inc. (US Division) council, highlighting another example of their activity in leadership or governance decisions of the divisions.

In October 1982, both the Netherlands Division and the German Division had established procedures to elect their leaders and councils. At that time and upon recommendation of the Executive Vice President and Europe Area Director, the WBTI Board granted chartered status to both divisions. In addition, and building on the work of someone who had previously served in Portuguese-speaking Brazil, the board granted permission to the Europe Area office to explore establishing a division (labelled as an 'Advance') in Portugal. The WBTI Board also gave approval to the Norway Division to join the Norwegian Mission Council. The WBTI Board approved the France Division to join the Federation of Francophone Evangelical Mission because it would help the division relate more effectively

[25] WBTI, "Board Minutes," May 1987, 4.

with the Christian public in France. In 1983, the New Zealand Division was granted charter status. The British Isles Division was permitted to become a Limited Company. Later the same year, the WBTI Board authorized the formation of a division in the Republic of Ireland, separate from the British Division, due to the political situation in Ireland. In 1985, the Swiss Division was granted charter status. In June 1990, the WBTI Board agreed to a provisional operational statement for starting WBT in Hungary. As the first Wycliffe Division in a formerly communist country in Europe, work in Hungary could proceed but needed to do so slowly to prevent being seen as a foreign organization attempting to make inroads, but instead ensuring it was a Hungarian initiative.

Meanwhile, interest was growing among Christians in South Korea. The WBTI Board decided that the Asia Area Director could form a home office in that nation and set up a local committee to give it oversight. The desire was to see new workers join from various church and denominational backgrounds. Consequently, new Korean members' pathways to WBT were created from the already established Korea Translation Mission (also known as the Korea Bible Translators), through church and denominational mission boards, and eventually, from the yet to be formed WBT Korea Home Office. At the October 1982 WBTI Board meeting, at the request of the Asia Area Director, the Korea Translation Mission was released from serving as the representative of WBT in Korea since the development of a WBT Korean home office was progressing.

WBT and SIL Relationship

The 1983 International Conference was held in Dallas. As WBTI's work continued to grow, the board enabled a larger group of representatives to attend the Conference. It gave official status (without vote) to delegates from Austria, Belgium, Denmark, France, Italy, Portugal, GILLBT (Ghana), NBTT (Nigeria), BTL (East Africa, Kenya), and South Korea. Representation was given to the unchartered divisions of Finland, Norway, Sweden, Switzerland, New Zealand, and Japan. The board also asked the Area offices to invite one representative from each affiliated national translation organization agency as an official observer to the conference.

The following people were elected to the WBTI Board: David Cummings, president, with board members Eric Brabham, Cyril Brigland, John Daly, Ken Gregerson, Richard Hugoniot, Carrie Kulp, Mildred Larson, Eugene Loos, Fred Magbanua, Bernie May, Paul Meier, Emmanuel Njock, Al Pence, Joeseph Profita, Burkhard Schöttelndreyer, and Peter Warkentin. The same members served on the SIL Board, except Ken Gregerson as the SIL President.

Delegates to both the SIL and WBTI Conferences further clarified the relationship between WBTI and SIL by describing what each focussed on:

> WBTI relates both formally and informally to Christian organizations. It does not normally have formal relationships with secular and academic organizations or governments.
>
> SIL relates both formally and informally with university and academic organizations and with governments. In certain circumstances it has formal or extensive informal relationships with religious entities where such relationships are appropriate to the fulfilling of its objectives.[26]

The WBTI Board decided that any actions taken by the SIL Board that the WBTI President, Executive Vice President, and Secretary thought to apply to WBTI would be adapted, adopted, and recorded in the minutes. While WBTI was financially dependent upon SIL, SIL was financially reliant on the individual Wycliffe divisions. That meant the WBTI Board wanted SIL to cover nominal operating expenses for the WBTI President, WBTI Board, costs of WBTI delegates to attend the Joint SIL-WBT Conference, and expenses of division representatives attending SIL Area meetings.

Leadership Transition

At its October 1983 meeting, the WBTI Board expressed its gratitude to Frank and Ethel Robbins for their faithful and effective leadership in the office of Executive Vice President as WBTI entered a new era. Robbins had overseen the growth and development of WBTI in the 'face of worldwide turbulence and difficulty.'[27] John Bendor-Samuel took over from Robbins. Both WBTI and SIL continued to use the title Executive Vice President (EVP). This use of EVP as the executive officer of the organization aligned with the use of 'president' to indicate chairing of the governing of the organization.

The International Headquarters at the ILC in Dallas increased in its importance for supporting the global work of WBTI and SIL. Consequently, priorities for the ILC's development in 1984 included building warehouse space, dormitories, classrooms for the Texas SIL school, extensions to childcare and administrative offices, and a cultural museum. Some new building space was designated for the US Division to support its members based in Texas.

Since the early 1970s, the International Administration was located at the

26 WBTI, "International Conference Extracts," May 1983, 5.

27 WBTI, "Board Minutes," October 1983, 2.

Dallas Center. However, after Bendor-Samuel became WBTI and SIL Executive Vice President, discussions concerning that location arose with the two boards in 1987. Bendor-Samuel was working out of the UK Division at Horsleys Green, a town about an hour from London. The WBTI Board decided that he could continue to operate from there rather than from Dallas. However, all other vice presidents were required to be based in Dallas, while area directors were in various parts of the world, closer to their areas. As with the other international administration officers, they served both WBTI and SIL. Representing an additional change, in 1987, various international administration functions at administration sections or departments and their respective heads and coordinators could be established in relevant parts of the world. This indicator showed an openness to limited decentralization from the traditionally centralized operations at the Dallas headquarters.

Strengthening Accountability

WBTI recognized that it was important for members of divisions to strengthen their relationships with prayer and financial supporters (individuals and churches). However, communication constraints in some difficult access regions such as Asia and Eurasia proved problematic. A member's furlough presented a significant time to reconnect with supporters. Nevertheless, the WBTI President noted a growing aggressiveness by the church for more involvement with and accountability from the missionaries it supported. He also observed that the WBTI Divisions were not yet taking this seriously.

The WBTI Board chose to promote these critical relationships by focussing on member furlough planning and member accountability to prayer and financial supporters. The International Administration reviewed, for key administrators, the role and implications of furlough and furlough workshops, study programs, teaching responsibilities at SIL schools, and service to international and division centres. This had consequences for the various divisions and the SIL field entities where WBT members served. It called for improved coordination of furlough plans and improved communication between a member's division, their field entity, and their constituency. This also related to how WBT members spoke of their financial needs. There were various cultural factors to consider. While the board wanted to continue the practice of not directly soliciting funds, there were likely to be nuanced cultural factors to consider in each country where WBT Divisions existed.

It was apparent that WBTI's leadership had a growing concern about the organization, and therefore, about all its divisions' relationships with churches. To understand this issue better, one must return to the formative years of WBT, Inc. and note how the organization lacked a clear understanding of its relationship with the local church. Over forty years later, the WBTI Board elevated the importance of this topic. The board called on the International Administration to research ways to improve relationships with members' home churches and churches in the field contexts and encourage major denominations to develop Bible translation programs.

WBTI recommended that its divisions work with church denominations to participate in Bible translation for the world's ethnic minorities, either directly or through WBT. Where there were significant doctrinal differences, denominations could create their own Bible translation organizations. Guidelines promoting joint membership with a WBT Division and a denomination's Bible translation organization were established. The International Administration took the principle 'that the task of Bible translation is the responsibility of the Church of Jesus Christ (Matthew 28:20).'[28] Consequently, WBTI committed itself to serving the home churches by enabling them to be involved in training and overseeing its members who chose to join WBT. WBTI required that all division members have at least one recognized home commending church body to which they belonged. WBTI divisions asked for the church's input at crucial points of the member's journey. These points included when the member applied to WBT, investigated an initial assignment with WBT or SIL, made furlough arrangements and assignment changes, or in times of spiritual or personal need.

Milestones

WBTI President David Cummings opened with a keynote address as the delegates gathered at WBTI's third International Conference in 1985 in Fort Worth, Texas. He stated,

> God has given us an awesome responsibility as leaders and representatives of the Corporation.... We must be sensitive to what God is telling us now, not resting on what has gone on before. We must watch for these things: (a) The spirit of this age: [Because] the world entices us... We must view leaders as our elders according to the Word of God. The heritage of a group must be communicated from generation to generation through effective training programs; (b) Spiritual warfare: We must frequently lay aside our personal rights in order to get the job done and we must guard against the tendency toward becoming comfortable; (c) The nature of God

[28] WBTI, "Board Minutes," November 1987, 24.

> working: What is the 'deep structure' God is looking for [within] the 'surface structure' of our plans and discussions; [and] (d) Ourselves: ... We are called to a life of holiness and we must live godly lives in a godless world. Let us be a renewed people looking for an ongoing renaissance.[29]

The area directors gave highlights. For example, Frank Robbins, Africa Area Director, reported that 'today is God's day for Africa' because of the open doors for Bible translation on the continent. Asia Area Director Al Pence reported more new members from Asian countries. Europe Area Director Earl Adams informed those present on progress in recruiting Europeans across the Continent. North America Area Director Aaron Hoffman mentioned new training programs in the Canada Division and a prayer network for unreached language groups led by the US Division. In the Pacific, Area Director Andy Gallman described the necessity for continuity in leadership and partnerships with various countries, national churches, and universities.

Vice President for Personnel Ron Rowland reported that by 1990, 50% of the membership would have joined in the 1980s, which reflected the peak of the Baby Boomer generation and the growth of the worldwide church. Thus, the focus would be on selection, training, and orientation of new members, as well as on leadership development.

The boards of WBTI and SIL were elected by the conference delegates, with elected members serving both boards. David Cummings was re-elected as WBTI President, and Ken Gregerson as SIL President. The other board members were WBT Division Directors Bernie May and Burkhard Schöttelndreyer; SIL Branch Directors John Daly, Dick Hugoniot, John Taylor, Ger Reesink, and Lambert Anderson; constituency members Emmanuel Njock, Joseph Profita, and Eric Brabham; members at large Millie Larson, Fred Magbanua, Eugene Loos, Paul Meier, and Samuel Escobar.

The developing topic of national involvement through the NBTOs drew attention. As a result of their conference in 1985, NBTOs wanted to be fully involved in the world-wide Bible translation effort. To this end, both the WBTI and SIL Conference delegates decided to commit to working in partnership with the NBTOs.

The International Administration presented its priorities by areas for the next two years. For example, newly appointed Africa Area Director John Watters included encouraging NBTOs in his list of priorities. Asia Area Director Al Pence included local recruiting (especially in South Korea, Hong Kong, Indonesia, and Malaysia) and the possible establishment of divisions, along with cooperation

---

[29] WBTI, "International Conference Extracts," November 1985, 1.

with NBTOs. Earl Adams, Europe Area Director, wanted to focus on developing the area, on leadership selection and development, on recruiting new workers, and on increasing prayer support. In Latin America, where there was only one NBTO, and the rest of the work was through SIL Branches, Area Director John Alsop included formal training of local citizens—both majority and minority groups. Aaron Hoffman, North America Area Director, included recruitment of personnel, maintaining of high standards in recruitment, and raising of financial resources. Ger Reesink from SIL PNG reported on Pacific Area priorities that included partnerships with sending churches, host governments and universities, and host churches and parachurch organizations, and consistent and balanced publicity (i.e., incorporating all aspects of SIL's efforts in WBT publicity). Special mention was made of the high level of maturity and commitment of so many of the recruited members. The emphasis on recruiting enough literacy workers to meet the global need was also noted.

A highlight at the close of this biennium was the milestone of WBTI and SIL's involvement in translation in the 1,000th language, ministry and members involved in or coming from 50 countries, and the 225th New Testament published and distributed.

Continued Growth

An update at the May 1984 WBTI Board meeting recorded 14 WBT Divisions in Europe. These divisions were active in discussions critical to their members assigned to SIL, including setting the cost-of-living quotas for members living and working overseas. The WBTI Board expressed concern about the growing number of US Division members assigned in the US and the addition of regional centres required to support them. The multi-faceted increase included those returning to the US for their children's education, for health reasons, or for retirement, but able to serve with the US Division.

As WBTI continued to grow, the administration, through newly formed area committees, helped guide the designing and running of conferences for Africa, Asia, Latin America, and the Pacific area directors, to be held in their areas in-between the corporate conferences.

As WBT Divisions became better known, they were also receiving greater undesignated legacies and deferred gifts from wills and trusts. Therefore, the WBTI Board instructed each division to follow the procedure of keeping the first US$10,000; of the remaining amount, 50% was to be allotted to SIL for field activities, and 50% was to be allocated to the division. Of the division's allocated portion, 50% needed to be set aside to assist its members in their retirement, unless there was another satisfactory provision. The US Division was the largest donor to SIL's operations, and it agreed to contribute at least US$500,000 to SIL annually. Funds coming into a division, in general, were subject to an assessment of 10%. The formula for distribution in 1987, for example, was: 9% to the division that received the funds, and 1% to the International Administration, divided as .7% for administrative costs, and .3% for the Corporation Travel Fund (for board meetings and international conferences). The incoming funds were under the control of the receiving division and could be directed to recipients such as SIL, NBTOs, other divisions or its members directly.

The relationship between the divisions and WBTI called for regular review. An inherent tension concerning lines of authority, as well as the extent of autonomy the divisions could exert, was always present. In 1987 the board clarified that divisions functioned as the members' employers, having authority over personnel actions required by national laws regarding incorporation, employment, taxes, etc. [30] In contrast, there were specific personnel procedures handled by the International Administration, such as acceptance, termination, and appeal. In exceptional cases, when a member did not have a home division, another organization could act as the responsible division. A growing pool of new members without bona fide divisions was joining, challenging the operating structure of WBTI, which relied on its divisions to handle all the recruitment and processing of new personnel, including those who would go on to serve with SIL.

Production of media communications and resources that accurately reflected the SIL field realities was a growing concern for both WBTI and SIL. There was an expressed desire to dramatize an SIL field story through film or in book form to stir interest and, ideally, recruitment, in the divisions. However, it was essential that these promotional materials respect the sensitivities of the cultures both WBTI and SIL served. Sometimes SIL field directors had to decide when such materials were anthropologically insensitive to the host culture and voice that decision, which caused tension. Therefore, the WBTI Board decided the Vice President for Public Affairs and the respective area directors would evaluate all new materials before circulating them among the divisions.

In Africa, complex political situations produced a challenging context for fledgling organizations. As a means of strengthening WBTI's work on the African continent, WBTI and Bible Translation & Literacy (East Africa) developed a cooperative agreement to establish an East Africa Bible Translation Centre aimed at furthering the work of Bible translation in Africa.

To advance Bible translation work in Panama, WBTI signed cooperative agreements with three Panamanian organizations: the Kuna Mission of Panama, the

[30] WBTI, November 1985, 11.

Pan America Mission, and the Crossroads Bible Church.

Interest in NBTOs was growing within the WBTI Board and International Administration, as was the number of agencies, presenting exciting possibilities for the ministry of Bible translation to expand beyond WBT Divisions and SIL field entities. However, some WBTI and SIL leaders were concerned about funding these new organizations, thinking it possible that financial donors could become more interested in funding nationals than those recruited and sent out by Wycliffe Divisions. The board adopted this guideline: 'No support should go directly from a WBT donor to a national translator.'[31] What it meant in practice was that all financial support needed to go through a WBT and SIL member who, in turn, could fund a local translator. In hindsight, this comes across as paternalistic. However, it may have had more to do with easing into a new way of working. Small steps forward allowed for time to create new operational and financial processes and for helping people prepare for further change.

Recognizing the growing role of the NBTOs and that they were not yet clearly placed within the membership structure of WBTI, the International Administration studied the performance and progress among NBTOs and learned about their respective goals and programs to improve how WBTI related to them. The investigation included examining what made an NBTO successful in its operations, identifying suitable training programs and techniques for NBTO leaders, and determining how NBTOs could be financed and developed further.

Divisions were also struggling to find their identities. Could a division affiliate with a national mission, church, or Christian association? Did these other organizations have aims and doctrinal positions compatible with WBTI? What were these associations' expectations of the divisions? The WBTI policy required that the divisions discuss any intent to join such associations with the area director, which would then be reported to the WBTI executive vice president. This example characterizes the ongoing challenge for WBTI and its board to establish guidelines intended to assist its divisions in knowing what kind of organizations they were and with whom they might best associate.

Membership Process

While the number of divisions grew, there was concern that the number of recruits across all the divisions was beginning to plateau, and SIL could not fill all its critical personnel needs. The WBTI Board discussed this concern at their November 1986 meeting, and they asked the International Administration to identify blockages or bottlenecks in the new member process. The strain was not found on the

31 WBTI, November 1985, 10.

field but rather as the divisions processed those at the Member in Training (MIT) level. This process included ensuring MITs received the necessary help from their divisions and supporting churches to keep moving along the career path. The administration encouraged the board not to panic but agreed that both board and administration must pay attention to the downturn in recruitment, with numbers too low to justify running all the field orientation courses planned for the upcoming years.[32]

Reporting to the WBTI Board in 1989, the executive vice president noted a definite decline in new member recruitment compared to the previous four years. As a result, the board wanted further work done to pursue innovative approaches to recruitment that would require greater collaboration between the divisions and fields so that WBT could 'sell [itself] to the new generation of the constituency.'[33]

Another contributing factor was that some divisions allowed their Short-Term Assistants (STAs) to extend their term of service beyond the two-year maximum without requiring them to apply for career membership. The International Administration recommended capping the STA category at a maximum service term of five years before requiring the person to resign or apply for career membership. Some SIL entities allowed STAs to fill leadership positions typically reserved for members, but in 1987 the WBTI Board decided that STAs could no longer hold these positions. Whether a person desired to transition from STA to membership application status or was applying as a new member, the International Administration instructed all divisions that all new members must attend the Intercultural Communications Course or its equivalent. There was an increasing recognition of the need to understand and relate across multiple cultures.

A growing number of current division member resignations, including those who served under SIL, presented a challenge with no clarity about why it was happening. Equally concerning was the significant percentage of initial assignments made to US Division and international administration roles and not to the SIL fields.

Additionally, the turnover of leaders and moral lapses among leaders were distressing. Was this due to poor discipleship or other factors? The International Administration believed it had more to do with identifying and training enough new leaders to lead and manage in both WBTI and SIL, given the expansion rate. Regarding effective member discipline, discussions at the international leadership level addressed how WBTI and SIL handled moral lapses or failures among their members, particularly regarding sexual misconduct. Given that these were Christian organizations, any time there was a lapse, for whatever reason, the administration needed to take suitable action to uphold the organizations' high moral

[32] WBTI, "Board Minutes," November 1986, 7.

[33] WBTI, "Board Minutes," May 1989, 1.

standards and to help those involved. This required an ongoing review of practices and policies by the organizations' counselling and personnel departments.

In 1987, the WBTI Board approved a Staged Member Acceptance Plan that covered four steps:

1. Application, technical evaluation, and orientation: This involved application for membership and referees; attendance of approved candidate course; passing a Bible knowledge assessment; submission of an acceptable doctrinal statement; and a physical examination. When a person was deemed suitable to proceed, it was because they also demonstrated spiritual maturity, biblical knowledge and application, physical and emotional health, interpersonal relationship skills, understanding and commitment to WBT's principles, motivation for the work, and appropriate academic or technical training and qualifications to fulfil a prospective assignment.
2. Technical training, assignment, and support discovery: After achieving the first stage, an applicant became a Member in Training (MIT) when they had done all pre-field technical training, had a good prayer and financial support basis, and had received an assignment.
3. Field training and national language study: The primary focus was on completing the appropriate field orientation and language study (for example, gaining a working knowledge of French if serving in Francophone Africa). Once these requirements were met, the person moved from MIT to Junior Member status.
4. Initial assignment: The person needed to satisfactorily serve for two years, complete all of stage 1–3 requirements, make a valid and satisfactory contribution to the organization's goals, and complete any conditions of the assignment entity.

Once these steps were accomplished, the person was given Senior Membership. If a person could not meet any of these initial assignment requirements, an administrator would work with them to find other assignment options.[34]

Concerns from Europe

The number of WBTI divisions around the world grew, prompting the board to request that the International Administration research WBTI's legal and financial responsibilities regarding the conduct and actions of the divisions. In particular, the board was aware of growing concerns within Europe, including that some European divisions faced requirements calling for greater legal separation from WBTI because of their own national laws and regulations. Also, WBTI's growth

[34] WBTI, "Board Minutes," May 1987, 13-18.

meant its budget and the income necessary for operations would likewise increase. Some European divisions reacted to this, wondering whether WBTI should also be financially separate from SIL. They were concerned about the demands being placed on them by WBTI's administrators and auditors. In response, the WBTI Board set up a task force of six specialists to examine this issue, concentrating on division autonomy, international responsibility in finance and accounting policies, standards, reporting, and funding the WBTI administration. The task force was to bring its recommendations to the 1988 International Conference.

Carrying on Despite Challenges

In Fort Worth, Texas, WBTI President David Cummings opened the 1988 International Conference with a keynote address to the 146 delegates and invited visitors. His focus was on carrying out WBTI's purpose in the face of difficulties and within varying contexts. Cummings pointed out that two conferences were running simultaneously for SIL and WBTI, and 70% of the delegates came from SIL Branches and Areas. This majority in SIL needed to be conscious of the challenges of the minority who served through the divisions and represented WBT to the home countries.

During the two years leading up to the conference, God provided for SIL and WBTI through gift income totalling $79 million from sources across the world. With 700 new members, membership totalled 5,500. According to Cummings, if each member had on average 100 supporting constituents, this meant another half million people were standing behind the organizations as they carried out their calling. In response, Jim Wilson led the delegates in a prayer of thanksgiving for all of God's benefits.

There were twelve NBTOs in attendance: Ghana Institute of Linguistics, Literacy and Bible Translation; Nigeria Bible Translation Trust; Bible Translation & Literacy (East Africa); Association Ivoirienne Pour la Traduction de la Biblia (Ivory Coast); Sudan Bible Translation and Literacy Association; Global Bible Translators (South Korea); Translators Association of the Philippines; Bible Translation Committee of Sabah; Indian Institute for Cross Cultural Communications; Papua New Guinea Bible Translation Association; the Solomon Islands Christian Association Translation Committee; and Associação Linguistica Evangélica Missionária (Brazil). It was a new development to have these additional and very diverse participants.

Executive Vice President John Bendor-Samuel gave his World Report highlighting developments affecting the work. He noted a 'trend of some sending churches or organizations to emphasize the replacement of missionaries with national workers, even though many times this is exaggerated or misinterpreted.'[35] There were assumptions that roles and structures could stay the same even if people from other cultures and backgrounds took on those roles. There were also assumptions that it would be 'cheaper' for national workers to do more of the work without recognizing the need for training regardless of where people came from.

Bendor-Samuel was concerned about the challenges of reaching the next 1,000 languages because many were in sensitive areas that precluded publicity and created difficulties for translation work and workers. He challenged the delegates to 'harness the prayers of God's people, which is the greatest untapped resource available to us.' [36] The 'moral decadence in the church in home countries' was also of interest. The challenge, therefore, was to unite 'under God [to] complete the task, giving a book that will change lives by the thousands, not just a book to put on the shelf.' [37]

The board of directors for WBTI and SIL was elected. Cummings was re-elected as WBTI President, and Ken Gregerson was re-elected as SIL President. SIL Branch Directors chosen were John Daly, Ger Reesink, Hans-Jurgen Scholz, Don Gregson, and Lambert Anderson. WBT Division Directors were Bernie May and Burkhard Schöttelndreyer. Constituency members were Eric Brabham, Fred Magbanua, and Emmanuel Njock. Members at large were Kemp Pallesen, Don Lindholm, Carolyn Miller, Don Robertson, and Morris Cottle.

Presenting the Vision

WBTI wanted to have an end-of-century goal statement which might begin, 'By the year 2000, and by the grace and help of God, members of WBT will endeavour to....' Further discussion refined this to encourage divisions to set goals for the end of the century that would reflect the essential priorities and program strategies of the SIL field entities.[38] The International Administration was entrusted with coordinating with the various area committees.

Three speakers addressed the theme of Partnership Development. Dr David Hocking, senior pastor of Calvary Church, Santa Ana, California—the largest supporting church of WBT members—presented his perspectives on supporting churches and constituencies. He touched upon the differing definitions of the church and mission agency and the responsibilities fulfilled through the selection and support of missionaries. He emphasized the relationships that must be fostered, especially in 'greater accountability to the Lord, each other, and the

35 WBTI, "Board Minutes," November 1987, 1.

36 WBTI, November 1987, 2.

37 WBTI, November 1987, 2.

38 WBTI, November 1987, 4.

Word,' emphasizing that 'the church is accountable to the agency and the agency to the church.' The next speaker was Clay Johnston, a regional director for the US Division. He focussed on the interdependence between WBT and SIL and the local churches. He included some frustrations expressed by local churches when bypassed in the recruitment and approval process, and their authority seemingly usurped in the sending process. Australian Division Director Darryl Kernick was the third speaker. He pointed out that the churches often saw mission agencies as 'takers' rather than 'givers' or 'partners'. The delegates discussed these presentations and recommended that the divisions consider these issues raised regarding partnership development with their staff and members.

Vice President for Personnel, Millie Larson, reported on the many open personnel positions that required special attention to fill in the areas of finance, secretarial, children's education, socio-linguistics survey teams, and literacy specialists.

Hyatt Moore, vice president for public affairs, hosted a session about presenting the work and called upon three speakers. Dennis Cochrane, the US Division campus recruiter, demonstrated that WBT was missing an opportunity created by the current trend of short-term overseas summer missions, available with other missions. The divisions and SIL entities needed to see short-term missions experiences as a potential part of the process of recruiting long term members. Next, Netherlands Division Director Auke Lemstra pointed out their success in recruiting people for specific roles, moving from recruiting more significant numbers of people to a more qualitative approach. Darryl Kernick, Australian division director, stressed the importance of divisions staying informed on SIL's field needs and their expectations for new workers.

President Emeritus George Cowan spoke on the importance of prayer, commanded in the Scriptures, and therefore not optional. He highlighted interdependence in prayer, which he defined as meaning we can't accomplish the task alone; that we should pray for those who pray for us, and let them know how God answers, whether positively or negatively; and we should bear one another's burdens, especially praying for leaders.

Concerns of the divisions were presented and discussed. The topics included speedy communication between SIL fields and divisions and the financial support quota system. Regarding personnel, issues of concern included accountability, recruitment, training, assignment, member care, furloughs, and children's education. How to relate to the new NBTOs, the role distinctions between WBT and SIL, and the fact that WBT and SIL were becoming middle-aged were also areas of interest. The latter issue drew particular attention since it could be associated with the death of a mission organization. Many divisions lacked the essential staffing required to cover critical operations. A rotating succession of SIL field members serving in their divisions for extended periods of time offered a possible solution.

Larrie Gardner of the International Counselling Department spoke on moral lapse matters and ministry. There was a call to holiness while remaining alert to temptations and vulnerabilities. There was an appeal to live by biblical standards, principles, self-knowledge, and accountability, both personally and corporately. The delegates commended the International Administration's efforts in addressing the area of moral purity. They recognized the importance of these efforts considering 'widespread breakdown in traditional Judeo-Christian values and the increase in materialism and the hedonistic lifestyle' in the cultures from which many WBT members came. This resulted in a call for leaders to be 'role models of personal holiness'. It required spiritual care for oneself and others, encouragement to maintain spiritual vitality for all members, and members ministering to one another. And it focussed on the Scriptures as the unchanging pattern for holiness.

Earl Adams, area director for Europe, presented a paper on WBTI's future, proposing a description of WBTI's structure as an 'association' of sending countries. With insufficient discussion time, the International Administration would explore the concept further through the various area committees and conferences and bring recommendations to the 1990 International Conference. In subsequent dialogue, the WBTI Board assured the divisions that they had complete autonomy to satisfy their national laws; that there wasn't any flow of financial responsibility from divisions to the WBTI Corporation or vice versa, and that the required financial audits were for WBTI, not SIL; and that the financial integrity of divisions was verified by the WBTI Comptroller and WBTI Board, as needed. WBTI monitored all the divisions' bylaws, constitutions, and incorporations to ensure they were updated as necessary. These measures were to ensure the integrity of WBTI as a legally incorporated body while upholding the individual autonomy of each division.

Setting Priorities

Priorities for WBTI for the next two years were set:

- Communication—pass on to constituencies the vision for the worldwide church's responsibility for Bible translation.
- Interdependence—emphasizes developing attitudes among the membership that promote interdependence with others, such as constituencies, churches, missions, government bodies, and NBTOs; attention is given to identifying

and training leaders.

- Partnering with NBTOs—done through developing appropriate ways of promoting the establishment and growth of NBTOs.
- Prayer—foster the importance of prayer for every aspect of the work.
- Recruitment—increase commitment to recruiting, involving both field and home entities.
- Spiritual vitality—provide spiritual counsel and other assistance to contribute to workers' spiritual, emotional, and moral health.[39]

Moving Forward

WBTI President Cummings opened the proceedings of WBTI's 1990 International Conference at the JAARS Center at Waxhaw, North Carolina, with his topic of 'Forces and Issues We Face in the World Today'. Cummings highlighted the dangers he viewed as approaching rapidly. This included the 'revolution of high technology—along with modernity and heightened legal structures.'[40] At the same time, WBTI and SIL needed to 'stay in business' through recruiting the 'right kind' of member.[41] Cummings pointed out that WBTI had necessities similar to a 'successful army' such as 'morale from an adequate mission statement, strength from quality training, [an] adequate source of supply, and knowledge of the enemy.' Cummings called on God to encourage all to 'keep moving' forward.[42]

Executive Vice President John Bendor-Samuel informed the delegates that during the 1980s, WBTI had gained 2,935 new members, an indication of answered prayer. Over the previous three years, the number of recruits had noticeably declined. However, loss through attrition stabilized as with other Christian organizations. He noted that the divisions continued to concentrate on core operations of recruiting new members, ensuring the divisions had adequate staffing, and helping members raise enough financial support to take up and stay in their assignments. He concluded that the challenge for the 1990s should be a focus on the following 1,000 languages and the hope of reaching them.

A vote taken of all the Senior Members concerning changing the cycle of International Conferences from two to three years passed, with 66.75% in favour (the required minimum to pass such legislation was 66.67%). As WBTI continued to grow, so did the cost of the event. Though the vote had barely passed, the next International Conference would be held in 1993 rather than 1992 and save significant financial resources.

---

39 WBTI, November 1987, 5.

40 WBTI, "International Conference Extracts," May 1990, 1.

41 WBTI, May 1990, 1.

42 WBTI, May 1990, 1.

WBTI adopted a new mission statement: 'Our mission is to glorify God in obedience to the Great Commission through a unique strategy that integrates Scripture translation, scholarship, and service so that all people will have access to God's Word in their own language.'[43] The statement was intended to help the organization's participants 'know what they are committing themselves to. With a clear purpose [e.g., "to glorify God by obedience to the Great Commission through scripture translation"] people can buy into our mission with real commitment and willing sacrifice.'[44]

The WBTI Board was elected (including those seated by having been elected in the SIL Conference) and consisted of David Cummings, president; Frank Robbins, SIL President; WBT Division Directors Bernie May and Burkhard Schöttelndreyer; SIL Branch Directors Don Gregson, Hans-Jurgen Scholz, Bruce Hollenback, Jim Swartzentruber, and John Taylor; constituency members Eric Brabham, Don Robertson, and Morrie Cottle; and at large members Don Lindholm, Carolyn Miller, Kemp Pallesen, Micah Amukobole, and Millie Larson.

As a follow-up to concerns expressed in the 1988 International Conference about the need for good leadership, the board set up a Leadership Task Force that produced a leadership philosophy. The conference accepted the document, which assumed an emphasis on effective leadership across WBTI. The philosophy itself covered many factors, including the importance of attitudes, skills, vision, ability to direct the corporate effort, and overall lifestyle of leaders that would help ensure their credibility with the membership. They chose leaders 'who manifest the God-given gifts that are necessary' for leading and developing the Wycliffe organization.[45]

Preparing for Restructuring

Following up from the 1988 International Conference, Europe Area Director Earl Adams reported on the proposal to restructure WBTI into an association of legally separate member organizations. The concept was that only divisions (or organizations) would be members of WBTI, rather than individuals (which was the SIL practice). Adams reported that WBTI would probably not continue to be a directing organization but more a facilitating, assisting, and organizing one. While all divisions supported this move, it primarily came from the European Divisions because they needed to show their governments clear legal separation from control of a foreign organization. Various models demonstrating how this would work included a House of Representatives based on population, a Senate of Member

---

[43] Millie Larson, *Intercom*, September 1990, 5.

[44] Larson, 5.

[45] WBTI, May 1990, 8.

Organizations (MOs) with voting delegates (the leader and board chair of each full MO), and observers (the leader and board chair of each developing MO).

Considering the WBTI Board, it could be a representative board, identical to the SIL Board, having a majority of overlap with the SIL Board. Or it could operate as an executive board, with seven members elected by the conference from among its delegates, responsible for appointing staff; reviewing goals, programs, and staff budgets; and acting for the conference between sessions.

Discussions around restructuring WBTI were significant and of interest to the delegates, resurfacing four times during the conference. After much debate and with multiple amendments effected, they reached and accepted the final motion. It reads as follows:

> MOVED to request the board to initiate the necessary legal steps to recognize WBTI as an association of legally separate member organizations, in accord with the following principles:
>
> The basis for organizational membership in WBTI will include agreement with WBTI purpose and strategy, doctrinal beliefs, membership and financial standards, and service philosophy. Factors such as these, basic to the unity of WBTI, will continue to be established, safeguarded, expressed, and monitored by the International Conference and Board.
>
> In regard to membership of individuals, Member Organizations will have the responsibility within their organizations for processing applications, granting and terminating membership, guaranteeing the right of appeal, and providing ongoing member care.
>
> Through a secondment procedure, individual members of Member Organizations may become members of SIL and/or may serve with other organizations with whom SIL or WBTI has a cooperative agreement.
>
> Each Member Organization will be responsible for its own income and will manage its finances in a way that safeguards the good name of WBTI.
>
> Further MOVED to request that the board continue investigating the possible restructuring of the WBTI International Conference and Board....[46]

Becoming an association of legally separate Member Organizations, the most significant change to WBTI since its formation in 1980, was a brave call by the

[46] WBTI, May 1990, 4.

conference delegates. It moved WBTI further away from operating as a traditional, hierarchical institution, with control over its operating units—the divisions/ Member Organizations.

Setting Course

Priorities for the next three years were set:

› Resource strategy of prayer focussed on those people who still do not have Scriptures, especially those in difficult access areas or where publicity is inappropriate; funding resources for implementing new strategies, helping 'fraternal organizations' and their development, training of local citizens and special literacy efforts; and partnership resource through networking and cooperation with other agencies involved in Bible translation.
› Recruitment, redeployment, and member care of personnel, with consideration of their abilities and what is called for to meet requirements of current field programs and strategies; and enabling personnel to find new assignments after completing their original assignments—so as not to lose them and their experience.
› Leadership strategy of identifying, mentoring, and developing leaders, including those elected to serve in various roles.
› Spiritual vitality through promoting spiritual growth and development of all members, including exercising God-given gifts, greater effectiveness in spiritual warfare through understanding and applying relevant biblical texts and the disciplined practice of prayer.
› Sharing the Bible translation vision by assigning significant human and financial resources to the effort of casting the vision for Bible translation with the church in areas of the world where it was not yet participating.[47]

Just as at the 1988 International Conference, the topic of NBTOs again received attention at the 1990 conference. First came a report from John Adive, Chairman of the Steering Committee of the International Fellowship of NBTOs, who held their second conference from 18–21 September 1989 in Mombasa, Kenya. Next, Africa Area Director Frank Robbins reported that efforts to develop NBTOs and support their programs would further the work of Bible translation around the world. Robbins suggested practical ways to help NBTOs, including training for constituency development, facilitating access to new funding sources, and building relationships with NBTO groups.

The pending restructuring of WBTI would give greater autonomy to all

---

[47] WBTI, May 1990, 13-14.

operations of a division, including how to access funding. As part of this financial development, work commenced to decentralize the Emergency Support Fund, used to supplement finances for members of all divisions whose support dropped below a recommended level. Many divisions were concerned that, as a result, they would struggle to raise the equivalent resources. Consequently, the US Division would continue as the major contributor to the Emergency Support Fund for another three years, giving the divisions time to establish new sources and methods for raising funds within their own contexts.

How information for publicity purposes was handled between the WBT Divisions and SIL Branches received further discussion. This resulted in a rededication to integrity and trust regarding ethical statements guiding media production and to enable communications specialists in both divisions and branches to cooperate on joint media projects. The aim was to make news and stories from the fields more readily available. Urged to recruit gifted communicators, including those found in SIL Branches, the divisions released them for special recruitment and publicity efforts.

Worldwide Fellowship

At the November 1989 board meeting, Executive Vice President John Bendor-Samuel gave his vision for WBTI in the 1990s. He thought WBTI should become a 'worldwide fellowship' instead of a 'tightly knit centralized western organization.' It would be a networking, cooperating, facilitating, vision casting, and training movement. It needed to be an organization relevant to 'completion of worldwide evangelization through proclaiming good news to the poor [and] open to greater participation by local sending churches.' It needed to be 'relevant to the hopes and outlook of young people.' It made prayer a high priority. It was committed to sharing financial resources between the North and the South. The Christian public needed to see it as 'dependent on God, both in word and in deed.'[48]

To encourage further autonomy and delineation between WBT, Inc. (US Division) and WBTI, Inc., the WBTI Board recommended that the US Division take steps to form its council without requiring an International Board appointee member.

An ongoing discussion topic regarded the WBTI and SIL Conferences and considered if the time had come to make significant changes. WBTI was now composed differently than it had been, with only organizations represented rather than individuals, like SIL. Also, jointly coordinating large events presented a challenge. Should they be held simultaneously, with or without overlapping sessions,

[48] WBTI, "Board Minutes," November 1989, 2.

or separated and held back-to-back? This question remained unresolved for many more years.

As 1990 ended, the International Administration submitted its Fiscal Year 1991 budget to the WBTI Board for approval. The executive vice president noted that only a few International Administration officers worked exclusively with WBTI. Most served with SIL but were available to WBTI as necessary. Consequently, WBTI's worldwide operations budget that year totalled only US$136,480.

As WBTI moved towards the end of the decade, the International Administration had projections that included recruiting 3,000 people to meet the extensive opportunities worldwide and to offset attrition. One-third of these recruits were to be support workers. There was to be a fourfold increase in prayer partners, including those addressing specific prayer strategies. In addition, income across the divisions was to double, primarily through new members' income.

Conclusion

The decade of the 1980s established that WBTI could become a catalyst for a worldwide Bible translation movement. Decision-making events of the twice-a-year board meetings and every-two-year International Conferences were avenues for discussions and decisions about WBTI's purpose. With more divisions forming, more Christians committed to this Bible translation movement in countries across Europe, Asia, the Pacific, Africa, and the Americas.

Three noticeable markers revealed WBTI's development in this decade:

1. The rise of NBTOs: While no clear strategy to assist NBTOs appeared, it is commendable that WBTI leaders saw their importance. Finding a way for NBTOs to integrate fully into WBTI's structure presented a challenge that remained unsolved during this decade.
2. The European drive for greater autonomy: The concerns originating in Europe forced WBTI to make structural adjustments to become an organization of autonomous organizations. However, doing so raised questions about the role of the International Administration and its strategies and goals since the divisions were now autonomous. These issues did not get solved during this decade, either.
3. The relationship with SIL: Though the International Administration encompassed both WBTI and SIL, by its admission, it concentrated on SIL's program, leaving WBTI with limited leadership. Measures to remedy this included strengthening the WBTI president's role or creating a new vice president role for the divisions. By the end of the decade, this too was still unresolved.

These three challenges would influence WBTI's development in the next decade. The new WBTI, now barely a decade old, was embracing its role in the future of Bible translation.

Leadership Theories and Practices

According to Peter Northouse, 'influence' was the most common description of leadership during the 1980s. However, scholars noted that this was not coercive or forced power but motivational. [49] In this era of WBTI's journey, we see evidence of its leaders using their influence to cast vision, create a strategy, and lead change. At the management level, numerous policies needed development to guide actions and decisions as the organization grew. The era's most relevant and prominent leadership theory was Transformational leadership, developed by James Macgregor Burns. It featured leaders who used influence to transform followers and 'provoke [them] to do more than what they [were] expected to do.'[50] Visionary leaders were transformational through the purpose, pride, respect, and trust they brought, and through communicating expectations, problem-solving, and coaching.[51] Many Western organizations practiced the theory. In WBTI, it was evident through helping build trust in the aims and activities within a growing and diverse group of leaders and their organizations.

In the mid-1980s, leadership theorist Bernard Bass took Transformational leadership further by highlighting how leaders motivated and developed followers by treating them as fully human and encouraging them 'to accomplish more than what is usually expected of them.'[52] Leaders raise followers' self-interests and help them move towards higher-level tasks that can include 'transcendental ideals such as freedom, justice, equality, peace, and humanity,' or more practical matters such as 'motivating subordinates to further work towards achieving the goals of the organization.'[53] Max De Pree states transformational leaders take an interest in their followers by exploring if they are reaching their potential, learning, serving, achieving results, managing conflict, and changing with grace.[54] Such leaders are 'concerned with emotions, values, ethics, standards, and long-term goals.'[55]

---

[49] Northouse, 4.

[50] Shahram Mollazadeh, Amir zadeh Mahmood, and Kamran Yeganegi, "A Review of New Leadership Theories and Its Components," *International Journal of Management Sciences and Business Research* 7, no. 2 (2018): 225.

[51] Bernard Bass, "From Transactional to Transformational Leadership: Learning to Share the Vision," in *Leadership: Understanding the Dynamics of Power and Infuence in Organizations*, ed. Robert Vecchio (Notre Dame: University of Notre Dame Press, 1997), 320.

[52] Northouse, 164.

[53] Mollazadeh, Mahmood, and Yeganegi, 225.

[54] Max De Pree, *Leadership Is an Art* (New York: Doubleday, 1989), 10.

[55] Northouse, 163.

Transformational leadership is the opposite of transactional leadership. As the name implies, the transactional leader uses contractual exchanges 'of rewards for effort, promises rewards for good performance [and] recognizes accomplishments.'[56] It's in the follower's best interests to meet the leader's expectations as the leader 'exchange[s] things of value with followers to advance their own and the followers' agendas.'[57] It is an exchange between the leader's aptitude to persuade and the follower's acceptance of authority. The leader may work in one of two ways: watching out for 'deviations from rules and standards' and then taking 'corrective action', or only intervening when 'standards are not met.'[58]

Sometimes transactional leadership becomes *laissez-faire*, the French term for 'let it go'.[59] The leader abandons responsibility, delays decisions, doesn't give feedback, and makes 'little effort to help followers satisfy their needs.'[60] But it's not necessarily a lack of leadership when a leader wants followers to take the lead.

During this era, we see all three leadership practices operating in WBTI: transformational, transactional, and *laissez-faire*. The organization's leaders were motivated to serve the broader agenda of WBTI. We see in WBTI's journey how at times, the International Administration or Board had to impose rules and standards and intervene when there were deviations by Wycliffe divisions or their personnel. Sometimes WBTI leaders led transactionally, and others took a *laissez-faire* approach when Wycliffe division leaders themselves needed to be decisive.

Journey Reflections (Influences and New Terrain)

This stretch of the journey beautifully illustrates the impact of external and internal influences in motion. As we travel through this time, we can see the waning effects of the industrial era. Leaders still talked about the 'need to stay in business', the 'intake of recruits', 'operating units', and needing to 'sell Wycliffe' to the next generation. They wanted people to 'buy into' Bible translation. The goals often referenced languages without mentioning the people who spoke those languages. Leaders may have been motivated from the heart, but they took their terminology and strategy cues from the corporate world. Yet, while big business ideas often drove them forward, they were also beginning to experience a change of climate and scenery: the European need for autonomy because of changing laws and

56 Bass, in *Leadership: Understanding the Dynamics of Power and Infuence in Organizations*, 320.

57 Northouse, 173.

58 Bass, in *Leadership: Understanding the Dynamics of Power and Infuence in Organizations*, 320.

59 Northouse, 174.

60 Northouse, 174.

practices, the growing national and local involvement in Bible translation around the globe, and the internal awakening of WBTI as something potentially much different from the WBTI that had begun this journey. Executive Vice President John Bendor-Samuel was one of those leaders, adept at envisioning what the future could look like and what sojourners might need to journey well. While the deep goals and values remained the same, it became apparent that the road ahead would look much different from what was behind.

Understanding the creation and growth of WBTI in this era helps us understand the challenges it would face in the future as globalization increased and the worldwide Church grew in leaps and bounds. The structures WBTI created served well for a time but became less helpful as the 20th century started giving way to the 21st. The closing years of the 20th century would find WBTI taking a new look at the path before them. The terrain was unlike any they had encountered thus far.

› What language and structures inhibit moving forward in your context? How do you see that changing and what is encouraging the change?
› What leadership models are you familiar with in your context? How have they been helpful? Are there other models that might be more helpful? Why?

Chapter 4
Maturing: 1991–2000

Historical Setting

As the 1990s began, geopolitical factors affected the development of WBTI. For example, Wycliffe South Africa, formed in 1973, was finally able to place recruits in overseas assignments. Previously they required non-South African passports as dual citizens with other countries, such as Australia. The situation changed when the political system of apartheid ended in 1990, and Wycliffe South Africa could freely participate in the worldwide Bible translation movement.

Until then, South Africa was in exile, isolated from the rest of the world. Apartheid was a political system to 'safeguard the privileges of a minority White community against the Black majority in the country.'[1] Many of the nation's white churches were part of the problem by not speaking out against apartheid. However, individual church leaders led the stand against the wrongs. A group of influential and mainly black South African theologians issued a call to action with the Kairos Document of 1985, highlighting the system's injustices. By the mid-1980s, South Africa had been affected by regional violence in protest of apartheid. The government declared a state of emergency that empowered the police to quell riots in black townships. The event caught the world's attention. The government was under tremendous pressure to dismantle the unjust system. A series of steps brought apartheid to an end in the early 1990s and led to a democratic government in 1994. The changes in South Africa had a worldwide impact.

During the 1990s, globalization was increasingly influencing events worldwide. Anthony Giddens defined globalization as 'the intensification of worldwide social relations that link distant communities in such a way that local happenings are shaped by events occurring many miles away and vice versa.'[2]

The 1990s saw the age of industry and technology merge into the age of information. Globalization was coming into prominence as multinational companies developed global workforces and markets. The global economic engine opened new trade relationships fuelled by goods that moved cheaply and quickly worldwide. The growing presence of international banks and governments willing to

---

[1] G. Jan van Butselaar, "The Role of Churches in the Peace Process in Africa," in *The Changing Face of Christianity: Africa, the West, and the World*, ed. Lamin Sanneh and Joel Carpenter (Oxford: Oxford University Press, 2005), 108.

[2] Anthony Giddens, *The Third Way* (Cambridge: Polity Press, 1998), 64.

remove financial barriers also contributed. News, ideologies, influence, and developments were able to spread more rapidly. Technology was on the rise, impacting all areas of life, particularly communication.

The 1991 collapse of the Union of Soviet Socialist Republics (USSR) was another geopolitical power shift. The interconnection of communication and globalization meant the rest of the world witnessed the event as it unfolded. This downfall ended the long political, military, and socio-economic stand-off known as the Cold War that began around 1950, characterized by the bipolar world of the USSR and the US. Out of this void, the US quickly became the dominant world power. The US and its Western friends wanted to promote freedom from tyranny. Many US Christians believed there was a biblical basis that indicated 'everybody wants to be free, politically and economically; God made human beings with the desire to be free.'[3]

Wycliffe's founder Cameron Townsend had a long-term interest in the USSR. He and his wife Elaine visited the USSR eleven times. Townsend was especially intrigued by the geographical area of the Caucasus with its great diversity of languages. The political dismantling of communism in the USSR meant that Christians in the Russian Federation could participate in worldwide mission agencies. By 1997 discussions were taking place with Russian Christians about the formation of Wycliffe Russia.

In mission theology, *missio Dei* (the mission of God) gained momentum through South African David Bosch's epic text, *Transforming Mission*. Bosch described the interpretation of mission through church history in four ways: (1) in the doctrine of salvation 'as saving individuals from eternal damnation'; (2) in cultural expressions as bringing the so-called 'blessings of the Christian West' to the rest of the world; (3) in ecclesiastical terms as the physical growth of the church or a denomination; and (4) in salvation history, as the way the world becomes 'transformed into the kingdom of God'.[4]

Bosch's theological work nurtured a broad acceptance of *missio Dei*, 'including Evangelicals, liberals, traditional Protestants, and Orthodox and Roman Catholics.'[5] Mission originates from the heart of the triune God, who acts as a 'fountain of sending love' because of God's love for all people.[6] The meaning of mission exists in the relationship within the Triune God in this progression: the Father sends the Son, the Father and the Son send the Holy Spirit. The Father, Son, and Holy Spirit send the church out into the world.[7] The church is missionary,

---

[3] Nicholas Wolterstorff, "Foreword," in *Evangelicals and Empire: Christian Alternatives to the Political Status Quo*, ed. Bruce Benson and Peter Heltzel (Grand Rapids: Brazos Press, 2008), 7.

[4] Bosch, 399.

[5] Kim, 26.

[6] Bosch, 403.

[7] Bosch, 399.

existing to be sent for God's mission. Bosch viewed the *missio Dei* as multifaceted, responding in several distinct ways to a growing agenda for mission that included '"the church-with-others", as "mediating salvation", "the quest for justice", "common witness", and "action in hope".'[8]

While Bosch's work helped develop mission theology in general, its effect on WBTI's development in this decade was unnoticeable. The prevailing view was that Bible translation was necessary for fulfilling the Great Commission but not associated with the broader plan of God's mission.

Christianity grew considerably during the 1990s. David Barrett's *World Christian Trends* reported in 1990 that there were 558 million people in the world who identified as Christian. That increased to almost two billion in 2000, making Christianity the most prominent world religion. [9] Mission efforts introduced the gospel to '58 percent of the world's people groups, especially the larger, more populous groups'.[10] Luis Bush and Thomas Wang initiated the AD2000 movement to evangelize all peoples by the year 2000. Bush wanted a movement to achieve this because it provided 'a place to foment harmony, common purpose, innovation, and renewal.'[11] AD2000 aimed to give 'all the gospel to all peoples in all places by the Church—Christ's Kingdom Come.'[12]

Western mission activity was influential across the globe. For all the good accomplished by Western mission, it still often carried the baggage of the past. These historical influences impacted the mission power dynamics. This included the ideological concept of *Padroado*, the 15–18th century practice of European colonial expansion coupled with 'the intimate relationship between cross and crown [that] shaped efforts at spreading Christianity.'[13]. There was also 'manifest destiny', the 'belief that God had chosen specific (Anglo-Saxon) nations, because of their unique or superior qualities, to fulfill his purpose in the world [which] resulted in a potent mix of racial superiority, territorial aggression or colonial expansion.'[14] Similarly, 19th century British evangelicals held to 'divine providence', the belief that their nation's overseas 'territorial possessions reflected God's providence and purpose.'[15] As well, the 'white man's burden' viewpoint was that modern Western culture should shape the world's culture, presuming the former was

[8] Kim, 27.

[9] Terry, and Gallagher, 297.

[10] Terry, and Gallagher, 297.

[11] Luis Bush, "AD2000 and Beyond: Toward a Conceptual Model," in *Working Together with God to Shape the New Milliennium: Opportunities & Limitations*, ed. Gary Corwin and Kenneth Mulholland (Pasadena: William Carey Library, 2000), 197.

[12] Bush, in *Working Together with God to Shape the New Milliennium: Opportunities & Limitations*, 199.

[13] Jehu Hanciles, *Beyond Christendom: Globalization, African Migration, and the Transformation of the West* (Maryknoll: Orbis, 2008), 92.

[14] Hanciles, 165.

[15] Hanciles, 164.

'destined to exercise dominance over others for the latter's own good.'[16] These ideologies were shaken as the church grew in the majority world. For example, the growing church 'entered into African religious cultures and Chinese Confucian cultures, and in each context, the local cultures [were] being remade.... This [was] a transformation shaped by local people, not foreign leaders.'[17]

The Latin American church and mission movement in the 1990s demonstrated significant mission engagement. In 1992, the third CLADE conference called together Latin Americans to engage outside of their region 'fully and without delay' in mission.[18] Within five years, almost 4,000 Latin American Protestant missionaries were serving around the world. Many would train as Bible translators and serve through WBTI's partners.

Towards the end of the 20th century, mainstream Western denominations were 'confronted with the stark evidence of plummeting membership rolls and a critical paucity of recruits to the ordained ministry.' Many became open to 'accept that evangelism must form at least part of the core of the mission of the church.'[19] At the same time, theologically conservative Christians 'no longer needed convincing that the gospel of the kingdom of God, which Jesus came to proclaim, must include an insistence on the social values of the kingdom, and hence on the priority of justice. Christian mission would never be quite the same again.'[20]

As the 1990s got underway, WBTI, too, faced increasing complexities, including the process of internationalization—the transition of a distinctly Western organization becoming an international body. How would a body of increasingly autonomous organizations be held together? How would WBTI's cultural diversity be reflected in its governance and leadership? How would WBTI incorporate interests from the worldwide church into its change processes? At the same time, managing the partnering relationship with SIL became more complex. SIL's substantial size and administrative requirements relative to WBTI compelled the joint International Administration to provide SIL with greater attention than it could give to WBTI. There was a great necessity to address administrative needs. WBTI would wrestle with these and other factors during this decade.

Immediate Challenges

Wycliffe Associates Canada and Wycliffe Canada hosted the first WBTI Board meeting for 1991 in May at the Baptist Leadership Education Centre in Toronto.

[16] Hanciles, 170.

[17] Sunquist, 151.

[18] Hartch, 187.

[19] Stanley, 214.

[20] Stanley, 214.

The 17-member board (the same people as those on the SIL Board) consisted of 15 men and two women, with only one person from the majority world—Micah Amukobole (Kenya). The rest were from the US (8), UK (2), Australia (2), Germany (2), New Zealand (1), and Canada (1). This membership structure was proportionally like that of the Wycliffe Divisions.

In his usual practice of reporting to the board, Executive Vice President John Bendor-Samuel gave an update on 'indicators of corporate progress' towards goals for the past fiscal year.[21] It was apparent that the divisions' recruitment of new personnel was declining each year. As a result, some translation projects under SIL remained incomplete. Assignments to new language groups were not increasing. Funding came through the recruits, resulting in inadequate funding for language projects. The implications were of concern because it meant that SIL, and therefore WBTI, could not take full advantage of an increase in new opportunities in many field contexts. Personnel numbers were in short supply, so attention to where and how current members served became even more critical. It was necessary to achieve a balance between people placed in new or continuing language programs, in academic research, in study programs, to assess and survey the remaining task, and in other 'highly specialized assignments'.[22]

Bendor-Samuel and WBTI President David Cummings grew more concerned about adequate development of the divisions, especially the newer ones, still small and under-resourced. To solve this dilemma, the International Administration created a new position of Vice President for Division Affairs. The board appointed David Bendor-Samuel (John's brother) to fill this position starting 1 January 1991.

WBTI faced four immediate challenges: (1) developing adequate staffing for the under-funded divisions (sharing staff among the various organizations offered one solution); (2) recruitment of personnel for SIL; (3) networking in sending countries to address the training requirements of new personnel preparing to serve in SIL field contexts; and (4) funding of SIL field strategies and operations (divisions needed to develop alternative funding sources).

The German and New Zealand home organizations asked the WBTI Board for greater authority to manage more personnel decisions handled by the International Candidate Secretary. In 1991, the board approved the German Division Council, and New Zealand Division Council could approve their Members-In-Training under the Secretary's supervision. Since New Zealand had greater capacity, it could also oversee its members' Leaves of Absence, Discipline, and Termination.

---

21 WBTI, "Board Minutes," May 1991, 1.

22 WBTI, May 1991, 3.

Funding New Opportunities

WBTI's leaders sought to address the shortage of personnel recruited through divisions for field projects. A solution was to employ people from countries where Bible translation was needed who had the training or experience to carry out language work. The divisions could raise funds for this, but they would have to manage the perception that foreign workers were no longer required.

The ten percent assessment of members' financial support was essential for funding the International Administration, divisions, and SIL entities. Each WO received and receipted funds for its members, retaining five percent of the total for the division's operations. Four percent went to the SIL field of assignment, with the remaining one percent to the International Administration.

The one percent received through the assessment process was insufficient for the International Administration to meet its budgetary requirements. Most of the budget came from Wycliffe US through undesignated legacy funds—gifts from donors' bequests and estates—that Wycliffe US passed on to the International Administration for its funding. At the time, both WBTI and SIL relied on these legacy funds, as neither organization was a fundraiser, and both found it challenging to find alternate funding. Because the International Administration required stable funding, the WBTI Board in November 1992 approached Wycliffe US to guarantee it would raise US$500,000 per year for at least six years. This request revealed the International Administration's vulnerability to funding its operations.

Until now, the financial support of division members assigned to serve in SIL funded all activities of both WBTI and SIL and accounted for 90% of WBTI and SIL's combined income. The members relied on funding from their networks of family, friends, churches, and the Christian public with whom they shared their needs. Fieldworkers' budgets included additional funds they needed to raise for their translation programs. This funding system, in place since SIL and WBT's founding, had worked reasonably well.

The growing operational requirements of the past decade showed that this funding and assessment system was no longer sufficient. Funding of national involvement and new WOs presented a challenge. Had the time come for a deliberate shift from a member-centred approach to a project-centred system? Would this better facilitate new strategies, promoting greater involvement of national colleagues and NBTOs? The board debated this during its November 1991 meeting. They chose to keep the member-centred system. And they wanted a new parallel and non-competing funding system that would not weaken the financial support base of the members and identify new sources of funding.

To address these increasing needs called for the divisions to expand their fundraising capacity to raise an additional US$10 million per year. Possibilities included setting up donor-invested foundations and offering churches and the Christian public ways to sponsor national Bible translators financially.

To put the new fundraising strategy into effect meant that divisions had to retrain existing staff or recruit specialized ones. Lengthy start-up activities could take at least five years to grow additional funding. Divisions doing fundraising needed greater accountability, and reporting expectations would apply to those receiving funds. The first division to take up the responsibility was Wycliffe US in 1993 when it asked its former president Bernie May to develop an initiative to fund national translator projects.

Leadership Analysis

The 1990 International Conference asked the International Administration to commission a study about an apparent lack of suitably qualified or experienced leadership across the WOs. In response, the area directors conducted research with the organizations in their regions. They processed this with the board in May 1991. Though described as critical in some organizations, the situation did not represent a crisis in all of them. Leadership development for the divisions stood out because it was different from what SIL required in field and translation contexts. Divisions couldn't assume that their members who were field leaders, often leading translation teams, could readily adapt to home country leadership roles. The latter had unique considerations such as speaking ministry, developing resources, and public relations with churches, missions, and the Christian public. While some people in the home countries could fulfill these roles, many were not recognized as 'real missionaries'—often defined as those serving overseas—and raising personal financial support proved difficult.

Members of WOs understood the ongoing necessity to develop a pool of people who could serve in various leadership roles in each division. For some members, this went against their view of the autonomous missionary who had no desire to be accountable to a leadership structure in their home country. After all, Cameron Townsend founded SIL as a field-driven organization with minimal regard to what the division leaders were communicating or doing.

WBTI's area directors were vital to addressing this need through their assistance to the divisions in developing leadership pathways for current and emerging leaders. The new leadership development plan included persuading current leaders to mentor new leaders. Some prospective leaders were encouraged to take formal leadership studies. Management training programs were set up under the International Administration to develop and support division managers, particularly those who were inexperienced.

Shorter Term Service

Leadership was just one of the personnel issues that required attention. Divisions noticed a growing interest in shorter terms of service, sometimes two years or less. In addition, many highly skilled people over 50 were expressing interest in membership. But a laborious, lengthy application process for longer-term membership often resulted in many looking at other mission agencies or giving up on missions altogether. The divisions and SIL entities required their skills and experience, making greater flexibility in membership options necessary. Therefore, in May 1991, the board approved an updated Short-Term Assistant (STA) plan that governed this membership category for shorter terms of service; or those over 50 who possessed the requisite skills. This comprehensive scheme covered all aspects of how an STA was accepted, how and where they served, and could even change their status to Career Member. The plan was evidence of WBTI's adapting to a changing workforce.

Official Language

An increasing number of organizations from around the world were joining WBTI. For most, English was not their national language. This necessitated a decision about what WBTI's official language would be. Recognizing English as the official language of most international organizations, in May 1991, the WBTI Board concluded an adequate knowledge of English would be a prerequisite for Senior Membership. However, SIL could choose a country's national language for official communication when working within that country, thus enabling local citizens to participate without being proficient in English.

Moral Conduct

As an increasingly diverse body requiring standards of behaviour for all people in all positions associated with the organization, moral conduct standards were developed and applied to all the divisions and WBTI administration. The standards addressed illegal activity and other forms of behaviour that violated biblical standards. It also outlined administrative protocols available when personnel conduct was in breach.

Unique Opportunities

Completing eight years of service, Executive Vice President John Bendor-Samuel gave his final address to the board in November 1991. He spoke of unprecedented opportunities in sub-Saharan Africa and language development needs in East Asia. But he also noted lower recruitment of new personnel throughout the WOs. For example, on average, during 1982–86, 300 new people were joining annually. Recruitment dropped dramatically to 171 new members in 1987, then to 97 by 1990, with 96 joining in language personnel roles. In 1990, there was only a net gain of 56 people because 40 had resigned, retired, or passed away. This was a shift from the 1970s when SIL started an average of 30 language programs each year, 40 annually in the 1980s, but only 25 each year in 1990–1991. What might God be saying with the unprecedented new opportunities but fewer people from the traditional contexts available to take advantage of the open doors? In response, Bendor-Samuel quoted from Isaiah 43, 'This is what the Lord says... See, I am doing a new thing....' Bendor-Samuel concluded that 'new messengers' were called for, but they would not necessarily come from the West. [23] They lived in Papua New Guinea, South Korea, Singapore, the Philippines, Nigeria, Kenya, Cameroon, Brazil, and Mexico. As an additional solution, teams finishing translations could move on to train and facilitate national translators, recruit new people as facilitators, and experiment with one team working in multiple language programs.

Bendor-Samuel concluded with a challenge for reaching the next 1,000 languages. Current WBTI and SIL strategies could be used in one-third of the remaining languages while experimenting with new approaches in the other two-thirds. The board enthusiastically asked Bendor-Samuel to share his vision in written and video formats with everyone associated with WBTI and SIL. As Bendor-Samuel stepped down from his role, his talents were still needed. Therefore, the board and incoming Executive Vice President, Steve Sheldon, gave Bendor-Samuel the title of 'Vice President at Large'. He could use this title when communicating about the challenge of the next 1,000 languages and when representing WBTI to other Bible translation agencies. The board thanked Bendor-Samuel for his service, especially his vision and passion for the task, his skill as an administrator and communicator, and his commitment to academic and professional excellence. The board thanked Bendor-Samuel's wife, Pam. They noted her 'selfless service in strengthening and supporting John [and] her successful balancing of home and teaching responsibilities.'[24] Pam taught various linguistic courses at SIL schools in the UK. Later, as a New Testament Greek scholar, she served as a consultant on several translation projects.

---

23 WBTI, "Board Minutes," November 1991, 2.

24 WBTI, November 1991, 11.

A New Season

Steve Sheldon's first board meeting as WBTI and SIL's new leader took place in May 1992 at the Dallas Center, with over one hundred staff and visitors present to hear his vision statement. WBTI International Administration officers in attendance included the five area directors (Americas, Europe, Africa, Asia, and Pacific) and five vice presidents (Academic Affairs, Finance, Wycliffe Organizations, Personnel, and JAARS). Interestingly, this meeting listed JAARS under the WBTI administration, though it was part of SIL structurally. Each area director served both organizations, apart from an SIL Area Director for Eurasia and a WBTI Area Director for Europe. Most vice presidents served both organizations, except for the WBTI Vice President for Division Affairs. These examples of numerous variations and anomalies illustrate the challenge of defining or explaining what belonged to WBTI and SIL under the joint International Administration.

All the vice presidents and area directors in this International Administration team were men. They came from the US (7), Australia (2), and the UK (1). Thus, 50 years after its founding, WBTI continued to be a Western male-led organization.

Sheldon's opening vision was called 'Stability with Flexibility'. He spoke of 'continuing strong in our current projects [and] expanding our focus toward the next 1,000 languages.'[25] In response, the board expressed its

> appreciation to [Sheldon] for his clear and challenging message [in the form of] his Vision Statement. We recognize the challenge given to us by God on behalf of the Bibleless peoples and we reaffirm our commitment [to the International Administration] as they lead us in carrying out God's commission. We commit ourselves to pray for [Sheldon] and his team for wisdom and strength in fulfilling this vision.[26]

This support from the board is a reasonable indicator that, once again, WBTI accomplished a successful leadership transition at the highest level. John Bendor-Samuel had made his mark on WBTI with his visionary leadership, leaving behind a sound foundation. Moving forward, Steve Sheldon charted a path for the organization's future. Successful leadership transition like this helps smooth the way for all involved.

Ongoing discussion took place between the board and International Administration concerning titles for senior officers. For example, the board used 'president' when referring to the board chair as the person who presided over board meetings. However, the president also held public relations responsibilities

---

[25] WBTI, "Board Minutes," May 1992, 2.

[26] WBTI, May 1992, 2.

and often represented WBTI to Christian publics and events. This went beyond the conventional role of a board chair. Likewise, the executive leader of WBTI and SIL (since it was a combined function) was called the Executive Vice President (EVP). Following conventional leadership practices and structures, the term EVP, and the relationship it stood for was confusing. The president, not the EVP, while not an executive officer, was the most senior leader. Reporting to the EVP were vice presidents and area directors. Some wanted the area directors to be called vice presidents for their respective areas. However, the area directors usually preferred 'Director' in their title because they did have to direct certain functions and responsibilities.

The board told Sheldon that he could use any of the titles: President, Chief Executive Officer, or Executive Vice President where appropriate, and depending on the cultural setting. However, Sheldon felt it was not the time to make these changes, given the focus and energy needed to lead WBTI through its reorganization process.

The International Administration and the WBTI Board communicated organizational values in the form of philosophy statements. These were the same as an organizational belief system expressing the foundations of both WBTI and SIL. The statements were to be 'living' and therefore regularly reviewed. There were statements on training, management, member care, and service.

Restructuring Continues

Starting in the early 1990s, the European divisions wanted changes to WBTI's structure. Even though the divisions were already autonomous, the European divisions had new requirements. They must demonstrate to their countries' authorities that they were independent organizations, not owned or controlled by the foreign and US-based WBTI. The European organizations had to take complete charge of their personnel and finances.

The restructuring had been discussed and debated within WBTI and SIL for two years. It was now ready for a vote of all Senior Members in WOs and SIL entities. The results of the 3,021 ballots were 87% voted in favour of the proposal to restructure, with 8% against and 4% abstaining. As a result, both corporations modified their bylaws to reflect this momentous decision. WBTI and SIL were now legally separate organizations. Structurally SIL would continue to be a sizeable corporation, with each field entity a subsidiary, and each individual a member, of SIL. On the other hand, WBTI became an 'international association of member organizations,' its membership comprising the WOs themselves.[27]

[27] WBTI, "Board Minutes," November 1992, 18.

The high approval of the voting membership would, in time, bring significant changes to everything about WBTI, adjusting in slow, steady stages. This transition would require that the International Administration give greater leadership attention to developing the WOs. Therefore, the new position of Vice President for Division Affairs (later renamed Wycliffe Organizations) was vital. In this role, David Bendor-Samuel brought two restructuring topics to the board: the purpose and format of the future WBTI International Conferences and the composition of the WBTI Board of Directors. Preliminary discussions addressed equipping the board with better representation from the wider Christian public and its interest in Bible translation.

The board was becoming aware that the next International Conference needed to be broadly characteristic of all the WOs. Asking both the director and board chair of each organization to attend could help accomplish this. In the past, only the director came. Inviting board chairs would help the organizations be better informed and bring external input to WBTI. The conference's primary purpose would be fellowship, presentations, and conversations about WBTI's goals and strategies. Preferably, the administration would handle legislative matters directly with individual divisions or at area meetings.

Scheduling the next International Conference for May 1993 provided the International Administration and board about 18 months to fine-tune its planning and purpose. As part of that process, at the May 1992 board meeting, Vice President for Wycliffe Organizations Bendor-Samuel described the enormous task ahead for reorganizing WBTI. This process included soliciting input from the divisions about changes to existing policies, with final changes and decisions to be made at the conference.

At this early stage of the restructuring, some critical areas emerged regarding standards for membership, financial standards, and the status of the WOs. Board members wanted these organizations to apply consistent membership standards to themselves. A WO could send its people to organizations other than SIL. However, Wycliffe US committed to SIL to provide human and financial resources. Perhaps other WOs would do the same. The board realized that the critical element of trust between the WOs and SIL ensured SIL would continue to receive the bulk of resources raised by the WOs.

Concerning financial standards, WO's financial officers were directly accountable to their governing board or an oversight committee and not to the WBTI Board. In other words, individual organizations in WBTI were to take full responsibility for their financial matters.

As of 1 November 1991, all chartered divisions of WBTI were recognized as Member Organizations (MO) of WBTI, provided their officers formally applied to the board corporation secretary for this status, and demonstrated adherence to the standards in WBTI's bylaws. There were also unchartered divisions and other entities recognized by WBTI that hadn't yet qualified for MO status. The International Administration was to help these organizations move towards MO status as quickly as possible.

WMOs had to follow three categories of standards to receive the rights of belonging to WBTI:

1. *Organization Operations*: covering adherence to the vision and purpose of WBTI, the function of being a WMO, organizational categories, ministry to supporting constituencies, attitude of Christian service, trusting in God for provision of needs, financial responsibility and accountability, interdenominational character (i.e. not aligned with any one particular church denomination), processes for accepting new members and caring for existing members, governance and leadership, handling discipline of members (including rights of appeal), and financially supporting WBTI and SIL with general administrative costs.
2. *Financial Standards*: covering financial procedures, audits, financial statements, management of financial systems that serve its membership, financial oversight at the governance level, and systems for raising, receipting, managing, and distributing funds.
3. *Standards for Individual Members*: ensuring that people accepted by a WMO were spiritually, emotionally, physically, and in other ways fit to be seconded to SIL for service, including orientation and training, and an adequate financial and prayer support base.

Because of significant changes featured in WBTI's restructuring, the International Administration created a consultative process on the new policies. In August 1992, WBTI hosted a meeting in Ede, Netherlands, with WMO leaders to process recommended changes in preparation for final presentation, discussion, and adoption at the 1993 International Conference. As that process continued through 1992, Sheldon reported to the WBTI Board about Vice President David Bendor-Samuel's remarkable efforts in managing the reorganization process. Noteworthy was how he handled views and opinions from the membership of WMOs and SIL. Leading a change process is seldom straightforward. Even when it slowed the process, to ensure people understood the changes taking place, WBTI's leadership team tried to be sensitive to perspectives expressed. The WBTI Board was supportive of how the process was going.

Later, at the November 1992 board meeting, Bendor-Samuel reported the feedback received from the Ede meeting. Members in both WMOs and SIL realized the significance of the proposed changes in restructuring WBTI, and many expressed their concerns. Did this mean the process should be slowed down, gradually making as few changes as possible and one at a time? If so, this could help dispel concerns about the process moving too quickly.

Three crucial policies related to the restructuring received the WBTI Board's attention at its November 1992 meeting:

- *The Partnership Between SIL, Inc. and WBTI, Inc. and MOs*: a comprehensive set of guidelines and protocols that provided the overall guidance to how SIL, WBTI, and its organizations sought to 'work together in close partnership' through 'bonds of common commitment'.[28]
- *Administrative Guidelines for Membership in Both a WMO and in SIL, Inc.*: procedures for accepting people in a WMO and in SIL, along with how Wycliffe members were seconded to serve under SIL.
- *Secondment by WMOs to SIL, Inc.*: procedures of responsibilities of the various parties concerned with Wycliffe members seconded to serve in SIL assignments.

Acknowledging legitimate concerns from across WBTI and SIL about the reorganization of WBTI, the board affirmed their 'sincere effort... to address these concerns'[29] through the three policy documents.

Organizational Categories

The process of reorganizing WBTI required clarity on different types of organizational categories, and therefore, the board approved these categories in its November 1992 meeting:

- *Representative* (an individual appointed by WBTI to represent it in a specific geographic location to individuals, churches, and other parties, and promote prayer and other forms of support for the work)
- *Agency* (an office established by WBTI to disseminate information about the work of WBTI and SIL and receipting of funds for the work, but not able to process individuals for membership for a Wycliffe Organization)
- *Sponsoring Committee* (approved by WBTI and formed where no Wycliffe Organization exists to sponsor an individual to serve with SIL and provide basic member care to that individual)
- *Applicant Organization* (an organization recognized by WBTI that intends to become a Wycliffe Organization, and WBTI helps with the process of becoming

[28] WBTI, November 1992, 19.

[29] WBTI, November 1992, 32.

a member organization)

- *Wycliffe Member Organization without Vote* (meets basic requirements for WBTI membership but has not had sufficient experience to qualify for voting representation at International Conference)
- *Wycliffe Member Organization* (has full membership status in WBTI and may vote on WBTI matters and at the International Conference)
- *Association Organization* (is involved in Bible translation and related tasks and wants an informal relationship with WBTI)
- *Cooperating Organization* (is not primarily involved in Bible translation but agrees to provide financial support and member care to people seconded to SIL)

WBTI's intentions to restructure added complexity as it sought greater diversity of organizational categories for agencies to participate with WBTI and second personnel to SIL. At the time, SIL primarily received personnel through one of these avenues provided by WBTI. Consequently, as SIL's valued partner, WBTI aimed to maximize the options for directing people toward serving in SIL.

Next Steps of Internationalization

In preparation for the 1993 International Conference, the board considered various names for it as WBTI restructured and wanted to signal that this event was different from previous International Conferences. The most popular options included 'Meeting' (though considered a weak term), 'Congress', and 'Convention' with preference to the latter. [30] The name change wouldn't occur in time for this event but would be adopted in time for the 1996 event.

This event's new purpose became more apparent. No longer primarily for dialogue, it needed to be a place to initiate changes to WBTI's Constitution, Bylaws, and Standards; elect the WBTI Board of Directors; discuss strategies, goals, and priorities for member organizations, and WBTI's cooperation with SIL. It needed to become a forum for dialogue, information, and inspiration for the member organizations. If ever called for, it needed to become a place of appeal on terminations of member organizations by the board.

To allow sufficient time to issue formal invitations to the conference, the WBTI Board decided on various categories of representation for organizations that were not yet fully functional or recognized as WMOs. The representatives coming from these organizations could participate in the conference but not vote on WBTI legislative matters. They were:

[30] WBTI, November 1992, 33.

- Non-Chartered Entity Director Delegates: The directors were delegates to both conferences and came from 14 groups in SIL and three in WBTI (France, Singapore, and Finland).
- Non-Chartered Entity Observer Delegates (able to participate but not vote): These were administrative officers from nine WMOs (Austria, Denmark, Italy, South Africa, South Korea (Global Bible Translators), Belgium, Hong Kong, Portugal, and Spain.
- Observer Delegates Council Chairpersons: These were the council or board chairs of WMOs who were not career members.
- Observer Delegates of NBTO Steering Committee: These were the office holders of the committee.

The conference ran from 14 to 27 May at the JAARS Center at Waxhaw, with the theme 'Reaching the Next 1,000 Languages'. On the first evening, the participants were transported to the Charlotte Convention Center to attend a Spring Harvest Celebration led by Wycliffe US President Hyatt Moore. The Christian public had also been invited to attend.

Altogether, 147 delegates, 55 observer delegates, and 20 alternates representing WBTI and SIL, as well as conference staff, attended the International Conference. Executive Vice President Steve Sheldon and his International Administration team presented a world report covered by regions and domains of responsibility in the opening session. Sheldon called for all to be 'people of prayer, committed to the work and to persevere in the midst of the myriad of challenges being faced in today's world.'[31] Recognizing the need for a vision from God, Sheldon drew from Joshua 2:25. He challenged those present to be committed to a right relationship with the Lord as people of the Word, committed to all kinds of partnerships in the work, and committed to developing and using new technologies.

Conference participants explored various topics of interest. For example, 'Mobilizing Members for Recruitment' addressed current members praying for, mentoring, and discipling new members and assisting their access to service opportunities in WBT or SIL. There was a call for shorter-term service options for young people who were less interested in longer-term membership. Research conducted by the Children's Education Department (CHED) showed that there were 608 Missionary Kids (MKs) now serving in Wycliffe and SIL. Out of these, 106 had parents who were members of SIL and WBT, meaning they were raised in SIL and WBT environments. These MKs returned to serve in these organizations, and for some, in the exact locations where they grew up.

The focus of another discussion was interactive cooperation among WMOs. This was already happening in Europe with well-established organizations

---

31 WBTI, "International Conference Minutes," May 1993, 2.

assisting and consulting with newer ones, helping them develop into mature organizations. The European experiment was a good one to promote internationally. The delegates supported a statement to ask the International Administration to encourage all the larger WMOs to help the smaller ones in financial assistance, partnership development, and counselling services for personnel.

During a session called 'I have a vision' led by Steve Sheldon and open to everyone, one delegate shared his vision about Old Testament translation. Seeing the Old Testament as critical to a living, vibrant church, he felt its translation should become more prominent than peripheral in WBTI and SIL's corporate thinking. He concluded, 'translating only the New Testament is translating for Old Testament obsolescence.'[32] While only a part of a vision session and not intended to lead to action by the two organizations, further discussion later resulted in just that.

The most prominent topic under consideration was WBTI's reorganization. Several years of work by the International Administration and the WBTI Board culminated in proposing this critical issue which would require lengthy exploration before reaching an agreement. Presentations arose from the floor, followed by small group conversations with reporting back to the plenary from these exchanges. Considered a democratic process, all participants had a voice to debate and improve the legislation. A committee processed this further until the Conference organizers decided the matter was ready for the delegates to vote. This process took all ten days of the event to work through.

Another topic looked at restructuring the WBTI Board to enable more effective governance of the reorganized WBTI. The board members were the same for both WBTI and SIL up until this time. Three options were under consideration: separate board membership, partially overlapping board membership, or majority overlapping board membership. The delegates debated the pros and cons of each option. While the boards moved toward greater separation, the EVP continued leading both organizations, keeping them moving in unison. There was already legislation mandating one person to be EVP for both corporations, and some senior leaders did not want to see that change.

Restructuring the Wycliffe Convention was divided into sub-topics, with formal business decided by a single vote from each WMO. Though the NBTOs did not have WMO status, finding ways to include them in the voting process was discussed with interest. A new category of 'Associate Organization' was proposed for the NBTOs. Another topic was to decide who should represent each WMO at the convention. While it was assumed this would be the director of each organization, some thought the organizations themselves could determine who could best represent them. Members of the board and officers of WBTI's International

[32] WBTI, May 1993, 40.

Administration would be delegates without voting privileges.

Among some participants, a debate arose about giving non-WMOs a status within WBTI, including voting privileges, leading to a contentious discussion on the relationship between WBTI and the NBTOs. Leaders representing NBTOs spoke up and pointed out that ever since 1990, they had been asking the International Administration to include them in WBTI. As one NBTO leader told the participants:

> Whether admitted or not, God has started a movement [i.e., the NBTOs] which will not be stopped.... This did not start yesterday, but rather [during] meetings at Yaoundé [Cameroon] in 1985, in Mombasa [Kenya] in 1989, and at Horsleys Green [UK] in 1991.... We know the majority [of SIL members and WMOs] want to have NBTOs along in the task, regardless of the risks on both sides.[33]

As the debate continued, some SIL delegates wanted more time to process the issue of NBTOs having membership and voting rights. Various scenarios were proposed; none gained enough support. Most of those who could vote voted in favour of NBTOs being accepted into WBTI as Associate Organizations with one delegate and, therefore, one vote in future conventions. Expressing a desire to work together, John Adive, from NBTT (Nigeria) and on the NBTO Steering Committee, challenged the delegates to have unity within WBTI 'to march forward to conquer the Goliath or Jericho of the Next 1,000 Languages.'[34]

When it was clear that all the legislative changes necessary for WBTI's reorganization received sufficient support, the committee handling the matter put this wording to the delegates for consideration: 'Having reviewed the 1990 Conference action initiating the reorganization of WBTI and recognizing the need for effective partnership within the newly defined relationship, moved to reaffirm our conviction that reorganization of WBTI is the will of God at this time.' Some delegates objected to the wording 'the will of God' because this could imply that some thought it was not God's will. After further discussion and amendments, the adopted final resolution changed the last part to 'Moved to affirm our support of the reorganization of WBTI as voted in 1991.' [35] In response, David Bendor-Samuel stated that he prayed that such a resolution could be supported by the delegates so that the reorganization could continue without further delays because it had first been raised by the European WMOs three years earlier.

At the end of the lengthy process, the delegates approved all legislative changes required to have WBTI's future event called a convention, held at the same time

---

[33] WBTI, May 1993, 53.

[34] WBTI, May 1993, 19.

[35] WBTI, May 1993, 31.

and place as the SIL International Conference. In addition to the WBTI delegates, each SIL entity represented would have one member from its delegation to the SIL Conference function as an observer at the WBTI Convention.

David Cummings was re-elected as WBTI President (and therefore board chair). Other elected positions onto the WBTI Board were Nico Daams (Wycliffe Netherlands Director) and Hyatt Moore (Wycliffe US President) in the Wycliffe Director slots. Don Robertson, Micah Amukobole, and Bill McIlvain were elected as constituency members. Bob Creson, Bruce Hollenback, Don Toland, Ray Gordon, and Scott McGregor were elected as SIL field directors on the WBTI Board. Carolyn Miller, Millie Larson, Don Lindholm, Earl Adams, and Theodore Williams were elected as SIL members on the WBTI Board. The breakdown of nationalities was US (11), Australia (1), Canada (1), Kenya (1), India (1), and Netherlands (1). Even though WBTI was becoming more culturally diverse, this was not yet evident in the board composition.

Implications of Reorganization

The consequences of the reorganization decisions of the 1993 International Conference were significant, but the impact and the understanding of all that was affected would take time to sink in. In summary, no longer would the same people serve as delegates to the SIL International Conference and the WBTI Convention. Motions passed in one meeting (including board meetings) were not automatically legislation or policy of both corporations. The two corporations, now fully separated, possessed unique policy manuals reflecting their individual natures, identities, and roles. Their distinctions increased in prominence and importance. Significantly, membership in SIL was now held by individuals, not by organizations, whereas in WBTI, organizations rather than individuals were members. Most SIL members were members of a WMO and therefore expected to be fully involved in decisions made by their WMO. But now, with this reorganization, it was apparent that WBTI was an organization of individual WMOs rather than an organization of individuals who were members of a WMO.

Even within the WBTI reorganization debate, SIL members participating in the discussions wanted to safeguard a requirement for WMOs to listen to their members in SIL when participating in WBTI matters. Individual SIL members desired to have the same influence in WBTI's decision-making as they did in SIL. For example, in the debate, an SIL member asked if 'power [is] only at the top' now that WMOs were autonomous. Responding in his official capacity, Vice President for Wycliffe Organizations David Bendor-Samuel observed that laws in most countries where WMOs existed recognized that duly appointed directors represented their organizations. Within WMO regulations, the membership was responsible for electing the governing body, which then decided policy.

WBTI, which had never been structured like SIL, no longer operated as if it were. WMOs were independent of one another and were responsible for their own governance. Their members played a role in choosing the governing boards and giving input into legislative matters. But these members no longer played a role in the affairs of WBTI as that was now in the hands of the WMOs. Based on input from some SIL members at the International Conference, this was a point of concern for them. Time would tell how long it would take for all existing SIL members to understand this change in WBTI.

The two-year term cycle of appointments of office holders in the International Administration was tied to the two-year cycle of the International Conferences. As an example of maintaining consistent policies and conforming to the International Conference, now being held every three years, at its May 1994 meeting the WBTI Board decided to streamline the process, and the executive director (executive vice president), vice presidents, area directors, officers of the board, and committees of the board were to be on this same three-year cycle. Simultaneously, the executive director's term limitation changed from eight years (a maximum of four two-year terms) to nine years (a maximum of three three-year terms).

Incorporation in Texas

In 1993, the board authorized the International Administration to move WBTI's incorporation from the State of California to the State of Texas. In May 1995, the board officially declared that, because it was a non-profit corporation, it had no assets to be distributed, transferred, or liquidated in California. Now, WBTI officially moved from its legal location on the west coast of the US (where it had started as WBT, Inc., later, Wycliffe US) to the ILC at Dallas. Its legal status was now aligned with SIL's incorporation (also in the State of Texas) and simplified meeting future legal requirements for both organizations through the International Administration and the two boards.

Funding National Involvement

In 1991, the WBTI and SIL Boards discussed issues relating to the next 1,000 languages and the likelihood of involving creative strategies to meet the need. Wycliffe US responded to this challenge in 1993 by creating 'Partners with Nationals' (in 1995 renamed The Seed Company) as an innovative fund-raising initiative for these projects. As President of Wycliffe US from 1980–1992, Bernie

May assumed leadership of this initiative. Under May, funding went to national translators (usually mother-tongue speakers who already knew the language and culture), so they could concentrate primarily on translation efforts. The new strategy did not abandon how WBT and SIL personnel had worked. Bernie May called this 'Paradigm A, the traditional member-driven system of fundraising [that] reflects a member-centric approach,' and had been a 'powerful method' of effectively managing resources and reporting to the funders. However, Partners with Nationals focussed on 'Paradigm B, the program-driven' approach set up to 'funnel resources directly from [funding] constituency to projects [allowing] for churches and foundations to relate to WBT in terms of projects.'[36] This new method attracted interest from funders, and it required a creative organizational structure because it differed from the 'A' approach. However, the 'B' approach called for well-defined projects that fit the new criteria. The emerging program of Partners with Nationals represented an updated example of this strategy.

Literacy and Promotion

At the November 1992 board meeting, the International Administration responded to a prior request to set up a task force to encourage SIL field leadership, WMOs, and the International Administration to create strategies that emphasized the importance of literacy and Scripture promotion for the success of a language program. In the SIL context, this involved 'all activities designed and carried out with the specific objective of achieving acceptance and use of vernacular literature' which included but was not limited to the Scriptures.[37] To achieve these goals, not only were local citizens to be trained in all aspects of this strategy but also to be pursued were partnerships with other organizations. This included partnering with non-print media such as the Jesus Film from Campus Crusade and the New Media Bible from the Genesis Project to make these available in languages where Bible translation was taking place through SIL.

For their part, WMOs were willing to strengthen their recruitment and fundraising efforts with their publics to support literacy and Scripture promotion. SIL fields needed to offer new members service opportunities (including shorter terms than those for existing translation personnel) as some literacy and promotion efforts could be completed in two-year terms. Because SIL fields addressed longer-term service times for language-related personnel, this called for a shift in thinking.

The work of this joint WBTI and SIL task force illustrated how WMOs embraced new ways of serving SIL through recruitment and fundraising,

---

[36] WBTI, "Board Minutes," May 1994, 6.

[37] WBTI, May 1994, 11.

proactively engaging in efforts to ensure the language communities would use the translated Scriptures. As this discussion with the two boards and the International Administration concluded, it was declared to be a 'momentous day' recognizing the importance of literacy and Scripture promotion and launching into an 'immensely broad and impossibly complex new era' for the two organizations.[38]

Associated Organizations

Newly created guidelines focussed on how Associate Organizations would be recognized in the restructured WBTI. These organizations sought to recruit people to do Bible translation in countries other than their homeland. While their standards were compatible with WBTI, they chose not to become WMOs. To qualify for this status, they had to 'second a significant number of their members to serve with SIL. Their members [could] also be supervised in field work by agencies other than SIL (including the Associate Organization itself).'[39] Their members could also be seconded to serve with a WMO or WBTI.

Like Associate Organizations, Affiliate Organizations differed in that they recruited and supervised people serving in Bible translation within their own country and closely cooperated with SIL in implementing field strategies. Recognition by WBTI showed that the Affiliate Organization had a close relationship with both WBTI and SIL. Affiliate Organizations would not be assigning their personnel to serve under WBTI, Wycliffe Organizations, or SIL. While Affiliate Organizations would assume responsibility for the financial support of their own members, administration, and operational requirements, they could receive these funds as income transferred from WMOs through their local SIL entity.

Both membership statuses revealed WBTI's genuine desire to recognize other organizations that were part of Bible translation who chose to keep their own identity and autonomy outside of WBTI but wanted a close relationship with WBTI and therefore SIL, too. Neither status was available to organizations that were already part of another Bible translation association like WBTI, such as the United Bible Societies (UBS). At the meeting of the NBTO Steering Committee in September 1995 in Manila, the participants welcomed WBTI's action in establishing the new status of Affiliate Organization, thus creating a place within its fellowship for qualifying NBTOs. The Committee encouraged all the qualifying NBTOs to begin applying for this recognition.

[38] WBTI, May 1994, 15.

[39] WBTI, "Board Minutes," November 1994, 15.

Status Changes

During 1994 various organizations, including the following, were approved by WBTI for status changes:

- Word Communication Berhad (Ltd.) in Malaysia: Applicant Organization status. Word was a new organization that already had a ten-member council and full-time administrator. It intended to proceed toward qualifying as a WMO.
- Wycliffe France (Association Traduire la Bible): Applicant Organization status because it had stabilized in structure and direction.
- Wycliffe South Africa: Applicant Organization.
- Wycliffe Bible Translators Hong Kong: WMO without vote.
- Global Bible Translators (GBT): Associate Organization with vote. It is worth noting that WBTI didn't at the time consider GBT to be a WMO. When GBT came on the scene, it was categorized as an NBTO, even though it did not do Bible translation within its borders. Because it was already under the Global Missionary Fellowship of South Korea, it was in the Associate category. GBT also didn't use 'Wycliffe' in its name. GBT wanted WBTI membership and approval so that it could send its members to SIL. But it also wanted to be able to send its personnel to other organizations.

Later and in preparation for inviting organizations to the 1996 Convention, the board presumed that all existing NBTOs would receive Affiliate Organization status before the meeting. Up until this time, the only organization with Affiliate status was GBT (Korea). The other organizations were: ANTBA (Burkina Faso), BTL (Kenya), CABTAL (Cameroon), GILLBT (Ghana), NBTT (Nigeria), ALEM (Brazil), TAP (Philippines), Kartidaya (Indonesia), IICCC (India), and BTA (Papua New Guinea).

Meeting of WMOs

The directors of the WMOs met in April 1995 at the Wycliffe Germany centre in Holzhausen. The International Administration sponsored the meeting under the guidance of Vice President of Wycliffe Organizations, David Bendor-Samuel. While discussing topics of mutual interest, the overriding feeling among the leaders was the necessity of holding this kind of meeting in between conventions. As the gathering was in Europe, it also included leaders of emerging Wycliffe Organizations in central and eastern Europe whose countries were now able to openly engage following the collapse of the communist era. Europe Area Director Darryl Kernick informed the WBTI Board of his concerns for some of these organizations which were enthusiastic for recruiting people for Bible translation but lacking the financial resources to support translators. This example illustrated some of the challenges the growing WBTI faced as it welcomed organizations outside its historical contexts.

Internal Relationships

Through the leadership of the vice president for Wycliffe Organizations and with the help of the WBTI President, WBTI was giving practical assistance for the development of all WMOs. These organizations had autonomy, but the smaller and newer ones still needed help in their development. WBTI would continue to explore ways to accomplish this.

Unlike the smaller, newer organizations, the larger ones enjoyed a different relationship with WBTI because they had administrative infrastructures, offices, and staff and were generally self-sufficient. Organizations like Wycliffe US openly shared policies they had developed (e.g., HR and financial) with the smaller organizations. The smaller WMOs could then adapt or learn from these as they established guidelines for their contexts. The largest organizations also benefitted from various privileges that the others did not have. For example, at the November 1994 board meeting, the two largest Wycliffe Organizations were present, along with their chairs. Wycliffe US Chair Don Kroeker and Wycliffe Canada Chair Roger Tompkins attended, and the newly elected Director of Wycliffe Canada, Jack Popjes, and Wycliffe US President Hyatt Moore (who was also a WBTI Board member). These leaders gave overviews and highlights of their organizations, and the WBTI Board responded by expressing its appreciation for the ongoing support by both organizations for WBTI and SIL's programs.

People Serving in the US

A study by the International Administration focussed on the percentage of people serving in home countries through the WMOs. Concerns were expressed by both the Christian supporting public and the wider SIL and WBT membership about how many people the WMOs had based in the sending countries. The study looked at the four largest Wycliffe Organizations—US, Canada, UK, and Australia. It calculated that the percentage of Junior and Senior members actively serving home operations varied between 25% and 39% of the respective organizations' combined memberships. A further 17% were home on furlough at any given time. The WBTI Board considered the numbers too high because fewer people were available for field assignments where the needs were critical. The number serving in the US was particularly high because it included staff at the Wycliffe US headquarters in California and its regional offices.

The many people assigned to JAARS at Waxhaw, SIL, and WBTI at Dallas added to the high number of members based in the US. The WBTI Board asked the International Administration to assess whether the services provided could be handled another way or discontinued. The thought was that this could release people currently based in the US back to SIL field assignments. The Administration reported back to the board that organizations such as Wycliffe US believed there weren't enough members in their organization to meet all necessities and expectations. More Wycliffe US members were required in assignments in the US to meet the personnel needs. Consequently, the board asked the International Administration to work with Wycliffe US to hold the percentage of the total Wycliffe US membership serving Wycliffe US at a maximum of 30% and the International Administration at a maximum of 25%.

This discussion demonstrated how the WBTI Board managed its concerns about the number of Wycliffe US members serving in the US through Wycliffe US or the International Administration. The board also wanted to safeguard that both Wycliffe US and the International Administration had enough people located in the US to enable them to be effective in serving worldwide needs.

Strategic Planning

Executive Director Steve Sheldon reported on WBTI and SIL's progress with the WBTI and SIL Boards at the May 1995 board meetings. The report described a continuing fall in recruitment and a negligible increase of active members. This downward trend caused concern for the WBTI Board as it 'indicate[d] a slowing down in the pace of Bible translation unless there [were] compensating increases in other organizations.'[40] The board asked for further analysis and application of this to the progress of Bible translation worldwide.

Sheldon updated the board on his administration's strategic plan, which looked at language projects, SIL entities, and Area level priorities. In response, the board commended the plan's 'good stewardship and appropriate accountability [that required] an ongoing focus on sound planning and responsible evaluation.'[41] The board asked for regular reporting on organization-wide progress. It also wanted to see 'all corporate entities [giving] priority to strategic planning and evaluation [including] goal setting and a system to monitor and report progress', starting and propelling an era of organization-wide strategic planning.[42]

---

[40] WBTI, "Board Minutes," May 1995, 2.

[41] WBTI, May 1995, 3.

[42] WBTI, May 1995, 3.

Bylaw Amendments

Following a process specified in the WBTI Bylaws, Senior members voted on WBTI re-organization legislation processed at the 1993 International Conference. Corporation Secretary Ken Davis reported to the board that 65.8% of the possible 4,017 Senior Members had voted (65% participation was required), with these results:

- Restructure International Conference: 84% in favour.
- Restructure the Board of Directors: 87% in favour.
- New Associate and Affiliate Organization categories: 78% in favour.[43]

It is of interest that, in this process, all Senior Members could vote (or abstain). These were the Senior Members of the Wycliffe Organizations, most of whom served in SIL assignments. As a result, they held a great deal of influence over the potential of restructuring WBTI and its future. In the end, enough Senior Members voted in favour of all these pieces of legislation. WBTI could now continue restructuring based on discussions first conducted at the 1991 International Conference, further processed at the 1993 conference, and approved and adopted in mid-1995. This vote was a culmination of this slow but thorough four-year change process.

Board Structure

In preparation for the 1996 International Convention with revised bylaws, the composition of the WBTI Board changed. Prospective candidates would be pre-processed by the Nominating Committee and then presented for election by the delegates of the WOs with vote at the convention, resulting in this revised board structure:

- President of the board (i.e., chairman): one person elected from a slate of two nominees.
- WO Directors: four people elected from a slate of eight people chosen by the WO Directors.
- Constituency Members: three people selected from a slate of six people nominated by the Wycliffe Organization governing bodies (i.e., boards or councils).
- Member of Associate or Affiliate Organization: one person from a slate of three people nominated by Directors of Associate and Affiliate Organizations.
- Career Member of a WO: one person from a slate of three people proposed by the WO.
- Representatives from the SIL Board: three people chosen from the slate of all SIL Board members.

[43] WBTI, "Board Minutes," November 1995, 2.

Board Purpose

Since the restructuring of WBTI was approved and the election of the new board would take place at the upcoming 1996 International Convention, the board took on a revised objective: 'To have final authority for the ongoing policies, business, and programs of the Corporation.'[44] The board's responsibilities now included the following:

- Appointment of specified officers, administrators, and committees.
- Granting members to or terminating members of WOs (including Associate and Affiliate ones).
- Handling the legal business of WBTI and establishing and reviewing agreements with other organizations.
- Monitoring the programs and operating budget of WBTI through reports from the president and executive director.
- Reviewing actions called for by the WBTI Executive Director concerning any WO and Associate and Affiliate organizations.

Role of the President

WBTI, which followed an approach like SIL's, still maintained the position of president. In the new WBTI structure, the role changed to 'provide vision and stimulus for completing the Bible translation task and provide spiritual leadership.'[45] The president held a public relations role representing WBTI to WOs, the Christian public, and other organizations, including serving as an advisor to WOs. The president also acted as chair of the board and in this capacity, assured the board and International Convention regarding completing all meeting preparations. Acting on behalf of the board, the president reviewed and monitored WBTI policies and programs and participated in global strategic planning sessions with the International Administration. Notably, the president nominated specific officers, including the executive director, for appointment by the board.

Function of International Administration

As part of the realignment process for WBTI, the purpose and function of the International Administration were to provide leadership to all of WBTI and manage the organization's operations with the primary focus of serving the WOs and helping them achieve WBTI's goals. To do this, the International Administration

[44] WBTI, November 1995, 5.

[45] WBTI, November 1995, 6.

developed the necessary expertise, reviewed its policies, proposed its strategies, and monitored resources to ensure achieving its goals. Even though WBTI had become an organization of autonomous organizations, the International Administration nevertheless bore the responsibility to represent all of WBTI, while final authority rested with the board.

Emergency Support

Until this time, Wycliffe US managed and funded the Emergency Support System, a program that benefited all WOs. It served members in financial relationship with their WOs, who also served in those organizations, or in assignments with SIL. When members' financial support fell below a certain percentage, emergency funds were made available.

As transitions took place in WBTI, this program required adapting. The emergency fund was slowly phased out with decentralization and progress towards autonomy among the WOs. By 1995, only four WOs had requested assistance for their members' support needs, totalling US$67,000 for the year. Five WOs, including Wycliffe US, provided these funds and now voluntarily contributed to the emergency fund, an encouraging development illustrating practical ways WOs were rising to the challenge of assisting each other.

WBTI also operated and approved other financial means of assisting the WOs, including a Ready Investment Account (RIA), held with SIL. Loans with low interest were available to purchase property by WOs through the fund. There was also the Loan Fund from which WOs could borrow up to US$10,000 at low interest for their special needs.

Increasing Internationalization

WBTI's development required a visual identity. Based on a decision made in 1977, WBTI had no official logo, though it encouraged every WO to create its own. After WBTI had reorganized and incorporated in 1980, the board and the International Administration decided to establish a standardized logo. As an individual and separate organization with its own growing identity, WBTI needed a distinctive symbol, and Wycliffe and related organizations wanted a recognizable emblem linking them to the 'umbrella' organization. Consequently, WBTI's logo went through various reiterations to capture the internationalization process.

In 1996, WBTI's International Convention was the first to be conducted as a restructured organization under revised bylaws which positioned it as an international organization. The meeting convened with the SIL International Conference at the JAARS Center in North Carolina from 25 May to 4 June. The Convention reflected the growing international composition of WBTI, grouped into these organizational statuses:

- WOs with vote, represented by two delegates per organization: 16—Australia, Canada, Finland, France, Germany, Japan, Netherlands, New Zealand, Norway, Singapore, South Africa, GBT South Korea, Sweden, Switzerland, UK, and US.
- WOs without vote, represented by one observer each: 4—Austria, Belgium, Denmark, and Hong Kong.
- Applicant Organizations without vote, represented by one official observer each: 6—Caribbean, Malaysia, Poland, Portugal, Spain, and Taiwan.
- Affiliate Organizations with vote, represented by one delegate each: 6—ALEM Brazil, ANTBA Burkina Faso, BTL Kenya, GILLBT Ghana, NBTT Nigeria, and TAP Philippines.
- Affiliate Organizations without vote, represented by one official observer each: 8—ACATBA Republic of Central Africa; AITB Côte d'Ivoire; ATALTRAB Chad; BTCS Sabah, Malaysia; BTA Papua New Guinea; CABTA Cameroon; Kartidaya Indonesia; and IICCC India.
- International Administration as official observers without vote: Steve Sheldon as executive director with his four vice presidents (Administration, Wycliffe Organizations, Personnel, and Finance) and four Area Directors (Africa, Asia, Europe, and Pacific).
- WBTI Board and international officers as official observers without vote: Ken Davis (corporation secretary), George Cowan (president emeritus), and Elaine Townsend (founder's wife).

Altogether, 37 voting delegates cast votes for the business at hand. While the official observers could not vote, they all had 'voice' in the proceedings and could contribute to the discussions.

Convention devotional speaker, widely published Yale University Professor Lamin Sanneh, made an impression on delegates with his 'strong and deep regard for vernacular Scriptures.'[46] Special reports from selected presenters acknowledged dependence on God. In his report, Executive Director Steve Sheldon addressed the convention theme, 'The Transforming Word of God', prioritizing stillness before God. He called on the participants to 'remember that there are eternal certainties in our uncertain world. The "Transforming Word" must be a fundamental part of our lives.'[47] David Cummings gave his final speech as WBTI President, reflecting on his 15 years of service. He noted how much the world had changed in this time and how 'things [had] become less comfortable' with human

[46] WBTI, "International Convention Minutes," June 1996, 2.

[47] WBTI, June 1996, 3.

wisdom presenting a discouraging element. Nevertheless, encouragement comes from God as we focus on his interests.[48]

Choosing the next WBTI Board was significant for the convention's voting delegates. It involved electing candidates pre-processed by the Nominating Committee. Of three candidates for president, John Bendor-Samuel (UK), already well-known to WBTI, was elected. Of eight nominees for the four slots for WO Directors, David Cummings (Australia), Hyatt Moore (US), Takashi Fukuda (Japan), and Richard Steinbring (Germany) were elected. Of nine nominees for the three slots for Constituency Members, Anne Henderson (Australia), Roger Welch (UK), and Don Robertson (Canada) were elected. Of five nominees for the Affiliate and Associate Organizations slot, Grace Adjekum (Ghana) was elected. Of 14 nominees for Career Member, Judith Schram (US) was elected. The final process was to choose three SIL board members to serve on the WBTI Board. Frank Robbins (US), Micah Amukobole (Kenya), and Barbara Trudell (US) were elected to fill these positions.

The 13 board members were from the US (4), Australia (2), UK (2), Canada (1), Germany (1), Japan (1), Ghana (1), and Kenya (1). Gradually, the WBTI Board was becoming more international, with 77% of the board coming from Western nations and 23% from majority world nations and a total of four women.

Barrie Wetherill of Wycliffe Associates UK and Martin Huyett of Wycliffe Associates US reported on the second international meeting of Wycliffe Associates held in the UK in 1996. There were now Wycliffe Associate organizations in the US, UK, Canada, Australia, New Zealand, Switzerland, and South Africa, with new developments underway in Malaysia and Singapore. Huyett informed the convention of Wycliffe Associates' desire to discover ways they could support Wycliffe in their labours through 'encouragement and enablement'.[49]

During a joint discussion between the SIL International Conference and the WBTI International Convention (since both events were held simultaneously with overlapping agendas and topics), a focus on 'Mobilizing the Total Team' arose. Fred Magbanua from the Philippines pointed out the growth of evangelicals in the 'mission fields' and that if WBTI and SIL were to mobilize the 'Total Team for the total task, [then] it should include every member of the Body of Christ who has a concern for the task of Bible translation.'[50] A representative of CABTA in Cameroon challenged SIL to think more of being a facilitator in helping local or national Christians to train and do Bible translation.

Other topics included strategies between WOs and SIL entities for short-term programs since the preference of those seeking to join was trending away from

[48] WBTI, June 1996, 4.

[49] WBTI, June 1996, 14.

[50] WBTI, June 1996, 14.

longer-term roles. A further issue calling for WOs and SIL field entities to work together, 'Strategic Thrusts in Literacy' required taking creative steps toward generating substantial resources for literacy personnel and funding.

Presentations on new strategies for training personnel for language and translation roles led to the WBTI Convention and SIL International Conference adopting this statement to address the rethinking of training throughout the two organizations: 'Our vision for WBT and SIL training is that: All members of the team, expatriate and national alike, will acquire the right training, in the right way, from the right people, at the right time and place, building upon their experience to that point, so that they will be able to serve effectively in their roles.'[51]

As WBTI grew and became more international, presentations centred on involving people from more nations. Delegates asked the International Administration and WOs to concentrate on strategies that 'encourage and help additional nationalities to be involved in carrying out the task [of Bible translation].'[52] There was also the necessity to find additional ways to raise funds. The convention asked the International Administration to establish joint forums for WOs and SIL field entities to develop alternative funding strategies.

Addressing various prayer needs during the closing celebrations, President Emeritus George Cowan led the participants in an hour-long 'Concert of Prayer'. Newly appointed WBTI President John Bendor-Samuel's closing address officially adjourned the convention, which would reconvene in three years.

Renewed Vision

When the new WBTI Board and International Administration gathered for their first meeting in November 1996, they adopted a three-year vision for WBTI that addressed three themes:

1. 'A well-functioning family of organizations' with indicators covering staffing for WMOs, financial support for smaller or applicant organizations, ongoing interaction and cooperation between all WMOs, and these organizations applying 'appropriate thinking, planning and evaluation.'
2. 'A full partner of SIL' with indicators covering effective interaction and communication between WMOs and SIL field entities and better systems to support cooperation, especially in personnel and financial matters.
3. 'An instrument God is using to involve the church worldwide in Bible translation' with indicators of financial assistance in countries where 'personal support is not possible', relevant sending organizations including in Latin

[51] WBTI, June 1996, 18.
[52] WBTI, June 1996, 19.

America and Eastern Europe, activities to spread the vision in new ways in countries not currently involved, and 'active cooperation with other agencies having common purposes.'[53]

This vision expressed new concepts not discernible in earlier statements, possibly due to the broader internationalization of WBTI and the changing worldwide contexts. Adoption of the term 'family of organizations' notably embraced all categories in WBTI and SIL and its field entities. Collectively, the WBTI and SIL Boards and International Administration were seeing this as a family. Before reorganization, WBTI existed for SIL's benefit. Now a maturing, more mutual relationship between two worldwide bodies, WBTI described itself as a full partner to SIL. WBTI was simultaneously becoming instrumental in serving the church to better engage with—and in—Bible translation. And finally, the intention to engage in Latin America, a region where SIL started its work but up until now held only minimal focus from WBTI.

Financial Needs

Ongoing discussion among WBTI's leaders was spurred by presenting financial requests to various publics. This controversial topic rested on the prevailing, unchanging principle of reliance on God's provision for all essentials. However, revised guiding concepts developed that recognized the necessity to better inform the 'whole church' of the 'needs with sensitivity and propriety.' Therefore, the various publics would be addressed uniquely and sensitively and made aware of the needs without conveying an obligation to meet them. Foundations and philanthropic agencies could at times be approached more directly with funding requests.[54]

Legal Separation

Even though the decision to legally separate the two corporations occurred at the 1993 International Conference, the process was deliberately slow. The administration structure was entwined and embedded in WBT, Inc.'s formation in 1942. Five years after the restructuring decision, the next stage was to ensure greater legal separation between WBTI, Inc. and SIL, Inc. through separate bank accounts, liability flow, and appropriate representation to the public. WBTI would make contracts with SIL to cover the leasing of facilities, sharing employees, and retaining accounting services as part of this process.

[53] WBTI, "Board Extracts," November 1996, 3.

[54] WBTI, November 1996, 11.

Priorities Ahead

In May 1997, Executive Director Steve Sheldon gave his first report for the new triennium to the WBTI Board. The International Administration had consolidated WBTI's focus into three initiatives for strengthening internal and external relationships:

Within the overall guiding strategy of deepening and enlarging partnerships both inside and outside our family of organizations, we commit ourselves to the following priorities:

› Strategic planning and use of resources
› Partnership
› Renewing our sense of urgency and focus[55]

Despite these intentions, insufficient staffing for core operations was hampering the effectiveness of many WOs. As well, smaller organizations in Europe were experiencing funding challenges. Creative approaches were called for to help the worldwide church become better engaged in mission while retaining WBTI's emphasis on Bible translation.

The International Administration planned a significant increase in its activity and involvement to support WBTI's vision. This included:

› Administrative support of WOs.
› Training and coaching their staff.
› Helping with their strategic planning.
› Subsidies for administrative needs in the smaller organizations.
› Improving systems supporting collaboration between WOs and SIL field entities.
› Spreading the vision for Bible translation in new countries.
› Interacting with other Bible agencies and providing support systems for people from 'less affluent countries'.[56]

To assure productivity and good stewardship of resources, ongoing attention to measure progress and evaluate the impact on the work was necessary and presented a challenge for the WBTI Board. To meet all stated goals required that WBTI's administration grow proportionately and raise additional funds to cover WBTI's support of the WOs. The solution was to ask all WOs to contribute financially to WBTI based on a percentage of the organization's total income, applied equally to all WOs, and conducting negotiations to gain their approval to pursue this further.

---

55 WBTI, "Board Extracts," May 1997, 1.

56 WBTI, May 1997, 4.

Challenges of Internationalization

Steve Sheldon's leadership team was composed of the area directors of Africa (John Watters, US), Asia (Dick Hugoniot, US), Pacific (Neville Southwell, Australia), and Europe (Darryl Kernick, Australia). The vice presidents were for personnel (Bob Creson, US), administration (Anton Bucher, US), finance (Dave Cram, US), Wycliffe Organizations (David Bendor-Samuel, UK/US), and the new positions of Vice President for Operations (Marvin Hyde, US) and Vice President for Legal Affairs (Bob Lipps, US). Later in 1997, Bendor-Samuel stepped down from his vice president role, completing a long tenure of leadership roles within WBTI and SIL. Although WBTI was truly international through its WOs, its leaders came from just three Western nations: US (8), Australia (2), and UK (1). While there were women serving in WOs, with many in leadership roles, this was not reflected in the leadership of WBTI.

At the end of 1999, Sheldon's third three-year term was concluding, having reached the nine-year term limit for an executive director. Allowing for a long lead-time and transition, the WBTI and SIL Boards had pre-processed their preferred candidate with the WMOs and SIL entities since this was a joint leadership role. There was 'strong favour' for the two boards to appoint John Watters as executive director-elect.[57] His term would commence on 1 January 2000.

As a means of stimulating new thinking around obstacles that challenged the development of WBTI, the board set up three task forces:

1. Funding of the International Administration.
2. Effective national partnerships.
3. Supporting individuals from less affluent or less politically open countries, including where there was no WO.

These task forces would meet over the subsequent months and make future recommendations to the International Administration and the 1999 Convention.

Area directors were observing changes within the worldwide church. For example, in the Americas, Marvin Hyde acknowledged some decline of members from Wycliffe Canada while at the same time, ALEM (Brazil) marked a growing interest in its ministry. Hyde also identified 'exploding interest in cross-cultural missions in many areas' of Latin America.[58] Dick Hugoniot noted that, in Asia, the Chinese church had a growing interest in unreached people groups. WOs in Asia were projecting a 35% increase of new members. WOs in Malaysia and Taiwan, including Kartidaya Indonesia, were also progressing in healthy ways. Darryl Kernick observed that small European WOs like Denmark and Norway were playing their

[57] WBTI, "Board Extracts," November 1997, 3.

[58] WBTI, November 1997, 9.

part on behalf of language programs. Exploratory efforts to recruit Russians were also in process. In the Pacific, Neville Southwell saw a thriving partnership emerging between Wycliffe Australia and BTA Papua New Guinea, concentrating on providing constituency development training.

Momentum for Reorganization

The International Administration needed expertise to mobilize people from the whole world, especially where there was no existing WO. In the Africa and Pacific Areas, WBTI required more staff to address WBTI issues. Cooperation was also needed between WBTI and SIL field entities to provide support and field assignments for personnel positioned to operate outside of established methods. The lack of Wycliffe leadership, in general, presented a significant challenge, especially if WBTI continued to grow and serve the WOs and partners. Improvement of regional representation on the WBTI Board called for the selection process to happen at the Area level rather than at the WBTI Convention. These issues reflected the challenges resulting from WBTI's reorganization and the growing worldwide interest.

As part of the International Administration's reporting to the May and November 1998 WBTI Board meetings, Africa Area Director John Watters expressed concern about African NBTOs' infrastructure, including financial management. In Cameroon, CABTAL marked progress in its development, and new WOs were emerging in Togo and Benin. The Africa Area had also held Targeted Information for Planning and Skills (TIPS) workshops to achieve strategic goals, which helped the Wycliffe side of NBTOs. Describing organizations as having sides, NBTOs appear here as embracing a Wycliffe side: addressing the national church, and an SIL side: emphasizing field work activities.

In Asia, Dick Hugoniot reported on global financial downturns affecting local currencies across Asia, prompting GBT to recall people from field locations back to South Korea to consolidate their financial situation. In Indonesia, Kartidaya continued to develop as an applicant Affiliate Organization, while a new WO was emerging in Thailand. A nationwide approach to the work of Bible translation gained attention in India while the training of Indians progressed, leading to 35 translation programs underway in the country. Wycliffe Malaysia continued to mature to the extent that it and Wycliffe Taiwan were granted WO without vote status, while Wycliffe Hong Kong achieved WO with vote status. Wycliffe Japan, celebrating its 30th anniversary, carried the historical significance of being the first Wycliffe Division to be established outside of the Western world. Much had happened over the 30 years that followed.

Darryl Kernick reported that the Europe Area related to 21 countries, though not all had a WO yet. Wycliffe Hungary and Wycliffe Czech Republic, however, received Representative status. Russian Christians, and other Christians around the world, expressed interest in starting a WO in Russia based in St. Petersburg. The Nordic WOs held a regional conference. Wycliffe Austria was granted WO with vote status. Wycliffe Caribbean, under Europe Area, was given WO without vote status.

In the Pacific, Neville Southwell reported that BTA PNG had completed its seventh New Testament program. There was a workshop on constituency development and church relations for Islanders involved in Bible translation, held in Vanuatu and attended by Islanders from PNG, Solomon Islands, and Vanuatu. At a recent forum, BTA PNG had a leading role in relating to Pacific Islanders showing interest in greater involvement in Bible translation. To accommodate these interests would require more informal membership categories.

In the Americas, Wycliffe US, located in southern California since its inception, decided to relocate its headquarters to have enough property to expand training facilities and have a decreased cost of living. Elsewhere in the Americas, contacts through COMIBAM from countries expressing interest in Bible translation led to discussions in Chile and Argentina. In Costa Rica, a training course was in the planning stage. There was the possibility of a sponsoring committee in Mexico for promoting Wycliffe activities. A national missions organization in Colombia showed interest in involvement in Bible translation. The growing opportunities in the Americas continued to press upon the International Administration. Until this time there was no area director for the region, though people like David Bendor-Samuel and later Marvin Hyde had been relating to Wycliffe US and Wycliffe Canada. In November, the board approved Steve Sheldon's plan to establish an Americas Area within WBTI. They appointed Marvin Hyde as interim area director while searching for a full-time person.

The WBTI Board had initiated three task forces in the previous year, and all were making progress in their respective areas of focus. In particular, the task force examining requirements where there was no WO received the board's approval to authorize the WBTI Areas to carry out the functions of a WO in initiating and supervising the member processes for recruits where needed and appropriate. The Areas choosing this approach implemented structures and processes to handle recruitment, processing, financial support, training, placement, and member care of personnel assigned to SIL field entities. As a result, where no WO existed, and neither were there any plans to establish one, the Areas could handle all essential requirements.

Board Composition

In preparation for the appointment of the next board at the 1999 International Convention, revised composition would mean there was: (1) the president (and therefore board chair); (2) five directors of related organizations (WOs, Affiliate Organizations, and/or Associate Organizations,) with one being the current director of any WO that had more that 50% of the worldwide membership of WOs; (3) five people from the constituency (which could be one per Area); and (4) three from the SIL Board.

Birthing of Vision 2025

The WBTI 1999 International Convention and SIL International Conference jointly took place from 1–10 June at the JAARS Center in North Carolina with the theme 'Together We Can'. WBTI President John Bendor-Samuel, in his opening address, spoke from Psalm 126, highlighting the 'celebration' of past blessings of 500 New Testaments translated and the 'great involvement of NBTOs'.[59] He spoke of 'desperation, an urgent cry to God [because] the task before us is enormous.'[60] He looked at 'expectation [of] hope in God, with joy and anticipation [and] a time in God's harvest for every language group.'[61] Devotional speakers were Min-Young Jung of GBT, South Korea; Fergus Macdonald of UBS; J.I. Packer of Regent College; and Don Carson of Trinity Evangelical Divinity School.

The selection by the delegates of the 13-member WBTI Board was an important responsibility, with the following results:

› *President:* Dick Hugoniot (US).
› *WMO Directors:* Sigmund Evensen (Norway), Takashi Fukuda (Japan), Marcel Gasser (Switzerland), and Roy Peterson (US—WMO that had more than 50% of the worldwide membership).
› *Associate Organization Director:* Min-Young Jung (South Korea).
› *Constituency:* Derek Fivaz (South Africa), Luis Pantoja (Philippines), and Roger Welch (UK).
› *Career Member:* Judy Schram (US).
› *From the SIL Board:* Carolyn Miller (US), David Ross (US/New Zealand), and Danjuma Gambo (Nigeria).

The composition of this board reflected a broader international representation than previously. From the Western world, there was 62%: US (5, including

[59] WBTI, "International Convention Extracts," June 1999, 1.
[60] WBTI, June 1999, 1.
[61] WBTI, June 1999, 1.

one with dual citizenship), New Zealand (1), also a dual citizen), Norway (1), UK (1), and Switzerland (1). From the majority world, there was 38%: Japan (1), Philippines (1), South Korea (1), South Africa (1), and Nigeria (1). The board's limited representation of women continued with only two, both from the US.

Leaders representing Bible agencies, missions, and churches, were asked to speak to the delegates for two days. These partner organization leaders included Luis Bush (AD2000 and Beyond), Fergus Macdonald (UBS), Denny Mulder (Bible League), Eugene Rubingh (International Bible Society), David Atkinson (Scripture Gift Mission), Avery Willis (International Mission Board of the Southern Baptist Convention), Paul Eshleman (Jesus Film Project), Dan Germann (New Tribes Mission), Gene Habacker (American Bible Society), Steve Douglass (Campus Crusade for Christ International), Luis Pantoja (of a church in the Philippines), Mutava Musyimi (National Council of Churches of Kenya), David Ruiz (COMIBAM), Paul Wang (of a Chinese church in Canada), Frank Barker (of a US church,) and Mike Frisby (of a UK church).

Summarizing the presentations and discussions, Gary Corwin, editor of *Evangelical Missions Quarterly*, noted these points:

› Your strength is your single-minded passion for translation.
› Establish liaison offices for distribution, media, church planting, development, etc.
› Continue using others to help carry out this task; respond from intentional partnerships to human needs; show boldness in strategic alliances and synergy while keeping passion for what God has called you to do; work toward synergism in partnerships, looking beyond organizational boundaries to the understanding that 'Together we can'.
› Vision 2025 is a bold plan, and the most significant obstacles are within and require the membership to sign on. Expect leaders to lead change.
› Be part of the church; recognize, communicate with, and listen to the friends you have in the churches; be open to new relational paradigms with churches; assess broader partnership with non-Protestant churches based on spreading God's Word.
› Use technology wisely.
› Foster the indigenization of responsibility in planning and implementation.
› Leave a legacy of translation training.

Approximately 350 leaders representing WBTI and SIL attended this triennial meeting. Outgoing Executive Director Steve Sheldon reported on the status of Bible translation, setting the stage for rigorous discussion on the matter. Sheldon pointed out that Bible translation progress was relatively slow throughout the first

18 centuries, despite significant milestones (the Septuagint, the Vulgate, John Wycliffe's English translation, the King James Version, Martin Luther's German translation, etc.). By the end of the 18th century, only 68 languages had access to a Bible translation.

According to Sheldon, in the 19th century, there was 'a six-fold increase in translation worldwide so that in those 100 years, an additional 450 people groups received Scripture in their languages for the first time, bringing the total number of language groups with SOME Scripture available to 522.'[62] This increase was attributed to the development of the so-called modern missionary movement and the formation of the British and Foreign Bible Society in 1804, with additional Bible Societies developing in other countries in the following years.

During the 20th century, Bible translation activity significantly increased, with translation begun in 1,690 languages. By 1999 the total number of language groups with some Scripture in their heart language was 2,212. It is worth noting that a primary issue of Bible translation concerns the language of the heart, which most effectively communicates personal and profound spiritual matters to most people in a given ethnolinguistic group. Ghanaian theologian Kwame Bediako states, 'whenever Western missionaries... made the Scriptures available to an African people in that people's own language, they weakened any Western bias in their presentation of the Gospel.'[63] Consequently, African Christians 'could truly claim they were hearing God speak to them in their own language. It amounts to the awareness that *God speaks our language too.*'[64] As more and more people become multilingual, the 'heart' language concept will vary depending on contexts, cultures, and individuals.

Sheldon's presentation noted that rapid progress in Bible translation could be attributed to the formation of SIL and WBT in the 1930s along with New Tribes Mission, Unevangelized Fields Mission, and other agencies that focussed on Bible translation for languages with fewer numbers of speakers. Additionally, indigenous translators were receiving training, usually to work in their vernaculars.

However, with further analysis of the 20th century, Sheldon observed that from 1981 to 1998 progress in Bible translation in new languages declined. He concluded that 'the estimate of how long it might take for all people groups to have SOME Scriptures in their heart languages COULD range from 100 to 150 years.'[65]

Incoming Executive Director John Watters presented his paper on Vision

---

[62] Steve Sheldon, "Bible Translation Status Worldwide: People Groups without Adequate Access to Scriptures," 1999, WBTI. 4.

[63] Kwame Bediako, *Jesus and the Gospel in Africa: History and Experience* (Maryknoll: Orbis, 2004), 58.

[64] Bediako, 58.

[65] Sheldon, 6.

2025, which he had prepared before the convention and conference, reflecting on the status of WBTI and SIL. The startling information from Sheldon and the challenge from Watters alarmed the participants, prompting thorough discussion that lasted the full length of the ten-day gathering. In the end, the delegates boldly set a new direction for WBTI and SIL in a resolution called 'Vision 2025' (see chapter 9).

The WBTI delegates also considered the International Administration's need for increased financial contributions from the WMOs to fulfil its budget, resulting in a plan for all WMOs to offer a voluntary contribution of 0.32% of their total income to WBTI starting in October 2000.

Europe Area Director Darryl Kernick led a presentation on broadening the nature of the family of WBTI organizations. More freedom and flexibility to describe the organizations was desirable, as the current descriptions were somewhat limiting. As a result, the board was asked to establish a new membership category that would allow other like-minded and partner organizations to affiliate more closely with WBTI. This request signalled to the incoming board and executive director that WBTI's reorganization was incomplete, and its structure still limited involvement for those seeking to participate in Bible translation. Another decision made by the delegates was to ask the International Administration to find ways to 'accelerate the decision-making process within the organization', especially regarding decisions made by the WBTI Convention or board.[66] There was concern among WO leaders that the change process for both WBTI and SIL could slow implementation, especially with Vision 2025's adoption.

As this was Steve Sheldon's last International Convention and Conference as executive director, he and his wife Linda were thanked 'with gratitude to God [for Steve's] contributions to Bible translation in his role of executive director of WBTI and SIL International.'[67]

Reframing as a Movement

The International Administration reported at the November 1999 board meeting the growing interest among young people from Costa Rica, Venezuela, Paraguay, and Argentina in involvement in Bible translation in Latin America. A new WMO was emerging in Russia, with Wycliffe US providing financial support for this development. The European WOs were working together to form a European Training Program to offer SIL-approved training for Europeans. In his final report to the board, Sheldon noted that interest among WOs for 'communicating

[66] WBTI, "Board Minutes," May 1995, 9.

[67] WBTI, May 1995, 9.

Vision 2025 was high.'[68] Discussions about Vision 2025 were stimulating new ways of working. However, Sheldon wanted these WOs to 'talk more about the Bible translation movement [and not] just our own work.'[69] This is noteworthy as the first reframing of Bible translation work as a movement, involving others in partnership beyond WBTI and SIL's conventional organizational boundaries. Two new organizations—Biblical Mission Association (Poland) and FEDEMEC (Costa Rica)—sought and received Cooperating Organization status, further illustrating WBTI was shaping up to become a movement.

Dave Ohlson was appointed to take the place of Fred Magbanua as Asia Area Director. Magbanua, chairman of Translators Association of the Philippines, had been filling in for six months after Dick Hugoniot, the previous Asia Area Director, was elected WBTI's President at the International Convention.

Restructuring

The board approved Watters's plan to alter the leadership structure to enable greater executive focus on the growing number of initiatives, provide greater focus on communicating and processing Vision 2025 internally and externally, and reduce the number of those reporting directly to the executive director. The newly established role of associate executive director for administration was filled by Don Lindholm, who would oversee the vice presidents for finance (Dave Cram), personnel (Larrie Gardner), strategy and information (Todd Poulter), and international communications coordinator (Carol Dowsett). In 2001 Darryl Kernick was appointed as associate executive director for operations (replacing the office of vice president for Wycliffe operations) with the area directors for Africa, the Americas, Asia, Europe, and the Pacific reporting to him.

Mission and Ends Statements

The new International Administration and board drafted revised statements to clarify WBTI's direction in the era of building a foundation for Vision 2025. The mission statement was 'Our mission is to glorify God by assisting the church worldwide in making disciples through Bible translation among people groups without adequate Scripture.'[70] The intentionality was clear: WBTI and all its organizations aimed to bring glory to God by positioning themselves to serve the church through Bible translation and its outworking of disciple-making.

---

[68] WBTI, "Board Extracts," November 1999, 1.

[69] WBTI, November 1999, 1.

[70] WBTI, November 1999, 4.

There were four Ends statements. WBTI exists so that:

1. 'The church worldwide is actively engaged in all aspects of the Bible translation task for people groups without adequate Scriptures.'
2. 'Sensitive and effective partnerships exist with SIL and other like-minded organizations.'
3. WOs 'function together as a unified whole.'
4. WOs 'function effectively'.[71]

The use of Ends statements, a new governance direction for WBTI, was influenced by John Carver's Policy Governance®, in which non-profit boards created criteria to determine when an organization's purpose was fulfilled and greatly clarifying a board's responsibility for monitoring the executive director's performance. In the WBTI Ends, there was an emphasis on engagement with the worldwide church; a desire for meaningful partnership with SIL, the inclusion of other organizations with similar goals as WBTI; and the intentionality that the body of self-governing organizations that made up WBTI would work together and function in a healthy manner. The board provisionally approved the wording and initiated a process involving input from the WOs.

WBTI's intentional emphasis on partnering went a step further when the International Administration made WBTI's doing-business-as name 'Wycliffe International' with the tag line of 'Partners in Bible Translation.'[72] This received good support from the WOs. The tagline would broaden the understanding of WBTI's identity, particularly as Vision 2025 partnerships increased.

Governance Responsibilities

The vice president for finance orientated the new board to its governance responsibilities for a non-profit organization. Already in place were many systems and much expertise to guide the board, such as the Board Committee on Finance, the Audit Committee, the External Auditor, the Administrative Committee, the vice president for finance, the treasurer, the controller, the Dallas Center finance manager, various existing policy and procedure manuals for finances and Wycliffe Organizations. Under the Policy Governance framework, the board's responsibility was to control budget values, ensure policies were in place to safeguard the organization's fiscal health, and monitor fiscal management, comparing current activities to board policies. The board's critical question concerned its accountability on behalf of WBTI and whether WBTI's total assets were sufficient for the organization to meet all its Ends. For now, the systems in place supported the

[71] WBTI, November 1999, 4.

[72] WBTI, November 1999, 4.

board's fiduciary governance responsibilities, but they would require greater attention in the future.

As part of WBTI bylaws, all Applicant Organizations and WOs needed to agree with WBTI's doctrinal basis.[73] Additionally, each organization had its own doctrinal statement, relevant to its local context and approved by the board, thus ensuring doctrinal compatibility.

Untimely Passing

John Watters's early days as WBTI Executive Director sadly coincided with the tragic death of Canadians Bob and Ruth Chapman in a Kenya Airways crash off the coast of Abidjan, Côte d'Ivoire in January, that included some national and regional leaders of Bible agencies. Chapman was appointed the previous year to succeed Watters as Africa Area Director. Now replacements had to be found at short notice. Dan Butler would serve from May 2000 to March 2001, followed by Tom Crowell.

Conclusion

Changes within WBTI characterized the decade of the 1990s. As subsidiaries of Wycliffe US, the divisions became independent non-profit charities in their home countries. These received a new name—Wycliffe Organizations (WOs). Most were from Western countries, but there were also organizations in Asia and Central and Eastern Europe by the end of the decade. They raised finances and engaged personnel and prayer support for Bible translation conducted worldwide through SIL International. WBTI adapted to include the NBTOs as Affiliate Organizations managing Bible translation programs in their own countries. WBTI was becoming more multicultural, with organizations in the Americas, Europe, Asia, Pacific, and Africa. WBTI established connections with a growing list of partner organizations. To better govern, lead, and manage the evolving WBTI, both the board and International Administration modified their structures. Holding this growing framework together represented a challenge.

The momentous decision by WBTI and SIL to adopt Vision 2025 occurred towards the end of this decade. This vision aimed to reassess and reimagine what the Bible translation task could look like if it realigned as a movement in closer partnership with the church worldwide.

WBTI's organizations were located worldwide, which helped WBTI become sensitive to global contexts. We started the era describing apartheid in South

[73] WBTI, "Board Extracts," November 2000, 5.

Africa, which illustrates how misreading and misinterpretation of the Bible can lead to the basis of a destructive worldview. Theologian N.T. Wright observes that this can happen when cultural bias influences a text's interpretation, noting that when 'endemic racism' exists in some cultures, 'neo-apartheid groups still try to base racial ideologies on scripture.'[74] Reading and misreading the Bible yields lasting consequences. Philip Jenkins describes how the government behind apartheid served a 'god who exalts the proud and humbles the poor—the very opposite of the God of the Bible who "scatters the proud of heart, pulls down the mighty from the thrones and exalts the humble" (Lk 1:51–52)'.[75] The apartheid era also 'gave a particular impetus to contextual Bible reading in South Africa... when socially engaged biblical scholars and ordinary Christians began to re-read the Bible together, yearning to hear a prophetic word from God.'[76] What happened in South Africa served as a wake-up call to WBTI to ensure that it held to values and practices of cross-cultural humility and servanthood.

Leadership Theory and Practice

This decade under review has observed the organizational cultural value of autonomy. For example, many WBT members didn't want to be under any formal leadership structure citing founder Cameron Townsend's values as their rationale. Townsend wanted the organization to be field and ministry-driven and gave less attention to actions or communications from WBT's leaders. Individual and organizational autonomy was in tension with WBTI's observations that leadership development called for attention—there was a growing and ongoing need to find new leaders. Some emerging leaders pursued formal leadership study programs, and to support less experienced leaders, the International Administration set up management training programs.

New leadership theories were being researched and developed during this decade. Servant leadership theory was one of the most notable. It was first mentioned as a business theory in a 1970 essay by executive Robert K. Greenleaf. In 1977, his book *Servant Leadership* was published. Drawing from his Judeo-Christian background, including becoming a Quaker in mid-life, Greenleaf described leadership that could serve all situations. He combined two words that were usually opposites—servant and leader—because he believed the 'two roles [could] be fused in

---

[74] N. T. Wright, *The Last Word: Beyond the Bible Wars to a New Understanding of the Authority of Scripture* (New York: HarperCollins, 2005), 107.

[75] Philip Jenkins, *The New Faces of Christianity: Believing the Bible in the Global South* (Oxford: Oxford University Press, 2006), 152.

[76] Gerald West, "The Bible and the Poor," in *Bible in Mission*, ed. Pauline Hoggarth et al. (Oxford: Regnum), 161.

one real person.'[77] Greenleaf noted how '*the great leader is seen as servant first*, and that simple fact is the key to [one's] greatness.'[78] This type of leader is primarily a servant who leads by example, is proven trustworthy, and whose servant attitude develops trust, in contrast with one desiring power and authority, and who is a 'leader first'.[79]

Servant leadership received scholarly attention in the 1990s, including from Peter Northouse, who summarizes it as a form of moral and ethical behaviour where leaders are 'attentive to the concerns of their followers, empathize with them [and] help them develop their full personal capacities.'[80] This model had and still has great relevance to WBTI. Further work on servant leadership by other theorists included James Laub's summary characteristics of 'values people, develops people, builds community, displays authenticity, provides leadership [and] shares leadership.'[81] WBTI, by its very nature, was a servant organization, serving Bible translation and serving its partner SIL. Consequently, servant leadership theory and practice could find a good home in WBTI.

Journey Reflections (Being and Becoming)

Every long journey requires its travellers to recall where they've been, focus on where they are going, and yet also watch the ground immediately beneath them as they continue putting one foot in front of the other. The years covered in this chapter provide a good picture of what that looks like. Past, present, and future came into focus as WBTI leadership sought to maintain continuity, keeping the support structures necessary to fulfill their commitments. Yet, at the same time, they were beginning to see those structures more as tent poles than marble pillars. Organizations were re-categorized, and board composition changed. A variety of systems were improved. And toward the end of this era, Vision 2025 was adopted. This would be a significant milestone marking the thinking of the time and recognizing the need to change for the future.

To '...remember that there are eternal certainties in our uncertain world... the "Transforming Word" must be a fundamental part of our lives.' David Cummings gave his final speech as WBTI President, reflecting on his 15 years of service. He

---

[77] Robert K. Greenleaf, *Servant Leadership: A Journey into the Nature of Legitimate Power and Grateness* (Ramsey: Paulist Press, 1977), 7.

[78] Greenleaf, 7.

[79] Greenleaf, 13.

[80] Northouse, 227.

[81] James A. Laub, "Assessing the Servant Organization Development of the Servant Organizational Leadership Assessment (Sola) Instrument" (Florida Atlantic University, 1999), 49-51.

noted how much the world had changed in this time and how 'things [had] become less comfortable,' with human wisdom presenting a discouraging element. Nevertheless, encouragement comes from God as we concentrate on his interests. This holds true in every era and on every leg of the journey. It is an ongoing process of being and becoming.

Being and becoming acknowledge the presence of God's Kingdom come and coming. It is a work in progress here and now and a shining vision of the future. Leadership that understands this is better prepared to help travellers not stumble on the stones beneath their feet while also still looking ahead to the horizon.

› What were some of the processes that needed to be maintained by WBTI in this era?
› What were some of the signs that change was needed?
› In your context, what do you see as needing to be maintained as-is? What could change? Why? What are some of the ways things could change?

Chapter 5
Moving: 2001–2010

Historical Setting

The socio-economic and geo-political forces of globalization, especially as covered in this chapter, influenced WBTI from its outset. However, globalization itself was not a new development. Thomas Friedman simplifies globalization into three eras, starting with 'Globalization 1.0', occurring from 1492 to 1800, and beginning with Christopher Columbus's sea journey that opened trade routes. This enabled Western nations to expand their boundaries and trade routes and claim new territories. A general question of the era was, 'Where does my country fit into global competition and opportunities?'[1] 'Globalization 2.0' continued from 1800 to 2000, with interruptions from the Great Depression, World War I, and World War II. Marked by the industrial revolution, this era observed multinational companies developing global workforces and markets driven by goods moved cheaply and quickly across the world, made possible by global banks and progressive governments removing financial barriers. Technologies such as the steam engine, telephone, airplane, personal computer, satellite technology, and the internet accelerated the pace of development. The big questions were: 'Where does my company fit into the global economy? How does it take advantage of the opportunities?'[2] 'Globalization 3.0' commenced in 2000 and continues today. The world seems smaller as individuals or groups interact around the globe 'easily and so seamlessly' thanks to widespread access to converging technologies of the smartphone, tablets, fast fibre-optic cable and Wi-Fi networks, diversity of apps, social networking, and robust cloud computing. These innovations enable individuals to access digital content inexpensively from their various locations. What were impenetrable barriers such as geographic location, language, and culture are now scalable in most if not all contexts. Friedman predicted that a greater diversity of 'non-Western, non-white' individuals would drive Globalization 3.0.[3]

This chapter takes place at the time when Friedman's Globalization 3.0 gets underway. While there is debate concerning Friedman's ideas on globalization, as we will see, WBTI's Western roots certainly become far more culturally diverse as

---

1 Thomas Friedman, *The World Is Flat: A Brief History of the 21st Century* (New York: Farrar, Straus and Giroux, 2005), 9.

2 Friedman, 10.

3 Friedman, 11.

they spread rapidly across the globe.

Another factor to consider was the changing demographic of Christianity. In 2002, Philip Jenkins brought to light information from the World Christian Database, noting that in 1900, 82% of Christians lived in Europe and North America, with the remaining 18% located in Asia, Pacific, Latin America, and Africa.[4] A study by the Pew Forum in 2010 found that 'more than 1.3 billion Christians live in the Global South (61%), compared with about 860 million in the Global North (39%).'[5] The shift over 100 years showed a dramatic increase in Christians in the majority world, from 18% to 61%, while the Western world saw a decline from 82% to 39%.

The year 2010 was significant because it marked the centenary of the Edinburgh World Missionary Conference of 1910. The conference participants had the 'expectation that other world religions would wither and die in the face of the triumphant worldwide spread of Christianity.'[6] A century later, while there is ample evidence that Christianity is a worldwide religion, 'other world religions have not only survived but have undergone significant growth and renewal.'[7] This type of shift caught the attention of mission organizations and leaders. Consequently, this and other topics important to the mission endeavour were discussed at four international conferences organized as part of the centenary of the 1910 event. Each conference was distinct from the other. Allen Yeh summarizes the intent and impact of each:

Tokyo 2010: The theme was 'Making Disciples of Every People in Our Generation.' It was the 'brainchild' of Dr Ralph Winter, founder of the US Center for World Mission. Winter never witnessed the fruit of his vision since he died the year before the conference.[8] The primary focus of the event was evangelism through 'frontier missions, that is, proclaiming the gospel to unreached peoples who do not have a missionary or church among them or a Bible in their language.'[9] An outcome of the conference, the Tokyo 2010 Declaration covered four areas: 'mankind's need (because we are sinners), God's remedy (Jesus Christ), our responsibility (missions—reaching all peoples through discipleship), and finishing the task.'[10] The outcomes of the conference came under the Global Network of Mission Structures (GNMS) that Winter had formed in 2005.

Edinburgh 2010: The Churches Together in Scotland and the University of

---

[4] Jenkins, 3.

[5] Pew Forum, https://www.pewforum.org/2011/12/19/global-christianity-exec/, accessed 5 January 2020.

[6] Todd Johnson, and Kenneth Ross, "The Making of the Atlas of Global Christianity," *IBMR* 34, no. 1 (2010): 12.

[7] Johnson, and Ross 12.

[8] Allen Yeh, *Polycentric Missiology: Twenty-First Century Mission from Everyone to Everywhere* (Downers Grove: IVP Academic, 2016), 65.

[9] Yeh, 66.

[10] Yeh, 90.

Edinburgh jointly organized this event. Nine themes were covered in the study process leading up to the conference, ranging from 'Foundations for mission' to 'Mission spirituality and authentic discipleship'.[11] By design, this was similar in process to the eight themes of Edinburgh 1910. Intentionally ecumenical, the conference presented the theme 'Witnessing to Christ Today' and included Roman Catholic and evangelical speakers and participants.[12] The primary statement of the conference was the 'Common Call' along with the 33 volume Edinburgh Century Series with its 'landmark missiology' published by Regnum.[13]

Cape Town 2010 (Lausanne III): The largest of the four events, with 4,500 participants from 198 nations, was organized by the Lausanne Movement with the World Evangelical Alliance (WEA). The emphasis was on an evangelical mission perspective. Because of its structure as a congress, the meeting allowed participants to take part in all presentations. The theme, from 2 Corinthians 5:19, 'God in Christ, reconciling the world to himself' set the tone of reconciliation for the congress.[14] The main document from the congress, the Cape Town Commitment, consisted of two parts: (1) 'For the Lord We Love' covered ten areas from 'We love God because he first loved us' to 'We love the mission of God'; (2) six themes covered in the congress from 'Bearing witness to the truth of Christ in a pluralistic, globalized world' to 'Partnering in the body of Christ for unity in mission.'

2010 Boston (the emphasis was on the year rather than the city): The final of the four events, held in November, had the theme of 'The Changing Contours of World Mission and Christianity'. The emphasis was on students, harkening back to the influence the Student Volunteer Movement had on the original Edinburgh 1910 Conference. The event centred on the eight original themes of Edinburgh 1910 but updated for today's context. It resulted in a comprehensive book of the proceedings titled *The Changing Contours of World Mission and Christianity*.[15]

Leaders from WBTI and individual WOs attended Tokyo 2010 and the Cape Town 2010 Congress as invited delegates. These Wycliffe representatives learned about the changing global dynamics of mission and contributed their voices and perspectives about the global Bible translation movement to the discussions.

As the new millennium began, WBTI awoke to the responsibility and privilege of engaging with the global church, showing signs of thinking and acting like a movement, or more accurately, as movements, for Bible translation. During this decade, substantial discussions at the WBTI Board and executive director levels would change the organization's direction, strategy, structure, and operations,

11 Yeh, 98.
12 Yeh, 119.
13 Yeh, 119.
14 Yeh, 139.
15 Yeh, 101.

redefining WBTI's path. To fulfill its mission and guide emerging strategies, WBTI needed its own leadership and board, separate from SIL International, resulting in numerous, and at times difficult, conversations with SIL leaders. WBTI faced the challenge of either remaining focussed solely on its partnership with SIL—providing it with resources—or exploring new opportunities that increasingly called for attention.

Strategic Direction

At their May 2001 meeting, the WBTI Board asked Executive Director John Watters to prioritize efforts for strategically allocating personnel and resources, developing evaluation processes and indicators of progress, and identifying factors that characterize authentic partnering. When the board met again six months later, new world events had come to the forefront. Watters reflected on the recent tragedy of September 11 and the terrorist attacks in the US, which had worldwide effects. He reminded the board from Psalm 46 that God is 'the source of our strength and hope. He alone has primacy in human affairs, whether the disaster is natural or man-made.'[16]

Short Term Missions

Individual WMOs, especially from Western and Asian nations, noticed the rapid rise of short-term missions (STM). Edward Smither notes how

> by 2005, over 1.6 million North American Christians were participating in short-term mission trips, with the average trip lasting about eight days. Many local churches, including youth groups, have added local and international mission trips to their outreach strategy. Christian high schools and universities have also promoted STM among their students.... The STM trend has helped church members gain exposure to the needs of the world and become globally focussed Christians—those who pray, give financially, and advocate for the needs of the unreached.... The STM phenomenon has also raised questions regarding the use of money in mission. For example, should a short-term team of ten Americans raise $20,000 to work at an orphanage in Haiti for a week, or would it be better for the group to send that money to the orphanage's long-term staff so they can enhance the work?[17]

---

[16] WBTI, "Board Extracts," November 2001, 1.

[17] Smither, 172.

The STM strategy was noticeably affecting WMOs who had relied upon longer-term personnel serving with them. This continuing shift to short-term missions challenged WMOs in their recruitment strategies since involvement in the Bible translation movement was considered a longer-term commitment.

Categories of Affiliation

The 1999 Convention called for revising organization categories to simplify WBTI's structure, streamline the organizations themselves, accentuate their commonalities, and emphasize that similarities and differences could strengthen and connect them. This resulted in two new classifications in 2001:

› *Accredited Organizations:* granted to an organization, individual, or group of persons approved to represent WBTI and its interests and provide essential functions of a WO in a given country. The status was intended to cover a range of options from representation to formal application for WO status. WBTI would assign staff to help the Accredited Organization in its ongoing development until it achieved WBTI standards. More than one Accredited Organization could exist in each country because they could be connecting to different audiences. But in such cases, the organizations would have to agree to cooperate and respect each other.
› *Associated Organizations:* in recognition of WBTI's unique relationship with other partners in Bible translation without their formal relationship or adherence to WBTI's standards and requirements. Its design enabled close fellowship with organizations that shared the vision of Bible translation; it facilitated direct dialogue, interaction, and mutual support; and it invited participation in WBTI's meetings and conferences.

The WBTI Board granting Kartidaya (a Bahasa Indonesia acronym of Yayasan Karunia Bakti Budaya Indonesia) a status change in 2001, from Applicant Organization to Affiliate Organization, is an example of the application of this new classification system.

Wycliffe Member Organizations (WMOs, also referred to as WOs, voting, non-voting, and Accredited) and Wycliffe Affiliate Organizations (WAOs) all had WBTI's authorization to use the name Wycliffe. Wycliffe Associates, classified as an Associate Organization, traces the use of Wycliffe in its name back to an informal agreement in 1967.

Refinements to the Board

Recognizing the variety of cultural approaches and taking the opportunity to express more inclusiveness, two types of positions on the board would no longer be selected by the delegates at the convention. Instead, the five Constituency Members would be chosen as one from each Area in a culturally appropriate manner by the WMOs through a process coordinated by the respective Area Director. The Wycliffe US President continued to be an automatically slotted position on the board because of the size of the organization.

Relationship with SIL

WBTI had the challenge of ensuring that people assigned to SIL met Wycliffe's personnel standards. Those coming from WMOs did not present a concern as these organizations followed WBTI's personnel standards, partly designed to make certain that they fulfilled SIL's criteria for service. But the situation was different with sending agencies that were not WMOs. If these agencies wanted to send their people to serve with SIL, it was WBTI's role to ascertain that the people were suitable for service with SIL. This required WBTI to set up cooperative agreements with other organizations, agencies, or churches to second individuals to serve with SIL. The agreement confirmed that the sending agency took legal and member care responsibility for its people sent to SIL. This process is an example of how WBTI managed its partnership with SIL in seconding people for service.

Another example of the relationship with SIL was Executive Director John Watters's desire for a closer cooperation between WBTI and SIL in Latin America. This region was experiencing considerable change, needing SIL's services less, and displaying an increase of interest by the Latin American mission movement represented through COMIBAM. Therefore, to ensure the region received the leadership it required, as a temporary arrangement, the SIL and WBTI Americas Area Director positions were combined. Dave Brooks accepted this role in 2001.

Honouring Kenneth L. Pike (9 June 1912–31 December 2000), who served for 37 years as SIL President, was another example of the partnership with SIL. SIL historian Boone Aldridge notes how 'Pike was a key player in SIL from the time it began to take shape... and he contributed much to making it the world's foremost institution of applied linguistics and Bible translation.'[18] His 'legacy of devotion to others' greatly influenced SIL's scholarly approach to serving 'indigenous communities, academia and governments.'[19] Seeking to commemorate the significance of

---

[18] Boone Aldridge, *Kenneth L. Pike: An Evangelical Mind* (Eugene, OR: Pickwick Publications, 2021), 209.

[19] Aldridge, 212.

Pike's service, the WBTI and SIL Boards made a joint resolution of gratitude to God for Pike's life and ministry of 65 years of membership in these organizations. The boards noted how he 'demonstrated a commitment to serve God with heart and mind' in his service as 'a pioneer in Bible translation, a champion of minority peoples around the world, and an innovator in the field of theoretical linguistics.'[20]

WBTI and SIL were also involved with The Seed Company (TSC), an affiliate of Wycliffe US developed in the 1990s. The International Administration viewed TSC as evolving from a 'Wycliffe type organization to a hybrid of Wycliffe and SIL.'[21] Initially, TSC sought to raise prayer and financial resources for national translators but began pursuing limited-goal translation projects, hoping to engage interest for longer-term projects. This included partnerships with the Jesus Film and translating the gospel of Luke, and with Scripture Gift Mission translating 100 verses of the gospel of Mark. Longer-term translation projects received technical support from SIL entities and some WMOs. The growth of TSC was a response to WBTI's desire to generate support for national translator programs.

Vision 2025 Three Years On

On 4 June WBTI President Dick Hugoniot called the 2002 WBTI Convention to order at the same time and place as the SIL International Conference. Their joint and separate sessions were held at the JAARS Center in North Carolina and concluded on 13 June.

The following categories classified those attending the Convention:

- *WMO with Vote:* Australia, Austria, Canada, Finland, France, Germany, Hong Kong, Japan, GBT (South Korea), the Netherlands, New Zealand, Norway, Singapore, South Africa, Sweden, Switzerland, UK, and US. Each organization was represented by its executive director and board chair or board representative. In a few situations, the organization also brought an alternate delegate at their own expense (who did not have voice or vote).
- *WMO without Vote:* Americas, Belgium, Caribbean, Denmark, Ireland, Malaysia, Russia, Taiwan, Thailand, and Togo. Each was represented by its executive director/administrator, an official observer (without voice or vote).
- *WAO with Vote:* ALEM (Brazil), ANTBA (Burkina Faso), BTA (PNG), BTL (Kenya), GILLBT (Ghana), NBTT (Nigeria), TAP (Philippines), and Kartidaya (Indonesia). Each organization was represented by its executive director who had vote and its board chair or board representative who was an official observer and therefore did not have voice or vote.

[20] WBTI, November 2001, 2.

[21] WBTI, November 2001, 5.

- *WAO without Vote:* ACATBA (Republic of Central Africa), AITB (Côte d'Ivoire), ATALTRAB (Chad), CABTAL (Cameroon), and IICCC (India). Each was represented by its executive director/administrator who was an official observer (without voice or vote).
- *Other Organizations:* FEDEMEC (Costa Rica), Wycliffe Czech Republic, Wycliffe Hungary, BMA (Poland), PROEL (Spain), and VCC (Vanuatu). Each was represented by its executive director/administrator who was an official observer (without voice or vote).
- *SIL Entity Representatives:* One person from each SIL entity who was a delegate to the SIL International Conference was given official observer status to the convention. There were 41 official observers from SIL.
- *Prayer Delegates:* A 17-person prayer team was present for the Convention and SIL Conference.
- *WBTI Board of Directors:* From the board, 12 members were delegates.
- *International Administration:* The 13-member team of the executive director, associate executive directors, vice presidents, and area directors were present as official observers.
- *Distinguished Members:* This group of eight people present as official guests included the president emeritus, the past president, the founder's wife, former executive directors, and other distinguished members.

The theme for both the Convention and Conference was 'Trusting God for the Impossible'. In Executive Director John Watters's opening speech, he reminded participants that this theme went back to the founding of the two organizations. He observed that as mission history evolved, the minority people groups whom WBTI and SIL served moved from the periphery to the centre of mission strategy, thanks in part to the Unreached Peoples Group concept coming out of the Lausanne 1974 congress. Even so, after three years, Vision 2025 was less attainable than initially thought due to various factors affecting missions, including the loss of critical leadership, the safety of personnel, and economic downturns. However, Watters reminded, 'God is able to accomplish His purposes despite these circumstances.'[22]

The topics presented were designed to stimulate discussion among the participants concerning the outworking of Vision 2025. Presentations focussed on member care, communicating well, and creative strategies (such as new approaches in training, involvement of the local community in Bible translation, and new technologies to assist in translation). Discussions were held on stewarding resources (people, technical expertise, leadership/management, and funds), engaging the worldwide church, serving unreached people groups, and strategic partnerships (with emphasis on the relational side of partnerships, being a good partner, and giving up control).

---

22 WBTI, "International Conference Extracts," June 2002, 3.

The executive director highlighted prayer as 'our greatest strategic response and our greatest resource.'[23] As a result, the delegates resolved to model and emphasize prayer in each organization, working with the International Administration to coordinate and strengthen prayer strategies. Darryl Kernick led a concert of prayer at the close of the Convention and Conference, inviting participants to pray in their languages. In addition, representatives from several countries read Revelation 5 in different languages. People present were reminded that 'someday every tribe and tongue and nation will sing these verses of praise to our Heavenly Father in all the languages of the world, including the last 3,000 to be reached as God works through Vision 2025.'[24]

A significant responsibility of the Convention was to establish and agree on WBTI's Doctrinal Statement. It covered nine points and would be the basis of agreement for people serving in WBTI and all organizations seeking to be associated with WBTI.

Professor Andrew Walls gave a special presentation on 'Demographics, Power, and the Gospel in the 21st Century'. He traced the movement of the church from its centre in Jerusalem, to Rome, to Western Europe and North America, and more recently to Asia, Africa, and Latin America. He stated that these newer contexts would be the primary mission senders and shapers of theology in the 21st century. He said it would be coming sooner than we think as leaders from these regions bring 'new understandings unhindered from Western thought.'[25]

The new board was elected to serve for the next three years:

› *President:* Dick Hugoniot (US).
› *WMO Directors:* Sigmund Evensen (Wycliffe Norway), Kirk Franklin (Wycliffe Australia), Justin Frempong (GILLBT, Ghana), and Kenneth Kok (Wycliffe Singapore).
› *Constituency Members* (chosen by each Area): Isidore Songaba (Burkina Faso), Daniel Bianchi (Argentina), Luis Pantoja (Philippines), Roger Welch (UK), and William Edoni (PNG).
› *Director of Large WMO:* Roy Peterson (Wycliffe US).
› *Members from SIL Board:* Danjuma Gambo (Nigeria), Judy Schram (US), David Ross (US).

The board was now more culturally diverse, composed of the following nationalities: US (4), Australia (1), Norway (1), UK (1), Singapore (1), Ghana (1), Burkina Faso (1), PNG (1), Argentina (1), Philippines (1), and Nigeria (1). In other words, 43% were from the Western world, and 57% were from the majority

[23] WBTI, June 2002, 9.
[24] WBTI, June 2002, 9.
[25] WBTI, June 2002, 5.

world. While this was a better representation of the diversity within WBTI, there was only one woman—a member of the SIL Board—perhaps reflecting on the limited number of women leaders serving in agencies associated with WBTI at that time.

Associated Partner Organizations

In 2001, the WBTI Board created a new organizational category called Associated Partner Organization (APO) for organizations that shared fellowship with WBTI through their mutual interest and commitment to Bible translation worldwide. Including the word 'Partner': (1) recognized these organizations were external to WBTI and therefore needed to be distinguished from the internal relationships with WMOs, and (2) demonstrated WBTI's respect and honour of these distinct ministries and affirmed their role in supporting or participating in the work of Bible translation.

Over the next two years, 12 APOs joined WBTI:

› Aramaic Bible Translators, US
› Wycliffe Foundation, US
› Wycliffe Associates, US
› Wycliffe Associates, UK
› Wycliffe Resources, US
› AITB (Associazione Italiana Traduttori della Biblia), Italy
› FEDEMEC (Federación Misionera Evangélica Costarricense), Costa Rica
› BMA (Biblical Missions Association) Poland
› LETRA Argentina (Latinoamericanos en Traducción y Alfabetización)
› Sukisa Boyinga, Democratic Republic of Congo
› ECS-TD (Episcopal Church of Sudan Diocese of Khartoum Translation Department)
› The Seed Company, US

Steps Towards Vision 2025

Executive Director John Watters challenged the WBTI Board at its 2003 May meeting, with research and insights on the worldwide church from Philip Jenkins's book *The Next Christendom*. 'Southern hemisphere churches remain invisible to churches in the North [but] by 2025, half of all Christians will be in the South.... The Southern church, compared to the West, is poorer, more conservative theologically, holds a high view of Scripture, and is somewhat Pentecostal in expression.'[26]

Watters shared highlights of an advisory council of Africans formed for

[26] WBTI, "Board Extracts," May 2003, 1.

WBTI Africa; 11 students in Peru were taking linguistic studies at Ricardo Palma University in cooperation with COMIBAM; progress in training, vision building, and language projects in India; and progress in fundraising and training programs for linguistic and translation roles in Europe.

Despite its adoption in 1999, Watters assumed it would take up to eight years to get Vision 2025 fully underway. Instead, as he visited WMOs and SIL entities, he found colleagues ready to engage in positive dialogue, often being ahead in new ideas. He noted the Southern church's readiness to be involved in the work and that the Western church would do well to continue with its commitment to Bible translation.

Compared to past methods and progress, Vision 2025 presented the challenge to quadruple the number of language projects in the next quarter century. Despite the use of new tools and methods enhancing productivity, language work and Bible translation continued to be personnel-intensive. To meet the goals required a significant increase in personnel. Three factors affected this:

› Recruitment from traditional Wycliffe sending countries for language-related personnel had declined sharply over the past decade.
› A large percentage of the new workers were anticipated from the church in the Southern hemisphere—thus, the Asian Diaspora, Latin America Initiative, and the African Recruitment Initiative, as well as the Asian WMOs, would play a significant role.
› The traditional recruitment model assumed that new members would raise their own personal and work-related support. Increasingly, however, new members were unable to raise their full support. In most cases, they could only raise a small fraction of the funds needed, requiring greater participation from local language communities and alternative ways to fund personnel.

Early planning for implementation of Vision 2025 revealed a funding need of about $25 million per year by 2005 and $40 million by 2010 to finance these new ways of working. In recent years the funding sponsored by WMOs as a percentage of the total amount requested had risen from about 50% before 2000 to 72% in 2002. However, the amount sponsored declined to 49% of the amount needed in 2003, and Watters predicted receiving only about 3% of the $14.1 million for 2003. This decrease in funding significantly impacted SIL Areas and field entities, and as a result, affected scores of language projects and creative strategies.

Though Wycliffe US raised 80–90% of this funding over the recent years, the sharp reduction in project funding occurred primarily from the US. Reasons for the decline included economic stagnation in the US, a significant drop in stock market values, increasing unemployment, and a decrease in giving to non-profit organizations and missions. European WMOs had increased project funding from

$660,000 in 2001 to $1.3 million in 2002 and had set a goal of $4.6 million by 2005. Most of this new funding was expected from governments and applied to literacy and development projects.

John Watters called for WMOs to give high priority to project funding through identifying new donors, maintaining current donors, and increasing staff levels to develop the donor base. He pointed out that the shortage of project funding through Wycliffe US meant that expanding engagement with the Global South church was affected. The most significant number of future language workers was expected to come from the Global South, thus necessitating what Watters referred to as the 'Greatest Strategic Question' of developing a strategy for fund-raising equal to the need.

Leadership Changes

A significant leadership appointment was made for WBTI after the 2002 Convention. For the first time, the organization would have its own Africa Area Director, John Bendor-Samuel, a familiar face to WBTI. The leaders of the Pacific WMOs supported a proposal by the International Administration to merge Wycliffe functions in the Pacific Area with those of WBTI in the Asia Area. The Asia Wycliffe Organizations also agreed with the proposal, and the new Asia-Pacific Area emerged, with Dave Ohlson appointed as Area Director. This meant the Pacific Area was no longer a joint WBTI and SIL Area. To ensure continued cooperation and continuity of leadership in Latin America, Dave Brooks' two-year appointment as joint WBTI and SIL Americas Area Director extended to December 2004, an exception to the WBTI Board's requirement for WBTI to have its own Area Directors in each of its Areas: Africa, Americas, Asia-Pacific, and Europe.

Takashi Fukuda was appointed as the next Asia-Pacific Area Director starting 1 January 2004, taking the place of Dave Ohlson. Fukuda was the first Asian to hold a senior role in the International Administration and the first Asian Area Director for Asia. Fukuda was instrumental in the formation of Wycliffe Japan in the 1970s. Taking the place of Don Lindholm, Peter Wang was appointed as Associate Executive Director for Administration, effective 1 September 2004. This was also the last board meeting for Bob Lipps as General Counsel, with Thomas Schneider taking his place.

Wycliffe Heritage

President Emeritus George Cowan met with the WBTI Board in 2002 to orient its new members to Wycliffe's history. He noted that many of founder Cameron Townsend's ideas, originally voted down by the board and later endorsed by them, are now considered normal practice. Townsend started a revolution in the world's perspective on minority languages. His unique leadership style, characterized by sensitivity to the needs and motives of host government leaders, was nonetheless powerful. In the early days, the organization faced unusual obstacles, including untrained, weak, raw recruits; opposition from church and mission leaders; extreme poverty during the Great Depression; lack of training materials; and opposition from Communism and other ideologies. In reflection, Cowan observed that God's hand was evident, his miracles abundant, and he should get the glory.

Relationship with SIL

Concerns emerged in 2004 about the SIL-run Dallas Center regarding all personnel, whether associated with SIL or WBTI, functioning under WBTI's moral standards as a religious organization since these standards didn't apply to SIL employees at Dallas. The solution accepted by the WBTI Board was that WBTI become the operator at the Dallas Center and thus the employer of SIL paid staff who worked there, under an agreement with SIL, with other international functions redistributed between SIL and WBTI. SIL would retain title to the land and buildings. Thus, Dallas staff would be under the same moral standards because WBTI, as a religious organization, could make this a requirement. This decision passed with four abstentions, revealing it as a controversial decision for the WBTI Board. Responsibilities continued to shift between SIL and WBTI depending on which presented the better fit for each situation. This solution ended up being unsatisfactory to WBTI, and within a few years, WBTI withdrew any responsibility for the Dallas Center.

The Wycliffe Affiliate Organizations (WAOs, the former NBTOs) had a close working relationship with their SIL field counterparts. A document called 'The Partnership Between SIL, Inc., WBTI, Inc., and Wycliffe Organizations' was developed in 1992 following the restructuring of WBTI. It described the expectations of the relationships of the WMOs with SIL International, but it did not have the WAOs in view. The historical basis of WAOs relating to SIL changed when they were brought into WBTI rather than left as NBTOs. The relationship called for redefinition as a partnership. It was critical to ensure WAOs, along with WMOs and their personnel, were in mutually respectful partnerships with their SIL counterparts.

A concern for both the WBTI Board and SIL Board and the International Administration was to examine the health of the partnership between the two organizations. The boards had processes that guided the monitoring of the partnership:

- The executive director was to include a statement on progress made in issues of conflict among the organizations and steps taken to resolve the dispute.
- The boards regularly reviewed the partnership statement.
- At each board meeting, the boards evaluated the partnership by asking themselves: How did the boards work together in partnership?
- The boards sought to model respect, understanding, and appropriate attitudes and behaviour toward one another.

Engaging with the Worldwide Church

Executive Director John Watters addressed the issue of the numerical and geographic growth of the church of the Global South and East, the necessity to engage it in Bible translation, and implications for WBTI's future. In reporting to the WBTI Board in November 2003, Watters noted these factors:

- Western churches and individuals were interested in Unreached People Groups.
- The nature of the church of the South and East with growing mission movements in Africa, Asia, and Latin America were mainly focussed on Unreached People Groups.
- A growing trend of cooperation among Western mission agencies.
- YWAM as an example of another operational model and structure for missions.
- The relationship of SIL and WBT where Wycliffe was growing in countries where only SIL had existed before.

In response to Watters's report, the board stated that effectively engaging and partnering with the church of the Global South and East in reaching the remaining languages of the world was essential to Vision 2025. Therefore, the board felt it needed to make this statement about the growth and maturation of the church of the majority world:

> Based on our growing excitement about what God is doing in the worldwide church, our sense of where we are in church history, and its significance in achieving WBTI End A [Worldwide Engagement of the Church], MOVED to foster an environment in which member organizations are encouraged and assisted to engage in appropriate

partnerships with churches of the South and East.[27]

The SIL Board adopted a similar statement at the same time: 'Whereas the WBTI Board has expressed its intent to continue an initiative whereby its member organizations will develop appropriate partnerships with the churches of the South and East, MOVED to express our support and encouragement for this initiative.'[28]

It was not apparent at the time, but the WBTI Board had set a new direction by expressing its intention to share the need for Bible translation with the church of the majority world (or Global South and East). This decision contrasted with founder Cameron Townsend's priority in engaging with the Western, especially the US, churches. The tide had shifted, and WBTI was moving into a deeper awareness of the church beyond the Western nations.

There were structural implications to this new course. Watters conceived of three models for WBTI's makeup:

- Model 1: a loose-knit membership organization for sharing information.
- Model 2: an alliance for strategy and policy formulation.
- Model 3: a significantly integrated family of organizations.

In the third model the WMOs would look at their responsibilities for informing and engaging not only the church within its borders but also the church around the world. In response, the board thought that Model 3 was the one to pursue.

Leadership Philosophy

The ongoing work on the Philosophy of Leadership, developed a decade earlier and covering qualities and expectations of leaders, was completed during the November 2003 WBTI and SIL board meetings. It defined leaders as:

> individuals who, by their spiritual gifts, attitudes, skills, vision, and overall lifestyles, have demonstrated maturity, credibility, and the ability to direct effort toward our organizational ends. Leaders strive to maximize the vision, gifts, and contribution of those they lead. Leaders who desire to extend the Kingdom of God will be committed to godly living and [an] exemplary lifestyle. They are accountable to God for the care of those they lead and to those who elect or appoint them.
>
> We believe that effective leadership involves respect for position,

[27] WBTI, "Board Extracts," November 2003, 2.

[28] WBTI, November 2003, 3.

> trust developed through credibility in the context of personal relationships, and authority equal to responsibility. We also believe that God works through women and men of every ethnic group and age level and calls them to be involved in leadership roles in all facets of our organizational life. Leaders should be chosen who manifest the God-given gifts that are necessary for effective service in a particular time and context.[29]

Both boards and the International Administration embraced the philosophy, whose intent was to guide the identification, appointment, formation, development, and support of leaders for both organizations.

Growing Diversity

The WBTI Board and SIL Board accepted Wycliffe Singapore's invitation to hold their May 2004 meeting in Singapore. Wycliffe Singapore Director and WBTI Board member Kenneth Kok thought it was an effective way to engage with the Singapore churches before and after the sessions. The boards were enriched, experiencing the environment in which a small WMO operated. The WBTI Board had no idea how significant Singapore would become within a few years.

Executive Director John Watters noted how Western, particularly American, values, worldview, and theological assumptions shaped WBTI. Now strengthened by cultural diversity, this broadened perspective would inform the organization's processes and structures. It involved making room at the table for everyone, with all learning to share power and participating in making decisions. WBTI needed to ensure that biblical values shaped it and not an overlay of Western values. Watters stated the necessity for WBTI and SIL to be agents of peace, learning to live as the family of God, demonstrating and experiencing his agape love.

Watters met with Peter Maiden, International Director of Operation Mobilisation (OM). Maiden was thankful for the variety of help and assistance received from WMOs. OM did well at recruiting and was interested in serving Wycliffe in this area. There was mutual interest in looking at what deeper cooperation could look like between Wycliffe and OM. The WMOs were encouraged to see how they could work more closely with their OM counterparts.

The International Administration held the first International Project Funding Sponsorship Meeting in Dallas. Representatives came from WMOs in Singapore, Australia, Germany, Switzerland, UK, US, and Canada, and APOs of The Seed Company, Wycliffe Associates US, and Wycliffe Resources (a short-lived organization to raise resources for the ILC). Unfunded projects became known and

29 WBTI, "Board Extracts," November 2003, 12.

gained sponsors from among those participating. The time together built greater unity and convergence among the various Wycliffe organizations, and there was a desire to make this an annual gathering.

The board approved Watters's request to establish a Vice-President for Scripture Promotion (VPSP) emphasizing translation, ethnomusicology, Scripture Use, and Orality and Storying. The SIL Vice President for Academic Affairs (VPAA) had served in this role from time to time. This new position would be filled by the VPAA, allowing that person to serve both WBTI and SIL more appropriately. Thus, the VPAA could switch to being the VPSP in Wycliffe or a church context. This example demonstrates the continued internal complexity of identity between WBTI, an overtly Christian mission, and SIL, with Christian mission in the background, using WBTI's identity to relate to the Christian public.

Also, at this Singapore meeting, the WBTI Board changed voting privileges and representation for WAOs to be the same as WMOs at the Wycliffe International Convention. This breakthrough gave the WAOs the same entitlements as WMOs for membership in WBTI requirements and expectations, and this gradually addressed the complex and multi-layered hierarchy and history.

Role in the 21st Century

During the May 2004 board meeting in Singapore, WBTI President Dick Hugoniot appointed a committee to discuss a paper titled 'WBTI in the 21st Century' written by Executive Director John Watters for the board's reflection. The committee, chaired by Wycliffe Australia Director Kirk Franklin, engaged in a free-flowing conversation using mental models to illustrate:

- WBTI's identity.
- the makeup of the WBTI Board, including overlap with the SIL Board.
- categories of membership in WBTI, with the suggestion to consolidate to a single category.
- possible changes to the administrative structure.
- implications related to the International Convention.
- structural issues presenting roadblocks to progress.
- the possibility of WBTI having its own executive director, separate from SIL.

Reporting on the committee's discussions to the board, Franklin stated they required more time to examine topics introduced in the paper. Because of the complexity of issues raised by the committee, Hugoniot formed a second committee to process matters further and report to the November board meetings. The committee would meet in September in Cairns, Australia.

Before that September meeting, aware of the gravity of what the committee would be looking into, Watters encouraged them to consider the longer term and wider world wherein they would recommend policies for WBTI. The committee in Singapore raised topics about organizational development issues rather than organizational growth or maintenance. One critical realization involved the likelihood that the WMOs had not fully grasped or understood the implications and possibilities of the creative freedom they already had and were still heavily influenced by limitations experienced before the 1992 reorganization.

The committee was to state how the executive director complied with these areas: leading WBTI in pursuing its Ends, complying with the Executive Limitations, or maintaining the Board-Executive Director Linkage. These constituted the foundational principles of Policy Governance that WBTI followed at the time and were measures of executive director success or failure. However, if the executive director's performance was lacking in these areas, Watters felt that meant the board had not clearly communicated this. If the issues were administrative, Watters wanted the WMOs concerned with these issues to bring them to the International Administration's attention.

Before 1968, there was no executive director in either organization because Cameron Townsend served as general director. Established in 1968, the International Administration had one executive director for both organizations. This solution seemed to have worked well for 36 years.

Under Watters, the executive director's office consisted of the Associate Executive Director for Wycliffe Operations, dedicated to WBTI, and the Associate Executive Director for Administration, shared with SIL. There had also been the creation of a WBTI Africa Area and the separation of the joint WBTI-SIL Pacific Area that resulted in a WBTI Asia-Pacific Area with SIL Pacific Area standing on its own. Rather than separating the executive director roles, more experimentation would occur with the current WBTI administration.

While WBTI and SIL were separate organizations, they differed significantly from typical corporations, based on their interconnection through shared vision, values, resources, and results. If a separation of executive directors occurred, the relationship would be at risk. WBTI's autonomous organizations agreed to abide by standards that included an agreement for WBTI to partner with SIL. The relationship between the two was more significant than each considered separately, more intimate and interdependent than most other partnerships. Combined, they represented something meaningful, often referred to as a family of organizations.

The financial cost of having separate executive directors was another concern. The WBTI Convention and Board had resisted a significant expansion of a WBTI administration. A separate executive director would necessitate separate vice presidents and offices, adding the challenge of finding individuals to fill these roles, increasing WBTI's budget.

Another cost was that the two executive directors would spend significant time collaborating to ensure the two organizations worked well together. Even with goodwill, situations could arise when the two leaders would be unable to get along, possibly due to changes in vision and programs, eventually leading to challenging, or even irreconcilable, differences between the two leaders. There were enough examples of this happening in WBTI and SIL's history. Within the International Administration, some believed that the two boards should not have to resolve such situations.

Considering the Future

The WBTI Board's ad hoc committee to explore the future met in September 2004 in Cairns, Australia, to discuss the implications arising from the Singapore Board discussion. Present were Danjuma Gambo, Kenneth Kok, Dick Hugoniot, Kirk Franklin, and Judy Schram as Chair, and Darryl Kernick from the executive director's team.

Before the meeting, Franklin wrote to the chair to recommend concentrating on WBTI's preferred future rather than reviewing WBTI's Ends and executive limitations (per Policy Governance processes). WBTI should be talking about becoming a movement rather than settle for being an institution. The committee didn't need to feel restricted by the current structure and policies. By releasing the status quo, the committee could dream about what WBTI could look like in the next three to ten years embracing and facilitating a worldwide Bible translation movement; and what the church of the South and East would look like when it was engaged in such a movement. Later, WBTI's core statements would provide a reality check for the board.

When the committee gathered, it discussed the composition of the WBTI Board. Of concern were the three overlapping members from the SIL Board who served on the WBTI Board. Separating the two boards would enable the WBTI Board to concentrate on what was essential to the movement rather than on the relationship with SIL. That relationship would need to take place through other means. A smaller 11-member board rather than the 14-person one with the three overlapping members would enable the WBTI Board to operate more efficiently with fewer board members.

Another issue concerned the WBTI President's responsibilities, including the role of board chair. Until that time, the president (a full-time role) was elected from a list of nominees put forward from all of the organizations. Now, however, the chair, a part-time position, would be elected from among the other board members, and would no longer hold this as a full-time position. This change would help the board stay focussed, and the executive director could handle the president's public relations commitments.

Also pondered were membership categories in WBTI. The statuses of the NBTOs reclassified as WAOs, and the newer APOs meant that, even if they were significant in the Bible translation movement, they couldn't fully participate in the same way as WMOs. Yet, it was within these two categories of organizations where future growth for WBTI would happen. The challenge for WBTI was how to integrate these organizations and moving toward a single membership category in WBTI could do that.

WBTI and SIL having separate executive directors proved the most complicated topic. Until now, WBTI and SIL theoretically worked together as equal partners because of the joint executive director. But changing ministry contexts revealed WBTI's need for its own executive director, devoting full attention to its development. The growth of the Bible translation movement and the church worldwide required a different approach. The executive director invariably came from SIL as the larger partner. A church leader from the Global South and East or someone with a missiological background characterized a more appropriate future WBTI Executive Director.

This separation of the executive director roles was timely. Completing the eight-year maximum term legislated by both SIL and WBTI, John Watters would step down on 31 December 2007. WBTI could then relocate its headquarters and leaders from Dalla to be near the church of the South and East.

As the WBTI committee worked through these significant issues, and since the boards met jointly, fully aware of what the WBTI committee was working on, the SIL Board became concerned about the discussions and the steps leading to dissolving what had existed until now as more than a traditional partnership. WBTI and SIL presented a symbiotic relationship where neither organization could continue without the other. The collaboration with SIL was mutually effective and cohesive. If WBTI proceeded to separate, then this was under threat. However, knowing it could offer input to the WBTI Board on any changes under consideration gave the SIL Board some assurance of a robust conversation at the next board meeting.

Worldwide Impact

Reporting to the board at the November 2004 meeting, Dick Hugoniot described having enjoyed his five years as WBTI Board Chair and President, working with the WBTI and SIL Executive Director and the SIL President. He prayerfully decided not to be considered for a third term as president. It was time for someone else to fill this leadership role, a lonely job at times as the president had no staff and limited resources.

Executive Director John Watters reported that God made it possible for WBTI and its primary partner SIL to impact about three-quarters of the current translation projects worldwide, with the rest handled by other Bible translation agencies. In Africa, new members were joining Wycliffe in Ethiopia and Togo. Also, Bible translation movements were emerging in Nigeria, including ten projects begun by Nigerians not affiliated with WBTI. In Asia, progress took place through guidance teams for Indonesia, East Asia, Malaysia, and the Philippines. In East Asia, training trainers in linguistics and translation and preparing training materials progressed within a house church Bible translation movement. Simultaneously, several WMOs, including Wycliffe US, saw an increase in recruitment.

WBTI in Latin America served a community of organizations at both local and national levels to promote, train, and offer advice about recruitment of Latin Americans for Bible translation. Though external to WBTI structures, these organizations demonstrated the building of a movement for Bible translation.

Collaboration and supportive networking among WMOs were fast becoming the norm in areas like communications, funding, partnering, and initiatives to engage with the churches of the South and East. For example, Wycliffe Australia partnered with BTA PNG in board governance training which helped bring BTA's board and administration relationship to a new level. And Wycliffe Australia learned about the unique challenges and opportunities BTA faced.

Living and working together harmoniously as a growing multi-ethnic family presented the challenge to understand and relate well with one another. Under the leadership of Takashi Fukuda, a small working group had the mandate to identify the issues facing WBTI and SIL as multicultural organizations and make recommendations that could lead to attitudes and behaviour that reflected healthy, effective working relationships in multicultural settings.

Three WMOs qualified to change their status, reflecting the maturing of these organizations:

- CABTAL (Cameroon) to WAO with vote.
- Wycliffe Malaysia to WMO with vote.
- Wycliffe Russia to WMO without vote.

The committee that met in September in Cairns made its report. As the two boards discussed the recommendations, WBTI reassured the SIL Board of its continued commitment to maintaining the close, unique relationship with SIL.

However, a misunderstanding between the two boards prevented a thorough discussion of the proposed WBTI directions. An environment of mutual support and safety was imperative. Nonetheless, the WBTI Board made these decisions:

› Start exploring the possibility of having separate executive directors for WBTI and SIL.
› Work toward a single organizational membership category in WBTI.
› Explore what the board structure should be to give it the governance it required in the changing environment for WBTI as it met the challenges of Vision 2025, including eliminating overlapping or crossover members with the SIL Board.
› Redefine the position of the president as only the board chair.
› Find ways to express the unique relationship between WBTI and SIL International and to ensure its continuation.

The change process was now underway, and the expected legislative adjustments for WBTI would take place at the International Conference the following May. Before that, all policies affected by the process required discussion and revision. With limited time, a joint committee of the two boards met in January 2005 to work through misunderstandings that arose in the board meeting. The committee members expressed their deep gratitude acknowledging the Holy Spirit for unity, clarity, and understanding.

The SIL Strategic Plan estimated that 2,644 languages were without a translation program in progress, and 2,168 of these languages (82%) were in the three major regions of the world with the greatest translation need: Nigeria and Central Francophone Africa (21%), Mainland Asia (29%), and Indonesia-Pacific Archipelago (32%). An estimated 3,478 people from WBTI and SIL, and 3,179 people from other organizations, were essential to start Bible translation in the remaining languages.

The Word in a Changing World

The WBTI and SIL Boards met together in May for two days immediately before the 2005 International Convention. A statement on the agenda which added to WBTI's policies declared their 'unqualified support' for SIL, expressing a 'Unity of Purpose with SIL' and demonstrated through:

› shared vision, resources, and beneficiaries.
› unreserved support of SIL's Purpose, Values, and Ends.
› thorough commitment to work together with SIL, respecting SIL's distinct roles and contributions.
› a desire for the good and success of SIL.[30]

30 WBTI, "Board Extracts," April 2005, 1.

The International Convention, referred to as ICON (a generic name for both organizations' respective events), was still held jointly with the SIL International Conference. This year's event, referred to as ICON05, was considered historic because it met in Asia at Chiang Mai. In the early days, these meetings were held in Mexico City and, until recently, had been held in the US. The theme for ICON05 was The Word in a Changing World. There were 46 official delegates (those who could vote) that included the directors and a representative from the boards of the WMOs. Executive directors represented their individual WAOs. There were 21 official guests from partner agencies, but none of those agencies were formally part of WBTI.

President Dick Hugoniot opened the Convention with the challenge that WBTI comprised a 'multicultural group who can meet the task by obeying Jesus rather than focussing on circumstances. Delegates should leave the Convention with a sense of purpose and excitement to do the will of God.'[31]

The WBTI Board elected for the next three years included:

› *President*: Dick Hugoniot (US) (he would not serve the full term).
› *WMO Directors*: Kirk Franklin (Australia), Sigmund Evensen (Norway), Mũndara Mũturi (Kenya), and Sung-Chan Kwon (South Korea).
› *Director of Large WMO*: Bob Creson (US).
› *Constituency Members (chosen by each area)*: Isidore Songaba (Burkina Faso), Daniel Bianchi (Argentina), Luis Pantoja (Philippines), Roger Welch (UK), and William Edoni (PNG).
› *Members from the SIL Board*: Barbara Trudell (US), David Ross (US), and David Bosma (Australia).

The composition of the 14-member board continued in the pattern of being culturally diverse with US (4), Australia (2), Norway (1), UK (1), Kenya (1), Burkina Faso (1), Argentina (1), South Korea (1), Philippines (1), and PNG (1). There was only one woman on the board.

The delegates had input into WBTI's operating budget for the next three years. They agreed that all WMOs make an annual contribution of 0.36% of their total income toward WBTI's fiscal needs. This slight increase from the 0.32%, decided at a previous Convention, indicated that WBTI's operational needs were growing, and the WMOs were willing to support this growth.

The worldwide church was the first main issue processed at ICON05. For example, The Ethiopian Evangelical Church Mekane Yesus (EECMY) was granted APO status for its Bible translation partnership in Ethiopia. Church representatives from Africa, Latin America, and Asia gave presentations followed by small group processing. These discussions resulted in WBTI's leadership working in

[31] WBTI, "International Convention Extracts," April-May 2005, 2.

partnership with the church worldwide, enabling 'a better understanding of the foundational role of Bible translation in the holistic mission of the church.'[32] The delegates asked the WBTI Board to 'continue to respond to the requests of the church of which Wycliffe Member Organizations are a part, by selecting and developing leadership, setting Ends and where necessary establishing structures that promote the building of capacity of the church so that [WBTI] can fulfill [its] unique role in the 21st century.'[33]

Another topic was multicultural teams and community. A presentation from Sherwood Lingenfelter of Fuller Seminary looked at multicultural teams and kingdom work, communication and conflict, leadership, and the challenge of resources.

The future in the 21st century was a significant theme for WBTI. Board members gave presentations focussing on the development of WBTI, its vision for the future, differences in responsibilities between WBTI and SIL, maintaining a unity of purpose between the two organizations, and structural changes to WBTI. As a result, the delegates approved the following:

- WBTI and SIL each having their own executive director: the two boards were encouraged to continue the process to move in this direction.
- Non-overlapping boards for WBTI and SIL: the WBTI Board was authorized to start the process to make the change to its bylaws.
- The WBTI President became the Board Chair: the board was asked to implement bylaw changes and prepare a job description to achieve this.
- A single category for Member Organizations: the board was to amend the bylaws eliminating WMO and WAO statuses, and every Member Organization shared equal status, voting rights, and standards.
- The Unity of Purpose Statement with SIL: this was affirmed as it reflected 'the heart and will of the entire family of organizations that [made] up WBTI.'[34]

WBTI delegates also approved WBTI's new core values, which until now were the same as SIL's. These new core values aligned better with who it was:

- The Glory of God among the Nations—Our motive for Bible translation is that some from all the peoples of the earth might pursue God and His glory.
- Christlikeness in Life and Work—Our quest is to be like Christ. We express this in the way we live and in the quality of the work we do.
- The church as Central in God's Mission—The church is sent by God to evangelize the world and disciple the nations.
- The Word Translated—The Word of God, translated into a language that

[32] WBTI, April-May 2005, 3.

[33] WBTI, April-May 2005, 3.

[34] WBTI, April-May 2005, 5.

speaks to people's hearts, transforms lives.

› Dependence on God—We depend on God for everything needed to complete the otherwise impossible task of worldwide Bible translation.
› Partnership and Service—We partner with others to complete the pressing task of translating the Word of God for the peoples of the earth.

The Convention affirmed the direction that the WBTI Board first started considering a year earlier at its meeting in Singapore in 2004. The board and its committees had worked hard since then to prepare the necessary changes. The delegates had spoken by affirming this direction, setting the course for the next two years. Before John Watters's eight-year term as executive director ended on 31 December 2007, the WBTI Board had a great deal to accomplish, including finding its own executive director separate from SIL.

Preparing for Changes

WBTI President Dick Hugoniot set up a committee of himself, Roger Welch, Sigmund Evensen, and Kirk Franklin, who met in July at the Wycliffe UK centre at Horsleys Green. Their efforts, to be presented at the November board meeting, would move WBTI forward by implementing changes approved by the Convention, especially in board composition, and appointing the next executive director.

The November meeting was the first for new board members elected at the May Convention. Executive Director John Watters stated that he and his team wanted to continue making WBTI a better servant of the peoples of the earth and partner with the worldwide church as it moved into the 21st century. He identified the continued importance of the issues of harmony and spiritual unity. Watters also noted how during the next three years, WBTI would be making significant adjustments that directly and indirectly impacted SIL International. WBTI's goals needed to strengthen both organizations because God's Spirit is one of unity. Changes were also happening within SIL, which would impact WBTI. They involved language project conceptualization, and holistic language development; research on Scripture use and multilingualism, as languages try to survive in a larger, socio-political environment; and how SIL can serve as an advocate for language communities in the context of the church and mission, governments, and others.

Indicators of Progress

The International Administration reported on WBTI's progress relative to its Ends. The funding goal for WMOs in Fiscal Year 2005 was US$14,188,874; the actual amount raised was US$14,983,167, an increase of 105.6%. For the Affiliate Organizations, the total raised through donations from churches, in-country sources, national sources, and income-generating programs totalled US$288,843.

Regarding prayer involvement, the number of names on the WMO's prayer mailing lists totalled 39,925. The number of prayer groups and networks WMOs related to totalled 658. The number of people registered to pray through the Bibleless Peoples Prayer Network was 35,722. Not included in these numbers are the largest sources of prayer: namely, the supporters of the nearly 6,000 members of WMOs, including many church groups. These might total more than 100,000 worldwide that would not necessarily be on formal prayer mailing lists.

Measuring each WMO's movement toward providing adequate resources for Bible translation offered another progress indicator. When estimating the resources in their countries, none of the organizations believed they were achieving their potential. Two-thirds rated themselves at 3–4 on a 1–5 scale (low to high), while 36% rated themselves at 2. The organizations struggled with weaknesses:

- Inadequate numbers of trained staff.
- Inadequate funds.
- Weak local funding for Affiliate Organizations.
- Weak boards.
- Old ways of working and thinking.
- The individualism of WMO members who had limited interest or concern for strengthening their WMOs through service during furlough or mutually determining with their WMOs what their assignment should be.

As the WMOs looked to the next five years, they set these goals: raising a total of US$56,000,000 per year by 2010; and recruitment of a total of 992 new personnel per year.

Ninety-two percent of all WMOs rated themselves as accepted and integrated as a valued partner in WBTI. Leaders of WMOs mentioned what their sense of value was within WBTI, including serving on the WBTI Board, the vision and global connection provided by WBTI, and the family atmosphere and supportive structures. When asked to rate whether WBTI presented an environment reflecting its multi-cultural diversity in its decision-making and leadership, of those same leaders, 5% believed it was unsatisfactory, 44% satisfactory, 36% very good, and 13% excellent. The leaders noted the growing diversity on the WBTI Board and appointments of WBTI Area Directors. WMOs received encouragement to create national-level solutions and to express their opinions. By contrast, decision-making processes, to some, still felt predominantly Western and Anglophone.

The board responded positively to the Indicators of Progress report noting that it was the first time the Ends-driven report included a summary of indicators of progress from WMOs. It was a complex process to measure indicators for all the Ends. In examining End A, the board asked that 'special attention be given to monitoring indicators that track engagement of the church of the South and the East, particularly in terms of prayer, recruitment of personnel and fundraising.'[35]

Executive Director Selection Process

Essential to the search process, a new job description for the executive director focussing solely on leading WBTI would replace what currently served for both WBTI and SIL. WBTI wanted to find a candidate called by God to the task with consideration of these qualities of character:

› Leadership style, missiological perspective of WBTI's work, vision-strategy, organizational experience, and fit.
› Relational and networking skills.
› The ability to analyze and synthesize current trends.
› Commitment to lifelong learning.
› Able to travel frequently with family situation allowing for this.
› Willingness to live outside of the US.
› Able to work effectively in all cultures and areas of world.
› Available for at least two three-year terms.
› Expected age range of 45-55.
› An established relationship with the SIL Executive Director (for the first time around).
› Adequate personal financial support.

There were considerations of whether the candidate was already a Wycliffe leader or someone without prior Wycliffe affiliation. Pros of insider candidates included knowledge of WBTI and WMOs, already enculturated, accepted within WBT, familiar with the way things work, and already supported financially. Pros of outsider candidates included someone who might be more willing to challenge the status quo, possibly more likely to think outside the box, wider experience beyond WBTI, perhaps more open to partnership, brings other contacts and networks (though may only be regional and country specific), and may feel freer to ask difficult questions.

The 18-month timeline created for the search and appointment of the executive director began in November 2005 and was to be completed in November 2006 when the board would make its appointment. There would be a well-managed

[35] WBTI, "Board Extracts," October-November 2005, 1.

overlap between the incoming and outgoing executive directors from March to December 2007. The new executive director would start on 1 January 2008. However, the outgoing executive director would lead the WBTI Convention in May 2008.

For the first time, because of the board's efforts, WBTI would have its own executive director. Recognizing the significance, the board declared:

> We, the WBTI Board, feel strongly that we are headed in the right direction toward selecting a new Chair and new Executive Director. We are going on with this process as mandated by the 2005 International Convention. We have come to this decision in the light of a common understanding that both organizations would have new respective Executive Directors.[36]

Changing Role of President

In a vote, the WMOs passed the bylaw amendment to change the president position to board chair. This position, to be elected by and from within the existing board at their November 2006 meeting, would require a new job description. In addition to chairing the board sessions and the Convention, the chair would work closely with the SIL President to ensure cohesion between the two boards.

One Membership Category

The WMOs, respected for their autonomy, unique character, and contribution to WBTI and Bible translation, passed the bylaw amendment to move the WMOs and WAOs to a single category. To preserve its unique heritage and maintain a standard of behaviour and single-minded focus on Biblical truth called for WBTI to confirm that the WMOs that ultimately controlled WBTI held the same objectives, values, and commitment to its long-term mission. Therefore, each WMO was defined by these characteristics:

- Agreed with WBTI's doctrinal position and embraced its standards.
- Aligned its primary objectives (stated in its official and legal documents) with WBTI's objectives (expressed in its Mission, Vision, Core Values, and Ends).
- Planned to maximize its capacity to impact Bible translation.
- Engaged with the worldwide church/Christian community through successful partnerships.
- Engaged in the gathering and facilitation of resources for Bible translation.

[36] WBTI, October-November 2005, 1.

› Prioritized developing harmonious and supportive relationships with the other WMOs.

Support of Multicultural Statement

The board affirmed SIL in the matter of 'SIL Conference's resolution committing to excellence in the way we work with multicultural teams and communities, and maintaining the Cross at the center of relationships, as expressed through humility, an attitude of learning, and grace.'[37]

Dissolution of WBTI California Corporation

In 1980, Wycliffe International incorporated in California. In 1994, after the International Administration moved to Dallas, WBTI incorporated in Texas. In 1995, the California corporation was moved to suspended status, creating some serious problems, including the rejection of visas and complications with State registrations. Hiring the California law firm of Yates and Yates, they formally dissolved the California corporation, so it no longer appeared on records.

Financial Contribution

The board held the contribution at 0.35% of WMO's total income. For the next Fiscal Year, the WBTI Administration estimated an operating and project income of $4,637,438 and estimated net operating and project expenditures of $4,679,326. The difference between income and expenditures would be financed from reserves.

New personnel included Eleanor Berry as vice president for finance beginning 1 April 2006 and Frederick Boswell as vice president for Scripture Promotion beginning 1 June 2005.

An Empty Seat

President Dick Hugoniot opened the May 2006 board meeting by acknowledging the vacant seat left by William Edoni, who unexpectedly went to be with the Lord on 28 February. The board held a time of remembrance and celebration of William's life, highlighting his unique perspective, which would be profoundly missed. PNG BTA celebrated 25 years, sadly without the presence of this beloved

[37] WBTI, October-November 2005, 4.

elder. Friends and fellow board members Kirk Franklin and David Bosma represented WBTI at William's funeral and memorial service in Port Moresby, PNG.

WBTI also celebrated 25 years in India, partnering with Indian missions in the cause of Bible translation. This celebration included the beginning of Word for All, the newest member of WBTI. These events in India and PNG pointed to the time around 1980 when considerable activity provided hope that Africans, Asians, Latin Americans, and Pacific Islanders could become part of the larger Bible translation process through leading translation projects. However, the long and often arduous journey showed mixed progress over the previous 25 years. As Vision 2025's end date drew closer, WBTI's prayer was for an extraordinarily different world to unfold in the next 25 years, one that fully included the worldwide church unlike any other time in history.

Supporting International Growth

John Watters pointed out how Wycliffe Member Organizations with Language Programs (the new name of the WAOs) differed significantly from the other WMOs, requiring that his team and Area Directors explore how to help them with their needs in engaging churches within their nations to build the 'Wycliffe side' of their operations. Having held early ties with SIL, the WAOs were generally stronger in their language program operations than in church relations.

Funding requirements and the variety of ministry contexts continued to grow. An Alternative Personal Funding Guidance Team comprised of Geoff Knott (Chair), Dave Brooks, Sung-Chan Kwon, Mũndara Mũturi, Wolfgang Binder, and Wayne Howlett were pursuing four different experiments: (1) minimum financial support quotas for people from Bangladesh, Cameroon, and Papua New Guinea; (2) matching funds in Wycliffe Africa, BTL, TAP, and Wycliffe Americas; (3) vision sharing in Kenya, South Korea, Wycliffe Americas; and (4) diaspora access in Wycliffe Americas with Hispanics.

Missiological Considerations

Watters attended a mission CEOs retreat where YWAM founder Loren Cunningham spoke. Cunningham raised his concern to bring the Word of God to the front of missions, not ignoring evangelism or discipleship. Watters suggested that Cunningham's approach could help WBTI as its WMOs communicated with churches. Until this time, the International Administration had primarily focussed on SIL's work, and WMOs did not necessarily receive the support they desired to connect with their audiences. Rather than using the term Bible translators, which put the emphasis on technical matters, Watters suggested describing those who provide and promote the Word of God among the nations, then progressing to more specific issues such as the complexities of making the Word of God available to all people.

Cultural and linguistic differences between peoples create barriers to the successful promotion of the Word of God. Researching those differences and applying the results to translating the Word and developing alphabets and literacy could overcome those barriers. Further research into multiple ways to communicate the Word with a people group, such as through audio and video, or using traditional oral communication methods, could also prove beneficial. In practice, Wycliffe Organizations were already experimenting with alternative ways of approaching their audiences, similar to what Cunningham was suggesting. For example, some organizations like Wycliffe US added the phrase 'partners in Bible translation' to their message, signalling a priority beyond a task and recognizing the collaborative nature of translation.

Leadership Transitions

The board was entering a season of making profound changes redefining the highest levels of leadership in the organization, impacting WBTI and its relationship to SIL International far into the future. They included: (1) no longer needing the position of president, and the board selecting its own chair; (2) redefining the board composition; and (3) selecting an executive director separate from the executive director of SIL for the first time since the inception of the International Administration in 1968. These enormous alterations called for God's wisdom.

The selection of the executive director and team would form WBTI's leadership and the way it related to the SIL Executive Director and team. The two new leaders needed a deep personal commitment to one another, and to be engaged in each other's lives in caring and supportive ways. The relationship they developed would serve as a benchmark for future generations of leadership. Therefore, the board required prayer when making their leadership selections and moulding the new executive director and leadership team with the SIL Executive Director and leadership team to function as a godly unit, bringing delight to God's heart.

After WBTI replaced the position of president with that of a chairperson, the first person elected to that role was Roger Welch. At the November board meeting, noting the magnitude of change the board had made in WBTI, Welch also expressed appreciation for Dick Hugoniot's service as president in a full-time capacity. Welch took on the chair position in a part-time volunteer capacity.

Progress Toward Ends

Executive Director John Watters informed the board how progress toward the Ends related significantly to how they integrated into the strategic planning of the WMOs. Consequently, strategic planning at the Area and WMO levels continued to be a significant initiative in this triennium. Watters noted collaboration and supportive networking among WMOs becoming standard practice. Exploring how Wycliffe-type activities could offer vision and service to the worldwide church was moving beyond national and geographic boundaries. Focussing on movements for Bible translation and not just on internal structures or the promotion of Wycliffe alone was crucial to achieving Vision 2025. And assuming partnership as a way of life was a trend away from the limits of an independent approach.

Other changes included the appointment of José de Dios as Americas Area Director. The board thanked Dave Brooks, who had held the position for both WBTI and SIL since 2001. With de Dios's appointment, the position was no longer associated with SIL. Going forward, WBTI now had its own Area Directors in all four Areas: Africa, Americas, Asia-Pacific, and Europe.

Identifying Best Contributions

The board altered the End designated effective relationships among WMOs with this addition: 'The full potential of each member organization with language programs to impact the Bible translation task is realized.'[38] Through this statement, the board sought to encourage WMOs to identify and then strengthen their best contribution toward Vision 2025.

Process for Next Executive Director

At the 2005 International Convention, restructuring WBTI to have its own executive director received the necessary support to continue the process. In November 2005, to manage the selection process, the board set up an executive director committee with Dick Hugoniot (Chair), Mũndara Mũturi (Director of BTL Kenya), Luis Pantoja (Constituency Member from Asia), and Roger Welch (Constituency Member from Europe). The committee sent a letter to WMOs and the International Administration asking for names of people to approach for consideration for the position of WBTI Executive Director.

The committee received 26 names. Three were from outside the WBTI world, and the committee decided not to contact them because the internal candidates

[38] WBTI, "Board Minutes," October-November 2006, 4.

were suitable. The chair contacted the remaining 23 either by letter, telephone, or personal interview. All of them responded, but only six said they were willing to go forward in the process. The committee wrote to the six with a list of 13 questions to be answered, as well as requesting references. The six who accepted the nomination had to make themselves vulnerable proceeding through the selection process. Each gave thoughtful and insightful answers to the questions. The committee recognized there were already leaders available in WBTI and SIL (two candidates were from SIL) who understood WBTI's ethos, were passionate to see Vision 2025 fulfilled, and desired effective engagement with the church of the South and East.

The committee had a teleconference in March and narrowed the list down to two candidates. The committee brought the two names to the board. After discussion and thorough processing, the board accepted their recommendation. The two candidates were: Sigmund Evensen, Director of Wycliffe Norway, and Kirk Franklin, Director of Wycliffe Australia.

A biographical summary of the two candidates was sent to all WMO directors and board chairs, requesting comments about the nominees. Over half of the WMOs provided responses and comments about the candidates. These were considered by the selection committee in its report to the board. Representatives of the committee then had in-depth interviews with both candidates and their wives.

Appointment of Next Executive Director

In its November 2006 meeting, the board met with the two candidates. In a closed session that followed, fully aware of the gravity of their decision, they sought God's direction in making the appointment. They voted, and when the results were known, the chair announced Kirk Franklin's appointment as executive director for the 2008–2011 triennium. Welch asked Sigmund Evensen to comment. He congratulated Franklin and thanked him for the friendship they had through the candidacy process. Franklin then gave his remarks and acceptance of the appointment. He echoed Evensen's sentiments regarding the journey to this point and affirmed his friendship with Evensen. A year earlier, Franklin said he never envisioned being chosen for the executive director role. But because William Edoni, his close friend whom he considered as one of his spiritual fathers, nominated him on behalf of the BTA PNG Board, he had to take the possibility seriously. To John Watters, he said he was committed to working with him and helping him to finish well. He asked the board for support and assured the SIL Board that SIL would remain a valued partner for WBTI. He asked for prayer for the Wycliffe Australia Board that would now launch its search for his replacement as their executive director. He thanked his family, his church in Melbourne, and WBTI Board members for their support. The board prayed for Franklin, whose term would start in 13 months, on 1 January 2008.

Global Leaders' Meetings

All of the WMO and WAO directors along with the International Administration met together in 2002. They now met for the second time, from 14–21 November, in Chiang Mai, Thailand. The executive director team, area directors, and vice presidents led the meeting. There were joint sessions with WBTI and SIL, separate meetings of the two organizations' leaders, and one day of Area meetings. The joint sessions included one day for prayer and reflection to build spiritual health and unity, and the next two days focussed on the following agenda items: Healthy Multi-Cultural Teams and Community, Language Communities in the 21st Century, Envisioning and Engaging the Worldwide Church, and Strengthening the Areas. During one of WBTI's separate sessions, the WMO Directors met with Franklin as their executive director-elect. Together they discussed ideas for the future structure of WBTI, endeavouring to better engage with the church worldwide.

New Board Structure

The first meeting of the WBTI Board without having three overlapping SIL Board members took place in May 2007. Having overlapping board members had proven a logistical challenge when the two boards met separately, as it meant the overlapping members weren't present. This new, smaller board configuration included Roger Welch (Chair), John Bennett (chosen as the Pacific Constituency member to replace William Edoni), Daniel Bianchi, Bob Creson, Sigmund Evensen, Kirk Franklin (who, because of his new appointment, would step down in 2007), Sung-Chan Kwon, Mũndara Mũturi, Luis Pantoja, and Isidore Songnaba.

Discovering the Mission of God

As a means of helping the board in its missiological reflection, John Watters quoted from Philip Jenkins's book *The Next Christendom* concerning the changing world and Christianity and the effects on missions.[39] Noting Jenkins's work, Watters observed that the foundation for world Christianity was the basic assumption underlying Vision 2025. Though Northerners may have been known for having wealth,

---

[39] Philip Jenkins, *The Next Christendom: The Coming of Global Christianity* (New York: Oxford University Press, 2002).

technology, linguistic specialization, and military and political predominance, Christianity has always transcended political, national, and cultural boundaries. Because of this, Watters hoped for great things to happen as historical movements unfolded before WBTI. Watters also referred to Christopher Wright's book *The Mission of God,* where Wright asserted that the canon of the Scriptures is a product of and witness to the mission of God. The Bible originated in the context of mission.[40] As a result of these reflections, the board affirmed this prioritization from Watters and encouraged him to develop the theme of God on mission further.

Watters discussed the implications for the WBTI Mission statement regarding God being on a mission. His presentation of WBTI's needs included dependence on God, not the US economy; commitment to steward and not to rule; recognition of who was the centre of all things and who should receive the glory. Bible translation would be at the level of the poor Christians rather than the prosperous ones in the future. Noting the continued necessity for increased project funds and the necessity to build confidence in their contributing foundations and other large-fund donors, Watters detailed the collaborative work between SIL, Wycliffe US, and other WMOs to improve project design and reporting methods.

New appointments to the International Administration included Joel Trudell as WBTI Africa Area Director, replacing John Bendor-Samuel, and Paul Frank as WBTI Vice President for Scripture Promotion (a new position).

WBTI Africa held an Area Conference in Yaoundé, Cameroon in 2007. In the Americas, church engagement improved, and partnerships were growing. In the Asia-Pacific Area, a helpful mobilization consultation had taken place. Europe's WMO's were seeing greater development and well-being, as well as growth in funding. Despite having no WMO, Romania expected substantial growth. In Belgium and Ireland, there were obstacles to overcome for these WMOs to be viable.

As WBTI sought to strengthen WMOs and improve collaborative efforts, there were also many responsibilities of the International Administration that needed to be separated from SIL while still maintaining good relations. For example, a WBTI Prayer Strategy began, each Area was developing WBTI Communication Hubs, and a meeting of Best Practices for communicators took place. IT support was in place. SIL and WBTI's finances were now separate. A joint WBTI-SIL Translation Conference held at the ILC in Dallas featured Scripture Promotion. And Wycliffe UK hosted an Andrew Walls and Lamin Sanneh series of lectures about the history of Bible translation.

---

[40] Christopher Wright, *The Mission of God: Unlocking the Bible's Grand Narrative* (Downers Grove: IVP Academic, 2006).

Planning for the Future

Incoming Executive Director Kirk Franklin presented the proposed new WBTI administration structure to the board. Discussion on a location change for WBTI's headquarters led to the board's decision to establish WBTI's operations in Singapore, effective after the new leadership team was in place. (Note: An office in Dallas continued to be maintained for WBTI because it had been incorporated in Texas.)

The board approved the budget with a total operating income of $1,240,600, with operating expense of $1,301,500, and estimated project funding income (and equal expense) of $1,197,820. The operating difference of $60,900 would be financed from funds available in reserves.

Transfer of Responsibility

The WBTI Board approved the International Administration's request that the International Operations at the Dallas Center be transferred back to SIL International, effective 1 January 2008, undoing the earlier decision that WBTI bore responsibility for the Center. With the changes in store for WBTI wherein it would no longer have much presence in Dallas, it was contrary to its purpose to be responsible for a Center it wasn't going to be using.

Elaine Townsend Memorial

WBTI recognized Elaine Townsend's significant role in the history and development of Wycliffe and SIL, as she supported her husband Cameron Townsend, the organizations' founder, and through her ministries of teaching and hospitality. Up until her death on 14 July 2007, she maintained a ministry of prayer and encouragement for Wycliffe and SIL colleagues around the world. The WBTI and SIL Boards expressed gratitude to God for the many years of faithful service Elaine Townsend gave to the two organizations and sympathy to her children, grandchildren, and great-grandchildren.

New Era Begins

On 1 January 2008, WBTI's first leadership team under Kirk Franklin (Australia/US) consisted of both new and continuing members:

- Continuing from the previous administration were Africa Area Director Joel Trudell (US), Americas Area Director José de Dios (Guatemala/US), Asia-Pacific Area Director Takashi Fukuda (Japan), Europe Area Director Frank Lautenschlager (Germany), Director of Finance/CFO Eleanor Berry (US). This last role continued to be shared with SIL International.
- New people and positions were Associate Director Min-Young Jung (South Korea), Director of Partnerships Dave Brooks (US), Director of Communication Susan Van Wynen (US), Director of Organizational Development Marshall Schultz (US), Director of Personnel Tim Feia (US), Director of Church Engagement Elisha Chua (Malaysia), Senior Advisor Darryl Kernick (Australia), Director for Research and Development Sung-Chan Kwon (South Korea), Missiological Consultant (part-time) Stephen Coertze (South Africa), Cross-Cultural Consultant Mary Lederleitner (US), Singapore Advisor (part-time) Tony Chan (Singapore), and Singapore Manager (part-time) Valerie Soo.

The new team was the most culturally diverse WBTI had ever seen at that level. It included four women which WBTI also had not seen before in leadership roles at this level. The team was spread across the world rather than concentrated in one location, and there was a small group operating out of Singapore.

A few weeks before the official handover from John Watters and his team to Franklin and his team, the Global Leadership Team (GLT) met for the first time, from 8 to 10 December 2007 in Singapore, with spouses included. Getting to know each other before preparing to lead WBTI was the primary purpose of this retreat. They identified characteristics to describe the new team:

- *How the GLT works together:* We respect each other with good interpersonal relationships and open communication, celebration, and trust. We are known for our fellowship and partnership, are outward looking, and celebrate diversity. We are nimble, flexible, cope with change, and are responsive to the opportunities God gives us. We eliminate 'silos' that take shape within our structure. We have alignment with each other in what we say internally and externally because we integrate our thinking within the whole team. We are always learning from one another and from our partners.
- *The kind of leadership the GLT provides:* We reveal godliness through praying together and are sensitive to the Holy Spirit. We demonstrate Christ's love in all we do and say. We are servant leaders and develop credibility with others, internally and externally. We are visionary and creative. We are capable and effective partners with a broad concern beyond our own people, strategies, and programs. We are people of both action and reflection.

International Administration to GLT

In his first report to the board, Franklin pointed out how the formation of the GLT meant that WBTI no longer had an International Administration situated in a centralized head office. Instead, it was a team of leaders spread across the globe, most of whom would work virtually. He spoke of the need to serve holistically, to examine their role in helping facilitate transformational change for the marginalized communities with whom they served. Reflecting on holistic mission, the call to a lifestyle of Bible translation, not a task of Bible translation, was revealed. In mid-2007, Franklin attended a retreat of the WMO BTA in PNG where its members candidly shared their feelings of being inferior to Westerners. He also noted recent experiences in Francophone Africa when French speakers voiced their feelings of inferiority because WBTI was an English-speaking organization. Franklin concluded that WBTI needed to deal with some of these issues if they wanted to experience the shalom of God.

Symbolizing what WBTI was becoming, a new logo was developed based on themes of currents, transformation, and dynamic movement, with colours each of the WBTI Areas felt expressed their spirit.

In their efforts to maintain their partnership, the WBTI and SIL Board continued to meet at the same time and location, with some joint sessions. In these early days of transition, not surprisingly, there were some missteps. The SIL President informed the WBTI Board that the SIL Board adjusted the SIL Ends without consulting with the WBTI Board, and for this, they apologized. Both the SIL Board and WBTI Board committed themselves to make no significant changes in their Ends statements without consultation with the other board.

The separation of SIL and WBTI was not the only difficult situation. Word for All (WFA), the WMO in India, also had trouble. WBTI investigated concerns expressed by various parties. On 31 January 2008, Franklin took the extraordinary measure of suspending WFA's WMO status, giving them six months to address their internal governance and structural problems. Within a few months, the Indian leaders had addressed Franklin's concerns. Therefore, discussions between WBTI and these leaders focussed on creating a completely different organization and structure to emerge in the next few months.

Another challenge occurred with NBTT, Nigeria, with its long-term issues of conflict in the administration, among board members, and with their staff. Dave Brooks was helping WBTI relate to NBTT in the growing crisis. While expressing concerns about the situation, the WBTI Board decided that the executive director should continue to build relationships with NBTT and that any action taken by the board at this stage may jeopardize these efforts. While continuing to monitor developments, the board asked the executive director to develop contextualized guidelines, indicators, and actions for how WMOs are disciplined when necessary.

Associated Partner Organizations

WBTI established the Associated Partner Organizations (APO) category, requiring no formal relationship with WBTI, but recognizing organizations with a mutual interest in and commitment to Bible translation worldwide. Each APO had its own standards and requirements. They were not subject to WBTI standards. The purpose for the APO status was to:

- provide fellowship with organizations who shared vision for Bible translation.
- provide opportunities for direct dialogue and interaction to motivate and encourage one another.
- provide mutual support through shared ideas, concepts, programs, and developments.
- participate in special meetings and conferences.

In March, two organizations requested and were granted APO status:

- Global PartnerLink (GPL) Canada, a subsidiary of Wycliffe Canada.
- Evangelical Churches Fellowship of Ethiopia (ECFE).

Granting APO status was seen as a positive development. However, Franklin recognized the necessity of adding value to both the APO status (granted by the board) and the MOU Partners (granted by the executive director). The number of organizations in these two categories totalled 27. Franklin set up a small group from within the GLT to study these issues:

- Is it possible to make the APOs and MOU Partners into one category, perhaps called Partner Organizations? By doing so, do we reduce the status of the APOs and therefore cause them concern?
- If we did this, MOUs would be customized to describe the relationship between WBTI and the partner.
- For some APOs and MOU Partners, SIL holds the key partnership. How do we recognize that factor?
- Do we deliberately make the Americas Area model of Bible translation movements as the WBTI default position, potentially affecting the purpose and viability of some WMOs?

Understanding and Knowing

Franklin began his role as WBTI Executive Director and Fredrick (Freddy) Boswell—who had served as Vice President for Scripture Promotion in WBTI and held a leadership role in SIL—as SIL International Executive Director on 1 January 2008. However, due to the long-range planning required beforehand and the timing of ICON (WBTI International Convention and SIL International Conference) in early May 2008, as outgoing executive director of both WBTI and SIL, John Watters was still technically in charge of ICON 2008.

ICON08 met in Chiang Mai the first week of May with the theme 'Understanding the Times—Knowing What to Do'. The following organizations were in attendance:

Wycliffe Member Organizations:

- Africa Area WMOs with Vote: ANTBA (Burkina Faso), BTL (Kenya), CABTAL (Cameroon), GILLBT (Ghana), and Wycliffe South Africa with a total of eight delegates. (Wycliffe South Africa, forming in the late 1970s, was recognized by WBTI in 1991. This occurred during South Africa's apartheid era, and in that context, the WMO related to Wycliffe's Europe Area. In time, the nation of South Africa was accepted into the global community, and by 2005, Wycliffe South Africa came under Wycliffe's Africa Area.)
- Africa Area WMOs without Vote: ACATBA (CAR), ATALTRAB (Chad), Wycliffe Africa, Wycliffe Benin, Wycliffe Togo with a total of ten observers.
- Americas Area WMOs with Vote: ALEM (Brazil), Wycliffe Canada, and Wycliffe US with a total of six delegates.
- Americas Area WMOs without Vote: Wycliffe Caribbean with a total of eight observers.
- Asia-Pacific Area WMOs with Vote: BTA (PNG), GBT (South Korea), Kartidaya (Indonesia), TAP (Philippines), Wycliffe Australia, Wycliffe Hong Kong, Wycliffe Japan, Wycliffe Malaysia, Wycliffe New Zealand, and Wycliffe Singapore with a total of 20 delegates.
- Asia-Pacific Area WMOs without Vote: Wycliffe India, Wycliffe Taiwan, and Wycliffe Thailand with a total of six observers.
- Europe Area WMOs with Vote: Wycliffe Austria, Wycliffe Finland, Wycliffe France, Wycliffe Germany, Wycliffe Netherlands, Wycliffe Norway, Wycliffe Sweden, Wycliffe Switzerland, and Wycliffe UK with a total of 18 delegates.
- Europe Area WMOs without Vote: Wycliffe Czech Republic, Wycliffe Denmark, Wycliffe Hungary, Wycliffe Poland, Wycliffe Russia, Wycliffe Slovakia, and Wycliffe Ukraine with a total of 12 observers.

Associated Partner Organizations:

- ACOTBA-SUBO (DRC), FEDEMEC (Costa Rica), LETRA Argentina, Episcopal Church of Sudan Translation Department, Ethiopian Evangelical Church Mekane Yesus (EECMY), and Evangelical Churches Fellowship of Ethiopia (ECFE) with a total of six observers
- Other Organizations: COMIBAM, FUMIG (Ecuador), LETRA Chile, LETRA Paraguay, LETRA Uruguay, and COMIMEX (Mexico) with a total of six guests.

The diversity of organizations and their geographic locations were an indicator of how WBTI was growing. Also in attendance were WBTI Board members, the GLT, and former executive directors and presidents (John Bendor-Samuel, David Cummings, Dick Hugoniot, Steve Sheldon, and John Watters).

WBTI Board Chair Roger Welch acknowledged the beginning of a new era with new opportunities and challenges ahead, stating in his opening remarks that 'WBTI is on a journey, and the journey is a good one. Structures have changed, and the leadership is different.' Two themes to be discussed during the Convention were: Engaging with the worldwide church in the 21st century and WBTI's partnership with the church.

Watters reported on highlights of his two years and nine months as executive director, touching on outcomes implemented from the 2005 International Convention. Franklin gave a 'State of WBTI' address in a joint session with SIL delegates. Travelling around the globe, he had seen how WBTI was 'positioning itself to help the church take the whole gospel to the whole world.'[41] For WBTI, the importance of understanding the mission of God grew, and WBTI assumed that 'God has a mission and the church has a crucial role in that mission. While Bible translation is important, glory should go to God, not to the process of bringing the Word.'[42] WBTI was now in a post-colonial era which meant it had to move away from an older mindset.

The new WBTI Board was elected:

- *Constituency Members:* Chantal Tehe-Yoa (Côte d'Ivoire), Daniel Bianchi (Argentina), Luis Pantoja (Philippines), Roger Welch (UK), and John Bennett (New Zealand).
- *WMO Directors:* Mũndara Mũturi (Kenya), Hannes Wiesmann (Switzerland), David Gela (PNG), Winston Chiu (Taiwan), and Bob Creson (US).

Once again, the WBTI Board was culturally diverse. However, it still had only one woman. The Board re-elected Welch as its Chair.

Both the WBTI Convention and SIL Conference delegates agreed to the

[41] WBTI, May 2008, 5.

[42] WBTI, May 2008, 5.

recommendation to move from a three-year to four-year meeting cycle, which allowed for a Global Leadership Meeting in between. It would also conserve financial resources since these global events were becoming more expensive as they grew in size.

Well-known and respected Indonesian pastor, Bambang Widjaya, presented the church's perspective of understanding the times, touching on issues of rising religious radicalism, the shift of the centre of gravity of Christianity, and the growth of the megachurches. Implications for missions to consider involved increasing participation of the local church and laity for mission work, including Bible translation, for which the local church collaborating with agencies like Wycliffe is responsible; implement synergy between gospel proclamation and community development, to eliminate impressions of imperialism; and recruiting Christians from the Global South into the global mission force.

Kuruvilla Chandy, a church leader from India, shared perspectives of the church and missions in India. Ajith Fernando, a leader of Youth for Christ in Sri Lanka, discussed the difficulties of communicating the gospel and promoting holiness in a shame culture. One complication was how to respond to post-colonial nationalism while fearing being controlled by others and with everything wrong being blamed on the colonialist. Christians in this environment must struggle to live a servant lifestyle.

Recognizing that in the future, most Christians will inhabit the same geographical areas as the remaining Bible translation needs, how should WBTI engage with them? Reflecting on the church and Scriptures in languages of the earth, Franklin described: the context of the church's relationship to mission and how an outward missional focus is now required; the translated Word as essential to church growth; the current context of church realities, where the church is both declining and growing, where the place of the Bible in some of the church is theoretical or more or less abstract in its importance, and where it is authoritative; and Wycliffe and the church today, and how WBT's past, which included minimal engagement with the church, has been changing.

This set the stage for interactive, community-based conversations, including both Wycliffe and SIL. Discussions at rotating table groups processed outcomes from the presentations about engaging with the church.

In his closing speech, Welch noted WBTI is good at analysis and at understanding the times, but not always in knowing what to do. Nevertheless, participants left ICON08 inspired by the vision of people from all tribes and languages populating the new heaven. Franklin reminded the participants of God's mission: the *missio Dei*. He emphasized the need to talk about the worldwide church rather than dichotomize it, to work on attitudes toward—and to appreciate—the local church.

WBTI Convention participants had a separate session for discussion regarding the needs for leadership development, facilitated by GLT member Tim Feia with table groups examining the issues. Participants generated a list of 59 ideas and requests on the topic:

- Mentoring, coaching, and ongoing training in leadership (19 topics, from funding contextualized leadership training to providing an ongoing process of modelling and mentoring).
- Practical skill development (16 topics, from help in learning English to learning best practices).
- Specific orientation to the organization (eight topics).
- Personal Growth (six topics, from developing listening skills to conflict resolution).
- Working with the board/governance (four topics, from how to motivate board members to training for the board chairperson).
- Preparing for leadership transition (two topics related to preparing for the transition).
- Reflective practitioners (four topics, from leaders needing time to reflect to recognizing that leaders are grown in processes that involve pain, bringing intimate contact with God).

Franklin committed the efforts of the GLT to develop strategies for addressing these needs and preparing the next generation of emerging leaders to be effective followers of Christ, both in society and as leaders of mission.

On May 9, the day after the Convention, WBTI hosted Affinity Group and Hot Topic meetings. There were five Affinity Groups for Member and Partner Organizations grouped according to these affinities: WMOs with Language Programs; WMOs with 100+ people; WMOs with less than 100 people (established); WMOs with less than 100 people (emerging); and APOs and MOU Partners. A GLT member hosted each group. Conversations centred on topics of mutual interest and produced various recommendations ranging from practical to strategic, offered to the GLT for follow up. For example, thinking the name was too long, the Affinity Group of WMOs with Language Programs sought another name for this organizational category. Among their most pressing concerns, the development of translation consultants required attention at the global, Area, and country levels to achieve Vision 2025. Though currently conducted by SIL, WBTI needed its own process of accreditation of international consultants for their WMOs with Language Programs.

GLT members hosted five Hot Topic groups: (1) What is a Bible Translation Movement? Definitions, Distinctives and Discussion; (2) Form, Function and the Future—WMOs and other Organizational Structures; (3) The Changing Church

Context—Implications for Today and Tomorrow; (4) Engaging with the Global Diaspora; and (5) Future Thinking for Personnel Funding. Since these were optional and potential participants had already engaged intensely in a week of meetings, attendance was low for most groups, yet each produced some recommendations for the GLT that would influence present and future development for WBTI. For example, leaders of APOs wondered what WBTI's expectations were of these organizations. A participant noted that by carefully examining its policies and listening to the APOs, WBTI demonstrated its openness to change. Referencing the Latin America model, which set up no WMOs, another participant wondered why WBTI continued to form WMOs in Africa and Asia rather than using the Latin American model. Did using the Wycliffe name for new organizations in these contexts present a problem since Wycliffe, as a foreign entity, was known to be a US organization?

Evaluation

The WBTI Board participated in a joint committee with the SIL Board to evaluate ICON08. Recommendations included:

- *Diversity:* Despite translation occurring in French and Spanish simultaneously during the conference, designing future conferences required broader input for the diversity of non-English speaking participants. Any papers presented required translation well ahead of time and called for timely distribution.
- *Participation of partners:* It was vital that WBTI include partners in all aspects of the conference, from presentations to table-group discussions. The current practice of seating them at the back of the room needed to change and bring them to sit together with the delegates.
- *Election process:* The election process for the board was too lengthy and needed to be handled in a more culturally appropriate way, considering the diversity of cultures in attendance.
- *Length of ICON:* Limiting the event to under seven days would allow better focus and less drop-off of attendance. Also, because of their other commitments, it was difficult for board representatives of Wycliffe Organizations to commit to such a long event.

Changing Terminology

An outcome of the changing dynamics with WBTI and SIL and the 2008 restructuring included controversy concerning terminology used between and within the two organizations. One example was the use of 'side' such as the Wycliffe or WBTI side and the SIL side. The myth was that the two organizations were two sides of the same coin. While that may have worked during their earlier history, it did not accurately describe their more recent relational dynamics. They were partners but were neither the same 'coin' nor on opposing 'sides' now that the organizations had separated. The acronym WSFO (for Wycliffe and SIL Family of Organizations), widely used by the previous administration, was a generic way of referring to all that was associated with the two organizations. Perhaps that worked when one administration ran both organizations, but it was no longer accurate, as WBTI had a completely different structure and leadership team from SIL. It was important to evaluate language use and terminology as WBTI's journey continued.

Meeting in Manila

In October 2008, the WBTI and SIL Boards met in Manila, hosted by Greenhills Christian Fellowship, the church led by board member Luis Pantoja. During the meeting, Darryl Kernick accepted the appointment as WBTI board secretary, with Irene Kernick to serve as assistant. Until then, Gene Burnham had capably filled the role for both WBTI and SIL.

The date for this board meeting was moved forward due to the timing of the World Evangelical Alliance (WEA) General Assembly, scheduled from late October to early November. The WEA had invited WBTI to be a Global Partner, and Franklin and some members of his leadership team would attend the Assembly and the Mission Commission Roundtable, which followed.

Franklin presented the WBTI Strategic Overview, describing it as a road map for an exciting future as the GLT and board considered where God had brought WBTI in his mission. The Overview was the work of the GLT in consultation with a dozen Member and Partner Organization leaders. The board carried the ownership of Vision, Mission, Core Values, Vision 2025 statement, Relationship with SIL statement, and Board Goals. The GLT held the responsibility of the Strategies and Tactics. In response, Board Chair Roger Welch stated that 'WBTI restructuring has been preparation for a new journey, but it is not the journey itself. The executive director's report helped the board to see the shape of the world we are moving into.'[43]

As the GLT settled into its roles, Franklin noted that in attempting to compile the annual Indicators of Progress report for the board, the data came from the WMOs, but many did not contribute. The GLT recognized the WMOs' growing weariness of contributing data. Some data, repeated from previous years, could

[43] WBTI, "Board Extracts," October 2008, 3.

indicate a lack of re-evaluation. Some rounding of figures by some WMOs could suggest they were making an educated guess. Gaining the WMOs' cooperation to complete the questionnaire became increasingly difficult. The GLT sent up to four reminders to most, and even then, a significant number did not answer, prompting the question, was the problem with the indicators? Franklin concluded that it was time for the board to review whether it even wanted indicators, and if so, what were the right indicators, and what did the board plan to do with, or about, the information gathered?

As the GLT began providing direction to WBTI, some developments with WMOs included the following:

› Wycliffe India was applying to become a WMO with Language Programs.
› Wycliffe Philippines was an emerging idea of WBTI Board member Luis Pantoja, focussed on recruiting Filipinos to serve across Asia and beyond and raising funds for Translators Association of Philippines (TAP). This created a new challenge for WBTI, with two WMOs operating in the same country, requiring both organizations to work closely together.
› Wycliffe Ireland closed its operations in 2008. Wycliffe UK provided representation and publicity assistance.
› Wycliffe Ukraine was having significant difficulties. The situation began deteriorating in 2008, and the Europe Area Director requested that this be addressed by the leadership. It wasn't, and the organization went dormant.

Unique Value of WBTI

As Franklin settled into his role, he took every opportunity to describe how the new WBTI brought unique value to three critical groups: the worldwide church and the global mission community, present and future Member and Partner Organizations, and language communities. WBTI and its GLT, because of the nature of its international identity, responsibilities, and relationships, was best positioned to exercise certain functions at the regional and global level and others at the country level. For example, at the regional and global level, WBTI brought influence, advocacy, partnering and facilitating partnerships, missiological reflection, etc. At the country level, WBTI brought organizational support, capacity building, lending credibility, encouragement, etc. At the language community and people group level, WBTI's benefit to these communities happened indirectly, as it came through the WMOs.

The above groups of functions each call for different skills, experiences, and relationships and could be combined into three distinct but interrelated roles:

- In role 1, visionary advocates were informed by missiological reflection regarding the vital role of the Word of God—in the most appropriate languages and media/formats—in the integral mission of God and His church and the transformation of people groups around the world.
- In role 2, WBTI and its Member and Partner Organizations served in partnership, not only as a means of accomplishing work but as an expression of the unity of believers. WBTI partnered formally and informally with other like-minded individuals and organizations at regional and international levels. Through such partnerships, WBTI catalyzed and sustained a global movement focussed on seeing individuals, communities, and nations transformed through God's love and Word.
- In role 3, WBTI brought practical support and assisted with capacity building with its Member and Partner Organizations so they could carry out their responsibilities more effectively and with greater impact. WBTI also facilitated and encouraged the efforts of the 12 WMOs with Language Programs that serve language communities in their own nations.

Managing Power

During 2008–9, as WBTI's new leadership structure became acclimated, Franklin encountered a range of expectations concerning how he should fulfill his role. For example, while meeting with African WBTI leaders, he was asked to be more directive to the Member Organizations and to use his authority to get them to do what was necessary to do. Area staff, he discovered, at times felt frustrated that they had no direct authority over the autonomous WMOs, and they wanted this changed. New GLT members initially articulated the same sentiment from time to time, concerned that though 'Director' may be in their title, their roles were only advisory.

Some WMO leaders expected the WBTI Executive Director and GLT to pressure or even discipline their organizations when thought to be uncooperative. The reality was that the only disciplinary authority that WBTI leadership had over WMOs was when they did not comply with WBTI standards.

Finding the right balance of influence was an ongoing challenge for WBTI's leadership. They discussed and applied a concept developed by Alex Araujo that used the metaphor of boats to describe paradigms of power in mission:

- *Rowboat* (low control): With minimal power inside the boat and in the hands of the person with the oars, it is slow, inefficient, and at the mercy of external elements.
- *Powerboat* (high control): A lot of power is inside the boat, in the control of the captain. It is confident, modern, powerful, noisy, and expensive. The

destination, and getting there fast, is often considered most important.

- *Sailboat* (shared control): The sailing team has some control and power, but it is subordinate to the wind. Success depends entirely on their cooperation with the wind. Some days the vessel will travel great distances. Other days the wind will be calm and the progress slow. But this may not matter, since it's the journey, not just the destination, that's important.

The executive director and GLT used these metaphors for the next few years. Many WBTI organizations identified with this and the aspirations of the sailboat, even if they thought they were a rowboat or powerboat. Sherwood Lingenfelter summarized this well: 'When we obey [God's] command to love first, relationship takes priority over control, and contextual leadership becomes possible.'[44]

Wycliffe Partners

Nearly 18 months into the new WBTI structure, a perceived division between Member Organizations and Partner Organizations grew increasingly evident. The current structure did not bring them together as it should. Many Partner Organizations were more engaged in the Bible translation movement than WMOs. An idea emerged from discussions among the GLT and the board that all organizations in WBTI be enabled to pursue their best contribution to Vision 2025. Redefining organizational categories could bring Member Organizations and Partner Organizations closer together. The next International Convention in 2012 would be the best place to adopt changes to the bylaws to make this possible. Insight into and input from Member Organizations and Partner Organizations on this issue was critical. The board encouraged the executive director 'to begin a consultative process with the Member Organizations and other partners in regard to the proposal for the realignment of organizations within WBTI.'[45]

In response, Franklin asked the WMOs for input on a proposal redefining how organizations relate to WBTI. All current categories (such as WMO with vote, WMO without vote, WMO with Language Programs, APO, MOU Partner) could be replaced with a single organizational category: Wycliffe Partner. Procedures for granting the current organizational statuses would be replaced by written Memorandums of Understanding (MOU) between WBTI and each Wycliffe Partner and would include adherence to WBTI Standards. This MOU would describe the relationship and expectations between WBTI and each Wycliffe Partner. It would be customized for each Wycliffe Partner, centring on their intended best contribution(s) toward achieving Vision 2025.

---

[44] Sherwood Lingenfelter, *Leading Cross-Culturally* (Grand Rapids: Baker Books, 2008), 112.

[45] WBTI, "Board Minutes," May 2009, 5.

It was Franklin's conviction that by enacting these changes, WBTI and its organizations would become more effective in managing the challenges of the 21st century while maintaining a focus on Vision 2025 through Bible translation movements.

Franklin reported to the board that area directors were noticing a common theme among a large percentage of WMOs concerning board governance and the lack of diligent scrutiny of their executive directors by some boards. Franklin intended, along with the area directors, to prioritize helping WMO Boards improve how they functioned.

The terms of service of the executive director and board officers needed better alignment with the cycle of the International Convention. The WMOs agreed to alter the Convention cycle from three years to four years, but that put the executive director's term of service out of sequence with the Convention. Franklin started his term on 1 January 2008, whereas John Watters resided as executive director for the Convention in May 2008. Rather than contending with a four-month gap, the handover between the incoming and outgoing executive directors would more appropriately occur during a ceremony at the Convention. The board also decided that the executive director's term limit would alter from a maximum of nine years (three three-year terms) to eight years (two four-year terms). Coinciding with the Convention cycle, board members served a four-year term, the board chair served for two years at a time, and the secretary and treasurer were appointed for four-year terms, ending after the board meeting which followed the Convention.

Singapore Office

The board's approval for establishing WBTI's operating headquarters in Singapore gained momentum, and with Wycliffe Singapore's assistance, WBTI registered in Singapore in 2009. The Singapore Board affirmed its willingness to co-locate with WBTI. In the capacity of Associate Area Director (Partnerships), Dave and Gwen Brooks moved to Singapore, rented office space in the same building as Wycliffe Singapore, and shared office resources such as an accountant and an administrative person. Appointed as Singapore Manager, Singaporean Valerie Soo brought her administrative experience. WBTI was now able to have a Singaporean bank account and apply for visas for non-Singaporean staff. WBTI kept its incorporation in the State of Texas, renting office space at the International Linguistics Center for a small Dallas-based team.

Leadership Development

Franklin developed a four-day event called Leaders Moving Forward. Based on an interactive model, it covered various foundational themes, including spiritual leadership, missiological consideration, leadership theory and practice in intercultural contexts, and orientation to the new WBTI. At its early 2009 trial in San Jose, Costa Rica, some GLT members facilitated leaders from Area Member and Partner Organizations in the Americas. It was successful and therefore was also conducted in Holzhausen, Germany for European leaders, Ruiru, Kenya for African leaders, and Bangkok, Thailand for Asia-Pacific leaders.

Revised Vision and Mission Statement

As they looked at revising WBTI's vision, the WBTI Board invited input from Member Organizations and the SIL Board, and at the May board meeting, processed the results. The Vision Statement, to be viewed in context with the Mission Statement, Core Values, and Board Goals, was intentionally broad and, together, the statements gave a clear picture of who WBTI was. The revised statement was: *Individuals, communities, and nations transformed through God's love and Word expressed in their languages and cultures.*

The WBTI Board followed the same consultative process in revising the Mission Statement with this wording: *In communion with God and with the worldwide church, we contribute to the holistic transformation of all peoples through Bible translation and compassionate services.* This statement defined the breadth of the whole community of WMOs. Each organization could frame its Mission Statement characterizing its unique focus, compatible with WBTI's vision and mission.

Member Organization Updates

Franklin informed the May 2009 board of these highlights:

- The executive director granted use of the name 'Wycliffe'—widely known as a reputable international organization—to 'Word for the Nations', now to be known as Wycliffe Romania. Thus, they gained credibility and the capacity to grow as a Member Organization without vote.
- Wycliffe Hungary and Wycliffe Russia celebrated their 10th anniversaries.
- Wycliffe Singapore and Wycliffe Austria celebrated their 25th anniversaries.
- Wycliffe Singapore launched their Reaching 200 Vision to encourage engagement of the Singaporean church in projects related to Vision 2025.

Partnership between WBTI and SIL

When the SIL Board spoke to the WBTI Board, it desired to frame it in the language of wanting 'cohesion' with WBTI. Because of this, 'cohesion' was monitored by the WBTI Board as a way of holding the executive director accountable for the relationship with SIL. The concept of organizational cohesion arose with the transition to new executive directors for both organizations. This raised questions for the WBTI Board: What does cohesion mean? What do we expect? The partnership between the two organizations was highly valued and important, affecting the successful implementation of strategies and practices between the two organizations. The topic of cohesion would continue between the two boards for a long time to come.

GLT's Identity and Role

In November 2009, during their final meeting of the year, the board raised the topic of the identity of the GLT. In contrast with the previous International Administration's management of WBTI and SIL, the GLT intended to be visionary, informed through missiological reflection, building the capacity of organizations in WBTI to pursue partnering opportunities for the Bible translation movement. These features describe the identity of the GLT:

› Team design—represented an ensemble (a mixture of gifting, experiences, and abilities).
› Team dynamic—expressed a positive attitude (the mission of God in the world was the motivating reason for being servant leaders).
› Team composition—reflected the diversity of the worldwide church (nine nationalities).
› Team structure—made up of 16 people (executive director, three senior leaders, four area directors, four specialist directors, and four consultants).

Two new people joined the team, including Strategic Networks Consultant Todd Poulter (US) and Director of Technology Kenneth Kok (Singapore).

'Last Languages'

Wycliffe US prepared to launch its Last Languages Campaign (LLC) from 20 to 22 November 2008, seeking help from WBTI to encourage the other WMOs in raising significant funding for Bible translation in the process. Despite the economic difficulty in the US due to the Global Financial Crisis, Wycliffe US trusted that the

Lord was leading them to proceed with this launch. The LLC required placement of current Bible translation projects under WBTI and SIL into Comprehensive Project plans that ran for multiple years. In many places, WBTI continued building capacity for WMOs to lead Bible translation projects, which could also benefit those organizations' participation in the Comprehensive Projects. The process of moving to Comprehensive Projects was called the Last Languages Initiative (LLI). SIL took the lead and asked WBTI to be an equal owner of it. The first three projects under the LLI and therefore funded by the LLC were Americas Area Comprehensive Project, Bangladesh Comprehensive Project, and Uganda-Tanzania Comprehensive Project. WBTI had only minimal involvement in the third, some in the second, and significant ownership in the first as it involved WBTI's Americas Area.

Due to the growing pressure on WBTI by SIL to fully embrace and co-own LLI, WBTI held a special conference on the LLI 14–18 September 2009 with Wycliffe UK hosting at its Horsleys Green Centre (see chapter 10). The conference itself provided the forum for presentations and discussions between representatives of WBTI and representatives from SIL to discuss the LLI. An overriding concern of the process was to produce large multi-year plans that the funders would pick up and cover for the project's duration. Expectations were placed on WBTI to engage in LLI projects at an operational level, but within the GLT, there was concern whether this was WBTI's best role and contribution. Many WMOs experienced confusion about how they or partners could be invited into the planning process for the LLI. Consequently, WBTI's Executive Director and GLT concluded that the LLI could not belong to WBTI, nor should it be considered a joint pursuit between WBTI and SIL, but that it was solely an initiative of SIL. While WBTI was supportive of SIL handling the initiative, individual WMOs could choose, without fear of reproach, whether they would promote, partner with, and/or participate in the LLI. WBTI's role was to create space for and recognition of the diverse groups that constitute WBTI and to strengthen their participation in Vision 2025. The LLI conversations, though difficult at times, provided WBTI with the opportunity to gain and articulate a clearer picture of their identity. Often, when discerning what you are not, you discover more about who you are.

Changing Ends to Goals

At its beginning, the GLT observed that the concept of 'Ends' was not easily communicated—did not translate well or easily—into many of the non-North American languages, contexts, and cultures represented by most of the Member Organizations and Partner Organizations within WBTI. At their October 2008 meeting, the board agreed with the GLT's observations, changed the Ends to board Goals owned and set by the board, giving direction for implementation strategies the GLT would pursue. The board adopted these Goals at their November meeting:

- God and His Church: Advocate Scripture translation, access, and use as vital to the integral mission of God and His Church.
- Language Communities: Facilitate partnering initiatives serving language communities that enable them to participate in the kingdom of God.
- Internal and External Relationships: Reflect, through all of our relationships and partnerships, God's desire to accomplish His mission through the unity of His people.

Revised Core Values

The board and GLT worked together to revise the Core Values to better serve WBTI, Member Organizations, and Partner Organizations. Since Core Values, stated as follows, should stand the test of time, these would not need revision for some time:

- The Glory of God among the Nations—Our motive in all we do is to see people of all nations able to know God and glorify Him.
- Christlikeness in Life and Work—We desire to be like Christ, following His example in who we are and what we do.
- The Church as Central in God's Mission—We believe the Church is created, called, and equipped by God to evangelize the world, and disciple the nations.
- The Word Translated—We desire to see people's lives transformed through the Word of God, translated into their languages and cultures.
- Dependence on God—We depend on God and His sufficiency to equip and sustain for life and mission.
- Partnership and Service—We serve in partnership to express the unity of believers and to further holistic ministry through the translation, access to, and use of God's Word.

Growth, Challenges, and Opportunities

As 2010 was underway, the GLT, now two years old, demonstrated that the goals of a multi-cultural team presence across the globe, supported by minimal infrastructure, had been achieved. As the team adapted to their new roles, it became abundantly clear that this was a journey requiring the GLT to think and act differently, make many adjustments, and create space for cultural differences and perspectives. The adjustments made today would periodically need review, as WBTI was moving away from being an institution and toward becoming a movement. Deciding the size of any necessary centralized administration and how to develop the operational headquarters in Singapore to accommodate it presented a challenge. At times the GLT discovered some WMOs were not functioning well; helping turn these situations around consumed the team's efforts and energy while simultaneously finding its way. Some matters had been inadequately addressed under the previous joint International Administration, illustrating the disadvantage of one administration managing two organizations with separate, unique structures. The WBTI Board rightly discerned that to remain faithful to its purpose and to the organizations it served, WBTI required its own leadership.

An ever-changing world revealed the complexities of keeping all of WBTI heading in the same direction, including leading a diverse alliance of 46 Member Organizations and 60 Partner Organizations and facilitating their best contribution to Vision 2025 and beyond. Providing resources for WBTI's operations and determining the quantity of staff necessary to respond to the opportunities God was giving to WBTI as an active partner in the Bible translation movement presented further complexities.

There were also encouraging signs. A movement occurring in parts of the global church, particularly in the majority world, indicated an embracing of the vision and need for Bible translation. One example was the joint effort with SIL called the Francophone Initiative, which served theological institutions in Francophone Africa using a standardized curriculum on the history and importance of Bible translation, embraced by 27 theological colleges so far. Ultimately, more pastors would seek training to understand the importance of Bible translation in their countries, leading to significant involvement in the Bible translation ministry from the church in these nations. There was a growing Bible translation movement in Latin America led by mission leaders that was not just raising awareness of Bible translation needs but distributing Latin American resources in the region and beyond. There was also a noticeable growing commitment from Eastern and Central European churches in Bible translation through their local Wycliffe Organizations in Russia, Hungary, Slovakia, Czech Republic, Poland, and Romania. Romania had the greatest potential due to the size of its church, and Wycliffe and others could encourage the church to see its calling as a sending body, not just a receiving body.

Dynamics of the WMOs

The WBTI Board and SIL Board met in May 2010 at BTL's International Conference Centre in Ruiru, Kenya. Franklin gave a missiological reflection based in part on the 1910 World Missionary Conference of Edinburgh. The relationship of the church's mission with trans-cultural mission created four dichotomies: Division between those churches that send and those that receive; between the home or Western country and the overseas mission field; between missionaries called to go and those at home; and between the life and the mission of the church. Reducing mission to a task accomplished by missionaries sent from 'Christian countries' to the 'mission fields' of the world resulted in these dichotomies. Nevertheless, as thinking continues to evolve, understanding emerges that all churches send and all receive, the whole world is a mission field, every Christian's call is to serve the Lord, and the Christian life in all dimensions bears witness to the universal lordship of Christ. This affects the WMO's view of their work and identity as not only to send but given the composition of various organizations (including denominations, etc.), they are sending, receiving, and ministering in these new dimensions.

Partnership for Language Communities

As the reshaping of administrative structure for WBTI and SIL continued to be felt internally and noticed externally, the GLT saw the necessity to clarify the partnership between the two organizations. They continued to share a common heritage and concern for the Bible translation and language development needs of minority language communities. Over the years, the organizations worked in close partnership as each grew and adapted its goals and strategies to address the global changes impacting minority language communities.

Wycliffe Member and Partner Organizations, as part of the ongoing partnership, act as advocates, develop funding, and recruit workers for language development and Bible translation efforts worldwide. Many of Wycliffe's Bible translation initiatives are carried out through partnership with SIL. And most of the SIL workforce was made up of members of WMOs.

The official partnership between WBTI and SIL had existed from the time of WBTI's formation in 1980. To date, WMOs shared resources (people, prayer, finances), training, and good will to facilitate work in more than 1,900 language programs with language development, Bible translation, and literacy. WBTI remained committed to maintaining a healthy and vibrant relationship with shared values of partnership, creative strategies, urgency, capacity building, and sustainability.

Changes in Leadership Team

WBTI's Director of Organizational Development Marshall Schultz resigned in 2010 due to health reasons. Adapted from the Organizational Development function, the Director of Strategic Initiatives role transferred to Francis Viscount.

When he became executive director, Franklin committed to the African Member and Partner Organizations to find an African to take on the Africa Area Director role. A process began in 2008 to identify suitable candidates, which led to a discussion with BTL (Kenya) to see if they would release their Executive Director Mũndara Mũturi for the role. BTL eventually agreed and negotiated a timeline for Mũturi to start on 1 January 2011. This required the WBTI Board's approval, which it gave at its November 2009 meeting. No stranger to the board, Mũturi was at the time its vice chair. He stepped off the board in 2010. Joel Trudell had willingly held the Africa Area Director role after John Bendor-Samuel retired in 2007 and for as long as it would take to find an African to fill it. Trudell was bid farewell with thanks at the 2010 WBTI Africa Area Conference for his willingness to serve in the role. Mũturi was welcomed as the new Africa Area Director, receiving support from the African WMOs and partners as the first African to hold the role. Mũturi kept the Area Office based in Nairobi, adding qualified Africans primarily from Kenya to the small-scale Area team. Mũturi's appointment made history as it pursued the concept of having area directors come from the same Areas for which they were responsible. It had taken a long time for this to happen in Africa. Since this created an opening on the WBTI Board, they appointed Boureima Ouédraogo, Director of ANTBA (Burkina Faso), to take Mũturi's place in the Member Organization slot.

Asia-Pacific would experience a transition of directors with Sung-Chan Kwon's appointment to officially take up the responsibilities from Takashi Fukuda as Asia-Pacific Area Director on 1 January 2011. Therefore, in late 2010, a ceremony at Fukuda's home church in Tokyo, Japan, acknowledged the fulfillment of Fukuda's leadership in the Asia-Pacific Area and marked the transfer of responsibility to his successor, Sung-Chan Kwon from South Korea. Fukuda was the first Asian to hold this leadership role and had given oversight to the Area since 2004, with most of his team based in Manila. He then became WBTI's Spiritual Ambassador to the GLT for a few years, gradually decreasing his WBTI role as he became more involved with Wycliffe Japan. With his small team based in Manila, Kwon, who continued to live in Singapore, had served at different times as Director for Research and Development with the GLT, as the director for GBT, and on the WBTI Board.

Developments with WMOs included Kartidaya's (Indonesia) founder and first Executive Director Nitya Travis retiring from the role. She was honoured by

Kartidaya for her long and faithful service. Also, Wycliffe Czech Republic celebrated its 10th Anniversary.

Celebration of a Life

A time of remembrance took place at the November WBTI Board meeting, recognizing Luis Pantoja from the Philippines, who served on the board for the previous nine years. Pantoja died suddenly on 6 September 2010 in Manila. Board Chair Roger Welch represented WBTI at the memorial service. Beloved and honoured, Pantoja's humility, wisdom, and grace touched many. His epitaph, penned by himself, reflects the man we remember: 'A handful of ashes now vaulted in this corner, with nothing to boast but grace from his maker.'[46]

Changing Perspectives

Franklin reported to the board in May 2010 noticeable changing perspectives of WBTI that included the following:

- Changing theological perspectives: from proclamation alone to integral mission (proclamation and demonstration of the gospel); and from local church emphasis and perspectives to global church (local church gaining perspectives of what was happening globally).
- Changing missiological perspectives: from the Western/Northern church to the global church; from an emphasis on task partnerships to a growing understanding of Kingdom of God partnerships (where the kingdom is what is prioritized); and from situations of high power and control moving to situations of shared power and control.
- Changing WBTI perspectives: from building an institution to travelling on a journey; from emphasis on individual members to a focus on organizations and movements; and from primarily being Western/Northern toward being global.

Reconfiguration

In October 2010 in Singapore, WBTI and SIL co-hosted the Global Leaders Meeting (GLM), a gathering of the GLT, SIL leadership team, SIL entity leaders, and Directors of WBTI Member and Partner Organizations—about 250 people in total. Both WBTI and Wycliffe Singapore had a core of people located in Singapore who efficiently and effectively ran the meeting logistics, making it a convenient

46 WBTI, "Board Extracts," November 2010, 1.

location. For WBTI, moving its operational headquarters to Singapore demonstrated that it had transitioned from being a North American-based organization to a global one, a realistic expression of the movements and organizations WBTI represented.

During the WBTI sessions, the GLT emphasized developing a common language and understanding among the diversity of leaders about WBTI's role in the world today. Highlighting initiatives and developments of Member and Partner Organizations accompanied orientation to WBTI's current structure, the roles of the GLT and board, and how WBTI partnered with SIL. Aiming to create a renewed context of unity and trust was needed because about 60% of the WBTI participants were new to their roles since the last GLM and had a limited understanding of how to relate to WBTI. About 15% of the WMO directors were new to their roles in the last 12 months, and most were still learning about the relationship between Member Organizations, Partner Organizations, and WBTI. A few WMO directors publicly questioned the necessity for WBTI since they primarily concentrated on sending their people and financial resources to SIL. Their reservations diminished as the GLM progressed, and they got to know the GLT and Partner Organization leaders. The biggest challenge coming into the GLM was to build unity and community within all of WBTI's diversity. Developing WBTI to its next reconfiguration level, preparing it to more effectively serve all who participated with it, represented the most significant opportunity resulting from the GLM. And the journey continued.

Franklin knew going into the GLM that he and the GLT had not thoroughly processed the reconfiguration concept with any of the Partner Organization leaders. Thus, the emphasis for WBTI was discussing the reconfiguration proposal. Up to this point, the directors of the WMOs with Vote (28 in total) held the power to determine the future of WBTI. Simultaneously at the GLM, SIL was addressing a topic of the reinvention of SIL. Many WMO directors were also engaging with that topic because it intrigued them due to their close partnership with SIL. The input on the reconfiguration proposal, including insights gained during GLM, meant that the board was closer to making the necessary policy changes.

Stewardship of Natural Resources

The Wycliffe Europe Area Committee called on the board to review WBTI's position on stewardship of natural resources. This affected travel, facilities, etc. They urged the board to include mention of stewardship of natural resources in WBTI's core statements. As a result of a discussion at the May board meeting, the executive director would assess the GLT's activities in this regard. A report given at the

November board meeting concerning a Carbon Footprint Assessment of the GLT explored the use of office air-conditioning, heating, lighting, and transportation to and from the office. The study found the 18-member GLT was a low user of energy for office needs. Many of the team worked from home offices. Six travelled to their office using personal vehicles, two of them used public transportation, and the rest worked from home. The significant level of international travel for all GLT members represented the larger carbon footprint concern, with no straightforward solution. Low-cost teleconferencing was in its infancy, and in many locations, there was poor internet bandwidth. Nurturing relationships, and thereby trust, was essential. Much of the interaction essential to the GLT was face to face, requiring travel. However, WBTI did release a statement on its website regarding the importance it placed on stewardship of the earth.

Conclusion

The world in 2010 was very different from the world in 2001 when this chapter began. Over the nine years in focus, WBTI also changed dramatically, adapting its structure to serve its evolving strategies. This was not unexpected, as the organization's leaders sought to discern and follow what God was accomplishing in the context of a complex and ever-changing world. Since its inception in 1980, WBTI was agile enough to adapt and adjust to new situations, helping to ensure an ongoing, positive impact and sustainability of its core purpose and ministry. The church worldwide, especially in the Global South and East, showed contextual change and growth. WBTI rejoiced in this, intentionally adapting to be helpful to the church that desired to participate in Bible translation and related ministries. This required cooperation in will and spirit and what David Bosch called 'bold humility'.[47]

Up until this era, WBTI measured growth in the number of people sent from WMOs to assignments in SIL, funds raised through WMOs, and the number of WMOs leading Bible translation programs (which was still low). Now, WBTI's growth was noticeable in the Partner Organizations that wanted to be formally identified with WBTI so that they too could be part of a global body working together. But this growth needed to take place with the development of the WMOs to ensure that they were encouraged and empowered to be effective.

After several years of painstaking work separating the International Administration and enabling WBTI to have its own leadership structure, in 2008, the new leadership team took up responsibilities for 48 Member Organizations and more than 50 Partner Organizations. Rather than seeking to establish a robust institutional structure, the new leadership team purposefully sought to participate

[47] Bosch, 501.

in the wider Bible translation movement. It wouldn't take long for WBTI to experience the joy of witnessing the energy and dynamism of this movement's 'ability to excite and enlist others as leaders and participants.'[48]

Built on the sturdy foundations of the International Administration under John Watters's leadership, the WBTI of 2008 benefitted from his well-organized creation of a road map to implement Vision 2025 after diligently counting the cost. People, systems, and finances from WBTI's large headquarters in Dallas accomplished this, and under their Vision 2025 Business Plan, they costed out the remaining task. As was typical of most business and Christian organizations in the previous era, their use of terms like workforce indicated that human resources were viewed and quantified more or less as commodities. Operating as an institution, they could implement institutional decisions, strategies, and structures to support what they believed God was calling them to do. And although structured very differently from the beginning, SIL International and WBTI were confident they could function effectively as a joint administration, for the benefit of all, without harming WBTI's future.

While this was happening, another development was gaining momentum when, at their November 2003 meeting, the WBTI Board adopted its commitment to engage with the church of the Global South and East (or the majority world). Though they could not have fully realized what they set in motion, from that time, much of the board's focus shifted to creating the organizational environment, framework, and structure for WBTI to thrive in pursuing this vision.

It is interesting that as the WBTI Board developed this vision, it faced constant scrutiny from its SIL counterparts. Little wonder, given the intertwined foundational relationship between the two organizations. Misunderstandings were easy to come by. It took grace and patience for all concerned in both organizations to allow WBTI to proceed into the, at times, murky future. As it continued its journey, it increasingly relied on the emergence of a slowly developing missiological foundation, which was also new territory. There were no road maps.

Perhaps a telling example occurred when I, Kirk Franklin, attended a weeklong course taught by missiologist Wilbur Shenk at Overseas Mission Study Center in April 2007. The topic was on Christendom and Empires, and I was there as part of a sabbatical, preparing to become Executive Director. After meeting me, Dr Shenk wanted to know why, as incoming Executive Director, I was attending a missiological conference. He said it was his first encounter with anyone from Wycliffe 'showing interest in the relevancy of missiology to a mission organization.' His words have never left me.

We pay tribute to those who served on the WBTI Board during the transition

48 Alan Hirsch, *The Forgotten Ways* (Grand Rapids: Brazos Press, 2006), 193.

years, and especially the two Chairs—Dick Hugoniot and Roger Welch, who steered the board when it often didn't know for sure where its decisions were taking it. Likewise, we pay tribute to John Watters, who, at the end of his tenure as Executive Director, oversaw the dismantling of what had been his legacy. He did this by splitting the joint WBTI and SIL Executive Director roles, which took grace and courage on his part. Supporting him was the SIL Board, with Carolyn Miller as Chair and Darryl Kernick as Associate Executive Director for Wycliffe Operations. We pay thankful tribute to these co-workers in Christ who supported what WBTI felt it needed to become, even though at the time, what the outcome would look like was uncertain.

Looking back provides perspectives that aren't obvious when they are taking place. We close with this insight from co-author Susan Van Wynen:

> We can become trapped in our structures and committed to what we think is necessary, so even when we can see God pointing elsewhere, we either knowingly or unknowingly lug those things behind us, which slows us down, or we push those things in front of us, which blocks our vision. It is a reminder to journey into the future as unencumbered as possible, to constantly reconsider what truly matters, with a willingness to let go of what doesn't.

Leadership Theories and Practices

During the era covered in this chapter, dimensions and types of leadership received further research and development by various scholars. Some work focussed on differentiating between leadership and management as 'two distinctive and complimentary systems of action' and 'both are necessary for the success in an increasingly complex and volatile environment.'[49] 'Management is about coping with complexity.... Leadership, by contrast, is about coping with change.'[50] C. Otto Scharmer stated that 'While management is about getting things done, leadership is about creating and cultivating the larger context—the fertile common ground and soil—in which things can happen.... The primary job of leadership... is to enhance the individual and systemic capacity to see, to deeply attend to the reality that people face and enact.'[51]

Craig Johnson in his book *Meeting the Ethical Challenges of Leadership* distinguished between leadership styles that are ethical and those that are unethical

[49] John Kotter, "What Leaders Really Do," in *Leadership: Understanding the Dynamics of Power and Infuence in Organizations*, ed. Robert Vecchio (Notre Dame: University of Notre Dame Press, 1997), 24.

[50] Kotter, in *Leadership: Understanding the Dynamics of Power and Infuence in Organizations*, 25.

[51] C. Otto Scharmer, *Theory U: Leading from the Future as It Emerges* (San Francisco: Berrett-Koehler Publications, 2009).

and the ensuing implications for the culture and performance of the organization affected. 'Good leaders... cast a *light* on the organization and "illuminate the lives of followers" and thus motivate the organization to both high performance and good stewardship. Unethical or negative leaders cast a *shadow* upon employees that covers them in darkness. A major ethical challenge of leadership is to avoid the temptations of wealth, power, and status that may lead to compromising one's values and casting a leadership shadow.'[52] Another example was the concept of Level 5 leaders by Jim Collins in his book *Good to Great in the Social Sectors* (2006). Such leaders are ambitious first and foremost for the cause, the organization, the work—not themselves—and they have the fierce resolve to do whatever it takes to make good on that ambition. A Level 5 leader displays a paradoxical blend of personal humility and professional will.

Timothy Laniak in his book *Shepherds After My Own Heart* describes another form of leadership influence, basing it on study of the Bible.[53] He describes Shepherd Leaders as compassionately using diverse skills and techniques according to the necessities of the context. The shepherd is one of the primary metaphors by which biblical authors conceptualized leadership. In Far Eastern animal husbandry, the role of the shepherd is to protect, provide, and guide. It follows that the role of pastor is based on being a 'shepherd of God's flock' (1 Peter 5:2). Like a shepherd, the leader has a variety of responsibilities. This style is a compassionate use of authority through a diverse and changing role because the responsibilities are constantly reassessed by the changing needs of the group in the leader's care.

The increasing complexities across the globe were creating contexts where rapid and adaptive innovation was becoming the key to survival for organizations. Theorists such as Donde Ashmos Plowman[54] and Mary Uhl-Bien[55] focussed on Complexity Leadership Theory which has these characteristics: it disrupts the organization's status quo by introducing uncertainty and by visibly addressing conflict; emphasizes inspiring others to solve problems and innovate; it manages words instead of managing people; and knows how to solve problems, learn in the process, and foster creative change. It is not just the act of an influential individual but is rooted in a multifaceted relationship that enables the use of intellectual assets through a network of distributed intelligence instead of relying on the limited intelligence of a few people in top-level leadership positions.

---

[52] Charles Tharp, "Book Review of Meeting the Ethical Challenges of Leadership," *Human Resource Management* 41, no. 4 (2002): 501-02.

[53] Timothy Laniak, *Shepherds after My Own Heart: Pastoral Traditions and Leadership in the Bible* (Downers Grove: InterVarsity Press, 2006).

[54] Donde Ashmos Plowman et al., "The Role of Leadership in Emergent, Self-Organization," *The Leadership Quarterly* 18, no. 4 (2007).

[55] Mary Uhl-Bien, Russ Marion, and Bill McKelvey, "Complexity Leadership Theory: Shifting Leadership from the Industrial Age to the Knowledge Era," *The Leadership Quarterly* 18, no. 4 (2007).

WBTI indirectly benefited from the development of and research into these leadership theories. WBTI's leaders were aware of some of the newer theories. For example, Franklin met Tim Laniak in 2008 and used some of his insights into Shepherd Leadership in WBTI's Leaders Moving Forward program. This included insights into the spiritual dimension of leadership. In general, WBTI was becoming aware of the responsibilities of leading in complex times. Concepts around Complexity Leadership Theory would shape WBTI's leadership team as they realized that while none of them had all the necessary solutions, working together and collaborating as a learning community would provide insights. The ethical demands of leadership were also taking root within WBTI, at times driven by individual WMOs' ethical challenges over the use of funds, personnel, or even the integrity of their leaders.

Journey Reflections (We've Never Been This Way Before)

For decades leaders in the corporate world, and in ministry contexts as well, have created structures and strategies designed to exercise control over their environments. It is considered part of being accountable, responsible, even visionary. Detailed plans mapping out the future 10 or 25 years in advance symbolized good leadership. But how do you draw a map of a place you've never been?

WBTI was entering uncharted territory, with terrain both unfamiliar and unexplored. At such points in a journey, it is essential to review your resources and to take a new look at your traveling companions. You may not know what the future holds, but you probably have some idea of who and what will help make the most of the journey. During the years tracked in this chapter, WBTI sought to discern how God was leading and to prepare themselves for the road ahead even as they were already on the move. This included leaving much behind, re-equipping for a different sort of journey, not meeting the expectations of some, and far exceeding the expectations of others. The expectation, or accountability, that matters most, however, is that of obedience. It is not as heavy a burden as some may think because the leader who obeys the call of God can rest in knowing the path ahead will be made clear, and the journey will end well.

Accountability to God and willingness to follow his lead require acknowledging that you aren't in control, but that you do lead through influence under his direction.

› What systems and/or structures did you observe changing in this chapter?
› What systems and/or structures are actually hindering your journey?
› What are some of the qualities of a missional leader?

Chapter 6
Birthing: 2011–2015

Introduction

As we move from the first decade of the 21st century, it is worth noting terminology used to describe the worldwide church. Two terms had become interchangeable: 'global Christianity'[1] and 'world Christianity'.[2] These expressions had gained significance in the lead up to the centenary of the Edinburgh 1910 World Missionary Conference and in sources like the *World Christian Encyclopaedia*. There were several ways to interpret what these terms meant. One is the evolving demographic of the church worldwide. As Lalsangkima Pachuau describes it, 'the majority of the world's Christians are now living on continents that were considered to be essentially non-Christian throughout most of the nineteenth century.'[3] This demographic shift was decades in the making and referred to in various ways, such as the church of the southern continent, the church of the South and East, or the church of the non-Western world. Pachuau preferred a 'more positive term': the church of the 'majority world'.[4]

A second interpretation is theological. In general, Christians across the globe share much in common such as worshipping the same triune God, serving the same Jesus Christ, being led by the same Holy Spirit, and drawing direction from the same Old and New Testaments. However, Douglas Jacobsen notes how global Christianity doesn't have an 'easily defined orthodoxy' or a 'geographic center, and no one authoritative leader'. [5] Instead, there is enormous variety, offering insights to participants of the Christian movement worldwide as they discover what has changed, including how the 'inherited language of Christianity, steeped in the Western cultural tradition' doesn't adequately describe 'the beliefs, values, practices, and affections of the global Christian community'.[6] From the global church emerge 'new voices... waiting to be heard, and fresh formulations of Christian

---

[1] Douglas Jacobsen, *Global Gospel: An Introduction to Christianity on Five Continents* (Grand Rapids: Baker Academic, 2015), ix-x.

[2] Lalsangkima Pachuau, *World Christianity: A Historical and Theological Introduction* (Nashville: Abingdon Press, 2018).

[3] Pachuau, 3.

[4] Pachuau, 5.

[5] Jacobsen, xv.

[6] Jacobsen, xv.

faith and life are ready to be uncovered.'[7]

Another way of interpreting the characteristic of global Christianity is its 'essential nature' of incarnating itself 'in any context to transform such contexts for the knowledge and likeness of God in Christ'.[8] When considering the Bible in the multitude of languages represented in world Christianity, this becomes evident. Global Christianity makes Bible translation in any language and culture essential. Lamin Sanneh refers to this as the Bible's 'translatability'. Without Bible translation the emerging global church is 'unrecognizable or unsustainable'.[9] God speaks in any vernacular, which is why out of all religions, the Christian faith, according to Kwame Bediako, is 'the most culturally translatable'.[10] The Christian faith can find its home in any and every culture and language. Bible translation has been a significant contributor to the phenomenon of global Christianity.

Reflecting on the early years of WBT, when its first recruits went to Mexico in the 1940s, reveals another factor of world Christianity. Few US churches were aware of the need for Bible translation among ethnic groups. Even fewer churches in Mexico were willing to participate in Bible translation among their ethnic groups. Beyond doubt, now 75 years later, global Christianity looks remarkably different. Christians, and their churches in the countries where Bible translation is underway or yet to begin, are increasingly involved in the movement, and in many contexts are the leaders, owners, and managers of this ministry. The remaining Bible translation needs are not, and never have been, solely Wycliffe's responsibility, but that of the global church, which calls for encouragement and support in its interest, involvement, and ownership of the Bible translation movement. As we will see, this factor significantly influences the reshaping of the next phase of Wycliffe Bible Translators International's development.

New Name

WBTI formed in 1980, adding 'International' to Wycliffe Bible Translators, Inc., thus differentiating the purpose and function of the international headquarters and its operations from the growing number of independent Wycliffe Divisions (later called Wycliffe Organizations) emerging around the world. The challenge facing the WBTI leadership team during 2009–2010 was attempting to define and describe the organizational make-up of WBTI. Ever since the Global Leaders Meeting of 2006, the word 'alliance' had been floating around leadership circles for consideration as

---

7 Jacobsen, xvi.

8 Pachuau, 3.

9 Lamin Sanneh, *Whose Religion Is Christianity? The Gospel Beyond the West* (Grand Rapids: Wm. B. Eerdmans, 2003), 97.

10 Bediako, 32.

an appropriate structural concept for WBTI. By late 2010, Executive Director Kirk Franklin suggested to the WBTI Board that a more accurate description for the organization was the 'Wycliffe International Global Alliance'. Franklin acknowledged the time had come for a formal name change to reflect what WBTI was becoming. The leadership sought transformation by addressing new realities in the global church. Franklin believed changing the name could do this because it signalled internally and externally that WBTI understood its global context.

At its November 2010 meeting, the WBTI Board approved changing WBTI's 'doing business as' name to Wycliffe Global Alliance and could include the tag line 'Partners in Bible Translation'. Because of its incorporation in Texas and registration in Singapore, the legal advice was to keep 'Wycliffe Bible Translators International' as the official registered name.

Until this time, the word 'international' in a mission organization's name was commonly associated with a headquarters in the US or UK with affiliated offices farther away but operations predominantly Western run or based. By contrast, WBTI's small primary office had located in Singapore, and its 15-person leadership team, originating from 10 nations, was located across the globe. WBTI had grown into an alliance of 105+ organizations with formal relationships and agreements, 45 of which carried the Wycliffe name in some form, recognizing Wycliffe's role in their beginnings. Most of the other 60+ organizations began because of local or national mission movements. These partner organizations had adopted Wycliffe's aims and therefore sought closer identification with WBTI. Changing the name would be the next obvious step.

The new name of Wycliffe Global Alliance went public on 1 February 2011, and to affirm a global perspective, was translated into these languages: Spanish (Alianza Global Wycliffe), Portuguese (Aliança Global Wycliffe), and French (Alliance Wycliffe Mondiale). Because organization names are often reduced to acronyms, and these would be different in other languages, when requiring brevity, the leadership referred to 'the Alliance'. However, for the purposes of brevity in this book, we often use 'WGA'.

Rolling out the new name happened quickly. The name change provided the opportunity to explain the numerous adaptations and alterations in the organization to both internal and external audiences. Other mission agencies were intrigued by the change and what it represented. The Alliance leadership described the deliberate use of terms chosen:

› *Wycliffe*: Input from stakeholders across most of the world emphasized the value of the Wycliffe name and reputation. In many people's minds, the name was linked, often instantly, with Bible translation for minority language communities. Keeping the Wycliffe name was crucial because of its recognition.

- *Global*: The focus was the entire world, not limited to being provincial in scope, transcending national borders, and bringing together a worldwide commonality. It was a bold indicator that this had become a global movement and was no longer an international institution tied to headquarters in historic centres of mission influence such as the US or UK.
- *Alliance*: The word means entering an agreement (usually formal) between two or more parties, made to advance common goals and secure common interests, and represented the heart of the organization's emerging structure. All organizations, churches, and movements wanting to be part of the Alliance would enter into a formal relationship with each other for their common good.
- *Tagline*: To address concerns about dropping 'Bible Translators' from this new name, the tagline 'Partners in Bible Translation' initiated a few years earlier would continue to be acceptable for use when necessary.

While choosing these key words in the new name was important, other realities affecting the Bible translation movement also influenced the decision, including the rapidly changing social, political, cultural, economic, and religious environments across the globe. Missiological research and discussions among academics and practitioners were gaining momentum and offering new perspectives. By paying attention to these perspectives, the Alliance entered into discoveries and new understandings, particularly observing the growth of the global church and theological reflection and development in Africa, Asia, and the Americas. The global church was changing and becoming more diverse, necessitating the holistic development of people and communities as a more significant part of the Alliance's thinking and actions. Bible translation facilitated transformational development of language communities confronting issues of spiritual and physical hunger, poverty, injustice, poor health services, environmental degradation, inadequate drinking water, while supporting quality education, reduction of infant-child mortality, and the prevention of the spread of HIV/AIDS, malaria, and other diseases.

Remembering John Bendor-Samuel

On 6 January 2011, long-time Wycliffe leader John Bendor-Samuel died from injuries from an auto accident near his home in Studley Green not far from the Wycliffe UK Centre. Bendor-Samuel held several leadership roles within Wycliffe, including Wycliffe UK Director, WBTI Executive Vice President, and until 2007, Wycliffe Africa Area Director. He was influential in the founding of several NBTOs in Africa (see chapter 8). At the May board meeting, the WBTI Board and SIL Board paid respect to Bendor-Samuel, also honouring his wife Pam, in appreciation for their years of dedicated and faithful service. SIL President John Watters led the boards in a reflection on the life of Bendor-Samuel.

First CFO

As WBTI gained greater autonomy from SIL in its leadership, it still shared a Chief Financial Officer (CFO) with SIL. The opportunity arose in 2010 for WBTI to have its own CFO, based at its Singapore operational headquarters. With the support of the current CFO and the board treasurer, Ah Chye Wong accepted the position.

The Alliance Board regularly examined the Alliance's financial position. At its May 2011 meeting, the CFO reported on the Alliance's good state of financial health and its adequate operating reserves and encouraged the leadership team to draw on these funds to cover any operation budget shortfalls. In their annual management letter about the organization's fiscal situation, the external auditors had no reason to raise concerns. New CFO Wong, working out of the Alliance's Singapore office, recognized the opportunities and challenges in learning US accounting. These included the complex system that integrated with SIL's finance operations at their Dallas headquarters and the geographical distance between the two. However, the audit report demonstrated progress.

First Steps to Structural Changes

The Alliance's name change set the stage for a new organizational structure inclusive for all organizations that had formal membership in WBTI and now the Alliance, as well as newer ones that filled the APO category, existing since May 2001. However, this category presented confusion for some organizations in the Alliance, and the leadership team wasn't always sure how to describe or deal with it either. Therefore, a decade later, at its May 2011 meeting, the board decided that this category, having served its purpose in its time, was no longer needed. Franklin also wanted the category of Wycliffe Member Organization with Language Programs changed. The title was too long and clumsy, often abbreviated as WMO with LP, and it set organizations in that category apart from others in the Alliance. Another intention was for Wycliffe Partner Organizations (WPOs) to feel at home in the Alliance. The broader goal for the Alliance concerned the eight different organizational membership categories. Franklin and the leadership team wanted a reduction to one category for all organizations. These would be called Participating Organizations (PO) and would include the WMOs with the original 'Wycliffe DNA' and the WPOs with a more 'diverse DNA' but still committed to the Bible translation vision. Agreements would express in detail the commitment of each PO.

Participation Streams

At the heart of necessary alterations was defining how current and future organizations participated in the Alliance. Franklin and the leadership team proposed describing this through Participation Streams as the criteria of activities an organization desiring to partner within the Alliance would fulfil. It was unlikely or unnecessary that an organization would engage in all seven Streams, but it was essential to participate in at least one of the following: Church engagement for the Bible translation movement; Prayer for the Bible translation movement; Fund raising for the Bible translation movement; Recruitment of people for the Bible translation movement; Recruiting and sending people to the Bible translation movement; Training in technical Bible translation roles, and/or Language program management in the Bible translation movement; and Specialty services.

An early observation of these Streams showed 30 of the Participating Organizations supervised Bible translation programs, notably more than when WBTI reorganized in 2008 when only 18 organizations managed Bible translation programs in their countries. Time would tell if this were a trend, with WGA taking a more significant role in leading and managing Bible translation, and if it would outpace its earlier purpose of providing resources for SIL.

Financing the Alliance

WGA required a reliable source of income to operate and to serve all its Participating Organizations. Up until this time, the 45 WMOs provided nearly half of the funding through their annual 0.35% contribution of their total income, though at times, meeting this contribution was problematic for them. For example, at the May 2012 board meeting, the Wycliffe US leadership informed the board about why it had missed two of its payments. The organization made its 0.35% contribution monthly from project funds. However, it had been experiencing an economic downturn that was affecting financial gifts for its projects. In the end, this was short-term and didn't affect future contributions. What's more, it alerted the Alliance Board and leadership of the challenges for some WMOs in fulfilling their financial obligations to the Alliance.

By contrast, at that time, the 50+ WPOs did not have to make financial contributions to WGA but would require attention if the WGA was to move toward a single membership category. All the organizations would contribute as equally as possible. But what criteria should be used? Among these organizations were church denominations and mission agencies, with Bible translation only a small part of a more extensive ministry. The same annual contribution of 0.35% of their total income couldn't be expected of them. Two possible approaches to establishing an appropriate fee structure for WPOs' contributions to the Alliance: (1) a fee based on the size of the organization and its contribution to the Bible translation movement through the Alliance. The greater the contribution (people, prayer, and funds), the higher the fee. The fee could start from US$100 per annum to a maximum of US$2,500 per annum; or (2) a fee based on geographical location. WPOs located in the North and West would pay more than those in the Global South and East. The fee for those in the North and West could be US$2,500 per annum and US$100 per annum for organizations in the rest of the world. While this would necessitate further discussion with the organizations over the next year, the overall topic of fees and the 0.35% contribution would frame an ongoing discussion and debate within the Alliance for the next decade.

The composition of the Alliance board reflected another area of the emerging Alliance structure, until this time based on two groups:

› Five board members represented the Christian constituencies of the five geographical regions of the Alliance (Americas, Asia, Pacific, Europe, and Africa).
› Five board members were CEOs of Wycliffe Member Organizations. One of these was the CEO of Wycliffe US, and one was the CEO of a WMO with Language Programs.

The proposed new board structure, using the Participation Streams as a basis:

› Three CEOs of WMOs that meet at least three of the Participation Streams. These three are chosen by the WMOs and granted voting rights by the board.
› One CEO of a WPO that meets at least three of the Participation Streams. This person will be chosen by the WMOs that have been granted voting rights by the board.
› The CEO of the Participating Organization that was the largest contributor to the Alliance. After considerable input, this was revised to 'The CEO of the founding organization, Wycliffe Bible Translators Inc. (Wycliffe US).'
› Five representatives of the Christian constituencies of the Alliance Areas to be chosen through a process led by the respective Area Director that involved the POs in that region.[11]

Managing a Change Process

Holding the organization firmly to its vision and values describes a significant responsibility of the Alliance Board. Intent on developing a structure to encourage and enable the Participating Organizations to contribute meaningfully to the future

[11] WBTI, "Board Minutes," November 2011, 10.

of the Alliance, the board's role required further thought, including possible reshaping of the Vision, Mission, and Core Values. The board could handle minor adjustments, but major adjustments could significantly alter the organization's direction. In the past, when making changes to core statements, the leadership and board processed them with the WMOs before a final decision. Accordingly, the board pursued a process enabling Alliance organizations to provide input to revisions.

Bylaws represented the highest level of policies. While responsible for keeping these up to date, on closer examination, the board realized the bylaws required significant reworking to reflect what the Alliance was becoming. Changes would not be straightforward as it involved the 29 WMOs with Vote to approve such actions, and they would first need to understand the reason for the alterations.

Substantial work occurred over the next 12 months, resulting in all revisions made to the bylaws by the May 2012 Wycliffe International Convention, including the move to a single Participating Organizations membership category, adoption of the Participation Streams, modifications to the board structure, and adaptations of the Convention's purpose and structure. A process of reviewing and re-writing the bylaws took place from May to September and involved some members of the board, the board secretary, and the executive director. The aim was to ensure that the policies reflected current direction and practice. The board approved the new bylaws by an email vote in September 2011. A referendum of the revised bylaws was promptly sent to the WMOs with Vote, who had until the end of February 2012 to approve them, which they did.

The Alliance Board primarily related to the WMO boards, thus encouraging each WMO to have their boards engage in revisions and decision-making processes. The executive director produced a video about these new directions for the Alliance, which circulated to the WMOs in late 2011. The executive director also travelled for face-to-face visits to explain the changes to WMO leaders, boards, and leaders of the WPOs. This involved a cross-section of organizations, including BTL Kenya, Wycliffe Singapore, and Wycliffe New Zealand. These interactions provided invaluable perspectives to further refine the proposed revisions.

A meeting with a dozen European WMO leaders and Area staff took place for two days in September 2011 in Frankfurt, Germany, to present the proposal and particularly to go through the revised bylaws. Alliance Board Chair Roger Welch and Executive Director Kirk Franklin hosted the meeting. The European leaders thoroughly engaged with all that was proposed, introduced other questions during the consultation, and indicated their appreciation for the chair's willingness to make time for the topics they wanted to talk about. This process worked well because when other WMO and WPO leaders heard of the thoroughness of the European leaders, they felt that all general concerns had been addressed, which was the case.

Reappointments and New Appointments

Reviewing the executive director's performance, it pleased the board to reappoint Franklin to the role for a second four-year term starting at the 2012 International Convention. A total of two four-year terms is the maximum the board's policy allowed, based on the previous policy jointly held with SIL. By its November 2011 meeting, concerned that the well-intended policy was now out of date, the WGA Board discussed the pros and cons of the eight-year limit and ways of adding flexibility that would permit the board to exercise its discretion in increasing the term if appropriate.

Its revised policy stated:

> The board appoints the executive director upon nomination by the chair. The appointment is for a maximum of four years at a time and normally for a maximum of eight consecutive years. The board may, at its discretion, reappoint the executive director beyond eight years if it deems it appropriate to do so and with the agreement of the executive director.[12]

Darryl Kernick was appointed for two more years as board secretary until the end of 2014. Bambang Widjaja of Indonesia was appointed to the board of directors, filling the role of Asian representative left empty by Luis Pantoja of the Philippines, whose sudden passing in 2010 had saddened all who knew him.

Relationship with SIL

Though the separation of the administrations of SIL and WBTI was now nearly three years past, the two boards continued to meet together twice a year, sometimes in joint sessions. During those times, the WBTI Board Chair sought input from the SIL Board on some of the vision and direction of WBTI, now the Alliance. For example, in the November 2011 meeting, the two boards discussed a 'Unity of Purpose Statement with SIL' that appeared in the WBTI policies since before the separation. Two sections of the policy discussed in particular stated how WBTI showed its partnership with SIL through 'unqualified support of SIL's Purpose, Values, and Ends' and 'unconditional commitment to work together with SIL, respecting SIL's distinct roles and contributions'.[13] The challenge before the two boards was to consider removing the words 'unqualified' and 'unconditional' because these were not the expressions of equal partnerships but reflected a previous paradigm of WBTI existing solely for SIL's purposes. As a result of this discussion, the WBTI Board revised this statement to read:

---

12 WBTI, "Board Minutes," May 2012, 3.

13 WBTI, "Board Extracts," April 2005, 1.

WBTI shares a unity of purpose with SIL, as demonstrated by:

- shared vision, resources, and beneficiaries.
- commitment to work together with SIL, respecting SIL's Purpose, Values, and Ends along with its distinct roles and contributions.
- a desire for the good and success of SIL.[14]

In summary, the changes made were minor in appearance but significant in practice and acknowledged the time had come to reflect the maturing relationship more accurately between the two organizations. Regarding its partnership with SIL, WBTI/the Alliance did not intend to provide unqualified or unconditional support but rather a continued commitment to work together with SIL.

Wellbeing of the Leadership Team

After four years as executive director, Franklin and the Alliance Board discussed the high demands of the leadership role, including frequent international travel and working virtually. These factors required careful management of both time and energy to ensure effective leadership over the long term, regardless of who served as executive director. The board was responsible for the leader's well-being, ensuring that person took the necessary intervals of leave from the role, including vacations, sabbaticals, and study leave. Likewise, the board instructed the executive director to make sure the Alliance leadership team received appropriate leave times. Establishing these safeguards would protect the long-term wellbeing and success of the leaders and the leadership team. As a result, Franklin planned to take a three-month sabbatical from February to April 2012. The other senior leaders, Min-Young Jung, Susan Van Wynen, and Dave Brooks, planned to do the same later in 2012 and 2013. This process of granting sabbatical leave for senior leaders was noted with interest by other mission agencies, viewing it as a sign of a healthy organization to encourage this to take place.

Divine Familial Terms Debate

Throughout the history of vernacular Bible versions, translation teams have encountered critically challenging issues of selecting the words that best express the intent, concepts, and content of the essential doctrines of the Christian faith. Since the Alliance worked in close partnership with SIL and other translation cooperatives, it was only natural that the Alliance would get drawn into theological debates around this particular issue, even though it did not have any direct activity in the translations that might be in question. It was not possible to simply withdraw from such a debate.

[14] WBTI, "Board Minutes," November 2011, 4.

In early 2012, the Alliance was quickly embroiled in an international debate over the issue of translation of divine familial terms—such as 'God the Father' and the 'Son of God'—in Bible translations for Muslim audiences. It became a missiological and theological issue of concern to some, with no straightforward solution at the time. This escalated to debates in the US, UK, the Netherlands, and Canada that began to affect the reputation of the Wycliffe organizations in those countries.[15] By February 2012, with no sign the issue was subsiding, the Alliance presented a twofold response. First, Franklin reached out to the leadership of the World Evangelical Alliance (WEA) to see if they could assist, and the WEA set up a theological study committee that eventually made recommendations on how to address this issue. And second, publicly, the Alliance made it clear that the Bible should not be translated in a way that would remove any message of Scripture that would cause an 'inaccurate, unclear translation that would mislead and result in needless offense or erroneous conclusions'.[16] Since Franklin had already planned on starting his sabbatical that month, his senior leadership team assured him that they had the Alliance's involvement in the crisis under control, which they did.

At the Lausanne Movement's Global Leadership Forum held in Bangalore in 2013, Franklin had many friendly encounters with church and mission leaders interested in the Divine Familial Terms debate. They were pleased to see how WEA lent its help, and all were hopeful that the Alliance and SIL could emerge from this without too much damage to their involvement in Bible translation. Franklin met two of the WEA panel members, as well as the heads of the WEA Theological Commission and Mission Commission, who were instrumental in assembling the panel. It became clear to him through these discussions that the partnership with WEA was quite unprecedented in the mission world. Few people could think of another time when this level of involvement had ever taken place by theologians and missiologists that WEA called together. It could describe a model of how WEA could serve the wider church and mission community in the future.

After the WEA's panel had completed its work, the Alliance Board, on behalf of the entire Alliance community, expressed appreciation for how the panel thoughtfully and conscientiously conducted the review of Divine Familial Terms best practices.

Look What God is Doing!

The most significant event for the Alliance in 2012, the Global Gathering, took place at the same time and location as SIL International's Conference. The

[15] It is beyond the scope of this chapter to go into details about the debate.

[16] Wycliffe Global Alliance Statement on Divine Familial Terms, 2011.

combined and jointly planned event called 'Look2012' was based on what God was doing around the world and, in the Alliance's case, through the Bible translation movement.

From International Convention to Global Gathering

A year before the Alliance's 2012 International Convention, the board decided to change the name to 'Wycliffe Global Gathering'. The name 'International Convention', in use for 20 years, carried historic associations of WBTI mirroring SIL's International Conference. For the newer Alliance organizations, that history was not even part of their experience. As the Alliance continued to develop and gain momentum, it was time for this event to have a new name. The purpose of the Global Gathering was to:

› celebrate what God is doing through the Participating Organizations on behalf of the language communities.
› provide a place to identify current and emerging opportunities for resourcing Bible translation movements among every people.
› enhance and coordinate communication between Participating Organizations.
› energize the participants with updates of progress toward WGA's vision.
› to offer a space to discuss missiological factors pertinent to the vision.
› present an opportunity to interact with SIL because of co-location with SIL's International Conference.
› give opportunity for input relating to the vision, mission, goals, and objectives of the WGA Board and leadership team.

Composition of Gathering Attendees

The board based the invitations for the Global Gathering on these criteria:

› The CEO (or equivalent) of each Participating Organization fulfilling a total of 3–7 Participation Streams.
› The chairman of the board of each Participating Organization fulfilling a total of 3–7 Participation Streams, providing that the organization had Bible translation (includes resourcing, managing, or both) as its primary function.
› A delegation representing Participating Organizations involved in 1–2 Participation Streams. The Alliance Area Directors worked with the executive director to determine which of these representatives to invite, based on the availability of Alliance funds to subsidize travel and accommodation costs.

Organizations represented through these criteria were:

- *WMOs:* ACATBA (CAR), ALEM (Brazil), ANTBA (Burkina Faso), ATALTRAB (Chad), Wycliffe Austria, Wycliffe Australia, Wycliffe Benin, BTA (PNG), BTL (Kenya), CABTAL (Cameroon), Wycliffe Canada, Wycliffe Caribbean, Wycliffe Czech Republic, Wycliffe Denmark, Wycliffe Finland, Folk & Språk (Sweden), Wycliffe France, Wycliffe Germany, GILLBT (Ghana), GBT (South Korea), Wycliffe Hong Kong, Wycliffe Hungary, Wycliffe India, Wycliffe Japan, Kartidaya (Indonesia), Wycliffe Malaysia, Wycliffe Netherlands, Wycliffe New Zealand, Wycliffe Norway, Wycliffe Philippines, Wycliffe Poland, PROEL (Spain), Wycliffe Singapore, Wycliffe South Africa, Wycliffe Romania, Wycliffe Russia, Wycliffe Slovakia, Wycliffe Switzerland, Wycliffe Taiwan, TAP (Philippines), Wycliffe Thailand, Wycliffe Togo, Wycliffe UK, Wycliffe US, and Wycliffe Ukraine.
- *WPOs:* ACOTBA-SUBO (DRC), AEL (Peru), Aramaic Bible Translation, Bridge to the World (Argentina), CET (Bolivia), CNBM (Mexico), COMIBAM, DOOR (US), ECS-TD (Sudan), ECEMY (Ethiopia), FEDEMEC (Costa Rica), GIDI (Indonesia), GMIM (Indonesia), GPID (Indonesia), GPM (Indonesia), Horizontes (Brazil), AITB (Italy), LAMM (Mexico), LETRA (Chile), LETRA (Paraguay), MissionAssist (UK), OM Sonora (Mexico), OneBook (Canada), PAAM (Panama), SIETE (Venezuela), TRES (El Salvador), UNTI (Mexico), Wycliffe Associates (US), YAJASI (Indonesia), YBI (Indonesia), YMP3 (Indonesia), YPA (Indonesia), and YPSA (Indonesia).

The board's convention travel fund covered air travel for these delegates, and when necessary, subsidized accommodation and meals. This first Global Gathering took place in Chiang Mai, Thailand, from May 3 to 9. Two hundred and twenty people from 67 nations participated. The Global Gathering included the Alliance Board; GLT; Area Staff from the Americas, Africa, Asia-Pacific, and Europe; and invited guests of SIL International. Combined with the SIL International Conference delegation, this encompassed communication, prayer, music, facilitation, event coordination teams, and a small security team, bringing the total number of attendees to over 450.

Executive Director's Challenge

Executive Director Kirk Franklin set the tone for the Global Gathering in two presentations on the first day. In his first presentation, with the SIL International Conference participants present, he captured the theme of Look2012—'Look what God is doing!' Franklin drew from Genesis 15:5 when God told Abram: 'Look up (look at, gaze, consider) at the heavens and count the stars.' Abram was to raise his sights higher to see and understand what God was revealing to him. The challenge to the Alliance's leaders was to courageously look up to God as they considered the changes taking place because of the complexities of contexts where God's mission was unfolding. In another example, from Genesis 22:8, Franklin used God's provision of a lamb for Abraham to sacrifice instead of his son Isaac. Abraham states: 'God will provide for himself the lamb…', meaning to look out for, to see to it, to provide. Abraham called that place *Jehovah Jireh* (v. 14), 'the Lord Will Provide'. The challenge to Alliance leaders was to look up to God, trusting that he looks out for and makes provision for his people.

With these insights as a foundation, Franklin gave an overview of the exciting journey of WBTI from its early beginnings and the shaping of the organization. Over time, however, the challenge of Vision 2025 and the resulting impact on global missions from the growth of the church in the Global South and East changed the mission's plan forever. WBTI was still a Western mission agency when Vision 2025 was adopted in 1999, with a small constituency of majority world nations. By 2012, 70% of the 100+ organizations that made up the Alliance were from the majority world. This changing demographic was also reflected in 60% of the Alliance Board and 50% of the Alliance leadership team coming from the majority world.

Transitioning from a predominantly Western organization to a global alliance was a deliberate recognition that no one agency owns the Bible translation movement. It was an acknowledgement that all participants in the Alliance were part of the global church. It was a belief that partnership and communion in unity expressed the biblical model for ministry. It was a viewpoint that required the Alliance to look beyond institutional structures and strategies to obey God's call. It was a statement that the future of missions was more likely to be realized in non-centralized, global, diverse, and dynamic organic structures.

Becoming the Wycliffe Global Alliance also brought to light the key role of each Participating Organization in fulfilling Vision 2025. The seven Participation Streams clarified the diversity of ways of being involved. Each organization had prayerfully discerned and identified the Streams that God had for them to fulfill as they sought his provision of resources, capacity, and creativity. Rather than competing to see who could do more, it promoted empowering each organization to make its best contribution to Vision 2025. The Vision 2025 Resolution closed with this statement: 'To this end, we commit ourselves to pray for the fulfillment of this vision, seeking God's guidance, and obeying Him in whatever new directions He may lead.' The challenge and opportunity shaping all Participating Organizations encompassed a commitment to God's purposes for those people groups being served, a compelling urgency for obedience to God and excitement in what he was doing, and a humble boldness as they participated in God's mission.

In a separate session entitled 'My Heart and Vision for the Alliance' held solely for the Alliance delegation, Franklin shared a message that emerged during his recent sabbatical, when he had time to reflect on the past and the future. He concluded his message with a transparent confession of some areas in his life as the leader of the Alliance in which he felt he had failed. These included his relationship with the Lord; times when he had spoken inappropriately about other people; how occasionally he had placed his work above his love for the Lord; how he had relied more on his organization rather than on his God; his weariness from a constant pursuit of working harder and not following a healthy pattern of rest, and thus setting a poor example; and his inclination to covet whatever he thought he had been deprived of by God. Those present easily identified with and personalized these confessed issues and rose to express their appreciation and forgiveness. Later feedback included some leaders stating they had never heard one of their leaders confessing and repenting in this way. It brought encouragement and a personal challenge to them about the need to cultivate their spirituality as they participated in God's mission.

Understanding the Alliance

As the Global Gathering progressed, through brief formal interviews with a panel of Alliance leaders (Roger Welch, Kirk Franklin, and José de Dios, facilitated by Eddie Arthur), followed by table group processing including on-the-spot video recordings of comments and ideas from the table groups, the Participating Organizations were taken on a journey to help give a clear understanding of what WGA was, the way it had developed, and how they could work together to achieve its vision.

Then followed seven five-minute presentations by participants from different parts of the world who spoke to the question: What does the Wycliffe Global Alliance mean to me? The presenters were: Fajak Avajani (ECS-TD, Sudan) Janice Moore (Wycliffe Canada), Marnix Riupassa (Kartidaya, Indonesia), Alex Mathew (Wycliffe India), José Carlos Alcantara (ALEM, Brazil), Decio de Carvalho (COMIBAM), and Helena Engkvist (Folk & Språk, Sweden). Ten-minute presentations followed from Luis Chavez (UNTI, Mexico), Wayne Freeman (Wycliffe New Zealand), and Rachel Narabe Ndjimalta (ATALTRAB, Chad). Their presentations demonstrated that in WGA, they had found the joy of belonging, the freedom to innovate, and the support of other Participating Organizations given during difficult times.

The Alliance Speaks

The short presentations, processed by table groups of six to eight people using flip charts, communicated their ideas to the WGA Board and the GLT. The facilitation team categorized these ideas presented in pictures, words, and diagrams and summarized them in the following four topics:

Leadership: appreciation for the direction WGA was taking; gratitude for the spiritual foundation modelled by the Alliance leaders; appreciation for the example of the humility seen in the GLT; and the challenge to WGA to lead with servanthood and a culture of faithfulness.

Missiological: ensure the missiological reflection foundational to WGA's development be shared with all Alliance organizations; creation of indicators to measure what the WGA valued, such as collaborative partnerships; what it looks like for God to be the centre of who the Participating Organizations were and what they did; and developing a Biblical worldview of funding that results in healthy models and systems of funding.

Complexity: acknowledging that what WGA means to various people and organizations is different; balancing the needs and the potential of newer with older established organizations; bringing clarity to what it means to be a Participating Organization; how does WGA and its organizations effectively partner with SIL; WGA isn't truly global since it doesn't exist in the Arab world; WGA should develop affinity groups or communities of practice in specific areas of the Bible translation movement; and continue to investigate and promote mechanisms for communicating needs for personnel and resources within the Participating Organizations so that they are known internally and externally.

Practical: in order to ensure that WGA lives up to its potential, the leadership needs to engage immediately with the practical realities of the Participating Organizations in their contexts; the Alliance's new name brings the need for new language; new terminology needs clarifying—for example, 'missiology' isn't understood by all of the church; a community response to the current funding crisis; coordination among Participating Organizations especially when there is more than one in a country; assisting WGA organizations develop diaspora ministry; starting dialogues about Human Resources processes; improved communication about personnel needs and recruitment processes; and being careful in placing rigid requirements for sending and placement of personnel upon Participating Organizations that were new to the Alliance.

A ten-minute video captured during table group discussions and viewed by the Global Gathering highlighted special comments and feedback. After this, Franklin and Board Chair Roger Welch responded with their appreciation for the invaluable input. Welch observed, 'the most moving thing about the videos is seeing people from the [majority] world say that they are feeling their value in the movement.'[17] Franklin and Welch agreed the input gave insights for planning to move forward. Relying on the Participating Organizations for their ownership of and involvement in the Alliance, the GLT served as a coordinator of the Participating Organizations' hopes and desires.

Addressing the challenge of mission funding, Franklin and Welch felt it had not been based on a biblical model and required attention. The current funding crises, indicated by a shortfall of funds raised for Bible translation, presented the opportunity to consider and explore a biblical and missiological model of finance. For example, Welch recognized the Alliance had an obligation to 'move away from dependence on a few wealthy and established sending nations including their major donors, toward something more equitable.'[18] Franklin affirmed how the GLT considered 'other funding models, not so much a "fix" but rather a [missiological] reflection on what is biblical.'[19]

The issue of sending and placing people to serve, whether in Participating Organizations or under SIL, was a concern requiring attention. WGA leader José de Dios shared about the difficulties and insensitivity of many current structures to global workers. Ruth Gracie from Wycliffe UK gave insights regarding sending organization perspectives. The two leaders presented issues, including the challenge of searching for jobs on Insite, an internal system shared by SIL and the Alliance. The system's information, often inadequate or outdated, hindered HR staff from finding appropriate matches between people and potential assignments. Staff shortages in Participating Organizations handling personnel complicated the task. There was also the member-care issue of Participating Organizations sending people to other Participating Organizations or to SIL, which also called for attention. Facilitating table discussions, Eddie Arthur invited input as to what could be done better and shared these insights with the whole group. In response, the Alliance leadership intended to focus on these issues in the coming months through a gathering of Alliance HR leaders later in 2012.

Recognizing Board Chairs

A special feature of the Global Gathering was Board Chair Roger Welch's hosting of a dinner for the sixty-five board chairs or representatives of Participating Organization boards in attendance. Several board chairs who had served at least ten years in their roles were recognized and presented with awards. They were Derek

[17] WGA, "Global Gathering Highlights," May 2012, 9.

[18] WGA, May 2012, 9.

[19] WGA, May 2012, 9.

Fivaz, Wycliffe South Africa; Andrew Tay, Wycliffe Singapore; Justin Songnaba, ANTBA (Burkina Faso); Jean Furter, Wycliffe France; Edwyn Kiptinness, BTL (Kenya), and Donat Gruber, Wycliffe Austria.

New Alliance Board

Four directors were elected to the board during the Global Gathering, while constituency members were appointed at the Area level before the event. Representing the founding organization, the Wycliffe US president was automatically seated on the board. The new board serving for the next four years included:

› *Constituency:* John Bennett (New Zealand), representing the Pacific; Ana Cristina Mejía (El Salvador), representing the Americas; Chantal Tehe-Yoa (Côte d'Ivoire), representing Africa; Roger Welch (United Kingdom), representing Europe; and Bambang Widjaja (Indonesia), representing Asia.
› *PO Directors:* Nicky Chong, Wycliffe Singapore; Bob Creson, Wycliffe US; Decio de Carvalho (Puerto Rico), COMIBAM International; Boureima Ouédraogo (Burkina Faso), ANTBA; and Hannes Wiesmann, Wycliffe Switzerland.

Worship and Biblical Teaching

The joint sessions of Look!2012 featured a daily experience of mixed SIL and Alliance table groups, bringing the two organizations together in a spirit of fellowship and sharing. These sessions involved worship through music led by the music team, prayer led by the prayer team, and God's Word led by Lindsay Olesberg from InterVarsity. She skilfully led the 500+ people through a study of 1 John using a discovery-oriented inductive Bible study method to help the participants slow down, centring their full attention on the text. This highly participatory process starts with observation—paying close attention to what the author has said; then understanding the author's message to the original audience; and finally, focussing on application, and being open to transformation by its truth.

Christopher Wright from Langham Partnerships International, presented on three occasions and was deeply appreciated for his biblical knowledge, exposition, and clear instruction. His topics addressed biblical foundations, studies in holistic mission, the church, and global mission. In summary, the starting point is with God and the mission of God, and Ephesians 1:9–10 and Colossians 1:15–20 give the cosmic plan of God for all creation. Three areas characterize our mission: evangelism and teaching (building the church), compassion and justice (serving society), and caring for creation. The Great Commission embraces all three of these areas. It is not as simple as 'go and evangelize', but rather, all the commands are built on the Lordship of Christ, which ultimately impacts individuals, *and* society, *and* creation. Wright considers holistic mission and global mission together, as both are intrinsically biblical. Holistic mission neither represents all the things we do in mission apart from evangelism, nor everything we do in mission including evangelism.

At the culmination of look!2012, SIL Board member Hans Combrink led a communion service with 500+ people celebrating the Lord's Supper together. All the participants lifted their voices to God in praise and prayer, each in his or her mother tongue, a fitting climax to the event.

The Global Gathering began with an emphasis on the centrality of God in our lives and mission. It concluded with the centrality of Christ in His redemptive work that is at the heart of our lives and mission.

Reviewing the Global Gathering

Soon after the event, the WGA Board provided a survey to the participants of the Global Gathering, with questions in English, French, and Spanish. The survey results showed that, in general, the participants were very positive about and satisfied with the Global Gathering.

There were also several issues mentioned requiring careful consideration for future Global Gatherings:

- The ten invited representatives from SIL would benefit from an orientation to the Alliance to better prepare them for participation.
- Event speaker Christopher Wright's contribution could have integrated more intentionally into the purpose and outcomes of the event.
- The French and Spanish speakers could have more effectively engaged in the sessions if communication barriers were better addressed.
- There were difficulties with the Spanish translation, which was not considered an acceptable standard.
- Due to the Alliance's decision-making process during the event, with voting rights given to some but not all organizations, there was awkwardness in the voting sessions when many delegates didn't know whether they had a vote or not.

These issues of language and voting would get further attention in the Alliance's development.

Orientating the New Board

Every four years, at its first meeting following the International Convention—later the Global Gathering—the board presented an orientation program to its new members at a retreat. Accordingly, how the board operated was covered on the first day of its November meeting. Topics included the Alliance's journey, its strategy, the corporate finance system shared with SIL, reflections from current board members, and the board's processes for governance.

Franklin took the opportunity to speak on the topic: The Alliance, Four Years from Now. The greatest influencing factor in how the Alliance understood itself since 2006, the date of WBTI's first missiological consultation (see chapter 8), had been its leaders' missiological awareness concerning the shift to the global church. While this influence and growing understanding slowly spread at the higher levels of leadership, Franklin considered it necessary to permeate the board and all Participating Organizations, as they became missiologically informed, adequately responding to global issues. Furthermore, such a missiological foundation provided a position to understand Vision 2025. It was the right moment for the GLT leadership and WGA board to re-examine and re-evaluate the missiological assumptions and implications of Vision 2025.

Franklin stated that the changing nature of the church becoming global had implications demanding that the Alliance's structure continue to 'evolve to truly be a global alliance of organizations rather than a singular and Western international body.'[20] Based on globalization issues, developing an organizational structure for the Alliance which enabled leadership from the majority world to provide a balancing influence on mission strategy would require further work. While there had been some progress, Alliance leadership was only in the early stages of understanding the implications of the global church. The areas Franklin identified as requiring more attention necessitated that WGA:

- consistently demonstrate transformational leadership through positive role models (especially in situations conditioned by hierarchical leadership models).
- appreciate and support courageous leadership that leads change and builds consensus in complex cross-cultural, multi-cultural, and inter-cultural paradigms.
- place greater priority and more resources in developing younger and new leaders across the globe.
- provide a growing understanding of spiritual, biblical, and missiological fundamentals that will positively impact the leaders and their followers.[21]

---

20 Kirk Franklin, "Wycliffe Global Alliance Board Orientation—the Alliance Four Years from Now," unpublished paper, (2012), 6.

21 Franklin, 6.

Developing Community

In late 2012, the WGA board, executive director, and the senior leadership team reflected on the development of 'body life' within the Alliance. They explored topics about achieving greater community within WGA.

The effects of autonomy: Was the concept of autonomy detrimental to building greater community within WGA? During the transition years following the restructuring of WBTI in 1991, functioning with autonomy was helpful when defining the relationship between WBTI and the newly shaped self-governing organizations that had been Wycliffe Divisions. The situation was different now. Participating Organizations were legally separate and self-reliant as required by their countries and operational needs, but the focus was on working together. This pursuit of interdependence did not necessarily conflict with autonomy since the latter was about the legal structure of the Alliance and the former was about behaviours and relationships among Participating Organizations and WGA as a whole. The preferred term in describing the organizations that now made up the Alliance was 'self-governing' rather than autonomous.

Reducing differences: Should belonging to WGA be more inclusive for all Participating Organizations? Undoubtedly barriers existed, including the different status of the WMOs and WPOs, contributors and non-contributors to WGA finances, and voting rights. Differences in each of these made the people in some Participating Organizations feel marginalized. The board wanted the leadership team to pursue a potential solution, investigating the possibility of Participation Streams being a way of 'determining greater involvement, including voting rights.'[22] This method was already in place and used when selecting someone from the Participating Organizations to serve on the board.

Managing Cultural Polycentrism: 'Polycentrism is defined as having a plurality of independent centres of authority, leadership, power, control, or ideology that may exist within a single political system.'[23] The topic was broad, requiring that the board and GLT conduct ongoing discussions about cultural polycentrism and its effects on the interdependent relationships of organizations within the Alliance. Some examples: Was polycentrism detected in the voices of mid-sized WMOs who considered themselves distinct from smaller WMOs, even those within their region? Did we see it in the Francophone Participating Organizations' expectations for greater support from the Alliance, contrasting with other African organizations? Did it affect how we assist Portuguese-speaking organizations, which were distinct from Spanish-speaking organizations, in Latin America? How

22 WGA, "Board Minutes," November 2012, 12.

23 WGA, November 2012, 12.

will these situations be managed so that WGA continues to be an interdependent community focussed on the Bible translation movement?

Change of Leaders

As 2012 drew to a close, several Alliance leaders were leaving their roles and others were starting in new ones. At its November meeting, the board recognized, thanked, and acknowledged the outgoing and incoming leaders:

- Ah Chye Wong (Singapore) completed two years as the Alliance's CFO and member of the GLT. The board acknowledged 'his significant contribution to the structure and processes of our finance systems which has set a sound foundation for the future CFO.'[24]
- Kee Ai Koh (Singapore), appointed by Franklin to replace Wong as the Alliance CFO, contributed substantially to this role through her knowledge of local accounting regulations in Singapore. Koh also served on the Wycliffe Singapore Board.
- David Cram (US) retired as the Alliance's Treasurer after thirteen years in the role. The board expressed appreciation to Cram and his wife Joan, presenting a plaque and acknowledging 'Dave's keen understanding of corporate finances and of legal issues as well as his thoroughness to detail in his management of WBTI finances.'[25]
- Hannu Summanen (Finland) was appointed as the new Alliance Treasurer, having managed his own accounting firm and served as Wycliffe Finland Board Chair.
- Nydia Garcia-Schmidt (Mexico/US) was appointed by Franklin to be the new Alliance Americas Area Director starting 1 May 2013. She had been Associate Americas Area Director under José de Dios (Guatemala/US), who had accepted the role of Partnership Consultant on the GLT.
- With the board's approval, Franklin created the role of Associate Director of Operations to which he appointed Judy Bokelman (US). This new senior GLT position reduced the number of direct reports to the executive director and placed greater emphasis on the technical and operational aspects of the Alliance.

Refining the Mission Statement

In late 2012, as custodians of the Alliance's purpose and direction, the board began reviewing the organization's mission statement of 'In communion with God and

---

[24] WGA, November 2012, 5.

[25] WGA, November 2012, 6.

with the worldwide church, we contribute to the holistic transformation of all peoples through Bible translation and compassionate services.' They circulated suggested revisions to the Participating Organizations for comment and input. The revised statement based on feedback was: 'In communion with God and within the community of His Church, we encourage and facilitate Bible translation movements that contribute to the holistic transformation of language communities worldwide.'[26] The changes reflected WGA's intention to demonstrate the Alliance's relationship with the church, the ministry of Bible translation, and the growing community of Participating Organizations.

Institution to Movement

Franklin presented his description of the Alliance at the Alliance Board's May 2013 meeting, hosted by Wycliffe Germany at its Holzhausen centre. He characterized WGA as 'like-minded organizations and movements who desire to act in community under God's direction. As a result, WGA and its Participating Organizations are providing meaningful leadership in the Bible translation movement worldwide.'[27] Franklin observed the board and GLT's challenge when explaining what WGA was becoming since it didn't fit conventional mission agency structures. Thirty-three years had passed since the formation of WBTI, and in that time, the world significantly changed as the church found new homes in the majority world. This spurred WBTI's transition to the Alliance as it developed and articulated its own identity while defining its place in the global context.

Historically formed as an institution with a well-defined and established framework, WBTI trained WMOs, accepted them, and granted them control within the organization. Because WBTI and SIL, for many years, had intertwined structures, policies, and procedures, the institutional characteristics of WBTI mirrored those of SIL. SIL-initiated programs and publications sometimes featured the Wycliffe name, though without any Wycliffe involvement. While the two organizations moved incrementally toward separate and distinct identities, when WBTI became WGA, the distinction was clear, and the name genuinely expressed their intention. With the separation came the realization that WGA is much more than just SIL's partner. As WBTI became the Alliance, the focus moved from institution to the journey of a Bible translation movement.

The Alliance's GLT believed it was time to introduce a more helpful way of understanding where WBTI had come from as an institution, and where it was heading as the Alliance and as a movement. In reality, WGA was neither functioning

[26] WGA, "Board Minutes," May 2013, 4.

[27] WGA, May 2013, 2.

solely as an institution nor a movement but was often flowing, back and forth, in the stream in-between. It was often 'caught in the in-between of who we already are and who we are yet to be.'[28] Before becoming the Alliance, WBTI had become very familiar with how an institution functioned. The lines of authority, structure, and how operational requirements took place were clear and straightforward. The organization had operated this way from 1942 to 2011. Now, the GLT believed that understanding the movement model was crucial. It answered spoken and unspoken questions about how WGA was led, operated, or behaved in various situations. The movement model would become the primary methodology of guiding how WGA developed its current and future policies, its financial procedures and practices, decision-making by the GLT, board governance, and how the GLT related to the Participating Organizations. It enabled a move away from the symbols and trappings of a 75-year-old institution with centralized structures, concepts, and expectations. The direction was now toward community-based relationships offered by a movement.

International Mission to Global Alliance

Mission structure and strategies must continually progress to allow for and encourage ongoing development, multiple partnerships, and diverse contexts. By design, traditional planning models helped to 'build' institutional structures for trustworthy and well-managed organizations. However, the GLT believed the metaphor of a journey was more appropriate for WGA because it needed 'to be versatile, flexible, and able to facilitate new or complimentary movements while at the same time maintaining its integrity and trustworthiness.'[29] The question arose whether the concept of journeying worked well across all cultures, with the likely answer that this metaphor would be useful but seen differently in various contexts.

The transition to becoming WGA began the shift in focus from operating as an institution for resourcing the activity of Bible translation to being on a journey as participants in Bible translation movements. This change required addressing the historical organizational understanding that WBT and later WBTI existed for one purpose: to resource SIL International. About a dozen national organizations (the NBTOs) leading and managing Bible translation and literacy programs in their own countries, though heavily reliant on SIL's good will, proved the exception. However, Franklin pointed out to the WGA Board that it was no longer wise or true to think of WBTI in these terms because the Alliance and its Participating

---

[28] Jason Ingram, Jeff Owen and Mike Donehey, Tenth Avenue North, "All the Pretty Things," 2010.

[29] WGA, May 2013, 3.

Organizations were now providing meaningful leadership in the Bible translation movement worldwide and regarded SIL as one of its strategic partners.

Autonomous to Interdependent

As WGA continued its journey, the Participating Organizations coming together as an interdependent community was a value of great importance. The board and GLT realized that through the ongoing process of change, the Participating Organizations, their leaders, and staff required careful nurturing from the board, GLT, and Area staff for the following reasons:

› The value of autonomy of the Participating Organizations, a carry-over from the previous structure of multiple WBTI Divisions, needed to be addressed because of its detriment to developing greater community. In response, the WGA Board agreed that the preferred term of 'self-governing' better described the organizations that made up WGA. 'Autonomous' was no longer an appropriate way of describing the relationships within the Alliance.
› Creating an atmosphere of belonging in WGA would fill a need and decrease the differences among organizations within WGA. One issue proving to be a stumbling block was the concept of status or voting rights in WGA. Differences in status had the effect of marginalizing some organizations and giving seeming prominence to others. Another issue was related to funding. Some organizations contributed financially to the operations of WGA, and others did not. A greater sense of community within WGA necessitated that the board and GLT deal with these issues.

Relationships of Global-Regional-Local

At this stage of WGA's development, healthy interaction between the various levels demonstrated a sense of community within WGA. While some linkages were common to all the levels, other levels experienced unique connections. Franklin defined these three levels for the WGA board:

› *Global:* The GLT, board, and Wycliffe Global Gathering focussed on the mission of God while listening to the 'wind of the Holy Spirit' for direction, vision, and purpose. WGA's ongoing missiological reflective process provided a place for discernment and guidance.
› *Regional:* The focus was on building trust and consensus among the Participating Organizations. Collaboration and formalization of partnerships happened here. The Participating Organizations and WGA Area leaders were

better known to each other at this level and were learning to trust each other. Integrated planning processes and visionary leadership guided this level.

- *Local:* Engaging with local churches and language communities through the Participating Organizations was the focus. Factors relating to funding were critical to organizations at this level. Therefore, organizational development, governance, financial integrity, ethics, and sustainable structures for the Participating Organizations required attention. Practical expertise and good partnering practices were essential.

Components of the Alliance

Some aspects of WGA were increasing in importance for supporting and sustaining a vibrant movement. These included:

- *Missiological foundations:* The ongoing process of missiological reflection was foundational to understanding how WGA should function, providing inspiration and momentum in defining and shaping the Alliance and guiding its future. Consequently, WGA leaders who operated as 'reflective practitioners' were better equipped to influence WGA's culture and practices. There was an urgent need to find sustainable ways of including more Participating Organization leaders in the journey of reflection.
- *Participation Streams:* WGA's missiological reflection provides a theological, missiological, and practical foundation for the shaping of WGA's journey. It opened the way for WGA's seven Participation Streams: Church Engagement, Prayer, Funding, Recruiting and Sending People, Specialty Services, Technical Training, and Bible Translation Programs. These Participation Streams were helping WGA identify ways God was calling WGA to participate together in His mission.
- *Communication:* The Participating Organizations required time and support from the GLT and Area staff to process change. Therefore, this called for the WGA leadership to communicate and encourage dialogue concerning the missiological and practical principles that inform the journey of transition that WGA is going through at all the levels of global-regional-local. It would take ongoing communication over time to understand and apply these principles, making it necessary for the GLT and board to over-communicate the principles of WGA.
- *Organizational Development:* Movements only move toward goals if the organizations making up the movements are healthy. WGA is healthy when all its Participating Organizations, as well as the leadership, are functioning well, and the development of each is a high priority. As the GLT endeavoured to encourage healthy Participating Organizations to come alongside those that might be struggling, this strengthened the community life of WGA.

- *Leadership Development:* WGA and its Participating Organizations would consistently require a growing pool of leaders at all levels, making it necessary to plan to strengthen current and future leaders' abilities to lead with a global perspective, including exploring the multicultural and intercultural dimensions of leadership. As well, building confidence in leaders would promote effective interaction in a global community.
- *Partnering:* Serving together among Participating Organizations and with external partners represents an essential value of WGA. Sharing together is critical, building relationships and community in partnerships that focus on the Kingdom of God. Seeking the goal of the exemplary role model in these kingdom partnerships, the GLT hoped to encourage and influence kingdom partnering among and between the Participating Organizations within WGA, its staff, and beyond.
- *Organizations in the Alliance:* For the WGA leadership, an awareness of and concern for the needs and aspirations of the Participating Organizations involves reminding them that they are the Alliance. As such, everyone benefits when the Participating Organizations develop an awareness of each other's needs and how best to assist each other. Consequently, it is essential for the GLT to facilitate and participate in forums for the Participating Organizations, Area staff, and others, exploring who they are, how they fit together, and how they partner in WGA.
- *Identity of the Alliance:* Many of WGA's audiences and partners worldwide—both within and outside the Alliance—did not understand the separate identities of WGA and SIL and their partnering relationship with each other. Within WGA, there was some slowness in clarifying the distinctions, including the administrative and leadership separation of both organizations. Referring to each other, including verbal and written references and policies, required sensitivity from both organizations to accurately reflect the relatively new paradigm.

Participating in the Alliance

By this time, WGA was composed of like-minded organizations, churches, and movements seeking to act as a community under God's direction. As a result, WGA and its Participating Organizations were providing meaningful leadership in Bible translation movements worldwide.

WGA was not structured like SIL or other organizations and rarely spoke as a singular voice for all the Participating Organizations, except in mutually agreed on essentials such as its mission, vision, values, and doctrinal and other standards. WGA wanted to help create space to serve as a think-tank for a diversity of voices and strategies, shaping an environment that values the Participating

Organizations and other partners and where the GLT consistently encourages and models thought leadership.

Within missions, WGA did not resemble typical organizational structures. Involvement in WGA was more important than its structure, which primarily existed to support it rather than to shape it.

Since organizational participation was key to the effectiveness of WGA, the GLT and board believed more work was called for to develop a structure that enabled all Participating Organizations to belong to the Alliance community without barriers to their involvement. Earlier progress of removing multiple categories and sub-categories of organization status was proving helpful to both the organizations and WGA leadership, but there were still these areas that the board and GLT believed required attention:

A single category of organizations: While internally, all organizations were referred to as Participating Organizations, in reality, the separation of WMOs from WPOs continued, and a sub-category of WMOs retained the exclusive right to vote on WGA affairs. Therefore, the board 'urged the executive director to continue to move in the following direction: the GLT will process the one category concept in their interactions with WMOs. The use of the term "Participating" should be seen as a transition title until the one category concept is established, after which it could be dropped.'[30]

Up-to-date Memorandum of Understanding (MOU) with all Participating Organizations: With the various categories of organizations came a variety of formal and informal agreements between these organizations and WGA and administrated through the area directors. This process would require streamlining. The board asked the executive director to bring a sample MOU to the next board meeting after first processing it with a few WMOs for their responses.

Voting issues in the business of WGA: The board recognized that deciding which organizations qualified to vote was of ongoing importance since this influenced who could serve on the board and provide governance, as well as upholding the purpose and core values of WGA. The board consulted with WMO and WPO directors on the board. 'They were of one mind that this direction should be pursued.'[31] Since this was a critical question, the board decided to revisit the issue at its next meeting. In the meantime, it wanted to better educate itself concerning what was required to govern the Alliance.

Funding WGA: The board considered the financial contribution of 0.35% of total income by each WMO to be working well, nevertheless recognizing the time had come for the executive director to ask all Participating Organizations—including WPOs—to make the annual 0.35% contribution. The board asked the

[30] WGA, May 2013, 5.

[31] WGA, May 2013, 4.

executive director to use the current fee structures as a starting point in discussions with WPOs when negotiating their financial contribution to the Alliance. The board assumed this process would lead to a uniform contribution from all Participating Organizations.

Home in the Land of Transition

Traugott Hopp, then Dean of Academy of World Missions, Germany, met with the board to offer some reflections on organizational transitions. During this time, Franklin introduced questions he and the GLT were hearing. When is the Alliance going to stop changing? When will we be done with all these transitions? The GLT's answer had been, Never, we hope! Because when the Alliance 'stops changing it becomes static and may be on the way to irrelevancy in a rapidly changing world.'[32] A willingness to be flexible and embrace change would keep the Alliance relevant in its desire to participate in God's very active mission. Hopp responded, 'we can make a home in the land of transition.'[33] Though still in the zone between institution and movement, additional transition elements would manifest themselves, requiring from WGA continued flexibility and willingness to adapt as God led.

With all the structural alterations underway from institution to movement, some Participating Organizations were asking the WGA leadership, 'How are you working to replace what we've lost? For example, the loss of the familiar, the security of established structures, the loss of control, or the loss of centralized international services (e.g., personnel). The assumption is that what's been lost must be replaced by the same thing or something similar.'[34] The GLT offered this challenge in response: 'All participants in the Alliance need to consider how to partner together in the Alliance rather than being dependent on centralized operational structures. In doing so, what is perceived as being loss, may in fact be the unfolding of much greater gain.'[35]

Reflecting on how the Alliance articulates its organizational evolution, Alliance Africa Area Director Mũndara Mũturi expressed a vision of the Alliance's future. He said the Alliance is 'like a big river [with] individuals and organizations coming in convergence or confluence and pooling resources for Kingdom purposes. Individuals and autonomous organizations disappear in the congruence of community.'[36] To be clear, individuals and organizations do not lose their unique

---

[32] Kirk Franklin, Susan Van Wynen, and Dave Crough, "Making a Home in the Land of Transition," *The Journey*, no. April (2014): 1.

[33] WGA, May 2013, 11.

[34] Franklin, Van Wynen, and Crough, 4.

[35] Franklin, Van Wynen, and Crough, 4.

[36] Franklin, Van Wynen, and Crough, 5.

identity in a nebulous mass called the Alliance. Nor do they disappear or stop being themselves when they enter into community. On the contrary, their identity acquires new dimensions—helping them to better participate in God's mission.

Reappointment of the Executive Director

The November board meeting hosted by Wycliffe US at its Orlando headquarters built on the growing realization of the importance of missiological reflection. The board added an extra day to missiologically consider the organization's historical development going back to its inception in 1942 as WBT up until the Alliance of today.

A significant responsibility for this board meeting was either to set in motion the process to appoint a new executive director to start in May 2016 or to reappoint Franklin for an additional two years beyond his current term. The board's policies allowed the board to extend the appointment of an executive director beyond the standard eight-year period by two years.

Since the Alliance Board held some joint sessions with the SIL Board, it was aware that the SIL Board had also begun its executive director appointment efforts with a list of names drawn up by its internal processes. There were some names on SIL's list of prospective nominees who were leaders filling crucial roles in WGA or Participating Organizations. Understanding that the strategic progress of one organization shouldn't hinder the action of the other in these appointments, this called for the WGA and SIL Board Chairs to keep each other informed of their process.

After considerable discussion in closed session and further discussion with the executive director, the board decided it would be in WGA's best interests to reappoint Franklin for the additional two years beyond his current term. With this decision, the board recognized the necessity of a succession plan to provide suitable candidates for consideration when selecting the next executive director. They requested that Franklin prioritize identifying and mentoring potential candidates. Other issues considered by the board included the critical lack of continuity facing the next board and GLT after May 2016 and the unfinished development of governance and structure for WGA.

Incorporating in Singapore

At the May 2013 board meeting, Franklin had raised the philosophical as well as the practical aspects behind his and the GLT's thinking concerning relocating WBTI's place of incorporation.[37] Currently, it was incorporated in the US state of Texas because WBTI's headquarters had been established there in 1980. However,

[37] WBTI was still the legal entity; Wycliffe Global Alliance was the 'doing business as' entity.

Franklin described how WBTI's legal presence in the US context prompted some audiences to confuse the Alliance with US organizations having 'Wycliffe' in their name (e.g., Wycliffe US and Wycliffe Associates). Franklin was also concerned that having this legal presence in the US could be misleading and indicate that the Alliance was not global after all but still heavily tied to its US roots. From a practical point of view, some duplicated processes occurred in the US and Singapore. Furthermore, the annual external audit called for by Texas law, as well as an annual audit and other legal requirements mandatory in Singapore, resulted in extra costs. Franklin's aim of keeping the GLT's administrative obligations to the required minimum meant it was time to explore the possibility of moving their incorporation from Texas to Singapore.

As a governance issue, the board explored the benefits of incorporating in Singapore, which would reduce the duplication of auditing requirements and the filing of Internal Revenue Service (IRS) reports in the US. By now, the Alliance had very little activity in the US, and the Texas incorporation was becoming decreasingly relevant.

After further investigation by the executive director and his team, they concluded that there were not enough compelling reasons to go through the process of trying to incorporate in Singapore. The board decided to retain WBTI's incorporation in Texas with a registered office in Singapore, and the issue of incorporating outside the US would remain in the background for now.

Core Values

Franklin requested that the board review the tagline of the Core Value, 'The Church as central in God's mission: Believing the Church is created, called, and equipped by God to evangelize the world and disciple the nations.' Feedback Franklin received from an indigenous leader of a Participating Organization referred to the use of the word 'evangelize', which raised concern, and could be misleading. For some, it carried overtones of imposition and colonial conquest, based on the experience of the church within their nations. The board agreed to this amendment to the tagline: 'The Church as central in God's mission: Believing the Church is created, called, and equipped by God to disciple the nations.'

Protecting the 'Wycliffe' Name

The names 'Wycliffe' and 'Wycliffe Bible Translators' were owned by Wycliffe US, but when used in the context of Wycliffe Global Alliance, Wycliffe International, or by a Participating Organization, were managed by WGA. The Alliance Board sought clarification with Wycliffe US to determine if there should be a simple written agreement or a legally binding agreement. Ultimately, the two organizations agreed to continue working together as they had historically in a spirit of faith and good will. Granting use of the Wycliffe name to other organizations in good faith presupposed that those organizations valued and respected the name's worldwide integrity. While dedicated to holding the Wycliffe name in high esteem among its Participating Organizations and various publics, WGA sought to negotiate fairly, respectfully, and impartially in any issue or dispute arising from use of the name, such as a Wycliffe organization withdrawing from the Alliance.

The board advised Participating Organizations using the name 'Wycliffe' or 'Wycliffe Bible Translators' to consider registering a trademark for it in their respective countries. This safeguarded the name's integrity and goodwill and demonstrated how WGA continued to navigate its intertwined history with Wycliffe US.

Reinstatement of Nigeria Bible Translation Trust

In November 2009, intending to encourage the Nigeria Bible Translation Trust (NBTT) to focus on resolving certain governance conflicts within the organization, and non-compliance with some WBTI standards, despite WBTI's attempts to intervene, the WBTI Board terminated NBTT's membership in WBTI. Since that time, members of the Alliance's leadership team and then Africa Area Director Joel Trudell had been relating to NBTT's leadership to assist them in working through the issues. Given the size of the remaining work in Nigeria, and the need to restore a healthy relationship with NBTT, Franklin emphasized the commitment of Alliance leaders to follow a process of rebuilding trust and relationships leading to NBTT's reinstatement in the Alliance.

Convinced that NBTT was ready to be reinstated as a Participating Organization, Franklin informed the board at its November 2013 meeting of his and current Alliance Africa Area Director Mũndara Mũturi's observations, and the WGA Board agreed to restore NBTT's status within the Alliance. In December 2013, Mũturi and Michel Kenmogne visited NBTT to convey the Alliance Board's decision. The members of NBTT received this news, according to the board chair, 'with a loud applause and regarded as glad tidings of great joy brought to us (NBTT and the Church of Nigeria).' At its reinstatement, NBTT was active in over 90 language programs.

New Organizations

In August 2013, a group of Pacific Island leaders met with WGA staff to learn from and encourage one another. They shared challenges and victories and prayed passionately together. The group ended the week with renewed enthusiasm, new ideas, and, most importantly, a sense that they were not alone in the ministry of Bible translation in the Pacific. The meeting culminated in the signing of MOUs between the Alliance and the Bible Translation and Literacy Partnership (BTLP) of the Solomon Islands and the Bible Translation Organisation (BTO) of Tonga.

At the May 2014 board meeting, Franklin reported on the Americas Area Director signing new MOUs that recognized new Participating Organizations: UNTI (Mexico), TRES (El Salvador), SIETE (Venezuela), ME (Venezuela), NHCLC (Hispanic Evangelical Association), AEL (Peru), and LETRA (Paraguay). These MOUs were temporary until all envisioned changes to Alliance membership categories and requirements were in place.

In Africa, with permission granted by Franklin to use the Wycliffe name and Ethiopian leaders requesting backing from the Alliance, plans were progressing to establish Wycliffe Ethiopia. Having formed a board and appointed Tefera Endalew as director, Wycliffe Ethiopia desired to engage the Ethiopian church, raise resources from Ethiopia, and planned to manage translation programs in Ethiopia.

Organizational Development

Many POs had been asking the GLT for assistance in organizational development (OD). When Dave Brooks of the GLT took up the challenge, he noted many of the more established POs were already responding and helping in organizational development, often holding and promoting a variety of philosophies and concepts. Though well-meaning, their assistance lacked coordination and did not always reflect the broader value of community in the Alliance. Brooks created an initiative to bring together those organizations wanting to provide OD support. Four organizations agreed to partner together in the Initiative: WGA, SIL, Wycliffe US, and The Seed Company. The aim was to follow the OD approach developed by the Americas Area, testing it with POs in other parts of the world. Four AOs wanted to participate in the initiative: GILLBT (Ghana), Wycliffe South Africa, BTA (Papua New Guinea), and Kartidaya (Indonesia). To participate, these organizations' boards and leadership agreed to a site visit with a diagnostic process covering a dozen aspects of effective organizational behaviour. The PO leadership received a report identifying the necessary improvements, along with a proposal for how to address the improvements. If the organization's leadership agreed, the OD team started a mutually accepted process that spanned 2–3 years. The OD team included: (1) lead consultants who oversaw the long-term engagement with each PO, and (2) domain consultants who brought specific expertise in different areas of organizational function (e.g., HR, governance, fund-raising, strategy and planning, etc.). These consultants were drawn from the resources of the five partners and were oriented, trained, and supervised by Maria Vega.

Future Governance and Structure

A discussion in the November 2013 board meeting explored the possibility of a single organizational membership category for WGA. There were many influencing factors such as voting and non-voting categories of organizations, WGA's Board structure and how board members were appointed, the financing of WGA, and agreements for Participating Organizations. The board and executive director made every effort to design solutions for the complex nature of these interrelated issues. As a result, Board Chair Roger Welch appointed an ad hoc committee to reflect on this further and make recommendations to the May 2014 board meeting. The committee met in Duncanville, Texas, in March 2014 and included board members Roger Welch, Decio de Carvalho, and Hannes Wiesmann; GLT members Kirk Franklin, Susan Van Wynen, and José de Dios; President of Wycliffe Canada Roy Eyre; and Wycliffe Africa Area Associate Director Michel Kenmogne. The committee's task was to investigate proposals for structures relevant to WGA community. These proposals needed to cover an appropriate governance model, board composition, executive director's term of service, and ways of Participating Organizations belonging and contributing to the Alliance. The committee brought their work to the board at its May 2014 meeting in San Salvador, El Salvador, hosted by Participating Organizations TRES and Miramonte Baptist Church. The committee grouped its recommendations in three topics: (1) belonging, (2) participating, and (3) governance and board structure. The board discussed the recommendations and made its decisions as follows:

1) *Belonging:* The board decided that WGA would become 'a covenantal community in which the relationships of organizations within WGA are managed by a covenant which expresses both the essential and practical elements of those relationships and the shared purpose of the Alliance.'[38] The implementation of this would occur at the 2016 Global Gathering, marking the official beginning of WGA as a covenantal community.

The board wanted to be sure that it owned the process of WGA becoming a covenantal community so that it gave oversight to the wording of the covenant that each organization signed. Therefore, the board required that every covenant established between an organization and WGA must include the values and beliefs of WGA (part 1, that included an organization's agreement to the mission,

[38] WGA, "Board Minutes," May 2014, 7.

vision, core values, and doctrinal statement of the Alliance); and implications of belonging to the Alliance (part 2, that included to which Participation Streams each organization committed). Other topics in this section of the covenant included integrity in communication, reference to the Bible Translation Programs Philosophy Statement, the organization's legal status, governance, and various behavioural expectations, including moral conduct, protecting personnel and corporate information, financial standards, financial contribution to the Alliance, and use of the name 'Wycliffe' (where applicable).

2) *Participation:* The board followed the ad hoc committee's recommendations to eliminate the multiple organizational membership categories in the Alliance, replacing Participating Organization (PO) with Alliance Organization (AO). However, since the WBTI Bylaws referred to POs, this required that the 29 WMOs with vote approve the change. This was addressed at the Voting WMOs consultation in 2015.

In its report to the board, the ad hoc committee recommended replacing the 0.35% financial contribution by WMOs with a voluntary contribution from all POs, presenting the Alliance's annual budget to POs, and seeking financial pledges from them to fund it. The concept of the 0.35% contribution, designed specifically for WMOs, currently provided US$704,000 in income or approximately 40% of the Alliance's total budget. The board decided to move toward a new method of financing the Alliance by replacing the 0.35% contribution. Its desire to see a new system based on a voluntary contribution from all POs would require presenting the WGA budget to POs annually and seeking pledges from them. However, changes could not be pursued until fiscal year 2016 at the earliest, when results of a planned referendum on amending the bylaws were finalized.

3) *Governance and Board Structures:* The term Board of Directors was considered standard under WBTI's Texas Incorporation. The ad hoc committee suggested the governance structure be called a council rather than a board. The board considered alternatives such as council or Governing Council. The term Governing Council polled strongly in a straw vote until recognizing that it might give the perception of being overly controlling. In the end, the board decided not to change its name.

The board determined that the authority to revise bylaws should not rest with them but with the majority of the POs and should be part of the amended bylaws sent to the current voting WMOs for approval. The board considered the ad hoc committee's proposal of setting up a Nominating Committee a good idea. It was also necessary to develop terms of reference covering a range of board governance matters, such as board member terms of service and term limits, maximum and minimum size of the board, gender balance, and regional representation guidelines.

Way Forward

The Wycliffe Global Gathering, scheduled for May 2016, required following a strict timeline and a significant amount of work from the executive director and GLT, as well as ongoing interaction with the board. The board chair and executive director called a special consultation in March 2015, asking that two people from each of the 29 WMOs with vote work through all the proposed changes. If that went well, the board could initiate a referendum for the voting WMOs to approve the amended bylaws, and by extension, the new directions for the Alliance. That process would take six months, and if successful, the 2016 Global Gathering could operate under the new bylaws. To meet this timeline required gaining the goodwill of the WMOs with vote and implementing the new bylaws within the next 12 months.

As the board and GLT prepared to embark on this next phase of the journey of the WGA community's development, two relevant observations arose: (1) the Alliance was continuing to realize that 'no single organization can leverage and institutionalize large-scale change on its own. In an increasingly networked world, creating a strategy that mobilizes and leverages a diverse array of organizations is essential.'[39] And (2) the Alliance experienced a sense of urgency about heading in this direction. The theme of urgency came to light during the February 2014 Wycliffe US-Alliance Missiological Consultation (see chapter 10). Participants spoke of a 'holistic urgency' describing it as 'God's priorities within His mission supersede the priorities of any one culture, organization, or individual.' This fitting description reflected that the entire Alliance community needed the opportunity to speak into and influence the change process.

Friendship in God's Mission

One direct outcome of the Alliance's missiological consultative process (see chapter 10) involved releasing philosophy statements covering topics of central importance to the Alliance's development, strategy, and how it functioned. Each of these statements flowed from input from leaders across WGA through a guided discussion process reflecting on the mission of God (*missio Dei*). They were intended to influence how WGA and its organizations participated in the Bible translation movement.

Exploring the value of relationships within the Alliance community offered one example of such discussion. Franklin and members of the GLT invited senior Participating Organization leaders from Wycliffe US and The Seed Company

[39] Josh Karliner, Gary Cohen, and Peter Orris, "Lessons in Forging Global Change," *Stanford Social Innovation Review* 12 (2014): 38.

to Addis Ababa, Ethiopia, for a two-day consultation in July 2014 on developing ministry relationships based on friendships. Ethiopian Evangelical Lutheran Church Mekane Yesus (EECMY) hosted the consultation. Topics included (1) developing a community of friendship in God's mission, (2) towards a missiology of friendship, and (3) implementing the Alliance's Principles for Community. The sessions included Bible studies developed from relevant biblical texts about friendship and community.

Changes in the Bible translation movement and the increase in participants from the majority world seeking to listen to and discern the movement of the Spirit led to exploring this theme of friendship in mission. These fresh voices arose, bringing ideas about ways to be involved, and with strength, vision, and experience not a result of their wealth but of their faith in a God who is able, a God who provides. What would the response be from the Western Participating Organizations who, until more recently, because of their wealth and influence, could act as 'gate keepers' and hinder these newer participants from finding their places in the movement? Those gathering in Addis Ababa faced this challenge from reading How Chuang Chua, who wrote that God 'continually invites us to participate in His relational life by calling us to a friendship, first with Him, and with other people.'[40] This call to friendship may lead to a community of shalom, which, according to James Davison Hunter, is 'a vision of order and harmony, fruitfulness and abundance, wholeness, beauty, joy and well-being.'[41] The importance of this cannot be overlooked because, as Chua notes, 'the profound invitation to friendship, divine and human, constitutes the primordial missiological principle!'[42]

Throughout WGA's new philosophy statements, there are explicit and implicit calls for a relational commitment among participants in WGA. For example, the Bible Translation Programs Philosophy statement declares, 'Building the necessary foundation of interdependent relationships required for Bible translation programs to contribute to transformation requires [POs] to model the character of God.' A mutuality or interdependency of a relationship is required, where each partner, regardless of social, educational, or economic status, contributes resources (funds, skills, materials, and knowledge) according to their ability to do so. Partners understanding that they need each other, and developing relationships of friendship, are essential to the Bible translation movement, illustrating how God's kingdom has come.

Those gathered in Addis Ababa took into consideration how to act justly, love

---

[40] How Chuang Chua, "Perichoresis and *Missio Dei:* Implications of a Trinitarian View of Personhood for Missionary Practice," 2010, OMF Mission Research Consultation.

[41] James Davison Hunter, *To Change the World: The Irony, Tragedy, and Possibility of Christianity in the Late Modern World* (New York: Oxford University Press, 2011), 228.

[42] Chua.

mercy and walk humbly with each other (based on Micah 6:8) as they reflected on these questions:

› Do we believe all others in the Bible translation movements are essential?
› Are there ways that we are doing things that hamper the participation of others?
› Are we willing to take a humble attitude and seek to learn and shift?
› Are we willing to let God redefine how He wants us to participate in his mission?
› Are we willing to let God take us beyond the images of 'go, give, pray', and let God redefine how He wants us to participate in the mission of God, serving humbly and in community, so that we might reflect His glory, even more so than presently?

Toward a Covenantal Community

The Addis Ababa gathering demonstrated the growing importance of living out the principles and attitudes of community in WGA as it became a global movement for Bible translation. The WGA Board examined the significance of keeping the Alliance's Principles for Community (see chapter 10) and the value of friendship central in who the Alliance was and how it functioned. The idea proposed at the WGA Board's May 2014 meeting of a covenantal community would require all organizations, their leaders and staff, and the Alliance's GLT and board to be characterized by the values of community and friendship.

The aim of being called a covenantal community was short-lived as six months later, at its November meeting, the board decided the concept required a more straightforward definition. In particular, the concern was that the use of covenant in the Bible was always exclusively between God and his people—the theological use of the word. However, another use of the word involved a formal agreement between two or more people or organizations. By suggesting a covenant could apply between organizations, it was reasonable to continue using the term and to pursue this valuable concept.

At this point, the wording 'covenantal community' was dropped. But a year later, the board decided to call WGA, as a whole, the Alliance Community, and the new agreement a Covenant/Statement of Commitment. As the ones primarily having discussions with the organizations, the Area Directors could use either or both terms, depending on the context they observed. Eventually, the agreement was translated into Spanish, Portuguese, French, and Indonesian. Negotiating the Covenant/Statement of Commitment with organizations had to wait until after the bylaw referendum passed, November 2015 at the earliest. The timeline for signing all agreements with all the organizations before the May 2016 Global Gathering was tight, an important consideration since organizations could only be invited to the event if they and their respective Area Director had already signed the agreement.

Retirement of Board Secretary

At the November 2014 board meeting, Darryl and Irene Kernick completed their term of service as Board Secretary and Assistant Secretary. A celebratory dinner took place, honouring the Kernicks' service to the board over the past six years, though it did not mark their retirement. They had accepted the board's appointment to be the Event 2016 coordinators (the combined SIL International Conference and the Wycliffe Global Gathering).

Voting Organizations

Looking back on the journey of the Alliance, one event stands apart from most others. It was not a large event, only attended by about 60 people, but the discussions and decisions made there took the Alliance in a direction inconceivable seven years earlier in 2008. When WBTI and SIL's administrations separated, the concept of WBTI as an organization without numerous membership categories seemed impossible because the WMOs with vote maintained control over WBTI and were unwilling to make concessions for the others—particularly for the partner organizations—to possess equal status with them.

While the WMOs with vote were significant to the Alliance, they were no longer the largest category, as shown in this table:

Type of organizations	WMOs with vote	WMOs without vote	WPOs
Total number	29	16	55

Table 2: Types and Numbers of Organizations

Regarding the restructuring of the organization discussed in this and the previous chapter, it always came down to how the voting organizations would feel about the proposal. The time had finally come to engage with these organizations more thoroughly.

There were 29 voting WMOs among the now more than 100 total Participating Organizations. The WGA Board decided that Chair Roger Welch and Executive Director Kirk Franklin, accompanied by the four Area Directors Mũndara Mũturi

(Africa), Nydia Garcia-Schmidt (Americas), Sung-Chan Kwon (Asia-Pacific), and Frank Lautenschlager (Europe), would meet with the executive directors and board chairs of the voting organizations. There would be no other participants. These leaders needed a safe, secluded space to debate with each other, the WGA Board Chair, the executive director, and area directors, their observations and concerns about the extensive restructuring process that the board had agreed to, that would fundamentally change WGA. The purpose and desired outcomes of the consultation were to help all who gathered do the following:

› Understand the underlying vision of WGA.
› Discuss how the envisioned covenantal community could look, where organizations can sense belonging and can freely participate in a community of mutual care and commitment to one another.
› Discuss what belonging to WGA will look like.
› Discuss what it means to participate in an alliance.
› Discuss proposals for a new board governance process and structure that best serves WGA.
› Discuss a funding model for WGA that will eliminate the current 0.35% contribution from WMOs with one based on sharing and funding the vision of the WGA by all Alliance organizations.

The 19–20 March consultation took place in Kusadasi, Turkey. Representatives from all the voting WMOs attended except NBTT (Nigeria) due to difficulties obtaining visas. Board member Hannes Weismann led reflections on body life from 1 Corinthians 12:12–26 and 13. As someone close to the purpose for the consultation, Weismann reflected on how

> the need for community is stronger than ever. Working in community is the foundational basis for the existence of the Wycliffe Global Alliance. We are not a community only because of our common goals, although Alliance organizations do share many common goals... it goes beyond that. My understanding of (1) Scripture; (2) the sovereignty of God; (3) my experience, our history and tradition in Wycliffe; (4) as well as a realistic understanding of human nature, points me to the importance of our community.

Roger Welch outlined the aims and purpose of the consultation. Franklin set the context by mapping out the journey from WBT to WBTI to WGA. Discussions centred around the Participation Streams and ensuring that the Alliance didn't drift from its mission. Welch facilitated the remainder of the first day, examining the governance structure. He outlined the board's recommendations about board composition, covering geography, gender balance, and a healthy mix of internal and external members. The founding organization, Wycliffe US, would retain a seat on the board through its president. Participating Organization Directors illustrated how they were implementing the Participation Streams. Questions from the leaders were about the composition and selection criteria of the board, the purpose of the Global Gathering, safeguarding the organization through the change process, and how new organizations join WGA.

On the second day, Franklin led a look at a vision for the future. He addressed the critical issue of how to fund the Alliance moving into the future. He suggested developing a three-year budget projection tied to a coherent vision for WGA to present to the larger funding organizations. For organizations to consider their contributions as meaningful, they wanted and needed to understand and embrace the vision. Questions and discussions from the participants centred around how to fund WGA, including the pros and cons of the current 0.35% contribution, a fee-based tier system, or a combination of the two. Despite numerous opinions expressed, the discussion was inconclusive with no alterations recommended, and the 0.35% contribution remained the most equitable to the majority of organizations.

Welch led a discussion on the proposed new bylaws that these organizations would have to vote to approve or reject. But that would come later. For now, it was time to work through all the detail and to raise questions. Discussions centred around aspects of belonging in the Alliance. Points made included the necessity for robust processes for entry into WGA and for upholding the values and standards of WGA. The benefits of being part of WGA ought to be clear to current organizations, and especially to those considering being part of the Alliance in the future. Feedback was given about the Participation Streams and ensuring their evaluative use in an organization's contribution to the Bible translation movement.

The discussion that followed addressed WGA governance issues, including the board member selection process. When board vacancies occurred, the initial stage would be through a new nominating committee to identify suitable potential board members. Questions from participants addressed ensuring gender balance, identifying suitable skills and experience required by the board, and pursuing a composition representative of the Alliance's five geographic Areas. In the final session hosted by Franklin and Welch, participants asked any questions not yet raised, which covered a range of topics. Some participants expressed appreciation for the Alliance's adaptability in pursuing its vision and doing this in a culturally sensitive way, given how diverse the Alliance was becoming. An organization's board member expressed that she was 'proud to be part of an organization that is so prophetic in the way it works.' Others expressed appreciation to the Alliance Board for all the effort it had taken to make this consultation a reality.

Franklin's feedback to the GLT after the consultation described how 'the Lord brought unity within the great diversity of people and perspectives represented.' As a result, the board and GLT had a more comprehensible direction for the future. Franklin and Welch felt this consultation had brought the commitment and solidarity essential to seeing the new bylaws adopted, setting in motion the next phase of the journey of WGA. Based on the Covenant/Statement of Commitment, it would comprise a single organizational category—Alliance Organization (AO)—and involve the discontinuation of the WMO and WPO categories.

Preparing for Change

At its May 2015 meeting, the board finalized all the input given through the voting organizations consultation that affected the new bylaws. Board Chair Roger Welch reported how the attendees embraced the themes of the Alliance community and inclusion. There was much discussion on how WGA will include emerging organizations, how organizations bring their strengths to WGA as a whole, and how the Alliance is funded and governed. Board Secretary Matt Dawson then initiated the process of the referendum. Each of the 29 WMOs with vote had six months, up to the November board meeting, to make their decision—either to affirm the new bylaws or to reject them.

The issue of the 0.35% contribution by all WGA organizations received further attention since the final wording would go into the new Covenant/Statement of Commitment. Though capped at a maximum contribution of US$450,000 per organization for fiscal year 2016, the board could lower this amount annually to lessen the financial burden for any organization faced with but unable to produce the payment. The minimum annual contribution per AO, set at US$250 for fiscal year 2016, increased to US$300 for fiscal year 2017 and US$350 for fiscal year 2018. Rather than calculating from their entire income, mission agencies whose ministry was broader than Bible translation movements, and churches and church denominations, were required to pay the 0.35% contribution calculated on their budget for involvement in Bible translation movements associated with WGA.

To maintain continuity in the Alliance leadership, the board reappointed Franklin as executive director from May 2016 to May 2018. This was critically important, as Welch planned to retire as board chair at the May 2016 Global Gathering, and it would be unwise for Franklin and Welch to vacate their roles simultaneously.

Role of the ALT

At the November board meeting, Franklin described how the leadership team acted as shepherds and servants on behalf of the Alliance community. They sought to be faithful in fulfilling their responsibilities. They did so as friends, consultants, facilitators, and advisors in these nine areas of regional-global initiatives:

› Deepening missiological reflection
› Nurturing leaders for the Bible translation movement
› Effective and timely communication
› Strengthening Alliance organizations
› Equipping for Bible translation
› Strengthening community
› Supporting collaboration
› Encouraging stewardship
› Ensuring a trustworthy organization
› Serving in unity

Franklin asked the board to change the name of the Global Leadership Team (GLT) to the Alliance Leadership Community and later to the Alliance Leadership Team (ALT) to align the name with the Alliance community. Franklin also informed the board of these leadership transitions:

› Hannes Wiesmann stepped down as Wycliffe Switzerland Director to replace Frank Lautenschlager as Europe Area Director effective 1 April 2016. Lautenschlager had served since 2007.
› Simon Wan from Singapore would be the new Asia-Pacific Area Director, commencing on 1 May 2016 when Sung-Chan Kwon completed his term of service.
› A new position on the leadership team was being created for Bryan Harmelink to serve as Director of Collaboration, effective 1 January 2016.

The board congratulated Franklin on completing his PhD at the University of Pretoria, South Africa, with the topic of a 'Paradigm of Missional Leadership: The Journey of the Wycliffe Global Alliance'. They encouraged Franklin to assemble a group of thought leaders to analyze his research, and from it to discover ways to enhance the Alliance's leadership development processes, and to find other ways to share the results.

The Journey Continues

The board learned that on 3 November 2015, the referendum on the new bylaws passed. According to the old bylaws, requirements for bylaw amendment stipulated that within six months of a board-initiated amendment, two-thirds of the Wycliffe WMOs with voting rights must vote in favour of the amendment after submitting the proposal to their respective boards. Since all 29 voting organizations cast votes in favour of the changes, the referendum carried unanimously. One of the resulting significant implications of this was the elimination of nine categories of organizations:

Member Organizations

1. Accredited Member Organization
2. Member Organization without Vote
3. Member Organization with Vote
4. Member Organization with Language Programs without Vote
5. Member Organization with Language Programs with Vote

Partner Organizations

1. Associated Partner Organization
2. Memorandum of Understanding Partner Organization
3. Other Partner Organization
4. Pending Memorandum of Understanding Partner Organization

In their place, there was now just one category: Alliance Organization. This extraordinary result represents the climax of years of discussions and decision-making processes.

Conclusion

The momentous decision to eliminate nine organizational categories and replace them with one traces its roots back to November 2003 when the WBTI board expressed its 'growing excitement about what God is doing in the worldwide church… to foster an environment in which member organizations are encouraged and assisted to engage in appropriate partnerships with churches of the South and East.'[43] At the time, the board had no idea their decision would ultimately result in the Wycliffe Global Alliance. At the start of 2011, WBTI was an institution with well-defined, established structures, into which WMOs were 'groomed, accepted, and granted membership'.[44] They had some degree of control over the vision and purpose of WBTI. But the tone and culture of WBTI primarily reflected the ideas and attitudes of an established, historically Western institution. And for many years, almost all the organizations in WBTI were Western in orientation.

When adopting Vision 2025 in 1999, WBTI's leaders had no clear understanding of where the organization fit into the future. However, it soon became apparent that WBTI needed to make greater efforts to develop meaningful partnerships

[43] WBTI, "Extracts," November 2003, 2.

[44] Franklin, Van Wynen, and Crough, 1.

with the worldwide church. This insight, combined with WBTI's characterization as an 'organization of organizations' rather than a monolithic institution, encouraged the leadership to see WBTI in a new light. Significant structural alterations introduced in January 2008 were followed by further strategic initiatives as WBTI transitioned to becoming the Wycliffe Global Alliance (the Alliance) in 2011. The name change represented a shift from a hierarchy to a community, from centralized control to polycentric collaboration, and a significant transition from when Wycliffe was viewed solely as a resource provider, with the principal influence on Bible translation originating from just a few sources. The time had come for WGA to declare its vision. While organizational complexities simplified with one category replacing nine, WGA was growing in complexities in other ways. Comprising a culturally diverse community, WGA encompassed a wide range of sizes of organizations, presenting a variety of purposes and scopes of ministry. All this required review and reconsideration for the Alliance leadership to effectively lead this community.

Leadership Theory and Practice

Leading the Alliance was a topic of regular consideration by its leadership team. From 2016-2020, they developed a leadership covenant that expressed essential values for all members of the team and provided orientation for prospective members. The covenant stated how team members, individually and as a group, fulfilled their responsibilities within the Bible translation movement. The values expressed a deliberate desire to serve the growing organizationally and culturally diverse community of the Alliance. The leadership team committed itself to the following values:

› I am learning to rely on the Holy Spirit to lead me in all situations.
› I am growing in my understanding of spiritual, biblical, and missiological principles, which guide my organization in fulfilling its vision.
› I am becoming a reflective practitioner with a broad worldview because I know how to reflect on, understand, question, and explore missional issues informed by cultural perspectives and the Bible.
› I am avoiding 'quick fixes' of complex leadership situations for which I am responsible.
› I am motivating and broadening the experience of those for whom I am responsible.
› I am encouraging those for whom I am responsible to raise questions, think creatively, act interdependently, and build community.
› I am spending adequate time with those for whom I am responsible.

- I am relating well to my supervisor.
- I am courageously leading change and building consensus and trust in complex cross-cultural, multi-cultural, and inter-cultural paradigms and in both global and local contexts.
- I am placing priority and resources on developing inter-generational, multi-cultural men and women as leaders.
- I am helping strengthen partnerships and partnering opportunities with leaders in the Alliance Organizations, SIL, and other agencies.
- I am growing personally, spiritually, and professionally through formal and informal opportunities.

The team members preferred to maintain this as an active discussion rather than making it a concrete document. The values expressed are worth considering, including those about sensitivity to the cultural perspectives existing on the leadership team and in the Alliance community, now representing over 85 nations. The leadership team was seeking to elevate and promote what David Livermore calls Cultural Intelligence (CQ).

Livermore defines CQ as one's 'capability to function in cultural contexts, including different national, ethnic, organizational, generational, and many other contexts.... It's a form of intelligence that can be developed and learned by anyone.'[45] In other words, it is about 'one's ability to understand, appreciate, and interact with people from different cultural backgrounds.'[46] Livermore observes how '70 percent of international ventures fail because of cultural differences.'[47] He suggests that performing too much cultural adaptation can create 'suspicion and distrust', nevertheless, 'inflexible behaviour' can be disastrous for most leaders and their organizations.[48] 'Uncritically accepting everything in a new culture and turning one's back on one's own birth culture is not culturally intelligent behaviour.'[49] So, there are two questions to consider: '(1) Is this a tight or loose culture [how strong the social norms are]; and (2) Will adapting compromise my organization or me?'[50]

Today WGA serves through offering global missional leadership. The WGA leadership's immediate priorities focus on promoting clarity of purpose and building unity of commitment within the community of organizations that make up the Alliance.

---

[45] David Livermore, *Leading with Cultural Intelligence* (New York: AMACOM, 2105), ix-x.

[46] Livermore, 33.

[47] Livermore, x.

[48] Livermore, 178.

[49] Livermore, 178-79.

[50] Livermore, 180.

Journey Reflections (People with a Purpose)

The gospel of John 17:20–23 states

> My prayer is not for them alone. I pray also for those who will believe in me through their message, that all of them may be one, Father, just as you are in me and I am in you. May they also be in us so that the world may believe that you have sent me. I have given them the glory that you gave me, that they may be one as we are one—I in them and you in me—so that they may be brought to complete unity. *Then the world will know* [emphasis added] that you sent me and have loved them even as you have loved me.

This span of years from 2011 to 2015 saw the shift away from multiple categories of organizations, the growth of global involvement, and the recognition of a widening spectrum of ways to be involved in the Bible translation movement. All of this, combined with a growing emphasis on discerning how God was leading in his mission, opened up a new opportunity to see the blossoming of what Christ depicts in his John 17 prayer: that when we are one in him—then the world will know. Recognizing this as *the* strategy for reaching the world with the message of God's love gives new weight and prominence to the importance of learning how to demonstrate unity in diversity, to live and serve authentically in community, and to genuinely understand and embrace the God-given best of all peoples and cultures. This is not a journey of random travellers who meet or pass each other occasionally, but rather a journey under God's direction, of God-ordained purpose and people, traveling together in and toward the Kingdom that has come and is yet to come.

- What transitions to community-thinking do you see in this chapter?
- What opportunities for greater unity do you see in your context?
- What do you see as key elements to being culturally inclusive in ways that will enrich your community/organization/context?

Chapter 7
Flourishing: 2016–2020

Introduction

This era under review coincides with the 500th anniversary of the Protestant Reformation in 1517. In 2017, many events around the world commemorated the significance of the Reformation. For the Bible translation movement, these memorials provided a reminder of the importance of faithfulness to Scripture. Purposeful remembering is essential, as the teacher in Ecclesiastes notes, 'No one remembers the former generations' (1:10). Theologian Alister McGrath describes how 'the study of history makes us alert to both the mistakes of the past and the alarming way in which they are repeated in the present.'[1]

How did the Protestant Reformation recall to memory the importance of faithfulness to God's Word? It helps to place the Alliance's history and its motivation within the Reformation's five pillars of *sola Scriptura* (Scripture alone), *sola gratia* (grace alone), *solus Christus* (Christ alone), and *soli Deo gloria* (glory to God alone) with '*sola fide*—the doctrine of justification by faith alone' as the trigger for the Reformation.[2] *Sola fide* is based on the foundation of *sola Scriptura*—'the affirmation that the Bible alone is the ultimate authority for life and doctrine.'[3] The doctrine of the authority of Scripture shaped the Reformers and gave them 'the courage to separate [from] Rome in their proclamation of the gospel.'[4] Since the 16th century, the 'affirmation of the divine inspiration and authority of the Bible has stood at the centre of Reformed faith.'[5] '*Sola Scriptura* acknowledges that there are other important authorities for the Christian, authorities who should be listened to and followed. However, Scripture alone is our final authority.'[6] Sola Scriptura and the Protestant Reformation serve as a historical reminder of the theological debates of the past that stressed the importance of and strengthened the cause of access to the Bible in all of the languages of the world's peoples.

At the start of 2020 emerged the unprecedented and unsettling time of what became known as the global pandemic of COVID-19. The crisis did not take our

---

1 Alister McGrath, *Historical Theology: An Introduction to the History of Christian Thought*, 2nd ed. (Oxford: Wiley, 2013), 14.

2 David Barrett, *God's Word Alone: The Authority of Scripture* (Grand Rapids: Zondervan, 2016), 11.

3 Barrett, 13.

4 Barrett, 13.

5 Barrett, 14.

6 Barrett, 23.

living God by surprise. Words of reassurance come from Psalm 117:1–2 (NLT), 'Praise the Lord, all you nations. Praise him, all you people of the earth. For his unfailing love for us is powerful; the Lord's faithfulness endures forever. Praise the Lord!'

Every nation connected to the Bible translation movement had to manage the effects of the pandemic, and most struggled to do so. With no clear, familiar, or customary pathways of response, each country did things differently, though the wearing of protective face masks soon became a global commonality. There was much uncertainty. Information about the virus and the medical advice on what to do was slow in coming and often varied. International air travel ground to a halt as countries closed their borders, and anyone travelling or living abroad unable to quickly heed their government's advice to return home remained stranded where they were. Many airlines and businesses went bankrupt. Widespread social and economic hardship resulted as people were required to work from home, schools were closed, and children had to learn online and remotely. Attempts to open back up were often futile as cities of millions of people were quickly put back into lockdown whenever the virus began spreading again. Eventually, the mass roll-out of quickly developed vaccines and increasing natural immunity held up glimmers of hope for a way out of the difficult times.

In the early months, as the virus spread from Wuhan, China, across the globe, due in no small part to readily accessible international travel, various opinions emerged about how long this pandemic would last. Some thought just a few months. Few at the time believed it would define all of 2020, yet it remained a significant problem in 2021 and into 2022.

Churches shut due to lockdown restrictions. Many were able to go online quickly, bringing the blessing of support to the community. Pastors and church administrators anticipated the challenge of what to do when their congregations could return to the physical meeting place. Would they come back? What would they come back to? Should it—or could it—be something different?

Christians could easily centre on their fear and uncertainty. Or, they had the opportunity be joyful and draw closer to the Lord through his grace. Sometimes they were doing both. Christians faced the opportunity to respond to the pandemic by exercising discernment, wisdom, and decisive action where needed. They also had the chance to lean into Scripture knowing God had led his people through crises many times before. This was evident in how he cared for the people of Israel throughout the Old Testament. In the New Testament, the Holy Spirit enabled the first disciples after Jesus left them (including some who initially felt abandoned by him). Many times, in the book of Acts, God intervened for his messengers when their lives were under threat. In similar ways, in 2020, the faith of many

Christians was unimaginably stretched. And the Bible translation movement went through some remarkable changes as God continued to carry out his mission.

Preparing to Celebrate

Final preparations for the 2016 Wycliffe Global Gathering represented the primary focus of the first half of the year. As custodian of the event, the Alliance Board oversaw who was invited to attend, which included all Alliance Organizations that had already signed the Covenant/Statement of Commitment and thus were part of WGA, as well as AOs in the process of and committed to signing by the time of the event, and thus were also able to attend. These organizations had both voice and vote at the Global Gathering, which helped communicate to all the AOs that the signing was a commitment to each other, not a contract between an organization and the WGA leadership. The board also invited to the Global Gathering those organizations that were interested in signing but as yet had no official links with WGA, granting them observer status with voice.

Based on a decision made between the WGA Executive Director Kirk Franklin and the board, implementing these signing requirements with the individual organizations largely fell to the area directors to sign each Covenant on behalf of the WGA Executive Director. The other signatory was the executive director, or equivalent, of each AO. The rationale that this responsibility fell to the area director was that it was this person's responsibility to maintain and nurture the relationships with each AO in each Area. With the approval of the referendum in November 2015 by the former WMOs with vote, the Alliance's relationship with the AOs now rested on each organization signing and abiding by the Covenant/Statement of Commitment.

Area directors followed a process of getting to know the applicant organization over time and through multiple interactions. This process could take several years with organizations that were new to the Alliance. The area director and the organization's leadership would take time to explore the benefits, and what it meant to be a part of the Alliance. These included:

› invitations to the Alliance's consultations, Area meetings, and Global Gathering.
› opportunities for input and confirmation of changes or modifications to the Alliance's By-Laws (the Alliance's highest form of governing policies).
› opportunities for input and confirmation regarding the Alliance's Board of Directors.
› invitations to provide input and discussion on the Alliance's Area and global strategy and budget.

- access to expertise, mentoring, and advice from members of the ALT, including the area directors and Area offices.
- listing of the AO on WGA's website, including prayer information, articles, and resources accessible by the Alliance's global audience.
- formal and informal networking with other AOs.
- recognition of an organization as being part of WGA, together with an expectation that such organizations were continually and conscientiously working at being trusted and healthy partners.

When the time came for the applicant organization to move forward in the process; the area director would talk to any other AO already in that country to determine if the new organization was relationally compatible with the existing one and whether the AO welcomed the new organization into WGA, thus avoiding relational tensions between multiple AOs in the same country. The final stage was the signing of the Covenant/Statement of Commitment, which outlined the expectations and benefits of being in WGA.

As the area directors met with the various leaders of the organizations interested in or planning to sign, the WGA leadership was particularly interested in how each organization embraced the values and ethos of WGA, expressed through the vision, mission, and core values of the Alliance, and also through the Bible Translation Programs Philosophy Statement and the Principles for Funding. The Principles for Community (see chapter 10) was, however, the most important of the statement documents for these new organizations because it outlined expectations of how AOs would relate with and behave towards each other and to the Alliance as a whole. The value of community remained fundamentally important for the Alliance to flourish as a movement in God's mission.

Crisis in Relationship

It was the Alliance leadership's commitment to and interpretation of these Principles for Community that would be the tipping point of a crisis with two key organizations in the Bible translation movement who were in the process of moving across from Participating Organization status to becoming AOs. These two organizations worked closely together, and at the time, held some degree of influence over each other. In both cases, the crisis resulted from the organizations' response to how the Alliance leadership interpreted the spirit of the Covenant/Statement of Commitment. The leaders of these two applicant organizations signed the document without hesitation, but due to ongoing concerns about these organizations' ability to live according to community values, the area director hesitated to sign. In both situations, the area director cited the need for more time, reflection, and dialogue. Both organizations, however, quickly responded by leaving the Alliance. One organization even turned to public media outlets to announce they had left the Alliance based on doctrinal disagreement over the Divine Familial Terms debate (see chapter 6). Though the other organization didn't use public media to convey it, they announced to their AO partners that the Alliance leadership effectively told them to leave, which meant they wouldn't be present at the Global Gathering. In the latter case, the organization eventually was able to join the Alliance after a meeting with the organization's board, leadership, and the Alliance leadership. In the former case, their separation from the Alliance was ongoing and indefinite.

Both organizations involved in this situation had been and continued working closely with many AOs. The crisis created misunderstanding between the AOs and the Alliance leadership, traversing the implications of these decisions. Rather than taking the easier path of signing the Covenant/Statement of Commitment with these two organizations, the Alliance leadership chose to uphold the community values that defined the Alliance. This test of defending values would shape the Alliance for the foreseeable future.

The New Community

In May of 2016 in Chiang Mai, Thailand, two major meetings took place simultaneously: SIL's ICON (International Conference) and WGA's Global Gathering. Unlike the interconnected global meetings of the past, these meetings fit and fulfilled the unique purposes, strategies, and structures of the two organizations and addressed topics critical to their participants, contexts, and development. SIL's ICON was a meeting of delegates and SIL's international leadership. The WGA meeting comprised AO Directors and Board Chairs and the ALT. Unfortunately, ten African AO leaders were unable to receive travel visas, leaving Africa under-represented in the Global Gathering. This factor would influence later discussions on future locations for Global Gatherings to give all participants a better chance to obtain visas.

While most sessions of the two meetings took place separately, joint sessions were held to hear introductory and closing reports from executive directors and board chairs of both organizations. Each day also included a joint time of worship with prayer, music, and time in the Word, reflecting on the theme of community. ALT member Mary Lederleitner coordinated these daily joint devotional sessions. She involved various leaders from the Alliance and SIL who gave reflections on these topics and Scriptures:

› Designed for community: community flows from the nature of God (Genesis

1:26–28; Matthew 5:43–48; John 13:34–35).

- Identified in community: as God's people we are called to community (Romans 12:1–21).
- Committed to community: differences and difficulties will never negate that calling (1 Corinthians 12:1–13:3).
- Community in action: community glorifies God, facilitates growth and illustrates the Gospel (Ephesians 3:14–5:2).
- The Attraction of community: community attracts people to God and his mission (John 17:1–23).

After the reflections, table groups of six to eight people with a mix of WGA and SIL members processed what they had heard. Feedback from these table discussions indicated participants found the devotional presentations deep and meaningful, and their discussions were rich and insightful. A noticeable warmth and kindness in the event carried through to meals and break times, an important indicator of the health of the event and of the community as the two organizations sought to relate well in new contexts and relationships markedly different from their historical experience of being known as a 'mirror image' pair of organizations.

More than 500 people from around the world sat together discussing God's Word and praying for each other and the global Bible translation movement. Some described these times of worship as 'a foretaste of heaven'. Strangers became friends. Those present in the room were representative of the global church. The worship team led the community in singing to God in many of the languages represented in the room. At one point, a song, translated into about 20 languages, was projected so that all could sing, and the delegates stood and praised the Lord in all those languages simultaneously. Described as a foretaste of Revelation 7:9–10, this illustrated John's vision from the throne room of God where he saw a great multitude that no one could count from all tribes and languages, standing before the throne and before the Lamb, crying out with a loud voice, 'Salvation belongs to our God who sits on the throne, and to the Lamb!' This moment of community worship expressed with confident hope that one day this Scripture would be fulfilled.

The devotional speaker was Piet Meiring from South Africa, whose input focussed on how love and forgiveness can impact a community of believers. It was a powerfully applicable message to the SIL and WGA delegates in their inter-organizational relationships.

In a joint session, WGA Executive Director Kirk Franklin presented an overview of the Alliance, providing an opportunity to celebrate what God was doing, and orienting those present who were unfamiliar with the Alliance's journey. A goal of WGA was to nurture an environment in which like-minded organizations and churches served together in God's mission through Bible translation movements worldwide. Franklin described three missiological themes critical to the current realities of the Alliance which shape its community and near future: (1) Polycentrism as an outcome of the community; (2) Friendship that strengthens the community; and (3) Generosity in the community.

In his conclusion, Franklin paid tribute to the WGA Board under Roger Welch's chairing, expressing the joy and privilege of serving under them with accountability to them. The entire ALT demonstrated genuine community, accountable to the Lord and to each other. Franklin also thanked his wife Christine, who stood by him through both good and challenging times, patiently supportive of his travels at the invitation of AOs, WGA partners, or Area leadership.

Franklin's desire for their time together was that the WGA community would grow in confidence in the Lord, knowing that God is at work perfecting his grace in everyone's lives. Just as Paul had the believers at Philippi in his heart because of their partnership in the gospel with him (Philippians 1:7), likewise Franklin encouraged each person present to have each other in their hearts, continually growing as a community in insight and revelation, discerning how to live to the glory of the triune God.

Celebration of Community

At the beginning of the Global Gathering, in the Alliance's first meeting on its own, Florence Wamae, the Africa Area Communication Coordinator from Kenya, emceed a celebration during which the four area directors—Mũndara Mũturi (Africa), Nydia Garcia-Schmidt (Americas), Simon Wan (Asia-Pacific), and Hannes Wiesmann (Europe) gave a brief overview of the process of the acceptance and signing of the Covenant/Statement of Commitment in each region. Projected maps indicated which organizations had signed the covenant, which had not yet signed but were in process, and in a couple of cases, which organizations, recognizing a ministry focus in areas other than Bible translation, wouldn't be signing and would no longer be WGA members. During this overview and time of celebration, along with the maps, organization leaders were asked to stand when their Area was presented, visually conveying who comprised WGA now.

A new AO leader spontaneously stated, 'this is the first time that we are here as real members of the Alliance,' a testament to the structural changes made just in time for the Global Gathering because the WMOs with vote decided to include all AOs, without distinction of category or status. When AO delegates took part in their first opportunity to vote for the new Alliance Board, many did so with dancing and rejoicing to and from the ballot boxes, celebrating that they were no longer on the outside or fringes. They were indeed part of the Alliance community. The structural changes and the new Covenant/Statement of Commitment enabled this to happen, and they were grateful.

In a separate session, WGA concentrated on two topics: Third Table Community Experience and Vision 2025. The discussions about Vision 2025 reminded the participants that in 1999 the original adopters of the vision had to discern God's guidance to move forward, often grappling with next steps to making that vision a reality while during the necessary though often halting organizational transition from institution to movement.

The Third Table discussions took place over three sessions during which participants explored how to strengthen healthy biblical communities in WGA. Sessions built on the daily times of worship and biblical reflection, which emphasized various aspects of community. During the first session, participants from five regions (Africa, Asia, Canada and the US, Europe, and Latin America and the Caribbean) identified five characteristic beliefs, values, attitudes, or practices from their region that they could offer as gifts to the rest of the Alliance to help build healthy biblical communities. The gifts from the five regions were combined to make a total of 15 gifts. In the second session, participants met in table groups to determine which of the gifts they were or weren't ready to receive, and why they were or weren't ready to receive them.

A clear majority of positive feedback went to 12 of the 15 gifts, which were then regarded as 'received' (see table below). Each participant then had an opportunity to vote on which four of these 12 gifts they felt were most important to the Alliance. Of the three gifts that received the most votes out of the approximately 630 votes cast, all were centred on relationships: Friendships, Relationships, *Ubuntu*; Working Well Together; and Trust in Relationships.

Received: Gift #1 *Simplicidad y Economia* [Simplicity and Frugality] (Offered by Latin America and Caribbean)	Received: Gift #2 Love to Celebrate (Offered by Africa)	Received: Gift #3 Accountability in Relationships and Resources (Offered by Canada and the US)
Not yet ready to be received: Gift #4 Boundless Optimism (Offered by Canada and the US)	Received: Gift #5 Respect for Leadership (Offered by Asia)	Not yet ready to be received: Gift #6 Transparency (Offered by Europe)
Received: Gift #7 *Trabalho Árduo* [Hard Work] (Offered by Latin America and Caribbean)	Received: Gift #8 Trust in Relationships (Offered by Canada, the US and Europe)	Received: Gift #9 *Flexibilidad y Adaptabilidad* [Flexibility and Adaptability] (Offered by Latin America and the Caribbean)

Received: Gift #10 Working Well Together (Offered by Asia)	Received: Gift #11 Value of Individuals (Offered by Canada, the US and Europe)	Received: Gift #12 Friendship, Relationship, *Ubuntu* (Offered by Latin America, Caribbean and Asia)
Received: Gift #13 Hospitality/Generosity (Offered by Asia, Canada and the US)	Received: Gift #14 Servant Leadership (Offered by Asia and Europe)	Not yet ready to be received: Gift #15 Value & Respect (Offered by Africa)

Table 3: The 15 Third Table Gifts

The three gifts the group was not yet ready to receive were Gift #4, Boundless Optimism, Gift #6, Transparency, and Gift #15, Value and Respect. Reasons for lack of readiness to receive these gifts included uncertainty regarding the meaning or intent of the gift, a desire for more clarity, wanting to put conditions on the gift, or queries about the Alliance-wide appropriateness of the gift.

During the third session, participants chose a specific gift and discussed how to put it into practice, showing the results of their discussion on chart paper. Small groups also met to discuss two of the three gifts that the group was not yet ready to receive (Gift #6, Transparency, and Gift #15, Value and Respect). They used this as a learning opportunity to explore what lay behind the lack of readiness.

The experience of the Third Table highlighted the cultural diversity present in the WGA community and the importance of dialogue and ongoing communication. It showed how WGA was better together. The exercise increased awareness of the uniqueness of each part of the community. Though likely their memory of the Third Table exercise and the gifts faded once leaders returned to their local contexts, observations and communications point to the continuation of the resulting incentive to deepen relationships within WGA.

New Board

An important function of the Global Gathering was to approve the members for the Alliance Board, as the nominating committee had already done the pre-processing and recommending of the board members. Now all the AOs had the right and responsibility to vote to approve the slate of candidates, rather than the previous structure of only the 29 organizations with vote having that option.

The AOs affirmed the board members as follows: Nestor Ahoyo Adjovi (Benin), Paul Bendor-Samuel (UK), Decio de Carvalho (Brazil) incumbent, Nicky Chong (Singapore) incumbent, Bob Creson (US/Founding Organization) incumbent, Marco Herrera (US), Agnes Lid (Norway), Lena Lim (Singapore), Ana Cristina Mejía (El Salvador) incumbent, Jayne Mutiga (Kenya), Bambang

Widjaja (Indonesia) incumbent. This new board was the most culturally diverse in the WBT-WBTI-Alliance's history. It also had four women representatives—the most in its history.

At a brief board meeting during the Global Gathering, Decio de Carvalho was elected as board chair, with Agnes Lid as vice chair. The board also addressed the topic of initial term length for the board members. The board had consulted with the AOs and decided to stagger the term of service for each of the board members. They could be reappointed at these intervals. Consequently, the process decided on was: one-year (2017): Nicky Chong, Marco Herrera, Ana Cristina Mejía; two-year (2018): Nestor Ahoyo Adjovi, Paul Bendor-Samuel, Agnes Lid, Lena Lim; and three-year (2019): Decio de Carvalho, Bob Creson, Jayne Mutiga, Bambang Widjaja.

Search for Next Executive Director

Franklin's term would end in 2018, and initiating a search process for the executive director was critical for the newly appointed WGA Board. The board's timeline included assembling a list of nominees for the role by mid-2016, appointment made by May 2017, an overlap time for the incoming and outgoing executive directors from November 2017, with the overlap completed by May 2018. To initiate this process called for the new board to form a search committee and update the profile of the executive director role from when the process was last used in 2006. Meeting the timeline required that they start the process immediately.

In a brief meeting held during the Global Gathering, the board explored the possibility of pausing the executive director search and selection process, extending Franklin's term to end in 2020 at the Global Gathering. Though unexpected, Franklin was open to further investigation of the proposal, and the board suspended their timeline, to be reviewed later in 2016. The board members committed to pray about asking Franklin to continue in his current role, and Board Chair Decio de Carvalho and Vice Chair Agnes Lid would meet with Franklin in September to discuss this issue. In the meantime, working groups were set up to:

› engage with the Franklins to determine their current situation and frames of mind regarding their roles so far, and to consider their perspectives regarding a transition to a new executive director within the next two years.
› work with the Alliance community seeking their input into the process and determining how better to support the executive director in the role.
› create a profile document for the executive director role.

Discontinuing Meeting with SIL Board

At a joint meeting in May of the SIL and Alliance Boards held immediately before the SIL ICON and the Global Gathering, the Alliance Board made known that the time was approaching for them to meet on their own rather than jointly with SIL as it had done since the 1940s. The Alliance Board wanted the space to work through the governance issues required by the new Alliance community, formed around the Covenant/Statement of Commitment. SIL was also embarking on a new era, with a new executive director, Michel Kenmogne, a new leadership team, and a new board. This May meeting was the last joint meeting of the two boards, ending a 74-year pattern of meeting for the same dates at the same locations, with joint and separate sessions. From now on, the boards could select dates and locations that better suited the requirements of their respective organizations and board members.

Another significant change took place after the SIL ICON and the Global Gathering. Franklin shared his observations with the WGA Board that when the Global Gathering was held at the same place and time as the SIL ICON, it created many challenges, especially for WGA. An example was Alliance delegates wanting to attend SIL sessions because their organizations worked closely with SIL. When the Alliance needed these leaders in its sessions and SIL simultaneously wanted them in the SIL meetings, this created tensions with some of these leaders and their partners in SIL. Attending both meetings was impossible for participants when the two organizations held their meetings simultaneously. Franklin proposed that the next time the Wycliffe Global Gathering met in May 2020, it called for an entirely different kind of event suited just for the needs and opportunities of WGA. The tradition of meeting with and at the same time as SIL was less important. Also, this change would better serve SIL, as meeting separately and at a different time and place would enable the Alliance to invite key SIL leaders to its meetings, and vice versa. Otherwise, the logistics of handling two separate events with joint sessions would continually become even more difficult. This was the direction the WGA Board wanted to take, and it called for negotiation with SIL leaders, which happened over the following months.

Franklin, de Carvalho, and Lid met with SIL Executive Director Michel Kenmogne and Board Chair Karel van der Mast to discuss the rationale for the WGA Board's request to be released from future joint meetings with the SIL Board, including the joint SIL ICON/Wycliffe Global Gathering. Concerns expressing how this could affect the SIL and the WGA partner relationship arose while also acknowledging that joint board meetings were not the only or the best way to maintain or nurture a partnership. Boards emphasized governance, but the partnership was managed at the administrative level.

New Board in Motion

The newly appointed board met for its first full meeting in November 2016, hosted by Wycliffe Germany at its recently developed Karimu Conference Centre at Holzhausen. The board spent a day in orientation activities and presentations for its new members. Franklin spoke on how WGA evolved, highlighting its missiological foundations. He then informed the board of upcoming changes to the ALT including:

› Stephen Coertze shifting from Consultant for Missiological Reflection to Director for Missiology.
› Susan Van Wynen departing from Communication to become Director for Strategy.
› Phil Prior (UK) was joining the team as the new Director for Communication.
› Mary Lederleitner, Consultant for Learning, was stepping down to pursue other ministry opportunities.

WGA Africa Area Director Mũndara Mũturi oriented the board concerning developments in his region, stating that there were 54 countries with 2,118 indigenous languages, five international linguistic blocks (English, French, Arabic, Spanish, Portuguese), and a population of 1.1 billion people with the average age of 19.5 years. There were 16 AOs, including two new ones: ITA (Guinea Bissau) and ACTB (Equatorial Guinea). The Area's leadership team focussed on developing Bible translation movements, coordinating, advising, guiding, training, and coaching Alliance Organizations, and providing an interface between the ALT and AOs, and between the AOs and the SIL administration in areas of partnering. The Area's strategic plan centred on organizational development, church engagement, and strengthening Bible translation programs for the AOs. Mũturi stated that these organizations faced many challenges such as discovering their identity and lacking 'Alliance-ness'—the concept of how these organizations lived out the values of the Alliance, including how to act and respond in community. Many AOs also expected much support from the Area. This posed a problem since the Area team was intentionally small, designed primarily for facilitation. Political instability and the high cost of travel within the continent, and difficulties for the Area team to obtain visas, presented additional challenges.

Other team members who met with the board to help them in their orientation process were Director of Missiology Stephen Coertze and Director for Strategy Susan Van Wynen. Coertze discussed the importance of missiology in the evaluation of mission practices expressed within the Alliance. Some examples include the shift in mission practices in Scripture and church history, missiology as evaluation of mission theory and practice, the process and history of missiological reflection within the Alliance, outcomes of the Alliance's journey of missiological reflection (see chapter 10), and thoughts about the future of missiology within the Alliance. Plans involved ongoing annual consultations, as well as special interest consultations on topics and themes of importance to the Alliance's journey. Van Wynen described how strategic planning could be rethought from a missiological perspective (see chapter 12).

Greatest Challenges Ahead

The board gathered for its meeting in May 2017 in San Juan, Puerto Rico, hosted by Board Chair Decio de Carvalho, who resided there. The board spent one evening meeting with friends of Bible translation in the San Juan area. In his report to the board, Franklin detailed the top three issues that could most significantly impact the Alliance and its organizations over the next three years. These were as follows:

- Developing and leading global-regional-local relationships: This included WGA leaders learning to think globally and act locally. This called for an increase in displays of generosity in funding and resource sharing across the Alliance, and welcoming shared ideas and expertise.
- Serving together in community in all of WGA's diversity: This meant that the larger, historical AOs needed to find their places in the WGA community and make their best contributions. Wider participation from AOs in the Bible Translation Program Stream and the Training in Bible Translation Roles Stream was required. Emphasis on developing community in WGA across geographical realities while recognizing language differences also called for attention.
- The WGA's ideology and ideas impacting its practice: This required helping the growing cohort of emerging leaders to develop their global missional mindset. It would involve the values of the Alliance (e.g., community, friendship, polycentrism, creating third spaces) positively impacting the broader Bible translation movement. And it entailed WGA learning how to serve with partners who may not share all of its ideas or values.

Challenges for African Community

In April 2017, the WGA Africa Area hosted a meeting with 40 AO leaders at Ruiru, Kenya. The theme of the meeting was 'Being of one mind and voice to glorify

God' (Romans 15:6). Its overall objective was to understand the values of WGA and put them into practice. Stephen Coertze facilitated a missiological discussion on funding as part of the meeting. In the process, the AO leaders identified their external partners, and thus gained a better understanding of the breadth of partnerships taking place. The results highlighted these organizations:

- Wycliffe US (15 mentions)
- Seed Company (18 mentions)
- Alliance Organizations outside of Africa, other than Wycliffe US and Seed Company (12 mentions), including Wycliffe Netherlands, UK, Canada, Hong Kong, Finland, and Switzerland
- Wycliffe Associates (4 mentions)
- SIL (3 mentions, plus 1 for SIL LEAD)
- JAARS (4 mentions)
- OneBook (5 mentions)
- Other organizations such as TearFund (a total of 5 organizations were listed)

The two AO partners outside of Africa most extensively engaged with African AOs were Seed Company, followed by Wycliffe US.

The AO leaders also discussed whether there were still noticeable effects of Western colonization on the African continent, and they offered this summary of hindrances:

- 'They taught us to eat the fish, not to catch the fish.'
- The education system was built on the Western system, but in the process, deprived many Africans of dignity.
- In many African minds, all solutions to problems and prosperity are in the West.
- Western stories of Africa often exaggerate or embellish stories of African realities.
- A perception that Africans need to portray themselves as ignorant and poor in order to be relevant within world missions.
- The languages from colonialism (French, Spanish, Portuguese, and English) dominate local languages.
- Educated people prefer English or French church services.

A summary of influences in Francophone Africa:

- Francophone Africa uses the French language, which has helped build the French economy at the expense of the local economy.
- There are still supremacist mindsets held by some Westerners.
- Some Westerners use the power of money to have their way in partnerships with Africans.
- There is a chronic dependence on external funding and expertise.

› Limited commitment is apparent for capacity building of Africans for future roles in the Bible translation movement.
› An 'ecclesiastical colonization' by the church remains.
› A complex superiority and inferiority mindset deprives Africans of the power to negotiate.

A final point:

› The structure of churches often duplicates imported models of polity. The culture and language of the colonizer became synonymous with Christianity and civilization. While Africans get upset by this, they don't offer missiological alternatives and supply no clear missiological influence on church structures in the *missio Dei*.

Through this exercise, the African AO leaders identified their perceptions of colonialism's lingering effects in their contexts, which, combined with their analysis of their AO partners external to Africa, encouraged deeper exploration of resolutions to these challenges. At this point, Franklin noted 'that the relational complexities [faced] inside and outside of the Alliance' made it necessary 'to think differently, so that we can act differently', which he described as 'creating Third Spaces'.[7] He considered it necessary to intentionally make space in WGA for voices from the majority world to be represented and heard by the whole WGA community. According to Franklin, these spaces would allow all to come together as equals and indicate 'deliberately wanting to hear from other parts of the world that we don't normally hear from or associate with.... What can we learn from them? What can they learn from us? When we deliberately do this more and more, we are creating new Third Spaces that in turn create new possibilities for participating in God's mission.'[8]

Hearing this, the African AO leaders asked Franklin to help them create Third Spaces with some Western AOs who were their main external partners. Franklin agreed to help, setting in motion a proposal that the Alliance leadership shared with Wycliffe US and Seed Company to see if they would be willing to meet with the African AO leaders. This process of dialogue and negotiation about a Third Space would continue through the end of 2017. In March 2018, in Johannesburg, the first Third Space forum in Africa took place (see chapter 10).

The entire Alliance community would benefit from a better understanding of the polycentric leadership centres emerging within WGA. What had been taking place for some time now in WGA was a deliberate movement away from centralized leadership structures so that there could be more expressions of leadership

---

7 WGA, "Board Minutes," May 2017, 8.

8 WGA, May 2017, 12.

taking place among and within a community that was learning together. Creating Third Spaces was a polycentric move, in which WGA continued to experiment with better ways of shaping community across the Bible translation movement. WGA's leadership believed this approach honoured God by visibly displaying unity. WGA had a unique opportunity to pursue this in Africa.

Types of Organizations

Historically, modelled after the original organization—Wycliffe US—all the AOs shared similarities, with modifications according to region. After the restructuring of WBTI to WGA was well underway, other models of organizational structure emerged among newer AOs. The growth and composition of WGA had become diverse, and with more organizations wanting to join WGA, this showed no signs of slowing. Four groups describe the different types of organizations:

1) *Institutions:* Most of the AOs were institutional in structure, with a centralized framework that included departments or specialists which managed various operations. The institution was usually registered with the government of its country and abided by national laws. The organization demonstrated control over governance, finances, and personnel. A board governed its ministry. AO institutions were found in Africa, Asia, Europe, Pacific, and the Americas. These institutions included church denominations and their mission boards who wanted to take a more active role in managing, equipping, or resourcing Bible translation programs in their nations or nearby regions. Thus far, these were present in Latin America, Africa, and Indonesia.

2) *Movements:* Unlike an institution, the essentials characterizing a movement include not being closely controlled, not likely established through legislation, and probably having an informal structure. It could be composed of individuals, AOs, and other partners in a given geographical region who chose to work together. Associations in countries where Bible translation had been underway for a long time, such as those found so far in Latin America, offer one illustration of a movement. These were usually indigenous language communities who believed they benefited by participating in the Alliance and being connected with and learning from a global body.

3) *Hybrids:* Some AOs didn't have a traditional institutional structure and were highly decentralized but maintained some vestiges of institutionalism for operational requirements, such as maintaining financial systems and standards, governance, and accountability. These requirements were more formal than those found in a movement. These hybridized organizations could have some aspects of a movement while simultaneously holding some degree of control and structure

more typical of institutions with a centralized hierarchy. More recently developing, and likewise found in Latin America (as in *Institutions*, above), their operations flowed back and forth between movement and institution.

4) *Unofficial/undocumented organizations/movements/networks:* A stipulation of signing the Alliance's Covenant/Statement of Commitment was that the AO operated within the laws of its country. However, in many parts of the world, AOs could not officially register or be recognized due to laws prohibiting their ministry. Recognizing that often these AOs existed in countries considered closed to Christian ministry—including parts of Asia, the Middle East, and North Africa—this called for working out a connection between the Alliance and these groups without jeopardizing the ministry in their contexts. This area necessitated further reflection and discussion by the board and ALT. (It is worth noting how earlier in 2011, the WGA Board had asked Franklin to explore ways to provide administrative support for countries and regions not currently within the defined boundaries of WGA Area structures but where a church was growing. For example, historically, WGA had little or no administrative presence or resources in regions including the Middle East and North Africa. Rather than creating new Area infrastructure, the board urged the WGA Area Directors to be creative and flexible in engaging with the church beyond the Alliance's conventional Area frameworks.)

Alliance Operations

When WBTI separated its operations from SIL in 2008, SIL still managed several areas of its day-to-day operations, including the email system, the intranet called Insite, and the finance systems. As WGA became more familiar with and accustomed to its mission, it continued with the process of separating operations. WGA Director for Operations Judy Bokelman led this process, working closely with the WGA CFO Kee Ai Koh and a new ALT position of Consultant for IT filled by Martijn de Vries (Netherlands). An operational change was to separate the email host domain from SIL. Efforts were also underway to have an HR system, that wasn't part of the old joint Wycliffe and SIL Insite intranet, that would serve AOs requiring something like this to meet their HR needs. WGA was in conversation with Wycliffe US about their plans to move to a new platform to see if this could serve the other AOs. Bokelman was also part of steering teams examining the finance system and other systems which depended heavily on Insite.

CFOs representing several AOs and the WGA CFO were looking at the complex finance system, including distribution of the 10% assessment from AO members' support. There were variances with AOs. For example, Germany assessed its members 10.35% to include the 0.35% contribution to WGA. Many AOs assessed their project funding income at more than 10%, while others did not assess any other income than member support.

Assessing Participation

As part of the process of signing the Covenant/Statement of Commitment, every AO identified the Participation Streams in which it was involved. In this way, the AO also determined the specifics of their contribution to the Bible translation movement through one or more of the seven Streams. From a governance monitoring perspective, the Alliance Board benefited from an environmental scan of how AOs were fulfilling specific Streams. The ALT surveyed AOs who were fulfilling the Funding Stream and compiled the results:

Region	Total no. of AOs	No. of AOs fulfilling Funding Stream	Total amount raised in 2016
Africa	16	4	US $147,288
Americas	30	11	US $168,148,948
Asia-Pacific	29	6	US $696,006
Europe	19	10	US $2,941,086
Total	**94**	**31**	**US $171,933,328**

Table 4: Participation in Funding Stream

According to WGA Africa Area leadership compiling the statistics, the amount of income raised could be as much as double the amount reported to the Area. African leaders pointed out that significant provision of and sharing of local resources for Bible translation occurs in the African context, suggesting data that cannot be counted or measured.

Another analysis examined how many AOs were fulfilling the Bible Translation Programs Stream. The data showed that out of the 91 AOs at the time, 31, or approximately one-third, were fulfilling the Stream.

Region	Total no. of AOs	No. of AOs fulfilling BT Programs Stream	Total no. of active Bible Translation programs
Africa	16	15	311
Americas	30	9	929*
Asia-Pacific	29	20	206
Europe	19	5	21
Total	**94**	**49**	**1,467****

Table 5: Participation in Bible Translation Programs Stream

* This amount included 839 projects with Seed Company involvement; up to half of these could encompass AOs also counted in the Africa, Asia-Pacific, and Americas Area numbers.

** Due to this overlap in counting, a more realistic total was approximately 1,000.

The measurements of the AOs' participation in the Funding and Bible Translation Programs Streams indicated the WGA community of organizations was providing better leadership and management of the Bible translation movement, compared with the time of restructuring WBTI in 2008. The growing involvement of AOs in the Bible Translation Programs Stream was a major topic of focus at the November 2017 board meeting.

New Directions in Bible Translation

ALT Director for Collaboration Bryan Harmelink presented an update in November 2017 to the board about newer developments in Bible translation, including tools for Oral Bible Translation, a Bible translation-related consultant approval process, training in Bible translation roles through a new program at YWAM's University of the Nations—Master of Applied Linguistics in Bible Translation—and a challenge from AOs to see a WGA-wide commitment to translating the 'whole counsel of God'. About this, Harmelink stated, 'we should be at a place where someone should have to argue why they only wanted to translate the New Testament and not the whole Bible.'[9] The board responded enthusiastically to the challenge from Harmelink's report. They recognized that the time had come for the Alliance to raise its own standards and to provide clear direction in areas previously overlooked or underdeveloped in the Bible translation movement.

The discussion included the thought that the ALT and Harmelink could simply give this direction to the AOs. But Franklin and Harmelink felt it would carry far more weight and authority as a directional statement from the board. The necessary expertise already existed, emerging throughout the Alliance community, needing only to be recognized and put into action. The board provided three directive statements:

1. The development of new Bible translation training: 'The board endorses, supports, and encourages the ALT in helping AOs and partners to work together to develop curricula for Bible translation training and processes that serve the changing contexts of Bible translation movements.'
2. A process to approve Bible translation consultants at the local AO level: 'The board endorses, supports, and encourages the ALT, together with Alliance

[9] WGA, "Board Minutes," November 2017.

Areas, Organizations, and partners, to develop appropriate guidelines for accrediting Bible translation consultants within the Alliance, and to review the concept and role of translation consultants within the translation process.'
3. Translating the whole counsel of God: 'The board endorses, supports, and encourages the ALT to: (1) "articulate the Alliance's commitment to the translation of the whole Bible"; (2) "encourage AOs to partner together with local communities to ensure that the whole Bible will eventually be translated and made available in the appropriate media"; and (3) "commit to establishing sustainable, community-based processes".'[10]

Until now, WGA had counted on other global Bible translation-related organizations to give direction to the more technical aspects of Bible translation, such as consultant development, Old Testament translations, and training for Bible translation roles. The WGA board's new directional statements were historic in their expressed desire to encourage AOs to apply dedicated leadership in these important areas.

Harmelink and Franklin sent out a communique to the AOs to share the board's statements and explain what each meant. For example, Harmelink stated, 'on the matter of accrediting or recognizing translation consultants, some AOs are already doing this, but others are not. This decision encourages all AOs to partner in ways that will contribute to increased capacity for translation consultancy in the global Bible translation movement.'[11] Regarding the topic of training in Bible translation roles, Harmelink spoke of the desire for the AOs to be playing an active role in 'partnership with others to develop training that is appropriate for their needs in the changing contexts in which they work.'[12] Concerning the whole counsel of God, Harmelink stated how this directive came 'in response to pleas for attention to the Old Testament as Scripture for the Church. This is already the expectation in many places, but this decision underscores the commitment of WGA to see this become normal practice.'[13]

The AOs were made aware that the ALT was not setting up formal structures to implement these directives. Instead, Harmelink, with the area directors and others on the ALT, would encourage and support AOs in taking leadership for Bible translation programs in their contexts. Within a year of announcing these directions, evidence of their positive impact on the AOs was emerging. For example, other institutions were looking at the YWAM program and exploring with Harmelink how to have something similar in other parts of the world. Paul Kimbi

---

[10] WGA, November 2017, 11.

[11] Bryan Harmelink with Kirk Franklin, "Communique from the Wycliffe Global Alliance: Announcing Directions in Bible Translation," November 2017, 1.

[12] Harmelink with Franklin, 1.

[13] Harmelink with Franklin, 2.

on the Africa Area team was helping create a process for consultant recognition in Africa. There was evidence that more AOs managing Bible translation programs were including the Old Testament in their goals.

Discerning Leadership

The entire process—raising Bible translation issues with the board, witnessing the board responding with its directives, followed by the ALT passing this information to the AOs, who then indicated their gratitude for the direction—presented a fitting illustration of WGA at work. It described an important issue ascending to the highest level of decision-making and governance, then rippling back through the entire WGA community, without the necessity to set up infrastructure and create new administrative positions to manage the process.

This process was very much in the spirit of a new purpose statement of the ALT that Franklin shared with the board. The ALT acted 'as a discerning community of global missional leaders that influences and inspires Bible translation movements, while encouraging AOs to fulfill, in community, their participation in God's mission [as it relates to] global Bible translation movements.'[14]

Helping leaders serve as discerning communities with a global missional mindset was also the focus of a new book that Franklin had written with Dave and Deborah Crough titled *Towards Global Missional Leadership* and published in 2017 by Regnum Books. The book, largely based on the Alliance's journey since 2008, emphasized globalization, leadership practices, and the *missio Dei*. A Spanish version, *Hacia un Liderazgo Misional y Global*, Regnum, 2017 was being distributed across Latin America. This version, revised in 2018 by the director of the Perspectives Program in Mexico, was used to help facilitate reflection on polycentrism and global mission with organizations there. Brazilian publisher Descoberta Editora released it in Portuguese, titled *Lideranca Missional e Global*. Released later in 2019 was the French version, titled *Vers Un Leadership Missional Mondial*, published by Regnum and printed by BTL's (Kenya) Tafsiri Press.

Consultant for Leadership Development Todd Poulter shared with the board a concept for sustainable leadership development processes that were characterized by: '(1) developing a *culture* of leadership development; (2) equipping leaders to lead with a global missional *mindset*; and (3) developing communities of leaders across cultures, regions, and generations.'[15]

At their November 2017 meeting in Singapore, Asia-Pacific Area Director Simon Wan gave an update to the board about the AOs in the region. He explained

[14] WGA, November 2017, 3.

[15] WGA, 2017, 5.

how vast the Area was, extending from India in the West to Tonga in the East. There were 29 AOs spread across sixteen countries, and 13 of these were in Indonesia. Since some contexts in Asia didn't allow for an established AO, the Area team was considering other strategies. The Area connected with the AO leaders to strengthen the Alliance community, help the AOs to remain relevant, create communities of reflective practitioners, and stay aligned with the Alliance's ethos.

Reviewing the Purpose

Those entrusted with governing an organization are responsible for ensuring that it is meeting its mission and following its vision. The ALT had been working on some revisions to foundational statements for the Alliance. These were processed and approved by the board in its May meeting. To demonstrate how these statements fit and flowed together, the ALT offered this progression:

> We are this: 'As a community of participants in God's mission, the Wycliffe Global Alliance provides leadership, influence, and service within Bible translation movements' (new Purpose Statement). So that we can do this: 'In communion with God and within the community of His Church, the Wycliffe Global Alliance contributes to the holistic transformation of language communities worldwide' (revised Mission Statement). So that this can become a reality: 'Individuals, communities, and nations transformed through God's love and Word expressed in their languages and cultures' (existing Vision Statement).[16]

The significant change of adding the new Purpose Statement was to signal that WGA was intentionally providing more effective and beneficial leadership, influence, and service within and to the movement. Though this provision was already happening, WGA's intention hadn't yet been emphasized in the defining statements. The ALT also released, through its foundational statements, descriptions of key terms that were essential to the Alliance community. This list of terms would continue to grow as they became part of the culture of the movement. The list included terms such as Alliance, Board Goals, Collaboration, Core Values, Friendship and Community, Global Missional Leadership Mindset, Holistic Mission, Integral Mission, Institution, Journey, *Missio Dei* (Mission of God), Missiological Reflection, Mission, Missional Intent, Polycentric Mission, Purpose Statement, Stewardship and Generosity, Third Spaces, Transformation,

[16] Susan Van Wynen, Dave Crough, and Kirk Franklin, "Foundational Statements of the Wycliffe Global Alliance," 2019, accessed 7 September, 2020, https://www.wycliffe.net/wp-content/uploads/2020/01/Alliance_Foundational_Statements_2019_09_EN.pdf.

Translation Movement(s), and Vision.

In each case, the description intended to explain how the Alliance's leadership interpreted or described that particular term. In other words, it took terms that were widely known and redefined them within the Alliance community. Here are a few examples:

> *Friendship and Community*—Friendship with God, with each other, and with those whom we are called to serve is a fundamental missiological principle for the Alliance because it gives God glory and serves as a visible demonstration of God's kingdom. Friendship takes place within and also creates and deepens community. The Alliance community shares common characteristics and commitments (Vision, Mission, Values, etc.) that bind together all of the Alliance Organizations.[17]

> *Third Spaces*—Deliberately creating safe spaces that enable different groups within the Alliance to come together to acknowledge, explore, discuss, understand, celebrate, reconcile, and create new friendships, ideas, and concepts, in and for God's mission. Each part of the body is needed, and our role has been to ensure that the body is healthy, growing, and effective. Rather than a binary approach to a conflict or decision—a 'right' way or a 'wrong' way—a preferred method is to negotiate a third way. This promotes interdependent cooperation of giving, receiving, and serving all across the global Bible translation movement, with all parties demonstrating respect and dignity in authentic partnerships based on genuine friendships in mission.[18]

Serving Bible Translation Movements

The ALT spent time in its January 2018 meeting held in Zacatlan, Mexico discussing how to describe its role of leading WGA as the Alliance served the Bible translation movements. This exercise had been ongoing since the WBTI and SIL International administrations separated in 2008. One key reason for creating WGA was the shift in the team's role from managing an institution to leading a movement. But this caused confusion for many AOs, still formed and functioning as institutions governed by complex management structures. In contrast, WGA had deliberately set a plan in motion to operate virtually, with a small leadership

[17] Van Wynen, Crough, and Franklin, 7.

[18] Van Wynen, Crough, and Franklin, 7.

team supported by a group of managers at various operational levels. The ALT decided it was time once again to articulate why it existed and how it operated.

The team reported to the board that the ALT's purpose 'when acting collectively' was to

- 'serve as a discerning community of global missional leaders;
- lead from a position of missiological reflection;
- influence and inspire Bible translation movements;
- support and encourage AOs as they fulfil, in community, their participation in God's mission as a part of Bible translation movements;
- attend to the wellbeing and effectiveness of the Alliance as a whole;
- operate with the delegated authority of the Alliance Board, on behalf of all AOs;
- serve as a catalyst to AOs in the growth and development of Bible translation movements; and
- serve the AOs by helping create environments and opportunities for every AO to be strengthened and able to serve well.'[19]

The ALT followed a framework of four areas of focus in an acrostic called ABLE:

- *A*: 'Alliance Organization community—AOs are able to contribute to and benefit from community life and practice'; this was carried out through serving in unity, supporting collaboration, and encouraging stewardship.[20]
- *B*: 'Bible translation capacity—AOs are able and equipped to participate in Bible translation'; this was focussed on the Bible Translation Programs Philosophy Statement and included priority given to the three-fold initiatives about Bible translation announced in 2017 (consultant accreditation, training programs for Bible translation, and translating the whole counsel of God.)[21]
- *L*: 'Leaders and leadership health—AOs are able to grow in sound leadership thought and practice'; this was accomplished through deepening missiological reflection, nurturing leaders, maintaining a vision for leadership development, developing leaders for the Bible translation movement, and creating a global missional leadership mindset.[22]
- *E*: 'Effectiveness—Alliance Organizations and the Alliance as a whole are able to function, share, and serve well'; this was achieved through supporting AOs, effective and timely communication, and ensuring the Alliance was trustworthy.[23]

---

19 Kirk Franklin, "How the Wycliffe Global Alliance Leadership Team Serves Bible Translation Movements," Unpublished paper, February 2018, 1.

20 Franklin, 1.

21 Franklin, 2.

22 Franklin, 2.

23 Franklin, 3.

Future Planning

There were two issues the WGA Board had to give attention to as it looked ahead: Global Gathering 2020, and coinciding with this, the transition of the executive director, as Franklin would be stepping down after 12 years in the role. Even though these two events were more than two years away, the board knew it needed to work on both. It set up a planning team, with Board Vice Chair Agnes Lid as its representative to the team and Dave Crough as event and program director. No longer tied to meeting in May every four years at the same location as SIL's International Conference at Chiang Mai, Thailand, the Alliance was now free to meet at a time and place of their choosing. After the ALT and board explored various possible locations in Asia, Africa, and Latin America, the decision was to hold the event in Johannesburg, South Africa, in September 2020.

Next Executive Director Search Process

The WGA Board took seriously its responsibility of ensuring the Alliance had an executive director, and in 2016, extended the term of service so that Franklin would serve until the Global Gathering in September 2020. At that time, he would have served for 12 years as the first executive director to lead WGA. In addition, looking back at the WBTI structure, Franklin was the longest-serving executive director in many years. In the past, board policy limited the terms and tied them to the WBTI Conventions (three-year cycle starting in the 1990s) and then Wycliffe Global Gatherings (four-year cycle starting in the 2000s).

Anticipating a two-year selection process, the board set up a search committee, chaired by Paul Bendor-Samuel, with five other board members, to represent themselves, the ALT, and WGA. The committee recognized this as a new undertaking for this board, none of whom had participated in WGA—nor been involved in the previous search WBTI conducted—in 2006–7. To a degree, the board felt like it was starting from scratch in the designing of a process to follow, as they set this timeline for the committee:

› May 2018: Search committee begins work.
› June 2018 (Ruiru, Kenya): Search committee meets with ALT to get input concerning desired characteristics for the executive director role.
› October 2018: Search committee makes a call across WGA for recommendations of suitable candidates.
› February 2019: The entire WGA community is asked to join in a week of prayer and fasting for the process and outcome. (This was in addition to the board

committee's process of a day per month for prayer for this process.)

- April 2019: Search committee processes the recommendations, then presents a short list to the board for consideration. The ALT is invited to give their comments. The short list is circulated to the AOs for comment.
- July 2019: Search committee has face-to-face interviews with the candidates on the short list. Spouses are included in the process.
- September 2019: Board has face-to-face interaction with the final one or two candidates recommended by the search committee. The board then makes its final decision and appoints the next executive director.
- March 2020: Outgoing executive director begins overlap with the incoming executive director.
- September 2020: Board oversees the handover to the incoming executive director at the end of the Wycliffe Global Gathering.

Europe Overview

At the May 2018 board meeting in Johannesburg, Europe Area Director Hannes Wiesmann gave an update on the AOs in his region. He indicated they were in stable societies with good infrastructure. The AOs were similar to one another in function. The Europe Area wasn't pursuing a strategy to create new AOs in countries where none existed. Instead, if any churches or other groups were interested in becoming part of the Alliance, the Area preferred to connect them with existing churches to build capacity for involvement in the Bible translation movement. A more recent development was that some European AOs were managing Bible translation projects in their countries, including projects involving diasporas of migrants from languages that still needed Bible translation. In all, European AOs were managing 20 Bible translation programs based in Europe.

Americas Overview

Americas Area Director Nydia Garcia-Schmidt updated the board at its September 2018 meeting. The Americas divided into four regions: North America, Latin America, Brazil, and the Caribbean. What was happening in the Bible translation movement in Latin America looked a lot like a social movement. Garcia-Schmidt's research found that factors contributing to the emergence of many of the movements included their dependence on the Holy Spirit's guidance. They also emerged out of a state or condition of dissatisfaction, which brought people together to find a solution. The Americas defined a translation movement as 'collective advocacy and action for Bible translation' and as a key aspect of the church's participation in God's mission. Bible translation movements are not owned or controlled by any one leader or group, but rather, they are 'guided and influenced by discerning, committed followers of Christ with the goal of all language communities having access to Scripture in a language they clearly understand.'[24]

The Americas Area was also exploring how the AOs were practicing generosity in their communities. They were discovering how the church was often not teaching about generosity but only waiting on donations. Recognizing that the subject of funding presented a challenge for AOs, the Area developed a financial diagnostic tool to help organizations see where they needed to improve.

Board Development

In July, between scheduled meetings, Decio de Carvalho resigned from the role of board chair and from the board. It was a critical time for the board as the search was already underway for the next executive director. In the midst of this, the board couldn't afford to allow WGA to drift from its mission, so they held virtual meetings to process what happened and chart a way forward. As a result, Vice Chair Agnes Lid stepped in as acting chair. She was elected as chair, with Marco Herrera elected as vice chair, at the September board meeting hosted by Seed Company at their Arlington, Texas headquarters. The board formally thanked de Carvalho for filling the role of Chair from May 2016 following previous Board Chair Roger Welch's retirement.

Financial Oversight

In 2018, Kee Ai Koh announced that she was stepping aside from her role as WGA CFO, which she held since 2012, and into the role of financial controller for the Alliance. Franklin informed the board of his intention to appoint current Board Treasurer Hannu Summanen as WGA CFO, proposing that this be combined with the role of treasurer. In this combination, as treasurer, Summanen would continue as a board officer reporting to the board chair, and as CFO, he would report to the director for operations and would work closely with the executive director. Combining the role brought synergy between the board's financial oversight responsibility and the day-to-day financial management through the CFO's role as part of the ALT. The board agreed to this change taking place in August. It ended a long tradition of having the treasurer as a separate function from the CFO, which WGA believed was no longer necessary. Furthermore, the board remained confident it could continue to carry out its responsibilities of financial monitoring.

[24] WGA, "Board Minutes," September 2018, 7.

New Appointments

From late 2018 to early 2019, many changes and additions took place among the ALT. This added new capacity and talent to the ALT, enabling some team members to reduce their involvement, allowing for other team members to take up these roles:

- New position of Associate Director (Regions), part-time: Mũndara Mũturi (Kenya) starting part-time in November. The four area directors would report to him.
- Director for Leadership Development, part-time: Mũndara Mũturi.
- Consultant for Leadership Development held by Todd Poulter (US), discontinued as an ALT position, and Poulter would assist Mũturi.
- Africa Area Director: Pauline Wairimu Irungu (Kenya). Irungu began the transition with outgoing Area Director Mũturi from October 2018 to May 2019.
- On 11 April, Wairimu Irungu became Africa Area Director.
- New position of Consultant for Prayer Advocacy: Jo Johnson (UK).
- Consultant for Bible Translation Programs: Paul Kimbi (Cameroon).
- Judy Bokelman's (US) responsibilities changed from those of Director for Operations to Consultant for Integrated Systems.
- Martijn de Vries (Netherlands/Switzerland) assumed the role of Director for Operations.

Third Face-to-Face Meeting

The ALT noticed concern arising within the team as it headed into the executive director transition period. Some existing team members were exchanging roles while new members were joining the team. There was uncertainty concerning whom the board would choose as the next executive director, and therefore their team leader. The team believed they would benefit from an additional face-to-face meeting each year, starting in 2018. Up until this time, to reduce travel and meeting costs, the team never met all together more than twice a year, though as a consequence, issues could build up between scheduled meetings.

In response, Franklin agreed to have more team meetings in 2018–2019. For example, in 2018, the team met in Zactalan, Mexico, in January; Ruiru, Kenya, in June; and Athens, Greece, in October. In addition, in 2019, the team was scheduled to meet in Budapest in February; then a retreat that included ALT spouses in Kangaroo Ground, Australia, was planned in June; and one more meeting would be held in Johannesburg, South Africa, in October. These additional meetings helped the team process the changes underway within WGA and functioning closely together as a leadership community would ensure the continuation of the Alliance as a whole.

Aligning Operations

Increasingly, WGA operational activities displayed effects of a gradual shift away from rented physical offices. During 2018, two changes occurred in this regard. In Singapore, WGA's operational headquarters was closed because the team was working virtually. Similarly, the board decided to close the Dallas office used by the board secretary and rented from the International Linguistics Center. The last vestige of a presence at that centre—one which began in the mid-1970s—departed when Board Secretary Matt Dawson and Assistant Secretary Janet Dawson began working from their home in Dallas by the end of 2018.

Another change occurred in WGA's communications functions, as the specialized team working under Director for Communications Phil Prior decreased in number. The function of communications at that point was (1) to assist AOs to simplify their message and effectively represent WGA and the Bible translation movement, (2) to resource AOs with communication information, (3) to resource AOs at a leadership level to better communicate about WGA, and (4) to build WGA image primarily through its website.

Next Cycle of Covenants

When the next cycle of the Covenant/Statement of Commitment rolled out in late 2015, the board policy stated that these needed to be reviewed and re-signed every three years. That was approaching at the end of 2018. However, the area directors and executive directors observed several concerns that called for attention, including wording that referred to the core statements, Participation Streams, AO financial contribution, and conflict resolution processes. The ALT recognized the likely outcome would entail major revisions to the Covenant/Statement of Commitment, necessitating a consultative process inviting all AOs to give their input to the draft revisions. To be done thoroughly would take time. Consequently, the board informed all AOs that the re-signing process would not commence until after May 2019.

Franklin hoped for completion of this before beginning the transition to the incoming executive director. Knowing all that this entailed, it seemed unwise to have a new Covenant/Statement of Commitment process occurring around the same time as the transition that would be well underway in late 2019. In the end, the May 2019 date proved unrealistic. To address the required changes called for further discussion with the AOs and processing by the WGA Board. A particular stumbling block, the 0.35% financial contribution from all AOs toward funding WGA was so problematic that the board and executive director called for a Task Force on Funding to meet in February 2019 in Singapore to discuss this topic and identify a solution (see chapter 10).

Partnership with SIL

This topic appeared on the WGA Board's agenda every so often. Just a few years previously, in 2016, topics concerning the relationship between WGA and SIL absorbed much of the board's attention. This made sense, considering the historical development of the two organizations, addressed throughout this book. In chapters 5 and 6, the development of the Unity of Purpose Statement between the two organizations took place. The time had come to remove it from the highest policy level for the organization and place something in board policy that affirmed the relationship. It was essential to include such a statement going forward. As time passed, fewer and fewer future board members would come along who possessed an awareness of or appreciation for the joint history and the close relationship between the two organizations. The board addressed the issue in 2018 with this statement:

> *Relationship with SIL:* Recognizing the historic relationship between Wycliffe and SIL, the Alliance collaborates with SIL International at many levels (e.g., through the Executive Director, members of the Alliance Leadership Team, Area staff, Communications team, Prayer team; as well as individual Alliance Organizations). Partnering together includes, but is not limited to, sharing of vision, insights, information, expertise, and resources.[25]

Ministering in a VUCA World

Franklin introduced the WGA Board at its joint meeting with the ALT at Männedorf, Switzerland, in April 2019 to the term VUCA (Volatile, Uncertain, Complex, and Ambiguous) as a description of the contexts in which WGA was ministering. Numerous themes relating to managing diversity within the movement summarized the WGA's contribution to these complex issues. This included bringing social cohesion to the wide variety of organizations and their leaders, which at times

[25] WGA, September 2018, 9.

involved organizations dealing with relational problems. Sometimes the ALT was able to use its negotiating skills to help bring change where needed. The ALT presented an example of leading in complexity through missional spirituality, discernment, and creativity, illustrating the ALT's understanding that, regardless of contexts and circumstances, this was still God's world, and he called them to work together as a flourishing community in service of Bible translation movements.

This joint board and ALT meeting, the first of its kind in WGA's history, traditionally only included the executive director, the board, and a few of the ALT. Therefore, the board and executive director believed the best way to allay concerns was for all the ALT to spend time together interacting with the board regarding the upcoming executive director transition. Through joint and separate sessions, the ALT observed the board at work and met board members informally. They attended a celebration of Bob Creson, outgoing president of Wycliffe US, who was stepping down from the board after joining it in 2002. He was the longest standing board member. John Chesnut, the incoming Wycliffe US President, also attended this joint meeting. Representing a unique situation for the board, whoever held the Wycliffe US President role was automatically on the WGA Board, a position tied to the role and not the person.

Polycentric Movements

At the joint meeting, Franklin noted WGA's awareness of the growing importance of polycentric movements within the Alliance, now suggesting they were also polyphonic, which the ALT described as follows:

> *Polyphonic Community*: The Alliance is many voices listening to and harmonizing with each other as friends in God's mission. God leads through his Spirit, and he speaks through any number of people regardless of their role, status, or culture. Consequently, the Alliance community experiences the beauty of diversity within the body of Christ and how each part blends within the symphony of chords of voices.[26]

As WGA reflected on its journey over the past decade, it recognized that there had been significant shifts in size, composition, and growing involvement in leading and managing Bible translation programs:

[26] Van Wynen, Crough, and Franklin, 7.

Year	2008	2018
Size	45 WMOs	100+ AOs
Bible translation management	15 WMOs with language programs	50+ AOs managing Bible translation programs
Total Bible translation programs	Approximately 150 language programs	Approximately 1,000 Bible translation programs

Table 6: Overview of a Decade of Development

The recent marking of milestones by AOs presented another indicator of organizational diversity in WGA. By late 2018, Wycliffe Romania celebrated its 10th anniversary, Wycliffe Hungary its 20th anniversary, and the first Asian Wycliffe organization, Wycliffe Japan, observed its 50th anniversary. Each milestone across the Alliance indicated another sign of God's blessing and goodness to all the faithful people of God associated with each AO.

WGA's growing role in the Bible translation movement continued to gain momentum. For example, more AOs were focussing on Old Testament translations. AOs who provided financial resources were also beginning to support translation and publishing efforts for the Old Testament. Paul Kimbi presented evidence of Bible translation consultant training and accreditation gaining momentum. AOs were setting up consultant development processes that would lead to appointing and accrediting suitably qualified Bible translation experts. Bryan Harmelink was seeing growing interest in developing new curricula for Bible translation training. The topics he had developed were unique and looked at the starting point for training for Bible translation roles as a theological-missiological one, then moving on to linguistics and culture. Topics included: 'how God uses language in his mission; listening and learning how to work with others in the mission of God; how language works; language ecologies in a globalizing world; theology as a local practice; introduction to translation studies; introduction to biblical languages and cultures for translation; and translation as a local practice.'[27]

Polycentric-Polyphonic Governance

Franklin led the board and ALT through a discussion during their joint meeting about WGA's current form of governance. The eleven-person board came from WGA's five geographical regions and displayed a mix of men and women, some with pastoral-theological backgrounds and others with business and not-for-profit experience. Those reporting to the board included the executive director, who managed the ALT; and the leadership team, whose purpose was to act as

[27] WGA, "Board Minutes," April 2019, 5.

a discerning community of global missional leaders that influences and inspires Bible translation movements while encouraging AOs to fulfill their part in God's mission.

It is generally agreed in good governance that boards exist to give oversight, input, and direction to an organization while also assuming a level of responsibility for the reputation, health, wellbeing, integrity, and legal and financial soundness of an organization. Going back to the late 1990s, the WBTI Board loosely followed John Carver's Policy Governance®, by which the board directed, controlled, and inspired the organization through written policies reflecting the organization's values and perspectives about goals to be achieved and means to be avoided.

As WBTI became WGA, it found weaknesses in its governance model, which did not fit what WGA had become. Struggling to reconcile the two while strictly following the governance methodology called for a detailed understanding of its approach, as well as monitoring the organization's activities in ways that were no longer applicable, leading to loss of interest from board members. At times the board found it hard to follow the policies it had inherited from previous eras. Governing an alliance of 100 organizations, each with their own boards, presented a challenge. Though WGA had become a movement supporting and encouraging movements, it held some institutional responsibilities such as legal and financial accountability. The design of traditional board structures preserved and protected institutional responsibilities, while a movement's imperative is to adapt and change—two very different sets of priorities. New board members had much to learn in a short time to understand WGA and how it differed from other organizations. WGA needed other voices, who might not see themselves as the typical board member, to speak into its governance process. As a missional movement, WGA required discernment at the board level concerning what is theologically and missiologically sound, not to automatically follow traditional corporate models.

All this provided context for discussion on a new governance model that would better serve WGA. Franklin drew from the work of Keith Carlisle and Rebecca Gruby, who express well the challenge the WGA Board faced, in that polycentricity describes 'a complex form of governance with multiple centers of semiautonomous decision making.'[28] Also discussed was the work of Anas Malik, who summarized a 'polycentric system [as] one where individuals [can] organize and devise rules for multiple government authorities at different scales' so that smaller units such as local governments fit inside the larger system and benefit from the 'overarching order' of that system and no one unit is 'allowed to exercise unlimited authority.' [29] This contrasts with monocentric governance, which oper-

[28] Keith Carlisle, and Rebecca Gruby, "Polycentric Systems of Governance: A Theoretical Model for the Commons," *Policy Studies Journal* 47, no. 4 (2019): 927.

[29] Anas Malik, *Polycentricity, Islam, and Development* (Lanham: Lexington Press, 2018), 19.

ates under 'a central authority [that] monopolizes collective choice [and acts] as a unitary sovereign rule-giver.'[30]

Malik's model is complex, relying on the use of 'metanorms'—the over-arching standards and values that support the self-understanding of individual organizations—while creating ways for organizations to relate to each other within the wider association of organizations.[31] These metanorms are pervasive and durable and act as powerful, though often unwritten, guides to what is acceptable and appropriate within the structure. Metanorms give space for a diversity of organizations to coexist within the same association while allowing for the autonomy of these organizations. They also serve the purpose of managing conflicts between organizations because they bring accountability through the norms.

WGA's biblical and missiological foundations described the metanorms that support community, generosity, mutual service, sacrifice for the sake of others, and recognizing the Alliance as a steward of God's mission. These metanorms, expressed in WGA's Philosophy and Principle statements, included the topics of Funding, Community, People, Translation Programs, and Church.

Developing polycentric governance in WGA required an explicit and intentional commitment, starting with the board and ALT. The result could create a much more deeply connected and richly diverse environment in WGA, where it drew upon and benefited from the knowledge, learning, and problem-solving skills as well as the spirituality embedded in each of the AOs.

A component of a system meeting the AOs needs, polycentric governance integrates conflict resolution between participants. It involves identifying and designating a group to monitor and evaluate what is taking place, and when necessary, granting the authority to intervene. In summary, rather than taking away an autonomous centre and replacing it with multiple autonomous centres, polycentric governance recognizes degrees and domains of autonomy that function well when guided by overarching metanorms.

The journey of exploring polycentric governance for WGA can be summarized as follows:

---

30 Malik, 53.

31 Malik, 19.

Model	Wycliffe International	Wycliffe Global Alliance	Polycentric Governance System (Carlisle and Gruby)	Polycentric Governance (Malik)
Characteristics	Based on Policy Governance® by John Carver	Missiologically informed, movement oriented	Processes of cooperation, competition, and conflict resolution	Smaller units fit within a larger, over-arching system
Structure	Broad written policies reflecting values and ends	Institutional responsibilities mixed with movement requirements	Connected, complex, coordination needed	Larger scale and smaller scale units limited in authority
Terminology	Ends, Expectations, Governance Process, Board-Executive Director Relationship	Board Goals, missional intent	Multiple, overlapping decision-making centres	Metanorms; multiple autonomous centres

Table 7: Overview of Models and Characteristics of Governance

Moving toward a polycentric system of governance in WGA wouldn't be straightforward. Nevertheless, rather than an extensive board, a minimal board structure for legal and financial requirements, operating as a 'wise' counsel, giving input, accountability, and direction depending on issues, topics, and needs, represented one possibility. There could be fluidity within the wise counsel group, with people coming and going depending on the topic involved and necessary expertise.

Discussions between the WGA Board and the ALT on polycentric governance were inconclusive in determining a way forward. There was much to consider, including legal requirements of being incorporated in the state of Texas. However, the board did agree on defining itself as a 'Governance Board that is visionary while it continues to work on its understanding of how to bring governance to our polycentric-polyphonic community. The Board casts vision, and it is up to the AOs to set strategy for their context.'[32]

Appointment of Next Executive Director

At its September 2019 meeting, the time had finally arrived for the WGA Board to make its most important decision to date: selecting the next executive director, who would succeed Franklin. The Executive Director Search Committee under Chair Paul Bendor-Samuel had worked diligently for over a year, holding multiple face-to-face and virtual meetings. Over a two-day period in early July in Frankfurt,

[32] WGA, April 2019, 7.

Germany, they conducted in-person interviews with the short list of four candidates and their spouses.

As their meeting got underway, Board Chair Agnes Lid expressed her desire for the board to continue to strengthen and develop into what the executive director and WGA needed. She spoke from Philippians 2 about loving one another and working together with one mind and purpose.

Now the board would hear each candidate's vision for WGA, followed by the board's questions on that vision, further interview questions, and an additional opportunity for each candidate to interact with the board. The board then spent considerable time in prayer and discussion before individually presenting their decision on the candidate. It was unanimous.

The board appointed Stephen Coertze of South Africa as the next executive director. Outgoing Executive Director Kirk Franklin was present when the board members prayed over Coertze. No stranger to the ALT, having served on it in various capacities since 2008, the transition would be relatively straightforward for Coertze, giving him until 31 March 2020 to do whatever he deemed necessary for personal space and preparation. From 1 April, Coertze and Franklin would have several days of face-to-face interaction followed by a few trips to key engagements. All of these served as opportunities for orientation. The official handover would take place at the Global Gathering in September 2020, coincidently occurring in Johannesburg, where Coertze and his family lived. The board chair was the one responsible for monitoring the transition process with the two leaders.

The board also welcomed its newest member, Susanna Muntz, Vice-President of Engagement for Wycliffe Canada. Muntz had served on the Executive Director Search Committee for the past 15 months, thus already becoming familiar with the board's responsibilities.

A *Shalom* Community

In the background, the ALT had been working on revisions to the Covenant/Statement of Commitment. The time was rapidly approaching when each of the AOs would be required to re-sign the document to continue to be identified as a member of WGA. Franklin and the WGA Area Directors had been processing input from the AO leaders, resulting in a complete rewrite of the document.

Participation Streams featured in the Covenant/Statement of Commitment. The Streams were streamlined from their original rendering to new and concise headings. The table shows the revisions.

Original (2011)	Revised (2019)
Church engagement for the Bible translation movement	Church
Prayer for the Bible translation movement	Prayer
Fund raising for the Bible translation movement	Funding
Recruiting and sending people to the Bible translation movement	People
Training in technical Bible translation roles	Training in Bible Translation Roles
Language program management in the Bible translation movement	Bible Translation Programs
Specialty services	Specialty Services

Table 8: Revision of Participation Streams

Emerging in the revision process was the plan for the Alliance community to be shaped by the Old Testament vision of *shalom*. The ALT had done some theological reflection on this and created a description that would guide WGA:

> *Shalom*—It is a vision of transformed communities where all manner of relationships between people and God, with oneself, with each other, and with God's creation are reconciled. It is an authentic and nurturing community that shows peacefulness, wholeness, and unity and where participants fully develop their potential because they are secure, cared for, and mutually respectful. It is a vision of peoples of all nations sharing equally in God's loving concern because no person, people group, language, or nation is above the other in God's eyes. It is a declaration that God uses the translated Word as a foundational means for holistic transformation.[33]

A new section of the Covenant/Statement of Commitment shows how *shalom* was included: 'Unity and *Shalom*: In their interactions with each other, Alliance Organizations [commit to upholding] attitudes and practices that promote unity and shalom and are characterized by mutual respect, integrity, humility, and generosity.'[34] An explanation of how this would function in the WGA community emerged from the outlined expectations of AOs towards each other, showing 'mutual respect, integrity, humility, and generosity'.[35] There were guidelines to follow in 'situations where unity and shalom are at risk', asking AOs to 'engage with the situation as soon as appropriate, in the most promising way(s), [with the goal of honouring] all involved parties' needs—humbly investing in mutual and deep understanding of all involved parties' positions, interests, backgrounds, and values.'[36]

[33] Van Wynen, Crough, and Franklin, 7.

[34] WGA, "Covenant/Statement of Commitment 2," 4 June 2020, 4

[35] WGA, 4 June 2020, 6

[36] WGA, 4 June 2020, 7

For many larger AOs, the financial contribution section represented the most controversial part of what would eventually be referred to as the new Covenant/ Statement of Commitment '2'. Rather than paying the 0.35% amount, they wanted a different system. With various models proposed, the board decided on a tier-structured fee instead of the percentage-based contribution. Later in June 2020, the board approved both the new financial funding model and the Covenant/ Statement of Commitment 2.

Preparing to Celebrate

Wycliffe Global Gathering Program and Event Director Dave Crough had been hard at work for the previous 18 months assembling a team of people to help prepare for this historic event. For the first time in the history of WBT-WBTI-WGA, in September 2020 in Johannesburg, South Africa, the organization would hold its own event, with approximately 300 people from the AOs, WGA Area teams, the ALT and board, and other invited guests expected to attend.

Crough brought his creative background to the fore and envisioned an event that glorified God through what the Alliance was becoming—a global movement for Bible translation serving the peoples of the world. The activities for each of the six days of the event were beginning to take shape. Then, the unexpected happened. In September, Crough was diagnosed with stage four sarcoma cancer. This devastating blow stunned Dave, his wife Deborah, and their family. It shocked the ALT, the board, and the Global Gathering Planning Team. The team had arranged to meet the following month in Johannesburg at the convention centre where the event was scheduled. But Crough could not join them, as he was receiving treatment in California. On short notice, the board and executive director organized a contingency plan and approached Karen Floor, Wycliffe South Africa Executive Director, to take Crough's place as Program and Event Director. She graciously agreed and led the planning meeting, following Crough's well-organized work and plans.

Celebrating a Life

The new year was hardly underway when the ALT and Alliance community lost its dear servant and friend Dave Crough to his brief battle with cancer. Dave had served on the ALT since 2011. He was often behind the scenes in helping the Alliance explain its values and beliefs. He called these its 'Alliance-ness'. His vision for the next Global Gathering was exciting. And now, he was gone. The ALT couldn't be there with Dave and Deborah, as another event was emerging: the global COVID-19 pandemic, immediately restricting the ALT's movements.

All this limited the team to processing their memories of Dave virtually at their February ALT meeting.

Cancellations

As 2020 began unfolding, some ALT members were aware that things were different and unsettling, including disrupted travel. For example, in late January on his way to meet with Board Chair Agnes Lid at her office in Oslo, Norway, Franklin passed through Singapore and Dubai. He realized something was amiss when he saw airport staff wearing face masks. He had gone through Dubai many times over the past months and had not seen this before. Then news began spreading as rapidly as COVID-19, and Franklin and the ALT knew that plans for their first face-to-face meeting from 10 to 13 February 2020, scheduled in Kuala Lumpur, Malaysia, might have to be postponed or cancelled. The greatest risk at that early stage is that team members could become carriers of COVID-19, picking it up on one of their flights and taking it back to where they lived. Sensing this, Franklin informed his board chair that WGA might have to cancel future engagements, not just the ALT meeting. The April board meeting scheduled for Bali, Indonesia, was at risk. And so was the unthinkable, the Global Gathering in September. Though still a long way off, it necessitated a decision within a few months. Thus began numerous cancellations of ALT meetings, board meetings, and Area Conferences, all replaced in one way or another with online equivalents.

At the board's virtual meeting in April, Karen Floor, Global Gathering Program and Event Director, reported on the status of Global Gathering planning. As a result, the board decided to reschedule the event for a year later, for 16–20 September 2021. But AO leaders were asked to hold the dates of 17–18 September 2020 for a virtual event.

Also affected was the planned orientation program for incoming Executive Director Stephen Coertze, who was to spend four days meeting with Franklin in the London area at the end of March, followed by several trips together to various events and meetings. All were cancelled. Instead, Franklin and Coertze spent several days in online conversations going over transition questions. This was the best they could do. At Franklin's request, during its April online meeting, the board agreed to bring the transition forward. Instead of occurring in September, it took place through a virtual meeting of the board and ALT on 3 June. The global context was one of crisis. It wasn't necessarily the best time to have a significant leadership transition. But that is what would happen. All concerned would get through this together in a way that glorified the Lord and testified to him being in control of the events of the world.

Assessing the Future

On 1 May 2020, WBTI, now WGA, was 40 years old. It had come a long way since its formation and was preparing to discern with God its direction and future as a participant in the Bible translation movement.

Recognizing COVID-19 as settling in for the long haul, the ALT contemplated its effects on the AOs. The leadership conducted an online survey with directors of AOs to identify what the Bible translation movement could look like during and after the COVID-19 pandemic as a means of determining how AOs were affected, thus far, by the crisis. Questions included: finding out each AO's primary needs, main goals, and unique contributions as they participated in the Bible translation movement; determining what was preventing the AOs from meeting these goals; how the AOs observed God working, and what new opportunities God was opening for them; and whether any goals called for reconsideration. The responses offered glimpses of how leaders were thinking about and preparing for the future. Overall, the results showed a remarkable degree of optimism in the face of increasing difficulties as direct and indirect results of the global pandemic. Encouraging evidence included:

> a willingness to follow, change, collaborate, and serve, [predating] the COVID-19 situation by years [and continuing] through the current tumultuous times and [conceivably] into the future, whatever it may hold. Leaders recognized the current context as another bend in the road or hill to climb but [held] steady on their journey. They bring the gifts God has given them and are also willing to let them go. They proceed in faith and yet are willing to survey the terrain and adjust course as needed. And, as one leader said, they '...trust in God that he would use this crisis for his glory and purpose'.[37]

Conclusion

The era under Kirk Franklin's leadership came to an official close on 3 June 2020 through a virtual handover ceremony held with the ALT and WGA Board. Documented on a video, Franklin, Stephen Coertze, and Agnes Lid offered perspectives and challenges to the Alliance community. No one could have predicted the events of 2020 or how they would play out for a movement like the Alliance. As the year unfolded, it was evident that God was in control, it was his mission they

[37] Kirk Franklin and Susan Van Wynen, "The Future of the Bible Translation Movement Survey Conducted by the Wycliffe Global Alliance Analysis and Report," 13 May 2020, 2.

were committed to, and it called for keeping their eyes focussed on him.

This experience of faith and trust was not new to WGA but had been apparent throughout its journey. Developing from its starting point in 1942, internationalization in 1980, restructuring in 1990, separating from SIL administrative functions in 2008, and adopting a new name in 2011 as the Wycliffe Global Alliance, it's been a journey of discovery and of experiencing God's faithfulness and patience. The more recent years have felt like an awakening, especially to those who have travelled through them.

Reflected in the Alliance's way of working have been many significant shifts such as the following:

› The ownership and responsibility for mission have shifted, spreading from Western countries toward polycentric areas of influence and spiritual vitality across the globe. These global spheres of influence help manage the dependency on Western resources through influence from the majority world by creating balance, providing new opportunities and practices, equalizing authority, rotating leadership, and incorporating these new areas of influence and spiritual vitality, all a reflection of what makes up WGA.
› WGA operates in an interconnected leadership web connecting many leadership centres.
› The circles of polycentric and polyphonic leadership within WGA are culturally diverse, creating mutual learning and an awareness of others.
› WGA's leadership and governance, somewhat polycentric in structure, demonstrates decentralization accompanied by limited control over the 100+ AOs, who collaborate as a community while retaining their distinctiveness.

These shifts are summarized in this table:

Paradigm	West to the rest	Western mission agency to an international organization	Centralized institutional structure to decentralized hybrid structure	Self-governing autonomous organizations to a global alliance in a community
Timeframe	1942–1979	1980–2007	2008–2015	2016+
Flow of resource	Resources sent	Resources sent and received	Resources shared	Collaboration
Structure	US HQ	US HQ with Divisions in other countries	Singapore HQ with Member and Partner Organizations	Virtual HQ with Alliance Organizations
Leadership	Western leadership	Western leadership	International leadership	Global (multi-ethnic) leadership

Table 9: Shifts in Structure and Leadership

In summary, WGA has moved from operating as an institution to journeying as an alliance within the Bible translation movement across the globe, so voices from all of its organizations and the church worldwide are involved in the vision. It has been a remarkable journey, and it continues.

Leadership Theory and Practice

In the era under review, newer models of leadership worth considering become known. A few are classified as formal theories, empirically proven through academic research. A few continue as informal theories since they are quite new and not yet researched or tested. All offer insights into—and a richer description of—global missional leadership.

R. Scott Rodin[38] and Kent R. Wilson[39] focus on Steward Leadership, a recently described leadership model with roots going back thousands of years. This model offers, perhaps, the greatest hope for the transformation and effectiveness of non-profit leadership. Such leadership varies according to individual personality and giftedness, the environment, organizational culture, specific challenges, and vision. The most important aspect is how the Holy Spirit influences the heart and dynamic journey of the steward leader. Steward Leadership compares closely to servant leadership, but the former addresses the role of the objectives of God, human owners, or stakeholders in how the leader makes decisions and manages others. Servant leadership does not adequately address many non-profit organizational issues such as non-owner leadership, resource management and growth, financial responsibility, organizational management needs, trusteeship, accountability (to God or stakeholders), and the rightful place of authority and power in leadership. Therefore, according to Wilson, servant leadership should be viewed as more of a subset within the larger and more inclusive model of steward leadership.

When Steward Leadership functions as an expression or practice of shalom leadership, the leader 'pursues reconciling relationships between people, people and God, people and their environment, and people and themselves. The leader works toward the well-being, abundance, and wholeness of the community as well as individuals.' In other words, according to Zenet Maramara, the Steward-Shalom Leader is

> one that seeks shalom in all areas of life and relationships. It embraces a fuller vision of biblical stewardship that takes into account

[38] R. Scott Rodin, *The Steward Leader: Transforming People, Organizations and Communities* (Downers Grove: IVP Academic, 2010).

[39] Kent Wilson, *Steward Leadership in the Nonproft Organization* (Downers Grove: IVP 2016).

> social responsibility, public engagement, care of God's creation, in addition to personal piety and worship of God. The God of abundance promises his people a life of flourishing in all its dimensions.[40]

Polycentric Leadership in an era of globalization provides a broader array of leadership voices, representing local and regional constituencies, empowered to self-organize within complex, adaptive, and self-regulating systems. This extends over all competing loyalties, whether ethnic, cultural, national, political, generational, denominational, or organizational, and offers a re-centring of a united polyphonic missional conversation. It has a communal nature—the community working together. Not centred solely on collaboration and partnering, but on a community's body life and how the members complement one another; empowering various centres of influence and integrating a diverse array of peoples within a movement can lead to enhanced decision-making and more effective operations.

The Humble Leadership theory, developed by Edgar and Peter Schein, aims at doing something new and better, and getting others to go along.[41] What is new and better will always depend on context, the nature of the task, and the cultural values of the group or organization doing the work. Aware of their limitations, even though such leaders know where they want to go, they are fully willing to listen to others, especially those who may be able to help them. They recognize that no leader has all the information required in any given situation, requiring more than what they have in terms of knowledge and skill, and they act on this. They ask for help and listen to others, including followers. Humble Leadership nurtures relationships with followers through a learning mindset, cooperative attitudes, and skills in interpersonal and group dynamics, reflecting both group phenomenon and individual behaviour.

Missional Leadership, according to Nelus Niemandt, is focussed on 'the transformation of people and institutions to participate, through meaningful relations and in the power of the Spirit, in God's mission.'[42] A missional leader understands that it's through God's grace that one leads in God's mission. The process starts with inner transformation and the release of an innovative spiritual gift of leadership to equip and guide God's people so they may effectively participate in God's mission in their specific contexts. A missional leader helps the church function as relational networks within the complex structure of the church to take her place in God's story and participate in the triune God's mission of transformation. This leader discerns and imagines with the Holy Spirit and God's community what God is doing in the world.

---

40 Zenet Maramara, "Shalom Leadership," *Christian Leadership Alliance blog*, 2018.

41 Edgar Schein, and Peter Schein, *In Humble Leadership: The Power of Relationships, Openness, and Trust* (Oakland: Berrett-Koehler 2018).

42 Nelus Niemandt, *Missional Leadership* (Cape Town: AOSIS, 2019), 73.

Christina Walker's research into Culturally Inclusive Leadership defines it as a relational approach that fosters learning, listening, and voicing so that team members sense they belong to the group and can contribute their unique perspectives to the group's process and outcomes. Leaders hold the tension that comes with diversity: Can we belong while retaining our uniqueness? Can we have stability (norms and boundaries) while retaining a sense of openness? Can we be safe while being willing to change? Leaders cultivate inclusion on their teams by creating attentive space supported by temporal space and proximate space. This understanding and use of space reflects the leaders' attention to physical environments that are also psychologically safe and open for diverse contributions.[43]

The journey of WGA intersects with the emergence of leadership with a global missional mindset. This behaviour has a diversity of influences. For example, we can see elements of humble, culturally inclusive, polycentric, missional, shalom-steward leadership at various levels of WGA. This healthy sign illustrates God at work, building people up and calling them to step into various leadership responsibilities that are now and will continue to be required. A key will be for WGA leadership to remain as a learning community as it studies and learns from its history and follows its journey with God into the future. There will be more leadership models and frameworks to draw from and develop in the process.

Journey Reflections (A Journey that Keeps on Going)

Traditional change strategies introduced the concept of a transition zone. Leaders learned how to manage change, guiding their organization from point A to point B, passing through the sometimes-treacherous transition zone, only to land in a new, safe and stable location. But then, while many of the followers attempted to rebuild structures very similar to those they left behind, the question would come, 'when will things settle down?' The leaders would try to reassure those around them, 'soon, very soon,' while deep down, they were beginning to realize they'd never really left the transition zone. It stretched out before them as far as they could see.

If you accept from the start that you are on a journey, change is no longer unexpected, learning becomes a lifelong pursuit, and your surety is in the leadership and the cause, not in the ground under your feet or the sign at your office entrance. As WGA ideology and ideas took shape, grounded in God's leadership and secure in the knowledge that the mission was his, Alliance leadership continued

---

43 Christina Walker, "Inclusive Leadership in INGO, Multinational Teams: Learning, Listening and Voicing in 'Attentive Space'" (Trinity International University, 2020).

to take in the landscape fast changing around them as they travelled. They took more notice of their place and role in the larger throng surrounding and moving along with them—the Bible translation movements. This journey was going to include more and more people and would continue for some time. Emerging leaders would need help to develop their global missional mindset so that WGA could continue to contribute.

WGA values and intentions require ongoing learning and reflection, as well as practical application. Community, friendship, polycentrism, generosity, and creating third spaces call for continued exploration and application. But they will look different in each new context and with each new group of travellers. There won't be a 'now we've got it all figured out!' moment. But there will be many moments of appreciation of the amazing God who invited each of us to participate in his mission on his journey. His footprints lead the way, his glory lights the path, and his grace will see us through.

› As you review the many transitions of WGA to this point, what patterns do you see?
› What types of changes seem to have the most significant positive impact? Which are the most challenging?
› How can you, in your context, help yourself and others prepare for ongoing change?
› What are some principles for determining what needs to change?

PART 2

KAIROS MOMENTS

Chapter 8
Embedding: National Bible Translation Organizations

By Kirk Franklin

Introduction

A unique aspect of WBTI's historical journey began in the mid-1970s with the development of National Bible Translation Organizations (NBTOs). This era presented many challenges and complexities. International mission agencies were unprepared, reluctant, and often unwilling to make the efforts required to find ways to be more inclusive of people and organizations that were not from the Western world. Major agencies also didn't know how to work well with national organizations or cross-cultural partners. WBTI faced similar challenges. Should these people be encouraged to form their own agencies outside of the WBTI structure? Alternately, could they be included as new types of Wycliffe divisions or some other organizational structure? Also, regarding qualifications, were Bible translation personnel from the majority world equal in their training and experience to their Western counterparts? The pathway for determining how to include the NBTOs into WBTI's organizational structure was not straightforward.

Nevertheless, NBTOs began to emerge, amidst influences of nationalism, embeddedness, and identity. All this occurred as Wycliffe Divisions progressed into the WBTI institutional structure, and eventually, into a global Bible translation movement.

The journey of the NBTOs' expansion was influenced by key people involved in the movement, including WBT and SIL founder Cameron Townsend. Some leaders in both WBT and SIL held a different view from Townsend, which provided encouragement and support to the NBTOs' development, particularly in Africa. WBTI and SIL's reasons for supporting or opposing the formation of NBTOs, as well as organizational dynamics and relationships between WBTI and SIL International, impacted the journey. Across the globe, sociological and missiological influences concerning the role of national Christians in international mission structures had their own effect. Each of these challenges tested the NBTOs as they set out to become established Bible translation organizations. Exploring these factors helps us understand the purpose of the NBTOs, and how NBTOs have played an important role in shaping the development of WBTI, SIL, and the Bible translation movement.

Call for a Moratorium

Dana Robert describes the early to mid-1900s as 'the greatest period of cross-cultural expansion in the history of Christianity.'[1] Also referred to as 'the tumultuous century'[2], worldwide events such as the World Wars, Great Depression, resurgent Islam, and rising nationalism all occurred during this period. It was a difficult time for mission agencies and their personnel.

Illustrating both the expansion and tumult, Robert observes, 'During the 1960s, the voices of young nationalists grew louder in regional and international church councils, and they accused missionaries of paternalism and failing to turn over church leadership structures to national control quickly enough.'[3] These and other factors were influential to a call for a moratorium on foreign missionary efforts in Africa. For example, in 1971 John Gatũ from Kenya, serving as General Secretary of the Presbyterian Church of East Africa, called for changes to how Western missions and the churches they started were conducting ministry in Africa. At a conference in New York he stated, 'We cannot build the church in Africa on alms given by overseas churches; we are not serving the cause of the kingdom by turning all bishops, general secretaries, moderators, presidents, and superintendents into good, enthusiastic beggars when we continuously sing the tune of poverty in Third World churches.'[4]

Gatũ championed 'principles of selfhood, self-reliance, and self-determination for the church and the nations of Africa', in what became known across the world as the Moratorium Debate. Later in his life, Gatũ observed how 'the call for a moratorium on missionaries... helped some missionary agencies re-examine their relevance in the changing world.'[5] He looked back on how many African leaders had been appointed to leadership roles with overseas mission organizations but managed to keep close links with their Western headquarters, returning there regularly to raise funds for the African work. Gatũ's principles had a definite impact, but change would be incremental.

A leading figure of the debate was Canon Burgess Carr, from Liberia, who attended the 1974 All Africa Conference of Churches (AACC) where the

[1] Dana Robert, *Christian Mission: How Christianity Became a World Religion* (Chichester, UK: Wiley-Blackwell 2009), 70.

[2] Terry, and Gallagher, 277.

[3] Robert, 68.

[4] John Gatũ, *Fan into Flame: An Autobiography* (Nairobi: Moran Publishers, 2016), 128.

[5] Gatũ, 129.

moratorium was discussed. The issue in focus was the African church's ability to 'speedily [move] towards achieving self-reliance.'[6] In Africa, there were some concerning challenges with the foreign missionaries. Carr called this 'exploitative aspects of the modern missionary enterprise [where a] considerable portion of the money allocated for "missionary work" by missionary-sending agencies [was] spent on the salaries and maintenance of their own personnel.'[7] Carr concluded that after 'a hundred years of missionary activity in Africa, the Churches are still not able to *stand on their own feet*.'[8]

Reasons for the Moratorium

Later in 1974, Gatũ held a press briefing that coincided with the International Congress on World Evangelisation at Lausanne, where discussion regarding the relationship between receiving and sending churches took place. Michael Cassidy outlines the four issues that Gatũ presented:

1. The uncertain relationship that exists between the sending and receiving churches
2. The need for selfhood and self-reliance of the church that has emerged on the mission field
3. The need for the national church to take the responsibility for mission with its own resources and its own people
4. The problem of institutions on the mission field—those that may or may not be desired by the church, the supervision of such institutions, and resources to sustain them.[9]

Two years later, in 1976, Pius Wakatama from Rhodesia (now Zimbabwe) popularized the moratorium call in his book *Independence for the Third World Church*, published in the US. A 1971 meeting of anthropologists in Barbados influenced him when they voiced their concern that missionaries should cease their ministry 'among the Indians of Latin America.'[10] These academics accused mission agencies of 'destroying indigenous cultures and helping to exploit native populations for the benefit of the West.'[11] While Wakatama makes it clear he did not agree with this group in what they represented, he did think it was worth determining if there

[6] Burgess Carr, "The Engagement of Lusaka," *Pro Veritate* June (1974): 8.

[7] Carr 8.

[8] Carr 8.

[9] Michael Cassidy, "The Call to Moratorium: Perspective on an Identity Crisis," *Churchman* 90, no. 4 (1976): 267, accessed 29 August 2020, https://churchsociety.org/docs/churchman/090/Cman_090_4_Cassidy.pdf.

[10] Pius Wakatama, *Independence for the Third World Church* (Downers Grove: IVP, 1976), 13.

[11] Wakatama, 13.

was any 'substance to the charge.'[12]

Wakatama wrote his book during the 1970s, when the British colony of Southern Rhodesia had become the self-declared independent country of Rhodesia under the white minority government of Ian Smith. (It later became part of independent Zimbabwe in 1979.) The church was the most credible and effective body pushing for independence since most freedom fighters like Robert Mugabe were either incarcerated or in exile.

Robert also observes that 'in the early 1970s, leaders of Christian Councils in the South Pacific, South Asia, Latin America, and Africa called for a "moratorium" on the sending of foreign missionaries so they could break long-term patterns of dependency that had been established during the colonial era.'[13]

In a tangential vein, E. Stanley Jones relates a conversation with Mahatma Gandhi, someone for whom Jones had great respect. He asked Gandhi, 'How can we make Christianity nationalized in India not a foreign thing, identified with a foreign government and a foreign people, but a part of the national life of India and contributing its power to India's uplift?' Gandhi replied, 'First, I would suggest that all of you Christians, missionaries and all, must begin to live more like Jesus Christ. Second, practice your religion without adulterating it or toning it down. Third, emphasize love and make it your working force, for love is essential in Christianity. Fourth, study the non-Christian religions more sympathetically to find the good that is within them, in order to have a more sympathetic approach to the people.'[14] Gandhi's admonishment provides a helpful perspective to the foreign missionary, creating the potential for greater effectiveness in their ministry.

Critics of the Moratorium

Many Western leaders were critical of the moratorium debate. Samuel Gatere notes how Stephen Neil, then at the University of Nairobi, 'once vilified [Gatũ] as an "ecclesiastic Idi Amin"' (after the notorious Ugandan dictator).[15] Johannes Verkuyl stated how the debate was causing Western young people to reconsider missionary service, and it was beginning to affect fundraising in Europe for mission in Africa. Herbert Works described the moratorium 'as a tragic concept which would turn the evangelical world away from [worldwide evangelization].'[16] In his opening address to the 1974 International Congress on World Evangelisation at

[12] Wakatama, 13.

[13] Robert, 68.

[14] E. Stanley Jones, *Gandhi: Portrait of a Friend* (Nashville: Abingdon Press, 1948), 51-52.

[15] Samuel Gatere in Gatũ, 295.

[16] Hebert Works, "Lausanne–a Catalyst for World Evangelization," *Church Growth Bulletin* 9, no. 1 (September 1975): 445.

Lausanne, Billy Graham called for the rejection of the very idea of the moratorium. Instead, he proposed that 'Churches of every land [should] deliberately send out evangelists and missionaries to master other languages, learn other cultures, live in them perhaps for life, and thus evangelize these multitudes.'[17] This statement from well-respected Graham greatly saddened the moratorium leaders who believed their intentions were misunderstood. Gatũ was in attendance and asked John Stott, co-leader of the Congress, to arrange a meeting with Graham. That eventually happened towards the very end of the Congress, and Gatũ was able to explain the case of the moratorium leaders.

Did this critique of the presence and activity of Western-based missionaries and their agencies in Africa, the Pacific, Latin America, and Asia affect the structures of all agencies? Did it affect the focus of the Bible translation organizations of WBTI with implications for SIL International?

Nationalism and Western Missions

Observing 20th century mission, Edward L. Smither notes its 'innovation and new strategies, [and how several] new organizations reflected this', including Townsend's founding of WBT and SIL.[18] Townsend and his colleagues were operating in the shifting winds blowing upon colonialism and ushering in nationalism.

After World War II, and especially from 1945 to 1965, many dependent nations began pressing for and gaining their independence from their colonizers. Since WBT was founded in 1942 and was internationalizing itself by the late 1950s, as it spread from its US roots to Australia, Europe, and Canada, it was going to be affected by the winds of nationalism. As well, these winds affected mission agencies in a variety of ways. To illustrate, Robert observes how 'many newly independent nations viewed Christianity as a Western religion closely identified with colonialism. Therefore, when they escaped the control of colonialism, they sought to limit the influence of Christianity as well.'[19]

The Case for WBT and SIL

In hindsight, this backdrop of Western colonialism and the call for a moratorium represented a conundrum for WBTI. However, at the time, it is likely that WBTI and SIL were more concerned about pragmatic implications of nationalism. For example, Townsend biographer Hugh Steven notes that

[17] Billy Graham, "Why Lausanne," Lausanne Movement, 1974, accessed 16 June 2020, https://www.lausanne.org/content/why-lausanne-print.

[18] Smither, 151.

[19] Terry, and Gallagher, 279.

> rising nationalism and reaction against American internationalism... made the securing of visas more difficult for SIL workers. Many governments were unwilling to allow expatriate mission workers into their countries unless they were highly credentialed.... Furthermore, many governments wanted their own people trained in linguistics and Bible translation procedures. They also wanted SIL to be in a position of accountability, and for translators to work under the authority of the recognized government agency.[20]

At the time, expatriate workers were sent from Western WBT Divisions to serve through SIL in places such as the then Territory of Papua and New Guinea, countries across sub-Saharan Africa, the Philippines, and nations in Central and South America. Naturally, WBT and SIL leaders were taking note of how most of these nations were in various stages of gaining self-governance and independence from their colonizers. Therefore, the question emerged regarding how to involve local citizens in Bible translation projects in these changing contexts.

As the national organizations developed, Cameron Townsend was no longer in active leadership, but as the founder of WBT and SIL, he had influence and respect in both organizations. In a speech to his staff in March 1977, Townsend encouraged the use of 'tribesmen' to do the translating. However, he stated, 'Now of course, those [tribesmen] will not become members of Wycliffe Bible Translators, at least not in the foreseeable future.'[21] Instead he said they should be employed by SIL members to do the translating. He did not believe that national translators should eliminate the need to recruit foreigners as the primary leaders and staff for Bible translation and other tasks of SIL.

These discussions were consistent with Townsend's expectation of his organizations to be held accountable to host governments. According to Steven, Townsend 'urged each field director to form a sponsoring committee of national leaders, educators, and scholars to speak on SIL's behalf and to offer advice and guidance through what sometimes were political minefields.'[22]

It is important to distinguish between who Townsend and others among his colleagues considered 'tribesmen' and 'national leaders'. These two groups were not the same in Townsend's eyes, particularly in a Latin American context, where very firm lines were drawn in history and society between the majority culture and indigenous people groups.

---

[20] Steven, *Yours for Finishing the Task*, 227.

[21] Cal Hibberd, "Quotable Uncle Cam," 2007, SIL International Townsend Archives.

[22] Hibberd, 227.

Forming National Organizations

In some parts of the world, SIL leaders helped initiate local agencies that are now known as National Bible Translation Organizations (NBTOs). Observing this new development, Townsend wrote a memo on 29 May 1979, asking that his leaders address the issue with 'extreme caution'. He perceived potential 'dangers inherent in hiring national translators or in investing foreign funds in national Bible translation organizations (NBTOs).'[23]

With this implication that Townsend was worried about rising nationalism where SIL was working, we gain insight by looking at what happened six years earlier at the 1973 International Conference of WBTI and SIL. There, leaders discussed a topic of flexible approaches that recommended SIL Branches encourage local citizens to become involved in furthering linguistic, literacy, and Bible translation work.

From the discussion, leaders decided on two options: (1) Where local Christian citizens held an interest in Bible translation and where there were still Bible translation needs, SIL should aim to encourage the formation of a national organization; and (2) Local citizens interested in working as members of SIL could be accepted as members only when there was a home division in existence, a local committee that would channel prayer and financial support, or a suitable alternative existed, such as another sponsoring organization.

The first option 'cleared the way for the formation of NBTOs, which would share responsibility for first-time translation.'[24] SIL and WBT wanted NBTOs to be structured under existing national church councils so that these bodies would be the ones to promote and oversee translation work. It was assumed that many 'SIL translators would shift from the traditional single-team approach to occupy the roles of facilitators and trainers of nationals who, under the care and sponsorship of the church, would do translation with the help of SIL translation consultants.'[25] ('Nationals' was the term used at that time to refer to people working in translation in their own countries.)

Concerns for Founder Townsend

This new direction chosen by the highest body for decision making in WBT and SIL—the Corporation Conference—troubled Townsend. Central to his concern was whether 'the Western church had abdicated responsibility to be the major

[23] Cal Hibberd, "Significant Events in the Life of William Cameron Townsend," 2015, SIL International Townsend Archives.

[24] Steven, *Yours for Finishing the Task*, 227.

[25] Steven, 227.

provider of translated Scriptures for the world's ethnic minorities.'[26] Townsend wrote this prayer that expressed his heartfelt concerns:

> Lord, is the day of expatriates doing pioneer Bible translation work past? Are we, the Christians of the United States and the West, to declare our independence of the command, 'Go ye into all the world and preach the gospel to every creature?' Are we to give as an excuse the anti-foreign attitude of countries that refuse to grant visas to missionaries? Are we to look to Him who told us to 'Go' and say, Lord, although it's true that there are many languages without the Bible in such-and-such country, the government won't let foreign missionaries in. Since we can't go, we have decided to give linguistic training to nationals and expect them to translate the Scriptures into those many, many languages. Please, Lord, don't think we have decided to 'pass the buck'. 'Let the nationals do it' really makes sense. The reality is that if they can get adequate training, they can do a better job than we can. Of course, we have always worked with the [nationals]. We wouldn't have gotten to first base without their help. Now, however, we'll leave them to work alone while we seek financial help for them and provide a certain amount of training and consultant help. But please, Lord, we aren't 'passing the buck.'[27]

Townsend held the 'conviction that nationals should remain independent of WBT-SIL control' because he believed 'his own colleagues would not treat nationals as equals.'[28] The solution to Townsend was to offer SIL's assistance to local citizens to form their own translation organizations that would then be apparently 'free of external control.'[29] These organizations would have full responsibility for their human and financial resource requirements. In this way, SIL avoided colonial attitudes and would keep in check cross-cultural tensions that Townsend believed would result under 'a mixed membership' and could lead to 'accusations of paternalism' if the foreign personnel were in control of the national organization, or the nationals were in control of the foreign organization. [30]

These were reasons why Townsend did not support NBTOs becoming structurally included in WBT or SIL. This created a dilemma for his colleagues who did want to see NBTOs become part of WBT or SIL. If they honoured the wishes of the founder, it meant that the NBTOs needed to be totally separate from WBT and SIL.

---

26 Steven, 228.

27 Steven, 228.

28 Boone Aldridge, *For the Gospel's Sake: The Rise of Wycliffe Bible Translators and the Summer Institute of Linguistics* (Grand Rapids: Wm B. Eerdmans, 2018), 203.

29 Aldridge, 203.

30 Aldridge, 203.

Challenges for Western Agencies

The challenge for Western missionaries was to be well qualified in cross-cultural communication, adopting the role of servant-trainer, totally devoid of racial prejudice and paternalism. Only then could local citizens be freed from being the 'recipient or assistant [and] rarely the co-worker.'[31] They would no longer be 'perpetual assistants'.[32]

A contradiction prevailed in the rising nationalism of the mid-20th century in education because, as Robert observes, 'Mission education had created the opportunities and climate for indigenous leadership, and a disproportionate number of leaders of newly independent nations had attended mission schools or been sponsored for Western education by mission scholarship funds.'[33] At the same time, Western missionaries had not completed their goal of training nationals. Wakatama valued formal training across Africa and believed that until this was widespread, mission agencies had 'a moral responsibility to sponsor nationals for overseas training.'[34] He further envisioned the national church and foreign missionaries working together, with the latter under the direction of the former until the national church took over all aspects of the work.

The 1960s–1970s marked a turning point in the internationalization of Christian mission, influenced by the growing list of countries being granted independence from European colonial powers. This was combined with other factors that Robert sees as 'external to Christianity itself, such as decolonization, population explosion, urbanization, migration, globalization, and improved transportation and communication networks.'[35] All were instrumental in the changing face of the worldwide growth of the church. Internal and external factors influenced Bible translation ministry in the majority world.

National Organizations and WBTI and SIL

Looking back, the 1973 joint International Conference of Wycliffe International and SIL is pivotal to understanding how the two organizations were grappling with the concept of national involvement. From that conference emerged a specific strategy of encouraging local citizens to be more engaged in Bible translation, and the new organizational category of NBTOs was finalized.

Later, in 1976, the WBT Board asked the International Administration to use

[31] Wakatama, 41.
[32] Wakatama, 63.
[33] Robert, 68.
[34] Wakatama, 40.
[35] Robert, 70.

its publicity channels to highlight national involvement in Bible translation, which included helping national translators get the necessary training and support. And by 1980, under Frank Robbins as Executive Vice President, the growth of national involvement became an ongoing objective as partnerships were growing in Africa, Asia, and the Pacific with national Christians who were committed to Bible translation.

Consequently, Townsend's vision of non-Westerners forming their own Bible translation organizations, separate from WBT and SIL, did not eventuate. Instead, WBT and SIL continued to engage with and help in the development of the national organizations.

Early Roots in Ghana

An example of this development occurred much earlier in 1960 when the late Ghanaian statesman John Komla Agama asked SIL to help translate the Bible into Ghanaian languages. At the time, Agama was studying in the UK, where he learned about the work of WBT. He met with the WBT British Council and asked them to consider sending translators to his country, because there were many languages that did not have any Scripture. The Council told Agama that WBT did not have any immediate plans to send trained personnel to Africa. But the need was noted, and within a year, the director of the British SIL school, John Bendor-Samuel, went to West Africa to evaluate the situation.

Bendor-Samuel arrived in Ghana in December 1961, 18 months after it had received its independence from Great Britain, the first African nation south of the Sahara to do so. He worked out a cooperative agreement between SIL and the Institute of African Studies at the University of Ghana. This stated that the two organizations would always work together in the development of Ghana's languages. Within a year, David and Nancy Spratt arrived and commenced linguistic and Bible translation work in the Kusaal language. At the same time, John and Kathleen Callow arrived to work in the Kasem language. Both couples were from the UK.

The agreement was built upon the vision of Ghanaian leaders like Agama, William Ofori-Atta, and Gottfried Osei-Mensah, with whom Bendor-Samuel had formed close friendships. These Ghanaian statesmen had national aspirations to develop and use the nation's languages as 'a platform for the intellectual, political, economic, and spiritual transformation' of their people.[36]

---

[36] Paul Opoku-Mensah, "Launching the Golden Anniversary in Tamale," 17 February 2012, GILLBT Admin Memo.

Complexities in Relationships

NBTOs supposedly developed under the guidance and assistance of both SIL and WBTI. However, it was SIL that supported their formation because these organizations had similar activities to SIL such as linguistics, literacy, and Bible translation work in their own countries. Most of their translators, usually trained by SIL, were 'mother-tongue', meaning that they served in their own language communities. Even with this close relationship, SIL chose not to include these organizations in its institutional structure. These national agencies needed to engage with the church in their countries, promote mother-tongue Scriptures, raise local funds, and recruit personnel and prayer support for Bible translation work. In this manner they carried out WBT-type functions.

Even with the emergence of NBTOs, there were two distinct and complimentary strategies taking place in the WBTI and SIL inter-relationship. WBTI oversaw Wycliffe functions or the home program that included: promoting and developing resources (people, prayer, and finance) for SIL; ministering to the church; partnering with the church, Bible colleges, and other mission agencies; taking care of members when they returned home; and partnering with field organizations (NBTOs and SIL) and advising them on strategic initiatives and joint goals. Then there were SIL functions or the field programs. These included: training members and nationals; technical tasks (Bible translation, linguistics, literacy, sociolinguistics, academic computing, etc); care of members on the field; host government and academic institution relations; and host church and mission relations.

NBTOs had their own functions: language program management and activities; administration (including relating to a board of directors/council); ministry, promotion, public relations, and fundraising with churches and their Christian public; and processing of new applicants, training members, and caring for their personnel. Their distinctive was the necessity to engage with their local churches, even though they were created in SIL's image rather than WBT's. NBTOs needed organizational development and to concentrate on fundraising to build that capacity. For NBTOs to develop, the historic organizational boundaries between WBT and SIL would have to be overcome.

The development of NBTOs prompted a call from WBTI to SIL to invest the latter's technical expertise into the national organizations, most of which lacked the financial and human resources that SIL possessed. This confirms how Bible translation 'tends to take the perspective of the missionary, who sees him- or herself as bringing the gospel from one place to another.'[37]

[37] Kim, 47.

The national organizations created a shift in what had been the simplistic perspective that organizations in WBT raised the resources for SIL to do its fieldwork. Now there were new players initiated by SIL that shared a vision for their own countries. A threshold had been crossed in the relationship between SIL and WBT because there were now others who shared the vision of Bible translation and had functions relating to both organizations. Up until this point, Bible translation was considered the domain of specialists, with expatriate linguists in charge, rather than the project being the responsibility of the local community. The rise of NBTO's changed this profile as mother-tongue linguists became the primary exegetes and translators.

Uniqueness of NBTOs

Up until this time, the history of WBTI and SIL had largely been written by SIL. This was because the emphasis was on the language communities which SIL served, and WBTI, through its organizations, supported. However, the emergence of NBTOs began to change this picture. For example, when John Watters was Executive Director of SIL and WBTI, he reported to the SIL Board in 2007 that the Wycliffe Member Organizations (WMOs) with language projects had usually started as NBTOs facilitated by SIL

> with the (implicit) promise that SIL would help [each organization] develop and eventually become the 'SIL' of the future within its nation. It would differ from SIL in its explicit Christian foundations and be similar in its pursuit of facilitating language-based development projects. That promise has been kept with varying degrees of commitment. In a number of cases there is significant division between the two. Experience has shown that SIL is not well qualified to build national institutions. Yet the reality is the WMOs exist.[38]

In 2015, Michel Kenmogne, SIL's newly appointed executive director, led a reflective process exploring key aspects of SIL's development. He noted how 1960–1975 was an 'expansion era' for SIL and how within SIL's field context

> nationalism advanced significantly in Asia and Africa. Many countries under colonial rule moved towards independence. This affected fieldwork, as many rethought their approach to missions (e.g., the Catholic Church adopting enculturation and indigenization approaches in order to make the church relevant to the people).[39]

[38] John Watters, "The Future of SIL and Some Implications for WBTI," 2007.

[39] Michel Kenmogne, "Observations and Thoughts on Sil's History," 2015, Current-SIL Internal Newsletter.

During this season, 'the threat of expulsion [of SIL personnel in some contexts] contributed to the creation of NBTOs, and more local citizens were trained' in linguistics and translation skills.[40]

SIL leader Paul Frank describes the formation of NBTOs as the crossing of a threshold within the context of WBTI and its relationship with SIL. Frank states, 'It was the beginning of the end of the simplistic model of "Wycliffe gathers the resources and SIL does the fieldwork."'[41] The emergence of NBTOs broke 'SIL's monopoly on field work' because there 'was another player on the field' (seemingly to imply that the NBTOs acted as a block or were uniform in character and outcomes).[42] The good in this was how 'SIL no longer had to think in terms of bearing the full load of accomplishing the Bible translation task. Others would share that load.' [43] (While the focus here is on NBTOs, SIL, and WBTI, other agencies like the Bible Societies had long been involved in Bible translation.)

Long-time WBTI leader Darryl Kernick notes how NBTOs were 'spawned by SIL in various countries, but SIL was unable to incorporate them within its structures.' NBTOs were effectively religious organizations because they related to the local and national churches. Consequently, Kernick remarks, 'they found a natural positioning within WBTI. This meant that WBTI now had some organizations that carried out field programs as well as those that provided resources.[44]

Growth and Development in National Contexts

Regardless of how Townsend, as founder, felt, NBTOs continued to grow in number, an indicator of how the Holy Spirit was and is already active in each language, culture, and context, thus demonstrating how 'the Christian faith is not imported but emerges out of local experiences.'[45]

NBTOs such as Ghana Institute of Linguistics, Literacy and Bible Translation (GILLBT) began forming in the 1960s. By the mid-1970s, more were appearing, and had distinctive names such as Nigeria Bible Translation Trust (NBTT), Bible Translation and Literacy (BTL), and the Bible Translation Association of Papua New Guinea (PNG BTA). Each organization was unique in its local aspirations.

---

40 Kenmogne.

41 Paul Frank, "SIL and WBTI in the 21st Century Some History, a Vision of the Future, and a Bit O' Fiction," 2007.

42 Frank.

43 Frank.

44 Frank.

45 Kim, 47.

First NBTO Conference

The NBTOs gathered for their first conference in Cameroon in May 1985 with 11 organizations represented. Cameroonian WBTI Board member, Emanuel Njock, presented insights from the event to the WBTI and SIL Conference later that year. He reported that the NBTOs realized they held dual functions, operating like a WBT division while carrying out field operations like an SIL branch. The NBTOs aspired to be more financially sustainable by raising local funds from churches, organizations, and individuals. They knew this would take quite an effort so until they were successful, they felt they still needed outside funding for small local projects. The WBTI and SIL International Conference delegates responded by expressing appreciation for Njock's report, noting the NBTO's desire to be fully involved in the world-wide Bible translation work. The conference went on record as being fully committed to work in partnership with the NBTOs, issuing this statement of intention:

> To maintain the present priority of seeking to facilitate the development of National Bible Translation Organizations in the spirit of the guidelines recommended by the NBTOs, and to seek opportunities for partnership and cooperation with nationals of the countries where we work in every way that is appropriate in each situation (both at the national level and in specific language projects).[46]

At the conference, the International Administration presented its priorities by areas for the next two years. Two leaders mentioned intentions to engage with NBTOs—Africa Area Director John Watters included 'encouraging NBTOs', and Asia Area Director Al Pence included 'cooperation with... NBTOs.'[47] After the conference had ended, WBTI President David Cummings wrote to friends to share some highlights, including the following:

> One special item of significance was to hear the report from the first International Conference of National Bible Translation Organizations. Several of the eleven groups are represented here with us and what a joy to hear how the Lord has been encouraging these groups in their own countries. As an organization we have committed ourselves to assist their endeavor to be involved in giving the Word.[48]

46 WBTI, "International Conference Extracts," 1985, 8.

47 WBTI, "International Conference," 1985, 8.

48 WBTI, "International Conference Extracts Addendum," 1985, 11.

Further NBTO Developments

In September 1989 in Mombasa, Kenya, WBTI President David Cummings led a two-week constituency development workshop. It was attended by NBTOs in Africa and representatives from the Pacific Islands and Asia. Representatives from yet to be fully established and recognized organizations in Africa also attended. Topics covered included the history of WBT, SIL, and JAARS; storytelling; and how to make a presentation about Bible translation for church and other audiences. This event demonstrated a significant effort by WBTI to equip NBTOs with skills to engage the church and build vision for Bible translation in their respective countries. Workshop participants planned to start units in their organizations, which would focus on church engagement and recruitment. However, the lack of any real attempts at understanding the national churches' perspectives and experiences regarding Bible translation or of finding the best approaches for building vision for Bible translation revealed limitations of the event.

Upon returning to their countries, three new African NBTOs developed that had not existed prior to the workshop: ANTBA (Burkina Faso), ACATBA (Central African Republic), and ATALTRAB (Chad). These resulted from the national vision for a national organization rather than from the initiative of SIL and WBTI.

Immediately after the workshop, the second NBTO conference took place in the same location in Mombasa. John Adive from Nigeria was the Chairman of the Steering Committee of the International Fellowship of NBTOs. He noted that insufficient financial resources, including some salaries, impeded growth for NBTOs. SIL leaders took note of growing evidence that efforts by SIL to develop NBTOs and support their programs would further the work of Bible translation around the world. The same leaders felt that SIL and WBT could help NBTOs in practical ways through training for constituency development, opening new sources of funding, and building relationships with NBTOs.

The WBTI and SIL International Conference of 1990 made decisions to strengthen the development of NBTOs, in part by understanding the NBTOs' existing strengths. This included their inherent capacity to integrate well qualified local citizens in the work of linguistic research, Bible translation, and literacy, which would strategically affect future efforts around the world. An impeding factor was the lack of financial resources (whether through SIL or NBTOs) that would enable more local citizens to be involved. The call went out to WBT Divisions to find considerable new funding sources for national involvement over the coming years. The Conference called upon the WBTI Board in consultation with the NBTO Steering Committee to explore the possibilities for long-term relationships between NBTOs and WBTI, especially regarding the nature and structure of this relationship, with recommendations to be brought to the 1993 International Conference.

In 1990, priorities for WBTI for the next two years were set, and some included specific mention of NBTOs. For example: (1) developing attitudes among the membership that promote interdependence with others, such as NBTOs, constituencies, churches, missions, and government bodies; (2) identifying and training up leaders for the NBTOs; and (3) developing appropriate ways of promoting the establishment and growth of NBTOs.

Part of WBTI's vision for the future involved helping NBTOs position themselves for growth and increasing effectiveness. In November 1990, the WBTI Board discussed the option for the NBTO Steering Committee to set up its own international infrastructure. The board saw potential disadvantages to setting up such a body, believing that this could divert limited resources of the NBTOs to sustain such a body. The board also believed it was premature to offer Member Organization status to any of the NBTOs, because the complete restructuring of WBTI had not yet been approved by its membership. The board did not want to 'prescribe or take the initiative with NBTOs, even though we are "family".'[49]

Agency of National Organizations

The development of NBTOs within the international mission agency structure of WBTI raises the question of another form of agency, namely the 'capacity to act or exert power.'[50] Graham Hill and Grace Ji-Sun Kim describe this type of agency as 'the freedom to make unrestricted and independent choices.' It occurs when 'individuals and groups... express themselves fully. They need agency to determine their own futures and forge their own identities. They need agency to contribute meaningfully.'[51]

The question that arises is whether NBTOs felt at that time that WBTI or SIL were giving them agency to chart their own courses for the future, establish their own identities, and make their own choices. A further possibility is that NBTOs did not think they were counted as equal with their international partners.

Another critical question is whether NBTOs had become financially dependent upon Western sources. If so, was their struggle for mutual respect hampered by this challenge? Albert Bandura states that agency is 'the human capability to exert influence over one's functioning and the course of events by one's actions.... To be an agent is to influence intentionally one's functioning and life's

[49] WBTI, "Board Minutes", May 1990, 15.

[50] Dictionary.com, "agency", https://www.dictionary.com/browse/agency?s=t, accessed 12 June 2020.

[51] Graham Hill, and Grace Ji-Sun Kim, *Healing Our Broken Humanity* (Downers Grove: IVP, 2018), 128.

circumstances.'[52] A further question is whether the international agencies were wise stewards with the resources they raised and then channelled to NBTOs. Kent Wilson states that steward leaders manage 'resources belonging to another person in order to achieve the owner's objectives.'[53] In other words, how were the intentions of NBTOs met by the stewardship of the resources raised for them by their Western counterparts? We will let these questions linger for now.

Overview of Historic NBTOs

The inclusion of 12 NBTOs at the 1988 WBTI and SIL International Conference marked a new development, as none had previously been invited. They included: AITB, ALEM, BCTS, BTA, BTL, GILLBT, GBT, IICCC, NBTT, SICA, SUBTALA, and TAP. From WBTI's perspective, these were the front-runners of a growing group of national organizations. Their individual development is described below in more detail.

Association Ivoirienne de Traduction de la Bible, Côte d'Ivoire (AITB)

Association Ivoirienne de Traduction de la Bible, Côte d'Ivoire (AITB) was formed in the mid-1980s with the rationale that a local institution would be necessary if or when SIL had to leave the country. This small association, created by SIL, represented a form of nationalization for Ivorians working in SIL language projects. However, it was not a grassroots indigenous movement because it was not empowered or equipped to do more. Literacy books and Scripture portions were published in the name of AITB, even if no one from AITB had any involvement in the project. Eventually, SIL leaders became concerned about the lack of development for AITB, even though other NBTOs were becoming more successful. In the end, AITB became dormant, and consequently, was never officially recognized in WBTI.

Associação Linguística Evangélica Missionária, Brazil (ALEM)

SIL (known as ILV, Instituto Linguístico de Verão) began working in Brazil in 1956. During the 1960s they established AWTB, Associação Wycliffe para a Tradução da Bíblia, (Wycliffe Association for Bible Translation) as a national organization for

[52] Albert Bandura, "Toward an Agentic Theory of the Self," *Advances in Self Research* 3 (2008): 16.

[53] Wilson, 36.

Brazilian participation. With an eye to the future, AWTB was based in the newly founded capital city, Brasília.

In 1958, ILV received an invitation from the Instituto Bíblico e Missionário Peniel, through its founder, Paulo C. Guiley, to present a course in linguistics to its first class of students, preparing to work with indigenous communities in Brazil. ILV linguist Ursula Wiesmann taught a three-month intensive linguistics course, the first SIL Linguistics course in Brazil. Rinaldo de Mattos, then a student at Peniel, was one of the participants.

During the 1960s, AWTB began offering linguistics courses to Brazilians. In 1973, the program was called Linguistic Methodology Course (CML), from which several Brazilians graduated. However, the program was closed after FUNAI, the National Indian Foundation, terminated its agreement with ILV in the 1980s.

In 1981, Rinaldo de Mattos was surprised and concerned to hear about the cancellation of CML. He raised the idea among CML alumni to form an association of Brazilian linguists to continue the program. He received many letters and phone calls from people in both ILV and AWTB supporting the idea. De Mattos decided to head up the movement, moving with his family to Brasilia, and was present in 1982, along with Wilbur Pickering and Pastor Gerson Camargo, when AWTB was offering its final linguistics course in Brazil. With the valuable collaboration of Isaac Costa de Souza, they laid out the statutes of ALEM (Evangelical Linguistic Missionary Association) to continue the work of translating the Bible into indigenous languages in Brazil and the rest of the world. Its first assembly was held from 12 to 13 August 1982. ALEM offered its first course, Linguistics and Missiology Course (CLM), in 1983.

In time, ALEM grew to lead linguistics training courses, as well being a missionary agency that sent and supported missionaries in linguistics and Bible translation service. It also created partnerships for Brazilians to serve other organizations in WBTI in translation and education in South Asia, Southeast Asia, and West Africa.

Bible Translation Committee of Sabah (BTCS)

The BTCS came into being in November 1979 through church leaders and other parties to promote and support Bible translation in the state of Sabah, Malaysia. Starting in 1980, it sponsored translation seminars to acquaint young people in local churches with the needs and opportunities for involvement in Bible translation. A translation workshop in 1983 attracted 45 participants from 19 different language communities with staff associated with BTCS and partners. The Committee ceased to operate after 1996.

Bible Translation Association, Papua New Guinea (BTA)

In 1973, SIL Director Karl Franklin wrote to some prominent Papua New Guineans asking them to consider serving on an SIL Advisory Committee (SILAC) that was intended to give guidance to SIL. All of them responded positively. The committee planned to bring Papua New Guinean Christians together to train as Bible translators, form prayer groups for Bible translators, and advise SIL on courses of action in literacy, adult education, and translation. Many of these committee members later became prominent leaders in PNG. In 1975, SIL hired Thomas Polume from Manus Province to work in its administration. In the same year, on 16 September, PNG gained independence from Australia. At that time, members of SILAC felt it necessary to form an independent organization to train Papua New Guineans to carry out translation work themselves.

Polume submitted a proposal to SILAC in 1976 to form a national translators association. As Chairman of SILAC, he stated, 'We believe in and are convinced that the Bible and the knowledge of it is important to the development of our country. We are convinced of the need of Bible translation and motivated to create an organization with the aim of assisting SIL translators to produce the Word of God in the languages of our people.'[54] SILAC dissolved in 1977 and BTA emerged, although it took until 1980 to be recognized by the PNG government. Polume decided it was time for him to move on to work with the PNG government, and thus he approached David Gela, a student at the University of PNG, about joining BTA.

In February 1980, based at the SIL Centre at Ukarumpa, BTA began to take shape as an organization. Using a borrowed office and staff housing, and with leaders lacking experience in developing an organization, BTA moved forward. David Gela served as the first director of BTA, and his wife Sineina assisted him. Gela had just graduated from university with teacher qualifications. He accepted a mandate from the Lord and the BTA Board to train and equip Papua New Guineans for Bible translation ministry.

From the outset, the BTA leadership wanted to establish the organization's identity. It had to consider its relationship with SIL in PNG. Was BTA going to merge with SIL, or would it operate as a parallel structure? The BTA leaders chose the latter, and the decision coincided with the new era of NBTOs with WBTI. From 1981 to 1983 there were small but significant developments for BTA, such as the start of the National Translators' Course for training Papua New Guineans for Bible translation. Gela describes the phase as 'growing by learning by/from

[54] BTA, "History of the Papua New Guinea Bible Translation Association," 2015.

looking, listening, talking, visiting, tasting, and feeling.'[55] BTA secured funding for construction of staff housing and an office at Ukarumpa. It invited existing Papua New Guinean Bible translators to join BTA, eventually managing 14 Bible translation programs, and celebrating the first fruit of the Zia New Testament.

The next stage of development took place from 1986 to 1991 when BTA decided to move its headquarters from the SIL Centre at Ukarumpa to the PNG capital of Port Moresby. It secured land at the suburb of Waigani and constructed two homes, offices, and conference and training facilities. The centre was dedicated in September 1991, and Gela's prayer was, 'Lord, you led us thus far. Take us on from here to where you want to establish BTA.'[56]

In 1996, WBTI granted BTA Wycliffe Affiliate Organization status. BTA's contribution to the Bible translation movement was gaining global recognition, including the Barai New Testament, managed under BTA, and acknowledged as the 400th to be completed in affiliation with Wycliffe and SIL worldwide. BTA Board Chairman William Edoni was elected by WBTI to serve on its board from 2002 until he unexpectedly died in 2006.

Stephen Thomas took over from Gela as BTA director from 2000 to 2006. The board brought Gela back after Thomas's term had completed. Gela served another 12 years until 2015. He describes this era as one of 'adjusting, tweaking, and reshaping' BTA as it acted locally, while it grew in the role it played in the global arena.[57] During Gela's entire tenure, from 1980 to 2015, he witnessed the organization that he and Sineina had faithfully helped birth and guide become a globally recognized part of the Bible translation movement, while retaining a strong Papua New Guinean identity. BTA was part of the original group of NBTO's, and Gela has been the longest serving leader from that original group. BTA represents an important part of the development of WBTI because it started in 1980, the same year that WBTI was formed.

Bible Translation & Literacy, Kenya (BTL)

In 1977, in association with the Bible Society of Kenya (BSK) and the Department of Linguistics and African Languages of the University of Nairobi, SIL began carrying out socio-linguistics surveys to determine the translation needs in Kenya. The surveys revealed the necessity for Scriptures in several small language groups in Kenya, though they did not yet have a written system. Because these languages were small, they were not in the scope of BSK's ministry, necessitating the formation of an organization prioritizing this challenge.

[55] David Gela, "Report to BTA Board," 2015, 2.

[56] Gela, 2.

[57] Gela, 3.

John Bendor-Samuel, SIL Africa Area Director at that time, did not think SIL should start this work. Instead, he turned to key Kenyan church leaders John Gatũ, John Mpaayei, and Gottfried Osei-Mensah who was then pastor at Nairobi Baptist Church. Bendor-Samuel met with these and other church leaders over a two-year period from 1978 to 1980 at the offices of the Bible Society of Kenya to discuss the way forward. These discussions led to the formation of BTL, which would focus on translation work among the small language groups of Kenya, while the Bible Society focussed on the larger language groups. On 4 March 1981 BTL registered in Kenya as a charitable Christian organization.

Gatũ's role in the decision to form a Kenyan organization is significant because he believed that Africans deserved the opportunity to contribute to Bible translation as a way of participating in worldwide evangelization. He pressed Bendor-Samuel on this because the African church, too, was called to this global responsibility. BTL honoured Gatũ for his influence by asking him to lay the foundation stone of the new BTL centre in Nairobi in December 1982.

SIL offered to kickstart the work through a team called the Kenya Working Group, and thus, in 1981, two language projects (Sabaot and Rendille) commenced. Kenyan General Secretary Micah Amukobole was appointed to lead the organization in November 1983 and served for 20 years. BTL's operations continued to be managed by the SIL Kenya Working Group until January 1987 when BTL assumed full responsibility for translation work in Kenya. BTL's Board very significantly decided to create a department wholly dedicated to engaging the Kenyan church. This was consistent with BTL's desire to involve the Kenyan church in the translation of the Bible, not only in Kenya, but also in East Africa. BTL became an Affiliate Organization of WBTI in May 1996. In 2000 BTL became the first former NBTO to have Wycliffe personnel directly seconded to it without those personnel first having to go through SIL.

To Amukobole's credit (and with the support of an active board), he set out to build BTL as an organization that sought to create a local constituency, utilizing Kenyan workers. One of his practices was to ensure that BTL engaged with the local community and church denominations before starting new projects. BTL would form local committees which partnered with BTL in recruiting those from the community who would join the Bible translation efforts with BTL. Consequently, BTL stood out for its professionalism, while in other Bible translation agencies local community members mainly worked as language helpers.

Ghana Institute of Linguistics, Literacy and Bible Translation (GILLBT)

In 1980 in recognition of its national identity, SIL in Ghana changed its name to Ghana Institute of Linguistics (GIL), and WBTI formally recognized GIL as an NBTO. At this point, GIL transferred from being under SIL to coming under WBTI. This made the situation in Ghana unique in the world of SIL. In 1982, GIL became GILLBT, adding Literacy and Bible Translation to its name. Although GILLBT was formally part of WBTI, it nonetheless retained a close relationship with SIL because of its historical roots. GILLBT's respected Ghanaian leaders included Kenneth Wujangi, Grace Adjekum, William Addai, and Justin Frempong.

GILLBT experienced a significant organizational crisis in 2008–2009 due to management and governance difficulties that resulted in a loss of confidence by overseas partners and funders. This crisis, unless addressed, would likely have led to the collapse of this nearly 50-year-old institution. In response, Paul Opoku-Mensah left his academic posting and became GILLBT's director because he wanted to reposition GILLBT to fulfil the vision of its founding fathers.

GILLBT existed within a global community of WBTI that worked together on a worldwide scale. Since GILLBT originally started as SIL's entity in Ghana, it still retained some core DNA of SIL, including a commitment for language development in Ghana. Thus, GILLBT's relationship with SIL remained important.

In 2010, a yearlong centenary celebration of Ofori-Atta's life took place, with GILLBT involved in the festivities. Ofori-Atta's legacy to GILLBT emphasized the importance of building relationships to transition to a truly national organization, owned and supported by Ghanaian Christians and their churches. Because of visionaries like Ofori-Atta, who gave of his time and resources to develop this organization, GILLBT benefitted from an all-embracing legitimacy.

Agama also had a strong passion for God's word in the local languages. Known to his church and other Christian organizations as a supporting pillar, and despite his busy schedule as an Assistant Superintendent of Police, Agama regularly found time to encourage GILLBT staff. GILLBT's heritage from its ancestors Agama and Ofori-Atta demonstrates that its aspirations of being a truly Ghanaian owned and led organization were well placed within the growing nationalization of the Bible translation movement.

Global Bible Translators, South Korea (GBT)

In 1974, Elmer Wolfenden from WBT visited South Korea to lead a seminar on Bible translation and linguistics at the Summer Institute of World Mission (SIWM), hosted by Korea International Mission (KIM). Donghwa and Hyunsook Kim attended this SIWM. Two years later, Ron Trail from SIL led a seminar on Bible Translation Principles at SIWM. Ron and his wife Gail remained in Korea for two years as a visiting lecturer at the East-West Center for World Mission. The Kims and Euijung (John) Kim took Trail's course. In 1978, KIM sent both Korean couples to attend SIL training in Dallas, Texas. In 1980–81, Steve and Marilyn Thrasher from WBT were invited by KIM to live in Korea in order to recruit Koreans, and to provide orientation to Bible translation. In 1983, Euijung (John) and Yeonhwa Kim were sent by KIM to serve in Indonesia. However, the relationship between KIM and WBT and SIL deteriorated, and consequently the Thrashers left KIM.

In 1984, Donghwa Kim started preparatory work to establish a new organization called GBT. Euijung (John) and Yeonhwa Kim joined Donghwa Kim in the venture. They invited influential church leaders to meet, hosted by Nam Seoul Church, to form a governing board for GBT. For five weeks Cal Rensch of SIL visited these leaders and organized various speaking engagements, giving presentations about Bible translation.

GBT started an annual recruitment and orientation event called Camp Wycliffe. In 1985 when the second Camp Wycliffe took place, 33 potential new members attended. These camps continued to be held annually, providing the main opportunity for those interested in Bible translation to learn about GBT. At this time GBT joined the Association of Korean Christian Mission Organizations. The GBT Board gained more members, with well-respected pastors also joining. In 1993, the board moved from managing to governing and appointed Donghwa Kim as Director.

GBT illustrates an oddity in how WBTI classified NBTOs. Why was GBT considered to be an NBTO rather than a Wycliffe Division, and later, a Member Organization? Perhaps this was because GBT already existed under another body, the Global Missionary Fellowship of South Korea. GBT also didn't use 'Wycliffe' in its name. For its part, GBT wanted WBTI membership and approval so that it could send its members to SIL, but it also wanted to be able to send its personnel to other organizations. When WBTI reclassified organizational categories in 1994, it gave GBT (and many other NBTOs) Associate Organization with Vote status. However, for the 1996 International Convention, WBTI gave GBT the classification of Wycliffe Organization with Vote (the same status as the former WBT Divisions).

Indian Institute for Cross Cultural Communications (IICCC)

In 1980, SIL staff and other linguistics experts helped initiate the IICCC as a training course for Indians wanting to serve in their own country in Bible translation, linguistics, and literacy. From the outset, those involved intended for IICCC to have Indian ownership. The Indian Missions Association (IMA) decided to make IICCC 'its training wing' to serve the Indian mission agencies.[58] In 1988, Jacob George became the director of the Institute and led it for 11 years. The number of Indians coming to IICCC for training and then establishing Bible translation programs was declining to the extent that by the early 1990s, George became concerned and initiated efforts to promote the Bible translation needs within his country. Eventually, he was instrumental in forming Word for All, that was recognized by WBTI in 2006. Word for All later disbanded in 2008, and Wycliffe India took shape that same year. Under Wycliffe India, the Institute for Linguistics and Languages developed, taking the place of the IICCC.

Nigeria Bible Translation Trust (NBTT)

In 1961, John Bendor-Samuel arrived in Nigeria to initiate SIL's language survey in preparation to serve Nigeria's minority languages. SIL was unable to secure land in Zaria where its teams were working, but purchased land in Jos in 1970, and consequently, moved there. SIL built its centre, equipping it with offices, a guest house, printing press, dining hall, and kitchen. It also set up an Institute of Linguistics to train Nigerians and shared the vision with church leaders and other interested parties. However, evoking interest in the training offered was a slow process.

In 1975, the government started a 'Nigerianization' policy, requiring that Nigerians hold full control of various enterprises,[59] which included the education sector, and therefore SIL's training institute. SIL Director Ron Stanford shared the vision of the Institute in August 1975 at the National Congress for Evangelisation. Prominent Nigerians attended, including Bitrus Pam, Bitrus Gani, Akanu Ibiam, O. Gani, Barnaba Dusu, and Byan Kato (later, Kato founded the Evangelicals of Africa and Madagascar). These Nigerian leaders did not consider that Nigeria was ready to develop a fully Nigerian Bible translation organization to take over the work of the Institute of Linguistics. However, they agreed to form a Council for the Promotion of Bible Translation in Nigeria.

---

[58] Warren Glover, *Making a Difference: Training Bible Translators in India* (Kangaroo Ground: WBT Australia, 2002), 40.

[59] NBTT, "Chapter 1—Brief History," unpublished paper.

In 1976, after a partial military coup in Nigeria, SIL leaders were asked to go to Lagos in March to meet with the Ministry of Internal Affairs. At that meeting, the SIL leaders were told that the Institute had not 'Nigerianized'; its work was focussed on minority groups that were of no interest to the government; the country did not require a specialized foreign group to do what the Nigerian churches and universities could do, and consequently, the Institute could be wound up as quickly as possible and turned over to Nigerians within a month. Barnaba Dusu led further negotiations with the authorities, and the council formally took over the responsibilities of the Institute, as well as 14 language programs. The new organization was registered on 1 July 1976 as NBTT, and the former SIL centre became the Nigeria Bible Translation Centre. Its first leaders were John Adive, Stephen Niyang, and Danjuma Gambo. Over the years, NBTT has developed into a reputable Nigerian Bible translation institution.

Solomon Islands Christian Association (SICA) and Solomon Islands Translation Advisory Group (SITAG)

SICA is an umbrella structure for all the mainline churches in the Solomon Islands. In the late 1970s and early 1980s, when SIL arrived in the Solomon Islands, SICA had been made aware of the need to translate the English Bible into Solomon Islands' Pidjin and the 70 languages of the country. Since SIL was an international organization, SICA wanted a local name that Solomon Islanders could identify with. They chose SITAG, which became an associate ministry organization of SICA, and received help in obtaining entry permits, residence permits, and work permits for foreigners coming to help in Bible translation, including the SIL personnel who came to work under SITAG.

SICA always desired to have an indigenous Bible Translation organization to take on the ministry of Bible translation for the country since SITAG and its overseas personnel were temporary. In 1993, a group of Solomon Islands translators working under SITAG came together and discussed the necessity of establishing a local Bible translation organization. After some prayerful thinking, they started to work on the name, constitution, and other matters. The rise in ethnic tensions in the Solomon Islands in 1998, when overseas SITAG staff returned to their home countries for safety, served as a confirmation of the dream for a local organization. In 2008, when presented with this dream, SICA embraced and endorsed the concept. The local ministry was initially called Solomon Islands Bible Translation and Literacy Partnership (SIBTLP) and later changed to BTLPSI (Bible Translation and Literacy Partnership of Solomon Islands). The organization continues to function.

Sudan Bible Translation and Literacy Association (SUBTALA)

In 1978, SUBTALA was founded, primarily through the efforts of John Bendor-Samuel. The organization brought together leaders of the southern Sudanese church in Juba to promote Bible translation and literacy under local ownership. Appointed as their first administrator, John Moi represented the organization at various SIL International and WBTI global and regional meetings. SUBTALA registered with the southern regional government in1982, which enabled it to obtain land. Due to the civil war, by 1987, all SIL personnel had left the region, leaving SUBTALA to function on its own.

Meanwhile, in Khartoum, a new organically grown association of translators emerged and eventually became part of the Translation Department of the Episcopal Church of Sudan. The main difference between SUBTALA and the newly formed Translation Department was their origins. According to Russ Hersman, 'One was imposed (with good intentions) and the other sprouted of its own accord.' Hersman, SIL Director at the time, when asked what should be done to promote the growth of the department, responded, 'Do nothing, but pray for and encourage the key players' because he 'did not want to overlay SIL on them as was the case for SUBTALA.'[60]

Translators Association of the Philippines (TAP)

In the early 1970s, SIL Philippines personnel envisioned forming a national organization to work alongside SIL. Then SIL Director Rev Morrie Cottle shared the concept with Filipino Colonel Silvino Primero, who also caught the vision.

In 1982, the Translators Committee of the Philippines (TCP), along with Filipino Bible translators, literacy specialists, and community development managers, met together to discuss the process for legally incorporating a Filipino organization. Incorporation resulted in April 1983 when Filipino government authorities recognized TAP. The original 17 members from TCP became the core of TAP. It was a long and sometimes difficult journey for TAP as it emerged from humble beginnings to serve the cultural communities of the Philippines, with the goal of translating God's Word into the heart language of the Filipino people.

At TAP's first conference, Rev Teodoro (Ted) Abadiano was elected as Executive Director, Attorney Gideon Cascolan as TAP's first Chairman, and Antonio Dasalla as Vice Chairman. Abadiano served as TAP Executive Director from 1982 to 1986 and 1992 to 1996. A decade after its formation, TAP's membership had grown

---

60 Russ Hersman, Email correspondence, 30 April 2020.

from its original 17 people to 55 who were serving and supporting ministry in 18 language groups in the Philippines. The first completed New Testament with TAP personnel was in the Tina Sambal language in 1999.

In 1998, TAP moved to its present office and training facility site at Quezon City in Manila. In 2004 TAP enlarged the facility to provide accommodation for members coming from field assignments to work on translation and literacy materials. TAP later expanded to better serve neighbouring Asian countries by training future specialists or consultants in translation, Scripture engagement, Ethno Arts, and Literacy Education and Development (LEAD).

Evolving Structures and Relationships

The year 1991 holds historic significance for WBTI due to its restructuring as an organization consisting of many individual organizations, sometimes explained as an umbrella organization of many organizations. Up until then, Wycliffe offices were called Divisions and linked with the first Wycliffe office, Wycliffe US.

After the restructuring, SIL changed its bylaws for its 14-member board of directors to include one member of an NBTO. Despite WBTI officially changing the name NBTO to Wycliffe Affiliate Organizations (WAOs), they were still widely being referred to as NBTOs in official meeting minutes. Understanding this name change and all it would impact would take time.

In 1992 WBTI and SIL created a partnership statement clarifying how WBTI, with its organizations, chose to partner primarily with SIL since that was the reason for the creation of the original Wycliffe Divisions—to raise resources of people, prayer, and finances for SIL. The leaders of the day wanted to ensure that the newly structured WBTI would remain committed to its partnership with SIL.

The partnership statement did not address the relationship between SIL and the NBTOs/WAOs because that relationship was not yet developed, even though NBTOs/WAOs primarily originated from SIL. NBTOs were given observer status, with members of the International NBTO Steering Committee attending the WBTI 1993 International Conference as delegates. At the Conference, Steering Committee member and BTL Executive Director Micah Amukobole was elected to the WBTI Board. Also, at that conference, the relationship between NBTOs and WBTI was discussed, with all the SIL delegates participating. Members of the NBTO Steering Committee voiced their concerns, such as, 'we would like a delegation with voice and vote'; 'to be serious, [WBTI] needs to invite, involve, and give ability to [the NBTOs to] actually participate in the Conference'; 'it is important to be a part of you'; and 'we need to be a part of you, your children, to come and participate with and learn from you.'[61]

[61] WBTI, "International Conference Minutes," May 1993, 2.

WBTI and SIL delegates realized the necessity to listen to the NBTOs that were asking to become part of the WBTI structure. NBTO representatives had been meeting with WBTI for the past eight years. NBTOs thought of themselves as the children of WBTI and SIL and wanted to be heard. With an air of consternation, one NBTO leader declared, 'this is not new, since we instructed the International Administration in 1990 to move ahead [for] us.'[62] In fact, the NBTO fellowship had met in Yaoundé in 1985, Mombassa in 1989, and Horsleys Green (UK) in 1991. As a result, delegates in both SIL and WBTI were calling for NBTOs to be recognized. The delegates appealed to the International Administration and boards of WBTI and SIL to find a way of recognizing NBTOs as associate organizations in WBTI and to extend to them the right of voting—'a symbol of equality' and inclusion.[63]

Even though the decision of the 1991 restructuring process within WBTI in conversation with SIL was to place the NBTOs under WBTI, the NBTOs struggled to fit in with WBTI, as well as to know where they fit in relationship with SIL. The NBTOs had unique challenges, and their concerns troubled their NBTO leaders, who sought to find ways to address these challenges effectively. Topics that concerned them and often dominated NBTO conferences included these:

› *Training needs:* In areas of technical and management responsibilities of NBTO staff, training was needed to help them effectively run their organizations and meet their mandate.
› *Relationships between NBTOs, local SIL entities, and WOs:* NBTOs lacked ways of directly relating with each other, as relational lines almost always flowed through SIL. In those instances where an SIL branch worked in the same country with the NBTO, there were perpetual tensions. As well, NBTOs were often in strained relationships with WOs that served as funders or resource providers.
› *Capacity building:* Capacity issues beleaguered NBTOs, especially in the areas of governance, ability to recruit and employ qualified management (e.g., financial management), communication personnel, and church engagement personnel.
› *Partial funding of projects:* Most translation projects under NBTOs received fewer funds from Wycliffe funders than what was budgeted, necessitating that the NBTO project managers recruit lower capacity staff or take longer to complete the projects.

[62] WBTI, May 1993, 53.
[63] WBTI, May 1993, 58.

Moving Out of the Shadow

When NBTOs were first emerging, most 'grew alongside their larger, stronger, more capable SIL partner [and] in many places, they lived in the shadow of their SIL partner.'[64] Due to a lack of clarity about where they previously belonged, some NBTO leaders had believed they were second-class citizens. By 1991, through a slow process, NBTOs relocated to WBTI, a more suitable home for them. As mission organizations, NBTOs fit within the purpose and values of WBTI, where they could now gain full acceptance.

NBTOs received a new category and name in 1991 as Wycliffe Affiliate Organizations (WAOs). However, another five years elapsed before the new term replaced the old. The NBTO name persisted because NBTOs did not fit the organizational model of the WOs—the WOs did not manage Bible translation programs, but the WAOs did. There would be further changes to their WAO name in the future as a wide range of structural and functional issues were addressed throughout WBTI.

At the next WBTI International Convention in 1996, in addition to the 20 WOs, each represented by two delegates, there were six applicant organizations and 14 Affiliate Organizations, each represented by one delegate. The latter were former NBTOs, along with some newer participants like ACATBA of Central African Republic, ATALTRAB of Chad, and Kartidaya of Indonesia. However, at the Convention, NBTO terminology continued to be used inter-changeably with the new WAO category.

In 2002, SIL and WBTI Pacific Area Director Neville Southwell reported to the International Administration his concern that if NBTOs became more aligned with WBTI entities, SIL could lose its connection in areas of mutual interest with NBTOs. SIL had been shifting its strategy from primarily seeking governments to sponsor SIL's work to situations where SIL's personnel were working under and with a new set of sponsors that included NBTOs, as well as churches, missions, and other organizations. By 1999, SIL's policy of 'national involvement' focussed on inspiring and facilitating local and national leadership to take primary responsibility for translation programs. At the 1999 WBTI Convention and SIL International Conference, WBTI President John Bendor-Samuel stated that the 'great involvement of NBTOs' was a reason for celebration.[65] At the same meeting, these organizations were officially referred to as Affiliate Organizations in WBTI.

---

[64] Frank, 1.

[65] WBTI, "International Convention Minutes," May 1999, 3.

Local Ownership of the Bible Translation Movement

Micah Amukobole was a key leader in the NBTO movement and held three overlapping roles that enabled him to give influence. (1) He served as leader of BTL, Kenya; (2) He served on the NBTO Steering Committee from 1985 until his retirement from BTL; and (3) He served on the WBTI and SIL International Boards from 1990 to 2002. Amukobole's vision was to ensure that the NBTO leaders invested in healthy, well managed, and well led organizations. He poured his energies into serving other NBTO leaders, including sharing with them BTL's constitution and policy documents. Unfortunately, many of these leaders didn't follow his advice and example, nor did they apply the necessary effort in developing both a local constituency and a strong organization. As a result, some NBTOs created dependency on their foreign partners in Wycliffe Organizations and SIL entities. Because of this, their organizations struggled to become resilient when times became difficult for their foreign partners to maintain financial support of the NBTOs.

The challenge of finding their appropriate organizational home—whether exclusively in WBTI, SIL, or in WBTI with partnership agreements with SIL—limited the NBTOs' development. The question of ownership at the local and national level emerged, especially in countries with a high degree of Bible translation activity and future needs, affecting each NBTO in different ways.

This chapter began with observations from the Moratorium Debate about expatriate missionary efforts in Africa. The debate included concerns: that Western missionaries brought the Gospel into Africa 'wrapped with cumbersome paraphernalia of Western culture'[66]; that Western mission agencies were not multi-racial or multi-cultural; that Western missionary leadership was detracting from the national church through financial and other types of control; and that some Africans felt Western missions had successfully discharged their responsibilities and could therefore leave.

A solution for Western missionaries that still had roles to play in partnership with the African church was the priority to be well qualified, have expertise in cross-cultural communication, and must not have 'the faintest vestiges of racial prejudice.'[67] Wakatama notes how 'centuries of racism in colonial times' made Africans intolerant of racism, especially from Western Christians.[68] Wakatama observes how 'the rising spirit of nationalism makes it imperative that nationals be trained to take over the work in their countries from missionaries.'[69]

---

[66] Wakatama, 13.

[67] Wakatama, 79.

[68] Wakatama, 79.

[69] Wakatama, 79.

While Wakatama was not directly addressing SIL or WBTI, he could have been. And if he was, the two organizations could have asked themselves whether it made any difference to the future of national translators within the WBTI or SIL contexts, such as (1) the linguistic qualifications necessary for national translators, and how these differed from requirements for expatriates; (2) funding of national translation programs; (3) the adaptation of the organizational structures of WBTI and SIL to accommodate non-Western participants or the assimilation of national translators into the future work of WBTI and SIL; and (4) the positive or negative impact of national translators upon recruitment of Westerners through WBT.

Despite progress made on some of these factors, there may have been less progress on the question of training of nationals, specifically if carried out half-heartedly, and mainly for expediency rather than as a necessity. Are resources for training released on a reward basis rather than the result of good planning, and for those who really deserve it? Perhaps a deeper question is whether national Christians should choose to maintain Bible translation structures left behind by Western missionaries, rather than working out the best way of conducting ministry in their localities. Otherwise, are the national Christians who want to participate left on the periphery of the Bible translation movement?

NBTOs that are now organizations in WGA may still have an identity challenge, requiring a new DNA decolonized from the era from which they arose. Some NBTO leaders felt as though their organizations had slipped between the structural boundaries of WBTI and SIL; while wanting to flourish in WBTI, they still looked to SIL for validation. WBTI recognized that knowing how best to help the NBTOs remained a complex issue.

Conclusion

Few leaders in WBTI and SIL supported and encouraged the development of NBTOs as much as John Bendor-Samuel did in his various leadership roles. This was especially true on the African continent, where he was known as 'Mr Wycliffe'. While he did work closely with African universities in establishing agreements for linguistic work, a strategy effectively used by SIL, he also worked tirelessly with church leaders because he believed the African church would not accept Scriptures produced by scientific organizations. They preferred religious organizations, and that is what WBTI stood for.

Bendor-Samuel's tireless work in supporting the development of the NBTOs received no recognition from WBT and SIL's founder, Cameron Townsend, which is understandable, as the two men worked and lived in two very different contexts.

Bendor-Samuel envisioned local Christians—especially in Africa, where he primarily worked—setting up their own functioning bodies to lead and manage Bible translation programs. This resulted in his legacy of being instrumental to the development of NBTOs worldwide.

The development of NBTOs, SIL, and WBTI are intertwined. When NBTOs grew in number and maturity, the international bodies of SIL and WBT that were the originators of these organizations did not have a clear strategy for them. It was a logical outcome for NBTOs to consider themselves second-class citizens in the larger WBTI and SIL relational dynamic. While SIL did create a position on its International Board for an NBTO Director, it was in WBTI that national organizations found a home where they were allowed to gain affiliation with WBTI. After 2008, they found full acceptance in the restructured WBTI, now WGA. In this process, showing themselves to be competent, NBTOs rose to the technical and academic challenges of Bible translation and became significant contributors to the Bible translation movement worldwide.

The journey of NBTOs has touched upon issues of nationalism, expressed in Africanization for those on the African continent, or nationalization of Bible translation in Africa and elsewhere. It has included an exploration of how the vision of Bible translation gets embedded into the national context while retaining a tension with its Western roots. The journey has mentioned the foundational role of the ancestors, which has been key to the formation of NBTOs. While Western pragmatism may have been a motive for some, national leaders aspire to national ownership, not only of the vision but also of the organizational structure necessary to carry out the vision.

The journey started by exploring the roots of the Moratorium Debate on Western missionaries and their agencies. While that happened in the early 1970s, it provides a framework to consider how the Moratorium Debate influenced international mission then and whether the issues and questions remain today, particularly within the Bible translation movement. We come to this point of the journey reminded of how complex it has become as new travellers join the journey—each must find their own pace, choose with whom they will walk, and find a way of belonging. It also demonstrates the necessity for those already on the journey to be inclusive, remembering that they don't 'own' the journey nor the plans showing how it should all take place.

Chapter 9
Perceiving: Vision 2025

By Susan Van Wynen

Introduction

How does God awaken his people to think beyond what they know, to unburden themselves of status quo, and to step out in faith? Looking back at 1999, we see at least two major milestones for WBTI. For one, there was the transition of the executive director as Steve Sheldon handed the role over to John Watters. Additionally, it was the year of the triennial WBTI International Convention and SIL International Conference, jointly called 'ICON99'. The theme was 'Together We Can'. In preparation for the transition of leadership, as well as for the Convention and Conference, John Watters presented a vision for the future to both WBTI and SIL. He had also prepared a twelve-page paper for the delegates of ICON99 to read before they arrived. It was titled, 'Vision 2025: A Vision for the Family of Organizations of WBTI and SIL International'. Many of the delegates came prepared to listen and to dialogue, having already had some time to read and reflect on the Vision.

The leadership responsibility of casting vision is often combined or associated with strategy and problem solving. Watters sought to introduce a vision that could lead to a new strategy that would address the remaining Bible translation needs.

Watters stated in the preamble to Vision 2025 that the highest goal 'is to glorify God and enjoy him forever.' Addressing the participating organizations, in the Vision proposal, Watters stated: 'We recognize that our ultimate goal is that every person in each generation have access to the Word of God in the language they understand best and be able to benefit from their language being used in various media.' The Vision addressed the goal of all peoples having access to God's Word in the languages that best communicated to them and acknowledged that at the rate of progress at that time, the goal would not be reached until 2150.

Watters began by outlining challenges that both WBTI and SIL faced as they looked to the future. He described the current situation as being at a 'crossroads [and] choosing between the status quo or walking in new ways. The status quo will leave us with impressive results, but those results will likely leave the local and national situations short of leadership to meet the needs of the next generation, and perhaps two thousand languages or more will remain without the Scriptures.'[1]

Watters offered a picture of the current path, based on the data available using current strategies. On this path, annual work begun in more languages would decline further than that experienced thus far, and the West would maintain control of the Bible translation movement. However, both Wycliffe and SIL would become less effective because of the decline in recruitment of the next generation of Western Christians, and because of the increasing and inevitable retirement of the current workforce. The current path would not even be able to maintain the status quo, let alone provide a way to increase the pace of the Bible translation movement.

The vision Watters sought to cast followed a second road. In consideration of this path, Watters presented six global factors requiring reflection and action:

› The first factor was the 'globalization of the church'—the demographic shift favouring the Global South and East.[2] One facet of this was the growing dichotomy between the source of future financial resources and that of future personnel. Financial resources came from the West while new people were coming from across the globe, yet neither WBTI nor SIL were equipped to manage this expanding global workforce. Another facet was the desire for the church from the South and East to assume greater partnership with the two organizations.
› A second critical factor was the 'problematic contexts where major translation needs remain.'[3] Many of the remaining Bible translation needs were in three geographical areas: the Indonesia-Pacific Islands region, central Africa and Nigeria, and mainland Asia from India to China. Many of these contexts were 'hostile to Christian activity', especially involving a 'large Western presence'.[4]
› The 'demographic growth of the future, favouring countries in Africa and Asia', was the third critical factor.[5] This was an additional East or West scenario as many nations in the East and South had growing, younger populations as compared with the aging population trend of the West.
› The fourth critical factor was the noticeable desire across the mission world, including the Bible agencies, for new partnerships that exhibited 'greater openness, vulnerability, and cooperation'.[6]
› 'Increased interest in the ethnolinguistic minorities of the world' was the next

[1] John Watters, "Vision 2025: A Vision for the Family of Organizations of WBTI and SIL International," 1999, 3.
[2] Watters, 3.
[3] Watters, 3.
[4] Watters, 7.
[5] Watters, 3.
[6] Watters, 8.

factor.[7] Mission agencies and others were showing interest in learning about local languages and cultures as 'a resource for communication, a medium for education, and a social reality deserving of their own rights, status, and attention.'[8]

› The final critical factor focussed on shifts in language use across the globe. English continued to grow as a preferred language in globalized contexts, and many nations were increasing their emphasis on both English and the majority language in their contexts, leading to increasing levels of multilingualism. Minority languages or languages considered less desirable by national leaders were often neglected, becoming endangered, or overlooked when it came to literacy and education.

These critical factors and Watters's challenge towards action set the stage for a rigorous discussion at ICON99. There were approximately 350 leaders as delegates representing both organizations at this triennial meeting.

The Emerging Vision

Outgoing Executive Director Steve Sheldon added to the foundation setting for Vision 2025. His presentation to the leaders at ICON99 highlighted the rate of progress of Bible translation over the previous 2,000 years. Progress was slow during the first 18 centuries, although major milestones were achieved (the Septuagint, the Vulgate, John Wycliffe's English translation, the King James Version, Martin Luther's German translation, etc.) By the end of the 18th century, 68 language groups had access to a Bible translation. The 19th century saw a six-fold increase in Bible translation. During the 20th century, Bible translation was underway in 1,690 languages. By 1999, 2,212 language groups had some Scripture in their heart language. WBTI and SIL had played roles in this rapid progress, along with other Bible translation agencies who concentrated on the world's smaller languages. In addition, training of indigenous translators took place, with an aim towards working in their own vernaculars.

Despite these signs of significant progress, the latter part of the 20th century wasn't showing such promise. From 1981 to 1998, there was a slowing down of progress in starting new Bible translation efforts. Sheldon concluded that 'the estimate of how long it might take for all people groups to have SOME Scriptures in their heart languages COULD range from 100 to 150 years.'[9]

7 Watters, 3.

8 Watters, 8.

9 WBTI, "International Convention Minutes," 1999, 6.

The startling information from Sheldon and the challenge from Watters fully captured the delegates' attention and resulted in thorough discussion. In the end, the delegates boldly set a new direction for WBTI and SIL in this resolution called 'Vision 2025':

> Motivated by the pressing need for all peoples to have access to the Word of God in a language that speaks to their hearts and reaffirming our historic values and our trust in God to accomplish the impossible, **we embrace the vision that, by the year 2025, a Bible translation project will be in progress for every people group that needs it.**
>
> We acknowledge that this cannot be accomplished simply by our working harder or doing more of what we are now doing. It will require us to make significant changes in our attitudes and ways of working.
>
> Our desire is to build capacity for sustainable Bible translation programs and Scripture-use activities. Therefore, we urge each entity within our family of organizations to give priority to strengthening present partnerships, forming additional strategic partnerships, and working together to develop creative approaches appropriate to each context.
>
> To this end, we commit ourselves to pray for the fulfilment of this vision, seeking God's guidance, and obeying Him in whatever new directions He may lead.[10]

The Vision was accepted unanimously by WOs, nearly unanimously by SIL entities, and was enthusiastically embraced by partner organizations as well.

It would take time to see the outcome or impact of Vision 2025 on WBTI and SIL's strategies, structures, and operations. But the very act of adopting the Vision was monumental in terms of how it was processed, debated over many days, and then agreed upon. The two organizations' leaders had prayerfully and thoughtfully re-examined the remaining Bible translation needs in the world, the current pace of starting new Bible translation projects, and the changing environment of resources required by mission agencies. The decision to adopt Vision 2025 appeared to be a renewed commitment and posture of openness to God's leading.

Bernice Ledbetter, Robert Banks, and David Greenhalgh point out the importance of vision in the life of an organization: 'Vision often calls for change and requires strategy for leading change toward the vision.... With increased levels of

[10] WBTI, 1999, 3-4.

responsibility, leaders depend mainly on their relational and conceptual skills to lead people and organizations through change, which requires strategy to move toward an inspiring and compelling vision.'[11] Both WBTI and SIL would rise to the challenge of grappling with the Vision and the creation and implementation of new strategies. ICON99 helped set them on this new path.

Presentations and discussions brought by various leaders present at ICON99 raised implementation questions and ideas related to the various scenarios represented across the world. Larry Jones, SIL Asia Area, gave a presentation that explored how SIL field strategies would need to change because of Vision 2025. Given the size and scope of work already in progress and the work that remained, such strategies would require a much larger set of partners than ever envisioned. Rick Brown and Don Gregson of SIL Eurasia spoke concerning partnering with other agencies and the implications of Vision 2025. They noted, 'by forming or joining a total team, we can each focus on the areas God has called us to.'[12] Russ Hersman presented recommendations of the Task Force for Effective National Partnerships as he addressed how Vision 2025 would affect partnership with the national workforce. Barbara Trudell from SIL Africa Area offered a presentation on how partnership with national institutions would help Vision 2025. She noted, 'substantial impact to language groups takes time, and so it is appropriate that SIL look to national institutions for long-term sustainability.'[13] Marvin Hyde, assisted by Darryl Kernick and Roger Welch, looked at how Vision 2025 required WBTI to change regarding the transitional sending church and its workforce. They noted how the relationship with the church was changing because, although the church cannot replace the mission agencies, there was a new set of relationships between supporting churches, the missionary, the field agency, and field leadership.

Audacious Goal

In the paper he developed as preparatory reading for the delegates of ICON99, John Watters made mention of how a 'vision such as Vision 2025 is a 'Big Hairy Audacious Goal' (or 'Bee-HAG').'[14] Watters was referring to the book, *Built to Last*, by Jim Collins and Jerry Porras. They explain a BHAG as 'a particularly powerful mechanism to stimulate progress.'[15] These bold goals help an organization aim for something not yet achieved. But they caution, 'a goal cannot be classified

[11] Ledbetter, Banks, and Greenhalgh, 116.

[12] WBTI, 1999, 5.

[13] WBTI, 1999, 5.

[14] Watters, 20.

[15] James Collins, and Jerry Porras, *Built to Last* (London: Random House Business Books, 2005), 93.

as a BHAG without a high level of commitment to the goal.'[16] Importantly, these audacious goals look towards the future in a time frame beyond 10–30 years. This means that the BHAGs provide the organization momentum long after its leaders have moved on. What's more, the organization's leaders require the 'ability to continually set goals for itself long into the future'.[17] Applied to the contexts of WBTI and SIL, Watters wondered how such goals could 'make the best use of our corporate resources over the next generation [by considering what it would take to] see a Bible, New Testament or relevant portions available in every language of the world considered viable, or [that] at least each has a program in progress.'[18]

Going forward from ICON99, Watters, his leadership team, and the delegates believed they were embarking upon a new path, implementing Vision 2025. The delegates returned to their locations around the world with the expectation that they would share the Vision and begin to work with their colleagues in identifying and developing strategies to implement the Vision. In doing so, they became 'characters' in the journey towards Vision 2025. Ledbetter, Banks, and Greenhalgh observe how 'vision can be thought of as story. Who are the characters, and what is the journey? The centrepiece of the story is an inspirational purpose. Why does this vision matter, and to whom?'[19] The emphasis of Vision 2025 was the language communities that still had unmet needs for assistance with Bible translation. It was an inspirational purpose because as Watters later elaborated,

> Vision 2025 is centered on the imagery of Revelation 5:9 and 7:9. God shows John a vision of who has been purchased by the blood of the Lamb, and who will stand before the Throne and the Lamb in heaven: a multitude that in quantity is beyond count and in quality comes from every tribe, language, people, and nation. God is the universal God. He is also the God of every locality. Vision 2025 is a trivial vision compared to the visions God provides in Revelation. God's visions are magnificent, inclusive, and range beyond boundaries most of us would never dream of going. Yet Vision 2025 does represent a contribution that he allows us to make for the peoples of the earth.[20]

Six months after ICON99, Watters and his leadership team updated the WBTI strategic plan to increase emphasis on implementing Vision 2025 through two initiatives: (1) Engaging non-traditional sending countries and agencies through innovative approaches for recruitment of new personnel to join the Bible translation

16 Collins, and Porras, 110.

17 Collins, and Porras, 107.

18 Watters, 8.

19 Ledbetter, Banks, and Greenhalgh, 116.

20 Watters, "Foundations of Bible Translation and Achieving Vision 2025," 2007, 3.

workforce that would take place alongside a major effort for recruitment in transitional sending countries; and (2) Building internal capacity to fund projects to provide for resources needed to implement Vision 2025.

As part of the first initiative, the WBTI International Administration was already noticing some prospects of Vision 2025 gaining traction: there were 'exciting developments in Latin America', a new priority on mobilizing the Asian Diaspora for Bible translation, and a growing partnership with the International Mission Board of the Southern Baptist Convention with its emphasis on unreached people groups.[21] Towards the end of 2000, Watters noted how among the WOs, there was great enthusiasm for the change brought by Vision 2025. When first adopted, the International Administration described Vision 2025 as an internal concept. However, Wycliffe Organizations promptly spread the word about the Vision among their church contacts, creating the necessity for new promotional and training materials, available in multiple languages, to better serve the Wycliffe Organizations' audiences. News of the Vision had now gone public.

Foundation Setting

Watters's focus was on implementing the directions outlined in Vision 2025, referred to as 'Setting the Foundations for Fulfilling Vision 2025'. This was neither a simple reorganization of the status quo nor a radical restructuring of WBTI. Instead, the first phase set the groundwork by investing time and resources in preparing WBTI to become a different kind of organization with changes in attitudes and ways of working. It was possible, even likely, that this phase would temporarily slow the current rate of progress of Bible translations due to the energy required for repositioning around the Vision.

Foundation setting had far-reaching implications and had to include consideration of greater complexities, diversity of the work force, and multiple types of partnerships. Therefore, the International Administration identified these essential components: (1) enterprise-wide coordination, collaboration, and integration through state of the art communication means that enabled all of the organizations to interact effectively; (2) reconsideration of all ways of working, abandoning what was no longer relevant, and in the process, focussing on recruiting and training Latin Americans, Asians, and the Asian Diaspora; (3) building new strategic relationships for potential partnership or strategic alliances; (4) stimulating innovation, experimentation, and new strategies, especially for field strategies in all five SIL Areas; (5) setting priorities and re-distributing funds to these priorities; (6) developing new competencies, and building capacity for

[21] WBTI, "Board Extracts," May 2000, 1.

partnership and training; and (7) building or revising systems and structures to support fulfilling Vision 2025, including in areas such as personnel, finance, and language programs; and enabling new recruits from Latin America and the Asian Diaspora to serve effectively.

One of the topics under consideration was what a 'Vision 2025 Worker' looked like. This ideal worker had these attributes:

- Conviction that God's Word is powerful
- Participation as a team player
- Commitment to relationships
- Zeal to see others succeed
- Motivation to share skills with others
- Genuine respect for other cultures
- Eagerness to serve under national leadership
- A high degree of flexibility and adaptability

Such characteristics were in alignment with the values expressed in the Vision but could, of course, vary in expression depending on context and culture. The attributes could also be growth opportunities for current personnel. Both current and future personnel could continue to grow in any of these areas. The aim was to find and encourage people with these attributes that would make them well suited to help in the implementation of Vision 2025.

2002 International Convention

The theme for both the 2002 WBTI International Convention and SIL International Conference was 'Trusting God for the Impossible'. In Executive Director John Watters's opening speech, he stated that, after three years, Vision 2025 was less feasible than originally thought due to many factors affecting missions, such as the loss of key leadership, issues around the safety of personnel, and economic downturns. Yet Watters believed that 'God is able to accomplish His purposes despite these circumstances.'[22] Consequently, he emphasized that prayer was 'our greatest strategic response and our greatest resource.'[23] The delegates resolved to model and prioritize prayer in each of their organizations and to work with the International Administration in coordinating and strengthening strategies for prayer.

A variety of topics were presented, intended to prompt discussion among the participants concerning the outworking of Vision 2025. Some of the presentations concentrated on stimulating ideas about Vision 2025, such as creative strategies

---

[22] WBTI, "International Conference Extracts," 2002, 3.

[23] WBTI, "Extracts," 9.

(e.g., new approaches in training, involvement of the local community in Bible translation, and new technologies to assist in translation), stewarding resources (e.g., people, technical expertise, leadership, management, and funds), engaging the worldwide church, serving unreached people groups, and strategic partnerships (e.g., prioritizing the relational side of partnerships, being a good partner, and giving up control).

Vision, Mission, and Strategic Plan

WBTI's foundational objective and strategy were updated during the Convention, resulting in greater alignment with Vision 2025. This was expressed in its Vision, Mission, Ends, Strategic Plan and Priority Initiatives, including making the summary of the Vision 2025 resolution as WBTI's new Vision statement:

Vision: By 2025, a Bible translation program will be in progress in every language needing one.

Mission: To glorify God by promoting and participating in a movement of the church world-wide to make disciples of all nations through Bible translation.

Ends: WBTI fulfills its Mission and Vision with three Ends:

A. *World-wide Engagement of the Church*
› The church worldwide is informed of the challenge of people groups without adequate Scriptures.
› The church worldwide is actively engaged to meet this challenge.

B. *Effective Relationships Among Member Organizations*
› The full potential of each member organization to provide adequate resources for the Bible translation task is realized.
› The member organizations function with harmonious teamwork and effective networking.

C. *Strategic Partnerships with SIL and Others*
› The partnership with SIL is mutually effective.
› The networking relationships with other organizations are mutually enabling.

The Ends guided the development and implementation of the strategic plan, which was extensive and included these six *Priority Initiatives* that would receive attention in the immediate future:

› Develop enterprise information systems
› Mobilize the worldwide church through national organizations
› Develop funding needed to implement Vision 2025

- Mobilize prayer worldwide
- Develop strategic information needed for mobilizing resources
- Develop strategic planning at the Area and Wycliffe Member Organization level

Each initiative had its own strategies. For example, 'Develop funding needed to implement Vision 2025' focussed on enabling WMOs to collaborate in funding projects. To figure out how to do this well, the executive director set up a guidance team to examine the personal funding system and an alternative system when traditional funding approaches were not working or no longer appropriate. A plan was also created to develop systems to support project funding including the International Project Registration system, the Universal Ranking System and the Project Evaluation System. These were to be integrated into the enterprise architecture (that included an internal intranet called *Insite*). The International Administration experimented with different guidance teams to lead the change process called for by the adoption of Vision 2025.

Implementing Vision 2025

John Watters reported to the May 2003 WBTI Board that he had assumed it would take six to eight years to get any new direction towards Vision 2025 underway. Instead, as he visited Wycliffe Organizations and SIL entities, he found colleagues ready to engage in positive dialogue, and often ahead in forming new ideas.

To achieve Vision 2025 goals would require WBTI and SIL to partner with others, including the church of the South and East. The number of qualified personnel available from the churches in the North and West was insufficient for current needs. The board felt the necessity to make a statement responding to the challenge occurring through the growth and maturation in the churches of the South and the East. After giving the SIL Board a lengthy opportunity to hear and discuss the statement, the WBTI Board made this declaration:

> Based on our growing excitement about what God is doing in the worldwide church, our sense of where we are in church history, and its significance in achieving WBTI End A [worldwide engagement of the church], MOVED to foster an environment in which member organizations are encouraged and assisted to engage in appropriate partnerships with churches of the South and East.[24]

[24] WBTI, "Board Extracts," November 2003, 2.

Vision 2025 Business Plan

Vision 2025 created the challenge of increasing the number of language projects by a factor of four in the next quarter century, compared to project numbers in the past. Although many new productivity-enhancing tools and methods were being used, language work and Bible translation were very personnel-intensive. To meet the estimated needs brought about by Vision 2025 required a major increase in personnel. As well, early planning for implementation of new ways of working indicated a call for funding of about $25 million per year by 2005 and $40 million by 2010.

In response, the executive director's team put together a business plan describing the personnel and financial resources required so that WBTI, SIL International, and other partners could understand what it could take to make Vision 2025 a reality. At their meetings, the board received the updated plan, which included these undergirding assumptions:

› The number of language communities needing a language development program wouldn't vary by more than 10% (from the potential 3,000 in 1999).
› 70% of the languages listed in the *Ethnologue* as having a 'possible translation need' would end up being a 'definite translation need'.
› Population size was a key factor in defining the scope and nature of language projects.
› The church within a country or region would provide leadership for language programs.
› WBTI and its WMOs, as well as SIL International and its entities, were committed to a common vision and partnership.
› The number of language programs SIL managed would decrease over time as the national workforce increased.
› By the year 2025, the majority (approximately 70%) of the workforce would be national rather than expatriate.

Interest Grows

As Vision 2025 became better known, WBTI and others anticipated that an extraordinarily different world would unfold over the next 25 years, one that fully included the worldwide church, unlike any other time in history. There were already signs of this. One could see God working through the meeting of missiological shifts and Vision 2025. For example, as a missionary sending continent, Latin America was experiencing significant growth. Many missionary movements there adopted Vision 2025, though some had little or no connection with WBTI. However, lacking any formal relationship with WBTI presented a challenge and would take time and dialogue for the WBTI Administration and Board to be able to establish new working relationships.

WBTI was growing in size while word of Vision 2025 was spreading around the world. WMOs needed attention. The WBTI Board called for '[t]he full potential of each member organization with language programs to impact the Bible translation task [be] realized.'[25] Through this statement, the Board sought to encourage WMOs to identify and strengthen their contribution towards Vision 2025.

Missiological Implications

Pragmatic business plans and implementation strategies were a priority in the early years of Vision 2025. Some WMO leaders began considering the Vision through a missiological framework, aware of the necessity for substantially more people of all nations to be involved. The mobilization of Bible translation resources was taking place—in individual nations and globally—in a rapidly changing social, cultural, economic, political, and religious environment. Wycliffe leaders required opportunities to reflect on Scripture, mission history, theology, and contemporary missiology, as these topics related to pursuing the ministry of Bible translation in a changing world. This led to WBTI's first missiological consultation, held in 2006 (see chapter 10).

In preparation for the consultation, issues specific to Vision 2025 and WBTI and its partners were identified:

› WMOs served as a window to the church regarding the needs, opportunities, results, ministry, and impact of Bible translation. What was the potential for a fresh understanding of the theological and missiological importance and implications of Bible translation in the global mission of the church?
› Now that Vision 2025 was at the seven-year mark, how had it impacted each WMO, and had this impact been significant in developing sound missiological strategies that helped communicate and implement the Vision?
› What was the likelihood that Vision 2025 was, in some places, being interpreted as yet another plan to evangelize the world?
› Given that, at times, the Great Commission had been reduced to proclamation alone, how could a holistic theology be developed that would address concerns of the marginalized peoples who were in focus in Vision 2025?
› Could dependence on technology get in the way of obeying the sacrificial incarnational calling of God if the church finally had the technology needed to

[25] WBTI, "Board Minutes," November 2006, 4.

'complete' the Great Commission?

› How could the church be helped to see Bible translation as mission?

During the 2006 consultation, participants indicated that WMOs and SIL entities were not all walking the same path, noting signs that some were starting to drift from the Vision. WMOs were recruiting around Vision 2025 themes while it appeared that many SIL Areas and entities were showing some ambivalence towards the Vision. What was becoming obvious were the various perceptions and interpretations of Vision 2025 and how it should be approached, leading to less unity of thought and action.

Vision 2025 had missiological implications calling for exegesis because it already had multiple meanings and interpretations. Was Vision 2025 a faith issue or a motivational issue, or both? There were biblical, theological, and missiological foundations for the Vision 2025 themes of partnership, sustainability, capacity building, and urgency. However, these were not yet fully developed or articulated.

Progress towards Vision 2025 would require accountability, reporting to stakeholders, and preparing them for the reality that some years may show more growth than other years. While a business plan may lead to the expectation of both greater reporting and progress, it also creates an inherent tension because Vision 2025 represents a vision rather than a goal.

Clarifying the Vision

In 2007, John Watters reflected on the eight-year mark since the adoption of Vision 2025. He noted that it was not a vow, political correctness, or a threat. It was a readiness for change, for risk-taking, and for success or failure, an opportunity for God to do new things in and through his people. It would only be achieved if God desired it. The date 2025 had caught a lot of attention since the Vision's adoption. Why 2025 and not 2020 or 2030 or something else? The ICON99 delegates had rigorously debated that very question. Watters noted that the date was arbitrary, intended to present a challenge and a call to the next generation to continue what God had been doing up to this point and to build upon the work of the previous generation of WBTI and SIL members, most of whom would retire between 2000 and 2025. For those in the Bible translation movement, the date encouraged prayer and humble dependence on God. No matter the calendar date, new opportunities to identify needs and develop themes and strategies lay ahead.

Leading WBTI and SIL towards Vision 2025, Watters made every effort to explain what the Vision was and was not. For example, he wrote an internal memo to present how Vision 2025 was, in fact, impossible to achieve. It was also not 'a test of God to see if he can do it' because God was free to do as he pleased. It was 'not a law or new legalism under which we must toil to prove ourselves to God' because all participants lived under God's grace. It was 'not a new burden of guilt' indicating that WBTI and SIL owed the world something even though God had invested an enormous amount of experience and knowledge in the two organizations and wanted them to be good stewards of that investment. Vision 2025 was 'not a selling of our birthright' because both organizations remained committed to providing 'meaningful translations, literacy materials, and other products' for the people who speak these languages.[26]

Instead, Watters stated how Vision 2025 was 'about an availability [and] a readiness to change', demonstrating the two organizations' openness to working in whatever ways God desired, acknowledging that all human and financial resources to accomplish the Vision belonged to him. The Vision was a call to 'freedom and creativity [with] joy, wonderment, and anticipation' to take risks and experiment with what God might do in and through the widening group of participants that included other Bible agencies, missions, and the worldwide Church 'as we journey with him'.[27]

Noting the increased pace of Bible translation start-ups through the 19th and 20th centuries, Watters considered that the date highlighted the 'continuation of God's action through time in regard to Bible translation.' He concluded that the organizations desired that 'God would allow that acceleration to continue on into the 21st [century].'[28]

Themes of Vision 2025

As WMO leaders sought to align their organizations with Vision 2025, some recognized a need to define themes that would guide them and WBTI as a whole. As a result, Watters developed these five themes that highlighted significant implications of the Vision:

› *Urgency:* Our sense of urgency is based on God's deep affection for humanity and His desire that individuals from every tribe, language, people, and nation on earth enter into a relationship with Him.
› *Partnership:* We will no longer do things by ourselves that could be done with others.
› *Capacity Building:* The results of capacity building include trained personnel, sufficient funding, and networks of people and institutions that can provide guidance, consultancy, and finances.

26 Watters, "Foundations," 1.
27 Watters, "Foundations," 1.
28 Watters, "Foundations," 1.

- *Creative Strategies:* We recognize that we cannot make our full contribution to Vision 2025 by working harder or doing more of the same. Instead, we must work differently, embrace new attitudes, and expand our repertoire of strategies so we can significantly increase our effectiveness.
- *Sustainability:* We commit ourselves to see that what has been started will be brought as close to a point of sustainability as possible.

Wycliffe Organizations Respond

In 2008, it was now more than nine years since the adoption of Vision 2025. The WBTI International Administration had recently determined that somewhere between the years 2031 and 2038, all remaining Bible translation programs would be started—a significant improvement upon the pre-Vision 2025 projection of somewhere between the years of 2125 and 2150.

One of the impediments to reaching the Vision was the matter of funding. Due to the assumed likelihood of employing a much larger group of local citizens to do most of the translating, the accompanying business plan contained various estimates of funds to be raised over the course of the Vision's lifecycle. Wycliffe US took the lead within WBTI, committing to raising US$1 billion over a ten-year time frame. They called this the 'Last Languages Campaign', and it was their financial portion of Vision 2025. Interestingly, the campaign launched the month after the global financial meltdown of October 2008. Even so, Wycliffe US received a significant gift that helped the campaign get underway. The WBTI Board viewed this major fundraising project as only one part of the whole effort for every WMO to contribute toward Vision 2025. Other WMOs set their own goals to help them do their share. For example, Wycliffe Singapore launched 'Reaching 200' with the aim of partnering with and funding 200 new Bible translation program starts in Asia and the Pacific.

WBTI Looks at Vision 2025

The International Administration, well organized under Watters's leadership, worked diligently to determine the cost of the remaining objectives of Vision 2025 and created a business plan to achieve them. From the headquarters in Dallas, Texas, they had people, systems, and finances sufficient to implement institutional decisions and strategies, and structures to support what they believed God was calling them to do. After the separation of the International Administration between WBTI and SIL, each organization appointed its own executive director. Newly appointed WBTI Executive Director Kirk Franklin and the new WBTI

Global Leadership Team (GLT) saw the necessity to update and clarify its position on Vision 2025.

Vision 2025 in Context

In 2010, WBTI's GLT met to review Vision 2025. This occurred two years into the new WBTI structure, during the GLT's first term of service, eleven years after the adoption of Vision 2025 by WBTI, WOs, SIL International, and other partner organizations, with fifteen years remaining until 2025.

The goal of this conversation was to encourage deeper reflection and comprehensive dialogue, and in the end, to clearly state WBTI's position on and commitment to the principles and foci of Vision 2025. In the process, the team reviewed the original Vision 2025 proposal and highlighted ideas and concepts which they believed required greater emphasis. They acknowledged the progress, challenges, and opportunities presented by Vision 2025. They also reflected on some of the changes of attitude, thinking, and behaviours in WBTI and among its partners since the presentation of the original proposal. Ideas and phrases in the original vision proposal required further reflection, possible adjustments, updating, or a new approach from the GLT, including how the Vision could facilitate WBTI's participation in God's mission. The intention was not to slow progress toward the vision but to ensure WBTI's development was based on sound missiological foundations rather than business tactics to achieve their goals, requiring further work and reflection in the years ahead. The following sections under the sub-headings of 'Goals', 'Key Factors', and 'What Matters', are a partial summary of the discussion, but without revisiting introductory material on the Vision already considered in this chapter.

Goals

Many people who were familiar with Vision 2025 knew it by the tagline: 'By 2025, in partnership, a Bible translation project in progress in every remaining language that needs it.' Several organizations had used such a tagline to present the essence of Vision 2025. However, because it represented part of an even larger vision extending beyond concepts of dates and projects, there was more to Vision 2025 than could be encapsulated in a tagline.

Vision 2025 grew out of a realization of the need for changes in hearts, minds, and ways of working was a necessity. The world had greatly evolved since the founding of both Wycliffe and SIL, bringing new opportunities and new challenges.

Key Factors

As mentioned earlier, Watters had listed six key global factors that called for thinking and working in new ways:

- Globalization of the Church
- Problematic contexts where remaining translation needs are located
- Demographic growth of the future, favouring Asia and Africa
- Increased desire for partnership
- Increased interest in the ethnolinguistic minorities of the world
- Significant language shifts in process

As important as these factors were and are, Watters's proposal also included three even more critical points, found in the first paragraph of the preamble to the Vision proposal. They were '… the biblical realities of Community, the Cross, and the New Creation.' In this preamble, he stated that we choose to evaluate and measure our decisions, actions, and relationships based on these three realities.

The participating organizations had repeatedly discussed, grappled with, and even strategized according to the first six factors. But the greater challenge came in using that same thoroughness within the context of these three biblical realities. Most would be quick to acknowledge these realities, but attention to them was often implicit rather than explicit. Rarely were these realities specifically referenced, particularly in relation to evaluation and measurement. It was worth further discussion to explore what that would look like and how it could be expressed.

WBTI leadership asked themselves, 'Who are we, how do we think and behave in light of the following?' And, 'What does it look like to measure and evaluate our Vision 2025 strategies and efforts according to these realities?' The statements, below regarding Community, the Cross, and the New Creation are from Watters's original Vision 2025 proposal.

> *Community:* We belong to the community of Jesus' disciples, the Church. We are sent out by that community, in many places work with that community, and are accountable to it and one another. Wherever that community is found, we pursue what is good for it and for all of its neighbours. We submit to one another in love, resisting personal ambition, humbly considering others better than ourselves, looking to their interests, delighting in the good in their hearts given by the Spirit.
>
> *The Cross:* We seek to imitate Jesus Christ and exemplify His act of self-giving love, where we put our bodies and lives at God's disposal,

> even in the face of human and spiritual opposition. In all our relationships, we renounce the use of power and privilege to coerce or manipulate others to satisfy our means or ends. We rejoice in God's gift of allowing us to be servants of the weak and poor, particularly those denied access to God's Word, serving them with respect and fairness, protecting their dignity and honour. We seek to make our service to others a service to the whole person.
>
> *New Creation:* We understand that change, growth, and transition mark God's action in the world as He brings the old-world order under His judgment and begins to implement His new creation, calling people from every tribe, language, people, and nation into His kingdom. We live under the truth that, through Jesus Christ, God conquered sin, death, and all the forces of evil allied against Him. All cultures stand under His judgment, as He empowers all His disciples under the New Covenant with the gift of His Spirit to begin transforming the status quo into a place for His light and life to be known.

The board goals of WBTI, adopted in 2009, echoed many of the thoughts expressed in the Vision 2025 proposal. WBTI chose to reflect the larger and longer-term goals in their vision and mission statements, but also included Vision 2025 in that context. As Watters stated in the original proposal, Vision 2025 was an 'audacious intermediate goal'.

This audacious intermediate goal addressed the question, 'what would we need to do so that by 2025 a Bible, New Testament or portions are available in every language of the world considered viable, or at least each has a program in progress?' The challenge to the participating partners was to be good stewards of God's abundant resources to 'make a significant difference in the ministry of Bible translation for the long term.'

Vision 2025 grew out of a desire for good stewardship of knowledge and resources in this generation for future generations. The leadership of WBTI sought to discern the times, to continue to encourage this kind of stewardship, and to seek to participate in the Vision with partners worldwide.

What Matters

It wasn't really about the date or the work of starting Bible translation in each remaining language community. Vision 2025 was really about the transformation to become the people God can use in His mission, to become the kinds of partners that can best serve as a part of the worldwide Church. It was about being willing to change, willing to take risks, willing to be obedient. It was only when being humbled before God, acknowledging this is His work, and resting in His hands that achieving Vision 2025's goals is possible.

Five themes emerged from the early-stage acts of processing and thinking through Vision 2025. The themes were partnership, building capacity, urgency, creative strategies, and sustainability. Much of the Vision 2025 dialogue and strategic planning taking place worldwide thus far had centred around these themes. Measuring progress in each of these areas considering the community, the cross, and the new creation would help keep efforts aligned, missiologically grounded, and prevent any one theme from dominating.

As they looked at the layered context of Vision 2025, the leadership saw a depth not revealed in the recitation of the one-sentence tagline. As they moved forward in trying to discern God's will concerning WBTI's participation in His mission, their desire was to:

› Glorify God and enjoy Him forever.
› Make choices, evaluate and measure who we are and what we do in keeping with the Cross, Community, and New Creation.
› Facilitate access to and engagement in God's Word, as a part of and along with the Church worldwide, particularly for those who do not yet have it in a language they fully understand. We realize access is not enough. There must also be engagement with Scripture, and transformational impact, for any of us to be truly changed by the Word of God.
› Serve as good stewards of the resources God makes available.

The team believed they could make their best contribution to Vision 2025 only through giving their attention to these concepts.

Progress, Challenges, and Opportunities

In the original Vision 2025 proposal, Watters offered comments and stated core values that encompassed both WBTI and SIL. At that time, this was appropriate, as the two organizations were under one international leadership team. Now that each organization had its own leadership, each needed to speak individually. The desire of both organizations was to continue in partnership as they shared a common concern for minority language communities and Bible translation.

As Watters stated in 1999, Wycliffe and SIL were both at a crossroads. Making critical choices for the organizations to continue to be an effective part of God's mission in the 21st century. Traditional ways of working, a primarily 'Western' workforce, and the corporate cultures all called for re-evaluation in light of the global context and theological and missiological understanding.

WBTI made significant changes in the years immediately following the 1999 Conference and the separating of the two organizations. The changes were not so much for the survival of WBTI but in response to seeing how God was working around the world. These changes, in many ways, were directly related to the biblical realities and the key global factors discussed previously. WBTI's then-current areas of focus and changes in the organization also took Vision 2025 and its themes into account, as reflected at that time in their Strategic Overview. The context of WBTI's numerous partnerships presented opportunities to grapple with the themes and implications of the Vision. One example was the discussion of the theme of urgency at the Last Languages Initiative Consultation in 2009 (see chapter 10). The following section is from a presentation at that consultation by WBTI Missiological Consultant Stephen Coertze.

Urgency in Service of our Patient God

Urgency in Vision 2025

When Vision 2025 was adopted, it was not a subject for debate, nor was it meant to represent an eschatological declaration. It was, however, adopted in one of the periods in Christian history when 'Christianity was running a high eschatological fever.'[29] Naturally then, explanations about this Vision received an added eschatological dimension. For example, under the heading, 'Themes of Vision 2025', WBTI referred to the urgency of Bible translation 'based on God's deep affection for humanity and His desire that individuals from every tribe, language, people, and nation on earth enter into a relationship with Him.' [30] This statement paraphrases part of Revelation 7:9, considered an eschatological text. A statement from Wycliffe US during this era explained the need to accelerate the start of new Bible translation projects: 'Working together, with God, Vision 2025 can be accomplished in this generation!'[31] Similar terminology had been attributed to both John Mott from the 1910 Edinburgh Missionary Conference and Luis Bush and the AD2000 Beyond movement. The Wycliffe US statement continued in this eschatological framework, declaring, '[t]he Bible reveals a picture of heaven with people from all nations and languages present. The translated Word will help to make this possible.'[32]

---

[29] Bosch, 504.

[30] WBTI, "Board Policy Manual," 2008, 5.

[31] Wycliffe US, http://www.wycliffe.org/Explore/WhenWillWeFinishtheTask.aspx, accessed 18 September 2009.

[32] Wycliffe US.

At the time, external claims made about the eschatological nature of Vision 2025 were unsurprising. For example, in response to a 2009 blog on recruitment for Bible translation, which references Vision 2025, one author ('SeekAndFind') was quite straightforward about when 'the end' would come. 'Scripture is pretty clear that once THAT JOB [Vision 2025] is done, Christ will return rather quickly thereafter.'[33] Other examples appeared of well-intended Christians who believed that the year 2025 was the year Christ could return because Wycliffe would have finished its job.

Stephen Coertze addressed the topic of urgency within the context of WBTI at a missiological consultation with this observation:

> The concept of urgency, both as a matter of focus and speed, is present in Scripture, though not used consistently. It is also present in both Western and African theological development, though more present in specific theological areas. As expressed in these theological frameworks, more so in the dispensational premillennial eschatology, it had an impact on the theory and praxis of mission. Though it was not the intention to interpret Vision 2025 from an eschatological perspective, it was framed in a heightened expectation of the return of Christ.[34]

Vision 2025 had captured the hearts and imaginations of followers of Christ worldwide, although the original Vision 2025 statement was primarily an internal document addressing Wycliffe and SIL. Many WOs found the Vision to be an inspiration and an encouragement to their supporters. These followers brought a wide range of theological backgrounds and enthusiasm. For example, it was not unusual for a time for Wycliffe US to receive letters from elderly supporters asking Wycliffe to 'hurry' and reach all the languages so Jesus would return sooner. A priority of the Vision 2025 document, however, was on the necessity to work with partners, encourage national leadership, build capacity in the church and language communities, and increase involvement in training, mentoring, and consulting. Watters referred to the importance of pursuing these as 'non-negotiable items'. These were all facets of the Vision that would take time and ongoing nurturing of relationships.

As they entered the second decade of the 21st century, WBTI was addressing these 'non-negotiables' through a wide range of strategies and through a repositioning of the organization that includes restructuring for the purpose of becoming an increasingly inclusive alliance of organizations. This would help in building a network of all types of organizations interested in minority language

---

33 http://www.freerepublic.com/focus/religion/2286246/posts, accessed 18 September 2009.

34 Stephen Coertze, "Urgency in Service of Our Patient God," 2009, 5.

communities and Scripture translation, access, use, impact, and in the growth of the Church. The GLT was also working to create an environment for true intercultural interaction and partnerships. This was a response to both the growth of the worldwide church and the leadership team's desire to contribute to and encourage the unity of believers. And as Jesus stated in John 17, '...then the world will know.'

As the GLT listened and learned in their Vision 2025 journey thus far, there were particular ideas and phrases in the original Vision 2025 proposal that required further reflection, possible changes, updating, or a new approach. Doing this would better equip WBTI to participate in God's mission through Vision 2025 and through whatever other means God allowed them to serve him.

A New Look at Vision 2025

About a year after the 2010 leadership discussion, another brief paper titled 'A New Look at Vision 2025' emerged to capture WBTI's ongoing conversations. It picked up on one of the primary keys to true participation in God's mission and in Vision 2025: the theme of community, Cross, and new creation. This reflected some of the thinking as WBTI moved deeper into missiological reflection, and multicultural, multifaceted partnerships and community. These factors were to help guide them in all they thought, said, and did, demonstrating respect for people, honouring Christ, and serving His Kingdom, as it comes, through His grace and justice.

The following portion of the original Vision 2025 proposal was a primary motivation for many on the WBTI leadership team and for many colleagues around the world:

> We acknowledge that this cannot be accomplished simply by our working harder or doing more of what we are now doing. It will require us to make significant changes in our attitudes and ways of working.
>
> Our desire is to build capacity for sustainable Bible translation programs and Scripture use activities. Therefore, we urge each entity within our family of organizations to give priority to strengthening present partnerships, forming additional strategic partnerships, and working together to develop creative approaches appropriate to each context.
>
> To this end, we commit ourselves to pray for the fulfilment of this vision, seeking God's guidance and obeying Him in whatever new directions He may lead.

The focus of these paragraphs is on willingness to change, partnership, and prayer. The GLT desires to continue with this focus. The following are some of their comments concerning aspects of Vision 2025 they believe are most critical:

› '...emphasizing inclusiveness and partnership (us partnering with the church, not the church partnering with us) rather than data and statistics.'
› 'Vision 2025 is not just about reaching language groups. It was introduced because we ourselves need to change and be transformed. It is a call to transformation...it is a call to deeper dependency on Christ.'
› 'Vision 2025 is not about reducing 150 years to 25 or about working harder. It is about faith in God and a willingness to take risks by making ourselves vulnerable.'
› 'WBTI is not trying to multiply itself, but rather be a part of the church.'

As the 'New Look' paper points out, the early Vision 2025 document focussed on 'our' organizations. Today, we focus on the diverse, multicultural body of the church worldwide and on seeing ourselves as a part of that church. Today we focus on building capacity *with* and as a part of the church, rather than 'building capacity in the church.' We still talk about 'building capacity through vision sharing, training, mentoring, and consulting', but rather than doing it from a framework of 'multiplying ourselves' we do it with the idea of the church multiplying itself and building capacity through local means, as opposed to external means only. We talk less about Wycliffe 'members doing the work', and more about partners, serving together, and Wycliffe personnel as a part of that larger picture.

We talk less about the historical 'family of organizations' and more about alliances, networks, and the larger family of believers. We respect the history of organizations and peoples and encourage good stewardship of the research, resources, and reputations through which God has enabled work to continue.

We are now past the crossroads where we observed the demographic shift of the church from west to south and east. We are well into an era in which the church is truly global and is also becoming more attuned to both proclamation and practice of the Gospel. This requires us to approach ministry holistically.

Our concern is not just to get projects started but to see the church engaged, and all of us working alongside minority language communities so they can thrive. This means caring about the whole person and trusting God to bring wholeness to individuals, families, and communities. This is the long view of Vision 2025 that motivates and encourages the leadership of WBTI. It's God's mission, but we are privileged to play a small part as he redeems and restores all creation.

As we continue to engage with Vision 2025, we desire to help create an environment for greater participation. We want to:

- Recapture the heart and essence of Vision 2025—we do not want to be so focussed on measuring 'project starts' that we miss many of the rich possibilities for what God may do in our midst and beyond us, and what we can learn along the way.
- Provide new perspectives from a repositioned WBTI—we want to hear, understand, and engage with the voices of many cultures and partners who are a part of God's mission.
- Deepen relationships with God and his people—we want to continue in and to foster corporate and individual spiritual growth, engage in theological and missiological reflection and dialogue, and develop richer relationships with the wider global church community.

All organizations measure something and are measured by something. We do not want to be measured by dates and deadlines. We do not want to be product driven. We want our attitudes, measurements, and activities to reflect the values of the Cross, of community, and of the New Creation—God's kingdom come and coming. We want to treasure relationships and trust God for the results. We want to be transformed by his power and his Word so that we reflect him in all we are and do. We want Vision 2025 to pull us closer to Christ so that we are aligned with him and can be used by him to share His Good News with the language communities of the world and with each other.

Wycliffe Global Gathering 2016

The paper referenced above reflects how WBTI continued to approach Vision 2025 contextually and with growing missiological understanding. By 2016, WBTI had become the Wycliffe Global Alliance (WGA). By now, there was a majority of organizations and leaders who had not been a part of the original adoption of Vision 2025 and who had not been a part of the joint Wycliffe and SIL structure. This growth and change, in many cases, represented the growth of the church worldwide and the responses to Vision 2025 over the past 16 years. Working differently, new partnerships, greater flexibility, and adaptability in response to what God was doing around the world had ushered in a new era for the Bible translation movement. It was once again time to bring the Vision before the entire body of global leaders.

As part of the WGA's triennial Global Gathering, Stephen Coertze led the representatives of more than 100 Alliance Organizations (AOs) in a two-day missiological reflection looking at WGA's journey in response to Vision 2025.[35]

---

[35] Adapted from: https://www.wycliffe.net/more-about-what-we-do/philosophy-and-principle-papers/the-alliance-journey-in-response-to-vision-2025-a-missiological-conversation/.

The reflection time began with an acknowledgment that Vision 2025 *served* as a reminder that, when participating in Bible translation, we need to both reflect on and respond to what we see around and before us. The purposes of the discussion were

› to revisit and reflect on the journey of WGA in response to Vision 2025.
› to explore some of the current questions AOs face in relation to Vision 2025.
› for each AO, in the context of their own unique contribution to Bible translation, to commit to engaging with the issues that could either hinder or enhance effective Bible translation.

The conversations were set around table groups with facilitators and emphasized the following areas:

› An overview of WGA's journey in response to Vision 2025.
› Missiological affirmations expressed in Vision 2025 (urgency: toward Kingdom-based partnerships, partnering as friends, partnering in the context of global realities; and dependency on God).

Missiological Affirmations

Urgency

The discussion of the topic of 'urgency' revealed a wide spectrum of views and a deep sense of concern for God's mission, our participation in it, and the needs of the people of the world.

The concept of urgency, as understood within the context of Vision 2025, appealed to those who view it as addressing a life and death situation. It called attention to the many language communities still without access to Scripture, to those who were dying without knowing the Saviour of the world. Churches cannot become strong and effective without the foundation of God's Word. God has commanded us to go; it is his will. Therefore, urgency is about completing translations as quickly as possible by partnering more, using available resources both locally and globally, and building more partnerships to engage with the work.

For others, urgency is about strategizing rather than speeding up the work. 'Focus' and 'priority' are considered more appropriate guiding words than *urgency*. Don't act in haste. Have patience to seek God's direction. Urgency is more about *how* the work is done than *when* the work is finished. Urgency should not supplant community involvement, partnership development, and church engagement but rather open opportunities for more involvement with less pressure.

Many organizations have been impacted by a sense of urgency. Some have identified specific goals in terms of the number of language communities to engage, or the number of churches to connect with language communities. Some have been more intentional about board training and church partnership development. Some WMOs have sought to foster closer relationships with WMOs in other parts of the world. Many are seeking to spend more time reflecting on God's mission and the role of Bible translation in it.

Tensions exist when issues of relationship and accountability are raised. Relationships take time, yet stakeholders expect quick, measurable results. Urgency will be defined differently in different contexts and languages. Our responses, then, should be context specific. Mission belongs to God. He is the one who is going to complete it in his own time. He has invited us to participate with him, but the success of his mission is not dependent on us. Our scale of urgency is measured by how well we understand God's mind, his will, his mission, etc. Therefore, urgency requires dedicated prayer.

As an Alliance, the consensus was that we need to pray, first and foremost, and then craft a strategy that addresses the needs and expectations of all partners involved. We need to depend on God to provide all that is needed to complete his mission. We need to build strong and healthy relationships; to communicate better—more often and more effectively—between ourselves and with constituents, partners, and local communities. We need to let go of control, thereby developing partnerships that offer the freedom to take more risks, to contribute whatever can be contributed, to pool resources, and to support one another in new ways. We need to think long term; think holistically; learn from our past, share our experiences with one another, and learn from one another.

Kingdom-based Partnerships—Partnering as Friends

Some say friendships grow out of partnerships, others say partnerships are built on friendships. Still others think the two do not need to be aligned at all. Some say friendship and partnership are commitments like a family. Others say they are not permanent, like a family, rather they are a choice, requiring commitment. Many people use the words 'friendship' and 'partnership' interchangeably, but then again, upon reflection, consider them to be different on several levels.

All agreed that friendship is culturally shaped and that our cultural definitions of and parameters surrounding good friendships are so different, they can cause deep conflict. But all also agreed that friendships that endure conflict together come out stronger and truer.

Friendships are more personal and individualized than partnerships. Friendships last; partnerships terminate. Friendship takes time and proximity and cannot happen easily where there are great distances, cultural differences, or gaps of time to be overcome. Friendships in WGA are costly both with time and money—for travel to visit, for helping one another with gifts of kindness (food, coffee, meeting one another's needs, etc.)

Friendships are built on the elements of biblical love. A person pursues a friend as the subject of the friendship rather than the object—to give rather than to receive; to celebrate with rather than compete with; to humbly know and to be known as equals. Good friends trust one another and are loyal to one another. Sincere friendships take time to develop well.

Partnerships, on the other hand, can be established more quickly as business agreements. Partnerships also require commitment, honesty, and trust, but can navigate the inconveniences of distance and time more easily. Partnerships are built on a common vision and clear commitments and goals. However, beyond simple productivity, we work together because it is God's will, and partnership in the ministry honours God. Partnership is a spiritual endeavour, reflecting God's call to live in community.

Partnerships between organizations can be practical. However, friendships between organizations are difficult to achieve and maintain, especially when leadership changes. Leaders model true friendship to the organizations. It is essential in building friendships within WGA that leaders lead the way.

There are many levels of friendship. Deep friendships are costly, and therefore precious, and they make life and work more beautiful. As an example of such friendship, God is not ashamed to call us his friends. Because one cannot manage many deep friendships, some believe it is more practical and sustainable to focus time, energy, and resources on only a few good friendships.

Kingdom-based Partnerships—Partnering in the Context of Global Realities

Understanding 'globalization' and 'glocalization' offers a better appreciation of how the WGA works. United in the Body of Christ, our shared beliefs, shared resources, and shared manpower allow WGA's community to form creative partnerships and strategies. In such partnerships, no one is less valuable than another, either locally or globally. When one is in need, resources are generously drawn from wherever the resource exists. Therefore, we are free to be more open, to talk about difficult things, to be vulnerable with one another. The strength of WGA comes from the relationships within its organizations; there is no control centre but multiple centres of influence, a democratization of power.

Globalization allows for fast access to information and encouragement from others. Something that proved successful in one place can quickly be made available to others. Globalization underscores the uniqueness of our contexts—makes us think of ways in which we can share and cooperate and learn from each other without losing our identity and distinctiveness. It creates a general sense of unity and friendships that we bring back to the local context. Polycentricism allows for better relationships between ourselves and with local churches. There are many local needs that require global partnerships and many local strengths that require a global system for expression.

Globalization and glocalization and polycentrism raise concerns, however. They could contribute to a dilution of individualism—a 'onenessization' of people, cultures, and organizations. Polycentricism challenges church government systems and churches' rising desire for more direct involvement in mission. This can cause concern for partners who fear losing control. Also, natural fears based on history can cause some to hesitate before entering a shared power system (consider the history of colonialism, or the historical position of SIL in many contexts). Some organizations prefer a hierarchical structure in their own context and therefore struggle to blend that with a fluid global structure. Furthermore, the difficulties one organization faces will impact others. For example, a financial crisis in one group will impact resources for others; or tensions from issues like the Divine Familial Terms (see chapter 6) controversy can impact many. The increased visibility of organizations in global partnerships and the proliferation of social media results in governments becoming more aware of activities happening in their nations. This creates an increased risk of exposure that can adversely affect people and projects in sensitive areas.

We need to ensure that our partnerships are balanced in time, authority, ownership, and competences both in giving and in receiving. We need a good platform for sharing best practices across organizations, systems to enable communication, technology appropriate to contexts, and strategies that address the seven Streams of Participation (see chapter 6). We need to acknowledge the wrongs made, ask forgiveness, and restore relationships in authentic reconciliation. We need to be humble, to listen more to God and to one another, to speak less and learn together, to be willing to give up rights, to embrace chaos, and to recognize the need for better coordination and communication on both the global and the global-to-local (glocal) levels. And we need to be intentional about meeting together to build trusting, interdependent relationships at all levels.

Dependency on God

Dependency is abandoning ourselves to God: We are dependent on God because our lives are not our own; we are dependent creatures. Secure in our identity as loved by God, we choose to live in total abandonment to Him. God becomes more important than anything else. We seek first his Kingdom, trusting that he will provide for everything else. We ask, 'What is urgent in God's eyes? What are his priorities?'

Dependency is balance: Dependency strikes a balance between waiting on God and in obedience acting on a plan. We make plans and then hold them lightly, always being willing to let them go if that's what God prompts us to do. We trust God in a deliberate, active way, not pursuing our own agendas, nor looking for quick and easy solutions, nor being lazy or inactive, but praying diligently, waiting expectantly, and acting obediently.

Dependency is freedom: Bible translation projects belong to God; transformation is God's work, not ours. Because all the work belongs to God, he is responsible for completing it. Dependency on God releases us from the worry of limited resources and time. We recognize our limitations and insufficiencies. We don't rely on ourselves. While we are accountable for and must be good stewards of what God has entrusted to us, dependency on God frees us from the pressure and stress of success. Knowing that God has faithfully provided in the past, we can have confidence that he will continue to provide for our needs in his work. Dependency and anxiety cannot coexist. Urgency should not ruin our dependency on God. Rather, there is an urgency for us to depend on God. We need to trust his timing.

Dependency is prayer: Prayer is action; it's an expression of dependence on God. Dependency is not just about funds or physical resources; it is also about seeking wisdom from God. It's about exercising self-discipline to limit our self-sufficiency or independence, which is sin. Humbling ourselves expresses dependence—demonstrating the ultimate test of intimacy with God.

Dependency is mutuality: Dependency on God frees us to have relationships or partnerships built on mutuality. Partnerships force us to trust God more. Partnerships are not based on material things but on God. One is not greater or less than the other. When we have needs, we can call on the global community, while at the same time being willing to sacrifice without expecting rewards or taking advantage of others. We are all frail and equally dependent on God. In partnerships, we model for one another our trust in and dependence on God. Sometimes one teaches and the other learns. Other times it is reversed. It is essential to intentionally build in time with God in our interactions with one another.

Missiological Reflections

An influencing factor in how WGA understands itself since its first missiological consultation in 2006 has been an awareness by its leaders of the increasing role of the global church. Adoption of Vision 2025 occurred at the peak of Western influence in mission leadership and strategy. Today, however, the Vision is taking effect in contexts where 'the predominance of one culture over others is no longer accepted, and where cultural polycentrism is a fact of our time.'[36] The 2016 discussion of Vision 2025 clearly depicts the deepening and enriching of dialogue and thought when a wider range of cultures and contexts are included. Polycentrism and polyphony were becoming a natural part of how WGA would express itself and how the Bible translation movement would go forward.

The actual Vision 2025 resolution has at least nine missiological implications:

- An awareness of the 'pressing need' that still exists for Bible translation.
- The adoption of a date as a means of motivating action.
- A realization that working harder is not what is required.
- An acceptance that different attitudes and approaches are needed.
- A focus on building capacity and sustainability is essential.
- A greater emphasis on partnering internally and externally is needed.
- An openness to new ways of working.
- A recommitment to accomplishing the task.
- An intentional desire to be led by the Holy Spirit.

The opening statement of Vision 2025 acknowledges that it is 'our trust in God to accomplish the impossible,' which is at least a partial acknowledgement of the mission of God (*missio Dei*). However, given the pragmatic history of WGA, the emphasis was likely intended or at least interpreted to be more about human involvement and responsibility than about the sending nature of the Triune God inviting people to join him in mission. The Vision 2025 resolution does, however, acknowledge that working harder (in the sense of a Protestant work ethic) or 'doing more of what we are now doing' will not accomplish the Vision. It is worth noting the changing understanding of the *missio Dei* in WGA and within various parts of the church and how it could influence a missiological reinterpretation of Vision 2025.

The sense of urgency depicted in the resolution with the specific reference to the year 2025 does have a hint of Mark 16:15 ('the gospel will be preached to the nations and then the end will come'). This is especially true if people use the year 2025 as an eschatological reference point to Jesus' return and the ushering in of

[36] Daryl Balia, and Kirsteen Kim, *Witnessing to Christ Today* (Oxford: Regnum, 2010), 255.

the end of the age as we know it now. Nevertheless, the focus of a particular year against the backdrop of the Great Commission texts (such as Matthew 28:18–20, Mark 16:15–20, Luke 24:46–48, John 20:19–23, and Acts: 1:8) conveys a sense of urgency towards obedience. These texts provide a biblical basis for this opening statement of the resolution: 'Motivated by the pressing need....'

When made aware of Vision 2025, many Christians and churches in the West, and especially those of the Global South and East, were challenged by it. For example, numerous missionary movements in Latin America responded by adopting it as their own. If this has created an understanding of the urgent nature of the kingdom of God arriving and transforming people and communities, and the role the Bible translation movement can play, then it is well placed.

The shift in global Christianity will continue to affect mission strategy. This shift is also significant in Vision 2025, as global plans for mission are increasingly initiated and led by Christians of the Global South and East. In this changing global context, Christians of the North and West continue to find their way. The emphasis on a specific date has always held more value for some than others. Nevertheless, it has served as a rallying cry and challenge to be open to God's leading.

The Alliance Journey in Response to Vision 2025

Reflection is critical. It offers a change of perspective. Are we willing to recognize when a door is closing, and are we willing to go through a new door in a direction we haven't gone before? Reflection must happen at all levels in the organization, from the board to the office and field staff. It's important to reflect on how things have changed and to consider what to do and how to respond to the new realities. Reflection demonstrates dependence and trust in God and allows for time to think creatively.

Interdependence is vital. The church, traditional mission, and methods will change because of context and their missiological understanding. We need to engage with the church: local, national, and elsewhere. There is more interdependence in mission today, consequently Wycliffe must be more interdependent with the local church in problem solving, resourcing, and sustainability. We need to get past binary identities of 'we receive' or 'we give' so that all are considered both givers and receivers.

Revisiting Vision 2025 now is timely. Because AOs have diverse histories, not everyone in Wycliffe fully understands the intent of the Vision, that it is about community transformation and about local ownership, not just about counting translation projects. The Vision offers the ability to include rather than exclude, providing a call for the church, and imparting a sense of urgency in building partnerships among the churches of the West and majority world.

We need partnerships. 'Together, we can.' We need to use the strengths we have to participate in the work of Bible translation. It's critical that we find our identity, know our strengths and weaknesses, so we know how we can serve one another. Small organizations can have a big impact on a region. Some organizations can serve as a model for other organizations in their own countries and beyond. Humanitarian mission goes hand-in-hand with Bible translation. Local involvement and ownership are essential. Senders must respect local needs; they should become trainers and helpers rather than doers. We need a strategy that uses existing structures. Funding organizations should recognize local and national decisions. We need more stories, different stories, of both failure and success. We can learn from everyone's story as being part of God's larger story.

Conclusion

Looking back at the composition of WBTI in 1999 (when Vision 2025 was adopted), it was still a Western mission agency (with a smaller component of non-Western nations) contributing their resources and personnel to Bible translation. By 2012 this had changed significantly, to the extent that 70% of the 100 organizations that made up the WGA were from the Global South and East. However, the question remains as to the role the church in Western nations will play in participating in and developing future strategies. Balance will be required, with dialogue from the Global South and East, as their perspectives will have a continuing and growing role in realizing the Vision.

An assumption we can make from this analysis of WGA's journey towards Vision 2025 is that, as followers of Christ, we should not assume that human endeavour is the primary factor in reaching a vision. Instead, we move more deeply into the conviction that it is the Triune God who achieves his vision. We are indeed privileged to be part of *missio Dei* and to participate in his instrument, the church.

This research has briefly examined WGA and Vision 2025 through missiological and theological lenses, noting the historical influence of North American evangelical fervour. It is commendable that this influence in mission has centred solidly on the involvement of people in planning and action. However, this has often occurred in ignorance of the *missio Dei* originating from God, reflecting his initiative and activity. As Christopher Wright helpfully explains, 'mission is God's... [and] the marvel is that [he] invites us to join in.'[37] As the global church

[37] Wright, 67.

becomes firmly planted in the soil of the Global South and East, it incorporates some new and much-needed voices. As it participates in God's mission with and alongside mission organizations such as WGA, the richness of God's people serving together as he intended is evident. The Bible translation movement will benefit like never before.

Some degree of caution is necessary when analyzing the progress of WGA in Bible translation (in terms of languages entered, work started, New Testament or full Bibles translated, number of new literates, etc.). Statistical progress is encouraging to the participants as well as the funders of the ministry, but history shows that what constitutes progress is often uncertain, and at times can be an illusion. WGA's journey includes ongoing exploration of the benefits and hazards of metrics and statistics, of quantitative and qualitative measurements. What does it look like to recognize relationships and collaboration of churches, mission organizations, and communities as metrics? Chapter 12 presents more history of WGA's journey of discovery related to metrics and measurements.

Leadership Reflections

When considering the adoption of Vision 2025, it is helpful to consider leadership researchers Bernice Ledbetter et al and their discussion regarding common tensions for leaders of Christian structures like WGA: 'the tensions between (1) tradition and adaptation, (2) preservation and innovation, and (3) stability and change.' [38] Within these tensions, leaders have to consider whether to take the organization in a new direction that may include adaptation that leads to abandoning tradition. Or, is it preferrable for a leader to 'call an organization to preservation rather than innovation?'[39] These were the challenges the leaders of the day faced when they considered Vision 2025.

When the Vision was adopted, the prevailing leadership theory and practice was transformational leadership, which seeks to lead with positive outcomes. The theory has various components: 'articulating a vision, providing an appropriate role model, fostering the acceptance of group goals, high-performance expectations, providing individualized support, and intellectual stimulation.'[40] Scholars have also categorized it into five components:

› 'Idealized influence (attributed) refers to whether a leader is perceived as ethical, confident, trustworthy, idealistic, and charismatic.'

[38] Ledbetter, Banks, and Greenhalgh, 42.

[39] Ledbetter, Banks, and Greenhalgh, 42.

[40] Muhammad Yasir, and Noor Azmi Mohamad, "Ethics and Morality: Comparing Ethical Leadership with Servant, Authentic and Transformational Leadership Styles," *International Review of Management and Marketing* 6, no. S4 (2016): 312.

- 'Idealized influence (behaviour) refers to the charismatic actions of the leader that focus on a collective sense of mission, beliefs, and values.'
- 'Intellectual stimulation [is] comprised of critical thinking about the solution of problems and stimulating creativity.'
- 'Individualized consideration [is] identified by providing a supportive climate for individual development, growth, and considering individual needs of followers.'
- 'Inspirational motivation refers to leadership behaviour that motivates followers by portraying optimism, inspires commitment to a shared vision, and communicates high expectations.'[41]

Since those tasked with leading vision in WBTI were ethical leaders, they sought input from a wide cross-section of participants rather than using their own personal vision to drive the change process. At various times they provided critical reflection on the Vision, even when some participants wanted to change the Vision to an operational goal or target to be achieved. While they led the Vision, they ensured that WBTI and later WGA kept to its core values, mission, and purpose.

A characteristic of transformational leadership theory first developed by James Macgregor Burns relates to how leaders act as strong role models for followers and followers want to emulate them. As the name implies, a transformational leader intends to transform followers and 'provoke [them] to do more than what they are expected to do.'[42] To do this, the leader is often visionary and gives 'a sense of mission, instils pride, gains respect and trust', 'communicates... expectations', uses 'careful problem solving', and gives individualized attention and coaching.[43] WBTI's leaders were trusted and ensured that Vision 2025 rested upon a strong foundation of trusting God for the impossible. They recognized that transformation comes from God. And they wanted to find ways for Wycliffe leaders around the world to carry the Vision forward.

As noted at the outset, the concept of a BHAG influenced John Watters's foundational thinking behind Vision 2025. James Collins and Jerry Porras, who developed the concept of BHAGs, state that they are about a paradox of an 'envisioned future... on the one hand, it conveys a sense of concreteness—something vivid and real; you can see it, touch it, feel it. On the other hand, it portrays a time yet unrealized—a dream, hope, or aspiration.'[44] Importantly, Collins and Porras state that 'a goal cannot be classified as a BHAG without a high level of commitment to the goal.'[45]

---

[41] Yasir, and Mohamad, 312.

[42] Mollazadeh, Mahmood, and Yeganegi, 225.

[43] Bass, in *Leadership: Understanding the Dynamics of Power and Infuence in Organizations*, 320.

[44] Collins, and Porras, 232.

[45] Collins, and Porras, 100.

Conceptualizing Vision 2025 in 1999 as a BHAG illustrates how it was a product of its times. Since then, WGA has shown a high level of commitment to the Vision, even as the organization continued to progress, change, and adapt to the changing contexts of its ministry. These were key factors in WGA's survival and adaptability demonstrated in its ability to lead and manage change in national, regional, and global environments. Change demands that the highest levels of leadership must deal with complex choices about the organization's direction while closely following its values. Leaders must overcome complacency though they realize that people can be fearful of the consequences of change. This calls for a sense of urgency, an ambitious determination to push beyond obstacles and create an emotional response to change. As John Kotter says, 'a true sense of urgency is a set of feelings: a compulsive determination to *move* [forward]… *now*.'[46] Leaders with vision enjoy the challenge of big ideas to protect the organization from failing and create a safe place for the best ideas to flourish. A leader with vision must 'fold a rational case directed toward the mind into an experience that is very much aimed at the heart.'[47]

As WGA's journey continued, it is significant to note that more than one era of leadership 'owned' and dealt with Vision 2025. As stated before, neither the date nor the deadline held the true value of Vision 2025. It was primarily about the motivation the Vision provided. Vision 2025 offered motivation to pray, to seek God's will, to commit to ongoing change and lasting values, motivation to seek out new relationships, to hold plans loosely, to collaborate, to take risks. In the early years of Vision 2025, there was a temptation to make it all about acceleration. But gradually it became apparent that the commitment to participate in God's mission meant it would happen at God's pace. Deepening relationships and learning to listen, think, and work differently sometimes requires less speed, more reflection. Even in the face of urgency—perhaps especially in the face of urgency—the measure of progress is as much about direction and depth as distance.

[46] John Kotter, *A Sense of Urgency* (Boston: Harvard Business Press, 2008). 45.

[47] Kotter, 47.

Chapter 10
Defining: Missiological Consultations that Shaped the Wycliffe Global Alliance

By Susan Van Wynen

Introduction

When is a meeting more than a meeting? It might be surprising that a series of over 30 meetings—referred to as consultations—provided some of the most defining, dynamic, and spiritually enriching contributions shaping the identity and impact of the Wycliffe Global Alliance, with each representing a significant step along the Alliance journey. These consultations, requested by many and attended with great enthusiasm, resulted in ongoing reflection, community, and collaboration. And everyone wants more.

Consultations welcomed participants from multiple countries, and several also included a wide range of participants from outside WGA. While held in locations around the world to encourage broad and varied participation and to provide the opportunity to experience diverse contexts, some consultation destinations were chosen for logistic convenience and to ensure that participants from a wide range of nations could obtain the necessary visas.

This chapter presents an overview of 28 missiological consultations held from 2006 to 2019, reflecting on some in greater depth, chronicling the events themselves, as well as the learnings. Examining what formed the content and context of WGA enables us to trace the path and progress of WGA's journey and its history in the making. It is a process that fundamentally shaped the character, identity, and practice of WGA.

Characteristics of a Missiological Consultation

Though the format of consultations took shape over time and varied according to the content, context, and participants, there were specific principles and goals established from the start. WGA missiologist Stephen Coertze led most of the consultations, and his description helps clarify why these were unlike other meetings.

In January of 2013, Coertze described a missiological consultation as when '...missiologists use their knowledge, skills, and understandings of the academic field of missiology to assist others (groups or individuals), through a consultative process, to understand or evaluate a certain topic pertaining to the group.'[1] Conducting a consultative process can take a variety of forms, including facilitating participation in discussion with an intended purpose and outcome and through research findings written up and presented to those who are involved.

Coertze outlined the critical missiological elements that should feature in a consultative process: (1) Understand the biblical message and its most significant themes; (2) Develop an awareness of how God is at work, both in history and in the world today; (3) Understand people in their environments; (4) Cooperate with the Holy Spirit; (5) Collaborate with others in community; (6) Understand the interdisciplinary nature of missiology.

Developing and cultivating certain necessary skills ensures that these critical elements are woven effectively into the consultative process. Coertze identified these as attitudes, resources, people, tools, and practices.

Depending on the topic and the needs of the participants, the purpose and outcome of a consultative process could involve ensuring an intended discussion process starts off on a sound biblical foundation, evaluating a set of documents pertinent to a group, setting direction, assessing or confirming current philosophies and practices, or introducing new learning. In addition, the nature of a missiological consultative process might potentially raise issues or awareness unintended as an outcome of the process.

Coertze advised thoughtful observation and reflection when designing a consultative process because, to a large extent, it would reflect the missiological soundness of the consultation itself, becoming even more crucial when taking place in a global context. Important factors involved participants, number of participants, geographical location, main consultation topic, framing of the discussion, and facilitation process.

By considering these factors when developing each consultation, further supplementary principles and guidelines continually emerged as the leadership and facilitation team gained experience in conducting the consultations.

[1] Stephen Coertze, "What is a missiological consultation?" 2013.

First Missiological Consultation, 2006

Background

The first missiological consultation was held from 29 to 31 August in Orlando, Florida and included 12 Wycliffe leaders from seven countries, gathered at the invitation of WBTI (and SIL) Executive Director John Watters. Several others had been invited but could not attend. Because of a prior commitment, Watters was also unable to attend, and WBTI Associate Executive Director Darryl Kernick came in his place. Bill Taylor, WEA Mission Commission Ambassador, facilitated the consultation, Wycliffe US President Bob Creson and his team provided logistics support and hospitality at their Orlando facilities, and the WBT US prayer team provided prayer support. Taylor and Wycliffe Australia Executive Director Kirk Franklin spoke about the consultation during EnterMission, the all-centre chapel for staff, thus informing the Wycliffe US leadership and staff and heightening enthusiasm for the event and the concept of missiological consultation.

Preparation

Consultation participants were seriously committed to engaging and participating in a robust conversation. Taylor supplied them with a reading list of articles and books to aid their preparation before the consultation. During the consultation, participants shared prepared summaries of their reading reflections, describing how the readings had informed their missiological understandings of Wycliffe and the mission of Bible translation. The pre-readings and the consultation itself would fuel discussions, encourage further reading, and have an impact for years to come. The missiological journey was underway with a new sense of purpose.

Processing Missiological Issues

A primary goal of the missiological consultative process was to define issues currently affecting WBTI, the Wycliffe Member Organizations (WMOs), and the WMO leaders. To begin this process, Franklin gathered a list of twenty issues affecting WBTI, sent it to the participants, who then prioritized the list items based on their contexts. A list of eight issues emerged, summarized as follows: (1) impact of short-term mission; (2) engaging the Diaspora in mission; (3) consumerism; (4) living in the Kingdom of God versus living in the kingdom of this world; (5) missiological importance of Bible translation; (6) saturation of information;

(7) challenges for non-western missionaries; (8) impact of the mega-church on missions.

Each participant presented issues they believed were affecting WBTI, WMOs, or their leadership. Forty-four issues were then submitted, grouped under eight headings, as follows: (1) the church in general; (2) the church and Bible translation; (3) the church and Wycliffe; (4) Vision 2025 today; (5) corporate unity; (6) importance of the mother-tongue; (7) regional issues; (8) missiological issues in training.

When the participants gathered in Orlando, they considered these issues, spending time in prayer and reflection to discern which of the issues the Lord was leading them to discuss at this time. Franklin recalled, 'Quite quickly and in an amazingly unifying way, three issues emerged as the most critical.' The shortlist, a synthesis of a number of the issues, would allow the participants to address them holistically. The three issues were:

› The church: ecclesiological significance and significance to WBTI.
› Bible translation: missiological basis and context.
› Vision 2025: missiological importance.

Through small group discussion of these issues an outline of the essential points emerged, which all agreed required further development, research, and reflection by the participants, WBTI Area Directors, and WMO leaders. Goals included involving more people in the conversation and eventually supplying articles on each topic that would help develop a global WBTI missiological perspective, thus serving the leaders of the organization as they grappled with these issues in their contexts.

The Reflective Practitioner

Taylor opened the consultation by talking about reflective practitioners. He defined them from a Christian perspective as 'women and men of both action and study; rooted in the Word of God and the church of Christ; obedient to the power of God's Spirit and to the Great Commission in all its fullness; servants who are globalized in perspective; citizens of their own cultures but also the world; leaders who are passionate of heart and who also reflect the heart of Christ.'[2] For Christians, this combination of action and study is rooted in the church, requiring a robust ecclesiology for those who truly desire to be reflective practitioners. This concept would bring new perspectives to WBTI, an organization founded in a pragmatic culture and context, steeped in decades of Great Commission 'go'

[2] *Global Missiology for the 21st Century*, ed. William D. Taylor (Pasadena: William Carey Library, 2000), 1.

motivation, focussed on 'task', and established as 'parachurch'.

As consultation participants grew enthusiastic about the reflective process, they began thinking about how they could live it out, share the concepts with their colleagues throughout the organization, and how it could impact their relationship with the church. The ripple effect continues to this day. Taylor's impact extended beyond his service as consultation facilitator. He made a significant and historical contribution to the development of WBTI thought and praxis. Franklin recalled, 'We were enriched through his biblical, theological, and missiological insights that were packaged in his own journey through life.'

Taylor began each day of the consultation with reflections on the missional triune God: God the Father in mission, God the Son in mission, and God the Holy Spirit in mission. Each reflection served as a theological and biblical basis for that day's discussions, a reminder of the role of each member of the Godhead—the *perichoresis*, that Taylor described as the integrated dance of the Triune missional community. Serving also as a reminder of the gift and need of community, using that understanding, leaders could nurture the discipline of listening to the Triune missiological community and to each other. With a growing unity among the participants as they began this journey, a deep exploration began into what it meant to participate in God's mission.

Over the next year, participants from this first consultation shared their discoveries and insights with other Wycliffe leaders and colleagues in partner organizations. They continued the journey as they looked more deeply into the three key issues. In November 2006, at the WBTI Global Leaders Meeting, all WMO directors were engaged in face-to-face missiological reflection, attending presentations, and participating in discussions based on the Orlando Consultation. The influence and impact continued to spread.

Second Missiological Consultation, 2007

Background

The 23 participants in this second consultation that met from 15 to 17 August in Singapore represented a diversity of cultures and backgrounds from Argentina, Australia, Cameroon, Germany, Guatemala, Korea, Papua New Guinea, Singapore, South Africa, and the US. Some had attended the first consultation, while others were new. Kan-Sang Tan, lecturer in Mission Studies at Redcliffe College, UK, served as facilitator. Wycliffe missiologist, Stephen Coertze, was one of the presenters. Wycliffe Singapore invited several other guests to participate on the first day. These included: Patrick Fung, General Director for OMF International;

Warren Beattie, Director of Mission Research for OMF International; Tang Shin Yong, Wycliffe Singapore Board member; Grace Toh, former missions lecturer at Trinity Theological College and former WBT member; Edwin Lam, Chairman of the Singapore Baptist Convention, pastor of Calvary Baptist Church Singapore, Chairman of Interserve Singapore, and Chairman of Forum of Mission Organizations of Singapore. The guests and their contributions to the missiological discussions were welcomed at these meetings, hosted by Wycliffe Singapore at their supporting church, Grace Chinese Church. Conducting this consultation in Singapore provided participants with a broadening perspective and a tangible reminder that these missiological discussions were global by nature. This pattern would continue as future consultations were held in diverse locations around the world, allowing for wider participation and an understanding of multiple and varied contexts.

Preparation

Pre-consultation reading, followed by reflections, also became a pattern of the consultations. This time the list included twelve articles ranging from an abstract of Thomas Friedman's *The World is Flat* to Tan's *Christology and Culture*. In his first plenary session, Tan drew from his own missiological reflections on the status of the mission enterprise and its global impact, including Bible translation. Tan encouraged the group to rethink their theology from new perspectives, considering the diversity, growth, and many voices of the church worldwide, mission as God's 'job description', and the role of Bible translation in holistic mission. Following each plenary session, participants met in small groups for discussion and reflection, then shared in the larger group. As they explored key missiological issues in their work and regions and began considering the unique contributions and strengths that any given culture could add, they raised an intriguing variety of thoughts, ideas, and questions.

Following are examples of the small group discussions:

- Korean participants reflected on the need to re-evaluate their mission's methodology, which they maintained had largely ignored their own cultural and historical patterns, taking the patterns and methods of others and adapting them instead.
- A group from Africa posed questions concerning how Bible translation could become an essential part of what African churches see as their responsibility. They also asked how history has shaped the current situation, and what changes are needed.
- Other table groups asked how Wycliffe's organizational history helps or

hinders our theology, our relationship with the church, and our desire for multicultural thinking. Some pondered how our structures, processes, and practices help or hinder us in the current world context, considering who we want to be and what we see God doing.

A New Vision

In his second plenary session, Tan presented a new vision of Wycliffe as a community of learners who are part of and serving the worldwide church through an example of missiological research, reflection, and practice. Participants were ready for the next steps on the journey of reflective practice. They looked at the vision, values, training, methodology, structures, and resources it would take to reach this vision. While this exercise appealed to many of the participants' problem-solving strengths, it also encouraged them to think more deeply about what might need to change and why.

Participants expressed a strong desire to conduct further missiological thinking in partnership with others, both inside and outside Wycliffe. They also wanted to ensure that the staff benefit from and take part in aspects of this reflection, including finding ways to help staff become aware of and understand the context and implications of the world, the church, and God's activities in the world. They agreed that though not every staff member would become a missiologist, each would benefit from having a missiological foundation.

While purposely avoiding setting up an administration and framing policy (pragmatic leaders are usually drawn to such activities), aiming instead toward a facilitating and awareness-building approach, the opportunity arose to discuss practical aspects of integrating missiological thinking into an organizational mindset. Consultation participants envisioned the steps involved in making reflective practice part of daily life and service.

Tradition and History

Tan's third presentation reinforced the value of studying globalization and multicultural realities. He urged participants to consider how these new contexts impact the understanding of spiritual transformation. Prefacing a discussion on looking at conversion as an event, a process, or relationship, Tan observed, 'Genuine conversion assumes a discipleship process of growth as the convert lives out the implications of being a follower of God.'

The consultation gave insights into the impact of Western perspectives and practices on traditional missions models and on Wycliffe's own established patterns. The key is not to reject this historical inheritance, nor to turn to some other geographically-based philosophy and theology, but to learn from the past and the present as we seek God's best from each time and place—or, as Scripture says, 'discerning the times'.

Missiology and Bible Translation

Missiologist Samuel Escobar said, 'It is time for a paradigm change that will come from a solitary return to the Word of God', which has tremendous implications for the missional ministry of Bible translation. Stephen Coertze quoted Escobar and, in his presentation, focussed on missiology in WBTI. He described a missiological framework for Bible translation as imparting a unified understanding of the biblical basis for Bible translation, with a reference point for discussing the importance of Bible translation on various levels, subsequently benefitting the church's recognition of Bible translation as their mandate, not belonging solely to a few specialist organizations.

In discussing the potential of a missiological framework, the temptation emerged to view missiology as a new program or department or as a solution to unresolved issues and topics. Consultation participants agreed that when developing a missiological domain, it was not to serve its own purposes, but to equip all levels of the organization in thinking, strategizing, and functioning following sound missiological understanding. A Wycliffe missiological strategy could include research, formal and informal training, orientation, consultancy, information and curriculum development and distribution, reflective culture formation, etc. Essentially, not only regarding missiology holistically but also its thought practice and dissemination is crucial.

Relating to the Church

Reflection on the church occurred when revisiting the application of missiological thinking to the three key issues determined in the first consultation: church, translation, and Vision 2025. Recognizing that WBTI and WMOs relate differently to the church in different contexts, participants discussed reframing the understanding of Wycliffe's responsibilities—so that the church identifies its responsibilities and Wycliffe helps it fulfill them. Participants expressed the necessity to rethink the understanding of the relationship between Bible translation and the Kingdom of God, including revisiting our theology of the Word of God. They asked, 'What is Wycliffe's theological position on the church, and how is this communicated to new workers? Is WBTI's ecclesiology biblical, and how does it impact the way we relate to the church and carry out mission in God's world? How do roles need to change?' They noted the Global South's readiness for increased responsibility and ownership of mission and the need to move beyond west-east-south classifications to interconnectedness. Participants called for further research and an apologia for Bible translation as mission to relate to the church.

Progress in Process

Although there were more topics than time, consultation participants had begun to see missiological foundations and expressions from a worldwide church perspective. Between the first and second consultations, additional leaders were welcomed into the discussion, showing that the impact was spreading. Involving outside facilitators in each consultation and including representatives of other organizations, such as OMF International, in the first day of meetings proved beneficial and encouraged the spread of missiological thinking across disciplines and boundaries.

Several recommendations resulted from the second consultation, many based on intentionally developing missiological and reflective thinkers, or a core group of missiological reflectors, to consider issues of partnership, stewardship, and contextualization from a reflective missiological perspective. There was a suggestion to explore possibilities for formal missiology training and scholarships, and a desire to stimulate missiological research, sharing and fostering of missiological discussion through a variety of forums and mediums, particularly encouraging research and thinking from Asian, African, and Latin American perspectives. A potential result from this could be a culture shift through missiological reflection and research in WBTI. Coertze agreed to help the organization begin this process. Other recommendations included inviting WBTI International Convention 2008 delegates to interact with the issues; holding regional forums for missiological think-tanks in WMOs and Wycliffe Area offices (and including local churches and inviting an external facilitator); and further developing and refining Wycliffe's three 'big missiological issues': the church, Bible translation, and Vision 2025.

Missiological thinking was helping Wycliffe leaders see the bigger picture of how God was at work in the world and what their part might be. Many leaders were developing as reflective practitioners, while others were at least gaining a better understanding of the value of this approach. The WBTI leadership had become advocates for this process. Well on their way to developing strategies and practices as missional thinkers and leaders, they were also exercising wisdom in their approach to missiology, as was apparent from the comments of several of the leaders at this consultation. They spoke of wanting to integrate the missiological consultative process within WBTI, not wanting it to become a purely academic exercise or a siloed 'program'. They also emphasized the need for global representation, local voices, and engagement with and as a part of the church. The WBTI leadership could see the path behind them that had brought them to this place, and they looked forward to continuing the journey with new enthusiasm, greater humility, and an expanded worldview.

Third Missiological Consultation, 2008

Process

This final consultation in a series spanning three years was designed to help Wycliffe leaders identify missiological issues related to Bible translation and the church and was purposely kept smaller in scale to allow time for deeper reflection and interaction with the South African guests and their presentations. The consultation was held from 19 to 21 August in Johannesburg, South Africa. Participants from each continent attended, as well as representatives from three WMOs, including one who was also a WBTI Board member and four WBTI GLT members, including Kirk Franklin. Each had previously committed to being part of the missiological contribution to WBTI. Stephen Coertze led and facilitated the event.

The theme of the consultation was understanding and participating with the church. Coertze opened the consultation with an overview of mission in his home country, South Africa: 'In many respects, South Africa is a rich country. Part of its wealth can be found in its mission history, mission contribution, and missiological reflection [which has] enriched the global community.' Coertze went on to cite South Africa's contribution to missiology, particularly through New Testament scholar David Bosch and the church's involvement in Bible translation. Participants were also privileged to learn from three distinguished guests, South African missiologists and church leaders, Piet Meiring, University of Pretoria; Maake Masango, University of Pretoria; and Ndaba Mazabane, Chairman of the WEA International Council, Missions and Outreach Pastor at Rosebank Union Church, Chairman of Evangelicals in Africa.

Each speaker, in some way, focussed on missiology, the identity of the church, and the role of the church. Meiring focussed on the whole Bible as a missionary text describing the history of mission and revealing that mission belongs to God. He summarized mission as expressed through the preaching of the Gospel (*kerygma*), the service of loving acts (*diakonia*), the communion among the saints while building up the church (*koinonia*), all connected to worship (*litourgia*).

Masango spoke of the need in South Africa to teach the next generation the stories of family and the stories of Jesus, told in the contexts of each nation, saying, 'If this doesn't happen, the people will spiritually perish.' Turning to the church in Africa, Masango cited three types of churches: The Dead Church, where people go only on Christmas and Easter because their grandmothers went there; The Alive Church, which has a message that everyone has to be rich and not poor because God has called us to prosper and where 'money seems to exceed Jesus Christ'; The Vibrant Church, a church that is poor (not just financially), where people come to offload their burdens.

Mazabane spoke from 1 Chronicles 12:32, referencing the men of Issachar who understood the times and knew what Israel should do. He presented this as a challenge to leaders today as they consider numerous global issues: a pluralistic society, increased materialism, disease and disaster, urbanization, increasing youth population, the persecuted and suffering church, the growth of the mission movement worldwide, tremendous change regarding the centre of Christianity, and the influence of China. Referring to Colossians 4:3, Mazabane stated, 'As long as heaven is open, the doors of opportunity are open for us. It is going to take people of integrity to walk through those open doors.' He went on to talk about the need for people who know God's Word, the need for intercessors, and the need for Christ-like people who are influencers. He spoke of the need for innovation, imagination, and inspiration from God, then outlined critical challenges, encouraging trends, and the contributions of the African church to the global church. In closing, Mazabane stated that a clear theology of God is the best starting point for the church to understand missions.

The thought-provoking input of the three South African guests, along with the pre-consultation reading and reflection, prepared the participants for an in-depth discussion of the two themes of understanding the church and participating with the church.

Understanding the Church

The conversation started with questions rather than statements. While statements about the church called for agreement or disagreement, given the changing nature and varied contexts of the church around the world, asking questions encouraged reflection. Questions included: Who is the church? What is the church? Why is the church? What do we mean by church? What is the understanding of mission by the church? Observing and contemplating the church in its past, present, and future included considering its contexts and diversity, trends and movements, challenges in relationships with mission organizations, common misconceptions, and its role and relationship with Wycliffe. Participants then addressed the necessity to change to better nurture and fulfill their relationships with the church.

Participating with the Church

'We cannot engage with the church if we do not first engage with the *missio Dei*. Otherwise, we engage with our own mission's agenda or the church's agenda rather than God's agenda.' This statement from the consultation demonstrates the participants' commitment to God's mission and to the role of the church in that mission. The participants identified terminology and practices requiring clarification to better align with this understanding and commitment. They also discussed qualities important to a relationship with the church. These included: listening, being relational, and serving as catalysts; being God-directed, and culturally and contextually appropriate; acting with intentionality, humility, honesty, and openness to new ideas and opportunities; and demonstrating advocacy, not agendas, relenting ownership, orientation toward the Kingdom of God and a servant model.

Outcomes

The decision emerged for the GLT to concentrate on these three areas: (1) working on the internal and external missiological messaging for Wycliffe; (2) framing statements about our recognition of the importance of the *missio Dei*; (3) exploring how this consultation changes our attitudes and behaviours.

Discussions regarding Wycliffe and the church would continue in the years ahead, but the Alliance leadership realized the significant step from this consultation occurred with the recognition that both Wycliffe and the church participate in God's mission, and God is in control. They also grew in their understanding of how attitudes and behaviours could change to better align Wycliffe and the church and how to nurture those relationships.

Last Languages Initiative, 2009

Background

The Last Languages Initiative (LLI) Consultation was held from 14 to 17 September at the Wycliffe UK centre at Horsley's Green, England. It was the first designed to address a specific current issue rather than starting from a broader theological theme, though it did follow a missiological approach. It was the first of several consultations that would move WBTI toward theological and relational approaches with partner organizations rather than transactional approaches which often dealt only with isolated issues.

Process

The subject at hand, the LLI, was a joint initiative of SIL and some of the WMOs. The goal of LLI was to develop a worldwide process for engaging in the remaining languages in need of Bible translation projects by 'doing strategic and comprehensive planning, designing of comprehensive projects, and eventual management and evaluation of funded projects.'[3] The purpose of this consultation was to provide WBTI with a theoretical framework to effectively engage with LLI.

The discussion included four topics: (1) the missional nature of God (*missio Dei*); (2) stewards of God's resources; (3) urgency in service of our patient God; (4) his kingdom come. Exploring these and other related topics and focussing on the mission of God led to thoughtful reflection, discernment, and direction for good practice. The first round of discussion on each of these topics happened electronically. Pre-consultation readings drew from David Bosch's perspectives on *missio Dei* and included an essay on *missio Dei* by Eddie Arthur. Through their reading, reflection, and responses, the participants heard from and considered one another's input. The electronic discussion began in April 2009, with the in-person consultation held from 14 to 17 September 2009. The 29 participants, consisting primarily of managers and administrators, were joined by another nine participants contributing virtually.

With animated discussion throughout the consultation, the WBTI team listened to and conversed with the numerous partners in attendance. Though conversations were not always comfortable, all involved came to a better understanding of next steps for planning and for working together. During the interactions, WBTI determined that their role was not to engage in the activities themselves but to help create environments where others could reflect and choose how and if they would engage in specific strategies. While acknowledging that not all Wycliffe organizations had to participate in every planned initiative, including WBTI, on invitation, WBTI would be willing to lead or participate in planning processes.

WBTI emerged from the consultation with newly stated principles for participating in comprehensive planning and a clearer picture of its future role, which would be helpful to WBTI, its organizations, and partners. This consultation sent a message to the WMOs that they were free to choose, partner with, or participate with strategies such as LLI, and WBTI would not commit to such initiatives on their behalf. But WBTI did have a role in encouraging solid theological and missiological reflection in all initiatives and offered principles that would help shape the future of Bible translation. WBTI's principles emphasized the importance of local community involvement, clarity in partnerships, forethought regarding diverse resourcing, and a high level of appropriate accountability.

---

[3] Stephen Coertze, "Final Report on the Theological and Missiological Consultation on the Last Languages Initiative," 2009.

Community Within the Alliance, 2012

Background

The theme of community, chosen for this consultation, described a foundational value of the Alliance (WBTI having now transitioned to the Wycliffe Global Alliance). Though there was no formal agenda, the goal was to explore key topics related to community. The 12 invited participants represented nine countries and met together in Accrá, Ghana, from 18 to 19 August, hosted by GILLBT. The subtitle of the consultation was 'Community... as an Expression of the *Missio Dei*.'

Preparation

Reading recommendations were sent to the participants beforehand, along with the following set of questions for reflection: How does Scripture describe community within the Trinity? Between God and those who are called into communion with God? And in the collective body of Christians worldwide? How do we as an Alliance respond to this? How do we express 'Alliance Life' in our local contexts? And, how do we, from our local contexts, respond to life within WGA?

Reading material included chapters from four books on missiology and papers on God and the church. From this, and as influenced by their contexts and experiences, participants exchanged and explored their thoughts, then developed a list of nine ideas which they narrowed down to three main topics for further discussion. Participants noted a significant difference in this consultation from many previous meetings they attended, in that there was no pre-planned agenda. Instead, they mutually created the agenda through conversation. The consultation was a model of community journeying together.

Discussion

The three topics for discussion were as follows:

- What is community?
- What is participation in community (as opposed to creating community)?
- How do we express community?

Small group discussions led to Scripture sharing, times of reflection, and thoughts on broadening the conversation to involve more of WGA. Discussions also resulted in a greater understanding that community is based on the relationship of and with the Triune God who created us to be in community. Our relationships are even more beneficial than our actions, and interdependency will lead to greater effectiveness.

The outcomes from this consultation would lead the way in reshaping WGA, guiding how it would relate both internally and externally moving forward.

Participants agreed that similar discussions were called for throughout the Alliance and should influence WGA's documents and conduct. They also recommended further discussion on several topics, including the Triune God, organizational discipleship, polycentrism, and rethinking the meaning of partnership. A philosophy and principles paper (see extracts in box below) was created based on the consultation participants' input and reviewed by them following the consultation. This paper has fostered ongoing conversation and reflection on the topic of community. An appendix to the paper offered comments on the intertwined nature of being and doing and included Scripture references that illustrate examples of being and doing as Kingdom living in community.

PRINCIPLES OF COMMUNITY

Community is the basis for the existence of the Alliance. We are not a community not only because of our common goals, though Alliance Organizations do share many common goals. Our participation in God's mission flows out of our communion with the Triune God and our fellowship within the Body of Christ. We are community because we joyfully share a common life in Christ.

We appreciate and encourage the interdependent and interconnected nature of all Alliance Organizations as we seek to glorify God and serve together in Bible translation movements.

Serving together in community, we love, respect, and honour one another. It is our collective responsibility to seek wisdom and discernment from the Lord and to encourage, mentor, assist, and advise each other. We seek to understand contexts and cultures. We create space to listen to one another and to speak truth in love. Our interdependence and interconnectedness create an environment where all Alliance Organizations generously give and graciously receive. We recognize we are not owners, but only stewards of the gifts God has given us. We affirm each other for who we are and not for what we contribute or for the quantity of the contribution. Our primary goal is to glorify God together.

1. We are created for community and called to community (creation and calling).
2. We are God's people, called to consistently and lovingly relate and behave according to the instruction of His Word and the example of Christ (identity—who we are together).
3. Living and serving in community glorifies God and provides a tangible example of the Gospel in action. We reflect the image of God through intentionally modelling authentic community (how we live together).
4. A community that glorifies God attracts people to God and His mission (what we do together).

The Community consultation is an example of how WGA decided what values, principles, and practices needed to guide them on their journey. New contexts, new discussion participants, and new challenges continued to add to ongoing reflection and praxis. This highlights the difference between a process with a pre-set agenda and pre-stated outcome, and a process of discovery when colleagues make the journey together. It also demonstrates WGA incorporating their learnings as more than topics for discussion. Stephen Coertze, who led this consultation, expressed it this way:

> As the organizations within the Wycliffe Global Alliance participate in Bible translation, they should be a tangible example of the Gospel community for all to see. And, therefore, being an Alliance should be more than an organizational model on how to function collectively as distinct organizations. The Alliance must embrace and reveal a community life that springs from our life within the Body of Christ.[4]

Funding God's Mission, 2013

Background

In retrospect, this consultation represented a major step forward for WGA. It was the first in a series of consultations announced by Executive Director Kirk Franklin at the Alliance Global Gathering in Thailand, April 2012. As WGA explored what it meant to function effectively as an interdependent, intrinsically connected alliance of organizations worldwide, noting that the local, regional, and

[4] Stephen Coertze, "Presentation to Consultation," 2012.

global contexts were also changing, it was the ideal time to look at global funding issues from a missiological perspective. Technological, geopolitical, economic, social, and religious factors required significant changes in thinking and evaluation of values and practices. As Stephen Coertze stated, it was 'a timely opportunity to revisit our understanding and participation as the body of Christ in funding God's mission.'[5]

The consultation held from 9 to 11 September in Antalya, Turkey, was the first phase of a two-phase approach. The subtitle of the consultation was 'Exploring a missiological response to undergird future practice.' The second phase would include four regional funding consultations in 2014. Out of these consultations, the leadership hoped to develop guiding principles on funding that would inform the WGA board and leadership and spread to the Wycliffe organizations and partners.

The goals of the funding consultations were to (1) deepen the individual and collective missiological understanding of the participants; and (2) articulate a fresh vision for funding practices for God's mission, based on a dynamic set of guiding principles that are missiologically sound, contextually relevant, sustainable, and globally respectful. The Antalya consultation's specific goals were to (1) identify existing funding practices and their underlying beliefs and values; and (2) explore missiologically sound guiding principles on funding.

Process

The approximately 40 participants representing a wide range of countries, WMOs, other mission organizations, and SIL took part in the pre-consultation reading and reflection, as well as biblical reflections presented during the consultation, designed to facilitate a community environment through formal and informal discussion. Each participant was encouraged to contribute in addressing four topics: (1) biblical foundations for funding God's mission; (2) God and man at work in history; (3) we all participate and share resources in God's mission; and (4) guiding principles. The following are summaries of those discussions.

Biblical foundations for funding God's mission: Discussion of God's attributes, provision for his people, the community of believers, and God's resourcing of his global mission led to the development of a picture of the process.

God and man at work in history: Participants were asked to identify the most common and influential practices and systems for funding God's mission locally, nationally, regionally, and globally. Participants also noted the diversity and the cultural specificity of these approaches as they discussed their experiences with these funding practices and systems. They then highlighted beliefs and values

[5] Stephen Coertze, "Funding God's Mission: Exploring a Missiological Response to Undergird Future Practice," 2014.

underlying these practices. Four themes emerged from this discussion: the need for community relationship grounded in love, the need for mutual understanding, the need to express generosity by following God's example, the need for responsible stewardship.

We all participate and share resources in God's mission: Participants developed guiding statements to summarize what they wanted to cover in this discussion. They spoke of wanting all partners (including local churches) in our mission communities to understand and participate in God's mission and recognized it would require intercultural responsiveness, giving voice, building dignity and community, and developing contextually sensitive and respectful accountability processes. They required a clearly articulated set of missiologically and biblically grounded values to guide those who participate in resourcing mission communities, calling for courage and wisdom when reviewing current beliefs and practices. Participants examined how issues of power and control explicitly and covertly influence funding systems and practices, considered what constitutes success in ministry according to the Scriptures, and contemplated how to evaluate and measure the qualitative and quantitative effectiveness of their ministry. They asked themselves how they might be valuing people based on how they receive personal funds.

Guiding principles: These included God's sovereign provision, our community, and our stewardship. Drawn from the wider conversation, they would lead to further discussions, regional consultations, and statements on funding principles.

Alliance Associate Director Min-Young Jung closed the consultation with a summary of observations. He highlighted that WGA was on a continuous journey of discerning and aligning themselves to what God was doing to fulfill his purposes. He recognized the consultation as an acknowledgment of the global church participating in all spheres of Bible translation, including funding. He closed by noting it would take 'a respectful recognition of each other in community as we participate in diverse approaches in our participation in the funding of God's mission.' Participants' comments reflected their realization that this was 'not an event to bring home a concrete result, but a journey we have started together' and that 'global mission may require a fundamentally different approach than just tweaking the conventional paradigm.' They spoke of the need to be relationship and community-based, rather than task-focussed; interdependent rather than individualistic; promoting dignity, not charity; focussed on obedience, not success.

Regional Funding Consultations, 2014

In 2014, four regional funding consultations followed the 2013 consultation on funding in Antalya. We will step out of chronological order to review those four consultations together. The locations and compositions were: (1) Asia-Pacific, 10–12 February, Bangkok, Thailand, with 50 participants from Alliance organizations within the Asia-Pacific Area, and leaders from SIL International and WGA. (2) Europe, 26–28 March, Holtzhausen, Germany, with 20 participants from Alliance organizations invited by the Europe Area Director, and leaders from WGA. (3) Africa, 8–10 April, Ruiru, Kenya, with 20 participants representing African Alliance organizations, an SIL entity, and WGA leadership. (4) Americas, 13–15 May, Mexico City, Mexico, with 40 participants from Alliance organizations in the Americas Area, SIL Americas personnel, and other partnering organizations invited by the Americas Area Director, along with leaders from WGA.

During the 2013 Funding Consultation in Antalya, participants identified existing funding practices and their underlying beliefs and values and laid the foundation for reflection and robust discussion worldwide. This led to regional consultations, with goals of building on outcomes from the first consultation, including local and regional perspectives and implications for contextualized resourcing practices.

The overarching purposes of the consultative process were (1) to deepen the individual and collective missiological understanding of the participants; and (2) to articulate a fresh vision of funding practices for God's mission based on a dynamic set of guiding principles that are missiologically sound, contextually relevant, sustainable, and globally respectful.

WGA operates in local, regional, and global contexts where many prevailing paradigms (including social, technological, economic, religious, and geopolitical) are being re-evaluated, revised, or replaced. Within the Alliance, members sometimes operate with a variety of diverging paradigms, which now call for re-visiting the understanding of and participation as the body of Christ in funding God's mission.

While the Alliance continued to explore how to function effectively as an alliance, the regional funding consultations stimulated significant new thinking about their beliefs, values, and practices. In July 2014, the GLT would act on the outcomes of these consultations, and regional and local discussions would continue as Alliance members worked together to understand their global commitment to participating in funding God's mission.

Reflective Process

The preliminary reading list for the regional funding consultations included the Alliance's notes on community, principal statements from the Antalya consultation on funding, and several articles about funding and theology. Participants were encouraged to draw from their own experiences and to ask critical questions such as: What new information have you learned from reading the material? What information would you like to explore further? What information causes discomfort? What information challenges current understanding? What information underscores current understanding and thinking? For future reference, they recorded their thoughts in writing, drawings, etc., condensed these into several belief statements, and summarized them into one central statement about the topic. Then they prepared and presented their reflections to the other consultation participants.

Consultation Discussions

Along with the biblical reflections and reading reflections, discussions intentionally addressed these four topics:

Biblical foundations for funding God's mission: Discussion focussed on attributes of God, expressions of God's direct provision and provision through His people, sharing in community, and biblical themes to promote understanding of how God resources his global mission.

Beliefs and values that underlie our understanding of funding: Table groups created drawings with imagery of both money and trees to stimulate their discussion and express their beliefs, values, and the principles influencing their understanding of participation in funding God's mission.

Funding practices that reflect holistic mission: Following a story about a funding initiative that developed from a relational context, participants told similar stories of their own. They explored underlying values and beliefs in these stories, reflected on current funding practices, and expressed their personal and organizational experiences and that of others with these practices. Discussion of these values, beliefs, and practices influenced further discussion on principles on funding.

Restating the biblical principles that should guide our funding practices: The facilitation team created a document featuring key input from the first funding consultation and reflecting biblical and missiological principles available to each regional consultation. Participants had the opportunity to evaluate this document, taking the biblical reflections, the reading reflections, and all the discussions in each consultation into consideration. Each consultation offered valuable ideas and information to strengthen the principles contained in the document.

Next Steps

With grateful appreciation expressed to all participants for their valuable insights, Franklin appointed an editorial team to process the information drawn from the global funding consultation and the four regional consultations. Encompassing all the suggested principles and statements and the raw data gained throughout, the resulting draft of guiding principles for participation in funding God's mission proceeded to the Alliance leadership team and board for additional input. Once approved, they were released as the Alliance's Principles for Funding (see box).

PRINCIPLES FOR FUNDING

Principles 1–4: God's mission belongs to Him

1. The mission of God is fulfilled by the Father, Son, and Holy Spirit in perfect unity.
2. Everything belongs to God, including all the resources necessary to fulfill His mission.
3. God invites and enables His global Church to creatively participate with Him in His mission.
4. God's love and generosity are without limits.

Principles 5–7: God provides for His mission

5. God creatively provides for His mission through a diversity of people, means, and resources.
6. As God's image bearers, and following His example, each person can joyfully and generously give according to the blessings God has given.
7. Recognising God's intention for provision through community, the sharing of God's gifts and resources, including money, is encouraged so that all may benefit.

Principles 8–14: God enables us to share His resources

8. All that we have is from God.
9. Participating in the funding of God's mission is an act of worship.
10. We give from what God has given us, acknowledging our dependence on Him through prayer and obedience.
11. No individual or group is self-sufficient. Sharing resources is an interdependent relational activity where all people and their contributions are valued and every person can graciously give and receive.
12. The sharing of resources needs to be sensitive and responsive to multiple cultures and contexts.

13. In the process of giving and receiving, the dignity of all is honoured and valued through respectful relationships and friendships.
14. When plans among funding partners work out differently than expected, it is an opportunity to come together in an atmosphere of grace to discern and align with what God is doing.

Principles 15–19: God expects wise stewardship of His resources

15. Stewardship and accountability are important to God; therefore, we are mutually responsible to use His resources ethically and wisely.
16. Stewardship values are developed and tested within community according to biblical principles.
17. A collective understanding of funding needs is determined through consideration of many factors including missiological and theological reflection and dialogue.
18. Transparent communication and trusting relationships are essential for dialogue regarding needs, and for avoiding issues concerning power, pride, and control.
19. Discernment in funding decisions includes prayer, reflection, diverse voices, and recognition of God's mission and His focus on the transformation and holistic restoration of people.

Regarding the funding consultations, Franklin observed 'We are on a continuous journey of discerning and aligning ourselves to what God is doing to fulfil His purposes,' noting that 'the global church is participating in all spheres of Bible translation, including funding. It will take a respectful recognition of each other in community as we participate in diverse approaches ... in the funding of God's mission.' Franklin noted that the 'contribution of all the participants in these consultations ... will strengthen the principles this Global Consultation effort seeks to reach. The process of reaching these principles was a missiological journey in itself and has contributed many unplanned outcomes that will be of benefit to the Alliance.'

Our Response to the Mission of God in Local Context, 2013

Background

Eighteen leaders from the Alliance and from SIL gathered from 27 to 29 August in Istanbul, Turkey, for the consultation on the theme of responding to God's mission in challenging religious contexts. The two organizations had been discussing the potential for this consultation for about a year. Like the Last Languages consultation, this event was designed to examine a particular context. This event examined the context of the changing face of mission in regions where other religions were dominant and traditional missions work was neither a viable nor a desired option. Participants looked at the characteristics of their local mission context, the external and internal factors (local and global) that were influencing their understanding of local mission contexts, the predominant challenges, and the main opportunities. Given the context, what mission efforts would work best?

Process

Preparatory reading included books on the mission of God and articles on mission in the Middle East and on Christian witness in a multi-religious world. The consultation, developed around the topic of the mission of God in context, had no pre-decided agenda or outcome. Experience had taught the leaders and facilitators that a well-organized, but less-directive process led to the participants developing keen new insights which would, over time, have a powerful influence on broader policies, philosophies, and practice, at least for the Alliance. The desire was for everyone to be enriched through the process and leave better equipped to take the conversation further in their own or other contexts. There was also the potential for the group to decide on any statements or follow-through that might come out of this consultation.

The participants also recognized that, even with good intentions, the danger existed of merely validating their mission efforts as relevant and important. As Bosch cautions, 'Our point of departure should not be the contemporary enterprise we seek to justify; but the biblical sense of what being sent into the world signifies.'[6] Emphasis on comprehending context from the perspective of Scripture aided understanding of how to respond to the mission of God. Group configurations considered the mix of participants for each conversation, and the discussion

[6] Bosch, 177.

process was designed to journey through Scripture and identify biblical principles that could inform the themes and the local contexts.

Statements referred to in this documentation, though well thought through and broadly agreed on, are best understood in the context of the specific discussion, and not regarded as official positions of SIL Eurasia Area or WGA. Though relevant and worthy of consideration, the conversations in this consultation took place in specific groups and contexts and were meant to be used for further reflection and conversation on the topic, then applied as appropriate in relevant contexts.

Discussion Process

- Discussion questions built one on top of the other, helping the group develop the detail and flow of the conversation and bringing clarity and focus to the topic. How is the mission of God expressed in various biblical contexts (Pre-Kingdom period; Kingdom period; Diaspora period; Pre-Ascension period; and Post Ascension period)?
- What principles can we identify from God's mission as expressed in these contexts?
- What is our understanding of our current local mission context?
- How do these identified principles confirm or challenge our approach to our local context?
- What changes should we make to our strategies and practice to reflect the principles identified?

Discussion groups reflected on three portions of Scripture: Psalm 32, shifting focus from self to focus on God as deliverer, protector, and giver of direction; Matthew 15:21–28, shifting focus from a limited, ethnocentric understanding of Jesus's disciples to focus on a kingdom understanding; and Matthew 28:16–20, shifting focus from kingdom task to kingdom relationship.

Participants shared from their preparatory reflection, participated in discussion groups, and brought their thoughts together collectively. Some of the summary reflections included:

- Mission calls us to reflect God's nature as a community, sharing in perfect unity as in the Godhead, shown in holistic concern for all creation, and in being ready to suffer.
- Do not avoid or seek suffering—suffering or persecution is not just an acceptable part of our lot; it should be an expected part.
- There is a need for vulnerability in mission.

- We need to look at the journey of the church through history.
- Our paradigm of the mission of God should, by definition, be the local and indigenous expression of the Kingdom of God.
- Our own culture/life experiences stunt our view of God and our message.

Participants agreed that the consultation had achieved the following desired outcomes: SIL Eurasia Area and the Alliance substantially and effectively reflected together missiologically on a topic of mutual interest. The consultation broadly addressed a particular mission context from a biblical perspective. And the consultation served as a valuable tool or methodology in evaluating their mission context.

Given the nature of the topic, the context, and the participating organizations, from the beginning, this consultation was not about solutions or immediate actions but about hearing each other and reflecting together. This pattern was the norm for the missiological consultations, but participants, accustomed to other types of meetings, appreciated the reminder. Much of the value of this consultation was that it could stand as an example, in future thinking, discussions, and actions, of how to hold other conversations and address other complex issues from a biblical perspective that reached deeper and broader than traditional meeting and partnership efforts as the journey continued.

Our Participation in *Missio Dei*, 2014

Background

This consultation consisted of 15 participants, some invited by Wycliffe US, some by WGA. It met from 4 to 6 February and was sponsored by and held at the request of Wycliffe US at its Orlando headquarters. The purpose was to seek discernment for what and how God wanted them to contribute to accomplishing his eternal purposes. The consultation opened with a time of reflection on a quote from Samuel Escobar:

> It has become evident that the new century will require a return to biblical patterns of mission. Radical shifts in culture, politics, and economics, as well as the growth of Christianity in the Southern hemisphere, have brought new scenarios. Traditional mission models inherited from the Christendom mentality and the colonial era are now obsolete. It is time for a paradigm change that will come from a solitary return to the Word of God.[7]

[7] Samuel Escobar, "The Global Scenario at the Turn of the Century," in *Global Missiology for the 21st Century*, ed. William D. Taylor (Pasadena: William Carey Library, 2000), 42.

Escobar's statement pointed to the need for new thinking about participation in God's mission. Over the years, it had become increasingly clear to mission agencies that values embedded in history and responses to those values and historical realities put some previously tried and tested practices at odds with current global realities and the contexts where mission agencies now served.

Functioning effectively as an Alliance was stimulating significant new thinking about beliefs, values, and practices, leading to a growing appreciation of the interdependent and intrinsically interconnected nature of the Alliance organizations. Wycliffe USA and many other Alliance organizations serve in local, regional, and global contexts in which multiple prevailing paradigms (i.e., social, technological, economic, religious, and geopolitical) are being re-evaluated, revised, or replaced.

Discussion Process

Prior to the consultation, participants shared reflections on the suggested reading material, including Alliance documents and other missiological texts. Discussions then centred around four topics: acknowledging that the mission belongs to God, recognition of our context within the mission of God, identifying our participation within the mission of God, and foundational missiological statements to evaluate and plan our ongoing participation accordingly.

Thoughts highlighted by participants included: the value of reflection; the need for continuous reformation; the importance of theological foundations to manage the tension between missionary, business, and academic culture; the necessity of focus given to both quantitative and qualitative evaluations; the need to relate to the church in its various dimensions; the importance of remembering and interpreting history; and the presence of globalization and the need to understand and relate to it.

Biblical reflection during the consultation centred on John 11:1–44, looking at the responses of each of the characters involved. Between Jesus and his unrestricted understanding and perspective of God's mission and the others with their limited vantage point, noting the contrast, participants applied this understanding of an eternal perspective to their own contexts, acknowledging that God is in control and can be trusted. The consultation used the following four themes that emerged in their study, as expressed in various biblical epochs, to identify guiding principles for participating in God's mission:

- Scope and purpose of God's mission.
- God's sovereignty in mission.
- God blesses his body to be a blessing.
- Expression of God's mission.

From the reflections and discussions on these themes, principles and statements emerged that would assist Wycliffe USA in evaluating and planning their participation in the mission of God, with an emphasis on God as creator, reconciler, and redeemer and on the importance of our relationship with God and each other. One participant's concluding reflection summarized the consultation's impact well: 'We must consider God's character, his Word, his movement in history and now allow these reflections to inform us as we place ourselves within his mission. Theologically-based progress—how God views his creation, his created people, and his mission—impact how we view our role, our plans, and our timing in his work.'

Bible Translation Philosophy, 2013

Background

As has been noted, the missiological reflective process began in 2006, impacting every area of the Alliance. With a renewed and more straightforward understanding of the reality of the mission of God and the central role of the church, the Alliance Board adopted a new set of core statements (Vision, Mission, and Board Goals). How WGA expressed their identity and attributes called for evaluation, and the activities and programs of Alliance organizations required alignment with the new core statements.

Language program work had become a significant part of the Alliance's efforts. By 2013, 42 Alliance organizations were involved in more than 970 Bible translation projects, demonstrating an important contribution to the broader Bible translation movement.

Because both the missiological reflection and the new core statements helped AOs better understand their unique identity and role in the Bible translation movement, this perspective also needed to be reflected in how Alliance organizations participate in language programs.

Language Programs (later renamed Bible Translation Programs) were a priority area requiring attention. Given their long history with SIL as the primary organization that carried out translation work, Wycliffe had relied on and adhered to the translation policies and principles established by SIL and by FOBAI. While those policies had served well and continued to inform the Alliance, Bible translation program work had grown into a significant part of the work of the Alliance itself. About a third of the Alliance organizations were directly involved in more than 200 translation programs around the world, not counting those involving Seed Company, also an Alliance organization. The Alliance now included Bible translation programs as one of the seven Participation Streams that defined its core purposes. The ministry of Bible translation that had birthed Wycliffe was now one of its major areas of direct involvement. Growth of the church worldwide vastly expanded the possibilities for further participation.

At the 2012 Wycliffe Global Gathering, during a special meeting hosted by Kirk Franklin and Dave Brooks, leaders from 33 Participating Organizations managing Bible translation programs met with Michel Kenmogne, Associate Director for Africa Area. Kenmogne presented a problem statement regarding Wycliffe organizations' involvement in language programs. This statement led to robust discussion, resulting in an agreement that the Alliance and its organizations with language programs struggled with their identity and ability to collaborate with other partners in language programs because of: the lack of a unified understanding of the foundations (theological and missiological basis) for doing language programs work; the lack of a Wycliffe description of the transformational impact aimed at through language programs; their struggle with the definition of the scope of their language programs' involvement and their positioning therein. The language program leaders requested that WGA take the initiative in formulating guiding principles for Alliance Bible translation programs. Franklin commissioned Brooks and Kenmogne to form a working group to develop a Bible translation program philosophy statement. A core team of nine people from various organizations agreed to work with Kenmogne and ALT member Francis Viscount to develop a draft statement. In the process, they agreed the Alliance should refer to its field programs as Bible translation programs rather than language programs, highlighting the central focus of the work.

The working group agreed to base the statement on the *missio Dei* with Bible translation understood as a reflection of incarnation which allows God's Word to indwell the community of speakers of a given language as the anchor point from which all language development will be considered. Moreover, WGA will intentionally emphasize the importance of theology in the process of Bible translation. They also addressed the centrality of the church, particularly as it related to Bible agencies as a functional part of the church and the churches' contribution to the development and practices of translation consultants. Also of importance, 'comprehensive quality' encompassed more than technical excellence, considering the relationships, processes, and behaviours of all those involved. It was on these principles that they created a draft philosophy statement.

The Consultation

From 24 to 26 September 2013, 29 participants gathered in Ruiru, Kenya, to read and reflect further on the values statement document, seeking to establish a solid foundation for WGA's participation in Bible translation programs. Participants responded to the request from the Alliance organizations in three ways: (1) foster a mutual understanding of the theological and missiological foundations for doing Bible translation; (2) recognizing the potential for ongoing development, establish a philosophy statement for WGA Bible translation programs that describes values and perspectives that should guide and influence Alliance organizations and the programs with Alliance involvement; and (3) discuss practical applications of the values promoted by the philosophy statement.

The outcome of the consultation, including work done before and after the consultation by the working group, was the Wycliffe Global Alliance Bible Translation Programs Philosophy Statement and Overview, which dealt with the topic of transformational impact and presented a rationale and key principles for Bible translation programs. The Philosophy Statement (see box) continues to guide organizations in their Bible translation program planning and work and is updated and revised as needed. As a member of FOBAI, the Alliance also continues to comply with their translation statements. There is collaboration and companionship on the journey as translation progress benefits from many partners.

EXCERPTS FROM THE WYCLIFFE GLOBAL ALLIANCE BIBLE TRANSLATION PHILOSOPHY STATEMENT

Introduction

The Wycliffe Global Alliance Bible translation philosophy is an expression of the Alliance Organizations' shared values and fundamental beliefs concerning:

- how Bible translation is a part of God's mission (*missio Dei*)
- the importance of contributing to the process of holistic transformation in and beyond language communities
- key principles that will guide Alliance Organizations in strategically responding to the widely varied contexts in which Bible translation programs occur

The transformational impact that God desires for language communities guides and shapes Bible translation programs.

Key Principles for Alliance Organization's Bible translation programs

1. *The ministry of Bible translation is built on the mission of God.*
 › Principle: Because mission begins with God, a primary response should be to seek to conform our wills to His will through prayer and supplication on the part of the Church and those desiring to engage in the Bible translation program.

2. *God calls the Church to participate with Him in advancing His mission.*
 › Principle: The present and future context of the Church is a critical factor guiding the planning and implementation of all Bible translation programs.

3. *Our Triune God calls us to reflect His character and attributes when we participate in His mission.*
 › Principle: Building the necessary foundation of interdependent relationships required for Bible translation programs to contribute to transformation requires Alliance organizations to model the character of God.
 › Principle: Growth and maturation are reinforced through humbly receiving and acting on the feedback of those with whom you have relationship.

4. *Following the example of Christ's obedience implies sacrificial vulnerability.*
 › Principle: For Bible translation programs to align with God's mission, spiritual unity is needed among Christian partners. Building and maintaining this unity is the highest priority for those involved.
 › Principle: Acknowledging and responding to God's sovereignty requires looking for how God is working when plans, schedules, and other goals are not achieved or when resources are (seemingly) not available.
 › Principle: Because the well-being of each member of the community working in a Bible translation program is essential, taking physical risks should be a shared rather than an individual decision. Vulnerability and obedience allow the spirit to work through many channels, including the unity of the community.

5. *The mission of God is both holistic and integral. God desires transformative change.*
 › Principle: Transformative change requires an expanding and deepening commitment from all those involved.

6. *The mission of God is to bless communities and those who serve them.*
 › Principle: Languages, cultures, identities, and being a community are all God-given gifts meant to bless humans.

Leaders Journeying Together, 2013

Background

The five-day consultation on Leaders Journeying Together was held from 14 to 18 October in Ruiru, Kenya, and began with each of the more than 30 leaders of Alliance organizations completing an Organizational Journey Survey that encouraged them to explore the heritage, identity, values, constituents, highs, lows, and turning points of their organizations. As a result, participants increased their understanding of their organizations, thus preparing them to share what they discovered with the other leaders and promoting unity of spirit and a greater awareness of each other's contexts and the global context.

Process

Each day had a different theme, and most days included biblical reflection, missiological foundations for global leaders, leadership issues and reflections, practical leadership experiences, and other activities. There were interactive sessions on leadership environment, global trends, and a biblical perspective on cross-regional cooperation and partnerships. Sessions focussing on personal, organizational, and Alliance journeys helped leaders integrate these facets of their lives. There was also time for interactive work on topics such as internships, women in leadership, intergenerational leadership, leadership succession, and virtual leadership.

Executive Director Kirk Franklin offered four key concepts related to leading from a global perspective and highlighted implications for WGA: (1) leading with a global perspective; (2) shifting from global to international; (3) understanding the *missio Dei* in light of contemporary mission; (4) developing a new paradigm of leadership for global mission. Franklin quoted Kwame Bediako, observing that 'Christianity has become a non-Western religion; meaning not that Western Christianity has become irrelevant, but rather that Christianity may now be seen for what it truly is, a universal religion.'[8] Therefore, mission agencies require wider pools of missiologically informed leaders who understand how to lead in the mission of God in a global context. Franklin also addressed WGA's need to develop a transformational leadership model.

Stephen Coertze's presentation reflected on four definitions of missiology, leading to a wide range of helpful insights from the participants as they expressed their desire for theological thinking, spiritual community, and cooperating with the Holy Spirit. The third day of the consultation highlighted the three journeys

8 Bediako, 3.

(personal, organizational, and Alliance) and the integration of the three in a leader's life. Franklin provided an overview of WBTI-WGA's history, emphasizing how this journey impacts leaders in the Bible translation movement. ALT members Judy Bokelman and Hannes Wiesmann led a discussion session on organizational journeys. Europe Area staff member Amy Barnes led a session on personal journeys, quoting C.S. Lewis, 'Be sure that the ins and outs of your individuality are no mystery to Him; and one day they will no longer be a mystery to you'[9]; and Jim Pluddemann (former SIM International Director), 'The primary stimuli for a leader's development are life challenges and situations that don't make sense.' Participants were invited to reflect on and describe significant markers on their journeys.

The last session, led by ALT members Todd Poulter and Bokelman, involved integrating the three journeys. The earlier presentations and discussions led to much reflection and potential for planning. Participants recognized that emphasizing community imparted a unified and connecting vision, significant in both forming and understanding our journey. They also noted God at work in each journey, providing faith and strength, intervening using change for his purpose, shaking us out of our comfort zones, and bringing our personal, organizational, and Alliance journeys together in His time.

Alliance Associate Director Min-Young Jung presented a session called 'Interaction with Global Trends: Some Implications for the Alliance', emphasizing the importance of discernment as a global leadership qualification. Jung referenced 1 Chronicles 12:32, the men of Issachar—200 chiefs—who 'understood the times and knew what Israel should do'. David Cardenas from the Americas Area presented 'A Biblical Perspective of Cross-Regional Cooperation and Partnerships'. He asked participants, seated at tables by Area, several questions, followed by asking each Area to share some of their strengths, needs, and weaknesses. As each Area told of their weaknesses, the other Areas expressed how their strengths could help. Cardenas led this activity, tossing a ball of yarn interconnecting the different Areas to illustrate how the resources for each need are present within WGA and demonstrating how they could help resource each other. The result was a wonderful, messy, visual representation of the network of connections.

Various activities gave participants opportunities to observe and reflect on key leadership issues: group and leadership dynamics, the importance of role clarification, taking risks, building community, and resolving conflicts or potential conflicts. One activity involved working together to plant trees on the Ruiru Centre. The project was purposefully organized in a way that required participants to share information and resources and to be patient. This became a memorable event, and several of the participants took pleasure in visiting 'their' trees,

---

9 C.S. Lewis, *The Problem of Pain* (New York: Macmillan, 1977), 147.

the fruit of their communal labour, in the following years. In keeping with the themes of both planting and leadership, Africa Area Director, and consultation host, Mũndara Mũturi, closed the meetings with this African proverb: If you want to eat for one year, grow food crops. If you want to eat for ten years, grow fruit trees. If you want to eat for a hundred years, grow people.

The Leaders Journeying Together consultation helped leaders grow in their understanding of leadership and WGA. They integrated experience and thinking from their own contexts and the global context. But the relationships built and the ensuing opportunities for collaboration and community were among the most enduring impacts of the consultation.

Bible Translation Philosophy Joint Consultation, 2014

Background

More than 50 WGA and SIL participants attended this joint consultation of a missiological exploration and response to the Bible Translation Philosophy Statement from 2 to 5 December in Kusadasi, Turkey. Approximately half were WGA leaders from around the world, the other half were SIL leaders, primarily from the West but representing their international language program services. WGA's Associate Director for Africa Area, Michel Kenmogne, and Alliance missiologist Stephen Coertze led the consultation.

The Alliance had released its Bible Translation Programs Philosophy Statement in November 2013. Members of SIL's executive leadership met with members from WGA's leadership on 17 March 2014 to discuss how SIL could interact with the Statement. The two leadership teams agreed to co-host a joint missiological consultation to equip and empower leaders in both organizations to use the Statement to guide their respective organizations' field programs.

Consultation goals established for Alliance and SIL leaders, facilitated through a reflective and consultative process, included the following:

- Understand the underlying tenets that support the Bible Translation Philosophy Statement, namely, the mission of God, holistic transformation, and the quest for comprehensive standards of quality in Bible translation.
- Embrace values and principles highlighted by the statement to influence the approach to field programs.
- Commit to identifying review processes for ongoing and future Bible translation programs in light of the Philosophy Statement.

Process

The discussion process included the reading reflections, an introduction to the Bible Translation Philosophy Statement, an opportunity to personalize the statement, the opportunity to explore three central tenets of the statement, and time to review Alliance Bible translation practices in light of the statement.

WGA and SIL are different in their nature, mandates, and overt positioning relative to the church. Questions for ongoing reflection include how the Statement could serve the diversity of organizations with their various streams of participation, how the Statement could serve SIL as it develops the infrastructure to facilitate language programs around the world, and how the Statement invites SIL and WGA to cooperate and collaborate as they both participate in the mission of God. The discussion of these topics would be ongoing in various contexts.

Drawing from several statement and principles papers that emerged from previous consultations, Franklin demonstrated (see box) how this process continued to inform and shape the Alliance, determining how it served in community with others, including SIL.

FROM THE BIBLE TRANSLATION PHILOSOPHY STATEMENT

Our Triune God calls us to reflect His character and attributes when we participate in His mission. By working through interdependent relationships, we demonstrate that we value and respect others for who they are and not only for what resources they have or tasks they can perform; we choose to build relationships and networks rather than work in isolation; we choose inclusiveness and promote participation in His Mission. In these ways, we seek to reflect His character and demonstrate love, humility, grace, forgiveness, reconciliation, and patience.

FROM THE PRINCIPLES OF COMMUNITY

Community in Action Principle: Living and serving in community glorifies God and provides a tangible example of the Gospel in action. The experience of participating in community should be one of mutual support and encouragement. We will respect and honour the diverse voices and gifts of each organization within the Alliance community. Together we seek to discern God's will.

FROM THE PRINCIPLES OF FUNDING GOD'S MISSION

Principles 8–14: God enables us to share His resources. No individual or group is self-sufficient. Sharing resources is an interdependent relational activity where all people and their contributions are valued, and every person can graciously give and receive. Discernment in funding decisions includes prayer, reflection, diverse voices, and recognition of God's mission and His focus on the transformation and holistic restoration of people.

Franklin concluded by stating, 'We respect and honour the diverse voices and gifts of each participant within the Bible translation movement. Together we seek to discern God's will. Because we value and respect all people and their contributions, we share resources and expertise in an interdependent relational activity.'[10] This particular consultation helped both WGA and SIL better articulate their perceived roles and opportunities and set the tone for WGA's future participation in the Bible translation movement.

Summarizing the consultation, Kenmogne observed that it was not a process to create, refine, or perfect a document, nor a practical exploration of applications of the Philosophy Statement. It was a moment to reflect on the guiding principles that undergird the Statement and to revisit and firm up our mission theology (normative), out of which flow our empirical mission philosophy, and resist the temptation of allowing mission science alone to guide our practices. He went on to say that mission is God's, not ours. While not an end in itself, Bible translation should be framed in the context of God's overarching plan for redemption, restoration, glory, rule, and *shalom*. Bible translation is 'body' work, done in community, by communities, and for the blessing of communities. The present and future context of the church is a critical factor guiding the planning and implementation of all Bible translation programs.

An additional highlight of this consultation was the participants' tour of ancient Ephesus, a reminder of the communities of believers who came before, and a call to continue building community among the consultation participants.

[10] Kirk Franklin, "Reflections on the Bible Translation Philosophy Statement," 2014.

Global Leadership Team Future, 2015

Background

WGA's leadership team had, for some time, engaged in conversations concerning the need for Alliance structures and processes to be flexible and open to appropriate change. Following their pattern of hosting missiological consultations to focus on major Alliance issues and topics, they decided to plan a consultation specifically for the leadership team regarding the substance and structure of WGA and its leadership. The team met from 3 to 6 February in Chiang Mai, Thailand.

Process

Stephen Coertze began with a presentation on how various understandings of *missio Dei* historically influenced the structures of mission agencies. Mission movements developed outside the structure or institution of the church. Coertze pointed out that much of evangelical mission structure was also moving more from institutional to movement structure. But WGA was shaped by an identity influenced by both movement and institution. WGA practice and their core documents reflect this. By adopting a broad perspective of mission historically, the question arises: what structure best facilitates WGA embedding within the mission of God? WGA is a community of organizations drawn together by God as part of His process to continue the transformation of Christ's Body into greater maturity, which involves reframing, refocussing, and refining.

Coertze pointed out that WGA's journey is taking place within a context where others are also journeying and involves a movement toward greater dependence and obedience, individually and corporately, which will require greater awareness and submission to God's work of redemption and transformation. WGA is called to be transformed and to act as a catalyst for broad transformation within the work of the church, specifically in Bible translation, but also inter-related with other aspects of a holistic transformation and movement toward *shalom* among minority language communities.

Table discussions included reflections on the God of mission, the church and its role in the mission of God, how WGA fits within the mission of God, how others see WGA, how the GLT sees WGA, and WGA's identity and the mission of God. Several statements made during the consultation expressed insights into WGA's nature, identity, and how it might be reshaping for the future:

Who we are: We need to be a humble, growing, covenantal community, a channel of God's *shalom* with emphasis on Bible translation in the world's language communities. With the church community, WGA is a fellowship of organizations that are part of the Bible translation movement, participating in the *missio Dei*. WGA, through reflective practices, is being transformed and becoming an instrument of transformation. We need to continually demonstrate a welcoming environment so that each organization, whether institution or movement, is a welcomed part of our community without loss of identity. The journey experience helps individuals and organizations become part of this vision and gain identity.

What we do: God is leading to new and uncharted territory; our primary role is to be obedient to the Lord, under the direction of the Holy Spirit. We encourage and strengthen as servant leaders, mentoring, caring, running interference to help connect and reconcile. Bible translation represents a crucial component for reconciling people to God. We can't miss this central element. We are a community coming together for a particular set of goals. Our vision, DNA, and goal of communicating the Word of God in the heart language is an inherent part of our identity as WGA in the mission of God. We must be aware, discerning where God is working and what he is doing, and we must be accountable—growing in our willingness to introduce deep spiritual practices.

This consultation, while not intended to offer concrete answers regarding the future of the WGA leadership team or WGA's structure, opened new doors for creative thinking, made the necessity for flexibility more apparent, and helped the leaders get on the same page concerning identity, purpose, and structure. Not a one-time exercise, this would describe part of an ongoing process as the WGA leadership continued their journey.

Leaders Journeying Together—Third Table, 2015

Background

The goal of this consultation was to gather a diverse group of leaders in a safe yet challenging community environment where participants could interact with one another across generations and cultures on issues relevant to their development as leaders in WGA, including some issues rarely discussed. The 24 participants selected for this event, in consultation with area directors, represented a cross-section of leaders holding various levels of responsibility. WGA Consultant for Leadership Development Todd Poulter ably led the participants, along with a facilitation team of younger leaders he had been mentoring. The participants met from 27 April to 1 May in Istanbul, Turkey, and came from Australia, Benin,

Brazil, Colombia, England, Ethiopia, Germany, Jamaica, Kenya, Norway, Papua New Guinea, Philippines, South Africa, Singapore, Slovakia, Trinidad and Tobago, and the United States. The youngest was 23, the oldest (Poulter) in his early 60s. There was a balance of men and women in this multi-generational, intercultural gathering. They also benefitted from Decio de Carvalho (director of COMIBAM and also on the WGA Board), and Peter Tarantal (Associate International Director for OM) participating with them for the week.

Process

Unlike the previous consultations, most participants at this event did not know one another before they arrived. However, with intentional space given for creating relationships in community, new friendships developed across generations and cultures, representing a significant aspect of this consultation. When participants had the opportunity to tell of their personal testimony and challenges, they spoke with remarkable vulnerability.

In reality, creating this community began four months before the event. Participants were divided into four 'Watching Jesus' groups, and each group was assigned a different gospel. Over the four months, group members read through their assigned gospel, focussing on a specific theme each month. By the time they came together in April, they had already been 'watching Jesus' together and sharing insights. Each day of the conference presented a different interactive method to help make the communication of Scriptures more meaningful. This included creating a psalm and a drama based on their reflections; and choosing participants to role-play disciples from the Gospel to be interviewed on a mock TV news program. This whole process made the biblical reflection particularly rich and enjoyable.

Franklin presented missiological foundations of 'The Alliance Journey', 'Community in the Alliance', 'Friendship in God's Mission', and 'A Paradigm for Global-Glocal Missional Leadership'. For some leaders, this was their first exposure to these themes. For others, it may have been the second or third time to address the topics, but each exposure deepened their understanding and appreciation of the issues and better equipped them for sharing with others.

When asked, 'How has God shaped us as leaders?' participants responded by telling stories of significant people and experiences in their development. Throughout the week, each individual or couple also had the opportunity to tell the group their response to the question, 'What do you sense God saying to you about being a leader and leading in His mission?' then receiving prayer. Those brief events turned out to be some of the most meaningful of the whole week.

Perhaps the greatest impact—what many called a 'prophetic moment'—was the 'Third Table' gift exchange. Participants separated into two groups: those from the Global South and East, and those from the Global North and West. Their first task was to identify characteristic attitudes or behaviours of their regions related to such things as leadership and decision-making, friendship and community, time orientation, use of money, trust and accountability, etc. This required filtering what might be more related to family or local culture, or just personal preferences. They then grouped these 'regional' characteristics into clusters of similar items. The next and more challenging task was to ask themselves: 'Which of these clusters of characteristics would we like to offer as gifts to others in WGA to make us a strong and healthy community?' They set aside items that didn't meet this criterion. Each group read one of their gifts, offering it to the other group. The group receiving the gift discussed it among themselves, asking: 'Are we ready to accept this gift? Do we need more clarification? Or do we want to send it back and ask the other group to make changes and then offer it again?' The groups, after much discussion, used all three options, depending on the gift. Each gift that was accepted was posted on a chart labelled Third Table. When they ran out of time, the group unanimously voted to extend the time to finish the exercise.

Two examples of the gift exchange:

- The Second Table offered the First Table the gift of a friendly, approachable community, allowing for collaborative input, and valuing inclusive rather than exclusive rights. The Second Table was pleased and amazed when the First Table willingly accepted this gift, recognizing their need for guidance in achieving community within the global context.
- The First Table presented the Second Table with the gift of dealing with conflict with love, respect, and doing so in a timely manner, which meant not avoiding or ignoring conflict, and leaving room for multiple ways of dealing with it. The Second Table graciously accepted the gift.

Even more important than the 'final product' of exchanged gifts was the interaction and learning that took place: first at the separate tables, and then together, as the two tables sought to create something new from the best of what they respectively had to offer. It was obvious how much each table felt valued when the other table accepted their gift, with or without questions. Both tables appreciated the affirmation that they had gifts to offer at the Third Table. They all grew in understanding of when it was best to express or to withhold their perspective for the good of the group. And both appreciated being carefully listened to and respected by their counterparts.

A goal for this gathering was to model and practice the quality of community the leadership desired to see reproduced throughout WGA among older and younger leaders, as well as within organizations and at national and regional levels. Poulter summarized the consultation saying,

> I strongly believe that the future will not be built on individual leaders, but on the relationships that are built between older and younger leaders. I sense that in our day, God is putting the pieces in place to unlock the collective potential of younger and older mission leaders around the world. Considering the disruptions, crises, and complexity that increasingly characterize our world, we will need both younger and older leaders to discern together how God is at work and what he is saying and to engage together in wise and courageous initiatives in response.

Review of Principles of Community, 2016

Background

Four years had passed since WGA's Missiological Consultation on Community was held in Accrá, Ghana, and ensuring that the resulting foundational principles were kept alive through ongoing missiological reflection was deemed important. Because the Principles of Community were developed through a missiological consultative process, reviewing them through a similar process seemed appropriate. The primary goal of the consultation was to review the biblical-theological basis for the Principles of Community. Inevitably, this would involve discussion of Trinitarian theology. The intent, however, was not to establish a Trinitarian position for WGA but rather to discuss and assess diverse perspectives in the Alliance. Ten participants were invited to this unique review-focussed consultation held from 7 to 9 December in Misano, Italy.

The goals for the participants were to (1) develop a deeper understanding of the biblical basis for community; (2) explore the interconnectedness of the Principles of Community and the Bible Translation Programs Philosophy Statement; (3) review and assess the Principles of Community; and (4) provide input for a possible update of the Principles of Community.

Process

The discussion process for this consultation, developed by Stephen Coertze and Bryan Harmelink, was designed to address the four goals listed above.

1. *Biblical basis:* The discussion process included two sessions of reflection on John 14–17. However, a participant mentioned the book of Ephesians and its important contribution to understanding community and unity in the Body of Christ, so they decided to reflect on Paul's letter to the Ephesians in the second session. For the participants, both times of reflection contributed significantly to understanding the biblical basis for community.

2. *Interconnectedness of the Principles of Community and the Bible Translation Programs Philosophy Statement (BTPPS):* While noting significant community aspects of the BTPPS, participants centred their discussion on the importance of relationships in community as the foundation for Bible translation programs. The translation process involves more than just the task of translating a text. It is essential to avoid the unfortunate dichotomy of relationship vs. task and to find ways to keep the relational and technical aspects of translation together in the process.

3. *Assessment of the Principles of Community:* All ten participants affirmed the four key principles resulting from the Ghana 2012 Consultation on Community. The participants in the December 2016 consultation acknowledged, however, that there are differences of opinion regarding some of the explanatory statements in the 2012 document. In light of this, the unanimous affirmation of the four key principles was significant.

4. *Input for a possible update of the Principles of Community:* This consultation, conducted to review the outcomes of a previous consultation, was especially significant since those outcomes had become an established document. Upon reflection, rather than referring to the Principles of Community as a 'living document,' perhaps it was more appropriate to refer to it as a snapshot or record of the conversation as it took place in 2012. Likewise, the outcomes from Misano would present another snapshot of the 'living conversation' taking place in 2016.

Another point of discussion during this consultation was that the purpose was not to correct or edit the document from the Ghana Consultation but to review and assess it. The key principles were, in a way, an invitation to local or regional reflection, with multiple reflections on these principles increasing learning and appreciation of diverse perspectives on the community God has created us to participate in together.

These three days offered a valuable opportunity to learn about the process of writing future documents and to assess current documents. Respecting the participants of the 2012 Consultation and recognizing that their outcomes represent a specific point on the journey leads to seeing this consultation as describing a specific point on the journey as well.

Global Leadership in Community, 2017

Background

As the nature of global mission changes, it affects what is required of the leadership in the Bible translation movement. WGA had already become a complex, global body of organizations from a greater diversity of contexts than ever in their history. Looking to the future, the WGA leadership team saw an urgent necessity to develop leadership with a global mission mindset, exposed to a wide variety of influences, including polycentrism, globalization, community, friendship, and other missiological, theological, and sociological themes and issues. To further this process, the WGA leadership set aside five days to work on these issues together and formulate ideas and plans toward becoming a global mission leadership community. More than 40 Alliance leaders, including representatives of AOs, the WGA Area staff, the ALT, and the Alliance Board of Directors, were invited to this consultation about Global Mission Leadership Communities, held from 13 to 17 March at Wycliffe Germany's Holzhausen conference centre.

Process

As in previous consultations, there were extended periods of biblical reflection, presentations, and group discussions. The resulting summary of the discussion topic statements offered by participants is, perhaps, the best overview of the value of this consultation:

Mission of God: The focus is on the God of mission more than on the mission itself. He owns the results, and he fully embodies his mission, bringing restoration to creation. It is all focussed on his glory.

Know the Times: Global realities affecting WGA can build or block our work. We need to keep up with changing times. If not, we will become ineffective, obsolete, and redundant. Jesus invites us to notice, listen, see, know, and respond together intelligently in community. We must ask the Holy Spirit for wisdom to understand, discern, and read the signs of the times, keeping alert and not being misled.

Next Generation: We need wisdom to humbly listen, change, and guide in making a place for next generation leaders to flourish. They need to be involved; they need to understand God's mission.

Community: The secrets of the Kingdom are seen and heard (discerned), not by the wise and learned, but by those who have soft hearts toward God and his community. We are God's people living and serving God in a community that glorifies God. When we agree to work together despite our differences and disagreements—even to the point of making ourselves vulnerable—God is glorified. There is safety in community decision-making, but it takes time and patience with resourceful listening. Communal leadership from diverse voices leads to good WGA decisions and enables risk-taking in a 'safe' environment.

Friendship: This is an attribute of God, expressed in the Trinity. Friendship with God is the basis of our friendship with each other, essential in accomplishing the *missio Dei*. Building friendship takes time and needs to be nurtured to have deep roots.

Unity: This is revealed in the Trinity; it goes beyond tolerance; it reflects the deferring of honour seen within the Trinity. Relational leadership reflects the Triune God; we can explore relationships within the Trinity to discover good principles for cross-cultural leadership in community. Unity, not uniformity; inclusive, not exclusive; unity does not imply less space for the individual. Relationship is necessary for creating unity; unity without friendship is not sustainable.

Instructions for Leaders: Participants looked at four areas: community praxis, friendship praxis, leadership praxis, and a general category of other points to remember. The instructions they compiled to guide leaders included the following:

› Seek collective wisdom and gifts from the community.
› Be flexible but do not compromise values—contextual in practice for his glory.
› Develop a theology of relationships. Study the biblical principle of friendship and its impact on cultures.
› Create an atmosphere conducive to friendship leadership.
› Go beyond organizational goals to pursue mission and friendship.
› Seek to build unity and friendship as a lifestyle.
› Intentionality is important in bringing about change.
› Learn to live with ambiguity and messiness.
› Find creative ways to implement learning in your context.
› In times of change, leaders must adopt strategies that give voice to all stakeholders in decision making. Otherwise, trust may be at risk.
› Willingness to reflect and to be flexible so that we find a place for change.
› Be global in thinking and detailed in execution.
› Global mission leaders need a new mindset and a relational skillset.
› Everyone on the team is important; the difference is role, not value.

Regional Global Leadership in Community, 2017

Background

This consultation focussed on Leading in Our Changing Mission Context with Asia and the Pacific. It was a regional adaptation of the previously held Global Leadership Community consultation. The majority of the almost 40 participants at this consultation were from Asia and the Pacific, although there was representation from several other parts of the world. They met from 5 to 7 July in Bangkok, Thailand. The consultation's objectives were to explore together, from a missiological perspective, how our changing global mission context is influencing leadership within the church and organizations engaged in the mission of God, and to discover together what leadership in community means, looks like, and how it functions.

The rationale for the consultation is as follows: As leaders, we function in a complex global society of greater diversity of contexts influencing our local contexts than ever before in our history. As we look to the future, we see the necessity for a growing body of leaders with a global missional mindset who understand the implications of friendship, community, globalization, polycentrism, and other issues impacting leadership engaging in God's mission.

Process

The recognition of challenging and changing contexts played a major role in this consultation. Stephen Coertze presented on the mission of God and global missional leadership, emphasizing five points:

- The Triune God initiates, owns, and fully reflects his mission.
- The mission of the Triune God has the whole of creation in focus.
- The Triune God is the ultimate example of unity and friendship.
- The Triune God in mission is the initiator, originator, and source of authentic giving, receiving, and generosity.
- My leadership is dependent on God's purpose for his mission.

Table groups then discussed the topic and brought up issues and ideas such as cultural differences in leadership, the need for discernment, appreciation for history, servants as leaders, relationships with God and others, and the example of Christ.

The later sessions of the day centred on how statements on the mission of God should shape leaders within God's mission. Participants reflected on prayer, trust, having a kingdom perspective, complementary gifts, friendship, and the church. They summarized with thoughts concerning the importance of valuing and encouraging others and becoming a continually reforming, learning, discerning community of leaders by influence and example in humility.

Participants were further challenged the next day as they reflected on Ephesians 3:14–21, observing, as in Paul's life, the global realities shaping them in their contexts and influencing their ministries. Topics representing the global realities included globalization vs. nationalism, religious persecution, technology, economics, media influence, generational differences, moral and ethical relativity, and migration. On the third day, participants indicated the three global realities that had the most significant influence in shaping their church or mission context and how, as leaders, they could positively respond to the identified realities or use them beneficially in their contexts. On the final day, focussing on John 17:20–23 and several passages related to friendship, Kirk Franklin presented a biblical reflection on leading in community, leading to continued discussion on the topic. Reviewing this consultation revealed a paradigm shift toward leading in community.

Together in the Mission of God in Europe, 2017

Background

Two separate sets of conversations led WGA's Europe Area to plan this consultation. In the Area's strategy process, they identified Wycliffe's 'positioning in the church' as a significant area of weakness, further described as follows: (1) Wycliffe is not known enough in the church; (2) Wycliffe often sees the church only as a resource provider; and (3) Relationships occur primarily through member/staff, not between Wycliffe as an organization and the church. In particular, the second item had missiological bearing, as it addresses the identities assigned to Wycliffe and the church: seekers of resources and providers of resources. With the goal of achieving a more thorough understanding of the Alliance's position in the church, a potential 'strategic project' was drafted (see below for further detail on the project).

In another set of conversations, when the Alliance Organization (AO) directors met in April 2016 to talk informally about various issues of concern, they independently identified the relationship with the church as the most significant topic to address. 'Church Engagement' was identified as the strategic topic of greatest interest at the October 2016 directors' meeting, reconfirming the topic's relevance.

Process

The consultation 'Together in the Mission of God' met from 9 to 11 May at Wycliffe Germany's centre at Holzhausen. The time together included reflection on Scripture as relevant to the mission of God, history of the church and mission, and current trends that impact the mission of God today. Discussion topics included the mission of God, the essence of the church, the relationship of the church, local churches and mission agencies, and practical steps for continued reflection on the mission of God in the various contexts in which we live and work. The consultation facilitators led the participants in reflective processes and large and small group discussions to deepen understanding of how we can participate together in what God is doing. There were two participants from each European AO and four pastors or church leaders invited to relate their experience and perspectives. Developed over several months, the schedule and discussion process for this consultation included input from Wycliffe Slovakia Director Jaroslav Tomašovský and Europe Area Director Hannes Wiesmann. Bryan Harmelink and Tomašovský served as facilitators.

A highlight mentioned by several participants was the extended time given for reflection on and discussion of the book of Ephesians and its significant message of unity, community, and the gift of God's grace for the church. Participants also appreciated time for individual reflection and the two panel discussions—one with church leaders, the other with AO directors. These, along with the table group discussions, brought a diversity of thought and voices to the consultation process.

From the perspective of the facilitation team, the consultation presented a forum for deepening understanding of the mission of God in Scripture, greater awareness of the complexity of the relationships between the church and mission agencies, better understanding of issues related to the church and mission in the European context, and regional group discussion of ways to build and strengthen relationships with the church in their context. This consultation was also an example of regional discussions feeding into global discussions as the three global consultations on ecclesiology followed shortly after this European consultation.

First Ecclesiology Consultation, 2017

Background

Twenty WGA leaders, plus facilitators, gathered from 20 to 22 September in Johannesburg, South Africa, to explore the relationship between the church and WGA. Through a reflective and consultative process, participants would: (1) explore the relationship between the church and mission; (2) inform WGA regarding its relationship to the church in mission, how it speaks about itself in relation to the church, and how it relates to the church in terms of Bible translation practices; (3) clarify and strengthen the ecclesiology of WGA.

Process

Participants designed six critical questions involving issues concerning their relationship to the church:

- How does the Bible translation movement relate to the mission of God?
- To whom does the Bible and Bible translation belong?
- How is mission understood by the church, churches, mission agencies?
- How can we speak about the universal church/the local church/mission agencies without making separate categories and what does it mean for us to say WGA is part of the church?
- What would the benefits be if the church and WGA work in unity?
- What are the elements/building blocks of healthy relationships between the church and WGA?

Discussions were recorded and collated into a single 'raw notes' document and later combined into a single document with the notes of the remaining two ecclesiological consultations.

Through concentrated efforts, consultation participants traced varying ways each individual described and related to both WGA and the church, making progress toward mutual understanding. Though WGA documents and statements describing WGA's relationship to the church were helpful, the need to better understand and express that relationship remained. For example, an AO could be representing a church body, such as in Ethiopia or Indonesia, where large individual churches (directly pursuing Bible translation and training for translation work) were members of WGA. These organizations would speak differently about their relationship to the church than would a traditional AO whose primary focus was on 'mobilizing' people, prayer, and funds from churches for work going on elsewhere. The multiple relationships of WGA to the church were also recognized, including WGA as a member of WEA; church denominations as AOs; individuals in AOs as 'sent' by their local churches; local churches directly involved in Bible translation projects; individuals in AOs holding clerical roles in churches; etc. Also, referring to the 'global' or 'universal' church and the local expression of 'churches' added a layer of complexity.

The consultation reached a consensus regarding WGA as it relates to the mission of God, as part of the body of Christ, and as created to participate in God's mission. Participants recognized the WGA's relationship to the church as a mystical union, viewing this unique bond in terms of Kingdom friendship rather than the fulfilling of a task. WGA, in its diverse forms, needs to continue to find helpful ways of expressing this relationship with the church, working out the relationship in all local contexts. WGA does not perceive itself as either being the church or as fulfilling the role of a church. It acknowledges that God has created his church for his mission. In this way, WGA and the church can participate together fully in Bible translation.

Second Ecclesiology Consultation, 2017

Background

Twenty-one participants took part in this consultation held in Europe from 28 to 31 November in Holzhausen, Germany, with representatives from Africa, Asia, Europe, the Pacific, and the Americas. Each ecclesiology consultation, attended by participants from all regions of the world, was conducted in a different region of the world.

Process

Adding to those topics addressed in the previous consultation, participants at this consultation added the following questions related to the mission of God, the church, and WGA:

› What are some of the main barriers to effectively working with the church?
› How do we as WGA address such barriers?
› If the church is created for God's mission, what is the role of WGA in that mission?
› What does it mean to say WGA 'serves the church'?
› What are the implications of WGA functioning independently of, or independently with, or dependent on the church?

› What attitudes and characteristics should WGA embrace to relate well with the church?

In each situation, the participants addressed the implications of their discussions on WGA thinking, integration for local contexts, and applied biblical reflections. The participants appreciated this process, as it demonstrated that WGA was serious in its efforts to hear the voice of AOs on these topics and not merely channel them in a specific WGA agenda. This hallmark of most WGA missiological consultations was, as previously mentioned, often surprising to participants. They might arrive expecting a fully developed program and agenda and instead encounter an interactive experience where their input was heard and valued. Again, discussions were documented, then processed with discussion documents from the previous and the following consultations.

Whereas in the Johannesburg consultation participants worked hard to understand and select terminology to use for both WGA and the church, participants in the Holzhausen consultation did not require many nuanced distinctions on their understanding of either the church or WGA. Perhaps because at least half of these participants were currently fulfilling active pastoral roles in their local churches, the multiple relationships of WGA to the church were assumed and recognized. In this consultation, they expressed the relationship of WGA and the church in the context of WGA working independently of, interdependently with, and, or through dependency on the church. They acknowledged that all the dependencies mentioned were, to a certain extent, multifariously present in the relationship between the church and WGA. They perceived that to disregard or negate the reality of any of these dependencies emphasized a dichotomy, as well as the often-present tension between the church and mission agencies in functioning collectively as expressions of God's mission.

The concept of 'multi-dependency' came into focus in further discussions. The integral relationship between the church and WGA was accepted, and of less concern was their mutual relationship within the Body of Christ. Attitudes were of greater concern, including how WGA portrayed these attitudes when relating to various expressions of the church. Acknowledging the church as the instrument created for God's mission, the onus is on WGA to recognize this, being mindful of expressing expectations of the church to participate in Bible translation. In addition, with awareness of the church's agenda, it would be important to find ways to link Bible translation to the church, not as an external resource, but from a relationship position within the church.

Third Ecclesiology Consultation, 2018

Process

This third and final ecclesiological consultation was held from 13 to 15 March in Bangkok, Thailand, and followed the same discussion topics and times of biblical reflection. The approximately 20 participants from around the world found a balance between the visionary and the practical as they centred on the basics of what church is, discerning the times, and WGA and the mission of God. They recognized the importance of 'flexibility, fluidity, and hybridity'. They extensively discussed the role of church leadership in WGA and the importance of connecting rather than having conflicting or competing agendas. An emphasis on humility led to discussing the participants' willingness to deconstruct the identity of WGA as it relates to the role of the church. They expressed their willingness not only to relinquish 'control' to the church but to disband altogether if the day came that the church willingly took leadership of the Bible translation movement. Though discussion pointed to the greater likelihood of working in unity, the willingness to accept a reduced role was a significant step.

A few quotes from participants offer highlights:

› One question: how do we grow together with the church in a shared understanding of God's mission? A great challenge!
› The diversity and complexity of the church and WGA are ASTOUNDING. But this does NOT mean we cannot find answers.
› Examining our relationships with churches or Christians is pretty important to help us better serve Bible translation and churches and to move forward!
› When Vision 2025 was being debated and adopted in 1999, we prayed that the church worldwide would own the Bible translation movement. Today, we recognize expressions of this occurring in UK, PNG, Brazil, Indonesia, China, Japan, Singapore, etc. PTL!
› We are unified around our vision and core values and then encouraged to apply these in a multifaceted manner within our contexts and spheres of influence.
› The church, expressed in local church congregation, must be in the driving seat of Bible translation, even if it needs assistance in the practicalities.

Participants in the three consultations faced the challenge of constructing discussion frameworks with some common understandings to describe WGA's relationship with the church. Following the three missiological consultations on ecclesiology, WGA leadership team members Stephen Coertze, Dave Crough, and Kirk Franklin compiled statements which became part of the continuing conversation and reflection on the topic. The necessity of finding multiple ways of understanding WGA's relationship with the church was apparent. This is part of what WGA does together, an ongoing journey of exploration and discovery.

Third Space Forum, 2018

Background

As the number of nations, organizations, and communities involved in the Bible translation movement grew, so did the evident need for change. It was insupportable for organizations and individuals to follow historical patterns of relationships and dialogue. Working in partnership—or not (otherwise referred to as working independently)—was traditionally considered a binary choice. Though some might claim to be in partnership, it might be unequal, with one party possessing more power and/or funds.

Such binary choices often impacted funding in God's mission. Dependence on an influx of large sums of money from affluent Western donors and the power associated with that in international mission partnerships describes one possibility. In contrast, those receiving the resources might feel controlled or even degraded because of a perceived loss of ownership, control, and decision-making, and the lack of recognition of their contributions. A binary choice of accepting funding in this way or not at all was considered too limiting. Instead, there should be a middle or third way.

Process

A Third Space was required where interdependent cooperation of giving and receiving across the global Bible translation movement is encouraged. In this way, all parties demonstrate respect and dignity through authentic partnerships based on genuine friendships in mission. A Third Space helps frame a missiological understanding of friendship, which deepens the value of partnering in mission. Confronting the realities of what interdependent partnerships called for reveals partnerships based on trust and friendship, focussed on what each one brings to the relationship, and emphasizing the kingdom of God rather than completing a task. True cross-cultural friendship calls for a long-term commitment among individuals and to places and includes the need to understand, respect, learn from, and live among another culture or religion.

Creating Third Spaces in Africa surfaced during a discussion facilitated by Franklin at WGA's Africa Leaders Meeting held in Ruiru, Kenya, in 2017. An outcome of the discussion was African leaders requesting a Third Space time with leaders of Wycliffe US. Therefore, from 21 to 23 April 2018 in Johannesburg, South Africa, WGA leaders Todd Poulter, Dave Brooks, and Mũndara Mũturi led and facilitated this discussion. The participants were African directors and board representatives from 16 AOs and nine Wycliffe US leaders. Africa Area staff also participated. Franklin, Stephen Coertze, Hannes Wiesmann, and Nydia Garcia-Schmidt represented the ALT. The consultation had the aim to create a Third Space with the African AOs and Wycliffe US with these factors in mind:

› First Space: Where African AOs are now.
› Second Space: Where Western AO resourcing partners are now.
› Third Space: Where we work together in God-honouring ways, for his glory, and for his kingdom.

Graphic 1: Third Spaces

This Third Space Forum brought together 24 leaders from African AOs and Wycliffe US to dialogue about the partnership dynamics of sending and receiving funds. As they participated in this consultation, they were not only discussing Third Spaces but experiencing one. Seeking to explore better ways to partner, African leaders invited Wycliffe US. Framing this conversation as a Third Space Forum challenged everyone to leave their respective spaces where they operated comfortably, to enter a neutral, less comfortable place for all, where no one knew what would happen, but which allows for common exploration.

Given the risky nature of such an endeavour, the willingness to show up was commendable—and the wholehearted engagement witnessed was remarkable. The positive change of atmosphere that occurred over the three days was palpable, and many expressed a desire to continue relating with each other in such Third Spaces.

This process represented a commitment to mutual respect, mutual learning, mutual influence, and mutual benefit. The beauty of the whole exercise reflected an honest quest for a deep win-win result. Franklin wrote,

We actually saw this emerging in Johannesburg as the two delegations expressed a vision for how they would like the partnership between them to look and then answered the question of how living up to these visions would benefit the partnership. The collection of potential benefits was exceptionally rich, and I've never participated in such an exuberantly joyful reporting session as when these were shared with the whole group.

People Serving in God's Mission, 2018

Background

From 21 to 24 August, 26 participants representing 22 AOs took part in this consultation. Most were either AO directors or personnel or human resources directors in their organizations. An affinity group discussion on 'Sending and Receiving People Well' at the 2016 Wycliffe Global Gathering resulted in those participants expressing a desire for a missiological consultation on a broader understanding of people in God's mission, which led to this consultation in Singapore. The topic, discussed previously in several forums and prioritized by WGA's leadership for further discussion, relates to the WGA's 'Recruiting and/or Sending People' Participation Stream. Therefore, it would be helpful for AOs to develop a deeper understanding of current issues around this topic, to assist personnel (new and experienced) in serving more effectively in their assigned roles

Purposes and Expected Outcomes

Participants, through the reflective and consultative process, could:

› clarify and strengthen their understanding of the kind of people God has always desired for His purposes in mission.
› explore the important realities impacting personnel serving in current and future Bible translation movement contexts.
› address challenges faced in the placement of personnel in other agencies—local and abroad—including the expectations and capacity of all agencies involved in such placement processes.
› discover necessary insights to strengthen the potential of organizations participating in the 'Recruiting and/or Sending People' Participation Stream. One practical outcome of this will be the drafting of guiding principles about People Serving in God's Mission.

- participate in up to two workshops relevant to current topics in the area of personnel-related work.

The four main topics were a biblical understanding of calling and sending, realities that impact serving in mission, spirituality in mission, and emerging models for people serving in mission. Stories were shared, key issues listed and discussed, Scripture explored, and a Statement on People Serving in Mission (see box) was developed as a guide for the ongoing journey.

EXCERPTS FROM STATEMENT ON PEOPLE SERVING IN MISSION

Important values that guide Alliance Organizations regarding people serving in mission:

- *We value God as the owner of his mission.* We are on mission because God has called us to join him in his mission. Jesus Christ has set the example of what it means to be sent by God. By following Christ's example, Christians can serve in his mission, wherever their location or whatever their context.
- *We value the Church's role in God's mission.* The Church is the body of Christ and Christ is head of the Church. The global Church carries out God's mission in a contextualized manner through its local expressions. Within these local expressions of the Church, God has uniquely gifted people to serve in Bible translation movements as part of his mission.
- *We value each person serving in God's mission.* On a global level, we value our fellow believers in Christ and their unique participation in God's mission. In our Alliance contexts, we equally value each person who participates in Bible translation movements in and through the organizations that are part of the Alliance, and through our partners.
- *We value spiritual well-being.* The spiritual well-being of people serving in God's mission is the foundation of their fruitfulness. The focus of this value is not on the task, but on the desired outcome of such service: transformed lives. In order to see transformed individuals and communities, the person serving in mission should be transformed to the likeness of Christ....

Short descriptions of ways of demonstrating values regarding people serving in God's mission:

- Communicating the importance of Bible translation as part of discernment....
- The assessment of people....
- Life in community and ensuring an environment of care....

Task Force on Funding, 2019

Background

At the consultation for WMOs with Vote held in Kusadasi, Turkey, in April 2015 (see chapter 6), these organizations discussed how WGA was funded based on a 0.35% contribution. After debating various other models for funding WGA's operating budget, without reaching a decision, they agreed to keep the 0.35% contribution and to ensure that all future AOs fulfilled this requirement. Now, three years later, entering a period of review and re-signing of the Covenants/Statements of Commitment, anticipating and preparing for likely questions and concerns that would arise in the review process took precedence. Some leaders of AOs had expressed a desire to discuss funding of WGA before the Covenants/Statements of Commitment re-negotiation and signing.

Purpose

In response, this consultation, gathering more than 30 leaders representing a wide range of AOs, the WGA Board, and the ALT, convened for a one-time Task Force. It met in Singapore from 25 to 26 February. In preparation for the consultation, participants read the Foundational Statements of WGA, the WGA Principles for Funding, the Benefits of Belonging to WGA, including background history, the WGA Income Overview, and a document that included the current funding model and other possible funding models.

The Task Force on Funding was designed to explore significant factors influencing and affecting the funding of WGA, including reviewing, in community, WGA's Foundational Statements (Core Statements). The advantageous timing of this Task Force preceded a review of the Covenant/Statement of Commitment, underway later in 2019, which included not only funding of WGA but also discussion of its future financial sustainability.

Topics for the Task Force included the following:

- Explore and propose models of financial sustainability for WGA. Such models must broadly represent AOs and their sources of funding.
- Consider proposals of alternative funding models or modifications to current models that aim for broad participation of all AOs in funding WGA.
- Observe how generosity is demonstrated within WGA, especially recognizing many forms of generosity are not quantifiable and therefore possibly regarded as of less value.
- Reflect on how WGA's Principles for Funding guide the discussion about the funding of WGA, including the ALT.
- Examine revised wording of the next version of the Covenant/Statement of Commitment that reflects any proposed changes
- Consider how to frame a final report soon after the Task Force's face-to-face meeting to be presented by the executive director to the WGA Board for discussion and approval at their April 2019 board meeting.
- Recognize that, contrary to most international or global mission agencies, and to ensure that WGA does not directly raise funds from the same donors that fund AOs, the executive director's responsibilities do not include fundraising.

There were also broader financial considerations, including the structure of the ALT (virtual, with little support staff and low overhead, but the necessity for a travel budget while also having a concern for ecological implications) and the inability of the current funding model to allow for growth of the ALT or Area staff. Additionally, the primary funders of WGA's budget were the larger AOs, yet often the organizations that most valued and might most require help from WGA were either smaller or new to WGA. This represented the growing edge of WGA in terms of new organizations, but not funding.

Process

Participants spent time in biblical reflection, giving attention to the story of God's provision for Elijah and the widow in 1 Kings 17:7–16. On the second day, they read and reflected on 2 Corinthians 8:1–15, considered what generosity looked like in their culture, country, or community, and sought to draw practical principles from the passage that would help impart 'the grace of giving' within WGA. Looking at the vision and future of WGA, they discussed and identified the focal point that would shape the future of WGA and how it could best respond to and invest in that focal point.

Each WGA Area held a conversation on the strengths and shortcomings of the current funding model. Seeing the differences and similarities among the Area responses shed new light on the issues and helped point out any facets that might be unclear to any of the leaders. Participants then broke into groups to discuss generosity in WGA. They looked at their contexts, identifying how their constituency or organization generously provided for the ministry of Bible translation. They listed examples of contributions not reflected in their financial systems and estimated and assigned monetary values to those contributions, which proved to be an effective exercise in understanding the nature of quantifiable and non-quantifiable resources. Contributions mentioned included relationships, encouragement, time, and prayer, as well as training, facilitation, and actual finances.

During the consultation, participants discussed why they valued WGA and presented their thoughts on funding models. Their ideas for models varied greatly, yet they strongly agreed about WGA's value and understood that funding represented one way for organizations to support what WGA offered. Participants had come to appreciate the missiological consultations, the ability to work in community, resolve disputes, and achieve together what couldn't have been done on their own. During the concluding open floor session, organizational leaders interacted with Executive Director Kirk Franklin and voiced their concerns, raised issues, and expressed preferences.

This consultation brought together key WGA leaders and board members for a unique time of reflecting on WGA values, budget, and strategies as an integrated whole. It was also an example of how WGA sought to hear a wide variety of voices and input and how they benefitted from taking them into account. Conversations from this consultation continued to have an impact on funding conversations. While the existing funding model would be retained for a while, the discussion resurfaced as the world and Wycliffe continued to grow and change and as the AOs continued their journey together.

Africa-Europe Funding, 2019

Background

Traditionally, in church and mission history, when it came to funds, Europe was the giver and Africa the receiver. But times have changed. The wealth of the West was vulnerable—it could collapse overnight. And even if that didn't happen, funding was more complex and not as readily available. More importantly, the African church had grown both in size and capacity for ministry. Many African AOs were rethinking their approach to Bible translation with less dependence on the West. They realized they did not always have to fund Bible translation through purely monetary means—there were other ways. A wide range of other issues had an ongoing impact on the relationship between European and African AOs. As Africa was becoming more self-sufficient, European AOs that had long supported Africa with both funds and personnel were questioning their future support relationship. Also, the ongoing impact related to the history of much of Africa's earlier colonization by various countries remained. This complex and varied history continued to shape and influence nations, organizations, people, and relationships.

Purpose and Expectations

This consultation was subtitled, 'A collective exploration of our understanding and application of the WGA Funding Principles.' The primary goal for this consultation was for leaders from AOs in Africa and Europe to meet each other in a new way, specifically related to, but not only about, funding. Not all the funding history among the organizations was negative, but this was a time to discuss misconceptions, to apply missiological thinking and WGA principles, to look at past and current contexts, and to discuss what had changed and what needed to change. Leaders of African and European AOs met from 24 to 27 March in Cyprus. Logistically and symbolically, Cyprus was the ideal location for this meeting between WGA's Europe and Africa Areas, with both coastlines almost within view as the two Areas reviewed their historical contexts, immersed themselves in biblical reflection and dialogue, looking for ways to meet and move forward together.

Participants met for the following purposes:

› Discovering and deepening our understanding of WGA's Principles of Funding and how to apply these principles in our funding practices.
› Understanding the complexities in which the other organizations in the two areas function concerning funding.
› Creating an environment for healthy and mutually beneficial relationships between the AOs in the two areas.
› Producing mutually accepted guidelines for continued future working relationships.
› Addressing the question of, 'what did we hear that we as an Area should address to improve our relationship with the other Area?'

Participants were asked what they expected from the consultation and hoped for the future. With both spiritual and pragmatic goals in focus, participants desired to see what God was doing and how they could be a part of it. They hoped to sharpen each other's calling. They wanted change in the patronage attitude between the funder and the funded and to gain a better understanding of the funding challenges between Europe and Africa, as well as the challenges AOs in Europe usually face in fundraising and funding. They wanted to share their experiences with the churches involved in Bible translation. They wanted to participate in and influence the conversations which sought to discover ways of funding partnerships appropriate to what might be an emerging mission paradigm. Together they sought a healthy, God-honouring way forward in how to relate and write (and fund), and new synergy, new perspectives, and new ways of thinking and working.

To inform future development, participants hoped to establish an overview of who was currently partnering with whom. They wanted to use clear principles to explore new funding practices for both continents. They wanted to be inspired to direct their organization's partnerships better and to discuss what partnership means—not only in respect to money (though that was a significant element to address). As one leader put it, 'Go back to the drawing board in how we approach our relationships, rather than trying to find temporary solutions for a funding model that poses problems in our relationships.' They wanted clarity on how Africa and Europe could work well together.

There was a strong desire to see situations from each other's perspective and to learn about each other's organizations, challenges, processes, new ideas, initiatives, and hopes. Many of their goals and desires were relational. They wanted to explore, build, and deepen friendships and enable honest feedback in culturally appropriate ways. For many, it was just the beginning of making friends with leaders from the other Area. They desired unity and understanding and wanted to get beyond a simplistic notion of funder versus those receiving funds. As participants shared and expanded on these goals and desires, they began to know and understand each other in new ways. The process of sharing also confirmed that they came to the consultation with the same heart and purpose.

Through Scripture and discussion, participants reflected on how God provides for his mission, then addressed the following question: As we continue working toward healthy and mutually beneficial relationships in funding, what guidelines would be helpful to direct our relationships? The following is a sampling of their statements and proposed guidelines (see box).

EXCERPTS OF STATEMENTS AND GUIDELINES

- We recognize that the old worldview of donors and recipients is no longer appropriate. We restate that we are together as partners raising funds for and carrying out Bible translation and associated activities.

- We determine to approach each new proposal with a partnership lens. We want to work to understand our respective contexts and to express our context, strategy, hopes, and concerns as honestly as we can. We agree to learn from one another. We agree to work together to move the mission of God in Bible translation forward to the best of our ability, stewarding God's gifts and offering them humbly to each other.
- Our organizations desire and intend to clarify our contributions, to make them with generosity, humility, and in a spirit of open-handedness.
- We want to understand and clarify the expectations we have of one another. We want to continue to deepen the extent to which we know one another through the process—donor, funding, field, recipient. We recognize that this will mean that we are not able to focus our partnership on some organizations—choices will need to be made. However, we also commit to intentionally relating to people as people, and not just staff members.
- We understand that it requires effort, cost, and time to meet face-to-face. We agree to make that effort, as far as we reasonably can, and to express our constraints and hindrances with openness if we are, for some reason, struggling with that.
- We will acknowledge communication and respond to all communications as a matter of respect and courtesy while also asking for and extending grace to each other in the pressures of our work.
- With our funding partners, we will move toward making specific commitments regarding visiting, Skyping, and responses to reports. Through discussion, we will come to that agreement together.
- We commit to pursuing mutual discovery of and with our colleagues, thus enabling us to let go of our assumptions and work together as peers.

Following additional presentations, another topic of discussion was how God enables us to share our resources. Facilitator Stephen Coertze offered participants the following question for discussion. What did we hear that we as an Area should address to improve our relationship with the other Area? Those from Africa Area responded with: sharing responsibility; communicating transparently; offering friendship before sharing needs; clarifying expectations; delivering timely reports; exercising good stewardship; raising local resources; contributing to local projects; being intentional in better understanding the Europe Area context. Europe responded as follows: commit to mutual discovery of our African colleagues, which will enable us to let go of our assumptions, apologize for them, and to work together as peers, with no hierarchy; recognize that we need to listen; we need to talk together; remember that we are colleagues—esteeming one another—we are together.

Young Leaders Initiatives, 2019

Rationale

Most AOs recognize the importance of inclusion of the younger generations. But as global changes have accelerated, so have generational changes, resulting in greater generational distinctions, for example, the striking changes between Millennials and Generation Z. Because Millennials are already involved in leadership in WGA, it is essential to take their contributions seriously.

Considering the unique perspectives a younger generation of leaders can bring to WGA, a consultation for young leaders to speak freely into the life and future of WGA was suggested and convened. It was held in Singapore from 31 July to 2 August. The consultation was limited to 12 participants from around the world. The small size of the consultation would help ensure time and space for in-depth dialogue. Kirk Franklin and Stephen Coertze acted as advisors to the event. Participants worked in three groups of four, with a facilitator for each group.

Purposes and Desired Outcomes

The stated purposes and desired outcomes for this consultation included: participants, together, seeking to discern the voice of the Lord to understand the vision for Bible translation; participants discussing how they perceive the future of WGA; participants considering what WGA will need to ensure that younger generations feel welcome and able to express themselves authentically and develop to their full potential.

Insights from this consultation would flow into discussions among the ALT, potentially affecting areas of strategy, communication, personnel, leadership development, etc. In the first discussion session, participants expressed their thoughts resulting from pre-consultation reading materials and any other sources that they deemed beneficial to the conversation. They mentioned the importance of work and life balance, a desire for mentoring and training, advantages and disadvantages of being digital natives (including easy access to information, but impatience when things don't come so easily), innovation, and the importance of collaboration and relationships.

The next discussion examined what differentiates younger leaders. Participants reflected on and responded to the following scenario and questions: Your organization's board seeks to understand younger leaders. How would you describe to the board the distinct characteristics of younger leaders? How would you express why younger leaders are crucial to your organization? Participants used descriptions like flexible, risk-takers, relational, influencers rather than controllers, teachable, willing to take input, energetic, impatient, open to change (personal and otherwise), holistic. Participants described an organization's need for younger leaders by observing that they have energy, they have fresh ideas for continuing an organization's vision and sustainability, they offer openness to global connection and communication, and their presence makes multiple generations a reality, all of which are vital for a healthy leadership team.

When asked, 'What would you as a young leader say to your board or leaders of your organization?' they responded, 'Honour us for our role, not our age; treasure us for our strengths and don't focus on our weaknesses only; trust young leaders and give them responsibility—God is in control! Leave it up to him! We as young leaders want a culture of honour, respect, and humility on both ends; we don't want to take your place, but work and learn with you. We need orientation and advice; we don't want to be seen or felt as a threat to you; we long for intentional leadership development.'

Participants were asked to consider, discuss, then answer the question: Is the organization in which you serve welcoming to younger leaders? Together, they shared their experiences, then presented and explained their answers. Responses varied greatly depending on their contexts. Some presented examples of younger leaders given opportunities in their organizations which included internships and intentional mentoring. Some spoke of flat structures where such opportunities were available to all, while others served in more hierarchical structures. Some had experienced high trust, and others, very little. Some felt the reality of inclusion did not match what they heard from leaders. Also, culture affected the way some organizations related across generations.

When asked what changes they would recommend, participants offered many suggestions, including:

- Listen, give space.
- Give young leaders space to develop new ways, to try things out, with safety to fail.
- Offer guidelines but let them function as they choose and select their mentors.
- In humbleness, believe young leaders are seeking the Lord's will just as you are.
- Don't feel threatened by younger leaders—they long to make an impact.
- Move from a narrower age perspective to an all-generation perspective.
- Invite young leaders to share in the community mindset and the big decisions—allow them to bring change and have an impact.

During the next two days, participants heard and interacted with presentations on the structure and ethos of WGA, introducing them to the Alliance context of their organizations. Results from this presentation and the discussions of the first day prepared participants for further discussions on the third day, prompted by the following questions:

› What is your vision for the future of the Bible translation movement?
› How would such an envisioned Bible translation movement capture the imagination of younger leaders?
› What should WGA (including its AOs) put in place to ensure that younger leaders could realize your vision for the Bible translation movement?

Invited to share their vision for the Bible translation movement, participants observed and experienced their value and their part in creating the future. One participant expressed gratitude in this way:

> I want to use this opportunity to appreciate all of you for trusting us and giving us the opportunity to meet with our friends from other countries... to reflect, dream together, and share our experiences. It was so enriching for me, and my organization will benefit from this consultation.

Exploring Generosity as a Way of Life, 2019

Background

The topic of generosity moved increasingly to the forefront as WGA grew in understanding God's mission, community, and friendship. This focus had already been acknowledged and expressed by many AOs that sacrificially helped one another and contributed to others in need. Along with funding, the expressed generosity included sharing staff, resources, and prayer. But there was also recognition that both organizations and churches could benefit from a greater understanding of what it meant to live a generous life. As the issue of generosity was a priority in the Americas, the suggestion arose for Wycliffe Americas Area to sponsor this global consultation, with most of the participants coming from the Americas, but with representation from the other Areas. It included 25 leaders from the Americas, one each from Europe, Africa, and Asia, five special interest and invited guest participants, plus staff and facilitators. This missiological consultation, with the heading 'Generosity that springs from the heart of God' took place from 2 to 4 July in Quito, Ecuador. Held in Spanish with translation for Portuguese and English speakers, it was facilitated by Stephen Coertze, with David Cardenas and Silvia Zelaya of the WGA Americas Area.

Rationale

As participants living and serving together in God's mission, generosity should be a natural response for WGA, demonstrating the habitual behaviour of friends in community in God's mission. As servants of our Lord, generosity encompasses all of who we are and includes time, service, compassion, and grace. It encompasses our whole being, not only our finances. Generosity envisions all of God's church as both givers and receivers. Generosity is not only a response from one person to another but also an expression of worship to God. An expression of our limitations before God, it also acknowledges that God provides all the resources his children require to serve one another, as well as those who need his redemption and transformation. Considering this as well as WGA's high value of the concept of generosity, it would be a worthy endeavour to explore together our understanding of generosity and how to develop a habitual behaviour of generosity that can lead to both the overall health of WGA and its impact on those it serves.

Through a reflective and consultative process, participants accomplished the following:

› Explored, from a biblical perspective, how generosity was understood and expressed by both the people of Israel in the Old Testament and the church in the New Testament.
› Had the opportunity to grow in understanding of what 'God is a generous God' means.
› Learned more about generosity as an expression of gratitude toward God and how generosity and stewardship go hand in hand.
› Discussed the importance of good stewardship and transparency.
› Had the opportunity to respond to these biblical discoveries, evaluate their own practices, and together, learn to cultivate a lifestyle of generosity, resulting in gratitude toward God, service toward others, and a healthy stewardship of receiving and sharing resources.

This consultation would also lead to developing resources for cultivating generosity in their own lives, in their organizations, and for sharing the concept of generosity with others.

Transformation as an Expression of the Mission of God, 2019

Rationale

From the time WGA embarked on its first missiological reflective consultation in 2006, a growing understanding of the concept of the mission of God increasingly influenced much of WGA's development. This understanding included an acknowledgement that, because of our human finiteness, and though we witness God's mission daily, it entails more than can be comprehended, can only be understood in part, yet encompasses numerous dimensions to be explored.

Scripture provides glimpses into various dimensions of God's mission. One of the dimensions is transformation. The foundational statements of WGA strongly reflect the importance of transformation. One way of viewing transformation is to see it as a goal of God's mission. True transformation in the context of God's mission entails the complete restoration of the individual's relationship with God, and in the broader context of God's restoration of all things, is expressed as God's *shalom*.

This consultation was a WGA and Seed Company sponsored event held at the headquarters of Seed Company, one of the US AOs, in Arlington, Texas, from 17 to 19 September. A missiological reflective discussion on 'Transformation as an Expression of the Mission of God' was considered a help in further unpacking participants' understanding of God's mission. Because a discussion on transformation itself can be very broad, the concept of how transformation directly intersects with the ministry of Bible translation became the priority. There were 18 participants, plus facilitators. Participants included several Seed Company leaders, ALT members, and two representatives from AOs in each Wycliffe Area. Bryan Harmelink and Stephen Coertze were the facilitators.

These represent the four main areas of focus for the consultation:

› *God effects transformation:* How do we think God perceives transformation? What does it mean to say that 'God is the biggest end-user of translation'? One example is God revealing himself and making himself known.
› *God's message of transformation:* What is the full message of the gospel? What is the whole council of God that leads to transformation? How does this affect which passages of Scripture we choose to translate? The Old Testament and the New Testament are both important.
› *God's message proclaimed:* What is the best way to present the gospel? What is the most appropriate way to make Scripture translation available, e.g., oral or

textual? How does the Bible translation process align with the proclamation of the gospel?

› *Transformation as the goal of God's mission fulfilled:* Together, the participants sought a biblical understanding of transformation originating from and expressed through the triune God; a vision for what transformed communities impacted by Bible translation will look like; and to recognize how understanding and vision impact our Bible translation practices.

Learnings from the consultation would feed into further discussion within the ALT and particularly among those AOs that participated in the Bible Translation and Training Streams (see chapter 6).

Makings of a Missiological Consultation

Through these 28 missiological consultations explored in this chapter, we gain the perspective of the importance of this consultative process in creating milestones, motivators, and fuel for the Alliance journey. There is value in recognizing what it takes to create and carry out a consultation, as well as appreciating the content and ongoing benefits resulting from the consultations. Without exploring in detail, here are some key factors.

Philosophy

› Create a community environment through formal and informal times of interaction that facilitate in-depth, heart-level communication, and make space for the quietest individuals to fully participate.
› Use reflective and missiological processes that enable significant interaction and engagement of all participants.
› Match the pace and content of the event to the participants' capacity to take in information and reflect on it. Use adult learning approaches.
› Ensure that everything in the program is aligned with and supports the consultation purposes.

Implications for the Program

› Don't fill every available minute, nor share every possible resource.
› Seek a balance between introducing new content and giving participants the time to interact with it and make it their own.
› Ensure the maximum participant mix at each table group.

- Use daily biblical reflection times to encourage individual and collective discovery (vs. 'preaching').

Implications for Facilitation

- Equipment and supplies (microphones, projector, paper, markers, sticky notes, etc.), furniture, and the room layout must all be considered.
- Translators may be required to translate presentations and other material. (Most, but not all, WGA consultations used English as the primary language, and many were conducted only in English because those participating were fluent in English. When necessary, every effort was made to accommodate the need for translation to ensure an inclusive environment.)
- Identify a logistics coordinator to assist with all logistic arrangements regarding the conference facilities and liaise with the conference staff.
- Identify table group facilitators and provide basic orientation before the consultation.
- Identify a note-taker for the consultation and one for each table group.
- Adapt the composition of discussion groups (table groups) to the issue in focus (e.g., regional or cross-regional groups).
- Table groups don't usually report everything to the whole group, but facilitators should collect and record significant issues, including those not included in the report to the whole group.

In addition to this short list of process-related tasks and reminders, there were, of course, much more detailed lists specific to each consultation. Other factors included all logistics and hospitality necessities. WGA was privileged to have efficient, qualified facilitators and logistics coordinators who managed these tasks and the consultations. The organizations and the staff at the sites hosting the consultations went to great lengths to serve well, and all benefitted from experiencing various venues, cultures, and contexts.

Another important element was the choice of materials recommended for pre-consultation reading. Often for the WGA consultations, this included WGA documents, missiological articles and texts, and data for WGA leaders engaged in missiological study programs.

Journey Thoughts

Impossible to fully recount, the value, richness, and depth of consultation conversations and discoveries consisted not only in the content. The contexts in which the consultations were held, the polyphonic contributions of so many pivotal voices, and the prayers and processes of creating community flourished long after participants packed their bags and headed home. Consultation milestones, documents, memories, and motivation mark the pathway of WGA. As has been said, it is a new journey. We have never been this way before. And in the words of an African proverb, 'we make our path by walking on it.' Looking over our shoulders, we see the footprints left by the consultations, enabling us to track this journey and face the future with both boldness and humility as we remember how good God has been to bring us thus far.

Chapter 11
Mapping: A Case Study of the Americas Area Journey

By Susan Van Wynen

Introduction

Wycliffe founder Cameron Townsend began work in Guatemala. The first Wycliffe organization originated in the United States, with the first members assigned to Mexico. Wycliffe's beginnings and rich history in the Americas might generate expectations of a solid institutional structure. Yet despite its heritage and history, the Bible translation effort in the Americas grew more as a movement than an institution as its leaders sought to determine the way forward under God's direction.

In 2017, the Wycliffe Global Alliance Americas Area leadership undertook a review process to honour their past, take stock of the present, and discern the best next steps into the future. In keeping with the desire to journey together with God and the ongoing efforts to view strategy and planning through a missiological lens, the Americas Area leadership conducted a two-day conversational consultation to examine their history and explore how to apply the journey concept as a historical strategy review process. The information and ideas in this chapter's case study were developed from that two-day conversation and are also the outgrowth of several decades of experience—close to a century when the years of experience of all the leaders who participated are combined. The purposes of the conversation included identifying, reflecting on, documenting, and sharing the process, progress, and decisions of the Americas Area Movement journey for the further learning of the Americas Area and informing and inspiring others on their journey. The consultation, titled 'Mapping the Americas Area Journey (thus far)' by Wycliffe Americas Area Director Nydia Garcia-Schmidt, took place from 1 to 2 September 2017, in Mexico City.

This case study, drawn from the report created on this consultation, includes much of the original report's content, plus additional notes which provide continuity and context and highlight ideas that are particularly helpful to understanding the Americas Area and its part in Alliance history.

Participants and Process

Americas Area leaders who participated in the conversation included:

- Nydia Garcia-Schmidt, Director for Wycliffe Global Alliance, Americas Area.
- Doug Baughman, Associate Director for Wycliffe Global Alliance, Americas Area.
- David Cardenas, Facilitator for Wycliffe Americas Area and President of COMIBAM.
- José de Dios, previous Director for Wycliffe Global Alliance Americas Area (2007–2013).
- David Brooks, Alliance Consultant, past Director for Wycliffe International and SIL Americas Areas, (2002–2006, this role predates the Alliance and represents the previous co-joined organizational structure).

Susan Van Wynen, Alliance Strategy Consultant, planned for the two-day consultation, co-led with Nydia Garcia-Schmidt, and wrote the original report for the Area from the more than forty-six pages of meeting notes taken by Gwen Davies, Wycliffe Global Alliance Communication Editor.

The conversation was shaped around these big-picture questions:

- *How will the past and present inform the ongoing Americas Area journey and future?*
- *What do you want others to know about the Americas Area journey?*
- *What will help others on their journey?*

In their discussions, to help the participants organize their thoughts, the conversation explored these aspects of the journey: Context; Identity, Vision, Values; People; Resources; Principles; Mindset; Decisions; Behaviours; Milestones; Lessons Learned; and Discernment/Goals.

Scope

For generations, God has been active in the Americas through his translated Word and the lives of his people. Consultation participants agreed that though they respect and honour this early translation history, there wasn't space or time to recount every event or story. They looked only as far back as the 1980s to explore and learn from this specific segment of the Americas Area journey. Tracing the journey that led Wycliffe Americas Area from a largely traditional missions model to becoming a Bible translation movement involved more than 100 organizations, movements, churches, and denominations in Mexico, Central America, and South America. (While Canada, the United States, and the Caribbean are also part of Wycliffe Americas Area, they were not the focus of this study and review.)

This case study, based on a conversational consultation, resulted in meeting notes which are not presented as quotes and do not identify specific speakers. The participant observations reproduced here may have been condensed or paraphrased in the notes. They may represent a thought contributed by more than one person. Some may appear in phrases rather than full sentences. In some instances, for clarity, contextual information has been added. Americas Area Director Nydia Garcia-Schmidt provided input to and approved this case study.

Garcia-Schmidt opened the consultation with a reflection on the past fifteen years of the Americas Area. She described it as living in two worlds: the world of traditional missions, predominately experienced through expatriate efforts, and the growing world of local church and indigenous mission. She talked about how things had been done and imagined what could be. She spoke of the need for contextualization and innovation and how these had already been key to their journey thus far. She expressed the goal for this consultation as having a conversation that could emerge as something appealing and not too academic, offering an example, not a model, something they could share with others who were asking, 'how did you do it?' And so, they began to share the stories of their journey....

Context

Exploring the context that has enabled or hindered the Bible translation movement in the Americas, consultant participants addressed the following:

What kind of terrain have we encountered? Terrain can include geographical locations crucial to the Bible translation movement; historical, political, sociological, and religious contexts; significant and lasting movement within movements, etc., that present opportunities or challenges.

What kind of weather have we experienced? Weather includes what made the timing 'right' for the movement to happen; what 'winds of the Spirit' were blowing; what 'rainfall' enriched opportunities and caused growth; what storms impeded progress?

While on a journey encountering different terrains, in any given location, terrain usually represents a constant (e.g., politics may change, but there will always be politics!) until encountering a new or different terrain. In contrast, weather can be a momentary event, fluctuating, then passing by.

Terrain (the ongoing contexts)

The participants noted that while Wycliffe Americas Area encompasses 26 nations in Latin America (including Brazil), North America, and the Caribbean, this consultation would primarily focus on the history of the Bible translation movements in Latin America. Each region has a very different history, many cultures, and contexts.

Describing the contexts of the regions they were looking into, participants noted that many countries have numerous people groups often referred to as *indigenous*, and others who may be referred to as *nationals* or the *majority culture*. They also remarked that indigenous people, enabled by God, were reaching other indigenous people, particularly when doors closed for others to serve among them. Early on, in places where there was violence or civil war, where missionaries had to withdraw, that is where they saw the more vibrant mission movement. In areas with ongoing dependency on the external church, the movements did not grow as quickly.

Weather (the momentary contexts)

Participants noted that identification of the 10/40 Window[1] had inspired a new generation, beginning in the late 1980s. Also, the appearance and influence of Liberation Theology, primarily in the Catholic Church, significantly impacted the culture and introduced a concept of a more humanitarian and integral mission. Other 'weather' trends mentioned by the participants included how COMIBAM[2] experienced tremendous growth in mission through a movement rather than an institutional model in the 1980s and ongoing. During the years 1999 to 2000, intent on gaining understanding concerning this movement, the leadership of Wycliffe International in Latin America took part in many conversations and meetings endeavouring to reach agreements on how to present the vision for Bible translation in the emerging COMIBAM mission movement.

COMIBAM, also sensitive to learning and understanding how to walk with the Bible translation movement, helped establish many structures and organizations that were both new and local. An increase in the numbers of missionaries sent to cross-cultural missions included those going to work in the 10/40 window. The number of missionaries active from 1996 to 2001 went from 2,684 to 4,849. There was formal training in eleven countries, with at least 250 students.

Participants told of how God was working in Brazil, describing mission there as more cohesive than in the Spanish-speaking arena, with the indigenous

[1] The 10/40 Window, a term coined by mission strategist Luis Bush, refers to the area of the world between 10- and 40-degrees north latitude; it includes about two-thirds of the global population and encompasses parts of Northern Africa, the Middle East, and Asia. A highly populated area, it is also characterized by the highest concentration of people groups without access to the Gospel. See also chapter 3.

[2] COMIBAM is the Ibero-American Missionary Cooperative, an alliance that brings together national mission groups and networks from twenty-five Latin American countries. COMIBAM is also a part of WGA.

movement also growing more and faster than in Spanish-speaking Latin America. One negative aspect of context that participants mentioned was the imposition of timelines that had put them in a mode of urgency to get Bible translation done quickly. They all asked, 'What is behind that kind of thinking?' David Cardenas presented another important question from this discussion of context: 'What is God doing and saying to us about how to walk together?'

Additional Context

Difficult terrain (in the form of geographical and political challenges) and changing weather (including new information, trends, and movements) awakened and encouraged the Americas Area on their journey, as they adopted new ways of working, sought stronger local involvement, and embraced an increasing number of new participants who were better informed than their predecessors. The mention of timelines above references Vision 2025, the corporate challenge issued in 1999 and adopted by Wycliffe organizations and SIL at that time (see chapter 9). It was a call to see Bible translation work begun in all the language communities that still needed the Bible in their language. But Vision 2025 was not always adopted holistically, with its call to a willingness to change, work differently, work in partnership, etc. What was often adopted was a 'deadline' sound bite—to have translation work begun by 2025 in all languages needing it. Urgency was often portrayed as about a task and on behalf of a product rather than as concern about building relationships that would lead to a lasting impact. While Vision 2025 has produced varying responses and both good and bad outcomes, the programs initiated because of it remain vital factors in the Americas Area journey. The participants' question about the Vision 2025 timeline focus serves as a reminder always to question and reflect on both motives and methods.

Journey Identity, Vision, and Values

Articulating the essential motivations and foundations for the journey, participants addressed these questions:

› *Where were we (the Bible translation movements, Wycliffe, the church in the Americas)?*
› *Where are we now?*
› *What were the vision and values in the beginning? Have they changed? How? Why?*

Consultation participants engaged in a robust discussion around these questions, with some of their observations of their past, present, and potential future listed below:

Inclusion—We don't want to leave people out. We find ways to be inclusive. When we have a consultation, all participants will have the opportunity to lead something. We value both men and women. It is an open space for young leaders and those from other cultures to work with more mature leaders. We want to see more people demonstrating and expressing intentional care for one another.

Trust and commitment—Significant trust was placed in the networks of partners, as there was no other option. The relationship with COMIBAM has survived four generations of leaders because of trust. There were times when one of us violated another's trust, and there were disagreements. But there was leadership commitment to partnership. We also need to focus on sacrifice.

Spiritual Focus—We want to continue establishing strong missiological and theological foundations for Bible translation. Prayer is critical. We want to respond to what's important to the Lord, not just our ideas. Importance of discernment. We always hope and pray for change that will lead to transformation. Remember the sovereignty of God. Though what is happening may be unpleasant, we are responsible for responding in a godly way without lowering our principles. It is a challenge, but he allows it. Having the Bible in our language brings value to us as a people. We are sensitive to Latin American spirituality, that is, how we express our beliefs and faith. Knowing this, we build on it from our experiences. There are times we want to move faster, but we make mistakes. As a consequence of the missiological learnings regarding the mission of God, we are learning patience, respect for how God is moving, and how to follow him.

Identity—It's important to know why you exist (as an organization, network, etc.); if that is unclear, others won't see it either. We are building together, sharing the knowledge and experience that comprises the Alliance Organizations. How do we promote the sharing of those experiences? We have mutual respect, exemplary at the leadership level. We support our leaders.

Relationships are core—It's important to go where people are (e.g., seminaries, churches, etc.). Informal conversations happen. A worthwhile principle or value is prioritizing connecting naturally with what's happening today.

A key comment from the discussion on Identity, Vision, and Values: 'What moves a movement? Shared vision, values, principles... that's what needs to happen!' (Nydia Garcia-Schmidt).

Deeper Conversations

During these conversations some values-related topics that arose were identified for further discussion. These included relating with churches, calling attention to how their mission is part of God's mission, and how the mission of Bible translation is an integral part of the whole. Polycentrism was another topic designated for further discussion. The participants cited examples of networks and organizations around the globe and in the Americas that have served and continue to serve as centres of influence. As one participant noted, these 'centres of influence impacted how we in the Alliance saw mission and Bible translation from the early days.' The participants mentioned, too, how networks have facilitated centres of influence, particularly indigenous networks in various countries, and how these connections have helped organizations be more eager to reach out globally in dialogue and partnership.

Most organizations, at some point, discuss identity and values with hopes that something concrete will emerge. Such conversations often go in circles and do not reach anything concrete. For the Americas Area leaders in this holistic conversation there was not a specific goal of reaching concrete statements of identity or values. However, the list of recognized values not only provided concrete statements but offered many in contexts that reflect on the past as they move forward or acknowledge the deeper reason for that value. The values discussion grew organically out of discussing their journey. It was not mechanical. There was little 'we used to be/do that, and now we have switched to being/doing this.'

The history discussed demonstrated how values did not simply 'switch' but grew and changed, illustrating missional intent and living the journey. Changes come through discernment and are purposeful yet organic. Traditional strategic planning often produces change in 'switch' mode, appearing as a sudden shift from one way of working to another, often without a comprehensive understanding of why and how. The conversation above was one of several that demonstrated journey progression exemplified by the participants' commitments to community and to purposefully listening to and following God. These commitments connect to both their heritage and their future and provide keen insights into the history of Wycliffe in the Americas.

People

Contemplating those whom God has called and worked through on the Americas Area journey, participants explored the following questions:

› *Who have the significant leaders and influencers been?*
› *Why and how were these people leaders and influencers?*
› *Who are the significant stakeholders?*
› *How has this changed, and why?*

The following are some of the participants' observations related to the above:

There have been notable individuals and notable groups of people, but in this discussion their qualities are of greater importance than their personalities. There is a ripple effect with relationship building, extending far beyond what we could have imagined. We are part of a community. Titles and position do not indicate greater consequence or worth, nor are they reliable indicators of success. However, examples of humility displayed by past and present Americas Area leaders have paved the way toward working in collaboration.

Significant influencers' principles had an effect, for example, not letting structures run the movement or organization but being vision-driven (missiologically, etc.). Annual retreats, while presenting no specific agenda and giving time to reflect on the previous year, proved productive and worthwhile. To maintain momentum, using innovative thinking, we ask ourselves, 'What can we do differently?' We must continue nurturing relationships with the indigenous church, showing them care, encouraging cooperation in intergenerational leadership, and inviting the youth to engage in the movement.

Among the numerous humble leaders cited who also demonstrated encouragement and a willingness to advise and mentor, the participants discussed a particular leader from the past who represented an important influence in the Americas Area. He could take general concepts and ideas and turn them into strategies and useful structures. He was relational but also had a practical approach and operational ability. He was a team builder. That's the whole basis of a team. Idea people, doers, and leaders who hold us to our principles. He wasn't afraid to say, 'That doesn't fit.'

A key comment from the discussion on People: 'Collaboration is God's way of enacting his vision' (David Cardenas).

Telling their Story

The participants honoured several leaders and colleagues in the process of the conversation, noting what they learned from them and how that knowledge could be applied in the future. While detailed information about these individuals is not required for this book, some of the qualities the participants referenced are included. Much of the discussion happened through storytelling. There was a free flow of conversation overflowing with reminiscing and reflecting. Although highlighting individuals, the conversation's overall emphasis was on the importance of being a team, being inclusive, and valuing all. Reflecting on the people on this journey thus far enabled participants to identify patterns, changes, and concepts that helped them in later conversations and to establish principles and priorities. They were able to see why they valued specific qualities because they could recall those who had modelled them along the way. Seeing where they had been revealed more about where they were at the moment and where they wanted to be.

Resources

To identify the resources God has provided, participants focussed on the following questions:

› *What resources have been important? Why?*
› *How have they been used?*
› *How were they provided?*
› *How has thinking about resources changed? How has the use of resources changed?*

Many provocative and interconnected thoughts emerged and are organized here, as much as possible, in the order of the questions considered, though they weren't necessarily expressed in the same order. This demonstrates how a natural flow of conversation on the journey can result in diverse insights that reveal rich patterns and practical observations, allowing participants to reflect on and often return to previously discussed concepts, resulting in increased understanding. As demonstrated here, all of this can then be organized in concrete, less conversational formats for further evaluation and for sharing with others. It gives a bird's eye view of the journey.

What resources have been important? Why? We must remember the value of generosity, not just with money but also with time (service) and relationships, being willing to share contacts and act as connectors. You do get a better 'return on investment' with relationships, but don't encourage relationships as a means to an end! Grow relationships, and live in community, because it's biblical. People tend to view money as the solution to their problems, but in true community, real partnerships work better than money. Funding, without necessary preparation and analysis, etc. can hinder the movement.

How have resources been used? Time, energy, and money have been spent on nurturing relationships. Investments have been made in technology (to support relationships). Resources have involved very little that was related to project funding. Besides reaching Scripture translation goals, results included transitioning to local leadership, increasing capacity, training, fostering vision in the movements, organization/leadership development, etc. There was an increase in long-term benefits, even with a decrease in funding. We now have stronger organizations and people with competencies they didn't have before.

How were resources provided? Sometimes less is more as we explore other ways of resourcing, focussing on generosity and being creative as opposed to just providing money. People can provide food for a meeting, housing, etc.—good principles that can work worldwide. When we felt there was a lack of resources because funding was reduced, people kept helping, and more consultants donated time, as they could work online. A church provided an office and other resources for LETRA Chile[3]. FEDEMEC[4] is now sharing its office with part of our Area team. A church in McAllen, Texas, gave Garcia-Schmidt office space. It happened because of relationships. When ALEM[5] hosted a meeting for the Alliance organizations in Brazil, they didn't charge for housing or food. We relate to 20–30 percent of the church in the Americas through COMIBAM; this is a major resource.

How has thinking about resources changed? How has the use of resources changed? Systems and Structures—Stewardship is not only asking 'where is our money going?' The former system and structure of branches/centres of operation seemed necessary at the time. Today they would be highly inefficient because of the money and people it took to keep them going and because there are now operational resources elsewhere. There was a strong reaction to seeing centres closed. But the world has changed.

Logistics—We have moved away from meeting in big hotels, involving conference amenities, etc. We listened to the movement and adjusted. One meeting was held at a camp in Argentina. At an Area meeting in Guatemala, indigenous leaders co-developed an agenda and co-hosted a meeting, endeavouring to include more people within the budget. It was held at a Bible school with up to eight people in each room. This was hard for a lot of people, but it established a lot of credibility with the indigenous leaders. This was crucial for those relationships, worth every discomfort.

Leaders—Some leaders are serving in combined roles. Participants gave examples of leaders serving in two or three roles. This enriches multiple environments (cross pollination). But it is challenging. Not everyone can or should do this.

Challenge as Opportunity—When we have experienced a shortage of funding, we felt the impact, but in a way, we welcomed it. It was challenging. We had to close some activities and stop some subsidies, but it also opened new opportunities.

Control—Control is a high value for many when it comes to any kind of resources, but to allow such thinking can lead to undermining Alliance values. Control issues (across partnerships) are a substantial hurdle to good stewardship.

Stewardship Priorities—How do we use money? To improve relationships.

One leader noted that 'outside of our circle, many don't understand how we

---

[3] LETRA Chile is a Chilean organization committed to Bible translation and literacy. It is a part of the Wycliffe Global Alliance.

[4] FEDEMEC is a Costa Rican network of churches and mission entities that helps equip and provides services for those wishing to participate in cross-cultural ministry. FEDEMEC is a WGA organization.

[5] ALEM is a Brazilian Bible translation organization involved in translation, church planting, and training of workers. It is a member of WGA.

use resources or why, how a movement has a ripple effect. A lot of people can't see that. It is important to communicate why this is effective.' For example, even other Alliance organizations may not understand our budget. Goal: how to better explain—to outside audiences and Alliance organizations—how the movements are working.

A key comment from the discussion on Resources: 'Stewardship of resources is a complex discussion. Like when you use airplanes to reach villages, it's efficient and a good use of resources in some ways, but you miss meeting all the people in-between...the people you'd meet if you went by canoe' (Dave Brooks).

This discussion on resources was a dynamic part of the whole journey conversation. It emphasized the need to think differently, think together, share stories and examples, rethink what is being resourced and why, and what it means to be successful. The comment above about not 'meeting all the people in-between' is a powerful call to re-examine 'efficiency' and 'good use of resources' considering what one is trying to accomplish and in light of valuing relationships and considering their success. This isn't to imply one should always take the canoe, but that it should be on the list of viable options.

Principles

Principles are guiding rules and beliefs, the outworking of identity, vision, and values. They should be embedded in the people in an organization or movement and set the stage for how people behave. Unfortunately, principles are often institutionalized and considered to be part of the structure of an organization rather than part of the character of its people. This hinders growth, flexibility, and compassion. When principles are a part of the people, both the people and the organization can flourish. Principles can be applied across many contexts, but the specifics of enacting those principles may vary by cultural interpretations, regions, or situations.

Because the original list of principles offered in this consultation conversation was quite long, it has been condensed and categorized. As with any list, it could be organized in various ways, but the following is an attempt to arrange the principles and comments provided by the participating Americas Area leaders so that the principles coordinate with the descriptions above.

Principles Representing the Value of People

Trust. Inclusion. Community. Unity. Diversity. Polycentrism. Working in collaboration. Humility. Be willing to ask forgiveness. Patience. Respect. Listen, listen.

Listen to multiple people and views. Readiness to respond to others. Relationships, relationships... Focus on people over finances. Within and across organizations, it is powerful when leaders commit to being friends, not just colleagues.

Principles Representing Commitment

Reliance on God as the leader. Missiological reflection is crucial. Commitment to being in the Word, individually and together. Prayer. Flexibility. Willingness to change as God leads and as circumstances change.

Vision-Focussed: Embrace both simplicity and complexity. Structures that serve (and don't drive). Outside-the-box thinking. Willingness to take risks. Change doesn't happen through a directive.

A key comment from the discussion on Principles: 'We struggle with the term "partner" in part because it is connected to transactional relationship. How do we state the principle "do nothing on your own"? It will be important how we state that' (Dave Brooks).

The participants' principles demonstrated both diversity and balance. They considered both reflection and practice, individual and community responsibilities, and avoided binary choices (such as choosing between simplicity and complexity). Almost every principle also included an implicit agreement to let go of control. Very few of the principles listed could be embraced or enacted by someone who was bent on power and/or control.

Mindset

Mindset is the habitual or characteristic mental attitude that determines how a person or group will interpret and respond to situations. Contemplating the past and the present, participants discussed what was needed for continued change and growth in the future. They acknowledged that mindset makes a significant difference in how individuals or a group approach various scenarios.

When reviewing the topic of mindset, it is helpful to remember that, before the creation of the Wycliffe Global Alliance, its predecessor Wycliffe International related much more closely to a partner organization, SIL. Today they function as separate, collegial organizations with many common values and considerable common history. Some Alliance Organizations second personnel to SIL. In the past, however, because Wycliffe International and SIL had a joint international leadership team and board, Wycliffe shared much of the SIL culture of that time. Both SIL and the Wycliffe Global Alliance have been undergoing many changes in recent years, so the former mindset must be considered as *former* for *both* organizations, and it does not necessarily represent the mindset of everyone involved, even in the past. Although SIL was not a part of the conversations featured in this case study, in the Americas, SIL and Wycliffe often look at their journeys together. The focus of this consultation was on Wycliffe's journey in the Americas, but it was noted that SIL has played a meaningful role in that journey. Among other services, SIL, for many years, served as the primary vehicle through which 'Westerners' could go out into the world to serve in Bible translation. As is common in missions worldwide, the Americas Area has moved on from 'the West to the rest' operational style (meaning US, Canada, and Europe sending out personnel around the world) to 'from everyone to everywhere'. But it has been and continues to be a journey.

Former Mindset

- We do it ourselves (Wycliffe and SIL) because no one else will (pioneers), no one else can (academics), it is less complicated to do it ourselves, we will have better control and better quality.
- This is our mandate, and we must maintain control because we are accountable to stakeholders.
- Partnership is good in theory, but all organizations have some quantity of individual priorities.
- We (SIL) don't have partners in this country, so there is no one else to work with.
- We (SIL) don't work with churches as it would endanger our other relationships.
- We (SIL and/or Wycliffe) provide the resources.
- Bible translation is very specialized, separate from other ministries and missions.
- We rely on external funding.
- We will create more organizations like those of the past.
- We are the experts.
- We bring, others receive.
- Institutional, hierarchical.

What has Changed? Why?

Acknowledging God's Mission—We have learned to respect how God is moving and how to follow. This is a consequence of a better understanding of missiology regarding the mission of God. We are learning patience; there are times when we want to move faster, but we make mistakes. We are learning flexibility, willing to change as circumstances change, as God meets us. In Latin America, there is a spiritual sensitivity to how we express our beliefs and faith. So, in our meetings, we acknowledge this and build on that from our experiences.

From Institutional to Community Thinking—We realized the term 'partner' can get in the way. It's about community. COMIBAM is a community. The Alliance is a community. It calls for another way of talking about partnership. It has too much baggage—for example, the implied 'I want you to partner with my agenda', transactional partnerships, etc. Leadership as a team is crucial—decision making together, bouncing ideas, etc. Moving from an institutional to a collaborative approach represents a significant transformation. There has also been a movement from Bible translation 'out there' done by expatriate experts to the community saying, 'We should own this.' Another aspect is inclusion. We value both men and women, as well as open space for other cultures and for young leaders to work with more mature leaders. A movement has to be led in a different way, inclusive, in community, through consultation—not totally reliant on 'let's plan the next three years.' We need to serve in humility as part of a community. A title doesn't make us better. We can acknowledge our mistakes and ask for forgiveness.

Narrow Focus to Big Picture—There was a shift from interest only in Bible translation by itself to interest in becoming part of a more holistic movement with the church. Before, the church felt it was on the outside. As long as we focussed more narrowly and treated Bible translation as a specialist discipline, that's how the church saw it. By recognizing the necessity of focussing on the big picture, we are becoming part of a broader mission movement. COMIBAM spurred endeavours to help integrate Bible translation into this movement. No longer transplanting our former model of creating organizations specifically focussed on Bible translation, we would be working with COMIBAM, who wanted us to help integrate translation as part of the mission of the church, not as a separate function. Now, this much more complete picture of the mission of God helps us engage as part of the church. It's not just about Bible translation but also stewardship of the earth and many other facets of ministry. As a body, it is necessary to be concerned about all of it. There have been monumental discussions about the social gospel, etc., that were part of the process. There is dialogue taking place, and we fit into that history. We have our identity, but we are part of something bigger. We used to set missiology aside, dismissing it with, 'we must keep focussed'; now that's shifted completely. We realized we also required thinking beyond existing structures, asking, 'Does the structure help or hinder?'

Encouraging Generosity in all Aspects—We don't talk about money as much as we used to; we discussed how the movement will be a church movement, not based on external funding and not with funding as the central focus. Today we are projecting an image of the Alliance that is more contextualized. Example: 'Before

I joined the Alliance four years ago, meetings were held in hotels. There was the perception that the Alliance had money. We must recognize that the church has local resources. We must project how Jesus participated in mission: his humility, and simplicity (as simple as possible). This is good for the Alliance journey.'

A key comment from the conversation on Mindset: 'We don't always do it right, but our intentions and commitment are to this vision' (unidentified participant).

The missional intent and journey mentality come through strongly in this discussion. The understanding of mission belonging to God, willingness to release control, to be flexible, to grow, and to change are all evident. There is a desire to continually re-evaluate structures in terms of their suitability and a recognition of the profound impact of shifting from institution to community/movement. The broader, more integrated emphasis on generosity also indicates a willingness to consider how God is working and to align oneself and one's organization to his leading and direction. The key comment is an excellent demonstration of the reality of the journey challenges and the humility mentioned. These are all significant factors in Wycliffe's history in the Americas Area.

Decisions

Decisions are the specific choices (one time or ongoing) that have had an impact along the way on the Americas Area journey. Participants discussed the following:

› *How, why, and to what degree did these decisions have an impact?*
› *What difference have they made?*
› *What environment and resources did they require?*
› *How did they affect the direction, pace, and scope of the movement?*

Some of the decisions below have been grouped and put in loose categories for easier reading and consideration.

Ground Rules—Every structure and process became open to examination.

Progressive Inclusion—We tried to give careful thought as to who else should/could be involved. 'As an expat, I tried never to attend meetings without being accompanied by a Latin colleague.' 'I made sure my job was short-term and a Latin leader replaced me.' We made an intentional choice to grow the Latin leadership through encouragement and mentoring. We intentionally sought to respect and honour our partners and their positions. We worked toward removing language barriers in meetings. We purposely exhorted and continue to exhort people to work together.

Rethinking Strategy Together—Asking and thinking through the questions: What is our focus? What are we here for? To encourage sending? Training? Other? Shift from a military model (bases, etc.) to a business model (transactional), to friendship in mission. Though some institutional functions are needed, so is careful thought and decision-making to keep them from overtaking you. How do you stay in the 'zone' without institutionalizing the movement and killing it? Choosing not to do operational things. We used to do very structured strategic planning but now have decided to do consultations. This allows everyone to be more involved. Allows people to share the issues and together figure out the next steps or solutions. More than a 'planning session'. People get to be active participants, ideas are listened to, and responsibilities and ownership are shared. We chose strategies that lessen the fears of our partners.

Choosing Community—We made it a priority to allow time and funding to build friendships. We chose to give up our meeting agenda and instead adopt the church's agenda. We are making room for meetings where we reflect on *missio Dei*. It is about mission in community and the importance of Bible translation for transformation. We bring people from Alliance organizations and the national church and missionary movement together. A mixture of people can make it transformational. It is not about mobilizing or showing statistics but about taking time for contemplation.

We did not have clarity about the future but knew it was time for a transition. We did our best. Prayer and input from the community are important, promoting a decision of not just one person or a few people. We've made it a priority to get Alliance organizations' input. The group will be able to determine what kind of leadership skills are needed.

We quit talking about being parachurch. It's more than a terminology change. Now we talk about being part of the body. We chose to send people (into Bible translation-related mission work) through church or local mission structures. There were internal struggles in 2003/4 concerning closing the Wycliffe Area function as a sending structure. We closed down the sending structure of Wycliffe Americas Area that was set up to handle finances, personnel, recruitment, etc. from countries without sending organizations. Closing it was a team decision; the decision fit our principles. We decided not to establish Wycliffe Organizations in Latin America on the advice of COMIBAM leadership, although some colleagues were very much against the decision. We chose not to establish Wycliffe as an institution. Instead, we chose to work in agreement with COMIBAM.

The relationship between Wycliffe and COMIBAM illustrates the choice to be a movement within a movement. Bible translation becomes a ministry where the church participates; it is not always associated with an organization. It becomes part of the outreach and cross-cultural ministry. Yet when the focus is on church planting and evangelism, the perception is that the church/movement puts Bible translation aside because of how it was done in the past (by foreign experts, etc.) and they don't know how it fits in their vision. There is strong motivation to try to work through the church so that Bible translation becomes integrated into the mission of the church, not something on the side.

Resource Allocation—Using funds and influence wisely to be a better partner to the movement, not establishing ourselves as an institution. Choosing to use funds to bring people together to build relationships. Choosing when to have joint comprehensive projects and when to disband. Choosing to use new technology and tools that help strengthen the movement, tools for monitoring and evaluation. Latin American organizations were weak in this. Now a culture of evaluation can help them appropriately assess how they can improve and have a greater impact.

A key comment from the discussion on Decisions: 'We chose to look at everything through the lens of our principles' (unidentified participant).

The journey approach to this conversation helped participants identify intentional changes along the journey. Without this sort of consideration, it would be easy to overlook the purposefulness and just say, 'Yes, because of new developments and contexts, things changed.' But in fact, very conscious choices were made that took the Americas Area down this path.

Behaviours

Behaviours are how an individual or group acts in various situations. Based on the previous discussions and additional reflection, the participants talked about and crafted a list of behaviours that characterize the Wycliffe Americas Area people and journey at their best:

Walk in humility. Resist defensiveness. Show respect and honour to others. Have the attitude of a servant. Let go of control so the global and local church can own the work. Develop a team and promote Latinos as leaders at the highest levels.

Invest in developing and maintaining personal relationships, making time for others, honouring relationships over efficiency. Talk to, consult with, and listen to everyone affected by changes, not just one side. Listen to partners' fears and respect their concerns. Do nothing on your own. Include partners as part of planning for events, conducting meetings so all partners feel valued and have the opportunity to speak—otherwise, people feel marginalized. Include and respect women. Take chances. Share as much information as possible. Then watch and see energy increase!

Prioritize friendship, friendliness as a behaviour, not overly formal. In Latin America, if we nurture a friendship, collaboration will follow. The Alliance has provided spaces for those face-to-face encounters. Recognize that we are a community, enter in, and nurture it. Don't artificially manufacture it, considering it a task! It's God's community and we're already part of it. We either mismanage it or learn how to do it well. While we communicate well with people in our own community, going to others can be difficult. When thrown into a foreign environment, community doesn't just happen. It calls for a missiological perspective.

Work in collaboration and community. Welcome new people to participate in consultations. Meetings can be natural or awkward, depending on how people are received. Develop friendships with the Wycliffe Area directors; get comfortable sharing ideas and holding annual or semi-annual retreats. Encourage collaboration to happen more naturally across areas. Keep short accounts with people and organizations. Don't talk behind their backs. When possible, unless requiring a third party in some cultures, go directly to the person.

Challenge the status quo. Keep evaluating everything. Is it worth doing? Is it necessary to change or adapt? Think outside the box—get missiological input not just from North America, Asia, Africa, and Latin America. Consider current thinking around the world as a resource.

A key comment from the discussion on Behaviours: 'Team leadership! We need diversity and people who are way out there with great ideas but don't fit. They're the only ones who can do it' (Dave Brooks).

These behaviours speak for themselves. One can note the consistency of values, principles, mindset, and behaviours, and how the decisions made flow out of them. Crises, new contexts, new partners, releasing of control, changing the status quo even when faced with intense criticism—none of these led to action without reflection or decisions made in isolation.

Milestones

A milestone is an action or event marking a significant change in the course of the journey or a stage of development. A milestone may or may not be directly correlated to the decisions referred to above. They may be tipping points, crises, miracles, crossroads, etc. What are the main milestones along the journey thus far?

The participants in this mapping consultation provided notable milestones from the 1930s through the present decade. Many of these would be difficult to understand without the full context of the conversation from this consultation and additional background, so only a few are mentioned in this chapter as examples. Milestones included the formation of numerous national mission organizations, collaboration efforts, meetings, and changes that signified the growth of a movement. Exact dates were not provided for every milestone.

Among the milestones referred to were the beginning of the AD2000 movement which engaged churches in mission, the influence of Lausanne conferences and Ralph Winters, and the growth of the 10/40 Window focus. Brazil, Mexico, and Costa Rica were also mentioned as making essential contributions to missiological development. According to José de Dios, 'We can't underestimate the influence of the Brazilian mission movement, and the depth of theology and missiology they've developed over the years. Argentina, too. Significant missiology—the backbone of the mission movement in Latin America.' Mexico has had tremendous influence within COMIBAM, with a multitude of indigenous groups. COMIMEX early on had an emphasis on working with indigenous churches and putting mission into practice cross-culturally within Mexico. Also of note, Costa Ricans were early pioneers in implementing some remarkable cross-cultural training for their people. So many Latin leaders in missions are Costa Rican. FEDEMEC was a model for extensive later development. There have been numerous centres of influence that impacted how we in the Alliance saw mission and Bible translation from early days.

Milestone Timeline

2006

› Discussion, dissent, then decision made *not* to start more Wycliffe organizations in the Americas, but to follow COMIBAM's advice and work in close collaboration with COMIBAM.
› For the first time, indigenous leaders are invited to one of the Americas Area meetings.
› Missiological/theological reflection process starts. Americas Area is one of the voices advocating for this.
› COMIBAM's new vision statement: All the church in holistic, global mission. This and collaboration create a broad channel of church involvement and ownership through which Bible translation can flow.

2007

› José de Dios is the first non-North American Area director in the Americas. (Takashi Fukuda led the way in Asia in 2004). Huge change.

2008

› The beginnings of the Wycliffe Global Alliance are recognized (Wycliffe International adopts the new name in 2011), and the structure continues to change from an institution to a movement. Also, a new multilingual website for the Alliance is consequential for the movement, demonstrating the diversity and value of all involved and making more resources available to the church worldwide.

2009

› Reflection on leadership. Different types of leadership are necessary for each season. Recognition that earlier in our history many pioneers/mobilizers were helpful, but today we require people who know how to collaborate.

2012

› CONPLEI[6] meeting. After a 500-year regional history of division among the indigenous and national (majority cultures of the Americas nations) peoples, at the 2012 CONPLEI congress, there is indigenous leadership of the congress, with national and expatriate people serving meals, cleaning bathrooms, etc.

2012

› Nydia Garcia-Schmidt is the first woman Area director in both the Alliance and the Americas.

2015

› Colombia Conference. Declaration of the importance of the indigenous church.

A key comment from the discussion on Milestones: 'Innovation became our tradition' (unidentified participant).

Milestones provide reference points along a road. Human-made physical milestones have existed at least since the time of the Roman Empire. They are meant to reassure travellers that they are on the right path and are used to indicate distance travelled or remaining distance to a destination. But if no one has yet been on this journey, it is the leader, not a stone marker, that instils confidence. So, it is not unexpected that, even with some mention of events and accomplishments, much of the conversation concerning milestones centred on leaders and leadership. Of particular interest, though organizations that discuss milestones typically concentrate on goals, metrics, and benchmarks to measure and compare, this discussion placed a higher value on relationships and progress in growing relationships. God's leading, godly leaders, and rich relationships led to the creation of milestones on a new journey. This is in sharp contrast to the traditional models of measuring against internal or external criteria. Such comparison becomes ineffectual when the criteria cannot take an everchanging context into account.

[6] CONPLEI (Consejo Nacional de Pastores y Lideres Evangelicos Indiginas) is the National Board of Indigenous Pastors and Leaders of Brazil, a missions organization committed to reaching the peoples of the Amazon Basin. CONPLEI is a WGA organization.

Lessons Learned

Discovering and articulating what they had learned on their journey thus far, participants were asked to reflect on and discuss:

- *How do we learn? Through trial and error, 'mistakes', hard experiences, surprising experiences...?*
- *What do we now think about differently, or do differently, or not do?*
- *How can these lessons inform the future?*
- *How can we share these lessons with others?*

The lessons learned are sorted by topics. Many could, of course, fit more than one category.

About God's Mission

It's a mix of three factors: time, place, and person. You may have the people but not at the right place or time. You may have the time but can't find the right people. Or have the place and people but not the right time. When these three elements come together, the Holy Spirit is present. It isn't necessary to force anything. We do have to be intentional but allow God to open the door. For the future of the Alliance and the movement, it has to be that way. According to David Cardenas, 'If we're saying that the mission belongs to God, we have to follow in his steps. But it does mean we have to interpret the times correctly and be ready to act. Because if we miss the Kairos moment, we'll miss our opportunity.' God takes us in a direction, and we don't know where it will lead. God puts things in our path—spend time processing why he allowed something to happen.

We have been learning about patience. There are times we want to move faster but we make mistakes. We've learned to respect how God is moving and how to follow. That's a consequence of the missiology regarding the mission of God. Start from missiology and an understanding that God wants us to participate in his mission. Then we can begin a commitment of church ownership of the vision, people, and resources. Mobilizers often talked about mission as a highly specialized task, done by specialists. The thinking was that the church can help support it, but it's not part of the church. But when you talk about the mission of God, it's a natural part of what the church is doing in the world, participating in God's mission.

About Movements

We learned the importance of becoming part of mission movements, caring about what others care about, and not only focussing on Bible translation. We continue to learn to be more aware of networks and the importance of looking at the terrain with a network lens. Movida, a youth movement in the Americas Area, is having influence not just here but also in Europe and may impact the Europe Area. We had to define partnership with COMIBAM: (1) not tied to finances; (2) can't be 'using' COMIBAM; (3) we must be willing to come under the leadership of the movement as equals.

Decreased funding can lead to increased creativity. An emphasis on finances leads to an institution, not a movement. If an organization stays based on an existing (older, institutional) donor base, they are likely to remain institutional and find difficulty in incorporating movement qualities. But if they consider a younger base, they might end up with more of a movement model.

We need to get past the binary thinking regarding institution/movement. Our reality is we have a board, financial and personnel accountability, etc. There are institutional elements, but we think and primarily operate more like a movement. We shouldn't pigeonhole organizations to choose to be one or the other. The journey is for each to determine what they are required to be and do, and to follow God's direction now and into the future. Have the courage to look at other networks, stand firm and keep persisting if we feel God is leading in a particular direction.

Experience in fieldwork and networks, an understanding of relating to partners, being a facilitator, and leading by influence, all have value but are hard to explain to someone who has never done it. As an example, YWAM people are training Jesus Film people, etc. We can get too stuck on identity and worry about losing it. Identity is good, but what identity? And holding too tightly to organizational identities can be harmful as well. Identity got in our way: 'I'm SIL', 'I'm Wycliffe', but where is it best for you to be to achieve the goals?

The Alliance was an institution and became a movement. COMIBAM started as a movement, then began institutionalizing, but wanted to maintain the ways of a movement, so they adjusted back to that approach. We don't get involved in the day-to-day functions of the institutions. We focus on the values: collaboration, friendship, unity, and trust. We are committed to serving but not intervening to prop things up in areas that weren't or aren't ready.

About Community

Relationship, relationship, relationship. Partnerships fall apart when investment in relationships is lacking. Learning how to disagree and still have a good conversation is essential. Some cultures do this better than others.

None of this can be done in isolation. Groups of indigenous leaders connecting and engaging with the mission leadership of COMIBAM, through Wycliffe's meetings, etc., all of this has motivated a greater dialogue. It is important to have Latin Americans evaluate projects. You get a whole different dynamic.

We need to keep designing new ways to do things but coordinate systems with other Areas. We want to process with our partners, but at the right time and in the right way, when all are ready, or we might create confusion. The process must be truly participatory. Merely producing a document is not helpful. People want interaction. Q&A. Public speaking, even videos.

It's good when different opinions are expressed. Find more ways to share those lessons, following Alliance themes, at the institutional level, not only in movement form. Not all we have in the Americas Area is relevant to everyone. The term parachurch hurt us.

About Leadership and Teams

Appreciate leaders with a network or movement mindset. Engage them.

In the previous (pre-Alliance) era the lack of leadership commitment to global cooperation slowed down the building of relationships and trust. If leadership changes, everything can change suddenly. We must do better at learning how to engage new leaders.

From the day we start, we can be thinking about who is going to replace us, what kind of person, pray about it, and ask God to bring that person forward. Recognize we all have limitations. Leadership transitions are crucial to the health of an ongoing movement. We try to avoid the former director casting too much of a shadow. It is necessary to determine how to do that better. Founders and other leaders need to know when to step down.

The formation of a team is critical. You only have so much emotional energy; you don't want to spend it on refereeing fighting among members, nor do you want just a bunch of 'yes men'. Choose people going in the same direction, on the same page. How you form a team has an impact on many. Consistency is required among the leadership team. Your partners will recognize if there is disagreement in the ranks. Avoid triangularization. Consult a variety of people and get their different versions. Sort out the essential issues discussed. Fully process it first as a team, then talk with partner organizations.

Use team members' special gifts. Find where your gifts are; delegate the rest. God has brought together people with certain skills and gifts. Be very intentional when investing in the professional development of the team. Connect them with opportunities, scholarships, training, etc. Consider it an ongoing learning journey. Develop new skills and strengthen existing ones. It is important to pray, discern, and wait for the 'right' people and the 'right' organizations.

General

- We can survive a lot if there is basic trust.
- There will be struggles on all sides, as it is hard for some to let go.
- We do not like it that anything good takes time, but it does.
- It's crucial to document things we might forget.
- We are not innovating enough with technology.
- Plan in cycles of three years instead of one. Much of what we do takes longer than one year. Have a plan but stay flexible.
- Systems thinking is helpful—a process approach. Respect the process.
- Seek to understand context, but don't assume you do.
- No one goes on precisely the same journey. People trying to do similar things won't have the same journey. Specific lessons are not always helpful, but the principles behind them will be.
- Don't disdain your reality even when it is not good. Learn along the way and have hope. It takes a great amount of work, and we must invest.

A key comment from this discussion on Lessons Learned: 'Each era has its own reality, and we presented the vision then for what we thought was best. But we have learned along the way' (unidentified participant).

Discernment and Goals

Discernment and goals are concerned with where and how we see God leading. Participants were asked to reflect on all they discussed as they considered the future and their next steps on the journey:

- *What significant endeavours do we sense God is doing related to the movement?*
- *What process of ongoing discernment do we need?*
- *What should our priorities be?*
- *What is our vision for the future?*
- *What are the challenges and opportunities in front of us?*

The following is a summary to help demonstrate the thought processes and outcomes of this discussion.

Area Focus

Area Director Nydia Garcia-Schmidt envisioned four areas as priorities for the next three years: seminaries, churches, prayer, and generosity. The priorities regarding churches and seminaries are closely tied together. Relating to seminary students and teachers could help the church think about Bible translation as central, instead of a separate or secondary program. The biblical foundations for Bible translation (missiological) could influence the vision from an early stage in seminaries, rather than only later in churches, providing an enormous impact.

Other topics included relating effectively to church denominations, prayer and discernment, keeping budgets low, keeping the movement growing and still allowing many voices to give input (polyphonic, polycentric), indigenous involvement, and resources for future Area facilitators. This resourcing involves people who are leading movements and have expertise in missiology, networking, etc. One criterion to be a facilitator is to be connected to a mission movement. That helps us know where to look for facilitators.

Global Focus

Is the Alliance sustainable? Why should we have a global budget when it is a movement, and anyone can participate?

Some people don't understand movements or movement models. It's a blind spot. It's not just about 'doing' but about missiology, about helping people understand movements and how they fit into God's mission. Those who have experience with the movements don't necessarily have experience with a different model, making it challenging in the Alliance, which has movements, institutions, and hybrids.

Working on better information coordination is called for, not communicating with leadership only, as it doesn't necessarily filter down. There is also the issue of lack of technical support.

Do we need to think beyond geography? Bible translation is not only a geographical issue—it's also collaborative. And countries with no Bible translation movement yet require some assistance. Consider combining efforts between Alliance organizations in one region with other organizations in other regions.

Another issue is the necessity of developing consultants. What role do Alliance Organizations have in that process?

Future Focus

Can we build on the current relationships? Is that one of our goals? And how do we cast vision? By being intentional in a few particular places. Our role is to be facilitators for organizations, connectors, not gatekeepers. Keep building relationships, keep moving forward. To relate to these organizations, take advantage of various points of contact. Invite yourself to meetings. Get to know them better.

Recognize the importance of Area and ALT working together to relate to organizations and institutions in the Area. As we look at the Area structure, ask, who else needs to be involved? How can we be more intentional as a team, communicating with each other as a global team?

A key comment from this discussion on the Future Focus: 'Who are we? You need to look at why you exist before you know what your structure needs to be, and your structure needs to be changing as you go' (unidentified participant).

Conclusion

There were rich conversations, discoveries, and many 'aha' moments in the course of this 'Mapping the Americas Area Journey' consultation. This case study offers a view of this consultation that used the journey concept as its primary structure for what would traditionally have been framed as a strategy review. A typical strategic planning review could not have unearthed the history, connections, or evidence of God at work in the same way as did this journey-focussed consultation. The following are comments from the participants:

> 'This discussion is helping to solidify positive aspects of the journey, and also helping us look toward the future (Nydia Garcia-Schmidt).
>
> 'That's the value of what we're doing, looking at what God has done and where he's going' (Dave Brooks).
>
> 'The journey has not been linear. But despite setbacks, there was a commitment to partnership on the part of all leaders' (José de Dios).
>
> 'We continue to see steps back and steps forward. We're not presenting a "model" but showing a journey. Others [Areas/Organizations] will have their own unique journeys. We are not seeking to be "The Model"' (Dave Brooks).
>
> 'We're a part of something amazing that God has done, we didn't see it coming!' (Nydia Garcia-Schmidt).

'We didn't see it coming!' is a good summary of what it's been like to be on this Alliance journey. It points to the fact of God's mission being under God's direction and according to God's timing. It also recognizes that the missional intent and participation of any person, organization, or movement, though determined by prayer, reflection, and discernment, is also very much under God's direction and subject to twists and turns that will inevitably surprise everyone but God.

Traditional strategy sets milestones in front of us and maps out our journey before our feet have touched the ground. But the Alliance leadership realized they were in new territory and the landscape required new ways of thinking, being, and working. We have never been this way before. This is apparent as we contemplate the Wycliffe Global Alliance history and journey as a whole, and the Americas Area journey in particular. On this uncharted journey, milestones are created and recognized as participants consider where and how they have been led. Maps can only be made in retrospect. A map, retracing a past leg of the journey, provides the opportunity for reflection and may advise future travellers, but the path will never be quite the same again.

The consultation participants were emphatic about not creating a model. They understood and hoped that others could learn from their journey experiences and lessons, but they also recognized that their journey, and each journey, is in some sense unique. No other Wycliffe Area or organization has quite the same history, nor the same leaders, context, or cultures. Mountain climbers will tell you that no two climbs, even up the same mountain, are alike. There are always variables. There is always something new. But there are many lessons to be learned and shared and history to be made.

Chapter 12
Measuring: Missional Intent of the Alliance Board

By Susan Van Wynen

Introduction

From the beginning of the Wycliffe Global Alliance in 2008, the leadership team took a somewhat unconventional approach to strategy and planning. In part, this was due to the nature of the organization—an alliance of many diverse organizations serving in a global context. WGA grew out of WBTI, which had operated more like a single organization for several reasons, including its history with SIL. It had also followed the institutional practices of early-mid twentieth century America, the culture in which it had been founded. The Alliance leadership quickly acknowledged the Alliance organizations' diverse nationalities, contexts, and cultures and the diversity of the leadership team and board's contexts, cultures, and experiences. They also recognized each Alliance organization's desire for a level of interdependence while maintaining some autonomy. Enveloping all this was the growing understanding of what it meant to participate in God's mission. Considering all these factors, the Alliance would need to plan and carry out its strategies differently and develop new ways of thinking about planning and strategy.

Over time, WGA's leadership began using the term 'missional intent' rather than 'strategic plans'. We describe missional intent as:

> A setting of direction, including the concerns, contexts, and/or causes an organization (group, or individual) believes God has called them to. The intent is clear, but the strategies and actions are flexible and constantly attuned to God's leading. Missional intent is the connecting of our identity (who we are) to God's purpose of blessing the nations, focusing our hearts and minds on a specific purpose or purposes (*how* we approach vision and mission) according to his leading.[1]

[1] Susan Van Wynen, "A Journey of Missional Intent: Organizational Strategy in the Context of God's Mission" (University of Pretoria, 2020), 44.

There were still planning and strategy efforts, but new terminology and ways of thinking and working recognized that mission is in God's hands. The emphasis was on discerning God's plans rather than WGA creating plans they then asked God to bless. Missional intent was about setting direction for how WGA would participate in God's mission, and this is what established the path for their journey. Strategies and plans would be steps on the journey and flow out of missional intent as leadership, including the board, listened, learned, and lived the journey of participating in God's mission under his direction. This approach would significantly impact how the WGA Board would fulfill its responsibilities.

Reflection and Realignment

From the beginning, WGA had qualities of both movement and institution and various influences on its philosophy and operational understandings. The most significant impact on WGA, even from before its official beginnings, was the concept of *missio Dei*. The missiological consultation in 2006 (see chapter 10) seeded this thinking that led to a deeper understanding of God's people as participants in his mission, invited to serve *with* him and under his direction, rather than seeing them as merely *tasked* to accomplish his work *for* him. In addition, there was a strong emphasis on the trinitarian nature of God and the Trinity's relationship with the church and all creation.

Noting the growth of the church worldwide, recognizing WGA's place as part of the church, and seeing the need for friendship-based relationships, the leadership began to understand change was required for the Alliance to better align with God's mission. As they continued learning, the leadership team sought to prepare for and undertake a journey appropriate to an alliance participating in God's mission, rather than pursue building a monolithic institution to accomplish a mission agenda. This led to reassessing the concept of strategic planning and developing the Alliance's concept of missional intent.

In the first few years of widespread change, as WGA was emerging, the leadership team and board thought it was best to continue to use some, but not all, of the more familiar, traditional strategic planning language and formats. But how they talked about planning and what they planned gradually altered as WGA developed. It also became essential to share their plans, motivations, and processes and seek the Alliance Organizations' (AOs) input. As WGA became more polycentric and polyphonic, with representation and leadership arising from many locations and many voices, conversation and community grew in importance. WGA was aligning its thinking, actions, and processes to better reflect its global nature and its desire to be positioned as participating in God's mission, not in pursuit of its mission.

As WGA openly shared its motivations and processes as it grew, changed, and developed, it began to shape and influence the Alliance culture beyond activities. The Alliance Leadership Team (ALT) and the leadership of many of the individual AOs realized that friendships, relationships, thinking, reflecting, and dialoguing together were essential if they were to go forward together. Standard policies and practices were not sufficient. They required common understanding and purposes, a common ideology that guided the movement and held it together. These elements were harder to chart on a spreadsheet or a graph. Strategies became less quantifiable and more qualitative. Stories often communicate more effectively than statistics. Progress needed to be 'measured' by quality and depth of relationships rather than ROIs (Return on Investment: a common business term listing a ratio between net profit and cost of investment, used to evaluate efficiency).

The case study presented in this chapter tells a portion of the story of WGA's journey thus far and how it carries out its missional intent. It focuses on the WGA Board's journey from primarily requiring quantitative reporting to encouraging qualitative reflection, covering the years from 2009 to 2012. Much of the content is adapted from unpublished reports of WGA's twice-yearly board meetings.

Early Days

While the board dealt with many issues during this period, for this case study, we will address issues that are, in some way, closely related to the topic of the board's discussion of measurement. The author/researcher of this chapter was present at each of these meetings and sat in on the Committee on Measuring Progress sessions.

In 2008, Wycliffe International (later named Wycliffe Global Alliance) began a new journey with a new board, executive director, and leadership team. The new leadership began to look at how God was at work in his church worldwide and how Wycliffe could best participate in his global mission. By 2009 the Wycliffe leadership was looking toward new ways of thinking and working. The board had developed three goals for the Alliance, replacing the previous 'ends'. The goals were:

1. God and his Church—Advocate Scripture translation, access, and use as vital to the integral mission of God and his church.
2. Language Communities—Facilitate partnering initiatives serving language communities that enable them to participate in the kingdom of God.
3. Internal and External Relationships—Reflect, through all of our relationships and partnerships, God's desire to accomplish his mission through the unity of his people.

These are the current board goals for the Alliance, with slightly updated wording from the 2009 goals (Wycliffe Global Alliance 2019).

Realignment and Revision

At its May 2009 meeting, the WBTI Board was asked to look at the realignment of Wycliffe Member Organizations (WMOs), revision of mission and vision statements, and board goals. Several serious administrative issues concerning WMOs were factors that encouraged the leadership and board to consider just what their responsibilities should be and why and how to execute them.

The board named a Committee on Measuring Progress, charged with exploring new progress indicators for WBTI goals. The administration (the executive director, backed by the leadership team) suggested they start over and not use the former indicators, which were primarily quantitative, reflecting what was deemed 'progress' in the individual Wycliffe organizations around the world. The committee's discussion promptly began focusing on how to measure qualitatively and quantitatively, particularly, but not exclusively, concerning Goal #1.

The committee decided the administration should develop a 'scorecard' for an initial trial with a few countries. The board would review the process before developing a system that would apply globally. The countries would receive a qualitative 'rating' for each of the criteria; the administration would propose action plans/strategies for each country to help them raise their score. The board would then review these plans, and reporting would be both quantitative and qualitative. By request, the leadership team began developing profiles for a given number of countries (10–20) based on the following criteria (these criteria were only suggestions; the board was open to other input):

› What is the potential of the church?
› What is already happening toward creating/promoting a Bible translation movement?
› Who is already participating?
› Relationships
› Attitude/Awareness/Vision

The board unanimously passed the motion to pursue this, requesting that the leadership team create a scorecard for each country (the 10–20 selected), attach strategies to each, and report back at the next board meeting.

These criteria were a significant step away from the former indicators of progress based on each organization's activities related to 'mobilizing' new personnel, fundraising, prayer, etc., now considered both outdated and impossible to track.

For example, of the number of prayer letters sent out by organizations, while some still mailed out printed information, most now sent information online. As a result, it was no longer possible to count the number of people reached. Even counting unique visitors to a given Wycliffe website left no way of knowing how many reposted the information, when, where, and shared it with how many people. These examples demonstrate that many of the previous indicators cannot be controlled or measured. The indicator did not demonstrate prayer activity or interest, nor took online activity into account, but merely reflected postage purchased. A new approach was needed. The leadership team was pleased to see the board moving toward more qualitative and realistic reporting. They were, however, not sure how the 'scorecard' method would work across cultures and given the many challenges many of the organizations faced. Most had very small teams for any sort of administrative roles and work.

Qualitative Reporting

Wycliffe's context was a significant point of discussion at the November 2009 WBTI Board meeting. Executive Director Kirk Franklin presented the following topics to the board for their consideration:

› Understanding Our Identity—Perceptions of our identity affect the effectiveness of our organization. There are different perceptions of our authority, and the Executive Limitations reflect certain expectations. Question for the board: What is the unique value that Wycliffe International brings to the groups it relates to? These groups were identified as the worldwide church and global missions, the member and partner organizations, and the language communities.
› Understanding Our Role—Wycliffe International's role with its member and partner organizations. How we relate to our member and partner organizations may be described as follows: Role 1—visionary advocate, informed by missiological reflection; Role 2—partner in global movement; Role 3—capacity building and organizational supporter. Questions for the board: Do these roles reflect how the board sees Wycliffe International? Are there additional ways the executive director and leadership team could effectively focus on these roles?

In this meeting, the sailboat metaphor was presented to the board under the topic of 'Managing Power in WBTI'. Questions for the board included:

› Does the board think the metaphors of power are helpful?
› Is the sailing boat metaphor suitable for Wycliffe International in terms of what it represents biblically, missiologically, and practically?

The Committee on Measuring Progress affirmed the May decision that a qualitative scorecard was probably the best way to measure progress. Their report to the board stated that while not excluding quantitative results, they needed to become more familiar with qualitative analysis—impact, not output, based on informed dialogue with people, partnering organizations, etc. Comparisons would not be made among countries but of the individual country's status quo as observed over time, along with assumed potential and development. A qualitative baseline would serve as a point of reference for each country. Representation of the status quo as described by the data could be summarized in grades (A–D or 1–10) to determine progress over time. Special care, it was noted, should be taken in developing a tool with which WBTI organizations and partners would feel comfortable.

As a next step, a committee subgroup working with the administration would define the process—creating the questionnaire, conducting a trial in no fewer than five countries, using the questionnaire with partners, church leaders, pastors, and community members. Analysis of the responses would lead to a 'score' for the country from which WBTI would subsequently develop a strategy for accomplishing goals. The subgroup would report back in May 2010.

Franklin's presentation and the notes on Wycliffe's context included above demonstrate the kind of input received by the board. To the board members, many with previous board experience, it was apparent that traditional indicators of progress were inadequate. Just as WBTI and its leadership were re-evaluating roles, board members recognized the necessity to re-evaluate their role and role fulfillment. Some were more comfortable with this than others, struggling to release status quo expectations and perceived control. But all shared a deep sense of responsibility and accountability.

Refining Measurements

A few members of the Committee on Measuring Progress sub-group, primarily members of the Alliance leadership team, had worked with an outside consultant for several months. Presented at this May 2010 board meeting was an extremely comprehensive, polished, professional model created to meet the board's requirements. It provided much more than the board had asked for, and after a lengthy discussion, the Committee on Measuring Progress felt it was too extensive. The organizations might not have the capacity or be willing to produce so much data that they were not already collecting. The leadership team was in complete agreement with this evaluation.

Both the leadership and the board realized the global organization could make only limited demands of the individual organizations, sensing the progress report would have a higher possibility of success if the administration primarily collected data the organizations had already produced. As a result, the committee proposed that the leadership team prepare a report for the board based on the WBTI goals stated earlier in this case study. The following questions were to be answered for each goal:

› What's working well/progress made?
› What's not working well and needs attention?
› Concerning the goal, what plans do you have?
› What barriers are there to progress?
› What other information is helpful for the board?

The expectation was a report, with these questions answered, from each Area (covering several organizations each) by the next WBTI board meeting.

The board had changed its expectations from its previous meeting, with more responsibility placed on the Areas, as they were to be in charge of gathering and organizing the information. The new questions were more focused and, at the same time, more open-ended than the first set of questions. The goal was to collect and compile already-existing data from the Wycliffe organizations. The board was also gaining more understanding of where accountability and responsibility lay. The pre-2008 structure had required the international administration to be responsible for many things over which they had no control. For example, how could Europe Area leadership be held accountable for Wycliffe Norway's recruitment strategies over which they had no say or jurisdiction? Even Wycliffe Norway would have had difficulty predicting numbers or quantifying 'successful' recruitment.

Redefining Progress

By this time, the Wycliffe Global Alliance was beginning to take shape. At this November 2010 board meeting, the name change was presented and unanimously accepted. Wycliffe Bible Translators International (WBTI), from 2011 onward, would be known as the Wycliffe Global Alliance (WGA).

In his executive director's report, Franklin presented some of the changing perspectives in the world of WGA.

› Changing theological perspectives: from proclamation alone to integral mission (proclamation and demonstration of the gospel); from local church emphasis and perspectives to global church (local church with global perspectives).
› Changing missiological perspectives: from the Western/Northern church to the church being global; from an emphasis on task partnerships to a growing

understanding of kingdom of God partnerships (where the kingdom is what is in focus); from situations of high power and control to situations of shared power and control.

› Changing Wycliffe International perspectives: from building an institution to travelling on a journey; from an emphasis on individual members to a focus on organizations and movements; from primarily being Western/Northern to being more global.

The Committee on Measuring Progress heard and affirmed reports from two of the four Areas. The other two Areas required more time to plan for and facilitate reporting. The committee recognized that qualitative reporting was, in some ways, more difficult to obtain than quantitative. Acknowledging that everyone's hard work was moving things forward, the committee recognized that measuring progress was an ongoing process. The administration would process the board requests and report to the May 2011 board meeting. The Area directors and two senior leaders, including the executive director, would meet in February to discuss the reporting needs. The Areas required their own measures of progress rather than simply reporting on how the organizations in their Area progressed. But they could choose to use organization-specific stories as examples of progress/health. In was expected that the Area directors' reports to the board would reflect taking 'ownership' of the level of progress within their Areas. The committee requested a preliminary report from the Areas by the May 2011 board meeting. In May 2011, the board would do an in-depth review of the two Areas that had submitted reports, and the other two Areas were to have preliminary reports.

This meeting marked another significant step in the board's journey. As they reflected on the implications of the changing perspectives the executive director had presented, it became apparent that the board and the leadership didn't 'control' what was happening in the various Bible translation movements worldwide. There was also a greater recognition that organizations had limited capacity to monitor and report on things that weren't already priorities, significant areas of interest, or concerns. If they weren't already gathering the data, stories, numbers, etc., for their constituency, the church in their country, and their donors, it was unlikely to be of prime importance. In a 2010 email, an Area director reported that of the questions the director had asked on the board's behalf, only three organizations in the Area responded. The director indicated the unlikelihood of receiving many responses as this type of request was low on the list of priorities. For many, this was a reality check. Lack of respect or desire to serve was not what limited the input. It was the reality of limited staff and time and a sense that they were already 'measuring what mattered' in their contexts.

In the previous era, Area directors set goals for people, prayer, and funds in the organizations in their regions. It was now apparent that it was not the responsibility of Area directors to determine these goals or for the board to monitor them. But everyone was still struggling with deciding what they could and should monitor. They started down a new path that would redefine 'progress' and concentrate more on organizational well-being than organizational activities. Activities might give clues about well-being, but they are not the essential measurements of progress.

New Way of Reporting

At its May 2011 meeting, the board approved the criteria and streams of involvement (Participation Streams) that would describe how organizations were involved in the WGA. By now, the name change to Wycliffe Global Alliance had received a positive response from around the world, with commendations from other organizations for this bold step. The reports from this board meeting also shared several instances of Wycliffe-to-Wycliffe cooperation and collaboration with others. Organizations saw the value of being a part of the Alliance as they shared resources and information.

In the Committee on Measuring Progress, two Areas were still unable to report adequately. They dealt with numerous issues during many transitions and could not provide cohesive information based on strategic plans. One of the other Areas (that had reported) resubmitted its report with updates and elaboration. Still, the Area director stated they were having difficulty connecting the goals the board had established with what was happening in the Area organizations. The other Area (that had previously reported) submitted an in-depth report that met all the criteria. The committee and board were pleased but realized there was too much in these reports (even though they were much less detailed than the reporting suggested by the outside consultant). They wanted a more straightforward report, with more consistency and a more uniform reporting format, showing diversity represented in the content rather than in the presentation.

Shifting their strategy, the board asked the leadership to produce a single report representing the uniqueness of each Area's context and plan, embedding the board goals for the Alliance in each Area plan. With no specific measurements given and combining both soft and hard measurements related to the goals, their expectation was an executive summary of two-page reports on each Area following a succinct template promoting consistency in style and format.

The streams of involvement concept and initiation accomplished many things, including affirming Alliance Organizations in their differing gifts, resources, and abilities, contributing to the board's understanding as they came to realize the diversity of the Areas. Each Area had its unique history and different previous structures. The Areas that had been dealing with crises or had more to undo before they could redo were in a different place than what the reporting criteria had been asking of them. The board realized that asking for uniform reporting, measuring like things in each Area, wasn't going to work.

The committee now recognized each Area's contexts, challenges, and uniqueness. The board was also growing in its overall understanding of the newly christened Wycliffe Global Alliance. Many realized this was far more than a new name; it was a new way of thinking about and being a part of God's mission. It was about many voices, being a part of the church, and multi and intercultural perspectives often contributing in ways no one would have previously imagined. Networks, relationships, and a deepening understanding of how God was working around the world created new ways of working and thinking—representing a more all-encompassing journey than the board had first envisioned.

Refining Reporting

At the November 2011 WGA Board meeting, Franklin presented a historical timeline from 1930 to the present, describing how the Alliance matured and changed, allowing for the inclusion of the Partner Organizations. At this time, there were traditional Wycliffe Member Organizations (WMOs) and Partner Organizations (WPOs), but both were considered Participating Organizations (POs). WGA was working out how to include the POs fully. Each PO committed to one or more participation streams: Church Engagement, Prayer, Fundraising, Recruiting and Sending, Specialty Services, Technical Training, and Language Programs. Franklin noted that twenty-seven per cent of the POs supervised language programs and that the number was increasing.

In their meeting, the Committee on Measuring Progress reiterated that simpler was better. They had concluded they did not need all the information they had initially thought necessary, nor all the available information. They reviewed the two Area reports not previously reviewed, noting the positive responses. In one case, the board asked if the Area plan was too ambitious, though they did appreciate the Area's new leadership, energy, and creativity. As for the other Area, the board was impressed by its missiological process and content and stated that they would like to see other Areas learning from that Area's best practices.

The board requested that future reports would again include the following questions for each goal:

- What's working well/progress made?
- What's not working well and needs attention?
- Concerning the goal, what plans do you have?

- What barriers are there to progress?
- What other information is helpful for the board?

The committee would not meet again until November of 2012. They commented that this should give the leadership team time to improve processes and refine reporting.

Comments from the leadership included the following:

The Senior Leadership Team (SLT) needs time to work with Areas, and some Areas need time to form. The SLT will get input from Areas at the February leadership team meeting, continue the building process, and improve and refine content. The SLT is requesting reports earlier so they can pre-process and better prepare. Currently provided information was the priority, but better information is now a higher priority. The SLT wants to get the Area directors together more often to build community and work together. The committee also felt this was necessary, establishing good accountability, developing best practices, and broadening cross-pollination. The Area directors have indicated they require a better understanding of giving input. This reporting affects the health of the organizations, their partnerships, etc. They want to know how to integrate this type of reporting into their planning. Everyone agrees that further work is necessary.

Sessions such as the executive director's presentation on the Alliance timeline continued to help the board grow in its understanding of the complexity and richness of Bible translation movements worldwide and the impossibility of controlling (or wanting to own) them. By this time, they had also shifted from thinking about what they would ask of the Alliance organizations to what they would ask of the executive director and, thereby, his leadership team. In terms of appropriate expectations and relationships in an alliance structure, this step of the board's journey was significant.

Missional Intent

Major topics of the November 2012 WGA Board meeting included: discussion of POs moving from autonomy to interdependence, modifying the mission statement, explaining core values, and modifying board Goal #2 in light of changing realities in WGA. Franklin reported on the global consultation on community held in Ghana. He presented an overview of the Alliance, including the following summary: The Alliance comprises more than 110 POs, including 45 WMOs and 70+ WPOs. They are bound together by their shared commitment to God's mission of reconciliation and the transformation of individuals, communities, and nations.

There were several new board members at this meeting. Franklin presented a summary of WGA's journey and talked about 'The Alliance Four Years from Now'.

A board member, now Area director, shared what he had learned in the past four years, and Susan Van Wynen spoke on *missional intent*. Franklin continued the discussion. He explained the use of the term missional intent for what was often called a 'strategic plan', clarifying that it wasn't just a shift in wording but a change in perspective and process. It did not mean the Alliance leadership was no longer strategic or making plans, but they were doing these things while staying centred on the fact that the future was in God's hands. Missional intent identifies the concerns, contexts, and causes we believe God asks us to observe. The strategies and actions need to remain flexible and attuned to him.

This discussion included considering whether to continue the Committee on Measuring Progress and whether there was a more appropriate way to reflect on accomplishing stages of the board's journey. With new board members, the question of quantitative measurements arose again, but after some discussion, the board again agreed to a more qualitative rather than quantitative approach. It stated that the board had found it challenging to find ways to measure progress despite the excellent work done over the last four years. The new quadrennium would begin to consider alternative ways of engaging with members and partners to move forward strategically.

In conclusion, the board agreed that, as WGA evolves, we all begin to understand more and more the ways of an alliance. Measuring progress in quantitative terms may not be the way that best fits the context, and qualitative reporting better reflects how progress is determined. Accordingly, the board requested the executive director focus on strategic reporting to the board based on the missional intent of the Global Leadership Team. There would no longer be a Committee on Measuring Progress. The board could request that the executive director address a specific theme within that strategy or determine the topics to report and reflect on.

Summary

Over three years and seven board meetings, this remarkable journey brought the WGA Board to a place of appropriate alignment, scope, and content of reporting. They moved from the concept of scorecard measurements of each Alliance Organization, with the responsibility primarily on those organizations, to a big picture, executive director-owned approach, revealing patterns, trends, challenges, and progress. This moved the responsibility to a place where the board could participate through response and action, ideally without being overwhelmed by details. Since the executive director reports to the board, it makes sense for this reporting to follow those channels. There was now the proper alignment of who had authority for what.

Initially, the board thought the individual organizations were responsible for reporting to them. They soon realized the diversity and limited capacity of the organizations made this very difficult, as did the new, more clearly defined Alliance structure. Accordingly, their focus shifted to the Area directors to gather and compile data from the organizations and from their Area strategies. But this emerged as unproductive since each Area differed in its development, growth, and capacity to gather data and report.

Both Asia and Pacific (considered one Area administratively) and Africa were, more or less, starting from scratch in terms of what information they could or wanted to report on and how to gather it. Uniform indicators just didn't work. There was also the challenge of connecting organization goals with board goals. It was not that they were incompatible; it was just a huge stretch to connect them directly. Areas wanted to work on organizational health, which was less production-oriented than what the board seemed to want in the earliest days of this journey. Everyone had the same desire to attend to the well-being of the organizations, but what would evidence of that well-being look like? Several attempts were made to address that through the reporting questions asked. Once examples of reporting as the board requested were possible and available, the board realized they didn't need that much information. But they now had the assurance that it was out there and that there were more than enough signs of progress.

By 2012, the executive director provided reports that integrated stories, information, issues, and evidence of various kinds of progress from around the world, specifically tailored to the board to encourage and enable its full participation. There was an understanding that indicators and strategy needed to be interwoven in a bigger picture rather than scorecard boxes to represent priorities for the Alliance as a whole and for its organizations.

Alliance strategy and progress reporting needed to be grounded in sound theology and grow from the Alliance's missiological thinking and values. Scope and content of reporting were increasingly better aligned with the new realities of Bible translation movements. And while the geographical constructs of Areas could be helpful, there was also much going on across Areas and through other affinities. Reporting was beginning to reflect that as well. The board had gained an understanding that progress was better observed and participated in than calculated and counted.

The journey continues. There are always new board members who, in their desire to serve well, seek something to measure. And there are always new questions, new challenges, and new ways of working that require the board to take stock of its purpose and place. It is important for the Alliance leadership to continue serving them well, inspiring them further, and journeying with them under God's direction.

In the words of Timothy Tennent,

> Missions always must unfold within the context of, and the anticipation of, God's work, which He alone initiated and which He alone can bring to final completion. This perspective if properly understood, should not render us passive or our work inconsequential. Rather, it puts all of our work within the larger and more ennobling context of God's action and the certainty of final outcome.[2]

[2] Tennent, 123.

Epilogue

By Stephen Coertze

This book is a missional leadership history explored in the context of the journey of the Wycliffe Global Alliance (WGA) as it developed from an institutional organization to a Bible translation movement. Where is that movement going?

On 1 April 2020, the Alliance launched its first Executive Director leadership transition, which would in many respects be a test for the vitality of the leadership model of WGA. This leadership model has evolved over 80 years, shaped by various leaders and organizational dynamics. Two distinct factors impacted this leadership transition, characterizing it as unique. It was the first since WGA emerged as a Bible translation movement, having the longstanding heritage of an institution. And this transition unexpectedly occurred amidst the unfolding global drama of the COVID-19 pandemic. We do not know what kind of world will emerge when the pandemic fades away. Though it will be a marker on the journey of WGA, our journey continues, shaped by multiple changing realities that we will face together.

The ministry of Bible translation continued to blossom amid the complex leadership transition. Therefore, it would be prudent to make a few observations on how earlier choices made by the WGA leadership that led to our current leadership philosophy played out in the context of this unique leadership transition.

One of the driving virtues of the missional leadership approach that guided us through the past years since 2008 was our firm belief that God is fulfilling his purposes. He is fulfilling his mission, and God calls us to participate with him in his mission. It soon became apparent that because of the pandemic and the global response, we could not, as a worldwide movement, envisage a future that would be a continuance of the past. We could consider a future that would be more uncertain, complex, and ambiguous. But this potential reality does not leave us disheartened. One thing remains certain: the pandemic did not catch God by surprise. He is still fulfilling his mission, and in dependency on him, we still joyfully participate with him in this. For this reason, we remain dependent on God and can be moved by his Spirit into new spaces wherever he wishes to take us.

Our leadership made many decisions as we developed into a global Bible translation movement. These choices served us well in the context of lockdowns, restrictions, and isolation. For example, our Alliance Leadership Team (ALT) operated primarily as a virtual team with minimal in-person interaction. We had already developed attitudes and competencies to work virtually, making it easier for the ALT to adapt to having only virtual interaction. A further example would include the previous leadership decisions to develop flexible structures that better suited a Bible translation movement. These gave us the agility needed to adjust many of our working patterns rapidly. Investing time in understanding issues such as the reality and impact of polycentrism on the Bible translation movement is another example. This understanding of polycentrism assisted us in cushioning much of the effect of the pandemic. This was seen in the Alliance Organizations' quick response to the pandemic, without the need to wait for instructions and directions from the ALT. They were, after all, best positioned and equipped to rapidly adapt according to the realities of the specific contexts in which they were operating.

The pandemic has impacted the whole of humanity in numerous ways. We are all dealing with losses and uncertainty about the future. All Alliance Organizations had to respond to new realities and often made bold and difficult decisions about their future. The WGA Board and the ALT had to answer questions never previously asked. During this, WGA has seen God at work in and through the Alliance during the pandemic and has continued to equip and encourage us.

In most cases, the Bible translation movement has flourished and continues to do so despite and because of the pandemic restrictions. New translation projects began, and the celebration of completed translations continued. More organizations joined the Bible translation movement, often with bold initiatives. There is a greater realization of the valuable contribution local communities make toward Bible translation. Innovations in virtual translation training and consultancy are under exploration. Organizations reach out to assist one another where needs arise. Bridging geographical constraints through virtual platforms provides more individuals with the opportunity to participate and connect. Meetings and events conducted in different yet effective ways have enabled people spread over the globe to meet constructively in the same room. For many individuals and churches, their understanding of the bigger picture of God's mission has expanded, and new ways of participating in his mission have become possible. Decisions made by leaders in the past continue to impact us and give us the tools to weather the storm of the pandemic. The pandemic will be etched in the memory of humanity for years to come and will be remembered by some as a pivotal time in the history of the Alliance's journey as it evolved from WBTI to WGA. All glory to God, who has uniquely equipped us to complete a leadership transition under unique circumstances.

The glaring question that remains before us is the future landscape of the Bible translation movement. Several current developments provide hints of what could lie before us, and several current realities particular to the Bible translation movement will still be relevant in the future. To name a few, these include the role of the global church in Bible translation; localization of Bible translation programs; holistic responses to Bible translation, calling for the translation of both testaments of the Bible; innovations in funding Bible translation programs; new understanding of language ecologies; and multi-modality products which include translation for the deaf as well as Oral Bible Translation. As we attempt to fathom the future before us, numerous global realities remain, impacting the context in which we serve. Two of these realities, namely the impulse for ideological and economic survival and global social movements, will continue to disrupt and shape the world we know. We will continue to see uprisings, revolts, suppression, conflicts, and disruption across the globe. It is only the depth of such turmoil and chaos that we cannot calculate at this stage. It is in this environment that Bible translation will continue.

The question is how the Bible translation movement will navigate through this growingly disruptive context. We are not stranded without a guiding compass, however. As suggested in the opening remarks of this book, we can appropriately navigate the future if we remain rooted in what has gone before. We have explicit references within our WGA history to help us on our journey. We will briefly refer to three historical markers that can guide us into the future.

God commissioned his church for his mission. We need to remain rooted in the mission of God. In response to God's calling, we have the joyful privilege of participating with him in his mission, particularly in the ministry of Bible translation. Those who have gone before us responded to God's calling to join his mission, and the same God who led them through the circumstances in of their time is leading us today.

We need to remain embedded in our history, which provides clear markers as we anticipate our future. We do have a rich history. Some of this history is espoused in this book, especially as it relates to decisions that our leaders made over the span of our journey. Traced from the days of Cameron Townsend, in 2020, we celebrated 40 years since the founding of Wycliffe Bible Translators International under the leadership of George Cowan, WBTI's first president. And in 2020, Kirk Franklin completed his role as executive director of Wycliffe Global Alliance, now widely referred to as a Bible translation movement. Today, we humbly recognise all those who have gone before us, responding to God's call in their contexts and times. *A Missional Leadership History: The Journey from Wycliffe Bible Translators to the Wycliffe Global Alliance* provides us with insights as to how our leaders in the past came to conclusions on perplexing questions with which they had to engage. Just as we don't have a roadmap before us to follow, neither did they. Serving as a reminder, the decisions we make today will become part of the continuing history of leadership that will impact and influence the future of the Bible translation movement.

We also need to remain rooted in our foundational statements. These statements include our Mission, Vision, Purpose, and Doctrinal and Value Statements, which form the core beliefs of the Alliance. These did not develop in a vacuum but over time on our journey. They indicate how we responded to God's mission in the past, providing light for our ongoing journey.

Past decisions by our leadership made in specific historical contexts over 80 years are still impacting us today. We are slowly emerging out of a pandemic and only starting to understand the new demands that this season of our journey with God in Bible translation asks of us. It is sobering to know that those leadership decisions made in our current context will continue to impact future understandings and practices of the WGA. As we look towards the ultimate destination, the missional leadership developed within the Alliance will continue to evolve. Our journey continues with hope!

Timeline

1917 Cameron Townsend, US, leaves California for Guatemala to sell Spanish Bibles.

1934 Townsend and L. L. Legters, US, found SIL.

1942 Townsend and William Nyman, US, found Wycliffe Bible Translators, Incorporated (in California) with a registered office in Los Angeles.

1942 First meeting of WBT, Inc. Board and SIL Board (composed of the same people), in Mexico City, 15 September. The two boards then meet jointly and monthly, usually in the Los Angeles Area.

1943 First Annual Meeting of WBTI, Inc. is held on 6 September in Cuernavaca, Mexico.

1943 WBT, Inc. Board approves Canada Division, the first Wycliffe presence outside the US.

1944 Townsend's wife Elvira dies after a long illness. Townsend meets Elaine Mielke and marries her two years later.

1954 WBT, Inc. Board approves the start of the Australian Branch of Wycliffe Bible Translators, an outcome of Ken Pike, US, teaching an SIL course there in 1950.

1959 Switzerland now has a Wycliffe representative.

1960 In May, after 18 years of service, William Nyman resigns from WBT as board secretary due to ill health.

1961 The British Advisory Council begins the process to be recognized by WBT, Inc. Board as a chartered Home Council of Wycliffe.

1962 Wycliffe.V. registers with German authorities to further the work of WBT.

1963 The New Zealand Council of WBT commences.

1963 Discussions begin to separate the international oversight of WBT from US domestic responsibilities.

1965 A Wycliffe representative is appointed for the Netherlands.

1965 The search begins for a new national and international adjoining headquarters in the US for Wycliffe Bible Translators.

1966 Ben Elson, US, is appointed as the Principal Administrative Officer of WBT and SIL, serving under General Director Cameron Townsend.

1967 Wycliffe US Home Council and Wycliffe Canada Home Council separate from each other, resulting in greater autonomy for each group.

1967 Wycliffe Associates is formed.

1971 Townsend retires as general director and becomes known as Founder and General Director Emeritus of WBT and SIL.

1971 Wycliffe US headquarters is established in Huntington Beach, California.

1973 WBT and SIL Boards approve plans to develop an international headquarters in Dallas, Texas.

1975 Frank Robbins, US, replaces Ben Elson upon the latter's retirement. Robbins' title is Executive Director of WBT and SIL.

1975 WBT Japan is founded, and Takashi Fukuda serves on Japan Division Council.

1980 Wycliffe Bible Translators International (WBTI) forms as a separate organization from WBT, Inc, with the latter becoming the legal body of the US Home Division, later known as Wycliffe US. George Cowan, Canada, becomes WBTI President. (Cowan first became President of WBT, Inc. in 1957).

1981 George Cowan retires as President of WBTI and becomes President Emeritus. David Cummings, Australia, becomes WBTI President.

1982 Korean home office for WBT commences..

1983 John Bendor-Samuel, UK, becomes Executive Vice President for WBTI and SIL, taking over from Frank Robbins.

1988 Twelve National Bible Translation Organizations (NBTO) attend the WBTI International Conference, marking the first NBTO presence at the conference.

1991 WBTI restructured with chartered Divisions becoming Wycliffe Organizations.

1992 Steve Sheldon, US, becomes Executive Vice President for WBTI and SIL, taking over from John Bendor-Samuel.

1993 WBTI encourages Wycliffe US to establish an organization, under the leadership of Bernie May, to fund national translator projects. (This eventually becomes Seed Company.)

1999 Vision 2025 is adopted; new Ends statements are created to guide WBTI.

1999 John Watters, US, becomes Executive Vice President for WBTI and SIL, taking the place of Steve Sheldon.

2000 WBTI collaborates with COMIBAM to encourage Bible translation movements in Latin America.

2001 Associate Partner Organization status created for greater participation in WBTI; 12 organizations presented with this new status.

2001 John Bendor-Samuel, UK, appointed WBTI's first Area Director for Africa Area. Dave Ohlson, US, appointed Area Director for WBTI's new Asia-Pacific Area.

2001 Burkhard Schöttelndreyer, Germany, is the first European appointed as Europe Area Director. George Cowan, Canada, was the first Europe Area Director (called Deputy General Director for Europe and Africa in 1963).

2002 In response to Vision 2025, WBTI Board asks International Administration to deliberately engage in appropriate partnerships with churches of the Global South and East.

2002 WBTI Board separates from SIL Board.

2004 Takashi Fukuda, Japan, is the first Asian appointed as Asia-Pacific Area Director.

2004 WBTI and SIL Business Plan for Vision 2025 is created.

2005 WBTI International Convention approves: WBTI having its own executive director, separate from SIL's; non-overlapping board members for WBTI and SIL; WBTI President title changed to Board Chairman; and the organizational categories of Wycliffe Member Organizations and Wycliffe Affiliate Organizations.

2006 Roger Welch, UK, becomes WBTI Board Chairman; the WBTI role of president, held by Richard Hugoniot, US, is discontinued.

2006 WBTI's first missiological consultation held in Orlando. This starts an annual reflective missiology process that continues to 2019.

2007 José de Dios, Guatemala/US, is appointed as Americas Area Director.

2007 WBTI Board discontinues having three board members overlapping with SIL Board.

2008 Kirk Franklin, Australia/US, becomes WBTI Executive Director after the role was separated from SIL.

2008 WBTI International Administration becomes the Global Leadership Team.

2009 WBTI's operational headquarters is established in Singapore. Global Leadership Team member, David Brooks, US, relocates from the US to Singapore to fill the Associate Director (Partnerships) role.

2010 Ah Chye Wong, Singapore, is appointed as WBTI Chief Financial Officer (before this, the position was shared with SIL and held by Eleanor Berry).

2011 WBTI's 'doing business as' name changes to Wycliffe Global Alliance and is accepted as Alianza Global Wycliffe (Spanish), Aliança Global Wycliffe (Portuguese), and Alliance Wycliffe Mondiale (French). The Alliance is composed of 45 Wycliffe Member Organizations and 50+ Wycliffe Partner Organizations.

2011 Mũndara Mũturi, Kenya, is appointed as Africa Area Director.

2013 *Philosophy of Bible Translation Programs* is released as the Alliance's ground-breaking statement, developed by a cross-section of leaders from Bible translation organizations in the Alliance.

2013 *Principles of Community* is released as the guiding statements of the Alliance's behaviour.

2014 *Principles for Funding* is released as guiding statements concerning the stewardship of financial resources within the Alliance.

2014 Seven Participation Streams are developed as the primary means by which Alliance Organizations indicate their involvement within the Alliance.

2015 The Alliance's *Covenant/Statement of Commitment* introduces how organizations are recognized within the Alliance, replacing five categories of Wycliffe Member Organizations and four types of Wycliffe Partner Organizations.

2016 Wycliffe Global Gathering takes place in Chiang Mai, Thailand, as the new Alliance configuration representing all organizations that had signed the *Covenant/Statement of Commitment*.

2016 Roger Welch retires as WBTI's first board chair. Decio de Carvalho, Brazil, is elected by the board as the new chair.

2017 Alliance Board announces three directional statements specifically about Bible translation, encouraging Alliance Organizations to place greater importance on developing new Bible translation training curricula, development and accreditation of Bible translation consultants, and translating the whole counsel of God (i.e., Old and New Testaments).

2018 Alliance leadership and board develop descriptions of key terms used within the Alliance. This list would grow as terms became enculturated into the movement. The list included terms such as Alliance, Board Goals, Collaboration, Core Values, Friendship and Community, Global Missional Leadership Mindset, Holistic Mission, Integral Mission, Institution, Journey, *Missio Dei* (Mission of God), Missiological Reflection, Mission, Missional Intent, Polycentric Mission, Polyphonic Community, Purpose Statement, Stewardship and Generosity, Third Spaces, Transformation, Translation Movement/s and Vision.

2018 Decio de Carvalho steps down as board chair, and Agnes Lid, Norway, is elected by the board to be the new chair.

2018 Board treasurer role and Alliance CFO role are combined, and Hannu Summanen, Finland, is appointed to the joint role.

2020 Stephen Coertze, South Africa, becomes executive director, succeeding Kirk Franklin.

Bibliography

Global Missiology for the 21st Century, edited by William D. Taylor. Pasadena: William Carey Library, 2000.

Aldridge, Boone. *For the Gospel's Sake: The Rise of Wycliffe Bible Translators and the Summer Institute of Linguistics*. Grand Rapids: Wm B. Eerdmans, 2018.

Aldridge, Boone. *Kenneth L. Pike: An Evangelical Mind*. Eugene, OR: Pickwick Publications, 2021.

Balia, Daryl, and Kirsteen Kim. *Witnessing to Christ Today*. Oxford: Regnum, 2010.

Bandura, Albert. "Toward an Agentic Theory of the Self." *Advances in Self Research* 3 (2008).

Barrett, David. *God's Word Alone: The Authority of Scripture*. Grand Rapids: Zondervan, 2016.

Bass, Bernard. "From Transactional to Transformational Leadership: Learning to Share the Vision." In *Leadership: Understanding the Dynamics of Power and Influence in Organizations*. Edited by Robert Vecchio. Notre Dame: University of Notre Dame Press, 1997.

Bediako, Kwame. *Jesus and the Gospel in Africa: History and Experience*. Maryknoll: Orbis, 2004.

Bosch, David. *Transforming Mission: Paradigm Shifts in Theology of Mission*. Maryknoll: Orbis, 1991.

Bosch, David. *Transforming Mission: Paradigm Shifts in Theology of Mission*. Maryknoll: Orbis Books, 2011.

Burns, James MacGregor. *Transforming Leadership*. New York: Gove Press, 2003.

Bush, Luis. "AD2000 and Beyond: Toward a Conceptual Model." In *Working Together with God to Shape the New Milliennium: Opportunities & Limitations*. Edited by Gary Corwin and Kenneth Mulholland. Pasadena: William Carey Library, 2000.

Carlisle, Keith, and Rebecca Gruby. "Polycentric Systems of Governance: A Theoretical Model for the Commons." *Policy Studies Journal* 47, no. 4 (2019): 927-52.

Carr, Burgess. "The Engagement of Lusaka." *Pro Veritate* June (1974).

Cassidy, Michael. "The Call to Moratorium: Perspective on an Identity Crisis." *Churchman* 90, no. 4 (1976): 265-80. Accessed 29 August 2020. https://churchsociety.org/docs/churchman/090/Cman_090_4_Cassidy.pdf.

Chua, How Chuang. "Perichoresis and *Missio Dei*: Implications of a Trinitarian View of Personhood for Missionary Practice." 2010. OMF Mission Research Consultation.

Collins, James, and Jerry Porras. *Built to Last*. London: Random House Business Books, 2005.

Deiros, Pablo A. "Historical Research." In *Introduction to Missiological Research Design*. Edited by Edgar Elliston. Pasadena: William Carey Library, 2011.

Escobar, Samuel. "The global scenario at the turn of the century." In *Global Missiology for the 21st Century*. Edited by William D. Taylor. Pasadena: William Carey Library, 2000.

Frank, Paul. "SIL and WBTI in the 21st Century Some History, A Vision of the Future, and A Bit o' Fiction." 2007.

Franklin, Kirk. "How Can the Reformation's Focus on Faithfulness to Scripture Inspire Us for Mission?", *HTS Teologiese Studies/ Theological Studies* 74, no. 1 (2018). https://dx.doi.org/10.4102/hts.v74i1.4817.

Friedman, Thomas. *The World is Flat: A Brief History of the 21st century*. New York: Farrar, Straus and Giroux, 2005.

Gatũ, John. *Fan into Flame: An Autobiography*. Nairobi: Moran Publishers, 2016.

Giddens, Anthony. *The Third Way*. Cambridge: Polity Press, 1998.

Glover, Warren. *Making a Difference: Training Bible Translators in India*. Kangaroo Ground: WBT Australia, 2002.

Graham, Billy. "Why Lausanne." Lausanne Movement. 1974. Accessed 16 June 2020. https://www.lausanne.org/content/why-lausanne-print.

Greenleaf, Robert K. *Servant Leadership: A Journey into the Nature of Legitimate Power and Grateness*. Ramsey: Paulist Press, 1977.

Hanciles, Jehu. *Beyond Christendom: Globalization, African Migration, and the Transformation of the West*. Maryknoll: Orbis, 2008.

Hartch, Todd. *The Rebirth of Latin American Christianity*. Oxford: Oxford University Press, 2014.

Hesselgrave, David. "The Great Commission." In *Evangelical Dictionary of World Missions*. Edited by Scott Moreau. Grand Rapids: Baker Books, 2000.

Hibberd, Cal. "Quotable Uncle Cam." 2007. SIL International Townsend Archives.

Hibberd, Cal. "Significant Events in the Life of William Cameron Townsend." 2015. SIL International Townsend Archives.

Hill, Graham, and Grace Ji-Sun Kim. *Healing Our Broken Humanity*. Downers Grove: IVP, 2018.

Hirsch, Alan. *The Forgotten Ways*. Grand Rapids: Brazos Press, 2006.

Hunt, Robert. *The Gospel Among the Nations: A Documentary History of Inculturation*. Maryknoll: Orbis Books, 2010.

Hunter, James Davison. *To Change the World: The Irony, Tragedy, and Possibility of Christianity in the Late Modern World*. New York: Oxford University Press, 2011.

Jacobsen, Douglas. *Global Gospel: an Introduction to Christianity on Five Continents*. Grand Rapids: Baker Academic, 2015.

Jenkins, Philip. *The New Faces of Christianity: Believing the Bible in the Global South*. Oxford: Oxford University Press, 2006.

Jenkins, Philip. *The Next Christendom*. Third ed. New York: Oxford University Press, 2011.

Jenkins, Philip. *The Next Christendom: The Coming of Global Christianity*. New York: Oxford University Press, 2002.

Johnson, John. *Mission Voices: Learning to Lead Beyond Our Horizons*. Carlisle: Langham Global Library, 2019.

Johnson, Todd, and Kenneth Ross. "The Making of the Atlas of Global Christianity." *IBMR* 34, no. 1 (2010): 12-16.

Jones, E. Stanley. *Gandhi: Portrait of a Friend*. Nashville: Abingdon Press, 1948.

Karliner, Josh, Gary Cohen, and Peter Orris. "Lessons in Forging Global Change." *Stanford Social Innovation Review* 12 (2014).

Kenmogne, Michel. "Observations and Thoughts on SIL's History." 2015. Current-SIL Internal Newsletter.

Kerr, David, and Kenneth Ross. *Edinburgh 2010: Mission Then and Now* Oxford: Regnum, 2009.

Kim, Kirsteen. *Joining in with the Spirit: Connecting World Church and Local Mission*. London: Epworth, 2009.

Kirk, Andrew. *What is Mission?* Minneapolis: Fortress Press, 2000.

Kotter, John. *A Sense of Urgency*. Boston: Harvard Business Press, 2008.

Kotter, John. "What Leaders Really Do." In *Leadership: Understanding the Dynamics of Power and Influence in Organizations*. Edited by Robert Vecchio. Notre Dame: University of Notre Dame Press, 1997.

Laniak, Timothy. *Shepherds After My Own Heart: Pastoral Traditions and Leadership in the Bible*. Downers Grove: InterVarsity Press, 2006.

Laub, James A. "Assessing the Servant Organization Development of the Servant Organizational Leadership Assessment (SOLA) Instrument." Florida Atlantic University, 1999.

Ledbetter, Bernice, Robert Banks, and David Greenhalgh. *Reviewing Leadership: A Christian Evaluation of Current Approaches*. 2nd ed. Grand Rapids: Baker Academic 2016.

Lewis, C.S. *The Problem of Pain*. New York: Macmillan, 1977.

Livermore, David. *Leading with Cultural Intelligence*. New York: AMACOM, 2105.

Malik, Anas. *Polycentricity, Islam, and Development*. Lanham: Lexington Press, 2018.

Maramara, Zenet. "Shalom Leadership." *Christian Leadership Alliance blog*, 2018.

McGrath, Alister. *Historical Theology: An Introduction to the History of Christian Thought*. 2nd ed. Oxford: Wiley, 2013.

Mollazadeh, Shahram, Amir zadeh Mahmood, and Kamran Yeganegi. "A Review of New Leadership Theories and Its Components." *International Journal of Management Sciences and Business Research* 7, no. 2 (2018): 223-34.

Neill, Stephen. *A History of Christian Missions*. 2nd ed. London: Penguin, 1986.

Newbigin, Lesslie. *The Open Secret: An Introduction to the Theology of Mission, revised*. Grand Rapids: Wm. B. Eerdmans, 1995.

Niemandt, Nelus. *Missional Leadership*. Cape Town: AOSIS, 2019.

Northouse, Peter. *Leadership: Theory and Practice*. 8th ed. London: SAGE Publications, 2019.

Oborji, Francis Anekwe. *Concepts of Mission: The Evolution of Contemporary Missiology*. Maryknoll: Orbis Books, 2006.

Opoku-Mensah, Paul. "Launching the Golden Anniversary in Tamale." 17 February 2012. GILLBT Admin Memo.

Pachuau, Lalsangkima. *World Christianity: A Historical and Theological Introduction*. Nashville: Abingdon Press, 2018.

Plowman, Donde Ashmos, Stephanie Solansky, Tammy E. Beck, LaKami Baker, Mukta Kulkarni, and Deandra Villarreal Travis. "The Role of Leadership in Emergent, Self-organization." *The Leadership Quarterly* 18, no. 4 (2007): 341-56.

Pree, Max De. *Leadership is an Art*. New York: Doubleday, 1989.

Rameka, Lesley. "Kia whakatōmuri te haere whakamua: 'I walk backwards into the future with my eyes fixed on my past'." *Contemporary Issues in Early Childhood* 17, no. 4 (2016): 387–98. https://dx.doi.org/10.1177/1463949116677923.

Robert, Dana. *Christian Mission: How Christianity Became a World Religion*. Chichester, UK: Wiley-Blackwell 2009.

Rodin, R. Scott. *The Steward Leader: Transforming People, Organizations and Communities*. Downers Grove: IVP Academic, 2010.

Sanneh, Lamin. *Whose Religion is Christianity? The Gospel Beyond the West*. Grand Rapids: Wm. B. Eerdmans, 2003.

Scharmer, C. Otto. *Theory U: Leading from the Future as It Emerges*. San Francisco: Berrett-Koehler Publications, 2009.

Schein, Edgar, and Peter Schein. *in Humble Leadership: The Power of Relationships, Openness, and Trust*. Oakland: Berrett-Koehler 2018.

Scouller, James. *The Three Levels of Leadership*. Cirencester: Management Books, 2011.

Self, Charles E. "Historical Research." In *Missiological Research: Interdisciplinary Foundations, Methods, and Integration*. Edited by Marvin Gilbert, Alan R. Johnson, and Paul W. Lewis. Pasadena: William Carey Library, 2018.

Smither, Edward. *Christian Mission: A Concise Global History*. Bellingham: Lexham Press, 2019.

Stanley, Brian. *Christianity in the Twentieth Century: A World History*. Princeton: Princeton University Press, 2018.

Steven, Hugh. *Doorway to the World*. Wheaton: Harold Shaw, 1999.

Steven, Hugh. *Yours for Finishing the Task*. Orlando: Wycliffe Bible Translators, 2004.

Sunquist, Scott. *The Unexpected Christian Century*. Grand Rapids: Baker Academic, 2015.

Svelmoe, William. *A New Vision for Missions* Tuscaloosa: University of Alabama Press, 2008.

Tennent, Timothy. *Invitation to World Missions: a Trinitarian Missiology for the Twenty-first Century*. Grand Rapids: Kregel, 2011.

Tennent, Timothy. *Invitation to World Missions: A Trinitarian Missiology of the Twenty-First Century*. Grand Rapids: Kregel Academic & Professional, 2010.

Terry, John Mark, and Robert Gallagher. *Encountering the History of Missions: From the Early Church to Today*. Grand Rapids: Baker Academic, 2017.

Tharp, Charles. "Book Review of Meeting the Ethical Challenges of Leadership." *Human Resource Management* 41, no. 4 (2002): 501-02.

Uhl-Bien, Mary, Russ Marion, and Bill McKelvey. "Complexity Leadership Theory: Shifting Leadership from the Industrial Age to the Knowledge Era." *The Leadership Quarterly* 18, no. 4 (2007): 298-318.

van Butselaar, G. Jan. "The Role of Churches in the Peace Process in Africa." In *The Changing Face of Christianity: Africa, the West, and the World*. Edited by Lamin Sanneh and Joel Carpenter. Oxford: Oxford University Press, 2005.

Van Wynen, Susan. "A Journey of Missional Intent: Organizational Strategy in the Context of God's Mission." University of Pretoria, 2020.

Van Wynen, Susan, Dave Crough, and Kirk Franklin. "Foundational Statements of the Wycliffe Global Alliance." 2019. Accessed 7 September, 2020. https://www.wycliffe.net/wp-content/uploads/2020/01/Alliance_Foundational_Statements_2019_09_EN.pdf.

Wakatama, Pius. *Independence for the Third World Church*. Downers Grove: IVP, 1976.

Walker, Christina. "Inclusive Leadership in INGO, Multinational Teams: Learning, Listening and Voicing in 'Attentive Space'." Trinity International University, 2020.

Walker, Ranginui. *Ngā Pepa a Ranginui: The Walker Papers*. Auckland: Penguin, 1996.

Walls, Andrew. "Afterword: Christian Mission in a Five Hundred Year Context." In *Mission in the 21st Century*. Edited by Andrew Walls and Cathy Ross. Maryknoll: Orbis Books, 2008.

Walls, Andrew. "Demographics, Power and the Gospel in the 21st Century." 2002.

Watters, John. "Foundation of Bible Translation and Achieving Vision 2025." 2007.

Watters, John. "The Future of SIL and Some Implications for WBTI." 2007.

West, Gerald. "The Bible and the Poor." In *Bible in Mission*. Edited by Pauline Hoggarth, Fergus Macdonald, Bill Mitchell, and Knud Jorgensen. Oxford: Regnum.

Wilson, Kent. *Steward Leadership in the Nonprofit Organization*. Downers Grove: IVP 2016.

Wolterstorff, Nicholas. "Foreword." In *Evangelicals and Empire: Christian Alternatives to the Political Status Quo*. Edited by Bruce Benson and Peter Heltzel. Grand Rapids: Brazos Press, 2008.

Works, Hebert. "Lausanne–A Catalyst for World Evangelization." *Church Growth Bulletin* 9, no. 1 (September 1975): 439-50

Wright, Christopher. *The Mission of God: Unlocking the Bible's Grand Narrative*. Downers Grove: IVP Academic, 2006.

Wright, N. T. *The Last Word: Beyond the Bible Wars to a New Understanding of the Authority of Scripture*. New York: HarperCollins, 2005.

Yasir, Muhammad, and Noor Azmi Mohamad. "Ethics and Morality: Comparing Ethical Leadership with Servant, Authentic and Transformational Leadership Styles." *International Review of Management and Marketing* 6, no. S4 (2016): 310-16.

Yeh, Allen. *Polycentric Missiology: Twenty-first Century Mission from Everyone to Everywhere*. Downers Grove: IVP Academic, 2016.

Name Index

Abadiano, Teodoro (Ted), 338
Adams, Earl, 63, 73, 89, 98, 100, 127
Addai, William, 334
Adive, John, 102, 126, 327, 337
Adjekum, Grace, 138, 334
Agama, John, 36, 322, 334
Ahoyo, Nestor Adjovi, 275-276
Amukobole, Micah, 100, 113, 127, 138, 333, 339, 342
Araujo, Alex, 201
Arthur, Eddie, 233, 235, 393
Bass, Bernard, 105-106, 378, 501
Bediako, Kwame, 147, 220, 411, 501
Bendor-Samuel, David, 53, 113, 120-121
Bendor-Samuel, John, 33-34, 36-37, 57, 72, 80, 86-87, 95-96, 99, 103, 107, 113, 117-118, 126-127, 131, 138-139, 142, 144-145, 166, 189, 195, 210, 222, 322, 333, 336, 338, 341, 343-344, 496-497
Bendor-Samuel, Paul, 275-276, 291, 301
Bennett, John, 188, 195, 236
Berry, Eleanor, 183, 191, 498
Bianchi, Daniel, 163, 177, 188, 195
Binder, Wolfgang, 184
Bokelman, Judy, 240, 283, 294, 412
Bosch, David, 9, 17-18, 22, 47, 110-111, 213, 364, 390, 393, 403, 501
Boswell, Fredrick (Freddy), 183, 194
Brabham, Eric, 85, 89, 96, 100
Brooks, Dave, 160, 166, 184, 186, 191-192, 203, 228, 251, 408, 432, 450, 459-460, 466, 474, 497
Burns, James Macgregor, 44, 105, 378, 501
Bush, Luis, 79, 111, 146, 364, 452
Cardenas, David, 412, 444, 450, 453, 456, 469
Carey, William, 18, 48
Carr, Burgess, 314-315, 501
Cassidy, Michael, 315, 501
Chan, Tony, 191
Chapman, Bob and Ruth, 151
Chesnut, John, 297
Chiu, Winston, 195
Chong, Nicky, 236, 275-276
Chua, Elisha, 191, 255, 501
Chua, How Chuang, 191, 255, 501
Coertze, Stephen, 191, 278, 280, 302, 305-306, 364-365, 368, 382, 385, 388-390, 393, 396-397, 411, 413, 416, 420, 424, 430, 432, 440-441, 444-445, 491, 499
Collins, James, 216, 349-350, 378
Cowan, George, 25, 28-29, 33, 35, 37, 45, 53, 61, 68, 72, 80, 82, 97, 137, 139, 167, 493, 496-497
Cram, Dave, 142, 149, 240
Creson, Bob, 127, 142, 177, 188, 195, 236, 275-276, 297, 383
Crough, Dave, 14, 247, 262, 287-289, 291, 297, 303-304, 430, 505
Crough, Deborah, 14, 287, 304
Cummings, David, 32, 53, 61, 81-82, 84-85, 88-89, 95-96, 99-100, 113, 127, 137-138, 153, 195, 326-327, 496
Dasalla, Antonio, 338
Davis, Ken, 134, 137
Dawson, Matt, 10, 260, 295
de Dios, José, 186, 191, 233, 235, 240, 252, 450, 467, 474, 497
de Mattos, Rinaldo, 330
De Pree, Max, 105
de Vries, Martijn, 283, 294
Dusu, Barnaba, 336-337
Edoni, William, 163, 177, 183, 187-188, 332
Elson, Ben, 28, 49-53, 57, 63, 495-496
Emmanuel Njock, 82, 85, 89, 96
Escobar, Samuel, 79, 89, 388, 405-406, 502
Evensen, Sigmund, 145, 163, 177, 179, 187-188
Eyre, Roy, 252
Feia, Tim, 191, 197
Fernando, Ajith, 196
Floor, Karen, 304-305
Franklin, Karl, 82, 331

Franklin, Kirk, 9-11, 20, 163, 171, 173, 177, 179, 184, 187-188, 190-197, 199-204, 209-212, 214, 217, 221, 223-224, 226-229, 231-235, 238, 240-243, 247-252, 254, 257-262, 269, 272-273, 276-279, 281, 283, 285-291, 293-299, 301-303, 305-306, 313, 359, 383-385, 390, 396, 401-402, 408, 411-412, 414-415, 418, 425, 430-432, 437, 441, 481-483, 486-488, 493, 497, 499, 502, 505
Frank, Paul, 189
Frempong, Justin, 163, 334
Friedman, Thomas, 155, 386, 502
Fukuda, Takashi, 57, 138, 145, 166, 175, 191, 210, 467, 496-497
Gambo, Danjuma, 145, 163, 173, 337
Garcia-Schmidt, Nydia, 240, 258, 273, 292, 449-451, 454, 458, 468, 473-474
Gardner, Larrie, 98, 149
Gatere, Samuel, 316
Gatũ, John, 314-317, 333, 502
Gela, David, 195, 331-332
Gela, Sineina, 195, 331-332
Goodner, E.S., 23-24, 28
Graham, Billy, 56, 68, 79, 317
Greenleaf, Robert K., 152-153, 502
Harmelink, Bryan, 261, 285-286, 298, 420, 426, 445
Hartenstein, Karl, 47
Hersman, Russ, 338, 349
Hoffman, Aaron, 89-90
Holzhausen, Andreas, 59, 81, 84
Hopp, Traugott, 247
Hugoniot, Richard, 85, 89, 142-143, 145, 149, 161, 163, 171, 173-174, 177, 179, 183, 185-186, 195, 215, 497
Hyde, Marvin, 142, 144, 349
Jacobsen, Douglas, 219-220, 502
Jenkins, Philip, 78, 152, 156, 164, 188, 502-503
Johnson, Craig, 215
Johnson, Jo, 294
Johnson, John, 9-10, 13
Jones, E. Stanley, 316
Jung, Min-Young, 145, 191, 228, 398, 412
Kenmogne, Michel, 250, 252, 277, 324-325, 408, 413, 415, 503
Kernick, Darryl, 97, 131, 142, 144, 148-149, 163, 173, 191, 199, 215, 227, 257, 325, 349, 383
Kernick, Irene, 199, 257
Kimbi, Paul, 286, 294, 298
Kim, Donghwa, 335
Kim, Euijung and Yeonhwa, 335
Knott, Geoff, 184
Koen, Piet, 56, 59, 81
Koh, Kee Ai, 240, 283, 293
Kok, Kenneth, 163, 170, 173, 205
Kwon, Sung-Chan, 177, 184, 188, 191, 210, 258, 261
Laniak, Timothy, 216-217, 503
Larson, Mildred, 54, 85, 89, 97, 100, 127
Laub, James, 153, 503
Lautenschlager, Frank, 191, 258, 261
Lederleitner, Mary, 191, 271, 278
Legters, L.L., 19, 77, 495
Lewis, C.S., 412
Lid, Agnes, 275-277, 291, 293, 302, 305-306, 499
Lim, Lena, 275-276
Lindholm, Don, 82, 96, 100, 127, 149, 166
Lingenfelter, Sherwood, 178, 202
Lipps, Bob, 142, 166
Livermore, David, 264, 503
Luther, Martin, 19, 147, 347
Macdonald, Fergus, 80, 145-146, 505
Magbanua, Fred, 85, 89, 96, 138, 149
Mahatma, Gandhi, 316
Maramara, Zenet, 308-309, 503
May, Bernie, 85, 89, 96, 100, 115, 129, 498
Mejía, Ana Cristina, 236, 275-276
Miller, Carolyn, 96, 100, 127, 145, 215
Moore, Hyatt, 97, 124, 127, 132, 138
Mott, John, 364
Muntz, Susanna, 302
Mutiga, Jayne, 275-276
Mũturi, Mũndara, 177, 184, 186, 188, 195, 210, 247, 250, 257, 273, 278, 294, 413, 432, 498

Neill, Stephen, 18, 504
Newbigin, Lesslie, 78, 504
Nida, Eugene, 22, 25, 28
Niemandt, Nelus, 309, 504
Niyang, Stephen, 337
Njock, Emmanuel, 82, 85, 89, 96, 326
Northouse, Peter, 44, 75, 105-106, 153, 504
Nyman, William, 11, 20, 22-23, 25, 28, 30, 43, 62, 77, 495
Ofori-Atta, William, 322, 334
Ohlson, Dave, 149, 166, 497
Olesberg, Lindsay, 236
Opoku-Mensah, Paul, 322, 334, 504
Osei-Mensah, Gottfried, 322, 333
Ouédraogo, Boureima, 210, 236
Pachuau, Lalsangkima, 219-220, 504
Padilla, Rene, 79
Pallesen, Kemp, 73, 96, 100
Pantoja, Luis, 145-146, 163, 177, 186, 188, 195, 199-200, 211, 227
Pence, Al, 82, 85, 89, 326
Peterson, Roy, 145, 163
Piet, Meiring, 56, 59, 81, 272, 390
Pike, Kenneth, 22, 25, 27-28, 30, 33-35, 160-161, 495, 501
Pluddemann, Jim, 412
Polume, Thomas, 331
Porras, Jerry, 349-350, 378, 501
Poulter, Todd, 149, 205, 287, 294, 412, 417-418, 420, 432
Prior, Phil, 278, 295
Profita, Joseph, 63, 82, 85, 89
Rensch, Cal, 335
Robbins, Frank, 51, 53, 69-71, 86, 89, 100, 102, 138, 322, 496
Rodin, R. Scott, 308, 504
Ross, David, 145, 163
Sanneh, Lamin, 109, 137, 189, 220, 504-505
Scharmer, C. Otto, 215, 504
Schein, Edgar, 309, 504
Schein, Peter, 309, 504
Schöttelndreyer, Burkhard, 85, 89, 96, 100, 497
Schram, Judy, 138, 145, 163, 173
Schultz, Marshall, 191, 210
Sheldon, Steve, 117-119, 121, 124-125, 133, 137, 141-142, 144, 146-149, 195, 345, 347-348, 496
Shenk, Wilbur, 214
Songaba, Isidore, 163, 177
Soo, Valerie, 191, 203
Southwell, Neville, 142-144, 341
Stanley, Brian, 12, 18, 48, 80
Summanen, Hannu, 240, 293, 499
Sunquist, Scott, 77-79, 112, 505
Tehe-Yoa, Chantal, 195, 236
Tennent, Timothy, 48, 78, 490, 505
Tomašovský, Jaroslav, 426
Townsend, Elaine, 110, 137, 190, 495
Townsend, W. Cameron, 11, 18-30, 41-43, 45, 51-52, 62, 68, 77, 81, 110, 115, 137, 152, 167, 169, 172, 190, 313, 317-320, 322, 325, 343, 449, 493, 495-496, 502
Trotman, Dawson, 23
Trudell, Barbara, 138, 177, 349
Trudell, Joel, 189, 191, 210, 250
Uhl-Bien, Mary, 216, 505
Van Wynen, Susan, 9-11, 57, 191, 215, 228, 247, 252, 262, 278-279, 288-289, 297, 303, 306, 345, 381, 449-450, 477, 488, 505
Verkuyl, Johannes, 316
Vicedom, Georg, 47
Viscount, Francis, 210, 408
Wakatama, Pius, 315-316, 321, 342-343, 505
Walker, Christina, 12, 310, 505
Walls, Andrew, 12, 48-49, 163, 189, 505
Wan, Simon, 261, 273, 287
Watters, John, 89, 142-143, 147-149, 151, 158, 160, 162, 164-166, 168-172, 174-175, 179, 184-189, 191, 194-195, 203, 214-215, 222, 324, 326, 345-352, 354, 357-359, 361-363, 365, 378, 383, 496, 505
Watters, Kenneth, 28
Welch, Roger, 62, 138, 145, 163, 177, 179, 185-188, 195-196, 199, 211, 215, 226, 233-236, 252, 257-260, 273, 293, 349, 497-498

Widjaya, Bambang, 196
Wiesmann, Hannes, 195, 236, 252, 261, 273, 292, 330, 412, 426, 432
Wilson, Kent R., 308
Winter, Ralph, 79, 156
Wolfenden, Elmer, 335
Wong, Ah Chye, 223, 240, 498
Wright, Christopher, 189, 236-237, 376, 506
Wright, N.T., 152, 506
Wujangi, Kenneth, 334
Wycliffe, John, 20, 43, 147, 347

General Index

0.35% Contribution, 224-225, 246, 253, 258-260, 283, 435

10% Assessment, 30, 71, 283

Acceleration, 51, 358, 379

AD2000 Movement, 111, 467

Africa, 9, 28, 34, 36, 56-57, 67-69, 72-74, 78-79, 85, 89-91, 94-95, 102, 104, 109, 117-118, 124, 131, 137-138, 142-143, 145-146, 149, 151-152, 156, 161-163, 165-166, 168, 172, 175-177, 184, 186, 189, 191-192, 194, 198, 208, 210, 222, 225, 231, 236, 247, 250-252, 258, 261, 271-274, 278-285, 287, 291, 294, 302, 304, 313-318, 321-322, 324, 326-327, 330, 333, 336, 342, 344, 346, 349, 361, 385-386, 390-391, 399, 408, 413, 418, 427-428, 431-432, 437-440, 443, 466, 489, 497-499, 501, 505

    Africa Area, 68, 72, 89, 102, 143, 151, 166, 172, 189, 191, 194, 210, 222, 247, 250, 252, 273, 278-279, 284, 287, 294, 326, 333, 349, 408, 413, 432, 440, 497-498

Age of Reason, 18, 22

Alliance Leadership Team, 8, 228, 232, 261, 296, 401, 479, 482, 491

Alliance-ness, 14

Americas, 82, 104, 118, 142, 144, 149, 151, 160-161, 166, 184, 186, 189, 191, 193-194, 204, 206, 222, 225, 231, 236, 240, 251, 258, 273, 282, 285, 292-293, 399, 412, 428, 443-444, 449-451, 453, 455-456, 458-459, 461, 463-465, 467-468, 470-471, 474-475, 497

    Americas Area, 6, 144, 160, 166, 186, 191, 193-194, 206, 240, 251, 285, 292-293, 399, 412, 443-444, 449-451, 453, 455-456, 459, 461, 463-465, 467, 470-471, 474-475, 497

Apartheid, 73, 109, 151-152, 194

Aramaic Bible Translators, 164

Argentina, 144, 148, 163-164, 177, 195, 231, 385, 458, 467

    LETRA Argentina, 164, 195

Asia, 32, 56, 69, 72-74, 78-79, 85, 87, 89-90, 104, 117-118, 137, 142-143, 149, 151, 156, 163, 166, 168, 175-177, 186, 198, 200, 222, 225, 236, 274, 282-283, 288, 291, 316-317, 322, 324, 326-327, 330, 346, 349, 359, 361, 424, 428, 443, 466-467, 489

    East Asia, 117, 175

Asian Diaspora, 165, 351-352

Asia-Pacific Area, 166, 172, 189, 191, 194, 210, 261, 287, 399, 497

Australia, 30-32, 35, 39, 43, 49, 53, 58-59, 61-62, 73-74, 81, 109, 113, 118, 127, 132, 137-138, 142-143, 161, 163, 170-171, 173, 175, 177, 187, 190-191, 194, 231, 294, 317, 331, 383, 385, 417, 496-497, 502

    Aborigines, 32, 59-60, 67

    Wycliffe Australia, 32, 73, 143, 163, 171, 175, 187, 194, 231, 383

Austria, 81, 84-85, 124, 137, 144, 161, 194, 204, 231, 236

    Wycliffe Austria, 144, 194, 204, 231, 236

Belgium, 73, 81, 85, 124, 137, 161, 189

    Wycliffe Belgium, 73

Benin

    Wycliffe Benin, 194, 231

Bible Translation, 9, 12-13, 19-21, 26-29, 33-36, 42-43, 45-46, 49-52, 57, 60, 63-64, 68-69, 72-73, 75, 77, 79-80, 82-84, 88-89, 91-92, 95, 98, 102, 104-107, 109, 111, 114, 117, 120, 123, 129-133, 135, 138-141, 143-144, 146-151, 153, 157, 159-162, 164-165, 168-169, 173-180, 182, 184, 186, 189, 192-193, 195-197, 202-206, 208-209, 213-214, 220-225, 229-232, 234-235, 240-245, 250-251, 253-256, 259-261, 263, 265, 267-270, 272-273, 278-279, 281-282, 284-290, 292-295,

297-299, 304, 306, 308, 311, 313-314, 317-327, 329-338, 341-348, 350-351, 353, 355-360, 362-366, 368-370, 373-377, 383-384, 386, 388-390, 393, 396, 398, 402, 407-409, 412-417, 420-422, 427-431, 433, 437, 439, 441, 443, 445-446, 449-455, 461-462, 464-465, 467, 470, 473, 480, 484, 487, 489, 491-494, 496-498, 505
Bible Translation Philosophy Statement, 413-414
Bible Translation Programs, 88, 151, 213, 224, 244, 253, 255, 270, 278, 282, 284-287, 290, 292, 294, 297, 332, 336, 341, 344, 348, 359, 366, 407-409, 413, 415, 420-421, 493, 498
Binary, 289, 375, 431, 460, 470
Bolivia
  CET, 231
Brazil, 57, 64, 73-74, 84, 95, 117, 131, 137, 142, 161, 194, 231, 233, 275, 292, 329-330, 418, 430, 451-452, 458, 467, 498
  ALEM, 57, 131, 137, 142, 161, 194, 231, 233, 329-330, 458
  Horizontes, 231
Burkina Faso
  ANTBA, 131, 137, 161, 194, 210, 231, 236, 327
Cameroon, 72-73, 117, 126, 131, 137-138, 143, 162, 175, 184, 189, 194, 231, 294, 326, 385
  CABTAL, 131, 143, 162, 175, 194, 231
Camp Wycliffe, 20, 22, 27-29, 335
Canada, 27-31, 39, 41, 43, 49, 52-53, 58-59, 61-62, 73, 81, 89, 112-113, 127, 132, 137-138, 142, 144, 146, 161, 170, 193-194, 229, 231, 233, 252, 274, 280, 302, 317, 450, 461, 495-497
  Global PartnerLink, 193
  OneBook, 231, 280
  Wycliffe Canada, 73, 112, 132, 142, 144, 193-194, 231, 233, 252, 302, 496
Caribbeans
  Trinidad and Tobago, 418
  Wycliffe Caribbean, 144, 194, 231
  Central America Mission (CAM), 24
Centralized, 50, 87, 103, 192, 208, 242, 247, 263, 281-283
Centuries
  21st Century, 163, 171, 178-179, 188, 195, 203, 219, 363, 365, 501-502, 505
  18th Century, 111, 147, 347
  19th Century, 111, 147, 347
  20th Century, 44, 48, 56, 107, 112, 147, 317, 347
Chad
  ATALTRAB, 137, 162, 194, 231, 233, 327, 341
Chile, 144, 195, 231, 458
  LETRA Chile, 195, 458
Christendom, 18, 49, 78, 164, 188, 214, 405, 502-503
CLADE, 112
Collaboration, 25, 80, 93, 141, 174-175, 186, 243, 261, 263, 285, 288, 290, 309, 330, 351, 377, 381, 409, 413, 441, 456, 459, 465-467, 470, 485, 499
Colombia, 67, 144, 418, 468
Colonialism, 11, 280, 317, 372
COMIBAM, 8, 79, 144, 146, 160, 165, 195, 231, 233, 236, 418, 450, 452, 454, 458, 462, 464, 467, 470-471, 497
Communism, 18, 45, 110, 167
Complexity, 76, 123, 171, 215-217, 234, 297, 420, 426, 428, 430, 460, 487, 505
Confucian, 112
Conquest, 17, 49, 249
Costa Rica, 144, 148-149, 162, 164, 195, 204, 231, 467
  FEDEMEC, 149, 162, 164, 195, 231, 458, 467
Côte d'Ivoire, 137, 151, 162, 195, 236, 329
  AITB, 137, 162, 164, 231, 329
Covenant, 79, 252-253, 256, 260, 263, 269-271, 273-274, 277, 283-284, 295, 302-304, 362, 435-436, 498
COVID-19 pandemic, 304, 306, 491
Czech Republic
  Wycliffe Czech Republic, 144, 162, 194, 211, 231
Decentralized, 50, 282

Democratic Republic of Congo
    ACOTBA-SUBO, 195, 231
Denmark, 73, 81, 85, 124, 137, 142, 161, 194, 231
    Wycliffe Denmark, 73, 194, 231
Dependency, 307, 316, 342, 367, 369, 373, 429, 452, 491
Divine Familial Terms, 228-229, 271, 372
DOOR, 231
ECFA, 69
Ecuador, 25, 65, 68, 195, 444
    FUMIG, 195
Ecumenical, 17, 47, 157
El Salvador
    TRES, 231, 251-252
Ethiopia, 175, 177, 193, 195, 231, 251, 255, 418, 427
    ECFE, 193, 195
    Wycliffe Ethiopia, 251
Eurasia, 87, 118, 349, 404-405
Europe, 17-18, 28, 32, 34-35, 43, 56, 73, 80, 84-85, 89-90, 94, 98, 100, 104, 118, 124, 131, 137, 140-142, 144, 148-149, 151, 156, 163, 165-166, 186, 191, 194, 200, 212, 225, 231, 236, 258, 261, 273-274, 282, 292, 316-317, 399, 412, 425-426, 428, 437-440, 443, 461, 470, 483, 497
    Europe Area, 73, 84, 89-90, 100, 131, 144, 148, 191, 194, 200, 212, 261, 292, 399, 412, 425-426, 440, 470, 483, 497
Evangel Bible Translators, 68
Evangelical, 11, 24, 48, 56, 67, 69, 79, 84, 145-146, 157, 177, 193, 195, 199, 229, 251, 255, 316, 330, 376, 416, 501-502
Finland, 58-59, 61, 73, 81, 85, 124, 137, 161, 194, 231, 240, 280, 499
    Wycliffe Finland, 194, 231, 240
Fluidity, 301, 430
FOBAI, 80, 407, 409
Foundational Statements, 288, 435, 445, 494, 505
France, 19, 58, 73, 81, 84-85, 124, 131, 137, 161, 194, 231, 236
    Wycliffe France, 131, 194, 231, 236
Francophone, 73, 84, 94, 176, 192, 208, 239, 280
Friendship and Community, 255, 288-289, 419, 499
Generosity, 273, 279, 288, 293, 300, 303, 311, 398, 424, 436-437, 443-444, 457, 462-463, 473, 499
Germany, 19, 34-35, 47, 49, 56, 58-61, 73, 80-81, 113, 131, 137-138, 161, 170, 191, 194, 204, 226, 231, 241, 247, 278, 283, 302, 385, 399, 418, 428, 497
    Wycliffe Germany, 131, 194, 231, 241, 278
Ghana, 36, 57, 72-73, 85, 95, 131, 137-138, 161, 163, 194, 231, 251, 322, 325, 334, 394, 420-421, 487
    Accrá, 394, 420
    GILLBT, 85, 131, 137, 161, 163, 194, 231, 251, 325, 329, 334, 394, 504
Globalization, 107, 109-110, 155, 238, 287, 309, 321, 346, 361, 372, 387, 406, 422, 424-425, 502
Global Leadership Team, 191, 261, 360, 416, 488, 497
Global Missional Leadership, 14, 264, 287-288, 290, 308, 424, 499
Global North, 156, 419
Glocal, 372
Governance, 24, 44, 51, 53, 83-84, 112, 121, 125, 128, 150-151, 172-173, 175-176, 192, 197, 203, 238, 242, 244, 246, 248-253, 258-259, 277, 282, 284, 287, 298-301, 307, 334, 340, 501
Great Commission, 17-18, 21, 48-49, 67, 74, 79, 100, 111, 236, 356-357, 375, 384, 502
Great Depression, 19, 45, 155, 167, 314
Guatemala, 11, 18, 191, 240, 385, 449, 458, 495, 497
Hong Kong, 72, 89, 124, 131, 137, 143, 161, 194, 231, 280
    Wycliffe Hong Kong, 143, 194, 231
Hungary, 80, 85, 144, 162, 194, 204, 208, 231, 298
    Wycliffe Hungary, 144, 162, 194, 204, 231, 298
Hybrid, 161
IFMA, 26, 30, 39

India, 18-19, 32, 57-58, 67, 73, 127, 131, 137, 143, 162, 165, 184, 192, 194, 196, 200, 231, 233, 288, 316, 336, 346, 502
- IICCC, 131, 137, 162, 329, 336
- IMA, 336
- WFA, 192
- Wycliffe India, 194, 200, 231, 233, 336

Indonesia, 60, 72-73, 89, 131, 137, 142-143, 159, 161, 175, 194, 210, 227, 231, 233, 236, 251, 276, 282, 288, 305, 335, 341, 427, 430
- GIDI, 231
- GMIM, 231
- GPID, 231
- GPM, 231
- Kartidaya, 131, 137, 142-143, 159, 161, 194, 211, 231, 233, 251, 341
- Yajasi, 231
- YBI, 231
- YMP3, 231
- YPA, 231
- YPSA, 231

Internationalization, 56-57, 61, 112, 123, 136, 140, 142, 307, 321

International Linguistics Center, 55, 203, 295

Ireland
- Wycliffe Ireland, 200

Italy, 85, 124, 164, 231, 420
- AITB, 137, 162, 164, 231, 329

JAARS, 41, 45, 55, 70, 99, 118, 124, 133, 137, 145, 161, 280, 327

Japan, 19, 57-58, 61, 73, 81, 85, 137-138, 143, 145-146, 161, 166, 191, 194, 210, 231, 298, 430, 496-497
- Wycliffe Japan, 73, 143, 166, 194, 210, 231, 298

Jesus Film Project, 80, 146

Journey, 9-10, 12-14, 45-46, 49, 74, 76, 88, 105-107, 153-155, 184, 187, 195, 199, 202, 207, 211-212, 214-215, 217, 232-233, 238, 241-244, 254, 257-258, 260-261, 265, 272, 279, 287-288, 297, 300, 306-308, 310-311, 313, 338, 344, 350, 358, 366, 368-369, 375-377, 379, 381, 383, 385, 387, 390, 396, 398, 402, 404-405, 409, 411-412, 416-417, 421, 431, 434, 437, 446, 448-451, 453, 455-457, 459, 461, 463, 465-466, 468-470, 472, 474-475, 478-479, 484, 486-489, 491-494, 499, 502, 505

Jungle Camp, 33, 50

Kenya, 85, 102, 113, 117, 126-127, 131, 137-138, 146, 151, 161, 177, 184, 186, 194-195, 204, 209-210, 226, 231, 236, 273, 275, 279, 287, 291, 294, 314, 327, 332-333, 342, 399, 409, 411, 418, 431, 498
- BTL, 85, 131, 137, 161, 184, 186, 194, 210, 226, 231, 236, 325, 329, 332-333, 339, 342
- Mombassa, 340
- Nairobi, 210, 316, 332-333, 502
- Ruiru, 204, 209, 279, 291, 294, 399, 409, 411-412, 431

Kingdom of God, 69, 112, 169, 207, 211, 245, 375, 383, 388, 392, 405, 431, 479, 484

Korean War, 49

Language Programs, 113, 117, 143, 184, 186, 197, 200-202, 209, 223, 225, 250, 262, 337, 352, 355-356, 407-408, 414, 486

Last Languages Initiative, 206, 364, 392

Latin America, 19, 25, 57, 73, 79, 90, 139-140, 142, 148, 156, 160, 163, 165-166, 168, 175, 177, 198, 208, 239, 274, 282-283, 287, 291-292, 315-317, 352, 355, 375, 451-453, 461, 464-467, 497

Lausanne Movement, 157, 502

Leadership Theories, 13, 44, 74, 105, 152, 215, 217, 503
- Charismatic, 44, 377-378
- Complexity Leadership, 216-217, 505
- Cultural Intelligence, 264, 503
- Culturally Inclusive Leadership, 310
- Humble Leadership, 309, 504
- Laissez-faire, 106
- Missional Leadership, 14, 261, 264, 287-288, 290, 308-309, 424, 491, 493-494, 499, 504

Path-goal, 74-75
Polycentric Leadership, 281, 309
Servant Leadership, 152-153, 308, 502
Shepherd Leaders, 216
Situational, 74-75
Steward Leadership, 308, 505
Steward-Shalom, 308
Traits-based, 44
Transactional Leadership, 106
Transformational, 105-106, 192, 222, 238, 363, 377-378, 408-409, 411, 464, 501, 506
Leaders Journeying Together, 411, 413, 417
Leaders Moving Forward, 204, 217
Linguistics, 11, 20, 22, 26-30, 33-35, 42, 45, 55, 60, 67, 72, 83, 95, 160-161, 175, 203, 285, 295, 298, 318, 323, 325, 330, 332, 334-336, 501
Literacy, 21, 68, 72, 90-91, 95, 97, 102, 129-130, 139, 166, 185, 209, 242, 251, 319, 323, 325, 327, 329, 331-332, 334, 336-339, 347, 358
Majority World, 48, 77, 112-113, 138, 146, 156, 163, 168-169, 208, 214, 232, 238, 241, 255, 281, 307, 313, 321, 376
Global South, 156, 166, 168-169, 174, 196, 213-214, 225, 232, 346, 375-377, 419, 497, 502
Malaysia, 89, 131, 137-138, 142-143, 161, 175, 191, 194, 231, 305, 330
BTCS, 137, 330
Wycliffe Malaysia, 143, 175, 194, 231
Metanorms, 300
Mexico, 11, 20, 22-25, 27, 33, 47, 57, 67, 117, 144, 177, 195, 220, 231, 233, 240, 251, 287, 289, 294, 399, 449-450, 467, 495
COMIMEX, 195, 467
Mexico City, 22, 47, 67, 177, 399, 449, 495
UNTI, 231, 233, 251
Mindset, 195, 279, 281, 287-288, 290, 309-311, 387, 422-424, 442, 450, 460-461, 463, 466, 471, 499
Missio Dei, 9, 47-48, 74, 78-79, 110-111, 196, 254, 281, 287-288, 374, 376, 392-394, 405, 408, 411, 416-417, 423, 464, 478, 499, 501
Mission of God, 9, 47, 110, 188-189, 195, 201, 205, 207, 236, 243, 254, 256, 288, 298, 374, 393, 403-407, 411, 413-414, 416-417, 422, 424-428, 430, 445, 454, 461-462, 469, 479, 493, 499, 506
Missiological Consultations, 381, 405, 416, 429-430, 437, 446
Missiologists, 9, 229, 382, 390
Missiology, 9, 78, 214, 255, 278-279, 330, 356, 382, 388-390, 394, 411, 461-462, 467, 469, 473, 497, 501-502, 504-506
Missional Intent, 7, 74, 288, 455, 463, 475, 477-479, 487-488, 499, 505
Missionary Kids, 124
Mission Conferences
Cape Town 2010, 157
Edinburgh 1910, 157, 219
Edinburgh 2010, 156, 503
IMC, 47
Tokyo 2010, 156-157
Modern Missionary Movement, 19, 48, 78, 147
Moratorium Debate, 314, 316, 342, 344
Movida, 470
Multi-ethnic, 175
NAE, 26
National Bible Translation Organizations, 5, 313, 319, 326, 496
Nationalism, 196, 313-314, 317-319, 321, 324, 342, 344, 425
Nationals, 36, 92, 129, 319-321, 323, 326, 342 343, 452
Netherlands, 56, 58-59, 61, 73, 81, 84, 97, 121, 127, 137, 161, 194, 229, 231, 280, 283, 294, 495
Wycliffe Netherlands, 127, 194, 231, 280
New Zealand, 12, 31-32, 43, 49, 58-61, 73, 81, 84-85, 113, 137-138, 145-146, 161, 194-195, 226, 231, 233, 236, 495
Wycliffe New Zealand, 73, 194, 226, 231, 233

Nigeria, 72-73, 85, 95, 117, 126, 131, 137, 145-146, 161, 163, 175-176, 192, 250, 258, 325, 327, 336-337, 346
    NBTT, 85, 126, 131, 137, 161, 192, 250, 258, 325, 329, 336-337
Non-profit, 22, 69, 128, 150-151, 165, 308
North America, 17, 33, 52, 54, 89-90, 156, 163, 292, 451, 466
Norway, 34, 59, 73, 81, 84-85, 137, 142, 145-146, 161, 163, 177, 187, 194, 231, 275, 305, 418, 483, 499
    Wycliffe Norway, 73, 163, 187, 194, 231, 483
Operation Mobilisation (OM), 170
Optimism, 17-19, 69, 73, 275, 306, 378
Pacific Islands, 12, 327
    Pacific Area, 90, 166, 172, 341
Padroado, 111
Panama, 28, 91, 231
    PAAM, 231
Papua New Guinea, 31, 73-74, 95, 117, 131, 137, 143, 184, 251, 325, 331, 385, 418
    BTA, 73, 131, 137, 143-144, 161, 175, 183, 187, 192, 194, 231, 251, 325, 329, 331-332
    SILAC, 331
    Ukarumpa, 331-332
    Waigani, 332
Paradigm, 129, 227, 245, 261, 388, 398, 405, 411, 418, 425, 439, 501
Paraguay, 148, 195, 231, 251
    LETRA Paraguay, 195
Participation Streams, 5, 295, 302-303, 485
    Bible Translation Programs, 244, 278, 284
    Church Engagement, 224, 285, 303
    Funding, 244, 304
    People, 224, 303
Partnership, 68, 83, 89, 96-97, 102, 122, 125-126, 141, 143, 146, 149-151, 158, 160, 167-168, 174, 177-179, 181, 186, 191-193, 195, 201, 205, 207, 209, 212, 227-229, 232, 240, 251, 273, 277, 286, 296, 326, 337, 339, 342, 346, 349, 351-353, 355, 357-358, 360-361, 363, 367, 369-371, 387, 389, 395, 405, 431-433, 439, 453-455, 461-462, 470, 474
Paternalism, 314, 321
Peru, 25, 165, 231, 251
    AEL, 231, 251
Philippines, 30, 32, 72-73, 95, 117, 131, 137-138, 145-146, 149, 161, 163, 175, 177, 194-195, 200, 211, 227, 231, 318, 338-339, 418
    TAP, 131, 137, 161, 184, 194, 200, 231, 329, 338-339
    Wycliffe Philippines, 200, 231
Poland, 80, 137, 149, 162, 164, 194, 208, 231
Policy Governance, 150, 172-173, 299
Polycentric, 263, 281-282, 288, 297, 299-301, 307, 309-310, 473, 478, 499, 501, 506
    Governance, 24, 44, 51, 53, 83-84, 112, 121, 125, 128, 150-151, 172-173, 175-176, 192, 197, 203, 238, 242, 244, 246, 248-253, 258-259, 277, 282, 284, 287, 298-301, 307, 334, 340, 501
Polyphonic, 297, 307, 309, 448, 473, 478, 499
Portugal, 84-85, 124, 137
Portuguese, 221, 256, 278, 280, 287, 444, 498
Post-colonial, 73, 195-196
Pragmatism, 43, 344
Principles for Funding, 270, 401, 435-436, 498
Principles of Community, 6, 420-421, 498
Protestant, 19, 75, 112, 267, 374
Protestant Reformation, 267
Reflective Practitioner, 263, 384
Republic of Central Africa
    ACATBA, 137, 162, 194, 231, 327, 341
Ricardo Palma University, 165
Roman Catholic, 157
Romania, 189, 204, 208, 231, 298
    Wycliffe Romania, 204, 231, 298
Russia, 19, 110, 144, 148, 161, 175, 194, 204, 208, 231
    Wycliffe Russia, 110, 175, 194, 204, 231
Seed Company, 128, 161, 164, 170, 251, 254, 280-281, 285, 293, 407, 445, 496
Shalom, 192, 255, 302-303, 308, 415-416, 445, 503

Short Term Missions, 97, 158-159
SIL International, 11, 63, 65-66, 71, 127, 136, 138-139, 145, 148, 151, 158, 161-162, 167, 176-177, 179, 185, 190-191, 194, 214, 231, 242, 257, 289, 296, 313, 317, 326-327, 329, 338, 341-342, 345, 352, 355, 360, 399, 502
SIL Branches, 36, 60, 64-65, 82, 90, 95, 103, 319
Singapore, 72, 84, 117, 124, 137-138, 161, 163, 170-173, 179, 190-191, 194, 203-205, 208, 210-212, 221, 223, 226, 231, 236, 240, 248-249, 261, 275, 287, 295-296, 305, 359, 385-386, 418, 430, 433, 435, 441, 497-498
Wycliffe Singapore, 163, 170, 194, 203-204, 211, 226, 231, 236, 240, 359, 385-386
Slovakia
Wycliffe Slovakia, 194, 231, 426
Solomon Islands
BTLP, 251
SICA, 329, 337
SITAG, 337
South Africa, 9, 56, 73, 109, 124, 131, 137-138, 145-146, 151-152, 161, 191, 194, 231, 236, 251, 261, 272, 291, 294, 302, 304, 385, 390, 418, 427, 432, 499
Wycliffe South Africa, 73, 109, 131, 194, 231, 236, 251, 304
South Korea, 57, 73, 85, 89, 95, 117, 124, 131, 137, 143, 145-146, 161, 177, 184, 191, 194, 210, 231, 335
GBT, 131, 137, 143, 145, 161, 194, 210, 231, 329, 335
Spain, 124, 137, 162, 231
PROEL, 162, 231
Student Volunteer Movement, 18, 157
Sudan
ECS-TD, 164, 231, 233
SUBTALA, 329, 338
Sweden
Wycliffe Sweden/Folk & Språk, 34, 61, 73, 81, 85, 137, 161, 194, 231, 233
Switzerland, 34-35, 49, 58-59, 61, 73, 81, 85, 137-138, 145-146, 161, 170, 194-195, 231, 236, 261, 280, 294, 296, 495
Wycliffe Switzerland, 35, 73, 194, 231, 236, 261
Taiwan
Wycliffe Taiwan, 143, 194, 231
Texas, 55, 61, 77, 80, 86, 88, 95, 128, 183, 190, 203, 221, 248-249, 252-253, 293, 301, 335, 359, 445, 458, 496
Thailand, 143, 161, 188, 194, 204, 231, 271, 291, 396, 399, 416, 424, 430, 498
Bangkok, 204, 399, 424, 430
Chiang Mai, 177, 188, 194, 231, 271, 291, 416, 498
Wycliffe Thailand, 194, 231
Theology, 9, 22, 78-79, 110-111, 163, 298, 356, 386-388, 391, 400, 408, 415, 420, 423, 452, 467, 489, 501, 503-504
Liberation, 452
Trinitarian, 78, 420, 478, 501, 505
Triune God, 78, 110, 219, 273, 374, 376, 385, 394-395, 423-424, 446
Third Spaces, 279, 281-282, 288-289, 311, 431-432, 499
Third Table, 274-275, 417, 419
Togo
Wycliffe Togo, 194, 231
Transformation, 112, 192, 201, 204, 221, 236, 241, 255, 288, 303, 308-309, 362, 367, 373, 375, 378, 387, 413, 416-417, 444-446, 454, 462, 464, 487, 499, 502
Turkey
Istanbul, 403, 417
Kusadasi, 258, 413, 435
Types of Organizations, 282, 365
Ukraine
Wycliffe Ukraine, 194, 200, 231
United Bible Societies, 130
United Kingdom, 236
Wycliffe UK, 73, 179, 189, 194, 200, 206, 222, 231, 235, 392
Unity, 70, 101, 126, 157, 171, 176, 178-179, 188, 201, 207, 212, 227-228, 232, 260-261, 264-265, 282, 290, 296, 303, 357, 366, 372, 384-385, 404, 411, 421, 423-424, 426-427, 430, 439, 459, 470, 479

Urgency, 36, 42-43, 141, 209, 232, 254, 357-358, 363-365, 369-370, 373-376, 379, 393, 453, 503
Uruguay, 195
 LETRA Uruguay, 195
USA, 59, 62, 406-407
 California, 11, 22-23, 30-32, 41-42, 49, 51, 54, 62, 64, 72, 96, 128, 133, 144, 183, 304, 495-496
 Dallas, 51, 55, 59, 61, 77, 80, 85-87, 118, 128, 133, 150, 167, 170, 183, 189-190, 214, 223, 295, 335, 359, 496
 Los Angeles, 23, 25, 41-42, 495
 Orlando, 42, 248, 383-385, 405, 497, 505
 Waxhaw, NC, 55
 Wycliffe Foundation, 164
 Wycliffe Resources, 164, 170
 Wycliffe US, 51, 62, 70, 72-74, 114-115, 120, 127-128, 132-133, 136, 142, 148, 151, 160-161, 163, 165-166, 175, 184, 186, 189, 205, 224-225, 231, 236, 248-251, 254, 259, 280-281, 282-283, 294, 297, 339, 359, 365, 383, 405-407, 432
Vanuatu, 144, 162
 VCC, 162
Venezuela, 148, 231, 251
 SIETE, 231, 251
Vietnam, 64
Vietnam War, 64
Vision 2025, 51, 145-147, 149-151, 153, 161-165, 168, 176, 186-188, 197, 199, 202-204, 206, 208, 214, 232, 238, 262, 274, 345, 347-369, 374-379, 384, 388-389, 430, 453, 496-497, 505
VUCA, 296
World Council of Churches, 47
World Evangelical Alliance, 157, 199, 229
World Wars, 11, 314
Wycliffe Associates, 51, 62-63, 112, 138, 159, 164, 170, 231, 249, 280, 496
Wycliffe Divisions, 68, 81-83, 86, 92, 106, 113, 220, 239, 313, 339
YWAM, 168, 184, 286, 470